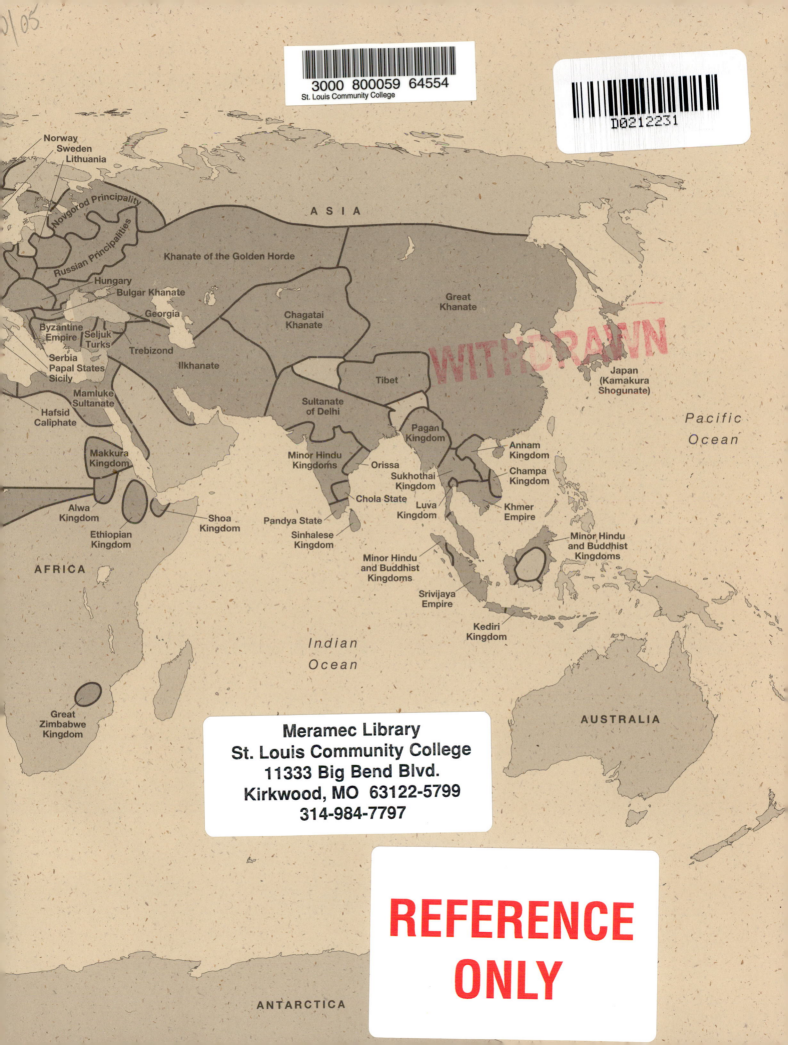

Norway
Sweden
Lithuania

Novgorod Principality

ASIA

Russian Principalities

Khanate of the Golden Horde

Great
Khanate

Hungary

Bulgar Khanate

Georgia

Byzantine
Empire

Seljuk
Turks

Chagatai
Khanate

WITHDRAWN

Trebizond

Japan
(Kamakura
Shogunate)

Serbia
Papal States
Sicily

Ilkhanate

Tibet

Mamluke
Sultanate

Pacific
Ocean

Hafsid
Caliphate

Sultanate
of Delhi

Pagan
Kingdom

Makkura
Kingdom

Minor Hindu
Kingdoms

Annam
Kingdom

Orissa

Champa
Kingdom

Sukhothai
Kingdom

Alwa
Kingdom

Shoa
Kingdom

Chola State

Luva
Kingdom

Khmer
Empire

Ethiopian
Kingdom

Pandya State

Minor Hindu
and Buddhist
Kingdoms

Sinhalese
Kingdom

AFRICA

Minor Hindu
and Buddhist
Kingdoms

Srivijaya
Empire

Kediri
Kingdom

Indian
Ocean

Great
Zimbabwe
Kingdom

AUSTRALIA

ANTARCTICA

WORLD

MONARCHIES

AND DYNASTIES

VOLUME 3

N–Z

CONSULTING EDITOR
JOHN MIDDLETON

SHARPE REFERENCE
an imprint of M.E. Sharpe, Inc.

Developed, Designed, and Produced by BOOK BUILDERS LLC

SHARPE REFERENCE

Sharpe Reference is an imprint of M.E. Sharpe, Inc.

M.E. Sharpe, Inc.
80 Business Park Drive
Armonk, NY 10504

Library of Congress Cataloging-in-Publication Data

World monarchies and dynasties / John Middleton, editor.
   p. cm.
Includes bibliographical references and index.
ISBN 0-7656-8050-5 (set : alk. paper)
1. World history. 2. Monarchy—History—Dictionaries. 3. Kings and rulers—History—Dictionaries. I. Middleton, John.

D21 .W929 2004
903—dc22   2003023236

Printed and bound in the United States of America

The paper used in this publication meets the minimum
requirements of American National Standard for Information
Sciences—Permanence of Paper for Printed Library Materials,
ANSI Z 39.48.1984.

BM (c) 10 9 8 7 6 5 4 3 2 1

Endpaper Maps: inside front cover: World Monarchies, 1279 C.E.;
inside back cover: World Monarchies, Present Day
(IMA for BOOK BUILDERS LLC)

Contents

Volume 3

List of Features . . . . *vii*

Nabopolassar 654
Nadir Shah 654
Nam Viet Kingdom 655
Nanchao Kingdom 656
Naples, Kingdom of 656
Napoleon I (Bonaparte) 657
Napoleon III 660
Nara Kingdom 662
Narai 664
Naram-Sin 665
Nasrid Dynasty 665
National Identity 666
Nationalism 668
Naval Roles 669
Navarre, Kingdom of 670
Nazca Kingdom 671
Ndebele Kingdom 672
Nebuchadrezzar II 673
Nefertiti 675
Nero 676
Netherlands Kingdom 677
Nevsky, Alexander 678
Ngonde Kingdom 678
Nguyen Anh 679
Nguyen (Hue) Dynasty 679
Nicholas I 680
Nicholas II 682
Norman Kingdoms 684
Norodom Sihanouk 685
Northumbria, Kingdom of 686
Norwegian Monarchy 687
Nubian Kingdoms 689
Nupe Kingdom 690
Nyoro Kingdom 690
Oaths and Oath-taking 691
Oda Nobunaga 692
Oldenburg Dynasty 694
Olmec Kingdom 695
Orange-Nassau, House of 696
Osei Tutu 697
Osman I 697
Ostrogoth Kingdom 698
Otto I, the Great 699
Ottoman Empire 700

Ottonian Dynasty 705
Oudh (Avadh) Kingdom 706
Pacal 706
Pachacuti 707
Paekche Kingdom 708
Pagan Kingdom 709
Pahlavi Dynasty 710
Pala Dynasty 711
Palaces 711
Palaeologan Dynasty 714
Palestine, Kingdoms of 715
Pandya Dynasty 716
Panjalu Kingdom 718
Papal States 718
Paramara Dynasty 719
Parks, Royal 720
Parthian Kingdom 721
Patent Letters, Royal 722
Pedro I 722
Pedro II 723
Pegu Kingdoms 724
Pepin Dynasty 724
Pepin the Short (Pepin III) 726
Perak Kingdom 726
Pergamum Kingdom 727
Persian Empire 728
Peter I, the Great 731
Philip II 732
Philip II of Macedon 734
Philip II, Augustus 735
Philip IV, the Fair 736
Phoenician Empire 737
Phrygia Kingdom 738
Piast Dynasty 739
Picts, Kingdom of the 740
Piedmont Kingdom 741
Plantagenet, House of 742
Polygamy, Royal 745
Pomare IV 748
Postcolonial States 748
Power, Forms of Royal 749
Powys Kingdom 751
Premysl Dynasty 751
Priests, Royal 752
Primogeniture 754
Prophets, Royal 754
Ptolemaic Dynasty 755

Ptolemy I 756
Pu Yi 757
Punjab Princely States 758
Pyu Kingdom 760
Qajar Dynasty 761
Queens and Queen Mothers 762
Radama I 763
Radama II 764
Rajasthan Kingdom 764
Rama Khamheng 766
Ramses II, the Great 767
Ranavalona I, Mada 769
Rastrakuta Dynasty 769
Realms, Types of 770
Rebellion 771
Reccared I 773
Regalia and Insignia, Royal 773
Regencies 775
Regicide 776
Reigns, Length of 778
Religious Duties and Powers 779
Richard I, Lionheart 780
Richard II 782
Richard III 783
Rights to Animals 785
Rights, Civil 786
Rights, Land 787
Ritual, Royal 788
Riurikid Dynasty 789
Robert I (Robert the Bruce) 790
Roderic 791
Roman Empire 791
Romanian Monarchy 796
Romanov Dynasty 797
Romanov, Michael 798
Royal Families 799
Royal Imposters 801
Royal Line 801
Royal Pretenders 802
Rudolf I 803
Rurik 803
Rus Princedoms 804
Russian Dynasties 805
Sabaean Kingdom 811
Sacral Birth and Death 811
Sacred Kingships 812
Sacred Texts 814
Safavid Dynasty 815
Saffarid Dynasty 815
Sa'id, Sayyid ibn 816

Sailendra Dynasty 817
Sakalava Kingdom 817
Saladin 818
Salian Dynasty 819
Samanid Dynasty 821
Samoan Kingdoms 821
Samsu-iluna 822
Samudera-Pasai 822
Sancho III, the Great 823
Sanusi Dynasty 824
Sargon II 825
Sargon of Akkad 826
Sasanid Dynasty 826
Satavahana Dynasty 827
Savoy Dynasty 829
Saxe-Coburg-Gotha Dynasty 830
Saxon Dynasty 831
Saxon Kingdoms 832
Scottish Kingdoms 834
Scythian Empire 835
Seclusion of Monarch 837
Second Empire 837
Seleucid Dynasty 839
Selim I, the Grim 840
Selim III, the Great 840
Seljuq Dynasty 841
Sennacherib 842
Serbian Kingdom 842
Servants and Aides, Royal 844
Seti I 845
Shah Dynasty 846
Shaka Zulu 846
Shalmaneser III 847
Shalmaneser V 848
Shamshi-Adad I 848
Shan Kingdoms 848
Shang (Yin) Dynasty 849
Sheba, Queen of 851
Shih Huang Ti (Shihuangdi) 852
Shilluk Kingdom 853
Shogunate 854
Shoguns 855
Shulgi 856
Shuppiluliuma I 857
Siam, Kingdoms of 857
Siblings, Royal 859
Sicily, Kingdom of 860
Sigismund 861
Sikkim Kingdom 862
Silla Kingdom 863

Sisters, Royal 866
Slavery, Royal 866
Sobhuza I 867
Sobhuza II 868
Sokoto Caliphate 869
Solomon 869
Songhai Kingdom 870
Soninke Kingdom 871
Sotho (Suto) Kingdom 872
Soulouque, Faustin Elie 873
South American Monarchies 874
South Asian Kingdoms 877
South Sea Island Kingdoms 883
Southeast Asian Kingdoms 885
Spanish Monarchies 892
Sparta, Kingdom of 895
Srivijaya-Palembang Empire 896
Stanislas I 897
Stanislaus II 897
Stephen 898
Stephen I (St. Stephen) 899
Stewart Dynasty 900
Strathclyde Kingdom 901
Stuart Dynasty 902
Subjects, Royal 904
Succession, Royal 905
Sui Dynasty 906
Sukhothai Kingdom 907
Suleyman I, the Magnificent 908
Sultanates 909
Sundjata Keita 910
Sung (Song) Dynasty 911
Sunga Dynasty 914
Sunni Ali 915
Susenyos 915
Sussex, Kingdom of 916
Swahili Kingdoms 916
Swazi Kingdom 917
Swedish Monarchy 918
Syrian Kingdoms 920
Tahitian Kingdom 922
T'ai Tsu (Taizu) 923
T'ai Tsung (Taizong) 924
Taifa Rulers 925
Tamerlane (Timur Leng) 925
T'ang Dynasty 926
Tarquin Dynasty 929
Tarquin the Proud 930
Taufa'ahau Tupou IV 930
Taxation 931

Tewodros II 932
Theater, Royal 932
Thebes Kingdom 933
Theodora 935
Theoderic the Great 936
Theodosius I, the Great 937
Thessalonika Kingdom 938
Thibaw 939
Thrace Kingdom 940
Three Kingdoms 940
Thutmose III 941
Tiberius 942
Tibetan Kingdom 943
Tiglath-Pileser III 944
Tikar Kingdom 945
Tio Kingdom 945
Titus 946
Tiwanaku Kingdom 947
Tokugawa Ieyasu 948
Tokugawa Shogunate 949
Toltec Empire 950
Tomara Dynasty 952
Tombs, Royal 953
Tonga, Kingdom of 954
Tonking Kingdom 954
Toro Kingdom 955
Toungoo Dynasty 956
Toyotomi Hideyoshi 956
Trajan 957
Tran Dynasty 958
Trastamara, House of 958
Treason, Royal 959
Tribute 960
Trinh Dynasty 961
Trojan Kingdom 961
Tsars and Tsarinas 962
Tshekedi Khama 963
Tudor, House of 963
Tughluq Dynasty 966
Tulunid Dynasty 966
Tupac Yupanqui 967
Turkic Empire 967
Tutankhamen 968
Tutsi Kingdom 969
Tyranny, Royal 970
Tz'u Hsi (Cixi) 972
Udaipur Kingdom 973
Uighur Empire 973
Ulster Kingdom 974
Umayyad Dynasty 975

United Arab Emirates 977
Urartu Kingdom 978
Ur-Nammu 979
Uthman dan Fodio 979
Utkala (Orissa) Kingdom 980
Uzbek Kingdom 980
Vakataka Dynasty 981
Valois Dynasty 982
Vandal Kingdom 983
Varangian Kingdoms 984
Vasa Dynasty 985
Venetian Doges 985
Victor Emmanuel II 987
Victoria 987
Vietnamese Kingdoms 989
Vijayanagar Empire 990
Viking Empire 991
Virachocha 994
Visigoth Kingdom 994
Vlach Principality 996
Vladimir Princedom 997
Waldemar I, the Great 998
Wang Kon 999
Wanli 1000
Warfare 1000
Weddings, Royal 1002
Wei Dynasties 1003
Welsh Kingdoms 1004
Wen Ti (Wendi) 1005
Wenceslas IV 1005
Wessex, Kingdom of 1006
Wilderness, Royal Links to 1007
Wilhelm II 1008

Wilhelmina 1009
William and Mary 1010
William I 1011
William I, the Conqueror 1012
William II (William Rufus) 1015
Windsor, House of 1015
Witchcraft and Sorcery 1017
Wu Tse-t'ien (Wu Zetian) (Wu Zhao) 1018
Xerxes 1019
Xia (Hsia) Dynasty 1020
Yadava Dynasty 1021
Yamato Dynasty 1021
Yaroslav I, the Wise 1025
Ya'rubi Dynasty 1025
Yemen Rulers 1026
Yi Dynasty 1027
Yi Songgye 1029
Yoritomo 1030
York, House of 1030
Yoruba Kingdoms 1031
Yuan Dynasty 1032
Yung Lo (Yongle) 1035
Zand Dynasty 1035
Zanzibar Sultanate 1036
Zapotec Empire 1037
Zara Ya'iqob 1038
Zimbabwe Kingdom, Great 1038
Zulu Kingdom 1040

Bibliography *1043*
General Index *I-1*
Biographical Index *I-21*

LIST OF FEATURES

Monarch Lists and Family Trees

Ashikaga Shogunate 61
Aztec Empire 85
Bourbon Dynasty 120
Byzantine Empire 136
Caliphates 144
Ch'in (Qin) Dynasty 177
Ch'ing (Qing) Dynasty 181
Chou (Zhou) Dynasty 184
East Asian Dynasties 252
Egyptian Dynasties, Ancient
 (Eighteenth–Twenty-sixth) 266
Egyptian Dynasties, Persian, Hellenistic,
 and Roman 271
English Monarchies 282
French Monarchies 318
Habsburg Dynasty 361
Han Dynasty 369
Hanover, House of 371
Hashemite Dynasty 377
Hawaiian Kingdoms 382
Hohenzollern Dynasty 406
Javan Kingdoms 459
Kamakura Shogunate 481
Koguryo Kingdom 504
Koryo Kingdom 509
Liang Dynasties 527
Ming Dynasty 618
Mughal Empire 638
Nara Kingdom 663
Ottoman Empire 702
Paekche Kingdom 708
Premysl Dynasty 752
Roman Empire 792
Russian Dynasties 806
Shang (Yin) Dynasty 850
Silla Kingdom 864
South American Monarchies 875
South Asian Kingdoms 878
Southeast Asian Kingdoms 886
Spanish Monarchies 892
Stuart Dynasty 903
Sui Dynasty 906
Sung (Song) Dynasty 914
T'ang Dynasty 928
Tokugawa Shogunate 949
Tudor, House of 965

Visigoth Kingdom 995
Windsor, House of 1017
Yamato Dynasty 1022
Yi Dynasty 1027
Yuan Dynasty 1033

Royal Places

Bourbon Dynasty: Versailles 119
Carolingian Dynasty:
 Carolingian Architecture 152
Ch'in (Qin) Dynasty:
 The Tomb of Shih Huang Ti 178
Habsburg Dynasty: The Escorial or
 the Monastery of San Lorenzo el Real . . . 360
Harems: Topkapi Palace 374
Heian Period: Mount Hiei 387
Irish Kings: Tara: The Sacred
 Place of Kings 441
Khmer Empire: Angkor Thom 497
Literature and Kingship:
 The Greek Theater 532
Louis XIV: Versailles 574
Maurya Empire: Pataliputra Palace 588
Meiji Monarchy: The Imperial Palace
 in Tokyo 600
Merovingian-Frankish Kingdom:
 St. Denis 607
Ming Dynasty: Ming Tombs 619
South Asian Kingdoms: Delhi 881
Spanish Monarchies: El Escorial 894

Royal Relatives

Alexander III, the Great: Olympias 29
Austro-Hungarian Empire:
 Franz Ferdinand 75
Bonapartist Empire: Marie Louise 115
Christianity and Kingship: Clotilda,
 Queen of the Franks 186
Divinity of Kings: The Divine
 Kings of Scandinavia 244
French Monarchies: Philippe d'Orleans 320
Habsburg Dynasty: The Empress Elizabeth . . 359
Hellenistic Dynasties: Sister-Wives 388
Inheritance, Royal: Eleanor of Aquitaine . . . 439
Leinster Kingdom: Arthur
 Macmorrough Kavanagh 523
Merovingian Dynasty: Clotilda 605

Napoleon I (Bonaparte): Josephine   659
Nicholas I: Constantine Pavlovich   681
Persian Empire: A Royal Imposter   729
Plantagenet, House of: Isabella   744
Polygamy, Royal: Kösem   746
Royal Families: Illegitimate Children   800
Russian Dynasties: Children of
    the Last Tsar   808
Tyranny, Royal: A Persistant
    Tyrant—Pisistratus   971
Yi Dynasty: Taewongun 1028

Royal Rituals

Accession and Crowning of Kings:
    Accession of King Baudouin   6
African Kingdoms:
    Polygynous Monarchs   11
Akbar the Great: The Jizya Tax   19
Aztec Empire: Aztec Sacrifice   83
Charlemagne: Jury System   166
Conquest and Kingships:
    Divine Right and Conquest   208
Descent, Royal: Mass at the
    Court of Louis XIV   233
Egyptian Dynasties, Persian, Hellenistic,
    and Roman: Rulers as Gods   272
European Kingships: The Royal Touch   293
French Monarchies: Reims Cathedral
    and the French Coronation Ceremony . . .   319
Funerals and Mortuary Rituals:
    Royal Mausolea   326
Gender and Kingship: An Anniversary
    as a Time for Criticism   331
Greek Kingdoms, Ancient: Theseus and
    the Minoan Bull Dance   345
Hirohito: Dating of Eras   400
Holy Roman Empire: The
    Charlemagne Connection   408
Inca Empire: Born of the Son-God Inti   431
Indian Kingdoms: Brahman Sacrifices   435
Khazar Kingdom: Legacy of the
    Khazar Conversion   494

Kingly Body: The Funeral of
    Henry VII of England   501
Koguryo Kingdom: Koguryo Burials   505
Marriage of Kings: Modern Royal
    Wedding Ceremonies   581
Mughal Empire: The Peacock Throne   640
Myth and Folklore: Indonesian
    Puppet Rituals   652
Oda Nobunaga: The Three
    Samurai Warlords   693
Ottoman Empire: Religious
    Authority of the Sultan   701
Regalia and Insignia, Royal: The
    Thai Coronation Ceremony   775
Roman Empire: The Games and
    Shows of Augustus Caesar   794
Sung (Song) Dynasty: Sung
    Landscape Painting   913
Swazi Kingdom: The Power of Ancestors . .   918
Toltec Empire: Toltec Art   951
Warfare: Aztec Coronation Rituals 1001
William I, the Conqueror:
    William's Landing 1014

Maps

African Kingdoms and States, 1500–1800 . .   12
The Aztec and Maya Empires   84
The Bonapartist Empire, 1812   116
The Byzantine Empire, ca. 565 C.E.   135
The Carolingian Empire   151
The Ch'ing (Qing) Dynasty, ca. 1800   180
European Colonial Empires, 1914   199
The Holy Roman Empire   409
The Inca Empire   432
The Macedonian Empire of
    Alexander the Great   560
The Aztec and Maya Empires   592
The Mongol Empire, Late 13th
    Century C.E.   632
The Mughal Empire   641
The Ottoman Empire, 1683   703
The Persian Empire   730
The Roman Empire   795

WORLD MONARCHIES AND DYNASTIES

VOLUME 3

NABATAEAN KINGDOM. *See* ARABIA, KINGDOMS OF

NABOPOLASSAR (d. 605 B.C.E.)

Founder of the Chaldaean dynasty of ancient Babylonia, who helped bring about the downfall of the Assyrian Empire. Nabopolassar (r. 626–605 B.C.E.) expanded the Babylonian Empire through extensive military conquest.

Born into a humble family and probably illiterate throughout his life, Nabopolassar was elected by the Chaldaean people in 626 B.C.E. to defend Babylon against an invasion from the south by the People of the Sea. The Babylonians at this time were governed by the Assyrian Empire, but the death of the Assyrian king Ashurbanipal in that same year provided Nabopolassar with an opportunity to break away from Assyrian governance and establish Babylonian independence.

Nabopolassar's own records show that he immediately adopted an aggressive stance toward the Assyrians, but it was not until 612 B.C.E. that he succeeded in creating an alliance between his armies, those of King Cyaxares (r. ca. 625–585 B.C.E.) of the Medes and those of the Scythians. Cyaxares and Nabopolassar also signed a treaty by which the Medes gained control of northern Mesopotamia, leaving Babylon in control of southern Mesopotamia. The combined armies attacked the Assyrian capital of Nineveh and destroyed much of the city, including the great library of Ashurbanipal and the splendid Temple of Ishtar. The fall of the city marked the end of the Assyrian Empire.

Much of the populace of Nineveh was slaughtered, although a few Assyrian nobles led by Ashur-uballit, a member of the Assyrian royal family, survived and fled to the west, where they took sanctuary with the Egyptians. This led to a second battle in 605 B.C.E., this time against the Egyptians at the city of Karchemish in the Levant. Once more Nabopolassar's armies were supported by the Medes, and once more the combined force was triumphant.

Shortly after this victory, Nabopolassar died, and the throne passed to his son Nebuchadrezzar II (r. 604–562 B.C.E.), who built a Neo-Babylonian Empire.

See also: ASHURBANIPAL; ASSYRIAN EMPIRE; CYAXARES; MEDES KINGDOM; NEBUCHADREZZAR II; SCYTHIAN EMPIRE.

NADIR SHAH (1688–1747 C.E.)

Peasant warlord who ended the Safavid dynasty of Persia, ruled as shah of Iran (r. 1736–1747), and briefly restored the Persian Empire through a prolonged series of brilliant military campaigns.

A member of the Sfshar tribe of Iran, Nadr Beg was born in a shepherd's tent in northeastern Iran in 1686. In 1704, he and his mother were captured and enslaved by Uzbek raiders. His mother died while in bondage, but Nadr escaped and became a highly successful bandit. Nadr led his robber band in capturing the cities of Kalar, Meshed, and Nishapur. He then declared his troops loyal to Tahmasp II (r. 1729–1732), the embattled Safavid claimant to the throne of Iran. In a series of brilliant military victories between 1729 and 1730, Nadir (having changed his name at this point) defeated the occupying Afghans and installed Tahmasp on the throne. The grateful shah named Nadir sultan of Khorasan and Kerman, and as ruler of these cities Nadir gained a reputation for skill and bravery.

Nadir next defeated the Turks at Hamadan in 1731 and placed Iraq and Azerbaijan under Iranian control. He crossed the newly won territories from west to east, a distance of 1,400 miles, to quell a revolt in Herat in northwestern Afghanistan. Meanwhile, left on his own, Tahmasp lost all that Nadir had gained in a quick war with the Turks, to whom he ceded Georgia and Armenia in 1732.

Frustrated and angered by Tahmasp's ineptitude, Nadir returned from Herat in 1732 and deposed Tahmasp in favor of the shah's infant son, Abbas III (r. 1732–1736). Nadir assumed the regency of the realm and then marched against the Turks. The Turks, however, were not surprised this time by the brilliant upstart, and Nadir suffered one of his few defeats in an enormous battle near Samara. Within a year, Nadir had raised and trained another huge army, and subsequently met and overwhelmed the Turks at the battles of Leilan and Baghavand in 1735.

Nadir now turned his attention to Russia, which succumbed to his threats and returned Caspian provinces and cities taken a decade earlier by Russian ruler Peter I the Great (r. 1682–1725). After accepting these concessions from Russia, Nadir entered the Persian capital of Isfahan, lauded by all as the restorer of the Persian Empire. Nadir named himself shah and began the Afshar dynasty in 1736, after ending the Safavid dynasty by deposing Abbas III.

Convinced that war would remain inevitable as long as the Turks and Persians practiced conflicting forms of Islam, Nadir produced a simple solution— he declared that, henceforth, all Persia would renounce the Shi'a faith and would become Sunni Muslim. For the next year or so, Nadir persecuted the Shi'a faithful. Then, bored with religious insurrections, he raised an army of 100,000 men and led it into Afghanistan in 1737.

Within a year, Nadir had conquered the Afghan cities of Kandahar and Kabul and continued eastward toward the rich prize of India. After crossing the Himalayas, he met the army of Muhammad Shah (r. 1719–1748), the Mughal emperor of India, on the plain of Karnal. Nadir defeated the Mughal ruler's troops in one day, then proceeded unopposed into the Mughal capital of Delhi. From that great city he removed all portable wealth, including the astounding Peacock Throne of the Mughals and the fabulous Koh-i-noor diamond. Returning to Persia, he attacked the Uzbeks and secured Persian dominion northeast to the River Oxus.

Harsh even in youth, Nadir Shah became progressively crueler, more tyrannical, and more paranoid as he grew older. Despite his brilliant military victories, his people came to hate him for the ruinous taxation he imposed on them, taxes made unnecessary given the extent of the spoils he won from India and other conquered states. Wherever he traveled, Nadir ordered massive executions to quell real and imagined rebellions. Even his own family fared no better; all his sons were killed either by his own hand or upon his orders.

A similar fate awaited Nadir Shah. In 1747, during a campaign against the Kurds, four members of his bodyguard attacked him in his own tent. Almost sixty years old, Nadir Shah killed two of his assailants before succumbing to the attack. Shortly after his death, civil war and chaos descended upon the empire he had forged. Despite Nadir's short reign and cruel final years, he is generally considered one of Persia's greatest rulers.

See also: SAFAVID DYNASTY.

NAM VIET KINGDOM

(207–111 B.C.E.)

Ancient kingdom in present-day Vietnam that many experts consider the first historical Vietnamese kingdom, marking the beginning of Vietnamese history.

The kingdom of Nam Viet was founded in 207 B.C.E., when General Trieu Da, a Chinese commander, overthrew the local Chinese authorities of Vietnam following the collapse of China's Ch'in dynasty. He killed all local Chinese who were still loyal to the emperor and declared himself king of the territory. Trieu Da took the royal name Trieu Vu Vuong, quickly enlarged his new kingdom through further conquest, and renamed it Nam Viet.

Encompassing present-day southern China and northern Vietnam, the Nam Viet kingdom incorporated the legendary state of Au Lac, which was located in the heart of the Red River Valley (in present-day northern Vietnam). Au Lac emerged out of the declining Hong Bang dynasty, the earliest Vietnamese dynasty, and it only lasted fifty years. Many Vietnamese historians consider the incorporation of Au Lac into Nam Viet to be the end of legendary accounts and the true beginning of modern Vietnamese history.

For the next 100 years after its founding, Nam Viet saw much conflict between King Trieu Vu Vuong and his successors and the Han emperors of China, who sought to expand their empire. Throughout the period, Nam Viet came increasingly into the Chinese sphere of influence, and in return for annual tribute, the Chinese offered Nam Viet protection from its enemies.

Finally, in 111 B.C.E., a Han Chinese army under the leadership of Emperor Wu-ti (r. 141–87 B.C.E.) reconquered Nam Viet and captured and killed its king. The Chinese renamed Nam Viet the kingdom of Annam ("pacified south") and went on to rule the kingdom almost continuously for more than 1,000 years.

See also: HONG BANG DYNASTY; SOUTHEAST ASIAN
KINGDOMS; VIETNAMESE KINGDOMS.

NANCHAO KINGDOM (700–800s C.E.)

Kingdom of unknown origins located in the southern region of China in Yunnan province.

The Nanchao kingdom was established sometime during the first half of the eighth century in western and northwestern Yunnan. The kingdom had a largely Thai population, even though its rulers were of a different ethnicity, most probably southern Chinese.

Between 757 and 763, armies led by the second Nanchao ruler, Ko-lo-feng (r. 748–778), conquered upper Burma and much of lower Burma. Soon after this conquest, Ko-lo-feng built a fortress in the upper Irrawaddy Valley to control the indigenous Pyu population, a number of whom were enlisted into his armies. Chinese records contain accounts of Pyu soldiers who served with the Nanchao forces that captured Hanoi in 863.

Ko-lo-feng's conquest of Pyu cities was successful in reopening the old trading road to India via upper Burma. The reopening of this route greatly contributed to the flourishing of trade and development in the region. Contemporary writers wrote of the production and trading of gold, amber, salt, horses, elephants, and other goods.

After Ko-lo-feng's death, his successor and grandson, I-mou-hsun (r. 778–808), continued to expand Nanchao's control over the neighboring states in the region of Burma. Nanchao armies twice invaded China and raided Tongking and Annam in Vietnam, which were then under Chinese control. In 791, I-mou-hsun acknowledged the overlordship of China; he sent an envoy there in 800 with a present of Pyu musicians.

Through the auspices of I-mou-hsun, relations between the Pyus and China were initiated and maintained.

Chinese histories make very little mention of the Nanchao kingdom after the region was subdued by the Chinese in the ninth century C.E. By the twelfth century, Nanchao was no longer mentioned in Chinese court records. In 1103 and 1106, Kyanzittha (r. 1084–1113), the king of Pagan kingdom in central Burma, sent two missions to China. The diplomats he sent requested Chinese assistance in subduing Tali, the successor of the old Nanchao kingdom, which was conducting regular raids on northern Burma.

See also: SOUTHEAST ASIAN KINGDOMS.

NAPLES, KINGDOM OF

(1100s–1861 C.E.)

Kingdom that occupied much of the southern portion of the Italian Peninsula between the twelfth and nineteenth centuries. A hotly contested area since its emergence in the twelfth century, the kingdom of Naples did not see lasting peace until its unification with the rest of Italy in 1861. Even today, the effects of centuries of continual struggle and exploitation can be seen throughout southern Italy.

The history of the kingdom of Naples is inextricably linked with that of the kingdom of Sicily, as the two were frequently united under the same rule throughout their existence. Consequently, it is difficult to attribute a precise date to the foundation of Naples, though many historians argue that the investiture of Count Roger II (r. 1105–1154) as king by Pope Innocent II in 1130 marks a crucial moment in the history of both kingdoms.

NORMANS, GERMANS, AND FRENCH

Roger II was the nephew of Robert Guiscard, a Norman nobleman who drove the Byzantines out of southern Italy in the eleventh century. Roger was granted most of the land taken by his uncle after a struggle over the papal succession made him one of the most powerful individuals on the Italian Peninsula.

The reign of Roger II was progressive and prosperous. But the Normans were displaced by the ascendancy of the German Holy Roman emperors at the end of the twelfth century, beginning with Henry VI (r. 1090–1097). Henry's son and successor, the powerful emperor Frederick II (r. 1212–1250), took over Naples in 1197 and became one of the most powerful figures of the German Hohenstaufen dynasty.

Hohenstaufen rule of Naples was effectively challenged in 1197, when Pope Clement IV named Charles of Anjou, who ruled as Charles I (r. 1266–1284), head of the kingdom. Clement had feared the power of the Hohenstaufens, and he also wanted to punish the family for its refusal to recognize papal supremacy over the lands conquered by Robert Guiscard.

In the dynastic struggles that followed the accession of Charles of Anjou, the kingdom of Naples separated from Sicily. The neighboring kingdoms warred intermittently until the late 1300s, when Queen Joanna of Naples (r. 1343–1381) granted limited sovereignty to Frederick III of Sicily (r. 1355–1377).

Questions surrounding Joanna's successor created more problems for the kingdom of Naples because she named Louis of Anjou heir to the throne over the objections of Pope Urban VI, who supported Charles of Durazzo. Charles had Joanna murdered and took the throne, ruling as Charles III (r. 1381–1386).

The Anjou (or Angevin) and Durazzo (the Spanish house of Aragón) lines continued to war despite Charles's apparent victory, setting the stage for an international struggle for control of Naples, with France and Spain each vying for supremacy. It was not until 1501 that the battles ceased, with Spain taking possession of Naples in accordance with the Treaty of Blois.

SPANISH RULE

The Spanish rule over the kingdom of Naples was brutally oppressive, especially as the overwhelming majority of the tax burden fell on the shoulders of poor farmers. The inability of farmers to reinvest their income in the land led to a steep decline in agricultural production, bringing with it widespread famine and social unrest.

Although some local uprisings took place in response to this situation—most notably in 1598, 1647, and 1670—these were all put down with vicious severity. It was not until 1707 that Spanish rule came to an end, as Austria took control of Naples in the War of the Spanish Succession (1701–1714). The two hundred years of Spanish rule between 1505 and 1707 left Naples economically and socially devastated.

Austrian control of Naples was brief. The Spanish returned to the kingdom in 1738, when the Spanish prince Don Carlos of the house of Bourbon took control of both Naples and Sicily in the wake of the War of the Polish Succession (1733–1735). Don Carlos, who became Charles III of Spain (r. 1759–1788), tried to establish some progressive reforms in Naples, instituting various economic and administrative changes. He became mildly popular for doing

so, but the years of misuse made his job difficult, and most of his aims went unmet.

More change in Naples was set in motion by the marriage of Charles's son, Ferdinand IV (r. 1759–1816) to Marie Caroline, the daughter of Maria Theresa of Austria and sister of Marie Antoinette of France. Marie Caroline was a powerful queen, who successfully purged Naples of Spanish influence and solidified an alliance with both England and Austria.

The French Revolution, in which Marie Caroline's sister, Marie Antoinette, fell under the guillotine, led Naples into war with Republican France. This began a disastrous series of battles that saw Naples change hands numerous times. This difficult period ended in 1816, with Ferdinand IV in control of a unified Naples and Sicily, known as the Kingdom of the Two Sicilies.

Both internal and external forces challenged this arrangement, however, and Ferdinand's successors did little to endear themselves to their subjects; fierce brutality and extravagant spending marked their reigns. The Italian movement for unification, or *Risorgimento,* led by Giuseppe Garibaldi and Victor Emmanuel II (r. 1849–1878), eventually conquered the Kingdom of the Two Sicilies and united the entire Italian Peninsula as one nation in 1861.

See also: ANGEVIN DYNASTIES; ANJOU KINGDOM; ARAGÓN, KINGDOM OF; FREDERICK II; HOHENSTAUFEN DYNASTY; HOLY ROMAN EMPIRE; MARIA THERESA; MARIE ANTOINETTE; NORMAN KINGDOMS; SICILY, KINGDOM OF; VICTOR EMMANUEL II.

FURTHER READING

Acton, Harold. *The Bourbons of Naples.* New York: Barnes & Noble, 1974.

NAPOLEON I (BONAPARTE)

(1769–1821 C.E.)

French military leader and emperor (r. 1804–1815), whose battlefield genius and passionate ambition for power enabled him to conquer nearly all of Western Europe in the early nineteenth century.

RISE TO POWER

Unlike many other men and women who rose to the throne, Napoleon Buonaparte (more commonly known as Bonaparte) was born into an aristocratic but not particularly powerful family. Napoleon's father, a lawyer and low-level political figure, and his mother, a minor noblewoman, raised the future emperor and his brothers and sisters on the Mediterranean island of Corsica, which was then controlled by France.

After being sent off to a French military school as a child, Napoleon was granted a military commission at the young age of sixteen and quickly rose through the ranks to become an officer in the artillery corps. The outbreak of the French Revolution in 1789 spurred the republican ideals of Napoleon and his family, as well as their support of French nationhood. As a result, they were forced to leave Corsica, which had few sympathizers for the revolutionary cause, and go to the French mainland. From this time forward, Napoleon was completely committed to the cause of France.

In France during the Revolution, Napoleon played a key role in repelling the British and Spanish forces that had invaded in an attempt to keep the Revolution from spreading to other parts of Europe. After this clash, known as the battle of Toulon (1793), Napoleon was given charge of a brigade and sent to Italy, where the French were driving out the occupying Austrian army, which had also been at war with France in the wake of the Revolution. A string of successes awaited him there, but not before events occurred in Paris that introduced his name to all of France.

MILITARY MIGHT

As post-Revolutionary France struggled to create and maintain a working government, a backlash movement began with the goal of returning the royal family to the throne. In 1795, royalist forces rose up in Paris to challenge the Republican government. Napoleon, at the head of the army opposing this revolt, utterly defeated the rebels and put down the uprising in one day's time. As a result of this victory, Napoleon was put in command of the entire French army in Italy, and he also won the hand of his wife, Josephine, whom he married in the spring of 1796.

In Italy, Napoleon overwhelmed the Austrian forces in 1796–1797 and was greeted by the Italian people as a liberator, though he did little to help improve their social situation. Napoleon's popularity rose in France as well, as word of his victories came back to Paris, along with captured money for the French treasury. Napoleon rather unexpectedly concluded the war with Austria in the autumn of 1797

After defeating the Austrians in Italy, the French general Napoleon Bonaparte crossed the Alps back into France, where he became ruler of the country. In this famous painting by French artist Jacques Louis David, *Napoleon Crossing the Alps,* the future emperor is in the heroic pose of a conquering hero.

with the Treaty of Campo Formio, which gave France the Austrian kingdoms. With Austria driven back, Napoleon next set his sights on Great Britain, the only European power remaining with the strength to issue a serious challenge to France.

Realizing that an invasion of Great Britain was not likely to succeed, Napoleon decided to wage indirect war on that nation in the spring of 1798 by conquering Egypt and cutting the British out of the Mediterranean and Indian trade routes. It was here, however, that the French navy suffered a setback at the hands of British admiral Horatio Nelson, who caught and annihilated the French fleet near the Nile Delta in August 1798. Napoleon, who had been defending the Egyptian mainland against an Ottoman attack, returned to France in 1799 when word reached him that the Republican government was rapidly losing the territories he had gained throughout the continent.

ABSOLUTE POWER

Napoleon returned to Paris to find a government riddled with corruption and a population eager for a

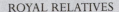

ROYAL RELATIVES

JOSEPHINE (1763–1814 C.E.)

A well-known beauty, Josephine married Napoleon largely because of his powerful position as head of the French army in Italy. Born Josephine de la Pagerie, the future empress was married to French general Alexandre de Beauharnais in 1779. Made a widow by the execution of Alexandre during the Reign of Terror in 1794, she was free to marry the increasingly powerful Napoleon, which she did in 1796.

Examination of their correspondence reveals that Josephine never had much feeling for Napoleon, and the extramarital affairs that each had, sometimes with the other's knowledge, certainly betray a difficult marriage. Since the union of Napoleon and Josephine did not produce an heir to the throne (she did have two children from her previous marriage), the empress was aware that she would likely be divorced and abandoned. Indeed, they did divorce, but Napoleon's enduring respect for Josephine's good sense led him to consult with her several times after their divorce. Josephine was a prominent social figure of the time, and her death was mourned by many of the prominent families of Europe.

replacement. Working with high officials, Napoleon staged a coup in 1799 and was named first consul of the new government, a position that, in effect, gave him authoritarian control of France.

Napoleon immediately set about consolidating his power, abolishing many of the democratic gains of the Revolution and putting all aspects of the state under a powerful central government. He was able to appease his internal enemies, especially in the Church, but he made this and other French institutions subject to government control. By 1802, Napoleon was sufficiently powerful to name himself consul for life, and he pushed through a new constitution that refigured France as an absolute monarchy.

Success to the East

With Napoleon at the helm, France was able to defeat, both militarily and diplomatically, all of its enemies on the continent by 1803, and was once again locked in a struggle with Great Britain for European supremacy. Although the French army was clearly superior on land, the British navy had controlled the seas since Nelson's first defeat of France in 1798; thus a stalemate occurred, with neither side eager to advance upon the other. This situation remained until

1804, when Napoleon was declared emperor of the French by a nationwide election. This move, and the extension of France further into Italy the next year, drew Austria and Russia back into the war.

Napoleon launched an offensive in the east in 1805 and drove back the Austrians and the Russians, who were under the command of Tsar Alexander I (r. 1801–1825). After a crushing defeat at Austerlitz in December of 1805, the Austrians withdrew from the war, and Napoleon was able to take the nearby Prussian territories with relative ease. By 1807, Napoleon had forced Alexander and Frederick William III of Prussia (r. 1797–1840) to give up much of their territory and join him in an alliance against the British, who had once again drawn the war in the west to a stalemate.

Trouble with Britain

The British defeat of the French fleet at the battle of Trafalgar in 1805, during which no British ship was lost, had convinced Napoleon of the necessity of an alternative means of warfare against the enemy. With this in mind, he created an arrangement to block British trade by sea through a European embargo known as the Continental System. Britain's naval supremacy and industry kept its economy aloft, however, and Napoleon's plans never achieved their goals.

The Home Front

With French power securely in place on the Continent, Napoleon set about ensuring his legacy in Europe. He filled several European kingdoms with his family members, and in 1809 he annulled his marriage with Josephine, who had not borne him an heir. Napoleon then married Marie Louise, a daughter of the Holy Roman emperor Francis II (r. 1792–1806). In 1811, the marriage yielded a son, François Charles Joseph, who later was hailed by Bonapartists as Napoleon II but never ruled France.

In governmental affairs, Napoleon's lasting contribution was the Code Napoléon, a new and complex legal system. Still in use in different forms today, the Code was an attempt to organize the French legal system into different sections governed by singular statutes. The Code Napoléon placed the numerous local French laws—many of which contradicted each other—under the authority of one clearly defined system. The Code was remarkable in that it was applied everywhere in France, thus making it one of the first national legal codes of the modern era.

DECLINE AND DEFEAT

The fortification of his empire through internal reforms was not enough to protect Napoleon. Trouble began in 1812, when the French, angry at Russia's refusal to adopt the trade blockade of England, invaded the western Russian territories. The campaign was a disaster, and Napoleon was forced to return to France just six months after he set out.

Seeing the French army weakened by its drive into Russia, a new coalition of nations sprang up against Napoleon, with Great Britain, Austria, and Prussia joining the Russian forces against the French ruler. By the spring of 1814, these allies beat back the overextended French army and captured Paris. Napoleon was forced to abdicate the throne and go into exile on the island of Elba, near the coast of Italy.

One year later, Napoleon escaped from Elba and marched on Paris with a huge army of supporters. He quickly reclaimed the throne and prepared to attack British and Prussian forces stationed in the Netherlands. With speed and surprise on his side, Napoleon hoped to divide the two armies and defeat them individually. This was not to be, however.

Crushed at the battle of Waterloo in June 1815, Napoleon was once again forced to abdicate the throne. This time he was imprisoned on the island of St. Helena in the Atlantic Ocean, where he lived in British captivity until his death in 1821.

See also: ABDICATION, ROYAL; BONAPARTIST EMPIRE; CONQUEST AND KINGSHIPS; MILITARY ROLES, ROYAL.

FURTHER READING

Asprey, Robert. *The Reign of Napoleon Bonaparte.* New York: Basic Books, 2001.

Schom, Alan. *Napoleon Bonaparte.* New York: Harper-Collins, 1998.

NAPOLEON III (1808–1873 C.E.)

President of France, emperor of the French, and last French monarch (r. 1848–1870), who was largely responsible for transforming Paris from a partly medieval city to a modern one.

Born in 1808, Louis Napoleon Bonaparte was the son of Louis Bonaparte, brother of Napoleon I (r. 1804–1815), and Queen Hortense of Holland. As a result of his uncle's defeat at Waterloo in 1815, Louis Napoleon spent most of his childhood in exile, first in Switzerland and then in England. With the deaths of his elder brother from measles in 1831 and Napoleon I's son, Napoleon II, in 1832, Louis Napoleon became the eldest surviving male of his family, making him the inheritor of the Bonaparte legacy and a contender for the throne of France.

VYING FOR POWER

A devoted follower of his uncle's politics, Louis Napoleon challenged the current king of France, Louis-Philippe (r. 1830–1848), through political writings and several failed attempts at armed rebellion. As a result of the second such attempt at rebellion, he spent most of the 1840s in a French prison. He escaped on the eve of the revolutions of 1848, a series of armed uprisings that began in Paris and spread to many other European capitals.

In the aftermath of the revolutions of 1848, Louis Napoleon won a seat in the new Constitutional Assembly, formed after Louis-Philippe's abdication, and he emerged as the leading candidate for president of the new republic. Running primarily on his family name, Louis Napoleon won by a wide margin, receiving five times the votes of his nearest challenger.

Limited to one term by the new constitution, yet seeking to remain in power, Louis Napoleon dissolved the National Assembly in 1851. The following year he took the title of Napoleon III, emperor of the French, inaugurating the Second Empire (1852–1870).

MODERNIZATION OF PARIS

Napoleon III's deepest impact on the shape of French history resulted from his desire to reshape Paris into the cultural and political center of Europe, while making the city better for its inhabitants. The strong economic growth of the 1850s enabled Napoleon III and the French government to fund widespread renovations of Paris's urban landscape. Such changes were badly needed, as the city had changed little since the Middle Ages but now accommodated a population that had more than doubled during three decades, reaching 2 million by 1870.

Under the direction of Baron George-Eugène Haussmann, Paris became a modern city. New sewers made city thoroughfares cleaner; nearly 1,000 miles of piping and 40,000 new gaslights made the city brighter, and by 1870 eighty million gallons of fresh water entered the city daily through newly constructed conduits. Many of the city's streets were widened and straightened, and they connected major monuments and institutions. The twisted and narrow streets common in medieval cities were now largely gone. In their place was a new and better-organized city, still evident in the Paris of today.

Not everyone looked kindly on these changes, however. The changes had caused the displacement of many poor residents of the city, and rents in the city center rose quickly. Efforts by Napoleon III to liberalize government in the 1860s, by extending voting rights and allowing open dissent, resulted in increased domestic instability and unrest. His brand of moderate monarchy pleased neither the working classes nor the entrenched aristocracy.

FOREIGN POLICY

One of the cornerstones of Napoleon III's foreign policy was the pursuit of an *entente cordiale,* or friendly relationship, with Great Britain. He believed that his country needed an alliance with Britain to reassert France's position in Europe. Unfortunately, this alliance drew France into the Crimean War (1853–1856) and facilitated the unification of Germany under German statesman, Otto von Bismarck.

In an effort to help Italy gain independence from Austria, Napoleon III sent troops to Italy in 1859, but the expensive venture lessened his popularity within his own country. Napoleon increased French territory by the annexation of Savoy and Nice in 1860 and by the acquisition of Cochin China in 1867.

Napoleon III's effort to gain international power changed the history of Mexico. In 1858, liberals in Mexico led by Benito Juarez took control of the Mexican government, but conservatives had taken most of the treasury. Napoleon convinced Britain and Spain to join forces with him to surround the Mexican coast until Juarez paid Mexico's international debts. The alliance had agreed that there would be no intrusion into Mexico or interference with its autonomy.

Soon, however, Napoleon became convinced that Mexico should be ruled by a foreign power. He thus sent 6,000 French troops into Mexico City in 1864 to secure it for Napoleon's chosen ruler of Mexico, Maximilian of Austria (r. 1864–1867), the brother of Austrian emperor Franz Joseph (r. 1848–1916).

Although the French had superior numbers and equipment, they were soundly defeated by the Mexicans at Puebla on May 5, 1864 (a date commemorated in Mexico as Cinco de Mayo). Napoleon then sent 20,000 soldiers, who succeeded in driving Juarez from the capital. In 1865, the United States demanded that French troops withdraw from Mexico, and Napoleon III acquiesced. Only two years later, Emperor Maximilian was captured by Mexican nationals, put on trial, and executed by a firing squad.

As a result of his ineffective foreign policies, Napoleon III found himself in a precarious position both at home and abroad by 1870. Growing tensions between France and Prussia, culminating in war in 1870, precipitated the end of the Second Empire. Napoleon III led his troops personally, and was captured by Prussian forces in September 1870. Soon after, Paris fell to the Germans, and France lost the regions of Alsace and Lorraine. Following the defeat and his eventual release by the Prussians, Napoleon III abdicated the throne in 1870 and joined his family in exile in Britain, where he died from kidney stones on January 8, 1873.

See also: BONAPARTIST EMPIRE; FRENCH MONARCHIES; LOUIS-PHILIPPE; NAPOLEON I (BONAPARTE); SECOND EMPIRE.

FURTHER READING

Price, Roger. *The French Second Empire: An Anatomy of Political Power.* New York: Cambridge University Press, 2001.

Smith, William H. C. *Napoleon III: The Pursuit of Prestige.* London: Collins and Brown, 1991.

NAPOLEONIC EMPIRE. *See*

BONAPARTIST EMPIRE

NARA KINGDOM (710–794 C.E.)

The period in Japanese history between the move of the imperial capital in 710 from Asuka to Heijo-Kyo (now Nara) in the Yamato district, and its move further north to Heian-kyo (present-day Kyoto) in 794. During this period, the Japanese elite looked to China for cultural and political inspiration in shaping a uniquely Japanese nation. The Nara decades were a rich cultural prelude to the brilliant, classical Heian period that followed.

During the Nara period, Japan maintained extensive contact with China via embassies of several hundred men and visiting priests and students. A distinct Japanese writing system based on Chinese characters evolved at this time because of this influence. Also during this period, the first historical chronicles appeared (the *Kojiki* in 710 and the *Nihon Shoki* in 720) to legitimize the divine descent of the emperors from the legendary Jimmu.

Reflecting the Japanese fascination with Chinese culture, the new capital in Nara was laid out in a grid pattern, copying the layout of the Chinese T'ang capital of Chang-an.

THE RITSURYO SYSTEM

During the Nara period, centralized governmental institutions set up during the Taika Reforms of 645 (the Great Change Reforms) rapidly evolved into a highly centralized system of administration known as

The main hall of the Todai-ji Buddhist temple and monastery in Nara, the eighth-century imperial capital of Japan, houses a bronze statue of Buddha (*Daibutsu*). It measures over 50 feet tall.

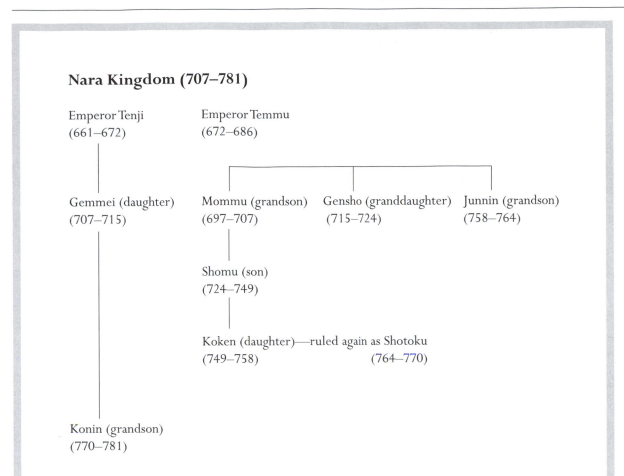

Nara Kingdom (707–781)

Emperor Tenji
(661–672)

Emperor Temmu
(672–686)

Gemmei (daughter)
(707–715)

Mommu (grandson)
(697–707)

Gensho (granddaughter)
(715–724)

Junnin (grandson)
(758–764)

Shomu (son)
(724–749)

Koken (daughter)—ruled again as Shotoku
(749–758)   (764–770)

Konin (grandson)
(770–781)

ritsuryo, which was copied from the Chinese model with significant Japanese modifications.

Under the *ritsuryo* system, administrators and officials were appointed and reviewed according to merit. The country was divided into hierarchical units. All land belonged to the imperial government and was allotted to farmer-peasants and important families for cultivation; in return cultivators were required to pay taxes in produce (rice) or labor. The government was in charge of roads and civil order.

The highly codified *ritsuryo* system remained the administrative framework of Japan for centuries. It was even woven into the new institutions of the *bakufu* system under the Kamakura shogunate established in 1192. Despite the centralized institutions, true centralized control was already problematical during the Nara period, as the imperial government was forcibly reshaped by economic reality and reacted pragmatically to shifts in local and regional power.

Unlike the case in China, rank and position in Japan had quickly become dependent on inherited family ties instead of personal merit. In addition, the peasants, who represented more than 90 percent of the population, bore an inordinate tax burden because of the practice of granting exemptions to courtiers, powerful religious institutions, and those who were willing to cultivate virgin lands. Those with exemptions exercised increasingly independent control over their own domains and constituted an ever-growing counterweight to imperial rule.

UNEASY RULE

At great expense to imperial and provincial coffers, the Buddhist religion gained new legitimacy in Japan during the Nara era. A devout Buddhist who blamed the suffering of the people on his own inadequacies, the emperor Shomu (r. 724–749) commissioned Buddhist temples for each province as well as the enormous wooden Todai-ji temple in the capital, Nara. In addition, Shomu commissioned an equally enormous bronze statue of Buddha to be housed in the Todai-ji. The bronze casting of the Great Buddha was extremely difficult, and Shomu called upon the people to make personal contributions to the effort. The new Buddhist centers were meant to be the physical instruments that unified the spiritual and political realms of Japan. Instead, they became a power base from which Buddhist monks could challenge Japan's rulers.

Emperor Shomu was a member of the powerful Fujiwara clan through his grandmother, who had been an imperial consort. In 729, Shomu married another Fujiwara daughter, the first empress who was not a princess of royal blood. This marriage established the tradition of Fujiwara marriages into the imperial house and reinforced the already considerable influence of the Fujiwara family at the court.

By the end of his reign, Shomu faced a dwindling tax base and growing resistance to central power. Beset by poor crops, famine, earthquakes, and disease (including the Great Smallpox Epidemic of 735–737), the peasants suffered greatly. Since the taxes on state lands were a heavy burden, many peasants simply abandoned their allotted fields and went to work on tax-exempt private estates, even though the legal demands of the nobles and temples might turn out to be equally or more onerous.

By 784, the imperial court was plagued by a depleted treasury and factional strife among the nobles. In addition, it was pressured by the growing interference of wealthy Buddhist monasteries in secular matters. Perhaps hoping to counter all these factors, Emperor Kammu (r. 781–806) moved the capital from Nara to Nagaoka in 784, and then again to Hein-kyo (modern Kyoto) ten years later. This latter move to Hein-kyo marked the end of the Nara period and the beginning of the Heian era. The capital remained in Kyoto for 1,000 years, and during the Heian period (794–1185), the imperial court reached its zenith in refined manners and artistic achievement.

See also: FUJIWARA DYNASTY; HEIAN PERIOD; JIMMU; T'ANG DYNASTY.

FURTHER READING

Bowring, Richard, and Peter Kornicki, eds. *The Cambridge Encyclopedia of Japan*. New York: Cambridge University Press, 1993.

NARAI (1632–1688 C.E.)

King (r. 1657–1688) of the Ayutthaya kingdom in Thailand (Siam), sometimes referred to as Narai the Great, who was best known for his efforts to advance the kingdom's foreign affairs and literature.

Narai was a successful ruler and great warrior who was able to resist his kingdom's long-time rivals in Southeast Asia. In 1662, his troops successfully invaded Burma and the kingdom of Chiang Mai in northern Siam. These and other triumphs exalted Ayutthaya military strength throughout Asia.

Narai also sought to involve his kingdom in the larger arena of world politics. Eager to end the Dutch East India Company's control over foreign trade in Siam, the king developed commercial relations with India and Japan and tried to establish contacts with the British East India Company and the French. When the British decided not to compete with the Dutch in the 1680s, Narai cultivated an alliance with France. The king was assisted in his diplomatic efforts by Constantine Faulcon, a Greek adventurer whose linguistic abilities enabled him to become Narai's chief minister and adviser in foreign policy.

Narai's attempt to court the French included sending diplomatic missions to King Louis XIV of France (r. 1643–1715) in 1680, 1684, and 1686. While on these missions, Faulcon led the French to believe that Narai would make territorial concessions and even convert to Christianity. As a result, the French dispatched progressively larger delegations to Siam in 1682, 1685, and 1687—the last one with six warships containing 600 soldiers.

Narai had thought that the French would be satisfied with his ceding to them the remote territory of Songkhla in southwestern Siam, but he was compelled to let them occupy the important city Bangkok as well. A significant anti-French and anti-Faulcon reaction arose as a result of this occupation. Consequently, when Narai's health started to fail (he suffered from an asthmatic condition), Faulcon was executed by opponents. After Narai died in 1688, his successors expelled the French from the country.

King Narai was a poet, and during his reign, he promoted a revival of Thai literature. Poets gathered together frequently at his court, and he commissioned one of them, Pra Horatibodi, to write a Thai language textbook. The book, *Chindamani,* was intended to counteract French cultural influence, and it ended up being used until the beginning of the reign of the Thai monarch, King Chulalongkorn (r. 1868–1910).

See also: AYUTTHAYA KINGDOM; CHULALONGKORN; SIAM, KINGDOMS OF.

NARAM-SIN (d. ca. 2218 B.C.E.)

King of the Akkadian Empire (r. ca. 2254–2218 B.C.E.) in ancient Mesopotamia, who was one of its greatest rulers and under whom the empire reached its peak of power.

Naram-Sin was the grandson of Sargon (r. ca. 2334–2279 B.C.E.), the legendary founder of the Akkadian Empire in ancient Sumer. Naram-Sin was the fourth king of Sargon's dynasty. He took the throne upon the death of his father, King Manish-tushu (r. ca. 2269–2255 B.C.E.), and reigned for nearly four decades. During his reign, Naram-Sin proved to be as successful a ruler as his grandfather. While at the height of his power, he called himself the "king of the four quarters," which implied that he ruled over all of the known world.

Naram-Sin spent much of his time in battle, quelling rebellions throughout his empire and conquering new lands throughout Mesopotamia. His conquest of the Lullubi tribe in the Zagros Mountains to the north is celebrated in a carved stele, or stone pillar, now at the Louvre Museum in Paris. On the stele, Naram-Sin is shown larger than life, a heroic figure rising up a steep hill as his adversaries fall.

Most of Naram-Sin's military campaigns were successful, and the empire of Akkad reached its greatest extent during his reign. Despite the frequent rebellions within the empire, the people enjoyed a time of relative stability throughout Naram-Sin's rule. Evidence suggests that Naram-Sin created the idea of a divine kingship for himself, a concept that was unusual for the time. Although he did not call himself a god, he credited his power with having come straight from the gods.

In addition to enlarging his domain, Naram-Sin unified the administration of the empire, appointing loyal family members and supporters to positions of power. He also encouraged the growth of trade and embarked upon an extensive public works program, building temples, fortifications, and various monuments celebrating his achievements. When Naram-

Sin died around 2218 B.C.E., he was succeeded by his son Shar-kali-sharri (r. ca. 2217–2193 B.C.E.).

See also: AKKAD, KINGDOM OF; SARGON OF AKKAD.

NASRID DYNASTY (1232–1492 C.E.)

Muslim rulers of the kingdom of Granada, a Moorish kingdom in the southernmost part of the Iberian Peninsula. The Nasrids were the last Moorish dynasty in Iberia, lasting much past the demise of the other Islamic dynasties there.

The Nasrid kingdom of Granada was built on the profits from the silk trade, and it became a great center of Moorish art. Its continued existence, however, was due largely to its tributary relationship with the Christian kingdoms of Castile and Aragón. The Nasrids' inability to muster a truly effective threat to the Christian kingdoms of the Iberian Peninsula made it easier to maintain this tributary existence.

The Nasrid dynasty began with the reign of Muhammad I al-Ghalib (r. 1232–1273), who established a small kingdom in Granada after the fall of the Almohad dynasty of Moorish Iberia. When Christian forces defeated the Almohads at the battle of Las Navas de Tolosa in 1212, most Muslim regions of Iberia were gradually overrun by Christian forces. Granada managed to survive, however, and the Nasrids eventually established their kingdom.

The kingdom of the Nasrids provided a significant haven for Christians and non-Christians alike as the rest of the Iberian Peninsula fell to Christians during the *reconquista* (reconquest). As Christian forces reclaimed territory, Granada received a flood of Muslim and Jewish immigrants who were unwilling to convert to Catholicism as demanded by the Christian monarchs.

Throughout its history, the Nasrid kingdom was continually threatened by the Christian kingdoms of Iberia. In addition to being the last stronghold of the Moors, it had crucial strategic significance, with ports that controlled the entrance to the Mediterranean Sea as well as traffic between Iberia and North Africa.

Over a period of more than two hundred and fifty years, the Nasrids faced numerous threats of invasion and conquest from the Christian kingdom of Castile. However, once Castile united with the kingdom of Aragón through the marriage of Isabella I of Castile

(r. 1474–1504) and Ferdinand II of Aragón (r. 1479–1516), the fate of the Nasrid dynasty was sealed.

The Nasrids faced threats not only from the Christian monarchies in the north, but also from the Muslim empires of western North Africa. At the same time, their location between these groups gave the Nasrids a major role in diplomacy between those groups, allowing them to play the Muslim North Africans off against the Christian rulers. This role helped Granada maintain its independence. The Nasrids were able to maintain sovereignty owing to the wax and wane of the Spanish reconquest and the inability of the Muslims in North Africa to muster a sufficient force to invade.

Through periods of relative peace, such as during the relatively long reign of Muhammad V (r. 1354–1359, 1362–1391), the kingdom of Granada was able to develop into a leading center of Islamic learning and culture. Its greatness is symbolically embodied in the legacy of the beautiful Alhambra palace, which survives today.

The late fourteenth century saw a renewal of the Christian reconquest, which contributed to a subsequent rise in hostility toward Christians in Granada. This provided motivation for the final battles of the Christians against the Nasrids, and it intensified when the Nasrids refused to pay tribute to the Christian monarchs in 1481.

During the final years of the reconquest, between 1481 and 1492, the Nasrids ultimately fell victim not only to Christian military forces, but also to internal wrangling that caused a split within the Nasrid dynasty. Control of the kingdom juggled between two rival Nasrid factions, one led by Muhammad XII (r. 1482–1483, 1487–1492) (known also as Boabdil) and the other by Muley Hacén (Abu-al Hasan Ali) (r. 1464–1482, 1483–1485) and his successor, Muhammad XIII ibn Sa'd al-Zaghal (r. 1485–1487).

By 1492, Isabella and Ferdinand had conquered the tiny kingdom of Granada. The last Nasrid ruler, Boabdil, first found refuge in the Alpujarras region of Andalucia (the southernmost province of Iberia). But he left there in 1493 to go to Morocco in North Africa, where in died in 1534. The end of the Nasrid dynasty and the conquest of the Moorish kingdom Granada paved the way for the Spanish monarchs to move on to other ventures, including the discovery and conquest of the Americas by Spanish explorers and adventurers.

See also: ALMOHAD DYNASTY; FERDINAND II; GRANADA, KINGDOM OF; IBERIAN KINGDOMS; MUHAMMAD XII.

FURTHER READING

Harvey, L.P. *Islamic Spain, 1250 to 1500.* Chicago: University of Chicago Press, 1992.

Lapidus, Ira M. *A History of Islamic Societies.* New York: Cambridge University Press, 2002.

Read, Jan. *The Moors in Spain and Portugal.* Totowa, NJ: Rowman & Littlefield, 1975.

NATIONAL IDENTITY

The culture, values, symbols, and traditions that characterize any specific nation and that can theoretically be understood and shared in by all members of that nation. Though the very idea that all people in a nation can have a common identity has been criticized as at least partially fictional, national identity has been a powerful force for historical change and remains so today.

EARLY FORMATIONS

Early efforts at generating national identity were thwarted by the limits of technology and distance, and people tended to identify more with small geographic areas and specific groups of relatives and neighbors. Some early empires, however, such as that of the Romans in Europe and the Han dynasty in China, made great strides toward the formation of widespread national identities through such projects as universal citizenship and the formation of state religion.

The most successful rulers of these empires, such as the Roman emperor Augustus (r. 27 B.C.E.–14 C.E.) and Emperor Wu Ti (Wudi) (r. 140–87 B.C.E.), took a very active role in promoting the unity of their people and consequently came to be seen as early national symbols. Images of both rulers, for instance, continued to appear on coins and in artworks long after their deaths. Although these empires lasted for remarkable lengths of time, both eventually collapsed, largely because of the difficulty of maintaining a cohesive identity across large geographic areas.

THE MEDIEVAL PERIOD

The early medieval period was marked by intense competition among local monarchs and kingdoms, as numerous groups sought to fill the void of power created by the collapse of the Roman and Han empires. This was true not only in China and in Europe, where feudalism soon developed, but even in areas where those powerful ancient empires had had little impact, such as India and Russia. As a result of the continuous territorial warfare that arose from this competition, national identities stagnated or returned to more localized domains for several hundred years.

Although monarchies were generally unstable throughout the medieval period, technological advances in the thirteenth through fifteenth centuries, especially the printing press, enabled the growth of widespread national identities. Improvement in printing technologies was instrumental in the development of national identity in Europe because it allowed for the spread of uniform information across large areas. As a result, it became much easier for distant individuals under the same monarch to identify with each other.

Standardized printing also hastened the consolidation of regional dialects into official national languages. This trend later reached its peak in France, where the French Academy was founded in 1635. To this day, the Academy, run by the French government, serves as the highest authority on the usage and grammar of French language. In 1674, King Louis XIV of France (r. 1643–1715) became the first monarch to head the Academy.

THE MODERN ERA

National identity became a much more prominent and powerful force beginning in the seventeenth century as a variety of changes swept across the world. In Europe, the Peace of Westphalia (1648) initiated the modern state system. In China and Japan, the Ch'ing dynasty (1644–1912) and the Tokugawa shogunate (1603–1868) began their long-lasting and relatively stable reigns. And in Russia, Tsar Peter the Great (r. 1682–1725) instituted a process of rapid Westernization that swept away old traditions and replaced them with new ones. These unrelated phenomena signaled the emergence of modern nations around the globe, and with them, widespread national identities.

Flags and Anthems

Modern national identities express themselves in a variety of ways. Flags, which local groups have used in a variety of forms for centuries, have become national symbols. For instance, the British flag, known as the Union Jack and adopted in 1801, is a representation of the crosses of the patron saints of the three kingdoms that made up the United Kingdom—England and Wales, Scotland, and Ireland—under the rule of one monarch.

Similarly, national anthems have evolved around the world and frequently extol the virtues of the monarchy or even a specific monarch. Britain's "God Save the Queen" is perhaps one of the most well known of these anthems, but Japan's "His Majesty's Reign," Spain's "Royal March," and the Netherlands' "William of Nassau" are other examples of such national anthems. In some countries where monarchies were overthrown, national anthems are specifically antiroyal, such as France's "La Marseillaise" (Song of Marseilles), which scorns the "hateful tyrants" of the French monarchy.

Most countries, however, have national anthems that ignore monarchy altogether, and instead celebrate the nation itself, such as Canada's "O Canada," Denmark's "A Lovely Land Is Ours," and Zimbabwe's "Blessed Be the Land of Zimbabwe." Both flags and anthems continue to serve as strong symbols of national identity today.

Religion, History, and the Arts

Less obvious, though no less important, elements of national identity include religion, history, and the arts. Although many nations in the modern era have discarded the idea of a state religion, domestic religious traditions are still a significant bearer of national identity. In Japan, for example, the Shinto state religion was abolished after World War II, but Shinto and Buddhist shrines and rituals still make up a major part of the lives of most Japanese citizens. A shared history, usually commemorated through national holidays and monuments, is also a critical part of national identity. India's Republic Day (January 26), for instance, marks the anniversary of the adoption of the first constitution of an independent India in 1950. In France, the annual Bastille Day (July 14) marks the day when the French Revolution began in 1789.

Achievements in the arts, both traditional and contemporary, form another crucial aspect of national identity. In Russia, for example, traditional Cossack dances from the sixteenth century are still practiced alongside ballet, which became a major art form in Russia only in the early twentieth century. Other important components of national identity include domestic wildlife, folklore, clothing, culinary traditions, currency, geographic landmarks, and political values.

See also: BODIES, POLITIC AND NATURAL; NATIONALISM.

FURTHER READING

Gillis, John R., ed. *Commemorations: The Politics of National Identity.* Princeton, NJ: Princeton University Press, 1994

Pecora, Vincent P., ed. *Nations and Identities: Classic Readings.* Malden, MA: Basil Blackwell, 2001.

NATIONALISM

A political ideology that considers the betterment of the nation before all other concerns, that holds one's own nation above others, and that inspires the loyalty of individuals to the nation. Nationalism has the potential to lead to national rivalries and conflicts, but it also serves as inspiration to liberate people from foreign oppression and rule.

ORIGINS

Many early kingdoms and empires—such as the Roman Empire—had some traits of nationalist ideologies. But nationalism as it is generally understood today is a phenomenon that began only in the eighteenth century.

The transformation of kingdoms into modern nations in the seventeenth century—especially in Europe, China, Japan, and Russia—established the foundation from which nationalism could develop. Stable nations led to the emergence of widespread national identities, thereby allowing disparate residents of a given nation to see themselves as not only similar in characteristics, but part of a larger body politic as well.

Although this trend had been evolving for several hundred years, it was the American Revolution that began in 1776 and the French Revolution that started in 1789 that ushered in the modern era of nationalist politics. The leaders of these revolutions emphasized not merely the shared destiny of all individuals living in the nation, but also the common end of all individuals and the nation itself. That is, the nation was seen as indivisible from its inhabitants, and

therefore the self-interest of the nation and the self-interest of individuals became one and the same.

Consequently, both revolutions were specifically antimonarchical. The French Revolution was especially influential in this regard because the revolutionary leaders attempted to export their nationalist ideology to other countries in Europe. Although the French revolutionaries were not overtly successful in doing so—France was ultimately defeated by other European military powers—the possibilities that revolutionary nationalism raised for people in other nations were made very explicit by the Revolution. That is, the French exported the idea of nationalism and universal citizenship, though not the actual policies of it.

TWO CENTURIES OF NATIONALISM

The nationalist ideologies of the French Revolution simmered across Europe for a few decades before boiling over in the revolutions of 1848. In one year, nationalist revolutions broke out in Germany, Italy, Poland, Denmark, Austria, Hungary, and France, which had returned to a monarchical form of government.

These new revolutions were nearly all antimonarchical, and they resulted in the overthrow of such royals as Louis Philippe of France (r. 1830–1848). They also forced other monarchs, such as Frederick VII of Denmark (r. 1848–1863), to accept liberal constitutions that severely curtailed the powers of the monarchy. Although none of the 1848 revolutions succeeded in establishing entirely new forms of government, they did liberalize existing governments a great deal and set in motion movements for national unification in Italy and Germany.

Germany

German unification finally occurred in 1871, and the disparate kingdoms of Germany emerged as one of the most powerful nations in Europe. For the next fifty years, Germany was in the grips of nationalist fervor, and these feelings tended to focus on the German monarchs, notably Kaiser Wilhelm I (r. 1871–1888) and Kaiser Wilhelm II (r. 1888–1918). German nationalism became the basis for tremendous military expansion under Wilhelm II, led to an arms race with Great Britain, and greatly increased international tensions throughout Europe by the start of the twentieth century, leading to World War I.

Austria-Hungary

Although nationalism worked to strengthen Germany, nationalist movements within the Austro-Hungarian Empire worked to break that empire apart. A nationalist movement known as pan-Slavism had been developing in the Balkan region throughout the nineteenth century, and it came to a head at the beginning of the twentieth.

Pan-Slavism advocated the national unity of all Slavic peoples, many of whom were under Austro-Hungarian rule. Slavs in the Balkans, supported by pan-Slavic nationalists in Russia and Serbia, were deeply opposed to the Austro-Hungarians, and began agitating for self-rule. These tensions erupted into the Balkan Wars (1912–1913) and ultimately into the assassination of Franz Ferdinand, the heir to the Austrian throne, in 1914. This event, coupled with the international tension surrounding German expansion, ignited World War I (1914–1918). Thus, historians frequently describe World War I as a nationalist war.

China

Chinese nationalism came into bloom at the same time that nationalism was creating a serious crisis in Europe. In 1911, a nationalist group led by Sun Yat-sen succeeded in overthrowing the last Chinese ruler, Emperor Pu Yi (r. 1908–1912), who abdicated the throne the following year. Chinese nationalism, however, sputtered soon after as a result of internal conflict and a Japanese takeover. It reemerged sporadically, most noticeably in the wake of the two world wars.

Japan

Japanese nationalism first emerged after the Meiji Restoration in 1868 and drove Japan on an expansionist track for the next several decades. Nationalism, as well as expansionism, abated briefly following World War I, but it returned quite forcefully in Japan in the 1930s and 1940s. Similar to the German nationalism of the pre–World War I period, Japanese nationalism was unrelentingly militaristic and centered on the emperor, Hirohito (r. 1926–1989). The expansionist policies supported by Japanese nationalists led the country into World War II (1939–1945), in which it was defeated by the Allied powers.

NATIONALISM RECONSIDERED

Although the twentieth century witnessed very violent and destructive nationalist movements, it also saw nationalism as a force of liberation. Many formerly colonized nations, such as India, Algeria, and the Democratic Republic of the Congo, gained their independence through nationalist agitation. Most of these types of nationalist movements achieved success only after World War II.

The twentieth century also experienced some organized international efforts to limit nationalism and offer opportunities for peaceful cooperation, most notably in the presence of the short-lived League of Nations and the current United Nations. The mutual consolidation of many European nations into the European Union in 1993 is a direct reaction to the negative impulses of nationalist politics.

See also: BODIES, POLITIC AND NATURAL; EMPIRE; NATIONAL IDENTITY; POSTCOLONIAL STATES.

FURTHER READING

Anderson, Benedict. *Imagined Communities: Reflections on the Origins and Spread of Nationalism.* New York: Verso, 1991.

Wiebe, Robert H. *Who We Are: A History of Popular Nationalism.* Princeton, NJ: Princeton University Press, 2002.

NAVAL ROLES

Importance of sea power in the reign of a monarch; function of a monarch in the establishment of a navy.

Before the twentieth century, large and small waterways provided the major means of travel. Monarchs endeavored to control navigation routes to protect their territory and the commerce they conducted with other realms. Victories or defeats at sea have changed the fortunes of monarchs and the course of history.

CEREMONIAL POWER

For the Western world, the Mediterranean Sea was the route to political and commercial power. The Greek and Roman empires depended on their naval power as well as their land conquests. An annual ceremony in Venice, first celebrated in 1177 and called The Wedding of the Sea, demonstrated the value placed on naval power. At this event, the chief magistrate would throw a golden ring into the sea and declare the city's right as a major port to exert maritime authority.

In ancient Siam (Thailand), the people depended on river barges for transportation. Kings often staged elaborate royal barge processions during festivals and royal ceremonies and to welcome foreign diplomats. Visitors to Siam in the eighteenth century reported that some of these processions included as many as 400 boats. The processions were occasions for celebration and for demonstration of the king's great naval power since the barges also served as warships. It is said that in the eighteenth century one could find 200,000 boats in the port city of Ayutthaya, attesting to the importance of navigation in the life of the country.

HE WHO RULES THE SEA

Throughout the Age of Exploration, which began in the fifteenth century, it was sea power that determined a nation's might. For example, although its land area is small, the superiority of the Netherlands on the sea in the seventeenth century enabled it to seize many Spanish and Portuguese colonies in the Americas and Asia and to establish itself as a major power.

As an island country, Great Britain also depended on the sea to establish its power. Henry VII (r. 1485–1509) is credited with planting the seeds for what would become the British Royal Navy. Recognizing the naval threats posed by Scotland and France, he constructed his own fleet of fifty-eight armed warships. Henry's successors were not as devoted to the navy as he, and the fleet decreased dramatically during the reigns of Edward VI (r. 1547–1553) and Mary I (r. 1553–1558). Elizabeth I (r. 1558–1603) did rebuild the fleet to some extent, but her major involvement in naval affairs was to decriminalize the activities of seamen such as Sir Francis Drake. This gave Drake and other privateers freedom to harass the ships of other countries. British fleets composed of both private and royal ships attacked Spanish vessels in particular, prompting Spain to form its powerful Armada to sail against English naval operations. Almost half of Spain's ships were destroyed in the ensuing conflict in 1588, drastically reducing Spain's international power.

As sea routes around the world were explored, knowledge about many of them was carefully guarded. Although Prince Henry the Navigator (1394–1460) encouraged the sharing of knowledge about sea travel among cartographers, shipbuilders, and instrument makers in Portugal, he did not want their knowledge to be widely disseminated. As long as other nations did not know how to reach distant lands, Portugal could keep a monopoly on trade with Africa and Asia. King Manuel I (r. 1495–1521) of Portugal declared a death sentence for anyone who shared navigation charts of routes along the African coasts.

Tsar Peter the Great of Russia (r. 1682–1725), who brought his country into the European mainstream, recognized the importance of a strong navy. He had traveled throughout Europe in 1697–1698, returning with plans to modernize his country and make it a great military power. To secure a port easily reached by European ships, Peter began what is known as the Great Northern War with Sweden in 1700. After nearly twenty years, Russia gained much of the Baltic coast. By the time of Peter's death in 1725, Russia had a fleet of more than forty ships and 800 galleys and was becoming a major sea power.

Although the navy has generally been a source of power for a monarch, in the English Civil War (1640–1652), the navy fought against King Charles I (r. 1625–1649). This loss of naval support was probably an important factor in his defeat and capture by the parliamentary forces of Oliver Cromwell in 1649.

See also: COLONIALISM AND KINGSHIP; COMMERCE AND KINGSHIP; CONQUEST AND KINGSHIPS; ELIZABETH I; MILITARY ROLES, ROYAL; PETER I, THE GREAT; POWER, FORMS OF ROYAL; WARFARE.

NAVARRE, KINGDOM OF

(1134–1515 C.E.)

An independent medieval kingdom comprising the modern Spanish province of Navarre and the French department of Basses-Pyréneés. The kingdom of Navarre played an important role in Spanish history because it controlled crucial mountain passes between France and Spain. Isolated from the rest of Spain, Navarre remained Christian as most of the rest of the Iberian Peninsula fell under Moorish influence.

RISE OF THE KINGDOM

In the late 700s and early 800s, the region of Navarre was part of the kingdom of Pamplona, which was ruled briefly by Charlemagne and the Franks. After the death of the first king of Pamplona, Iñigo Arista

(r. ca. 824–851) in 851, Pamplona and the neighboring dukedom of Vasconia were united as the kingdom of Navarre. In 860, the Crown of Navarre went to Arista's son, Garcia I Iñiguez (r. 851–880), who established ties with the Christian kingdom of Asturias and zealously defended his kingdom from Moorish invasion from the south.

When Garcia I was killed in battle against the Emir of Córdoba in 880, the throne passed to his son, Fortun Garcés (r. 880–905), who was captured by the Moors and held prisoner for fifteen years. After a twenty-two-year reign, Fortun entered a monastery, and the Crown passed to Sancho I Garcés (r. 905–925). By the time of his death in 925, Sancho I had succeeded in driving all the Moors from Navarre and in extending his own domain to include much of the region of La Rioja. His son and successor, Garcia I Sanchez (r. 931–970), also engaged in numerous conflicts with the Moors, who still threatened Navarre and other Christian kingdoms in Iberia. Garcia II ruled until 970 and was succeeded by his son Sancho II Garcés (r. 970–994).

PERIOD OF GREATNESS

The most notable ruler of medieval Navarre was Sancho III, the Great (1004–1035), during whose reign the kingdom attained its greatest prosperity and extent. Sancho substantially enlarged his territory through conquest, eventually ruling almost all of Christian Spain. Because of its size and power, the kingdom of Navarre played a central role in the Christian reconquest of Spain from the Moors. Sancho's empire was short-lived, however. At his death in 1035, he divided his territory among his four sons, with the eldest, Garcia III (r. 1035–1054), receiving Navarre.

Garcia's son and successor, Sancho IV (r. 1054–1076), was murdered by his brothers in 1076. From then until 1134, Navarre came under the rule of the kingdom of Aragón. Under Alfonso the Fighter (1104–1134) of Aragón, the combined kingdoms reached their greatest territorial extent as a result of numerous conquests against the Moors. Alfonso had no heirs, and upon his death the kingdoms of Aragón and Navarre separated, with the throne of Navarre going to Garcia IV Ramirez (r. 1134–1150), a descendant of Sancho the Great. Garcia was an ineffective leader, but his son, Sancho VI, the Wise (r. 1150–1194), fortified Navarre and was undefeated in battle.

FOREIGN RULE

From 1234 to 1274, Navarre was united with the French county of Champagne. It was ruled directly by France until 1328, when the kingdom declared its independence and called Juana II (r. 1328–1349) to the throne. Her grandson, Charles III (r. 1387–1425), was called "the Noble" because he brought peace and prosperity to Navarre by instituting governmental reforms and improving transportation throughout the region. Because Charles outlived his sons, the throne went to his daughter Blanca (r. 1425–1441), who was married to John II of Aragón (r. 1425–1479).

After years of civil strife between Blanca's son Charles and his half-brother Fernando, Blanca's grandson Francis Phoebus (r. 1479–1483) eventually succeeded to the Navarrese throne. At this point Ferdinand II of Aragón and Castile (r. 1479–1516) sought to gain sovereignty over Navarre by arranging a marriage between Francis's sister Catherine and Ferdinand's oldest son. Instead, in 1494, Catherine wed a French count. Ferdinand never gave up his hope of ruling Navarre, however, and he annexed most of the region in 1512. The French portion of Navarre, however, remained independent until 1589, when it became part of France.

See also: ARAGÓN, KINGDOM OF; CASTILE, KINGDOM OF; SANCHO III, THE GREAT.

NAZCA KINGDOM

(flourished 100s–600s C.E.)

Pre-Columbian civilization of Peru that flourished prior to the rise of the Incas. Together with the Moche civilization, the Nazca belonged to the Wari culture.

Among the most famous civilizations of South America because of the remarkable Nazca Lines created near the coast of southern Peru, the Nazca are also among the least understood people in the region. Like the Moche people, the Nazca left behind a wealth of ceramic and textile artifacts, along with an important urban center at Cahuachi and a cemetery in Chauchilla.

Working with clues from burial sites at Chauchilla, archaeologists theorize that the Nazca were a stratified society, probably headed by a priestly class. The spread of their distinctive cultural elements, particularly pottery, suggests that the Nazca dominated the southern coastal region of Peru, although this distribution could indicate an economic, or trading, dominance rather than a military one. The Nazca developed a sophisticated system of aqueducts and dams to support their agriculture, and Nazca culture reached its peak between the 100s and 600s.

Of all the archaeological evidence that the Nazca left behind, the most impressive and intriguing are the Nazca Lines. These are a series of some thirty-two huge geoglyphs, which are depictions of figures (spider, monkey, dog, fish, and so forth) created on the surface of the earth by removing dark-colored surface rocks to expose lighter earth or stone beneath. The Nazca images are huge and can only be identified when viewed from a great height. The geoglyphs were never even noticed in modern times until the first airplanes flew over the Plains of Nazca near the Peruvian coast, where the images are located.

The meaning and purpose of the Nazca geoglyphs remain unclear, although there has been no shortage of theories offered to explain them. One of the more fanciful suggests that the lines and figures could only have been created by visiting extraterrestrials, and are intended to be read from space. Another theory holds that the geoglyphs were created on such a huge scale and oriented to a celestial viewer because they were intended to be seen by the gods. More mainstream theorists suggest that the figures served as calendars or as maps of the constellations. In the absence of a written record (the Nazca appear never to have developed a written language), there is no way to prove or disprove any of these theories.

As with many other civilizations in Mesoamerica and South America, the Nazca enjoyed a brief period of cultural ascendancy before abruptly disappearing from their settlements and urban centers. Like the Moche, the disappearance of the Nazca seems to have had no natural external cause: there is no evidence of disaster or war to explain why the people seemed suddenly to abandon their cities. Some experts believe that perhaps the Tiahuanacans of the Lake Titicaca region began intruding upon Nazca territory and that the people abandoned their cities in the face of a more powerful invading force. This is only speculation, however.

See also: INCA EMPIRE; MOCHE KINGDOM; SOUTH AMERICAN MONARCHIES.

NDEBELE KINGDOM (1830s–1890 C.E.)

Kingdom founded by Mzilikazi (r. 1830s–1868) during the violent years of demographic upheaval that also gave rise to the Zulu kingdom.

In the 1830s, southern Africa was the scene of great upheaval. The Dutch had claimed a colony centered at Cape Town, and its settlers, called the Boers, were rapidly moving inland, evicting the native occupants and claiming vast tracts of land for their farms. British settlers, enticed by reports of great mineral wealth, were also claiming territory throughout the region, attempting to displace the Boers and African peoples alike. In response to these threats, a powerful leader named Shaka Zulu (r. 1816–1828) amassed a great army to drive the Europeans away, while simultaneously enriching himself and his followers by raiding cattle from the Bantu peoples of the region.

FORMATION OF THE KINGDOM

Among Shaka's generals was Mzilikazi, who had not joined Shaka's forces by choice. Mzilikazi's people had been allied with the Ndwandwe, against whom Shaka had led a successful military campaign in the early 1800s. The victorious Shaka demanded that Mzilikazi and the defeated Ndwandwe submit to Zulu rule. On the strength of his military prowess, Mzilikazi was made a general and sent out on a cattle raid. Instead of turning the captured animals over to Shaka, however, Mzilikazi kept the animals for himself and headed north, declaring himself a king.

Nzilikazi's new kingdom, like the Zulu kingdom of Shaka, was not geographically based but was centered upon the person of the leader. Also like Shaka, Mzilikazi recruited subjects through conquest. As he and his followers moved through an area, the peoples they encountered were given a choice: become allies or face attack. At first, Mzilikazi enjoyed great success, and his following grew to dominate the region. In 1837, however, his beleaguered neighbors had had enough. An unlikely alliance of Boers and local African peoples of the region expelled Mzilikazi and his Ndebele, forcing them to retreat northward across the Limpopo River.

Entering these new lands, Mzilikazi led his forces against the Shona people, who until this time were the dominant power in the region. Mzilikazi and the Ndebele conquered the Shona, and by this time they also had defeated, or outrun, Zulu troops who pursued Mzilikazi on orders from Shaka. Mzilikazi at last felt secure enough to establish a permanent capital for his Ndebele kingdom at Bulawayo (in present-day Zimbabwe).

Mzilikazi maintained his powerful army, using them to mount raids against neighbors and defend his territory against the expansion of Boer settlements. By 1852, however, his increasingly unsuccessful campaigns against the Boers forced them to acknowledge defeat. The peace that followed did not last long, however. The discovery of rich gold deposits in this part of southern Africa touched off a gold-hunting frenzy among Europeans.

EUROPEAN THREAT

The influx of Europeans, in turn, touched off waves of migration, as indigenous peoples fled the violence and disruption that the gold hunters left in their wake. Many of these refugees came to settle in Ndebele lands but were unwilling to submit to Mzilikazi's rule. Mzilikazi was able to maintain order only through military force, and the years from 1860 until the king's death in 1868 marked a time of great internal strife in the Ndebele kingdom.

Mzilikazi was succeeded on the Ndebele throne by his son, Lobengula (r. 1868–1893). But Lobengula secured the throne only after two years of factional violence had wracked the Ndebele kingdom. Lobengula lacked the personal charisma of his father, and he never managed to reunify the kingdom. He also faced the ever-growing threat of European incursions into Ndebele lands. In an attempt to stabilize his kingdom, Lobengula sought to establish diplomatic relations with the British, entering into an agreement in which the British promised to provide military assistance in return for exclusive mining rights in Ndebele lands.

Unfortunately, this alliance with the British ultimately proved to be the undoing of the Ndebele kingdom. The treaty between Lobengula and Great Britain became the basis on which his new "partner," the British East Africa Company, engineered his overthrow. Mining expeditions sent by the company were escorted by British military troops, whose presence inspired resentment in Ndebele villages. In 1890, some Ndebele attacked the British, precipitating an all-out war that Lobengula was powerless to forestall.

In 1893, after three years of violence throughout Ndebele territory, the British attacked Bulawayo and burned the Ndebele capital to the ground. Loben-

gula and his supporters were forced to flee for their lives. Lobengula spent the next year trying to muster a big enough force to strike back and reclaim his kingdom, but he never got the chance. He died in exile, and with him died the hope of reestablishing the Ndebele kingdom.

See also: AFRICAN KINGDOMS; LOBENGULA; MZILIKAZI; SHAKA ZULU; ZULU KINGDOM.

FURTHER READING

Oliver, Roland, and G. N. Sanderson, eds. *Cambridge History of Africa from 1870 to 1905*. New York: Cambridge University Press, 1985.

NEBUCHADREZZAR II

(d. ca. 562 B.C.E.)

The greatest ruler (r. 604–562 B.C.E.) of the short-lived Chaldean or Neo-Babylonian Empire in Mesopotamia, who is known to history largely for conquering the Hebrew kingdom of Judah and for rebuilding the ancient city of Babylon, transforming it into one of the most magnificent cities in the ancient Near East.

Nebuchadrezzar (also referred to as Nebuchadnezzar) was the son of Nabopolassar (r. ca. 625–605 B.C.E.), a Babylonian leader who revived the Babylonian Empire from his base in Chaldea along the Persian Gulf around 625 B.C.E. Trained to leadership from an early age, the young prince Nebuchadrezzar led an army that crushed the Egyptians under Pharaoh Necho II (r. ca. 610–595 B.C.E.) at the battle of Carchemish in Syria in 605 B.C.E. Learning of his father's death while on that campaign, Nebuchadrezzar sent his army home via a route through northern Mesopotamia, while he took a shortcut through the desert, arriving in Babylon twenty-three days after his father's death to claim the throne.

When the Neo-Babylonian Empire was formed from the remnants of the Assyrian Empire, it took control of all the former Assyrian territories and client states. Among these dependencies was the Hebrew kingdom of Judah. Like other regional rulers caught between the great powers of Mesopotamia and Egypt, the kings of Judah had to play a balancing act that did not always succeed. Encouraged by promises of support from Egypt, Judah rebelled

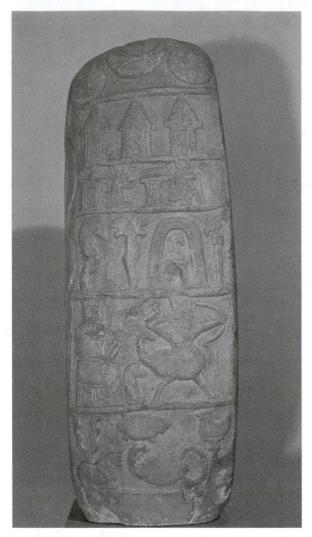

The greatest ruler of the Chaldean Empire, Nebuchadrezzar II is known for his territorial conquests and extensive construction projects, including the fabled Hanging Gardens of Babylon. Inscribed boundary stones, or *kudurrus,* were placed at significant sites and served as records of royal decrees, transactions, and other notable events.

against the Babylonians in 598 B.C.E., only to be defeated by Nebuchadrezzar's forces the following year. King Jehoiachin of Judah (r. 598–597 B.C.E.) and 3,000 of his subjects were exiled to Babylon, but Judah was left intact.

A second Hebrew revolt in 586 B.C.E., started against the advice of the prophet Jeremiah, brought Nebuchadrezzar with a large army to lay siege to the city of Jerusalem. The Babylonians destroyed the city, including Solomon's Temple, and forced many thousands of citizens into exile. This event is bitterly recorded in the Bible (where the Babylonian king is called Nebuchadnezzar and is seen as an instrument of Divine punishment from the Hebrews' god).

Nebuchadrezzar's alliance with the kingdom of the Medes, a powerful state located on the Iranian plateau to the east, was cemented by his marriage to Amytis, daughter of the Median king, Cyaxares (r. 625–585 B.C.E.). According to legend, Nebuchadrezzar built the famous hanging gardens in Babylon to relieve his wife's longing for her mountainous homeland. The alliance with the Medes gave Nebuchadrezzar a free hand to subdue and incorporate all Assyrian lands from the borders of Egypt in the south well into Anatolia (present-day Turkey) in the north.

Under Nebuchadrezzar, an effective bureaucracy governed the Chaldean Empire. Heavy taxes were collected from the people to offset military expenditures and to support Nebuchadrezzar's ambitious construction program, which focused largely on the city and region of Babylon. Nebuchadrezzar built temples, lavish palaces, and massive fortifications. He strengthened and extended the walls of the city, constructed broad processional boulevards, and restored old canals and built new ones for purposes of defense, sanitation, and irrigation. Hundreds of rooms and courtyards were added to the royal palace, and brilliant tile reliefs were used to decorate the palace and other buildings.

In his documents and inscriptions, Nebuchadrezzar claimed universal kingship, granted by the Babylonian god Marduk, who was actually revered throughout Mesopotamia. He also claimed to be a descendant of the Akkadian king, Naram-Sin (r. 2254–2218 B.C.E.), who had ruled nearly two thousand years before. Nebuchadrezzar also claimed the mantle of reformer and fighter for civic justice.

By all evidence a pious follower of the ancient gods of Babylon, Nebuchadrezzar engaged many thousands of workers in rebuilding and adorning temples. One of these was the massive Etemenanki complex in Babylon, which housed an astronomical observatory as well as a temple to Marduk. The Etemenanki may have been the model for the Tower of Babel mentioned in the Bible. Nebuchadrezzar also gathered antiquities into a museum, and he encouraged the arts and literature.

After a long reign of forty-three years, Nebuchadrezzar died peacefully of natural causes in 562 B.C.E. He was succeeded by his son, Amel-Marduk (r. 561–560), the first of a series of weak and ineffective rulers who presided over the rapid decline of the empire. The Book of Daniel in the Bible relates an account of Nebuchadrezzar's madness, but historians discount this story. This probably referred to a later successor, Nabonidus (r. 555–539 B.C.E.), whose eccentric behavior may have led to the fall of Babylon to the Persians less than twenty-five years after Nebuchadrezzar's death.

See also: AKKAD, KINGDOM OF; ASSYRIAN EMPIRE; CYAXARES; JUDAH, KINGDOM OF; MEDES KINGDOM; NABOPOLASSAR; NARAM-SIN.

FURTHER READING
Roux, Georges. *Ancient Iraq.* 3rd ed. New York: Penguin, 1992.

NEFERTITI (ca. 1416–1350 B.C.E.)

Chief wife of Pharaoh Akhenaten (Amenhotep IV [r. 1350–1334 B.C.E.]) of Egypt's New Kingdom, and stepmother of the young pharaoh Tuthankhamun (r. 1334–1325 B.C.E.), who helped her husband launch a period of religious reform in ancient Egypt.

A noblewoman from either the Mitanni kingdom of the Middle East or from the Egyptian royal family, Nefertiti married her husband before he became pharaoh. After he took the throne, Akhenaten gave his wife the additional name Neferneferuaten, which associated her with the sun-god Aten, whose worship became the defining feature of their reign.

From the beginning of Akhenaten's rule, Nefertiti assumed important religious functions, as can be concluded from many portrayals of her alongside her husband in Egyptian sculptures and reliefs from the period. In many portraits, Nefertiti is shown dispensing *maat* (order or truth), a quality said to keep the world in balance by defeating the powers of chaos. One shrine at the temple of Karnak in Luxor was dedicated to Nefertiti alone. She is the only person other than the pharaoh to be depicted being embraced by the divine rays of Aten, the sun-god.

THE AMARNA REVOLUTION
Early in their reign, Akhenaten and Nefertiti staged a religious and political revolution. They imposed exclusive worship of the sun-god Aten and suppressed the powerful priests of Amon-Ra, the supreme Egyptian deity. At their new capital city Akhetaten (Tel-el-Amarna), they appointed many commoners to the administration.

Under Akhenaten and Nefertiti, the royal art of Amarna became less formal and more natural than the previous style, and the official literature of the new regime reflected the actual spoken language. The royal couple imposed these and other reforms by means of absolute power, building a cult around themselves as the center of public art and worship. In fact, the royal family became the virtually exclusive subject of all art at Amarna, even in private homes.

Early portraits of Nefertiti at the temple of Karnak show her with physical features similar to those of her husband, but she later appears as an individual with her own features. One of the most famous portraits of Nefertiti is an elegant painted bust sculpure found at Amarna. Nefertiti is often featured together with the pharaoh and their six daughters in intimate family scenes. She sometimes appears with royal regalia—she was the only one of Akhenaten's wives ever de-

The wife of Pharaoh Akhenaten, Nefertiti helped her husband introduce new religious beliefs in Ancient Egypt, and her likeness appears in numerous portraits and sculptures. This painted limestone bust was discovered at the ruins of Amarna, the capital of Akhenaten's kingdom.

picted with a crown, and many scholars speculate that Akhenaten eventually named her as co-regent.

DECLINE AND FALL

Some twelve years into Akhenaten's reign, Nefertiti seems to have left public life. Some scholars speculate that she opposed her husband's belated compromises with their opponents. Others believe that she returned to Thebes, the old capital of Egypt, to try to win over the dispossessed priests of Amon-Ra.

According to some evidence, Nefertiti outlived her husband and later planned to marry a Hittite prince in order to maintain her power and keep the cause of Aten alive. Or she may have taken on a male persona and ruled herself for two years, with her daughter Meritaten as her official wife. Still other archaeological evidence, however, indicates that Nefertiti died before Akhenaten.

In any event, soon after Akhenaten's death, their religious revolution was forcefully overturned, and the old order was restored. Nefertiti's name and picture were removed from many monuments, as were those of Akhenaten. However, enough of her sensitive, beautiful portraits have survived to stimulate continuing historical and romantic speculation about this remarkable queen.

See also: AKHENATEN; EGYPTIAN DYNASTIES, ANCIENT (EIGHTEENTH TO TWENTY-SIXTH).

NEPAL, KINGDOM OF. *See* SHAH DYNASTY

NERO (37–68 C.E.)

Emperor of Rome (r. 54–68) during a period of great cultural achievement, who in contrast is remembered mainly for his cruelty and his cowardice.

Originally named Lucius Domitius Ahenobarbus, Nero was born on December 15, 37. His father was a Roman consul, Gnaeus Domitius Ahenobarbus, and his mother was Agrippina, the great-granddaughter of Emperor Augustus (r. 27 B.C.E.–14 C.E.). His uncle was the emperor Caligula (r. 37–41), who also ruled Rome for a time and whose instability and cruelty were mirrored in Nero's own reign.

When Nero was eleven years old, his ambitious mother took her fourth and most prestigious husband, Claudius (r. 41–54), then emperor of Rome. Although Claudius already had a son, Brittanicus,

from a previous marriage, Agrippina managed to talk her new husband into adopting Nero as his successor. To strengthen his claim to the throne, Nero married his stepsister, Claudius's daughter Octavia, in 53, and Claudius then died the following year. Nero claimed his imperial inheritance, but he was still very young (he was only sixteen years old). Agrippina therefore exercised a great deal of influence over the early years of Nero's reign, serving as one of his advisers along with his tutor, Seneca the Younger, and Burrus, who led Nero's Praetorian Guard. (The Praetorian Guard was the personal security force sworn to protect the emperor.)

As emperor, Nero quickly discovered that at last he had the opportunity, and the power, to indulge himself as he wished. He is remembered for his decadence, his devotion to spectacles and performances, and his passion for the arts. He fancied himself a singer, ordering the public to attend his performances. This behavior gave rise to the legend that he "fiddled while Rome burned." Nero is also remembered for his unvarying response to those who stood in his way: he had them

The fifth emperor of Ancient Rome, Nero was a cruel, unstable, and decadent ruler who enjoyed grand spectacles and performances. An enthusiast of art and architecture, he spent much of his treasury rebuilding Rome after a devastating fire swept through the city in 64 C.E.

murdered. For instance, in 58, Nero began an affair with a woman named Poppaea Sabina, although he was married to Octavia. His mother did not approve of his affair, and in retaliation he ordered Agrippina killed. He was also responsible for the deaths of many of the major Roman writers of his era, including Lucan, Seneca, and Petronius.

The death of Agrippina marks a period in which Nero's dissolute behavior intensified, perhaps due, in part, to the encouragement of Poppaea. When Nero decided to marry his lover in 62, he had no patience with the inconveniences involved in getting a divorce, he simply ordered Octavia killed. Meanwhile, he moved further and further away from the counsel of his advisers, neglecting his armies and the duties of his office, and turning instead to sycophants and hangers-on who encouraged him in his debauchery.

In 64, the city of Rome suffered a devastating fire, which many believed was set by Nero himself. Nero had developed an enthusiasm for architecture and was frustrated that there was not enough space within the city to accommodate his designs. Nero, however, laid the blame for the fire on the city's Christians and initiated a period of brutal reprisals against the still young religious sect. For the powerful families of Rome, for the army, and even for the Praetorian Guard, Nero had clearly become a problem that could no longer be ignored. In 65 a conspiracy was formed to oust Nero and replace him with a new ruler of their own choosing.

Nero discovered this plot and retaliated in the only way he knew how—killing everyone he suspected of involvement. Following this incident, his instability became ever more blatantly exposed, and revolts became widespread throughout the empire. In 68 Nero's armies, and even his own Praetorian Guard, determined that their loyalty belonged to the office of emperor, not to the man who held it, and that Nero was a danger to the throne. They joined the cause of the rebelling factions, and Nero fled in a panic. With no safe place to turn, he committed suicide on June 9, 68. He was the last of the Julio-Claudian emperors.

See also: CALIGULA; CLAUDIUS; JULIO-CLAUDIANS; JULIUS CAESAR; ROMAN EMPIRE.

FURTHER READING

Grant, Michael. *The Roman Emperors: A Biographical Guide to the Rulers of Imperial Rome, 31 B.C.—A.D. 476.* New York: Barnes & Noble, 1997.
Nardo, Don. *The Roman Empire.* San Diego: Lucent Books, 1994.
Starr, Chester. *A History of the Ancient World.* New York: Oxford University Press, 1991.

NETHERLANDS KINGDOM

(1813 C.E.–Present)

A constitutional monarchy created in 1814 from territories that had been under Napoleonic control, including Belgium, Luxembourg, and the seven provinces that had formed the independent federation of the United Netherlands.

Before their annexation by the revolutionary French government in 1795, the seven provinces of the United Netherlands had been governed by a hereditary *stadholder,* or governor general. The son of Prince William V of Orange (r. 1751–1795), the last *stadholder* became King William I (r. 1813–1840) after commanding Dutch forces in the French Revolutionary wars. William I governed autocratically and soon faced rebellion from Belgium, which declared its independence from the Netherlands in 1830.

William I abdicated in 1840 in order to marry a Catholic countess, which was unacceptable to the Protestant citizens of the Netherlands. His son, William II (r. 1840–1849), met opposition from those who agitated for political and economic reforms. In 1848, with revolution threatening all over Europe, William II accepted a new liberal constitution, which made ministers responsible to the States-General (parliament) instead of to the monarch.

William II's son, William III (r. 1849–1890), was opposed to the liberal constitution and wanted to renounce his right to rule. But he ended up succeeding his father on the throne when William II died in 1849. During William III's long forty-one-year reign, the major force for reform in the Netherlands was the prime minster, Johan Rudolf Thorbecke.

When William died in 1890, his only surviving child, ten-year-old Princess Wilhelmina, inherited the throne. Luxembourg seceded from the Netherlands kingdom that same year rather than accept a female ruler. Because Wilhelmina was too young to rule on her own, her mother Emma acted as regent until 1898.

Queen Wilhelmina (r. 1890–1948) was known for her grasp of affairs of state. In May 1940, when the Netherlands fell to the German Nazi invasion, the royal family fled to England, where Wilhelmina inspired the Dutch resistance through radio broadcasts. In 1948, the ailing Wilhelmina abdicated in favor of her daughter, Juliana (r. 1948–1980), whom the people had come to love for her relief work in a war-ravaged country. As queen, Juliana was known for her social concerns; she continued her postwar relief operations and became president of the Dutch Red Cross. In 1980, Juliana abdicated in favor of her oldest daughter, Beatrix (r. 1980–present), who proved to be more aloof than her mother and who adopted a more managerial style of rule.

As constitutional monarchs, the rulers of the modern Netherlands, like the queen of England today, enjoy only symbolic power. They exercised their only significant political power during World War II, when Queen Wilhelmina had to make decisions in the absence of the States-General and ministers. The monarchy has remained popular among the Dutch citizens of the Netherlands as a symbol of national unity.

See also: JULIANA; ORANGE-NASSAU, HOUSE OF; WILHELMINA; WILLIAM I.

NEVSKY, ALEXANDER (1220–1263 C.E.)

Prince of Novgorod and Vladimir (r. 1252–1263) who defeated the Swedes and, most notably, the Livonian Knights, but who cooperated with the invading Mongols in their subjugation of northern Russia.

Born Alexander Yaroslavich, Nevsky was the son of Yaroslav II (r. 1238–1246), grand prince of Vladimir and one of the most powerful of Russian rulers. Alexander became military commander (prince) of Novgorod at age sixteen. For the next four years he fought the Finns and Lithuanians in the Baltic area, where Novgorod ran its profitable shipping lanes. Then, in 1240, he defeated a sizable and organized army sent by the king Erik Eriksson of Sweden (r. 1234–1250). This victory came near the River Neva and thus earned him the surname of "Nevsky."

After this important battle, Alexander Nevsky had ongoing disputes with the municipality of Novgorod, and the hero was exiled a short time later. In 1236, Pope Gregory IX conspired with the Livonian Knights—an order of knights in the southeastern Baltic area who also had a growing empire in the region—and gave his blessing for a crusade against the prosperous Novgorodians. Faced with this threat, the city fathers of Novgorod thought better of their earlier decision and called back Alexander Nevsky, their heroic military commander. Alexander met and defeated the powerful knights in a fierce battle on the ice of Lake Peipus (near Pskov) in the winter of 1242.

Nevsky returned from this victory to rule a grateful Novgorod. However, during these struggles with the Finns, Lithuanians, Swedes, and Livonian Knights, enormous Mongol armies had subjugated most of eastern and southern Russia. Alexander's own father had agreed to serve the new Mongol rulers before his death in 1246.

Alexander, the great hero who had secured the Baltic, never fought the invading Mongols. Instead, over the next sixteen years, he made three trips to meet the great khan in the Mongol region of Karakorum in Central Asia and developed a close friendship with Batu (r. ca. 1227–1255), the local khan of the Golden Horde (the name of the Mongol state that ruled Russia). However, Alexander did fight against his brother, Andrew, who revolted against the Mongols, and he fought against other Russian principalities that rebelled against them as well.

Eventually, in 1252, Alexander followed his father as grand prince of Vladimir (appointed by his friend, Batu). Through a policy of diplomacy and cooperation, he was able to save Novgorod, Kiev, and several other Russian cities and principalities from bloody reprisals by the Mongols. He also was consistently praised by the Russian Orthodox Church, which was left intact and untaxed by the Mongols. During a diplomatic mission to settle tax disputes with the Mongols in 1263, Nevsky died. He was succeeded as prince of Vladimir by his brother, Yaroslav III (r. 1264–1271). Popular tradition in Russia made Alexander Nevsky a great hero, and he was canonized by the church in 1547.

See also: RUS PRINCEDOMS; RUSSIAN DYNASTIES; VLADIMIR PRINCEDOM.

NGONDE KINGDOM

(ca. 1500–late 1800s C.E.)

Kingdom in eastern Africa that was founded around 1500, when immigrants from what is now Tanzania came into northern Malawi in search of a place to settle.

The founders of the Ngonde kingdom were a Mbundu-speaking people, and, as such, they shared a relationship with the kingdoms known by that name that rose later in Angola. In fact, the rulers of Ngonde, like those of the Mbundu kingdoms, bore the title of *ngola,* from which the modern nation of Angola takes its name.

The Ngonde state was originally organized in small, independent chieftaincies. But around 1600, these individual states united to form a kingdom, most likely in order to participate more effectively in the regional trade that flourished in east Africa. The ruler of the kingdom took the title *Ngola a Kiluanje,* probably a reference to the king's ritual responsibilities for rainmaking shrines.

The Ngonde never achieved dominance in the region; that fell to larger or more militant states such as the Lunda and the Undi. They did, nonetheless, manage to remain independent of their more powerful rivals, at least until the 1800s. At that time, the Ngonde kingdom lost much of its revenues, derived from brokering trade, when neighboring trading partners began dealing directly with the Europeans. By the late 1800s, the British had established the Central African Protectorate, under whose jurisdiction Ngonde fell, and the kingdom was subsumed under colonial rule. Its kings became figureheads, cultural icons rather than political figures.

See also: AFRICAN KINGDOMS; LUNDA KINGDOM; MBUNDU KINGDOMS.

FURTHER READING
Pachai, Bridglal. *Malawi: The History of the Nation.* London: Longman, 1973.

NGUYEN ANH (d. 1820 C.E.)

Founder of the Nguyen dynasty of Vietnam, who took the imperial name Gia Long (r. 1802–1820). A nephew of a Nguyen warlord, Nguyen Anh was the only member of the Nguyen family to survive the Tay Son rebellion, a rebellion against oppressive landlords and overlords of the kingdom of Dai Viet (in present-day Vietnam).

By the end of the 1700s, peasant revolts over oppressive policies and taxation had begun to break out in both the northern and southern parts of the kingdom of Dai Viet. Capitalizing on this civil unrest, two brothers from the village of Tay Son in Binh Dinh province led a rebellion from 1771 to 1802 that ousted the last monarch of the Le dynasty and the ruling lords of the Trinh and Nguyen families. The Tay Son brothers sought to restore national unity and redistribute land and property to the poor.

During the rebellion, all of the Nguyen ruling family were killed except the sixteen-year-old Nguyen Anh, who fled to the Mekong River Delta and began gathering supporters to stage a counterattack. Around 1778, Nguyen Anh led an attack against the Tay Son, whose control over the country was weakening. He relied on help from a French missionary by the name of Pigneau de Béhaine to finally defeat the Tay Son forces in 1802.

Nguyen Anh ruled as Emperor Gia Long for the next eighteen years. Because of his close relationship with Pigneau de Béhaine, he implemented policies of tolerance for Christian missionaries that would be atypical of his successors. When Nguyen died in 1820, he was succeeded on the throne by his son, Minh Mang (r. 1820–1841). The Nguyen dynasty that Nguyen Anh founded continued to rule Vietnam until 1945.

See also: LE DYNASTY; NGUYEN (HUE) DYNASTY; TRINH DYNASTY; VIETNAMESE KINGDOMS.

NGUYEN (HUE) DYNASTY

(1802–1945 C.E.)

Last ruling dynasty of Vietnam, which was finally forced to cede power to the French after World War II.

The Nguyen (or Hue) dynasty of the kingdom of Vietnam was founded in 1802 by Nguyen Anh, who took the imperial name Gia Long (r. 1802–1820). But the Nguyen family had a long and illustrious history before becoming the ruling dynasty of Vietnam. As early as the mid-sixteenth century, with the partition of Vietnam into northern and southern states in 1545, the powerful Nguyen family ruled the southern half of Dai Viet in the name of the Le dynasty. In 1620, the rivalry between the Nguyen and the Trinh families erupted into open warfare, with hostilities continuing intermittently for the next fifty years. By 1673, both families accepted a de facto division of Vietnam.

At the end of the eighteenth century, a revolt known as the Tay Son rebellion erupted and nearly ended the powerful Nguyen family's reign. In 1771, two brothers from the village of Tay Son in Binh Dinh province revolted against the Trinh and Nguyen families and sought to unify the country. With the support of the peasants, the Tay Son brothers implemented land reform policies, redistributed wealth to the poor, and restored national unity. Nguyen Anh, the nephew of a Nguyen warlord, retook control of the country in 1802 with the help of the French and changed its name to Nam Viet. (It was the Chinese who began using the name Vietnam.)

The French invaded Vietnam in 1858 and forced Tu Duc (r. 1847–1883), the last of the Nguyens to rule the kingdom as an independent state, to cede the three eastern provinces of southern Vietnam to France. Later in Tu Duc's reign, the French established the colony of Cochin China and the protectorates of Annam and Tonkin in the region. During the following years, until 1945, the Nguyen family still ruled over the northern and central regions of Vietnam, but it was the French who had real control of the country.

See also: LE DYNASTY; NGUYEN ANH; TRINH DYNASTY; VIETNAMESE KINGDOMS.

NICHOLAS I (1796–1855 C.E.)

Russian tsar (r. 1825–1855) who stifled civil liberties in Russia and instigated the Crimean War (1853–1856).

The grandson of Catherine II the Great (r. 1762–1796), Nicholas Pavlovich was the third son of Tsar Paul I (r. 1796–1801) and Maria Fedorovna. Catherine intended Nicholas's eldest brother Alexander to succeed her rather than her own son Paul, so she separated Alexander and his younger brother Constantine from the family to educate them as she desired. However, Nicholas, the youngest brother, remained in his parents' austere court, where his father's infatuation with the military strongly influenced him.

When Nicholas was four years old, his father appointed a Russian general, Count Lamsdorf, as his tutor. Nicholas studied classical languages, law, and philosophy, but Lamsdorf was a poor teacher and Nicholas increasingly rejected his studies, instead indulging his fascination with strategy and the military lifestyle.

When the Russian army defeated the French forces of Napoleon Bonaparte in 1812, Tsar Alexander I (r. 1801–1825) did not allow his younger brother to participate in the conflict. But Nicholas was permitted to join Alexander's triumphant march into Paris in 1814. Recognizing Nicholas's love for the army, Alexander gave him a ceremonial commission as a staff officer and arranged for him to tour the European capitals. Thus, although he served in the army, Nicholas never entered combat, and his lack of experience presaged the poor military decisions he would later make as tsar.

Alexander I died in 1825, leaving no direct heir. Next in line of succession was Nicholas's older brother, Constantine, but intimidated by threats from a rebellious group called the Decembrists, Constantine refused to take the throne. After some hesitation, Nicholas took the throne as Nicholas I and brutally suppressed the Decembrist uprising. The group's actions, coupled with Nicholas's memories of the assassination of his grandfather, Paul I, created a deep fear of revolution in Nicholas that would dictate many of his future actions.

An autocrat who denied basic civil liberties to his people, Tsar Nicholas I of Russia made little attempt to improve the lives of the Russian peasantry during his thirty-year reign. His policies contributed to crippling social problems that fueled the Russian Revolution in 1917.

ROYAL RELATIVES

CONSTANTINE PAVLOVICH (1779–1831 C.E.)

Constantine Pavlovich was the younger brother of Tsar Alexander I and the older brother of Tsar Nicholas I. When Alexander and Constantine were children, their grandmother, Catherine II, separated them from their parents and assigned the Swiss republican Jean Francois de La Harpe to educate them. La Harpe taught his pupils the benefits of a republican government and stressed the need to increase civil liberties in Russia. Constantine, however, ignored this lesson. When Alexander I appointed him as ruler of Poland in 1815, Constantine brutally suppressed any uprisings and allowed Polish citizens little personal freedom. Constantine greatly enjoyed living in Poland, even divorcing his first wife to wed a Polish princess. Therefore, when Alexander I died in 1825, Constantine refused to succeed his brother because his wife wished to remain in Poland. Moreover, Constantine believed that Russia was more susceptible to a rebellion than Poland was. He was initially correct in this belief. In 1825, a group called the Decembrists, consisting of members of the St. Petersburg regiment, tried to seize the Russian throne, even slyly using Constantine's name in their rallying cry, "Constantine and Constitution." After some confusion, Nicholas I crushed the rebellion and then became tsar of Russia. Ultimately, however, Constantine misjudged Poland's stability. A huge uprising exploded across the country in 1830. A dejected Constantine died in 1831 before the uprising was defeated.

Nicholas's distaste for government bureaucracy was as virulent as his fear of revolution. Shortly after his accession, he commissioned the Committee of December 6th, a group of independent counselors, to evaluate the status of Russian society. Unfortunately, the Committee concluded that no major overhaul of Russian society was necessary. Consequently, during the thirty years of his reign, Nicholas made no significant attempts to resolve the issue of serfdom, Russia's lack of economic development, or inequalities between the nobility and peasant class.

Instead, Nicholas and his advisers developed the Nicholas System, a series of measures designed to stabilize the entrenched Russian social structure. To prevent interference from the bureaucracy, Nicholas established His Majesty's Own Chancery, a separate body formed to fulfill his edicts. Within this body, Nicholas created agencies, called Sections, to enact his reforms. Initially, the Sections provided some positive results. The Second Section, headed by Michael Speransky, a reformist minister whom Alexander I had banished to Siberia, codified all Rus-

sian laws dating to 1649. The Fifth Section, although it never considered eliminating serfdom, did emphasize education for all peasants and promoted the implementation of modern agricultural methods. Nicholas hoped that private landowners would follow the state's example and educate their own serfs.

The Third Section became the most notorious branch of Nicholas's government. Spurred by his fear of revolution, Nicholas formulated the doctrine of Orthodoxy, Autocracy, and Nationality. This doctrine asserted that Russia was a devoutly Orthodox society led by a ruler whose authority came directly from God, and that support for the emperor provided Russians a moral and intellectual superiority to other Europeans. The Third Section's mission was to ensure that all members of Russian society upheld the doctrine.

Nicholas genuinely hoped that the Third Section's actions would benefit Russian society. He believed that a corrupt government official was committing the same offense against the doctrine as a radical revolutionary because both individuals endangered society's stability and ignored the emperor's divine authority. However, the Third Section rewarded its members for the volume of people they indicted rather than the veracity of the indictments. Thus, many innocents were accused, and often convicted, of betraying their society. The Third Section eventually became a secret police force that menaced any individual who openly disagreed with Nicholas's policies.

This police force damaged Russia's cultural institutions. Censorship of all publications was one of the Third Section's primary duties; therefore, works that praised Nicholas's policies were printed, while those critical of the Nicholas System were suppressed. Censors, wanting to please their superiors, began to discover seditious messages in seemingly innocuous works. Eventually, the Third Section's administrators considered themselves to be the protectors of Russian art and literature. In reality, they disillusioned many writers such as the poet Pushkin, who had originally supported the Section, and forced many artists into exile.

Nicholas's deep fear of revolution also dictated his foreign policy. In 1833, he signed a treaty with the rulers of Austria and Prussia that presumably ensured stability in Western Europe. The three nations agreed to jointly quell any rebellions that occurred in their territories and to support the faltering Ottoman Empire. The treaty was successful, and when the Revolutions of 1848 erupted across Europe, the uprisings largely failed to threaten Russia and its allies. When Hungary rebelled against Austrian rule in 1849, Nicholas sent a million troops to eradicate the Hungarian forces. His victory earned him the appellation of "The Gendarme of Europe."

At the same time, the victory weakened Russia's position among other European countries. Austria and Prussia resented the massive debt they owed to Russia, and France and Britain feared the strength of Russia's army. These countries thus formulated a plan to attack Russia and decrease its military dominance. Russia's rulers had long desired to gain control of Constantinople because the city was recognized as the birthplace of Orthodox Christianity. Recognizing this desire, the European monarchs urged the Ottoman sultan to aggravate Nicholas by expelling all Orthodox monks from the Ottoman Empire. When Nicholas attacked the Ottoman armies in 1853, he initiated the Crimean War, and Austria, France, and Britain openly supported the sultan, Abdulmecid I (r. 1839–1861).

Nicholas's campaign was initially successful. But by 1855, the stagnant state of Russian society, which Nicholas had misguidedly preserved, undermined the army. Nicholas had resisted the development of railroads, viewing them as an evil import from Western Europe. But without them, he was unable to supply his troops fighting the war. Although Russia was far closer to the front lines, the French and British troops were much better fortified. Late in 1855, the allied forces destroyed the Russian naval base at Sevastopol, effectively winning the Crimean War.

Nicholas did not witness this ignominious defeat. A cold he contracted in February 1855 when he insisted upon inspecting troops that were departing for the Crimea developed into pneumonia, and he died shortly afterward. Before he died, Nicholas told his son and heir, Alexander II (r. 1855–1881), that "I wanted to take everything difficult, everything serious, upon my shoulders and to leave you a peaceful, well-ordered, happy realm." Instead, he left a badly defeated Russia that still had not resolved its increasingly crippling social problems.

Historians differ over the nature of Nicholas's character. Although the Nicholas System was overwhelmingly oppressive, it stemmed from Nicholas's deeply paternal attitude toward his nation and an initial desire to see it prosper. But despite Nicholas's intentions, his system could not resolve the overwhelming problem of serfdom, the demand for greater freedom and representation among the Russian middle class, and the encroachment of European events in Russian affairs.

See also: ALEXANDER I; ALEXANDER II; CATHERINE II, THE GREAT; ROMANOV DYNASTY; RUSSIAN DYNASTIES; TSARS AND TSARINAS.

FURTHER READING

Lincoln, W. Bruce. *Nicholas I: Emperor and Autocrat of All the Russias.* DeKalb: Northern Illinois University Press, 1990.

Westwood, J.N. *Endurance and Endeavour: Russian History, 1812–2001.* 5th ed. New York: Oxford University Press, 2002.

NICHOLAS II (1868–1918 C.E.)

The last tsar of Russia (r. 1894–1917), who was executed during the Russian Revolution.

Nicholas Aleksandrovich was the son of Tsar Alexander III (r. 1881–1894) and Maria Fedorovna, a Danish princess. As a child, Nicholas studied foreign languages, history, and military strategy. When he was twenty-one years old, he joined the State Council, the tsar's primary advisers. The following year, he both oversaw the construction of the Trans-Siberian Railroad and headed the Special Committee on Famine Relief, which was designed to counter a devastating drought in Russia.

Consequently, when Alexander III died in 1894, Nicholas had already acquired substantial leadership experience. Yet, surprisingly, the new tsar displayed an ignorance of public sentiment that would plague him throughout his reign. Embracing Russia's traditional autocratic government, Nicholas, in 1895, flatly rejected any expansion of power for the elected *zemstvos,* popular rural assemblies that functioned as municipal governments. The next year, during his coronation festivities, a riot exploded among the thousands of citizens who had assembled to celebrate the event, and nearly 1,500 people were trampled. Despite this tragedy, Nicholas attended a lavish ball that same night, adding to the public perception that he was indifferent to the suffering of the Russian people.

Rural and urban poverty also exploded during Nicholas's reign. Because of overpopulation, the land available for farming had steadily shrunk, and farmers saw their incomes rapidly decline. In Russian cities, industrial workers bemoaned poor working conditions and wages. In addition, in 1904, Russia suffered a crushing defeat in a war with Japan when the Japanese navy routed Russia's vaunted Baltic fleet.

Agitated by these crises, terrorist groups launched attacks against prominent government officials. After several assassinations, Nicholas severely limited public freedoms. In 1905, during protests against new martial laws, a riot erupted at the Winter Palace in St. Petersburg. Soldiers fired upon the crowd and killed 150 rioters in an incident now known as "Bloody Sunday." Later, in October of that year, workers staged a national strike to denounce the shootings.

Alarmed by the public turmoil, Nicholas signed the Fundamental Laws in 1906. These laws finally created an elected legislative assembly and ensured basic civic liberties. However, Nicholas still exercised his authority; he alone appointed the assembly's leader, and he could dismiss the assembly whenever he wished. When the Duma, the new assembly, convened in 1906, its members demanded total democracy and massive land reform. Unwilling to comply, Nicholas halted the session. He repeated his actions

later that year when the Second Duma forwarded similar demands. To appease the public, Nicholas did adopt some suffrage reforms, an action that mollified the upper classes and the third Duma, but not the bulk of the population.

Nicholas then enjoyed several peaceful years. But in July 1914, Russia found itself at war with Germany as World War I erupted across Europe. Initially, the public rallied behind Nicholas's call to protect "mother Russia." But after several minor victories over the German army, the Russians experienced a crushing defeat at the battle of Tannenberg. By the end of 1914, the Russian army had lost a million soldiers and faced a massive shortage of supplies. When the campaign resumed in 1915, the Germans and Austrians scored another major victory in the region of Galicia (in present-day Poland and the Ukraine). Faced with rapidly declining civilian and military morale, Nicholas assumed personal control of the Russian army.

Rising public unrest accompanied Russia's military failures. In return for their support of the war, members of the Duma expected Nicholas to permit widespread social reforms. Nicholas grudgingly appointed moderate reformist ministers. But when Nicholas took command of the army in 1916, he left his wife Alexandra in virtual control of the country, and she replaced many of the new ministers with others more loyal to the monarchy. Advised by her spiritual consultant, the notorious Rasputin, Alexandra forcefully asserted the power of the monarchy. The Russian public, aware of Alexandra's German lineage and Rasputin's influence over the tsarina, believed the two had conspired to undermine Russia's stability.

In December 1916, a group of conspirators murdered Rasputin. This action precipitated a wider revolt against the government, and on February 27, 1917, the Russian capital fell to the revolutionaries. Recognizing the strength of the revolt, Nicholas abdicated the throne and was succeeded by his brother, Grand Duke Mikhail Aleksandrovich.

The Russian Revolution continued, however, and soon deposed the provisional government in November 1917. In 1918 Nicholas and his family were taken to the city of Ekaterinburg for their safety. The revolutionaries, known as Bolsheviks, originally planned to bring Nicholas to trial, but when antirevolutionary forces sought to free the former tsar, the new government ordered his execution. On July 17, 1918, Nicholas, Alexandra, and their children were shot and their corpses burned in the cellar of the house they were staying in at Ekaterinburg. The death of Nicholas and his family marked the end of the Romanov dynasty as well as the end of the Russian monarchy.

See also: ALEXANDRA; ROMANOV DYNASTY.

FURTHER READING

Carrere d'Encausse, Helene. *Nicholas II: The Interrupted Transition.* Trans. George Holoch. New York: Holmes & Meier, 2000.

Warth, Robert D. *Nicholas II: The Life and Reign of Russia's Last Monarch.* Westport, CT: Praeger, 1997.

NORMAN KINGDOMS (1130–1268 C.E.)

Kingdoms on the island of Sicily and in the environs of the city-state of Naples that were ruled by knights of Norman descent and were combined into one kingdom between 1130 and 1268.

Located in the Mediterranean Sea between the headlands of modern Libya and the toe of the Italian Peninsula, the benighted island of Sicily has suffered invasions of conquering foreigners since time immemorial. Greeks, Romans, Carthaginians, and Arabs all claimed the island in ancient times. By the eleventh century, European nobles became the latest group to set their sights on controlling Sicily and southern Italy.

FORMATION BY THE NORMANS

In 1059, Pope Nicholas II thought it the better part of valor and political wisdom to grant the Norman noble, Robert Guiscard, title and seigneury to Sicily's sun-drenched valleys and mountainsides. Robert, fresh from victories in Apulia, Calabria, and other parts of southern Italy, decided to leave consolidation of this portion of his allotment to his younger brother, Roger, who had also participated in the conquests of his brother.

A year later, in 1060, Roger turned his attentions to his new kingdom. By 1072, the Norman adventurer had fully subjugated Sicily, and he ruled the island kingdom as Count Roger I (r. 1072–1101) until his death in 1101. With control of Sicily, the Normans were firmly in control of the straits of Messina—the fifty miles of water between Europe and Africa.

In granting Sicily and Naples to the Normans, the Church consolidated its hold on Sicily and the south of Italy, since these were officially papal fiefdoms.

The Greek priests of Magna Graecia (as Sicily and southern Italy was known), placed there under the auspices of the Byzantine Empire, were soon replaced by Roman prelates.

EXPANSION OF THE REALM

Roger II (r. 1105–1154), the son and successor of Roger I, eventually added Naples and Capua to the kingdom of Sicily. With these additions, he felt so successful that he changed his title from count to king in 1130. Roger II was opposed on all sides, however. The Saracens, or Muslims, wished to recapture fertile Sicily. The popes in Rome feared encroachment in the Papal States. The Byzantine Greeks had not completely forgotten their ancient colonies in southern Italy. And the Germans had imperial designs of their own in southern Italy.

Roger II fought all of these opponents and usually won. Between 1135 and 1153, he extended his domains into North Africa by taking Cape Bona, Tripoli, and Tunis. His greatest triumphs, however, were probably in Sicily itself. Unlike many of his fellow Westerners, Robert did not hesitate to use the talents of the Muslims and Jews in his territories, and both of these groups were generally better educated and more adept at administration than any of their European contemporaries.

As a result, Roger's court became the most civilized on the European continent, paving the way for the even more resplendent rule of Emperor Frederick II (r. 1212–1250). The Muslim biographer, Idrisi, described the capital city of Palermo under Roger as beautiful beyond compare, with towering palaces and pleasure gardens lovelier than could be found anywhere else in the world. Under the Normans, Palermo was also unique in that it contained mosques, churches, and synagogues side by side, reflecting a broad religious tolerance.

PERIOD OF DECLINE

Roger's son and successor, William I (r. 1154–1166), did not have his father's ambition or industry. He became known as "William the Bad," probably because his hands-off approach to rule unfortunately coincided with a successful Muslim revolt in Tunis that ended Norman rule in North Africa.

His son and successor, William II (r. 1166–1189), though known as "William the Good," was little different from his father in tastes or inclinations. But he was perhaps more fortunate in his timing and his biographers. When William died in 1189, he left no heir, and his dashing cousin Tancred (r. 1190–1194), the bastard grandson of Roger II, was chosen king.

The death of William was not overlooked by the German Holy Roman emperor, Henry VI (r. 1190–1197), who had married William's aunt, Constance. Henry thus felt his claim was just as legitimate as Tancred's, and he accordingly claimed the Sicilian throne for himself. Through clever political maneuvering and reasonable generalship, he went to Palermo in 1194 with a sizable army, demanded his rights, and was subsequently crowned king of Sicily—thus ending Norman rule of the island.

GERMAN RULE

Henry VI's son, Frederick II, made Palermo his capital when he succeeded his father as Holy Roman emperor. Frederick became the most powerful and unusual ruler of the thirteenth century, known as the *stupor mundi* ("Wonder of the World").

Frederick excelled in every endeavor he pursued. He founded a Sicilian university that included Jewish and Muslim faculty. He wrote books and spoke six languages fluently. When Frederick finally, though reluctantly, succumbed to the pope's insistence on a crusade, he so impressed the Muslim sultan of Egypt, al-Kamil Muhammad II (r. 1218–1238), that he was allowed to name himself king of Jerusalem and return home from that gore-drenched soil having never spilled a drop of blood.

After Frederick's death in 1250, the opposition he had faced in his German domain was directed to his son and successor, Conrad IV (r. 1250–1254). Revolts broke out nearly everywhere in the realm. The pope took Naples, but Conrad took it back. Chaos ruled as Normans, Germans, and popes all laid their claims to the Italian and German territories. In this maelstrom, Conrad died in 1254, only four years after taking the throne. His illegitimate brother, Manfred (r. 1254–1266), was left in command of the Norman forces.

Manfred had inherited much of his illustrious father's charm and intelligence, important assets in the impossibly complex political situation in which he found himself. He fought continuously, mostly against the papacy, for the next twelve years. This left little time to play music and hold court, which was a pity, as even the dour Italian poet, Dante Alighieri, remarked on Manfred's rare musical talents.

The popes despaired at Manfred's gaiety and competency, and in 1264, Pope Urban IV decided to join with France to overturn the impious Manfred. Charles of Anjou, the brother of King Louis IX (r. 1226–1270), responded to the papal call. He marched through Italy with 30,000 troops, defeated Manfred's outnumbered troops, and killed the valiant Manfred, who had thrown himself into the midst of the fray.

FRENCH AND SPANISH RULE

In 1266, Charles of Anjou declared Naples and Sicily to be French, inaugurating the new kingdom of Naples, ruled by the French Angevin dynasty. As Charles I (r. 1266–1285), the disdainful Charles of Anjou ruled with an autocratic hand. Consequently, in 1282, a general revolt rose spontaneously in Sicily to overthrow the hated French rule. Beginning after the hour of evening prayer, the "Sicilian Vespers" (as the uprising came to be called) resulted in the death of almost all Frenchmen on the island. Charles of Anjou was understandably furious and swore a "thousand years" of vengeance; the pope declared a crusade. The Sicilians responded by offering their island to Pedro III of Aragón (r. 1276–1285). He accepted, and the brief French rule was ended. From 1282 to 1410, Sicily was ruled by the kingdom of Aragón.

See also: ANGEVIN DYNASTIES; ANJOU KINGDOM; ARAGÓN, KINGDOM OF; FREDERICK II; NAPLES, KINGDOM OF; SICILY, KINGDOM OF.

FURTHER READING

Power, Daniel, Rosamund McKitterick, Christine Carpenter, and Jonathan Shepard, eds. *The Norman Frontier in the Twelfth and Early Thirteenth Centuries.* New York: Cambridge University Press, 2004.

NORODOM SIHANOUK (1922–)

Episodic ruler (r. 1941–1955; 1960–1970; 1993–2004) of Cambodia (Kampuchea), whose reign coincided with the tumultuous Vietnam War era.

Norodom Sihanouk was born in the Cambodian capital of Phnom Penh on October 31, 1922, to Prince Norodom Suramarit and Princess Sisowath Kossamak. Both of his parents were of royal blood, each representing one of the two traditional dynastic families of the region: the Norodoms and the Sisowaths. At the time of Sihanouk's birth, the throne was occupied by his maternal grandfather, Sisowath Monivong (r. 1904–1927).

Sihanouk received his primary education in Phnom Penh at the Ecole François Baudoin. Upon graduation he went to Saigon (now Ho Chi Minh City) in Vietnam to complete his secondary schooling. He was then sent to France to attend a military school but was called home in 1941 because the current Cambodian king, Monivong (r. 1927–1941), had died and Sihanouk was under consideration as the royal successor.

The choice of successor fell to a royal council, but because Cambodia was a French protectorate at this time, it was Parisian, not local, politics that weighed most heavily in the selection of the new king. The French considered Sihanouk to be the royal candidate least likely to cause trouble, so the eighteen-year-old prince was given the Crown in September 1941. Soon after taking the throne, Sihanouk found himself rendered powerless by the outbreak of World War II and Japan's rapid conquest and occupation of much of Indochina. When the Japanese occupational forces captured the Cambodian capital, Sihanouk was taken prisoner, having ruled for less than a year.

After the withdrawal of the Japanese at the end of World War II, France once again took control of Cambodia, but Sihanouk had other plans. In 1947 he established a limited monarchy that ruled with the collaboration of an elected parliament and a prime minister (a role he retained for himself). In 1953 he declared martial law and dissolved the national parliament, believing that its current members were too beholden to French interests. In November of that year he declared Cambodia's independence.

For a five-year period, from 1955 to 1960, Sihanouk stepped down from the Cambodian throne in favor of his father, but he remained in political control as prime minister. From 1960 to 1970, however, he once again took charge as Cambodia entered a new and dangerous era in which America began its involvement in the civil war in neighboring Vietnam.

At first, Sihanouk maintained Cambodia's neutrality, but as time passed he saw that the Viet Cong were likely to win. Hoping to ingratiate himself with the probable victors, Sihanouk offered them

the use of Cambodian territory, enabling the North Vietnamese forces and their allies in the south to receive supplies from China and to stage attacks against their adversaries. This, in turn, induced the United States to begin carpet-bombing Cambodia's border region in 1969 and to attempt to undermine Sihanouk's regime.

With the support of the Central Intelligence Agency (CIA), a pro-U.S. general named Lon Nol staged a coup in 1970 that ousted Sihanouk from power. Sihanouk fled to Beijing, China, where he established a government in exile and waited for the opportunity to return to Phnom Penh. In the Cambodian countryside, meanwhile, a guerrilla faction known as the Khmer Rouge had arisen. These guerrillas were led by Pol Pot, a brutal revolutionary who hoped to establish a communist government in Cambodia. Sihanouk allied himself with the Khmer Rouge, and when Pol Pot's forces were victorious in 1975, he was rewarded with the restoration of his title as king. Within a year, however, Pol Pot had placed Sihanouk under house arrest. For the next four years he could only watch as Pol Pot's thugs brutalized Cambodia, ultimately killing some 1.7 million people.

Pol Pot was finally ousted by Vietnamese forces, which invaded Cambodia in December of 1978 and remained in control there until 1989. During these years, Sihanouk once again lived in exile. Only after Vietnam withdrew, and under the condition that he denounce the Pol Pot regime, could Sihanouk return to his kingdom but not yet to his throne. In 1993 a new constitution was drafted that restored Cambodia to a monarchy, and Sihanouk was once again installed as king. Until his abdication in 2004, Sihanouk ruled Cambodia as a constitutional monarch with no executive powers.

See also: CAMBODIAN KINGDOMS; SOUTHEAST ASIAN KINGDOMS.

NORTHUMBRIA, KINGDOM OF
(547–827 C.E.)

One of seven early Anglo-Saxon kingdoms of Britain, located in the northeastern part of the country, that was once one of the strongest kingdoms in Britain. Settled by Angles around 500, Northumbria was originally two separate kingdoms: Bernicia, which stretched from the River Tees to the Firth of Forth, and Deira, which covered the territory from the Tee River to the Humber River.

King Ida of Bernicia (r. ca. 547–559) established the foundations of Northumbria when he took the throne of that kingdom in 547. Under his rule, Bernicia included what is now Berwick and Roxburgh in southeastern Scotland as well as Northumberland and Durham in northeastern England. Meanwhile, King Aelle of Deira (r. ca. 569–599) ruled a territory now occupied by the northeastern part of Yorkshire in England.

In the mid-sixth century, Aethelfrith of Bernicia (r. 592–616), a descendant of King Ida, formed Northumbria (which literally means, the land north of the Humber) by joining the kingdoms of Bernicia and Deira. Aethelfrith also added territory in Wales and Scotland to the kingdom. King Aethelfrith was removed from the throne by Edwin of Deira (r. 616–633), who built Northumbria into the strongest kingdom in England. Edwin was also noted for bringing Christianity to the kingdom after he converted to the faith in 627. Northumbria became an important center of Christianity and learning, and was home of the Venerable Bede, the first English historian.

In the seventh century, wars with the Anglo-Saxon kingdom of Mercia and its Welsh allies endangered Northumbria's rulers and the supremacy of the kingdom. King Edwin was killed by Cadwallon, a Welsh ally of King Penda of Mercia (r. 626–654). His successor, Oswald of Bernicia (r. 634–642), was killed by Penda. Under Oswald's successors, Oswiu (r. 642–670) and Ecgfrith (r. 670–685), Northumbria was eclipsed by the rival kingdom of Mercia.

By 827, the kingdom of Northumbria had accepted the supremacy of the kingdom of Wessex. In the mid-ninth century, Danish invaders occupied south Northumbria and pushed the Northumbrians northward, confining them to a small area bordered by the Tees River in the south and the Firth of Forth in the north. In the eleventh century, conquering Danes installed Danish earls in the region. Although the Northumbrians expelled the Danish earl Tostig in 1065, the Danes returned soon after and took full control of the kingdom.

See also: ANGLO-SAXON RULERS; MERCIA, KINGDOM OF; WESSEX, KINGDOM OF.

FURTHER READING
Stenton, F.M. *Anglo-Saxon England.* New York: Oxford University Press, 2001.

NORWEGIAN MONARCHY

(ca. 800s C.E.–Present)

Scandinavian monarchy whose existence stretches back to the early Middle Ages and continues today.

From the early Middle Ages until the ninth century, Norway consisted of a number of small, frequently warring kingdoms. Around 872, Harald I Fairhair (r. 858–928) succeeded in uniting much of Norway under his rule. From that time forward, although various regions sometimes chose their own kings or rose up against rulers they disliked, the trend in Norway was toward a single monarch.

The Icelandic historian Snorri Sturluson (1179–1241) wrote one of the best medieval national histories, the *Heimskringla,* which relates the sagas of the Norwegian kings from Halfdan the Black, who preceded Harald Fairhair, to Magnus Erlingsson (r. 1161–1184) in the late twelfth century. Although the accuracy of Sturluson's account can sometimes be questioned, his *Heimskringla* provides a vivid account of life in Norway during the Viking era and of the types of conflicts the kings had to face.

In the early 1100s, Olaf II Haraldsson (r. 1016–1030), son of a minor king, conquered Norway and promoted Christianity as the official religion. After his death in battle against rebellious earls and lesser kings supported by Cnut the Great of Denmark (r. 1019–1035), who had driven him out of Norway in 1028, Olaf became Norway's first patron saint. His half-brother Harald III Hardraada (r. 1045–1066) continued the work of establishing a strong monarchy in Norway; he also claimed the throne of England but died in battle against English king Harold II Godwinson (r. 1066) in 1066.

In 1319, Norway and Sweden were united under Magnus VII Eriksson (r. 1319–1355), although the two kingdoms were separated again under his sons, the younger of whom, Haakon VI (r. 1355–1380), ruled Norway. His brother having died in 1359, Haakon was also elected king of Sweden in 1362, but he lost that kingdom to Albert of Mecklenburg (r. 1364–1389) the following year.

Haakon was married to Margrethe, daughter of

The current king of Norway, Harald V, is a constitutional monarch whose role is primarily ceremonial. His 1968 marriage to Sonja Haraldsen, a commoner, triggered heated debate about the future of the monarchy, but the majority of the Norwegian people have since accepted Queen Sonja enthusiastically.

Waldemar IV of Denmark (r. 1340–1375). After the deaths of Haakon and Waldemar, Margrethe (or Margaret) united all three Scandinavian countries in the Kalmar Union of 1397. Norway's union with Denmark endured until 1814.

As a result of the upheaval of the Napoleonic Wars in Europe, Denmark ceded Norway to Sweden in the Treaty of Kiel in 1814. In the years that followed, Norwegian nationalism increased but was suppressed by the Swedish monarchy. Swedish kings of the House of Bernadotte continued to rule Norway until 1905.

In June 1905, the Norwegian ministry of the Swedish government declared the union of the two countries to be at an end. After much negotiation, in which war was narrowly averted, the union was officially ended in the autumn of 1905, when Oscar II of Sweden (r. 1872–1907) ceased to be king of Norway.

After its break with Sweden, Norway remained a constitutional monarchy. The government considered inviting either a Swedish prince from the Bernadotte dynasty or a Danish prince of the House of Glücksburg to take the throne. The invitation was finally offered to Prince Carl, grandson of Christian IX of Denmark (r. 1863–1906), who accepted only after a referendum by the Norwegian people approved.

In November 1905, Carl was elected king by the Norwegian government, taking the name Haakon VII (r. 1905–1957). During World War II, while Norway was occupied by Germany, King Haakon VII and the cabinet maintained a government in exile in England. Upon Haakon's death in 1957, his son, Olaf V (r. 1957–1991), took the throne. Olaf was succeeded as king of Norway by his son, Harald V (r. 1991), in 1991.

In 1990 the constitution of Norway was changed to allow the eldest child of the monarch to succeed to the throne, regardless of gender. This change applies only to members of the royal family born after 1990, however. As a result, Harald V's son Haakon is the Norwegian crown prince even though he has an older sister. But should Haakon's first child be a daughter, she will be the heir to the throne.

See also: DANISH KINGDOM; HAAKON VI; HARALD III HARDRAADE; HAROLD II GODWINSON; KALMAR UNION; MARGARET OF DENMARK; OLAF II (SAINT OLAF); OLDENBURG DYNASTY; SWEDISH MONARCHY; WALDEMAR I, THE GREAT.

FURTHER READING

Butler, Ewan. *The Horizon Concise History of Scandinavia.* New York: American Heritage, 1973.

Larsen, Karen. *A History of Norway.* Princeton, NJ: Princeton University Press for the American-Scandinavian Foundation, 1948.

Toyne, Stanley M. *The Scandinavians in History.* 1948. Reprint, New York: Barnes and Noble, 1996.

NOVGOROD, PRINCIPALITY OF.

See RUS PRINCEDOMS

NUBIAN KINGDOMS (c. 850–663 b.c.e.)

Kingdoms that existed during a relatively short period when the rulers of Nubia (formerly called Kush), an ancient state south of Egypt, conquered their northern neighbor and reigned as pharaohs of Egypt.

After dominating Nubia for centuries, Egypt gradually weakened after the rule of Ramses II (r. 1279–1212 B.C.E.). Around 1070 B.C.E., after the end of the period known as the New Kingdom, internal strife between pharaohs and priests eventually splintered Egypt into a number of petty kingdoms, and Nubia regained its independence. In fact, a large number of Egyptians left the country and took refuge in Nubia during that period.

Little is known about Nubia between c. 1000 and 850 B.C.E., but its importance grew in the ninth century B.C.E. when the capital city of Napata served as a religious and political center. During this time, the Napatan dynasty, a family of Egyptianized kings, ruled the country, assisted by an influential priesthood based at Gebel Barkal, a holy mountain that was considered the home of the god Amun.

Nubian rule over Egypt began around 767 B.C.E. under Pharaoh Kashta (r. 760–747 B.C.E.) of the Napatan dynasty. His reign marks the beginning of Egypt's Twenty-fifth (or Nubian) dynasty. Around 730 B.C.E., Libyans from the north invaded Egypt and Nubia during the reign of Piye (r. 747–713 B.C.E.), Kashta's son and successor. Piye's troops crushed the Libyans, and Piye then left Egypt and returned to Napata. In 716, Piye's successor, his brother Shabako (r. 713–699 B.C.E.), marched north to put down an uprising in Egypt; he remained there and reasserted Nubian rule over both kingdoms.

The Nubian pharaohs encouraged economic and cultural recovery in Egypt as well as the revival of ancient traditions during a period of Egyptian decline. Disintegrating ancient religious texts were recopied, including the famous Memphite Theology, a creation story recorded by Shabako's scribes. The Nubian pharaohs also hired Egyptian architects and artists to restore old temples and construct new ones throughout both Egypt and Nubia.

Nubian rulers also combined Egyptian practices with their own customs. Royal costumes used features of both cultures. Nubian rulers were mummified and buried in pyramids like Egyptian pharaohs. However, royal succession followed the Nubian matrilineal tradition, with the Crown passing to the king's maternal brother or nephew rather than from father to son as in the Egyptian custom.

The most famous Nubian pharaoh was Taharqa (r. 690–664 B.C.E.), who constructed many commemorative temples in both Egypt and Nubia as part of an attempt to unify and bolster the kingdom. Toward the end of his rule, continual assaults by the Assyrians into Egypt forced him back to Nubia around 667 B.C.E.

Taharqa's successor, his nephew Tanwetamani (r. 664–656 B.C.E.), returned to Egypt from Nubia and drove out the Assyrians in 664 B.C.E. The following year, however, the Assyrian king Ashurbanipal (r. 668–627 B.C.E.) launched a devastating attack on Egypt's capital city of Thebes, slaughtering the people, ransacking the city, and looting its temples.

Ashurbanipal's invasion marked the end of Nubian rule over Egypt. The Nubians retreated to Napata and then, around 530 B.C.E., moved their capital to Meroe. The Nubian culture that developed in Meroe was a combination of Egyptian and Southern African traditions. The Nubian dynasty survived in Nubia until around 350 C.E., when it was defeated by the Axumite Empire centered in Ethiopia.

See also: AKSUM KINGDOM; KUSH, KINGDOM OF; RAMSES II, THE GREAT.

NUPE KINGDOM

(ca. 1400s–early 1800s C.E.)

Kingdom of central Nigeria, one of many Yoruba states, which was reputedly founded by a culture hero named Tsoede.

According to Nupe tradition, sometime between 400 and 500 C.E. a great hero named Tsoede reportedly came to the people of the Nupe region to teach the people skills and a civilized way of life. Tsoede is credited with introducing everything from bronzeworking to social institutions, such as marriage and the family. All Nupe rulers were thought to have descended from Tsoede.

The Nupe achieved acclaim throughout the region for their fine craftwork, and when long-distance trade became common, their reputation spread even further. Bronzework and weaving were the primary craft items produced by Nupe artisans, and the very formation of a centralized, unified kingdom may well have been a response to increased demand for Nupe craft items. Whatever the reason, the Nupe kingdom arose in the fifteenth century, with its capital at Bida.

The royal court of the Nupe kingdom was similar in form to the courts that characterized other Yoruba states prior to the arrival of Islam to the region. In the early 1800s, however, Fulani Muslims came into Nupe territory and conquered the kingdom. What was once an independent and unified kingdom became a collection of three emirates, centered at Bida, Agaie, and Lapai, respectively.

See also: AFRICAN KINGDOMS; YORUBA KINGDOMS.

FURTHER READING

Nadel, S.F. *A Black Byzantium: The Kingdom of Nupe in Nigeria.* New York: Oxford University Press, 1973.

NYORO KINGDOM (1300s C.E.–Present)

African kingdom of west-central Uganda, also called Bunyoro (Bu- is the Bantu prefix signifying a geographical entity or territory), and the oldest of the four traditional kingdoms of the nation of Uganda.

The Nyoro kingdom was founded sometime in the fourteenth century by people who migrated into the region from the Congo in the west. The newcomers were probably looking for fresh pasturage for their cattle, and they eventually settled in the lands surrounding Lake Albert.

ORIGINS AND ASPECTS OF KINGSHIP

The Nyoro myth of origin centers on a possibly mythological figure named Kintu. Analogous to the Judeo-Christian Adam, Kintu is thought to be the first man and is credited with founding Bunyoro. The Bunyoro kings all claim to have descended from this founding ancestor.

The Bunyoro king is called the *omukama,* which roughly translates as "the greatest of all men." Today the *omukama*'s role is more or less ceremonial, his function being to serve as an exemplar of cultural identity. In the past, however, he was the absolute ruler of his territory. At the height of their power, until about 1600, Bunyoro kings controlled a vast expanse of territory that extended west into Congo and eastward all the way into Kenya.

Within the royal court, the king stood at the apex of power, assisted by two important councilors, the *okwiri* ("official brother") and the *kalyota* ("official sister"). Administration of the empire was delegated to appointed officials, usually drawn from the powerful Hima pastoralists who formed a noble class within the kingdom. The Hima ruled at the dictate of the king rather than autonomously.

Bunyoro's fall from preeminence in the region began with a breakdown in central control over the empire. There was no strict rule of succession, beyond the provision that a king must be of the Babito line (that is, must be descended from Kintu). This arrangement resulted in frequent battles among rival claimants to the kingship.

Similarly, the king had no extraordinary charter by which to justify his right to rule, for the Nyoro did not believe their kings to be divinely ordained or to possess supernatural abilities. The Nyoro king had only as much power over his subordinate territories as he could personally ensure through his appointment of regional governors. As the empire expanded, the Nyoro kings lost control over many of these governors. As a result, the peoples of the kingdom often rebelled against the rule of the kings, which weakened the power of the kingdom.

THE RISE OF THE GANDA KINGDOM

In the 1600s, the subject territory of Buganda successfully broke away from Bunyoro control and reclaimed its territorial autonomy. Within a century, it grew strong enough to eclipse Bunyoro in power, and Bunyoro began a slow decline. A long succession of Nyoro kings were forced to spend their time and resources in an effort to keep other parts of the kingdom from following the example of Buganda. With the Nyoro rulers thus occupied, the Ganda kings were free to concentrate on increasing the extent and wealth of their own realm.

Best-known of all the Bunyoro kings is one who arose on the eve of Bunyoro's final eclipse in the late nineteenth century. This was Kabarega (r. 1870–1894), who began his rule in 1870 after a bloody war of succession against his brother, Kabigumire (r. 1869–1870). Kabarega lacked the support of the nobility, but he had the enthusiastic backing of the military and the common people, whose will prevailed.

Kabarega was not content with putting down local rebellions. Instead, he adopted the expansionist ambitions of the earlier Bunyoro kings. He created a massive army and sent it forth to conquer neighboring territories. One frequent target of his military campaigns was the kingdom of Toro, which lay to the south. Over a period of several years he succeeded in severely disrupting that kingdom's stability. His soldiers captured two successive Toro kings and killed a third. It was only with the arrival of British military assistance that Toro succeeded in ending its long conflict with the powerful Nyoro army.

Kabarega, however, did not easily acquiesce to British colonial rule. He mounted a determined and initially successful resistance throughout the 1870s and 1880s. In 1894, however, British forces conquered the Nyoro capital of Mparo. Kabarega fled to lead a guerrilla campaign from the Ugandan forests. His intransigence against his much more powerful enemy was ultimately to no avail, however, for in 1895 he was captured by British forces and exiled to the Seychelles Islands.

COLONIAL AND POSTCOLONIAL ERA

Kabarega's resistance to British colonial rule earned a sorry fate for his kingdom. Although it was once the preeminent power among Uganda's four traditional kingdoms (the others being Toro, Ganda, and Ankole), the British refused to deal with Nyoro's kings. Instead, the colonial authority chose to work through the Ganda, whose rulers were more cooperative. Bunyoro became just one of several minor kingdoms subordinated to Ganda rule.

When Uganda gained its independence in 1962, the Nyoro entertained some hope that they might be restored to their earlier power. In the mid-1960s, however, Ugandan prime minister Apolo Milton Obote abolished all the traditional kingdoms. It was only in 1993 that the Ugandan government restored the traditional kingdoms, including Bunyoro, albeit as apolitical institutions. The once formidable power of the Nyoro *omukama* is now gone, and the Nyoro kingdom stands as a symbol of cultural identity rather than as a political actor on the national stage.

See also: AFRICAN KINGDOMS; ANKOLE KINGDOM; GANDA KINGDOM; KABAREGA; TORO KINGDOM.

FURTHER READING

Beattie, John. *Bunyoro: An African Kingdom.* Fort Worth, TX: Holt, Rinehart & Winston, 1988.

OATHS AND OATH-TAKING

A solemn promise or affirmation of loyalty and duty or responsibility made by a ruler to the people; a pledge of loyalty made by a vassal to a lord.

The practice of giving and receiving oaths began in ancient times when lords or kings conquered another ruler or when two leaders consolidated their power. The oaths defined the relationship between the two and stipulated the responsibilities of each party. Evidence of such oaths exists in many cultures.

The oath was often made first by the person with lesser power or the person who had been defeated by a more powerful individual. The role of the ruler was to accept the oath and pledge his protection to the weaker oath-giver. Kings, nobles, and common people swore oaths. Naturally, the form and articles of the oaths differed among classes and cultures, but several common characteristics of oath-taking can be identified:

- An invocation to a deity and/or the use of a sacred object or symbol of power.
- Specific promises that are to be honored.
- Consequences of failure to uphold the oath, sometimes including the evocation of a curse to befall upon the oath-taker.
- Acceptance of the oath by those to whom it is made.

Monarchs were expected to make oaths to their subjects during the coronation ceremony, which was generally held in a sacred place under the auspices of the kingdom's highest religious leader. The oath might be taken either before or after the people's acclamation of the ruler. A medieval English king's oath, administered by the archbishop, included promises to keep the peace, to be faithful to God and the Church, to use justice and mercy, and to uphold the laws and customs of the nation.

An oath, whether taken by a king or a commoner, places great importance on the acceptance of personal responsibility. Of course, not all individuals, including monarchs, kept the oaths to which they swore. A panel of the medieval Bayeaux Tapestry (1066) depicts King Harold II of England swearing an oath of allegiance to William of Normandy in 1064. As he raises one hand and rests the other on sacred relics, he promises to help William capture the English throne. Instead, upon the death of King Edward the Confessor in 1066, Harold accepted the throne of England for himself, which led to the Norman invasion and conquest of England by William that same year.

In an effort to consolidate their power, rulers often required subjects to take oaths renouncing their own religions in favor of that of the ruler. Under Visigothic rule in the Balkan region and Spain between the fourth and sixth centuries, Jews were required to take oaths promising not to participate in Jewish rituals and to pronounce their belief in the Christian tenets of the Nicene Creed. Queen Mary I of England (r. 1553–1558) required her subjects to take oaths renouncing Protestantism in favor of Catholicism, condemning nearly three hundred individuals who did not do so to death.

Rulers have also expected personal oaths of allegiance from their subjects. In some instances, all vassals were required to attend a public ceremony, typically in a sacred place, and individually swear their oaths of fidelity. These visible and verbal displays helped the ruler, especially one whose legitimacy was in question, to establish and maintain control of his or her kingdom.

Oaths sworn to lords in Anglo-Saxon England (449–1066) reveal the close bonds between secular and religious power. The vassal swore on the name of God that he would be loyal to the lord, would honor what the lord honored, would follow all the lord's commands, and would never perform any deeds that might displease him.

Oaths demanded of subjects are not a purely a Western custom but have been an important part of Eastern cultures as well. For example, immediately upon assuming power in 1002, the Cambodian ruler Suryavarman (r. 1002–1050) brought together as many as 4,000 officials for a public oath-taking ceremony.

Vestiges of ancient oath-taking ceremonies survive today not only in the investiture rituals of the remaining monarchies of the world, but also in the protocols of the inaugurations of many modern heads of state.

See also: ACCESSION AND CROWNING OF KINGS; FEUDALISM AND KINGSHIP; SUCCESSION, ROYAL.

ODA NOBUNAGA (1534–1582 C.E.)

Japanese feudal warlord who nearly succeeded in unifying Japan and ending the constant military clashes between opposing clans that marked the *sengoku,* or Warring States, period from the mid-1400s to late fifteenth century.

FAMILY AND CHARACTER

Though the son of a local *daimyo,* or feudal warlord, Oda Nobunaga came from a relatively modest provincial family. Nonetheless, his career as a military commander shaped Japan for the rest of its history. The motto on Nobunaga's personal seal, *Tenka Fubu,* translates as "a nation under one sword" or "a unified realm under military rule." He was audacious and ruthless in achieving this goal, and was haughty and sometimes contemptuous of his subordinates.

Brash and crude as a youth, Nobunaga is said to have behaved disgracefully even at his father's funeral, where he acted rudely toward others and angrily threw incense at the mortuary tablet during the funeral ritual. Such behavior greatly frustrated his father's loyal retainer, Kirate Kiyohide, who had been given the task of helping Nobunaga rule. Eventually reaching the limit of his patience, Kirate felt pushed to "remonstration through suicide." Reportedly, the old samurai's urgent appeal to honor and his death by Japanese ritual suicide, or *seppuku,* greatly impressed Nobunaga and helped curb his dishonorable ways.

LEADERSHIP

By 1558, Nobunaga had secured control of the Oda family after having his disloyal younger brother, Nobuyuki, murdered for his role in a plot against him. The killing sent a powerful message to any other family members who might be considering treason.

Brilliant at warfare, Nobunaga amassed great power through a series of successful battles and campaigns over rival *daimyo.* In 1560, he consolidated control of his province, Owari, by leading his greatly outnumbered troops to victory at the famous battle of Okehazama. By 1568, he was able to take over Kyoto, the imperial capital, in support of and in con-trol of Ashikaga Yoshiaki (r. 1568–1573), the ruler of the Ashikaga shogunate—whom Nobunaga forced out of the capital in 1573.

In 1571, Nobunaga crushed opposition from the Buddhist monks at Mount Hiei by burning the monastery and slaughtering 3,000 people, regardless of age or position. Three years later, in 1574, he forced the opposing fanatical Ikko sect of Buddhists into their own fortifications and then burned their Nagashima complex, massacring an estimated 20,000 men, women, and children.

Oda Nobunaga was shrewd in choosing his allies and his subordinates, while the battles and intrigues of his rule never ceased. Early on, in 1562, he entered into a sometimes uneasy alliance with Tokugawa Ieyasu, who, with Toyotomi Hideyoshi, was one of the two reforming warlords who subsequently built on Nobunaga's successes. Ieyasu eventually established the Tokugawa shogunate, which ruled Japan from 1600 to the Meiji Restoration in 1868. Toyotomi Hideyoshi rose to power as one of Nobunaga's finest warriors.

DICTATORIAL RULE

After 1568, Nobunaga exercised almost total administrative and political control of Japan, and he was unquestionably a dictator. Oddly, he never had himself named shogun. Some historians say this is because shoguns had to belong to the house of Minamoto, and his family line was Taira. Others say that Nobunaga was confident that asking for legitimization would diminish his power and put him in a

ROYAL RITUALS

THE THREE SAMURAI WARLORDS

The period of the Warring States, or *sengoku,* in Japan (mid-1400s to late 1500s) was brought to a close by the military and political accomplishments of three successive samurai warlords whose destinies were closely entwined: Oda Nobunaga (1534–1582); Toyotomi Hideyoshi (1536–1598); and Tokugawa Ieyasu (1542–1616). A much-quoted, popular Japanese story describes the reaction of each of these warlords (reflecting their personality and style of rule) when faced with a songbird that will not sing: Says Nobunaga, "I will kill the bird." Says Hideyoshi, "I will persuade it to sing," forcibly if need be. Says Ieyasu, "I will wait for it to sing."

position inferior to the agent who conferred the title of shogun.

Nobunaga was the first Japanese warlord to understand the strategic use of the new firearms brought to Japan by the Europeans, most notably at the battle of Nagashino in 1575. Through conquest and governance, the Nobunaga regime redrew the map of feudal Japan. Nobunaga redistributed conquered domains to his commanders and vassals, upsetting patterns of local power. He instituted a survey of agricultural lands under his control, presumably to assess the obligations of his vassals. He worked to rebuild Kyoto's economic status and maintain order within his growing territory. He also standardized weights and measures, closed many of the numerous toll booths along the roads—a move popular with ordinary citizens—and began a campaign to disarm all peasants.

Probably to counter Buddhist power, Nobunaga became friendly with Jesuit missionaries in Japan and protected them from persecution or hostile acts. Clearly, he found them sympathetic, and through them he became the first Japanese ruler to become known in the West. On a lakeside in Azuchi, he built the finest castle in Japan as a symbol of his power. He also built a fleet of six large seagoing ships, all unprecedented in size.

Schooled in the rituals of the Japanese tea ceremony, Nobunaga collected tea implements and gave them as gifts to those he favored. He loved poetry and was known to be jealous at times of others' talent.

END OF HIS RULE

By 1582, Oda Nobunaga began a military campaign to bring western Japan under his control and finally unify the country. Instead of achieving victory, Nobunaga was killed in June 1582 when one of his retainers, Akechi Mitsuhide, turned against the dictator. On the morning of his death, after entertaining a group of nobles in the Honnoji temple in Kyoto, Nobunaga woke to find the temple surrounded by forces gathered by Mitsuhide. Trapped in the building, Nobunaga either committed suicide or died in the fire that was started by the troops surrounding the temple.

In the clashes that ensued among the samurai clans after Nobunaga's death, his loyal retainer, Toyotomi Hideyoshi, proved himself a better soldier and a better politician than his rivals and rose to be first among equals. By 1590, Hideyoshi had become the undisputed ruler of Japan, building on Nobunaga's successes and consolidating control through a network of powerful personal loyalties.

See also: Shogunate; Tokugawa Ieyasu; Tokugawa Shogunate; Toyotomi Hideyoshi.

FURTHER READINGS

Henshall, Kenneth G. *A History of Japan: From Stone Age to Superpower.* New York: St. Martin's Press, 2001.

Oldenburg Dynasty

(1448–1863 C.E.)

Scandinavian dynasty that ruled in Denmark and Norway from 1448 to 1814, in Denmark to 1863, and in Sweden 1457 to 1521. The Oldenburg dynasty had its roots in the state of Oldenburg, a region in northwestern Germany bordering the North Sea. During the twelfth century, the counts of Oldenburg became princes of the Holy Roman Empire.

The first member of the Oldenburg dynasty to rule in Scandinavia was Christian I of Denmark (r. 1448–1481) and Norway (r. 1449–1481). Christian's younger brother Gerard and his successors continued to rule as princes of Oldenburg in Germany until the 1600s. Although Christian also became king of Sweden in 1457, the country never accepted his rule or that of his descendants. The Swedes threw off Danish rule in 1521 under Gustavus I Vasa (r. 1523–1560), the founder of Sweden's Vasa dynasty.

In Denmark and Norway, the Oldenburgs oversaw times of great change, ruling from the late Middle Ages into the mid-1800s. During this time, Scandinavia and the rest of Europe changed from an era in which coalitions of nobles could overthrow kings to an age of absolute monarchy and then to a time of fear of republicanism following the French Revolution.

In the Treaty of Kiel (1814), Denmark ceded Norway to the Swedish Crown, ending Oldenburg rule of Norway. In Denmark itself, however, the Oldenburgs continued to rule, their kings' names alternating since the 1500s with monotonous regularity in a series of monarchs named either Frederick or Christian.

The last Oldenburg king of Denmark, Frederick VII (r. 1848–1863), ruled during war with Prussia over the duchy of Slesvig, the possession of which Denmark and Germany had contested for centuries. Frederick died childless in 1863, ending the direct Oldenburg line. He was succeeded by Christian IX of Glücksburg (r. 1863–1906), a member of the Sonderburg-Glücksburg dynasty.

See also: DANISH KINGDOM; GUSTAVUS I (VASA); NORWEGIAN MONARCHY; SWEDISH MONARCHY.

OLMEC KINGDOM (1400s–400 B.C.E.)

The earliest known Mesoamerican civilization, located in Mexico, and thought to be the progenitor of all of the later high cultures of the region.

The people known today as the Olmec first appeared in Mesoamerica around 1400 B.C.E. They settled in the lowlands of eastern Mexico, where they learned to domesticate maize, the staple of their economy and a central element of Olmec culture. Very little is known about the early centuries of Olmec settlement, but the Olmec are known to have developed irrigated agriculture, for they constructed great stone aqueducts and drainage systems.

The Olmec were the first people of Mesoamerica to develop a writing system, which employed both pictographs and syllabic elements. They also developed a complicated calendrical system. Both of these developments seem to have been motivated in part by the central role that maize played in the Olmec culture. The calendars were developed to chart the growing and harvest seasons, whereas the writing system enabled the Olmec to keep records for the allocation of the grain harvest.

As the Olmec grew more efficient at agriculture, they were able to support a larger and more specialized population. By about 1200 B.C.E. they had become the most powerful people in the region, and their leaders began a campaign of conquest, bringing the neighboring tribes under their control. It is believed that this control did not extend to political stewardship but was limited instead to the extraction of tribute in the form of maize and slaves.

The Olmec rise to dominance took many centuries, but they eventually spread from the Chontalpa lowlands in the east to the Tuxtlas Mountains in the west. The Olmec established a number of important ceremonial centers: La Venta, in the present-day Mexican state of Tabasco; San Lorenzo Tenoctitla, in the state of Veracruz; and Laguna de los Cerros, also in Veracruz. Olmec ceremonial centers were notable for their pyramids, which probably originated as simple platform mounds. The centers also contained ball courts, leading some scholars to suggest that the Olmec invented the ball games that became ubiquitous in the cultures of Mesoamerica.

It is unclear how urban Olmec ceremonial centers were. It is certain that they were used for rituals, but it is not known whether or not they supported markets or a large residential population. The ceremonial aspect of their existence has been demonstrated by the discovery of a great deal of Olmec art that appears religious in nature. Examples of this art include representations of what must have been the chief deities of the Olmec, especially figures of a jaguar god with human features and the feathered serpent that later became known as Quetzalcoatl. These figures were carved or sculpted in wood, jade, and basalt.

Basalt was only mined in the western reaches of Olmec territory, but basalt sculptures have been found throughout the kingdom. The most impressive

Artifacts of the ancient Olmec civilization of Mesoamerica, these colossal stone heads with carved features range in height from 5 feet to more than 11 feet and weighing thousands of pounds. Since the first head was unearthed from a Mexican jungle floor in 1862, a total of 170 heads have been discovered.

of the Olmec basalt sculptures are huge heads that stand from five to eleven feet tall. These are, in fact, only a portion of the original sculptures: the heads were toppled from their perches on equally monumental bodies. These huge sculptures are thought to represent Olmec rulers. The production of the statues must have been of great importance, for there are many of them: more than 170 Olmec heads have been found to date. Many of the heads have been mutilated. Individual statues may have been constructed during the reign of the king that they represented, then decapitated and otherwise mutilated after that king died and was replaced by a new ruler.

The Olmec kings likely resided in the ceremonial centers because the structures that are commonly identified as altars seem also to have served as thrones. Some of these structures have dates incised on them, possibly signifying the reign of the particular kings who used them. It appears that once a monument or statue was deemed no longer useful, it was recycled to make a new one.

Scholars know little more about Olmec society beyond the likelihood that it contained two classes: elites and commoners. The elites most likely comprised the priestly hierarchy and the nobility, and lived in or near the ceremonial centers. The commoners were largely farmers, who were essential to the maize-based economy. Sculpted figurines provide a glimpse into certain cultural practices that are echoed in later Mesoamerican civilizations. For instance, the Olmec appear to have practiced intentional cranial deformation, strapping the heads of their infants to boards in order to force the bones to reshape into an elongated form. This same practice was found among the Maya, who came to the region much later.

The Olmec built burial pyramids, and these do not seem to have been reserved only for royal burials. The ball courts also appear to have had ritual significance. Blood sacrifice is also attributed to the Olmec. However, it is not known conclusively whether this meant human sacrifice (as practiced by later peoples, such as the Toltec and Aztec), or simply nonlethal bloodletting done by members of the priestly and noble classes.

Because the Olmec writing system has not yet been fully deciphered, scholars are not certain of the number of kings, their names, and the dates of their respective reigns. It is known that sometime around 400 B.C.E. the Olmec abandoned their ritual centers,

and a new culture, that of the Teotihuaca, began its rise to dominance.

See also: AZTEC EMPIRE; MAYA EMPIRE; TOLTEC EMPIRE; ZAPOTEC EMPIRE.

FURTHER READING

Coe, Michael D. *The Aztecs.* Norman: University of Oklahoma Press, 1973.
Davies, Nigel. *The Ancient Kingdoms of Mexico.* New York: Penguin, 1990.

ORANGE-NASSAU, HOUSE OF

(1747 C.E.–Present)

Ruling house of the Netherlands from the mid-eighteenth century to the present day.

In 1747, after a forty-five-year interregnum (a period between reigns, when no king was on the throne), William IV (r. 1747–1751) of Nassau succeeded his distant cousin, William III (r. 1672–1702), as *stadholder* (viceroy) of Holland. In tribute to his ancestors, William took the dynastic name Orange-Nassau. (In 1554, William I, the Silent [r. 1472–1584], count of Nassau, had received the princedom of Orange through inheritance and was proclaimed stadholder of Holland and Zeeland.)

William IV had previously been stadholder of Friesland, one of the seven provinces of the Netherlands. Upon his death in 1751, William IV was succeeded by his son, William V, the Batavian (r. 1751–1795), who declared war on France in 1793. Two years later, when the French republic conquered the country, William fled to England.

From 1795 to 1806, Holland was renamed the Batavian Republic, but the country was a republic in name only and was, in fact, dominated by France. In 1806, Napoleon Bonaparte transformed the country into the kingdom of Holland, with his brother Louis Napoleon (r. 1806–1810) as king.

By the time the Napoleonic Empire collapsed in 1813, William V had died in exile. However, his son, also named William, returned to Holland. Since the office of stadhllder had been abolished, William became prince of the Netherlands in 1813. Two years later, as William I (r. 1815–1840), he became king of the Netherlands and grand duke of Luxembourg. During his reign, which restored the House of

Orange-Nassau to the throne, the southern province of the kingdom separated, forming the independent kingdom of Belgium.

William I abdicated the throne in 1840, after his Dutch subjects forced him to revise the nation's constitution and make it more liberal. He was succeeded by his son, William II (1840–1849), during whose reign calls for reform increased, and the Netherlands became a constitutional monarchy. Upon his death in 1849, William II was succeeded on the throne by his son, William III (r. 1849–1890), the first king to rule the Netherlands as a constitutional monarch.

With the death of William III in 1890, the male line of the House of Orange-Nassau came to an end in the Netherlands. William III was succeeded by his daughter, Queen Wilhelmina (r. 1890–1948), who ruled during the German occupation of the Netherlands in World War II. Wilhelmina fled to England in May 1940 and spent the remainder of the war in exile.

Following the war, Queen Wilhelmina abdicated in favor of her daughter Queen Juliana (1948–1980) who, in turn, abdicated and was succeeded by her daughter, the present ruler, Queen Beatrix (r. 1980–present).

See also: JULIANA; NETHERLANDS KINGDOM; WILHELMINA.

ORISSA KINGDOM. *See* UTKALA

(ORISSA) KINGDOM

OSEI TUTU (ca. 1636–1717 C.E.)

First king (r. ca. 1697–1717) of the Asante kingdom of Ghana, who created a distinctive form of governance that survives to the present day.

Born into the Oyoko clan, Osei Tutu was the nephew of the ruler of Kumasi, a small state located in what is today the nation of Ghana. When his uncle died in the late 1600s, Osei succeeded him as ruler of Kumasi and embarked upon a campaign to extend the borders of his realm. At that time, the region was home to several small, independent states, the most powerful of which was that of the Denkyera, who monopolized local access to the trans-Saharan trade.

Osei knew that he could not challenge the Denkyera alone, so he forged a military alliance with the other Asante states. With this additional force, he succeeded in conquering the Denkyera after waging a war that lasted from 1699 to 1701. Building on the success of this alliance, Osei formalized the arrangement, thus creating a unified Asante Empire that soon became the dominant political and economic power of the region. At its height, the Asante Empire encompassed nearly all of Ghana and extended well into present-day Cote d'Ivoire (Ivory Coast).

Osei used various rituals to legitimize and consolidate his power through the region. Chief among these was the ritual of the Golden Stool. Throughout Asante territory, the installation of a local ruler was traditionally accomplished through a ritual that employed a stool. The stool was a symbolic item, not to be mistaken for a royal throne. It was seen as the repository for the spirit of the local people. Osei established a supreme stool, ornamented in gold, which was understood to incorporate all the others, thus coming to symbolize the unity of all the Asante peoples.

Osei also reconfigured other ceremonial occasions, most notably the *odwira,* a harvest festival, and instituted them on a national scale. This, too, was another way to provide a ritual enactment of Asante unity. Osei Tutu's unified Asante kingdom proved exceptionally enduring, lasting to the present day.

See also: ASANTE KINGDOM.

OSMAN I (1259–1326 C.E.)

Anatolian Turkish ruler (r. 1280–1324) who founded the Osmanli dynasty of the Ottoman Empire. Osman was a bey, or lord, and although he is sometimes called the first Ottoman sultan, the first Ottoman ruler to use the title of sultan was his son Orhan (r. 1324–1362).

Born in Anatolia (present-day Turkey) in 1258, Osman was the son of a clan ruler called Ertugrul. A talented warrior and leader, Osman inherited a small principality in the 1280s. Around the 1290s, he declared his territory independent of the Seljuk Turks, whose crumbling dynasty was leaving a power vacuum in Anatolia. Osman married the daughter of a holy man and raised his son Orhan to succeed him as a military and political leader.

Osman's army was a collection of seminomadic

ghazis, or Muslim warriors. They fought in the name of Islam, but also for material and territorial gain. Despite the religious basis of his leadership, Osman proclaimed a policy of religious tolerance that was to become a hallmark of the Ottoman Empire.

In the early decades of the fourteenth century, Osman gained territory at the expense of the Byzantine Empire, as his troops conquered lands north and west of the central Anatolian region. Near the end of his life, he laid siege to Bursa, a prosperous Greek Christian city near the Sea of Marmara (which lies between the Black and Mediterranean seas). Osman's son Orhan conquered the city, and the infirm Osman lived long enough to hear of the victory.

After his death in 1324, Osman was buried in Bursa, which became the first capital of the Ottoman Empire. His dynasty and the empire it ruled are known as Osmanli (in Turkish), deriving the names from their first ruler.

See also: BYZANTINE EMPIRE; OTTOMAN EMPIRE; SELJUK DYNASTY.

OSTROGOTH KINGDOM

(200s–552 C.E.)

Kingdom of the Ostrogoths, the eastern branch of the Germanic Gothic peoples, originally located in Eastern Europe, later moved to Italy, and eventually conquered by the Byzantine Empire.

According to tradition, the ancestors of the Goths were the Gotars, a Germanic people from the area of southern Sweden and the southern Baltic area. By the 200s, the Goths had settled in the region north of the Black Sea. They soon split into two groups, the Ostrogoths (or East Goths) and the Visigoths (or West Goths).

After the Goths split, the Ostrogoths settled in the area of the present-day Ukraine and established a kingdom there. One of the early Ostrogothic kings, Ermanric (r. ?–375), was defeated and conquered by the Huns around 375. From then until the death of the Hun leader, Attila (r. 445–453), in 453, the Ostrogoths were subject to the Huns, although they retained some degree of autonomy.

After the death of Attila, the Ostrogoths moved westward and settled in the ancient Roman province of Pannonia (roughly present-day Hungary), where they became somewhat troublesome allies of the Eastern Roman or Byzantine Empire. Their most important king at this time was Theodoric the Great (r. 474–526). After ravaging the Balkan province of Thrace in the 470s, Theodoric, through the Eastern Roman emperor Zeno (r. 474–491), diverted his attention westward. Zeno commissioned Theodoric to overthrow Odoacer, a former barbarian mercenary who had overthrown the last Roman emperor in the West, Romulus Augustulus (r. 475–476), in 476 and taken the title king of Italy. After marching to Italy, Theodoric quickly overcame Odoacer and killed him. Theodoric then established an Ostrogothic kingdom in Italy, with its capital at the city of Ravenna in northern Italy.

The Ostrogothic kingdom in Italy was the most civilized of the post-Roman barbarian kingdoms in the western Mediterranean region. The kingdom was marked by the persistence of Roman civilization and the continued acknowledgment of the rule of the Eastern Roman emperor at Constantinople. Even the Roman Senate continued to meet (as it had under Odoacer), and many of its senators served in Theodoric's government.

Unlike other barbarian states, the Ostrogothic kingdom in Italy did not have different sets of laws for Romans and barbarians, although Goths were tried by Goths in military courts and Romans by Romans in civilian courts. Like other barbarian states, however, Ostrogothic Italy did face the problem of religious differences. The Ostrogoths were Arian Christians, an early form of Christianity that denied the equality of Christ with God the Father. But most of the Roman subjects in the kingdom were followers of the Roman branch of Christianity, which accepted the doctrine of the Trinity.

While Theodoric ruled, his strong personality enabled him to keep tensions between Ostrogoths and Romans in check. Toward the end of his reign, however, he adopted a harsher policy toward the Senate and leading Romans for fear that they were conspiring with the emperor. After Theodoric's death in 526, the Ostrogoth-Roman relationship began to fray and show more strains.

Theodoric was succeeded by his young grandson Athalaric (r. 526–534), but the real power lay with Athalaric's mother and regent, Amalasuntha, who was Theodoric's daughter. Many traditional Ostrogoths believed that Amalasuntha was too "Roman" in her actions and beliefs, and that she favored the

Roman subjects of the kingdom to the detriment of the Ostrogoths. She also lacked Theodoric's fame as a war leader, which was an important attribute to the Ostgrogoths.

In 534, Amalasuntha was imprisoned and murdered by her cousin, Theodahad (r. 534–536), who took the Crown of the Ostrogothic kingdom for himself. At this time, the Ostrogoths were in the path of the Roman emperor Justinian (r. 527–565), who wanted to destroy the influence of Arianism. Justinian used the murder of Amalasuntha as a pretext to deal with the Ostrogothic kingdom. Proclaiming themselves avengers of Amalasuntha, Roman legions under General Belisarius landed in Italy in 535.

The Romans deposed Theodahad, a poor leader, in favor of General Witiges (r. 536–540), who was captured and taken to Constantinople in 540. (The Ostrogoths had offered to make Belisarius their king, but he refused.) Witiges was succeeded by the brief reigns of Hildibad (r. 540–541) and Eraric (r. 541), both of whom had the support of the Romans. When Belisarius returned to Constantinople in 541, the Ostrogoths rebelled under the leadership of Totila (r. 541–552), who took the Ostrogothic throne.

A fairly capable leader, Totila retook Rome, but he was eventually defeated and killed in the battle of Busta Gallorum in 552 by the Roman general Narses. Soon after the defeat of Totila, the Ostrogothic kingdom of Italy came to an end, and control over Italy passed to the Byzantines and then the Lombards, another Germanic people who invaded northern Italy in 568 and established their own kingdom.

See also: BYZANTINE EMPIRE; JUSTINIAN I; LOMBARD KINGDOM; THEODORIC THE GREAT.

FURTHER READING

Burns, Thomas S. *A History of the Ostrogoths.* Bloomington: Indiana University Press, 1984.

OTTO I, THE GREAT (912–973 C.E.)

German King (r. 936–973) and Holy Roman emperor (r. 962–973) of the Saxon dynasty, who defeated the Magyars, consolidated and extended German rule even to Italy, and created a highly efficient church-based ruling bureaucracy for the German Empire.

The son of German king, Henry I (r. 919–936),

Otto I succeeded to the German throne upon the death of his father in 936. He was twenty-four years old. After taking the throne, Otto faced rebellions by his brother Henry and Duke Eberhard of Franconia. Otto defeated the Franconians at the battle of Andernach in 939, and he forced Henry to submit in 941. Meanwhile, Otto also campaigned against King Louis IV of France (r. 936–954), who had assisted the rebels.

In 951, Adelaide, the widowed queen of Italy, appealed to Otto for help from her incarceration at the hands of the new Italian king, Berengar II (r. 950–963), who wanted to force Adelaide to marry him. Otto responded to Adelaide's plea by invading Italy. He defeated Berengar, rescued and married Adelaide, and forced Berengar to swear fealty to him. Otto also assumed the title king of the Lombards.

In 953, Otto's son, Duke Ludolf of Swabia, and his son-in-law, Conrad the Red, led a rebellion against him and were later joined by the Magyars in the revolt. Otto quickly returned from Italy to defeat the Magyars near Augsburg in 955, and his victory freed Germany of threat from that quarter for generations. Meanwhile, he curbed the powers of the German dukes by forming a close alliance between the Crown and the Church.

In the meantime, Pope John XII appealed to Otto I to help defend the Holy See against the resurgent Berengar II, who had renewed aggressive actions against the papacy. Pleased to comply, Otto returned to Italy and once again easily dispatched the forces of Berengar. Otto then successfully pressed the pope to revive the imperial title held by the Carolingian kings, since it was the papacy's right to bestow the title of emperor.

Otto was crowned Roman emperor of the West in 962, as a result of which he is often considered the founder of the Holy Roman Empire. In addition, Otto's coronation helped legitimize the German claim to imperial power. But Pope John XII soon thought better of this coronation, finding the new emperor too powerful. Not one to hesitate, Otto marched on Rome, called a synod of bishops, and established his own pope, Leo VIII, who was installed in place of John XII. Otto also took as imperial property all the papal lands except the immediate environs of Rome and some of its surrounding territory.

Otto had his son, Otto II (r. 973–983), crowned co-emperor in 967 as a way to ensure the imperial succession. In 972, he secured his son's marriage to

Theophano, daughter of the Byzantine emperor, Romanus II (r. 959–963). By the time Otto died in 973, he had united his empire from the Baltic Sea to the Mediterranean Sea. He had developed strong ties with the Empire of the East (the Byzantine Empire) and had subjugated the papacy to the will of the emperor. Most importantly, he had created an efficient, loyal, and assiduous bureaucracy by his creative use of the Church's structure and training of intelligent and capable young men. This government did not look for war to fill its coffers but instead promoted a peace and prosperity that Germany enjoyed for generations. For these accomplishments, Otto has been given the honorific "the Great."

See also: HOLY ROMAN EMPIRE; SAXON DYNASTY.

OTTOMAN EMPIRE (ca. 1300–1923 C.E.)

Powerful and wealthy political entity that dominated much of the eastern Mediterranean for nearly six hundred years. From its capital at Constantinople (present-day Istanbul) in Anatolia (present-day Turkey), the Ottoman Empire extended its reach north into Crimea, west to Morocco, south to Yemen, and east to Iran, incorporating parts of Arabia, North Africa, and Syria. Ruling this vast expanse of lands was the Ottoman, or Osmanli, dynasty, which ruled over its empire longer than any other single dynastic clan known to history. The empire's eventual rise to wealth and power, however, could hardly have been predicted from its origins, in one of the small, scattered emirates that littered the landscape of Anatolia (Asia Minor) in the eleventh century.

RISE OF THE EMPIRE

The rise of the Ottoman Empire began with the peoples of the Asian steppes region, nomadic tribes called Yoruk (from which later came the word "Turk"), who, prior to the 700s, traveled south and east to find fresh lands free of the depredations of Mongol raiders. Herders and fierce fighters, these tribes eventually made their way to the Anatolian plains. In Anatolia, they came into contact with Islam, and over the course of the eighth and ninth centuries, most converted to this religion. Most, however, also retained the social organization, warlike culture, and nomadic lifestyle of their ancestors.

One group was different, however. These were the Seljuks, who took advantage of the hospitable Mediterranean climate of the region and settled into villages. With the advantage of agriculture, they soon grew numerous and powerful and ultimately took control of the region, establishing their capital in the city of Isfahan, in Iran, in 1077. Across their western border lay the wealthy and powerful Byzantine Empire, with its capital at Constantinople. It was not long before the Seljuk rulers began to look jealously upon their neighbors' lands.

A series of skirmishes between the two occurred as the Seljuks tried to expand into Armenia, which was then part of the Byzantine Empire. In the last decades of the eleventh century, the Seljuks finally succeeded in ousting Byzantine defenders from the region. This success, however, set the stage for the decline of the Seljuks. With a powerful enemy on the western border, the Seljuk rulers were unprepared to face an additional threat from the north, which came when Mongol raiders swept into the area in 1243. The Mongols devastated the Seljuk Empire, only to return to the north as swiftly as they had come.

With the empire in tatters and the Seljuk dynasty demoralized, many of the smaller tribes of Anatolia were free to establish themselves as autonomous emirates. One such tribe was led by a warrior named Osman. A follower of the *ghazi* tradition ("warriors of Islam"), Osman began a series of military actions against other principalities, and by 1299 he had taken control of nearly all of Anatolia, while the Seljuk dynasty faded into obscurity. It is from Osman that the term *Ottoman* was later derived (from the Turkish *Osmanli*). Osman, now called Osman-*ghazi* I (r. 1280–1324), established a capital city in Bursa in Anatolia, and then set out to do what the Seljuks had tried but failed to do previously: conquer Byzantium.

Osman's military successes were due in large part to his ability to attract volunteers for his armies. These volunteers came from throughout the Islamic world, drawn into Osman's service by the promise of a share of the wealth gained through conquest. With help from these "warriors of Islam," Osman soon extended his empire well beyond the borders that the Seljuks had established.

Osman died in 1324 and was succeeded by his son Orkhan-*ghazi* (r. 1324–1359), who continued the work of expanding the lands under Ottoman rule. However, it was not until the reign of the third Ottoman ruler, Murad I (r. 1359–1389), that this expansion took on dramatic proportions. Sultan Murad created a new military force, the Janissaries, which consisted of former slaves and, later, Christian captives who were required to pay tribute in the form of military service. Unlike the *ghazi,* who fought from horseback, the Janissaries were foot soldiers. With their incorporation into the sultan's army, they offered greater military flexibility as well as a huge boost in manpower. The Janissaries swore their allegiance directly to the Ottoman sultan himself, and from their ranks he chose the best to serve as advisers in both peacetime and war.

From 1362 to 1363, Murad's powerful new army helped achieve the greatest military expansion to date, enabling him to capture Thrace (the northeastern portion of Greece), southern Bulgaria, and northwestern Turkey. This was Byzantine territory initially, but Murad followed a practice that his grandfather Osman had initiated earlier: he offered the services of his Janissaries to the Byzantine Empire to aid in its defense. Then, with his troops in place, he followed up with an invasion of his own.

EXPANSION AND CONSOLIDATION

With the capture of Thrace, the Ottoman Empire gained its first toehold in continental Europe, raising fears that Christian Byzantium would be next to fall. These fears led Pope Gregory XI (r. 1370–1378) to call all Christian lands to launch a crusade to take back the territories lost to the Turks and to defend the Byzantine capital of Constantinople. This crusade failed, and in its wake the Ottoman Empire expanded further, laying claim to Serbia and Bulgaria in the Balkan region of southeastern Europe.

The reign of Mehmed II (r. 1451–1481) was a time of such unprecedented military success that the sultan is remembered as "Mehmed the Conqueror." In 1453, Mehmed succeeded in capturing the greatest prize of all, the city of Constantinople, which he made his new capital and site of the imperial court. Three years later, the ancient Greek city of Athens fell to Ottoman forces, and by 1478 the empire stretched northward to include Bosnia, Wallachia (now part of Romania), and the Crimea. In 1480, Otranto, in Italy, was forced to join the empire, and even Rome was threatened with conquest.

Although the Ottoman Empire would expand further, massive territorial gains declined with the end of Mehmed II's rule. His successors became more preoccupied with consolidating control of the territories they held. This proved difficult, not only because the empire was so vast, but also because of administrative factors and disputes over the imperial succession.

Of all the Ottoman emperors, the one best known to the Western world is Suleyman I, the Magnificent (r. 1520–1566). His reputation derives from two sources. First, he more than doubled the land-

ROYAL RITUALS

RELIGIOUS AUTHORITY OF THE SULTAN

Unlike dynastic houses that claim descent from the gods, as was true in Japan, the Islamic Ottoman dynasty derived its validation wholly from the temporal world. Without popular support and a loyal retinue of palace guards, the sultan could be easily deposed and replaced. Nonetheless, as caliph (supreme temporal leader of Islam), the sultan had two important religious duties. The first was to maintain Islamic orthodoxy among his people, which meant that he had to root out all improper religious beliefs and practices. His second responsibility was to ensure the safety of travelers on the road to Mecca in Arabia. This was of grave importance, for the single most important ritual occasion in the lives of most Muslims is to make a *hajj* or pilgrimage, to the holy city of Mecca, which is the birthplace of Islam.

Ottoman Empire

OSMAN I*	1280–1324		IBRAHAM	1640–1648
ORKHAN	1324–1359		MEHMED IV	1648–1687
MURAD I	1359–1389		SULEYMAN II	1687–1691
BEYEZID I	1389–1403		AHMAD II	1691–1695
SULEYMAN ÇELEBI	1403–1410		MUSTAFA II	1695–1703
MEHMED I	1410–1421		AHMAD III	1703–1730
MUSA	1410–1413		MAHMUD I	1730–1754
MURAD II	1421–1444		OSMAN III	1754–1757
MEHMED II*	1444–1446		MUSTAFA III	1757–1774
MURAD II	1446–1451		ABD AL-HAMAD I	1774–1789
MEHMED II*	1451–1481		SELIM III*	1789–1807
BEYEZID II*	1481–1512		MUSTAFA IV	1807–1808
SELIM I	1512–1520		MAHMUD II	1808–1839
SULEYMAN I*	1520–1566		ABD AL-MAJID I	1839–1861
SELIM II*	1566–1574		ABD AL-'AZIZ	1861–1876
MURAD III	1574–1595		MURAD V	1876–1876
MEHMED III	1595–1603		ABD AL-HAMID II*	1876–1909
AHMAD I	1603–1617		MEHMED V	1909–1918
MUSTAFA I	1617–1618		MEHMED VI	1918–1922
OSMAN II	1618–1622		ABD AL-MAJID II	
MUSTAFA I	1622–1623		(AS CALIPH ONLY)	1922–1924
MURAD IV	1623–1640		*Indicates a separate alphabetical entry.	

holdings inherited from his father, Selim I (r. 1512–1520). His armies conquered most of Greece and Hungary, threatened Rome, and even captured lands held by the powerful Holy Roman Empire. Second, Suleyman was a great builder and a patron of the arts. During his reign, a number of great temples and public works were built, including the Dome of the Rock in Jerusalem. Within Islam, Suleyman is honored as the "Lawgiver," because he achieved the final codification of the *kanun,* or "sultanic law," that evolved over centuries as a result of decisions by the sultans.

A Fractious Ruling Family

Succession to the imperial throne in the Ottoman dynasty was a highly contested affair. There was no rule of primogeniture, in which the firstborn child, often a son, is clearly recognized as heir. Thus, the death or expulsion of a ruler was likely to be followed by a struggle among several contenders for

THE OTTOMAN EMPIRE, 1683

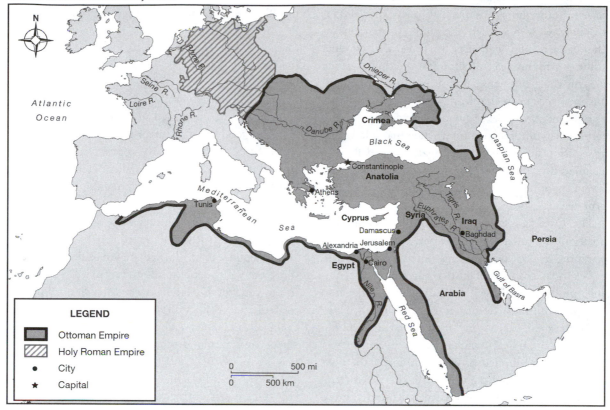

LEGEND

▰ Ottoman Empire

▨ Holy Roman Empire

● City

★ Capital

---

the throne. These power struggles endangered the safety of the empire, which at times was left leaderless as factions fought for supremacy. In addition, there were frequent plots and schemes hatched among the nobility, most of whom were heir to the warlord tradition and likely to betray their allegiance to the sultan to further their personal interests.

Murad II (r. 1421–1444; 1446–1451) was the first Ottoman ruler to attempt to make his position more secure. He did this by reorganizing the military and forming a personal armed force from the Janissaries, which he elevated in status so that they ranked higher than hereditary warlords and nobles. The problem with this solution was that he merely replaced one set of power brokers with another. In time, the Janissaries themselves often toppled a weak emperor.

Mehmed II (r. 1451–1481) turned to the law to strengthen the emperor's position. He decreed that upon the enthronement of the eldest son of a dead or deposed ruler, all other contenders to the throne were to be murdered. This meant killing not only the siblings of the newly enthroned emperor but also the brothers of the previous ruler. In terms of political

expediency, this law had at least the merit of simplicity, and it remained in force for more than 150 years.

Nonetheless, there was no guarantee that a sultan's rule was secure. Deposition was always possible, as Beyezid II (r. 1481–1512) learned to his dismay. His son, impatient to rule, deposed him in 1512 to become Sultan Yavuz Selim I (r. 1512–1520). Selim I's brief eight-year rule was followed by the reign of Suleyman I, whose own sons also tried to overthrow their father. Suleyman, perhaps recalling Beyezid II's experience, resorted to a simple solution to end the threat to his reign: invoking the law passed by Mehmed II, he attempted to have his three sons killed. His son Selim survived and eventually took the throne as Selim II (r. 1566–1574).

Life Within the Empire

The Ottoman Empire, though predominantly Islamic, consisted of a remarkable diversity of peoples. Within its borders lived Persians and Mongols, Slavs and Greeks, Jews and Christians. Perhaps more remarkable was the official attitude of tolerance for differences in beliefs and lifestyles. Although Christians and other non-Muslims had to pay special tribute, they were accorded the same protections as other citizens and were free to travel and conduct business without fear of molestation. In fact, one role of the Janissaries was to ensure that non-Muslims were protected from violence from followers of Islam. A vivid example of this tolerance comes from the late fifteenth century, when many Jews fled persecution in Spain and Portugal. Beyezid II, who occupied the Ottoman throne at that time, welcomed these refugees into his empire and gave them a safe haven.

The Ottoman state was under the absolute authority of the sultan, whose primary purpose was to guarantee *adalet* (justice). This not only referred to the Western concept of justice, meaning the equitable application of law, but also included the idea that the weak must be protected from harm. Thus, the sultan's chief duties included overseeing the operation of the *ulama* (courts) to make certain that laws were fairly applied, as well as imposing the *siyasset*, a specific form of punishment levied on corrupt officials who overtaxed or mistreated the peasantry. The sultan also made public announcements of all new laws and taxes, so that the populace was less likely to be swindled by corrupt officials. To make certain that his officers were behaving properly, the sultan made periodic tours of the empire in disguise, visiting local bureaucracies to see that they were all fulfilling their obligations.

The Ottoman Empire was hierarchical, with the top level composed of military leaders and others whose families had been raised to noble status. Most of the wealth and property was concentrated in the hands of this elite class. The remainder of the population consisted of tradesmen, craftspeople, farmers, and others who held little real property. Membership in either class, however, was not an inevitable result of the fortunes of birth. A simple peasant, by performing a valued service to the sultan, could be elevated to higher rank. Conversely, an official who betrayed the sultan's confidence could easily find himself stripped of rank and property.

THE EMPIRE IN DECLINE

In the 1800s, the nations of Europe began expanding, and Russia also sought to gain new territories. It was from Russia that the Ottoman Empire faced its first serious challenge. In particular, Russia hoped to gain the territory of Crimea, which offered access to the Black Sea. Claiming outrage that the Ottoman Empire gave rights to Catholic France rather than to Orthodox Russia in the Holy Land, Russia launched the Crimean War (1854–1856). The Ottomans won, but only with the help of an alliance with Britain and France. The once seemingly invincible empire now realized that its continued survival depended on the help and goodwill of loyal allies.

In 1905, the Ottoman Empire was challenged from within. Rebels in the Balkan states of Bosnia and Herzegovina rose up to demand independence, and they were soon joined by like-minded factions in Bulgaria, Serbia, and Montenegro. Seeing an opportunity to gain Ottoman territory, Russia lent the rebels support in an alliance known as the Pan-Slavic movement. The rebellion lasted from 1875 to 1878; in the end, the Ottomans were forced to relinquish control of all Balkan territories.

In 1911, danger came from a new quarter. The European scramble for colonial territories in Africa was in full swing, and both Italy and France had their eyes on Libya in North Africa. Italy invaded that Ottoman-controlled territory first. The Ottomans, whose control over North African territories was only tenuous, were unable to hold onto the province because the sultan was preoccupied with attacks from Greece, Serbia, Bulgaria, and Montenegro, all of which took territory once held by the empire.

The final blow came in 1913, although it would be another nine years before the Ottomans were finally ousted completely. This was the year of the Second Balkan War, a regional conflict that brought renewed hostilities from Greece, Serbia, and Montenegro. Although the war was short-lived, the unrest among rival factions led directly to World War I. At the close of that war, the Treaty of Versailles (1919) resulted in the loss of Syria, Palestine, Arabia, and Mesopotamia from Ottoman control. Only three years later, in 1922, a group of Westernizing rebels known as the "Young Turks" toppled the Ottoman sultan, Mehmed VI (1918–1922), and declared Turkey a republic. The centuries-old Ottoman Empire now ceased to exist.

See also: ABD AL-HAMID II; BEYEZID II; BYZANTINE EMPIRE; OSMAN I; OTTOMAN EMPIRE; SELIM I, THE GRIM; SELIM III, THE GREAT; SULEYMAN I, THE MAGNIFICENT.

FURTHER READING

Braude, Benjamin, and Bernard Lewis. *Christians and Jews in the Ottoman Empire: The Functioning of a Plural Society.* New York: Holmes & Meier, 1982.

Shaw, Stanford J., and Ezel Kural Shaw. *History of the Ottoman Empire and Modern Turkey.* New York: Cambridge University Press, 1995.

Wheatcroft, Andrew. *The Ottomans: Dissolving Images.* New York: Penguin, 1993.

OTTONIAN DYNASTY (919–1024 C.E.)

Medieval German dynasty that ruled Germany and the Holy Roman Empire.

The Ottonian dynasty, also known as the House of Saxony or the Liudolfing dynasty, began with Duke Henry of Saxony (Henry the Fowler), who was elected King Henry I of Germany (r. 919–936) in 919. Only one German king, Conrad I (r. 911–918), had preceded him since the end of the Carolingian dynasty.

Conrad I had designated Henry I his successor while on his deathbed. This designation was confirmed by Henry's election by the German princes and his consecration by the clergy. Henry, in turn, designated his son, Otto I (r. 936–973), as his own successor.

Hereditary succession to the German kingship was not automatic, since monarchs needed the approval of the German princes to rule. However, it seemed as though the succession might become hereditary in this period, as the Crown passed from father to son through four generations.

In 961, Otto II (r. 961–983) was made co-ruler with his father Otto I, and he ruled alone after his father's death in 973. Otto II was succeeded by his three-year-old son, Otto III (r. 983–1002), whose grandmother and mother served as regents until Otto III reached his majority in 995.

Otto III died without an heir at the young age of twenty-one, and was succeeded by his cousin, Henry II (r. 1002–1024), the duke of Bavaria. Henry II also died without an heir and was the last ruler of the Ottonian dynasty. His successor, Conrad II (r. 1024–1039), was the first ruler of the Salian dynasty.

The Ottonians ruled not only as German kings but also as Holy Roman emperors. Although Henry I was never crowned emperor, his son Otto I was crowned at Rome in 962. Otto II, Otto III, and Henry II were all crowned emperors at Rome in their turn. Although the name Holy Roman Empire is sometimes used to refer to the empire at this period, "Holy Empire" did not come into use until the reign of Frederick I Barbarossa (r. 1155–1190) and "Holy Roman Empire" appeared only in the thirteenth century.

Though their rule was relatively brief, the Ottonian accomplishments were not insignificant. Perhaps their main achievement was in preventing the German dukes from gaining autonomy and Germany from fragmenting into a number of minor principalities linked only by common language.

The Ottonians also suppressed a number of rebellions. Henry I, for example, put down rebellions by the duke of Bavaria in 921 and the duke of Lorraine in 925. Throughout the reigns of his successors, warfare against rebellious dukes was an ongoing occurrence. Otto I spent the entire thirty-six years of his reign in near-constant warfare, fighting rebellious German dukes as well as rebellious Italians and the Byzantine Empire. Otto I also expanded the kingdom to the north and east, although the main period of German colonization of these areas came later, during the reign of Otto II.

Partly to counter the ambitions of the German dukes, the Ottonian kings gave monasteries and bishoprics greater administrative functions within the kingdom. They also exercised power through the appointment of counts, who served as administrators for the Crown. During the reign of Otto III, the *ministeriales*—unfree servants of the Crown, administrators and knights—became an important part of government. Otto III preferred to rely on them rather than the nobility.

In their relations with the Church, the Ottonians pushed for greater control. Henry II, for example, claimed the right to both appoint and invest bishops. The papacy later contested this right, however, since it implied that the bishops owed allegiance to the emperor and that the emperor had religious authority and was more than purely a secular ruler.

The Ottonians succeeded in making the German king master over the dukes or princes of Germany and the empire. In doing so, however, the dynasty failed to institutionalize the means by which they governed, relying on ties of personal loyalty rather than any clearly established administrative system to hold the kingdom together.

See also: CONRAD II; HOLY ROMAN EMPIRE; OTTO I, THE GREAT.

FURTHER READING

Barraclough, Geoffrey. *Origins of Modern Germany.* 3rd. ed. (1947). Oxford: Basil Blackwell, 1988.

Holmes, George, ed. *Oxford Illustrated History of Medieval Europe.* New York: Oxford University Press, 1988.

Leyser, Karl. *Medieval Germany and Its Neighbours: 900–1250.* London: Hambledon Press, 1982.

OUDH (AVADH) KINGDOM

(ca. 500s B.C.E.–1856 C.E.)

Kingdom of religious and political importance, located in the central part of northern India, which is now part of the modern state of Uttar Pradesh.

According to ancient Hindu myth, the city of Ayodhya was the birthplace of Rama, the incarnation of the Hindu god Vishnu. As such, it was one of the seven sacred cities of the Hindus. No one knows when the name of this ancient city came to be applied to the surrounding area, as Avadh, or when the name Oudh came into use for the kingdom that developed in the region.

In the sixth century B.C.E., King Prasenajit of Kosala (d. 568 B.C.E.) was a formidable rival of the kings of Magadha, Bimbisara (r. ca. 603–541 B.C.E.), and Ajatasatru (r. 541–519 B.C.E.). Gautama Siddhartha, the Buddha, was born in northern Kosala and sometimes resided in the city of Ayodhya, then called Saketa. By the fifth century B.C.E. there were more than one hundred Buddhist monasteries in Ayodhya.

The region around Ayodhya, which became known as Oudh, eventually become part of the Magadha kingdom.

Over the centuries, however, Oudh changed hands many times. Around 155 B.C.E., it was overrun by Menander (r. ca. 155–130 B.C.E.), the Indo-Greek king of Bactria (part of present-day Afganistan). Later, in the fourth and fifth centuries B.C.E., Oudh became part of the Gupta Empire. In the seventh century C.E., it was part of the Empire of Harshavardhana, and in the ninth century it was ruled by the Gurjara-Pratihara dynasty.

In 1192, Oudh came under Islamic rule when it was conquered by the Delhi sultanate. Oudh's governor, Ain-ul-Mulk, revolted against Delhi in 1340. The revolt was suppressed, but by that time a large portion of Oudh had been annexed by the kingdom of Jaunpur.

When Jaunpur fell to Delhi in 1479, Oudh's previous boundaries were restored. Oudh came under Mughal rule in 1526, when Delhi was conquered by Babur (r. 1526–1530), who established the Mughal Empire.

Oudh continued to be an important province of the Mughal Empire under Akbar the Great (r. 1556–1605). It remained under Mughal control until 1724, when its governor, Saadat Khan, declared independence. Saadat Khan (r. 1724–1739) established the Nawab dynasty of Oudh. He was followed on the throne by Safdar Jang (r. 1739–1754) and Shuja-ud-Daulah (r. 1754–1775).

In 1764, Shuja-ud-daulah, who took the title Nawab Wazir ("first minister" of the Mughal Empire), fell to the British East India Company at the battle of Buxar. Seeking to make Oudh a buffer between them and the dominions of the Maratha Confederacy, the British left the Nawabs in charge of Oudh, but they made it a feudal state under the protection of the British East India Company. This marked the beginning of the end for the kingdom of Oudh. In 1856, claiming continual misgovernment by the Nawabs, Britain annexed Oudh and it became part of the British Indian Empire.

See also: DELHI KINGDOM; GUPTA EMPIRE; GURJARA-PRATIHARA DYNASTY; KOSALA KINGDOM; MAGADHA KINGDOM; MARATHA CONFEDERACY; MUGHAL EMPIRE.

PACAL (603–683 C.E.)

Ruler of the Maya (r. 615–683), who inspired the grand art and architecture of the Mayan city of Palenque.

The Mayan monarchy was typically patrilineal (descending through the male line), but Pacal came from a line of strong women and inherited the throne from his mother, the Lady Sak-K'uk.' He later explained this deviation from tradition by claiming that his rule had been divinely ordained. Pacal also proclaimed that his mother was the human embodiment of the Mayan creator-goddess, the First Mother. Pacal may have needed to use these divine references in order to secure his hold on the throne; Mayan inscriptions in Palenque reveal that he was only twelve years old when he became king.

Pacal's city of Palenque was probably constructed during his reign and that of his son and successor, Chan-Bahlum (r. 683–702). The construction of the city was careful in its attention to structural and aesthetic detail. The main palace was filled with distinctive vaults in what has been termed the Palenque style. The walls were coated in plaster to give them a smooth, almost glossy finish, and the interiors of the buildings were filled with elaborate terra cotta and stucco images.

The Temple of Inscriptions in Palenque provides a number of excellent examples of these carvings. Among other things, they hint at the lifelong romance between Pacal and his wife, the Lady Tz'ak-Ahaw. Married on March 22, 626, according to the Maya calendar, their marriage lasted almost fifty years, until her death in 672.

Pacal survived his wife by eleven years, dying at the age of eighty in 683. He was placed in an ornate tomb under the Temple of Inscriptions. Pacal's five-ton carved limestone sarcophagus weighed so much that it was set in place beneath the temple before construction began. He and his jade funerary mask and breastplate were found undisturbed by archaeologists in 1952.

See also: MAYA EMPIRE.

PACHACUTI (ca. 1471 C.E.)

Incan emperor (r. 1438–1471) who established a tradition of rapid conquest that was taken up by his son, Topa Inca (r. 1471–1493), which formed the foundation of the Inca Empire.

Pachacuti was born Cusi Inca Yupanqui, son of the Inca ruler Viracocha Inca. As Viracocha began to consider retirement in his old age, he chose one of Cusi Inca Yupanqui's brothers, Inca Urcon, to be his successor, despite the fact that various important members of the Inca military preferred Cusi Yupanqui.

When the Inca capital city of Cuzco was threat-ened by the advancing armies of the nearby Chanca people, Viracocha and his chosen heir retreated to safety in the mountain sanctuary of Calca. Cusi Inca Yupanqui, the two generals who supported him, and several nobles remained behind in Cuzco to defend the city, which they did successfully. Once joined by other allies, Cusi Inca Yupanqui pursued the Chanca army and won two more decisive victories.

After Cusi Inca Yupanqui tried and failed to reconcile with his father, he established himself as emperor in Cuzco and named himself Pachacuti ("reformer of the world"). Through shrewd military alliances with the Chanca and resourceful generalship, Pachacuti soon encircled the stronghold of his father in the Andes Mountains. Viracocha Inca died during this time, and rule of the Calca faction passed to Inca Urcon. When Inca Urcon was killed in a minor clash with Pachacuti's forces in 1438, the Calca faction fell apart and the Inca people were united once more.

Taking advantage of the military framework already in place, Pachacuti proceeded to conquer several provinces to the south and west. Skirmishes with the Chanca continued until one of Pachacuti's sons, Topa Inca Yupanqui, acting under his father's orders, decisively subjugated both the province of the Chanca and that of the Quechua. He then proceeded to conquer territories as far north as modern-day Quito in Ecuador.

Pachacuti swiftly instituted new policies to help unite the many divisive sections of his suddenly expanded empire. He instituted a system of forced ethnic resettlement, which helped downplay the strength of former ethnic ties. He established a regularized state religion and set up a system of corporate land ownership. Pachacuti also instituted new building programs, allegedly designing many of the elaborate temples and palaces of Cuzco himself and most likely ordering the construction of Machu Picchu.

During this period of advanced administration, Pachacuti chose to hand over the reigns of power to his son, Topa Inca Yupanqui, who continued the tradition of conquest and building begun by his father.

See also: INCA EMPIRE.

FURTHER READING

Niles, Susan A. *The Shape of Inca History: Narrative and Architecture in an Andean Empire.* Iowa City: University of Iowa Press, 1999.

PAEKCHE KINGDOM (ca. 250–660 C.E.)

Kingdom that developed in Mahan, the southwest region of the Korean Peninsula, during the third century.

The Mahan region initially consisted of a series of self-sufficient walled cities that were subservient to China. In the third century, under the leadership of King Koi (r. 234–286), these cities established a confederacy that threatened to overthrow Chinese control. China responded by attacking the region from its northern strongholds. Koi then sought assistance from the Puyo princes of Manchuria. The Puyos defeated the Chinese but then assumed control of the region and named it Paekche.

One of the more important Paekche kings, Chogo (r. 346–375), consolidated Paekche by subduing all of the Mahan communities. Then in 371, he led an invasion into the kingdom of Koguryo, Paekche's northern neighbor, during which he killed Koguryo's king and annexed a large portion of the Korean Peninsula. Assured of his authority, Chogo made significant changes in Paekche society. Before his ascendancy, the Paekche leader had been elected from among the leading families of the kingdom's major cities. But Chogo now declared that the kingship would be inherited, thereby retaining the position for his family. Chogo also commissioned an official written history of Paekche, supported the introduction of Buddhism, and established diplomatic ties with Japan.

Over the next century, Paekche developed social institutions. The walled cities became sizable fortresses that protected the kingdom's borders. Originally, each city maintained its own agricultural economy, but as the authority of the king increased, all land came into his possession. Paekche's rulers used this wealth to protect their security, granting ownership of the land to the kingdom's most powerful families in exchange for their allegiance. During this process, the local inhabitants were converted into a powerless, though nominally free, peasant class.

Paekche's rulers also developed a bureaucratic system to accompany this new, hierarchical social stratification. The kingdom was divided into a series of units, each with its own governor and administration. The governor in each district collected newly instituted grain taxes, which were used to finance military and construction projects. Unfortunately,

Kings of Paekche

ON-JO	18 B.C.E.–28 C.E.
TA-RU	28–77
KI-RUQ	77–128
KAE-RU	128–166
CH'O-GO	166–214
KU-SU	214–234
SA-BAN	234
KO-I	234–286
CH'AE-GYE	286–298
PUN-SU	298–304
PI-RYU	304–344
KYE	344–346
KUN-CH'O-GO	346–375
KUN-GU-SU	375–384
CH'IM-YU	384–385
CHIN-SA	385–392
A-SIN	392–405
CHON-JI	405–420
KU-I-SIN	420–427
PI-YU	427–455
KAE-RU	455–475
MUN-JU	475–477
SAM-GUN	477–479
TONG-SONG	479–501
MU-RYONG	501–523
SONG	523–554
UI-DOK	554–598
HYE	598–599
POP	599–600
MU	600–641
UI-JA	641–661

the peasant class paid the majority of these taxes. In addition, peasants faced mandatory military service and could be conscripted at any time for local civic projects.

Although Paekche had rejected Chinese control, the kingdom and its two neighbors, the kingdoms of Silla and Koguryo, remained highly dependent upon Chinese culture and commerce. The three kingdoms jointly developed *idu*, a Korean syntax that used Chinese characters, as their language system. Paekche art, architecture, and dress all displayed direct Chinese influence, and Paekche imported the majority of its manufactured items from China. Most importantly, the three kingdoms adopted the Buddhist religion. Buddhism held a special appeal for emerging kingdoms such as Paekche because it emphasized a harmonious unity among its believers. Paekche's rulers emphasized that such unity should also exist among their own subjects.

Although Paekche, Koguryo, and Silla shared a common heritage, relations among the three were rarely peaceful. In 475, Koguryo, still bitter over its defeat a century earlier, invaded Paekche, killed the king, and razed the Paekche capital of Hansong. The Paekche kingdom was greatly reduced and forced to regroup. Two factors allowed the kingdom to survive temporarily. First, the capital was moved to a much more secure location at Sabi. Second, King Song (r. 523–554) of Paekche formed an alliance with Silla.

In 554, however, Silla, fueled by its increasing power, betrayed the alliance and seized the vital Han River basin from Paekche's control. Enraged, the Paekche kingdom turned to its traditional enemy Koguryo for support. Alarmed by the combined power of Paekche and Koguryo, Silla enlisted the support of the T'ang dynasty in China. The two alliances created a stalemate that lasted just over a century.

Continued aggression by Paekche and Koguryo finally ended the confrontation between the two alliances. During the reign of King Uija (r. 641–660), Paekche launched frequent attacks against Silla to regain the land it had previously lost. In retaliation, Silla mounted a massive invasion across the eastern border of Paekche, while T'ang forces landed on Paekche's western coast. In 660, the two forces crushed Paekche's army and killed King Uija, ending Paekche's autonomy. With Paekche's defeat, Silla became the predominant power in southern Korea. Although eventually subjugated by Silla, Paekche

occupied a historic position as one of the three kingdoms that gave rise to modern Korean culture and nationalism.

See also: KOGURYO KINGDOM; SILLA KINGDOM; T'ANG DYNASTY.

FURTHER READING

Eckert, Carter J., et al. *Korea Old and New.* Cambridge, MA: Harvard University Press, 1990.

PAGAN KINGDOM (1044–1287 C.E.)

Kingdom in Myanmar (Burma), located on the Irrawaddy River Delta, which flourished from the mid-eleventh century until its collapse in 1287.

The Pagan kingdom was established in 1044 when the Burman ruler, King Anawrahta (r. 1044–1077), conquered the Pyu peoples and consolidated all of central Myanmar under the supremacy of the Burmans of Pagan. The kingdom flourished culturally for two centuries before collapsing as a result of a Chinese invasion from the north.

In 1057, King Anawrahta led the Pagan kingdom to victory over the Mon kingdom, capturing its capital of Thaton. Following this conquest, Anawrahta deported Thaton's king, Manuha (r. ?–1057), and its entire population to outlying regions. The conquest of the Mons marked the beginning of a long-lasting struggle between the two kingdoms that ran throughout much of the history of Myanmar. Thaton's defeat also gave Pagan a gateway to the sea, and Anawrahta quickly gained control of the Irrawaddy Delta. Under Anawrahta, Pagan adopted the Mon alphabet and Theravada Buddhism, which thrived and eventually became the most powerful element in Myanmar life.

In 1084, King Kyanzittha (r. 1084–1112) succeeded to the throne of Pagan. Kyanzittha brought a higher level of prestige to the Myanmar kingship than it had ever reached before. He erected a new palace, created a series of inscriptions, and began to send missions to China. His kingship was recorded in an inscription erected by his grandson and successor, Alaungsithu (r. 1112–1167) in 1113. The inscription, discovered by scholars in 1911, has been called the Rosetta Stone of Myanmar, since the text appears in the Pyu, Mon, Burmese, and Pali languages.

After a succession of kings who failed to cope

with revolts and disorder within the kingdom, King Narapatisithu (r. 1174–1211) took the throne after restoring peace in 1173. Narapatisithu, who was the longest-ruling Pagan king, erected temples, developed irrigation, and introduced Sinhalese Buddhism to the kingdom.

After refusal to pay tribute to Emperor Kublai Khan of China (r. 1260–1294) led to a Mongol invasion of Pagan, King Narathihpate (r. 1254–1287) fled his capital, sealing the fate of his kingdom. With no central leadership, the people of Arakan in the north and the southern Mon people rebelled and claimed independence from Pagan. Narathihapate attempted to return to his capital in 1287, but he was murdered by one of his sons, marking the end of the Pagan kingdom.

See also: BUDDHISM AND KINGSHIP; BURMESE KINGDOMS; MON KINGDOM; PYU KINGDOM; SHAN KINGDOMS.

PAHLAVI DYNASTY (1925–1979 C.E.)

Iranian dynasty whose two shahs, Reza Shah Pahlavi (r. 1925–1941) and his eldest son Muhammad Reza Shah Pahlavi (1941–1979), were Iran's last royal rulers.

In 1921, Reza Khan, a career military officer, led a coup against the ruling monarchy of the British protectorate of Iran. Reza seized Teheran, the Iranian capital, and took control of the armed forces as minister of war. By 1923, he had consolidated enough power to become prime minister, and, in 1925, when the weakened Ahmed Shah (r. 1909–1925) of the Qajar Dynasty was deposed by the national assembly, Reza Khan was elected shah and founded the Pahlavi dynasty.

Reza Shah Pahlavi implemented many ambitious reforms in an effort to modernize Iran and diminish the influence of the country's Muslim leaders. He centralized government administration, built a strong modern military, and encouraged industrialization by building thousands of miles of new roads and the Trans-Iranian Railroad. He also reduced the number of clerics in the legal system, instituted a Western dress code for all men and women that was enforced by the police and the military, and opened all public places and educational institutions to women.

During World War II, although Reza Shah Pahlavi declared an official policy of Iranian neutrality, he maintained a close relationship with Germany. This proved to be his undoing. The relationship was seen as a potential threat to the Soviet front, and, in 1941, Soviet and British troops invaded Iran and occupied the country. On September 16, 1941, Reza Shah Pahlavi abdicated the Peacock throne, naming his eldest son, Muhammad Reza Pahlavi, the next shah.

Muhammad Reza Shah Pahlavi attempted to continue the reforms begun by his father, but he faced a struggle for control of the government with Prime Minister Muhammad Mossadegh. The struggle culminated with the shah fleeing the country in August 1953. But the shah returned to Iran within a few days as Mossadegh was ousted in a coup led by monarchist supporters of the shah, aided by the United States.

At this point, the shah's power began to grow significantly. He maintained this power over the years by destroying or silencing his opposition, often bru-

The second and last ruler of Iran's short-lived Pahlavi dynasty, Muhammad Reza Shah Pahlavi worked to modernize his country. His increasingly oppressive rule, however, led to an Islamic revolution in 1979 that transformed Iran into a theocratic state. The shah died in exile a year later.

tally. In 1961, Muhammad Reza announced the White Revolution, which attempted to further stimulate the economy and modernize and secularize Iranian society. Most boldly, however, the White Revolution mandated a series of land reforms that angered the landowning classes. As before, the shah stifled the uprising and thousands of people died.

Muhammad Reza Shah's goal was to turn Iran into one of the foremost economic and military forces in the world. Aided by tremendous increases in oil revenues, he supported further industrialization efforts in the country, and, in January 1973, he nationalized Iran's oil industry. This rapid growth had economic consequences, however. The people of Iran were forced to deal with soaring inflation, shortages of consumer goods, and rampant corruption. Beginning in the late 1970s, the discontent of many sectors of Iranian society created a powerful protest movement that demanded the deposition of the shah.

On January 16, 1979, Muhammad Reza Shah Pahlavi fled Iran as protests against his rule grew. Soon after he left, revolutionaries led by exiled religious leader Ayatollah Khomeini overthrew the shah's government and established a new religiously based government. Muhammad Reza Shah Pahlavi never returned to Iran and died in exile in 1980. The overthrow of his government marked the end of over four hundred years of monarchy in Iran.

See also: ISLAM AND KINGSHIP; QAJAR DYNASTY.

PALA DYNASTY (750–1169 C.E.)

Rulers of the Indian states of Bengal and Bihar, who built canals and monasteries and left an enduring artistic and cultural heritage.

In the mid-eighth century, following more than a century of anarchy and confusion, the feudatory chieftains of the Indian state of Bengal asked Gopala, the son of a military chief, to stabilize the kingdom. Gopala (r. ca. 750–770) did so by gaining and consolidating political authority over all of Bengal, ensuring peace and prosperity in the land. Gopala was the founder of the Pala dynasty.

The most famous Pala leaders were Gopala's son and grandson, Dharmapala (r. 770–810) and Devapala (r. 810–850). During his reign, Dharmapala expanded the Bengal kingdom westward across northern India and from the Himalaya Mountains in the north to the central

Indian states of Malwa and Berar in the south. For a short time, he also controlled the strategic city of Kanauj. After Devapala took the throne, he carried out raids throughout northern and southern India. His armies even defeated Amoghavarsha (r. 814–877), a powerful ruler of the Rastrakuta dynasty of Maharasthra.

The reigns of Dharmapala and Devapala were among the most spirited chapters in the history of Bengal. Great supporters of Buddhism, the two rulers financed the building of monasteries and promoted learning and religion. They also supported the building of temples to several Hindu gods. Many public works, including waterways, also date from this time. With the dynasty's support, a distinctive school of art, the Pala School, was developed in Bengal. Pala paintings featured illustrations of the life of Buddha on palm leaves. Pala Bronze was a distinctive style of metal sculpture, usually of religious figures.

After Devapala, the Pala dynasty declined in power and importance. Vigrahapala (r. 850–854), Devapala's son or nephew, ruled for only a few years before abdicating the throne to become an ascetic. His successor, Narayanapala (r. 854–908), a religious pacifist, was reluctant to lead the Bengal army.

When Narayanapala lost a key battle with the Rastrakuta dynasty around 860, the Pratihara dynasty of Kanauj took advantage of Pala weakness and pushed eastward, conquering the state of Magadha (or southern Bihar) and the northern part of Bengal. Before Narayanapala's death in 908, the Rastrakutas defeated the Pratiharas, and Narayanapala was able to regain control of all of Bengal and Bihar. However, with the spirit that had been the strength of his people now broken, the dynasty and kingdom continued to decline.

The Pala dynasty continued to crumble in the eleventh and twelfth centuries. When Ramapala (r. 1077–1120), humiliated by rebellious subjects and dramatic defeats, was unable to stop the dynasty's decline, he committed suicide in the Ganges River. Only one brief reference, an inscription from 1175, notes the rule of Govindapala (r. ca. 1161–1174), the last king of the Pala dynasty.

See also: INDIAN KINGDOMS; RASTRAKUTA DYNASTY.

PALACES

Royal residences, typically imposing in size, grandiose in design, and lavish in appointments.

Throughout history, monarchs have reserved or constructed palaces and other types of palatial homes as a way of enjoying the spoils of their rule and intimidating their subjects with the size and grandeur of their residences. Although most monarchs today have only symbolic rather than political roles, many still maintain large and magnificent royal residences. Many palaces throughout the world today are open to public viewing, a fact that reflects the democratic forms of government that now exist in place of, or alongside, monarchical rule.

ORIGINS AND ANCIENT PALACES

Since most early monarchies derived from military power, many monarchs occupied residences that were, in some way, militarily strategic, with extensive natural or man-made defenses, such as natural cliffs, thick stone walls, or surrounding moats. The construction of palaces as military fortresses became a tradition that continued for thousands of years.

The Egyptian Age

Written records from ancient Egypt indicate that many Egyptian pharaohs had palaces built by slave labor. These palaces often were built in connection with sacred temples, so that the pharaohs, who were considered high priests, could perform religious duties in or near their residences.

Unfortunately, little physical evidence of most of these early Egyptian palaces survives. One notable exception is the palace complex at Medinet Habu, which was built by Ramses III (r. ca. 1182–1151 B.C.E.) in the twelfth century B.C.E. This palace complex was designed as a military fortification, with a protective wall surrounding various buildings.

The Post-Egyptian Age

As time went on, royal palaces grew in function, size, and opulence. Many ancient palaces, such as that of Nebuchadrezzar II of Babylon (r. ca. 604–562 B.C.E.), became legendary in their own time for the skill and cost required for their construction.

Over the course of 500-plus years, twenty-four Chinese emperors of the Ming and Ch'ing dynasties ruled from the mysterious confines of the Forbidden City in Beijing. The world's largest palace complex, the Forbidden City contains nearly 10,000 buildings and is enclosed by a wall more than 30 feet high.

A royal palace, fortress, prison, arsenal, mint, zoo, and repository of crown jewels, the Tower of London has been the setting of historic events for nearly 1,000 years. The oldest part, the square, central building known as the White Tower, was begun by William the Conqueror in 1078 C.E.

Centuries of warfare and neglect have left few of these palaces standing, though archaeologists have recently uncovered remnants of some of the major palaces of the post-Egyptian age. Visitors to Rome, for example, can see traces of the famous palaces of the Palatine Hill, where rulers such as the emperors Augustus (r. 27 B.C.E.–14 C.E.) and Tiberius (r. 14–37) built imposing residences.

In ancient China, the rulers of the Ch'in (Qin) dynasty (221–207 B.C.E.) began constructing royal residences at Xi'an in the third century B.C.E., and this work was continued by the Han dynasty (207 B.C.E.–9 C.E.). These royal Chinese palaces were actually fortified cities, with enormous networks of buildings and streets surrounded by defensive barriers.

Later Chinese monarchs continued this tradition of palace construction, which reached its peak with the Forbidden City of Beijing, constructed in the fifteenth century and occupied by rulers of the Ming (1368–1644) and Ch'ing (Qing) (1644–1912) dynasties. Today, the Forbidden City, a vast royal complex of palaces and buildings, is one of the most popular tourist destinations in Asia. Similar royal cities can be found elsewhere in the world, including the Kremlin in Moscow.

Many of the palaces built by monarchs in the medieval, Renaissance, and early modern periods are still in existence. Among these are the Topkapi Palace in Istanbul, which housed the sultans of the Ottoman Empire; the Palace of Versailles in France, built by King Louis XIV (r. 1643–1715); the Schönbrunn Palace in Vienna, completed in the eighteenth century as a summer residence for the Habsburg rulers of the Austro-Hungarian Empire; and the Tower of London, a grim-looking fortress begun in the eleventh century that became the home of several English monarchs and later served as a royal prison and place of royal execution.

MODERN PALACES

The tradition of large and magnificent palaces continued into the modern era. One of the most notable palaces of more recent date is Sans Souci in Potsdam, Germany, designed and built by Frederick II the Great of Prussia (r. 1740–1786) in the mid-eighteenth century. Frederick used Sans Souci to host elaborate dinner parties for the leading intellectual lights of his day.

Similar in size to Sans Souci is Buckingham Palace in London, England, which at one time was actually the private residence of the duke of Buckingham, who built it in the early eighteenth century. King George III of Great Britain (r. 1760–1820) purchased the building from the duke in 1761, but the royal family did not begin using it until 1837. Japan's Imperial Palace in Tokyo also dates from the modern era, with construction beginning under the powerful shogun, Tokugawa Ieyasu (r. 1603–1605) in 1603.

Among the most famous royal palaces in the world is Versailles. Like many royal residences, it is actually a compound of several buildings and open areas, including a large park, gardens, numerous fountains, and galleries displaying works of art. Fittingly, Versailles, a monument to the power and splendor of French monarchs, became the site of the beginning of the French Revolution in 1789, when the Estates-General revolted against Louis XVI. Revolutionaries attacked the palace, stealing or destroying many of its treasures.

The spread of democratic government in the years following the French Revolution led many nations to enact symbolic controls over the monarchy, in order to represent the power of the people over the outdated authority of kings and queens. One of the things they also did to represent the newfound power of the common people was to open up royal residences to the general public.

See also: ARENAS, ROYAL; ART OF KINGS; COURTS AND COURT OFFICIALS, ROYAL; HAREMS; LOUIS XIV; PARKS, ROYAL.

FURTHER READING
Conti, Flavio. *Homes of Kings.* Trans. Patrick Creagh. New York: HBJ Press, 1978.

PALAEOLOGAN DYNASTY

(1261–1453 C.E.)

Greek dynasty that ruled the Byzantine Empire from 1261 to its final conquest by the Turks in 1453.

The first emperor of the Palaeologan dynasty was Michael VIII Palaeologus (r. 1261–1282), who helped restore of the Byzantine Empire after a period of decline. Appointed regent for Emperor John IV of Nicaea (r. 1258–1261) in 1258, Michael Palaeologus became emperor after defeating Baldwin II (r. 1228–1261), ruler of the Latin Empire of Constantinople, and recovering the city of Constantinople.

During Michael's reign, he negotiated peace with the Tartars and Mamluks, as well as a temporary union between the Eastern Orthodox Church and the Western Christian Church. His successor on the throne was his son, Andronicus II (r. 1282–1328), whose policies renewed the schism between the Eastern and Western churches and lost most of Asia Minor (present-day Turkey) to the Seljuk Turks. During the reign of Andronicus III (r. 1328–1341), the fourth ruler of the Palaeologan dynasty, the Turks gained almost complete control of Asia Minor.

Upon the death of Andronicus III in 1341, his son John V (r. 1341–1376, 1379–1391) acceded to the throne. But due to family and political dissension, he was prevented from ruling by John VI (r. 1347–1354), also known as John Cantacuzene, the chief minister under Andronicus III who proclaimed himself emperor. John VI finally abdicated in favor of John V in 1354.

John V lost the throne again twenty-two years later, this time to his own son, Andronicus IV (r. 1376–1379), who deposed him in 1376. However, John V regained the throne three years later and held it until his death in 1391.

During his rule, John V tried in vain to heal the religious schism between East and West. Meanwhile, the Ottoman Turks continued to gain power at the expense of the Byzantine Empire. When John V died in 1391, he was succeeded by his son, Manuel II (r. 1391–1425), who ruled alone until 1399 and then shared rule with his nephew, John VII (r. 1399–1408). During their rule, the Byzantine Empire lost more ground to the Turks, eventually holding on to only Constantinople and a few small dependencies.

Manuel's son and successor, John VIII (r. 1425–1448), tried in vain to enlist Western European aid against the Turks, who posed a tremendous threat to the empire. In an attempt to gain support, he agreed to the union of the eastern and western churches at the Council of Florence in 1439.

Upon John's death, his brother, Constantine XI (r. 1448–1453), succeeded him on the throne. But Constantine was killed a few years later when the Turks stormed and conquered Constantinople in 1453, a defeat that marked the end of the Byzantine Empire. Branches of the Palaeologus family survived, however, and continued to hold power in parts of Europe. One branch of the dynasty ruled the Italian marquisate of Montferrat from 1305 to 1536.

Best known for their love of culture and education, the Palaeologan dynasty was instrumental in ensuring that the Greek people retained their cultural identity after their conquest by the Ottoman Turks.

See also: BYZANTINE EMPIRE; OTTOMAN EMPIRE.

FURTHER READING
Speck, Paul. *Understanding Byzantium: Studies in Byzantine Historical Sources.* Brookfield, VT: Variorum, 2003.

PALESTINE, KINGDOMS OF

(ca. 1100 B.C.E.–1948 C.E.)

Series of kingdoms that ruled in Palestine, a region on the eastern shore of the Mediterranean Sea. Palestine has long been an important region because of its many holy sites, which are revered by Jews, Christians, and Muslims.

ANCIENT JEWISH KINGDOMS

Four nearly successive kingdoms of Jewish people were founded in ancient Palestine in the first and late second millennium B.C.E. The first of these kingdoms, the kingdom of Israel, began with twelve tribes of Jewish people who formed a kingdom around 1100 B.C.E. The first ruler of the kingdom was Saul (r. ca 1020–1010 B.C.E.), whose victory over the Philistines paved the way for the foundation of a stable kingdom.

Saul's successor, King David (r. ca. 1010–970 B.C.E.), grew to become a king of legendary status who turned the kingdom of Israel, with its capital in Jerusalem, into a powerful, prosperous, and important state. David's son Solomon (r. ca. 970–931 B.C.E.), another powerful leader, succeeded him on the throne of Israel around 970 B.C.E. But cohesion among the Jewish tribes fell apart after Solomon's death, and the country was divided into two separate kingdoms: the kingdom of Israel and the kingdom of Judah in the south.

JEWISH KINGDOMS AND FOREIGN RULE

The kingdom of Israel never managed to become a stable entity during the nearly two hundred years

that it continued in existence. In 722 B.C.E., the kingdom fell to the powerful Assyrian Empire.

The kingdom of Judah survived more than one hundred years longer, but it also was eventually made a vassal of Assyria and later paid tribute to Babylonia. Judah repeatedly attempted to rebel, and was eventually destroyed by the Babylonians around 586 B.C.E.. Both kingdoms were incorporated into the Babylonian Empire.

For the next nearly four hundred years, Palestine was ruled by a succession of invading empires. After the Babylonians, the region was ruled by the Persian Empire from 539 B.C.E. Alexander III, the Great (r. 336–323 B.C.E.) of Macedonia incorporated Palestine into his empire around 332 B.C.E. After Alexander's death, the region was ruled by the Ptolemaic kings of Egypt and later by the Seleucid kings of Syria.

When the Seleucids restricted the religious practice of the Jews in Palestine, they sparked a revolt by a religious family called the Hasmoneans, also known as the Maccabees. The Maccabees managed to gain control of Jerusalem by 164 B.C.E., and by around 100 B.C.E., the Hasmonean leaders were calling themselves kings of Judaea and the fourth Jewish kingdom was established.

Not long after the establishment of this new Jewish kingdom, however, dissent began to grow among various political factions in the country. This led to civil war, which erupted in 67 B.C.E. Sensing weakness, the Romans entered the war, conquered Jerusalem, and by 37 B.C.E. had put an end to the Hasmonean dynasty.

The Romans ruled Palestine as part of the Roman Empire and later as part of the Byzantine Empire. Roman and Byzantine rule lasted from 63 B.C.E. until the early 600s C.E. During the early period, Jewish kings, chosen by the Romans, were nominally in charge of Palestine during the reign of the dynasty of Herod. The last Herodian ruler of Judaea was Herod Agrippa II (r. 49–92). After his death, Judaea and Palestine were ruled only by Roman officials, and the kingdom of Judaea ceased to exist as a state.

When Roman emperor Constantine I, the Great (r. 307–337) recognized Christianity as the state religion of the empire, Christianity spread and Christian pilgrims began to travel to Palestine, the birthplace of their religion. By the early 600s, however, rulers with a new religion would come to dominate Palestine and the Middle East—the Muslim Arabs.

MUSLIMS AND CHRISTIANS

In the battle of Yarmuk in 636, Muslims from Arabia under Caliph Umar (r. 634–644) decisively wrested control of Palestine from the Byzantines. From then until 1099, Palestine was ruled by a series of Muslim dynasties led by political and religious leaders known as caliphs. The Umayyad dynasty of Damascus ruled from 661, followed by the Abbasids of Baghdad in 750. In 1070, the Muslim Seljuk Turks arrived from the east and took over Jerusalem. They killed many Palestinian Christians and cut off the route to the Christian holy places from Europe, setting the stage for a series of confrontations with European Christians.

In the late 1000s, European Christians began taking action to gain control of Palestine from the Muslims, engaging in a series of military expeditions known as the Crusades. Christian Crusaders successfully captured Jerusalem in 1099 and then established new states, including a Christian kingdom, the kingdom of Jerusalem. After less than a century of Christian rule, however, the Muslims regained Palestine.

In 1187, Sultan Saladin (r. 1175–1193) of the Ayyubid dynasty of Egypt gained control of the region, and Palestine became a province of Muslim Egypt. Palestine remained under rule of the Mamluk dynasty of Egypt for more than three hundred years. The Jews and the Christians, as the minorities in Palestine, were treated poorly by the Mamluks, and Palestine in general was in decline at this time.

The next conquerors of Palestine were the Ottoman Turks, who defeated the Mamluks in 1517 and made Palestine part of their Ottoman Empire. Palestine remained part of the Ottoman Empire for 400 years.

After World War I, the League of Nations divided much of the Ottoman Empire into mandated territories and, in 1920, Great Britain received a mandate over Palestine. The British relinquished control of Palestine in 1948, when the modern Jewish state of Israel was established.

See also: CRUSADER KINGDOMS; DAVID; HASMONEAN KINGDOM; HEBREW KINGS; HEROD; ISRAEL, KINGDOMS OF; JUDAH, KINGDOM OF; JUDAISM AND KINGSHIP; SALADIN; SOLOMON.

FURTHER READING

Hitti, Philip K. *History of Syria, Including Lebanon and Palestine.* Piscataway, NJ: Gorgias Press, 2002.

PALLAVA DYNASTY. *See* MYSORE KINGDOM

PANDYA DYNASTY

(ca. 300 B.C.E.–ca. 1550 C.E.)

Ancient dynasty of Tamil traders from the southernmost part of India, whose kingdom and culture were destroyed by military conflict with the Chola dynasty in the tenth century C.E. and again by the Delhi sultanate in the fourteenth century.

The Pandya dynasty was centered in the city of Madurai on the extreme southern coast of India. Early years of prosperity and peace, from about 300 B.C.E. to 700 C.E., were followed by centuries of warfare that have made it difficult for scholars to learn about the dynasty's history.

EARLY CONTACT WITH GREECE AND ROME

A few records remain from the early days of the Pandya dynasty, written by Western authors and explorers such as Scylax of Caryanda, the Greco-Egyptian geographer Ptolemy, and the Italian explorer Marco Polo. In 300 B.C.E., the Greek historian Megasthenes wrote that the Pandyas were Tamil-speaking people who lived in a kingdom with 365 villages in the south of India.

By the first century B.C.E., the Greeks and Romans were actively trading pearls, shells, and fine cottons through Pandya ports, and some colonization was taking place. The Pandyas sent an emissary to the Roman emperor, Augustus (r. 27 B.C.E.–14 C.E.) to facilitate trade and immigration.

CULTURAL HERITAGE

The Pandya dynasty encouraged and supported many cultural activities in their kingdom. In the first century C.E., marathon artistic festivals called Sangams were held at Madurai. The poems recited at these festivals were remarkable because of their secular nature at a time when the rest of Indian literature had a heavy religious orientation.

These ancient poems described social conditions in a time before the Aryan peoples arrived from the north, and they included detailed descriptions of commercial life and foreign trade, as well as undated references in praise of various kings.

The literary tradition of the Pandya kingdom seemed to have continued for a few centuries: a few poems of love and social life have survived. As late as the fifth or sixth century, Pandya's literary academy produced literature of very high quality. Unfortunately, by the time of the Pandya ruler, Kudungon (r. ca. 590–620), the Pandyas had become indifferent to culture and learning and were focused primarily on trade and commerce.

MILITARY EXPANSION

In the late seventh century, the Pandya ruler Arikesari Maravarman (r. ca. 670–700) expanded from the southern tip of India, conquering some of the territory of the neighboring Cheras people along the Malabar coast of southwestern India. The Pandyas also engaged in struggles with the Pallavas dynasty on the southeast coast of the Indian subcontinent.

Arikesar Maravarman was a great soldier who won a spectacular victory against the Cheras at the battle of Tinnevelli. He was succeeded on the throne by Kochchadaiyan Ranadhira (r. ca. 700–730), who conquered Kongu, a region of southwestern central India whose access to the sea was blocked by the Cheras dynasty.

Kochchadaiyan's son and successor was Maravarman Rajasimha I (r. ca. 730–765). Taking advantage of rival claims to the throne of the Pallava kingdom, Rajasimha I fought a prolonged war against the Pallavas on behalf of one of the rival claimants, Chitramaya, and defeated the Pallava king, Nandivarman II (r. ca. 731–795). However, the Pallava general, Udyachandra, arrived and rescued Nandivarman, and Chitiramaya was killed.

Although defeated in Pallava, Rajasimha I conquered more of the southern interior of India, and he defeated the western Calukya dynasty at their capital city of Badami. Under his immediate successors, the Pandya dynasty pushed its imperialist forces further northward. In the face of this threat, the Colas (Cholas), Pallavas, Kalingas, Magadhas, and other dynasties formed a confederacy, but their combined forces were unable to hold back the ever-advancing Pandyas.

DEFEAT, CONTAINMENT, AND FOREIGN RULE

Srimar Srivallabha (r. ca. 815–862) continued the Pandya policy of aggression and invaded the island of Ceylon. The confederacy of dynasties allied against the Pandyas attacked again from the north, and at the battle of Tellaru in the late nineteenth century, the Pandyas were defeated and pushed back into their own country.

Srimar's son and successor, Varagunavarman II (r. ca. 862–880), followed the expansionist policies of his father and tried to regain Pandya prestige by attacking the Cholas. Once again, however, the confederacy repulsed the Pandyas.

During the reign of Varagunavarman's grandson, Maravarman Rajasinha II (r. ca. 900–920), the Cholas invaded and defeated the combined forces of the Pandyas and their ally, the king of Ceylon, at the battle of Vellur in 915. The Chola dynasty then ruled the Pandyas for thirty years, until their defeat at the battle of Takkolam in 949 at the hands of the Rashtrakuta dynasty of the Deccan region.

A Pandya leader, Vira Pandya, claimed victory over the Cholas after the Rashtrakuta victory and attempted to reign as an independent ruler. But he was killed by the Cholas, who established a joint Chola-Pandya dynastic line to rule. In the years that followed, the Pandyas made other attempts to revive past glories. But the Cholas and a military occupation of Pandya territories stopped all such efforts until the Sinhalese armies of Ceylon invaded Pandya in 1175.

END OF THE PANDYA DYNASTY

The Pandya dynasty's downfall was the result of repeated attacks from the north and a family dispute over succession to the throne. Scholars have little reliable information about dates and details of the Pandyas during this time period. Adding to the confusion is the custom whereby Pandya leaders often had the same names as their predecessors.

Sometime in the late twelfth century, Kulasekhara Pandya, with support from the Cholas, killed his brother Prakarma Pandya, who was backed by the king of Ceylon, over a succession dispute. The Cholas responded by attacking Ceylon, whose king asked for Kulasekhara's support in return for recognizing him as the true king of the Pandyas.

Kulasekhara allied with Ceylon, and the Cholas sent an army to defeat Kulasekhara and limit his power. The victorious Cholas sent Kulasekhara into exile and replaced him with Vira Pandya, the son of Prakarma Pandya. Vira then joined with Ceylon against the Cholas, but he was defeated, and Vikrama Pandya came to the throne.

The Chola ruler, Kulottunga III (r. 1178–1218), attacked again around 1216 and overpowered the reigning Pundya ruler, Jatavarman Kulasekhara (r. 1190–1216). Kulasekhara's successor, Sundara Pandya I (r. 1216–1238), then attacked the Cholas, defeated Kulottunga III, and drove the Cholas out of Pandya territory, ending Chola control of the kingdom.

The Pandya dynasty continued to rule until Ghivath-al-din Muhammad Shah I (r. 1325–1351) of the Muslim Tughluq dynasty, the ruler of the Delhi sultanate, invaded the south of India in 1325 and made the Pandyas vassals. By the mid-sixteenth century, all the Pandya territories had passed into Muslim hands.

See also: CALUKYA (CHALUKYA) DYNASTY; COLA KINGDOM; DELHI KINGDOM; INDIAN KINGDOMS; KALINGA KINGDOM; MAGADHA KINGDOM; SOUTH ASIAN KINGDOMS.

PANJALU KINGDOM

(ca. 1041–1222 C.E.)

Relatively short-lived Buddhist kingdom in east Java about which little is known other than some of its sculpture and its ornamental writing style.

The Panjalu kingdom was one of the two kingdoms into which the island of Java was divided by King Airlangga (r. ca. 1019–1041), ruler of Kediri, just before his death in 1041. Of these kingdoms, Janggala (also known as Malang) controlled the north and east of Java, while Panjalu ruled the south and west.

Panjalu is sometimes known as Daha, the name of its probable capital, but the name Kediri is more commonly used than either Panjalu or Daha. Kediri was probably the popular name for the kingdom, while Panjalu was mainly an official or sacred name used primarily by the elite. The name Gelanggelang also appeared in the thirteenth century along with the name Daha.

The precise location of Panjalu's capital is unknown, but it is likely that it was situated somewhere near the modern city of Kediri. Culturally, Panjalu (Kediri) soon came to outstrip the Janggala kingdom in its influence. Although no architectural remains have been firmly identified with either kingdom, the Kediri area is known for its sculpture. Kediri also developed a highly ornamental style of script.

The division of Panjalu and Janggala (or Kediri and Malang) came to an end in 1222, with the formation of the unified kingdom of Singasari, the capital of which lay in the lands formerly belonging to Janggala, north of Malang.

See also: JANGGALA KINGDOM; JAVAN KINGDOMS; SOUTHEAST ASIAN KINGDOMS.

PAPAL STATES (754–1870 C.E.)

Area of central Italy historically administered and controlled by the papacy, also known as the "Church States." These provinces and cities were a legacy from the so-called Donation of Pepin.

In 754, the Frankish king Pepin III (r. 751–768), the father of Charlemagne (r. 768–814), went to the aid of Pope Stephen II and began to oust the Lombards from the north of Italy. The pope had recognized Pepin as the rightful king of the Franks, and Pepin agreed to help the pope in return. Pepin also promised to turn over to the pope all the lands he recovered. This bequest of territory, known as the Donation of Pepin, comprised the majority of the lands that became the Papal States.

The Donation of Pepin included most of central Italy, including all the areas around both Rome and the Exarchate of Ravenna. The Donation also extended along the coast of the Adriatic Sea from Rimini to Ancona. These lands were augmented in 1077 as a result of an alliance with the Normans, who granted the popes the duchy of Benevento, which was contiguous to the existing holdings of the Normans in Italy.

From the reign of Holy Roman Emperor Frederick I Barbarossa (r. 1152–1190) through that of his grandson, Frederick II (r. 1212–1250), the papacy maintained firm control over these core holdings of territory. However, it struggled unsuccessfully to extend its temporal sway throughout Christendom.

Then, in 1309, the so-called Babylonian captivity began, when King Philip IV of France (r. 1285–1314) coerced the papacy to move to Avignon, where it remained for over a hundred years (until 1417). When the popes finally returned to Rome, they found that the "Papal States" had become a proud lot of independent city-states accustomed to making their own decisions. These city-states were not inclined to accept anything other than spiritual guidance from the papal administrators.

The popes in Rome ruled a large territory in Italy known as the Papal States for more than 1,000 years. In 1870, Pope Pius IX witnessed the dissolution of the Papal States, as the regions of Italy united to form a single nation. Pius IX also claimed the distinction of being the longest-serving pope, heading the church for thirty-one years and seven months.

However, a series of worldly wise and powerful popes emerged on the papal throne, culminating with the warlike Julius II (r. 1503–1513), who reasserted and even extended the temporal control of the papacy to Bologna in the north and down the Adriatic coast to the Campagna.

With the death of Julius II, the onset of the Counter-Reformation, and the reasserted independence of the central Italian city-states, the papacy's political control rapidly waned in the fifteenth and sixteenth centuries. Now unaccustomed to warfare, even the pope's Swiss Guards offered no resistance to the incursion by Napoleon Bonaparte into Rome in 1796.

Pope Pius IX (r. 1846–1878) witnessed the final dissolution of the Papal States during the movement for Italian unification known as the *Risorgimento*. First Bologna and Romagna, then Marche and Umbria broke away from the Papal States, joining the kingdom of Sardinia.

Finally, King Victor Emmanuel II of Italy (r. 1849–1878) captured Rome from the papacy in 1870. Helpless, but proud, Pope Pius IX (r. 1846–1878) refused to recognize defeat and became a voluntary "prisoner" within the Vatican until his death in 1878. His successors maintained this unusual and ambiguous political position until 1929, when the Lateran Treaty between the kingdom of Italy and the papacy defined the Vatican City as an independent state within Italy.

See also: CHRISTIANITY AND KINGSHIP; FREDERICK II; HOLY ROMAN EMPIRE; PEPIN THE SHORT (PEPIN III); VICTOR EMMANUEL II.

PARAMARA DYNASTY

(ca. 820–1235 C.E.)

Rajput rulers of the Indian kingdom of Malwa, who declared independence from neighboring imperial powers and allowed religion, the arts, and learning to flourish.

The name Paramara means "slayer of the enemy." The first known king of the dynasty was Upendra (r. ca. 800–818), who was a vassal of the Rastrakuta dynasty of the Deccan region of India.

Malwa, a fertile plateau region in central India, was surrounded by the kingdoms of the Rastrakuta and Pratihara dynasties, two of the most powerful Indian dynasties in the eighth and ninth centuries. During that period, Malwa often bore the burden of clashes between those two great imperial powers, who both sought to control Malwa.

When the Pratihara ruler, Mahendrapala II (r. ca. 893–914), died around 914, the Pratihara vassals began to fight among themselves, and their kingdoms began to disintegrate. Eventually, the Paramara ruler of Malwa, Siyaka II (r. ca. 948–973), took advantage of the situation. Siyaka sacked the Rastrakuta city of Manyakheta in 972, a decisive first step in the extinction of the Rastrakuta Empire. However, it was not until the rule of Munja (r. 973–995), the successor of Siyaka II and one of the greatest generals of the age, that the Paramaras actually achieved independent rule in 974.

The Paramara dynasty of Malwa reached its height under Bhoja I, the Great (r. 1018–1060). Under his strong arm, Malwa enjoyed peace, prosperity, and the pursuit of learning. Taxes were low, the central government was competent and efficient, and local governments had a substantial voice in the management of their own affairs.

Bhoja, like other Paramara rulers, supported religious and educational institutions. Large temples, built by the kings or by the rich in Malwa society, were used not only for religious and secular instruction, but also as community centers for the poor, where people could enjoy fairs, festivals, and performances of literary drama.

After Bhoja I, the Paramara dynasty began to decline. While he ruled, Bhoja relied on a well-paid regular army, which marched against the great Muslim leader, Mahmud of Ghazni (998–1030), stopping the Muslim advance and protecting the Deccan plateau from the Muslim aggressors for another 300 years. However, subsequent Paramara rulers returned to an army of hereditary military officers, who did their best to protect the kingdom and maintain Paramara cultural legacy, but ultimately failed to rally the Hindu leaders to defend against the Muslim invaders. In 1235, the sultan of Mandu, a city in central India, captured the last Paramara ruler, Siladitya (r. dates unknown), and Ujjain, the seat of Paramara power, passed into Muslim hands.

See also: MAHMUD OF GHAZNA; MALWA KINGDOM; RASTRAKUTA DYNASTY.

PARKS, ROYAL

Parks and gardens built by rulers in various cultures and periods of history. Throughout history, monarchs around the world have built elaborate gardens and parks. These have varied in appearance according to the cultural values of their time and place, but they seem to have served many of the same purposes in countries as varied as Aztec Mexico and Renaissance Italy.

No one knows the historical origins of gardens and parks, although the flowers found buried in ancient Neanderthal graves suggest a deep-seated human appreciation for natural beauty. Just as the gathering of wild grains, herbs, and fruits led to the discovery of agriculture, so an appreciation of nature in the wild may have led to the discovery that people have the power to re-create such beauty at a place of their own choosing.

The religious role of early monarchs usually included rituals and prayers to assure fertility and adequate water supplies. In Peru, for example, the Inca rulers would use a golden plow to turn the earth for the first corn planting of the year. In Japan, the emperor to this day plants rice shoots in the imperial paddy in the spring. The first royal gardens may have grown from such ritual practices.

The royal parks and gardens of monarchs often boasted trees brought from great distances, massive landscape formations, and water features reminiscent of exotic climes. In this fashion, a king displayed his earthly powers to command vast labor resources, as well as his sway over the countries where the plants originated—"the entire world" in much monarchic propaganda. This also allowed kings to associate themselves with the divine powers that imposed order and harmony on a chaotic, unpredictable world. The Aztec royal gardens described by early Spanish observers in the fifteenth century C.E. contained trees, flowers, birds, and animals from all over Mexico. Chinese poets during the Han dynasty (206 B.C.E.–220 C.E.) described the imperial parks as portraits of the empire in miniature. These Chinese gardens often included symbolic "mountains" and "islands," recalling the dwelling places of the "Immortals" of Chinese legend; the dynasty itself claimed immortality by association.

At least some Egyptian pharaohs planted gardens at temples and tomb complexes. The powerful Queen Hatshepshut (r. 1503–1483 B.C.E.) had massive terrace gardens built at temples at Madinat-Habu, with ponds, flowers, and scented trees expressly brought from the faraway land of Punt (possibly the Somali coast). Ramses II (r. 1279–1212 B.C.E.) included public gardens in his new royal capital of Pi-Ramesse, located at the Nile River Delta.

Perhaps the most historically important royal gardens were those of ancient Persia, which influenced the European, Islamic, and Indian cultural worlds. When they conquered Mesopotamia in the 500s B.C.E., the Persians inherited ancient traditions of civilization, including royal gardens. These may originally have included sacred "trees of life," such as are found in the description of the Garden of Eden in the Hebrew Bible.

The kings of ancient Assyria had menageries of exotic animals in their gardens, while the famous hanging gardens of Babylon, built by Nebuchadrezzar II (r. 605–562 B.C.E.), had been built to satisfy the longing of the queen for her mountainous homeland in Media. To this tradition, the Persians added large hunting preserves, at first left in their natural state and then altered with rows of trees, strategically placed shade, and sweet-smelling flowers.

These Persian parks, which were used as official throne rooms, so astonished ancient Greek writers and so impressed the great conqueror Alexander the Great (r. 336–323 B.C.E.) that monarchs in Europe and elsewhere for generations to come would draw inspiration from their accounts. The English word "paradise" derives from the Persian word *paridaeza,* which means "walled garden."

The Persian gardens wielded even more influence via the spread of Islam. In the Koran, the Prophet Muhammad described the afterlife as a well-watered garden with fruit trees, lush patches of green, and pleasure pavilions. This was an apt description of the gardens of Persia discovered by conquering Arab tribesmen who surged out of the desert in the seventh century C.E. Thereafter, every Muslim ruler strove to display his piety by reproducing paradise gardens, often following a standard model. Four channels, representing the main rivers of paradise, divided these gardens into quadrants, punctuated with cypress trees symbolizing eternity and surrounded by high walls to ward off the hot winds. This pattern was often enhanced with the use of brilliantly colored tiles.

Perhaps the peak of Muslim royal gardening was reached under the Mughal emperors of India in the sixteenth and seventeenth centuries C.E. Their gardens combined the balance, order, and human scale of the Islamic tradition, with the extravagant colors and luxuriant excesses of Hindu architecture and crafts. The Mughal ruler Shah Jahan (r. 1628–1658) graced his Taj Mahal, completed in 1643, with a public park, to benefit even his poorest subjects.

Similarly, the royal parks of European kingdoms, created to display monarchical splendor and wealth, were gradually opened to broader public access. By the nineteenth century, most of these royal parks belonged to everyone in the nation. Hyde Park in London, the Tuileries in Paris, Schönbrunn in Vienna, and many others became the great public parks that made urban life bearable in the modern industrial era.

See also: HUNTING AND KINGSHIP; PALACES.

FURTHER READING

Adams, William Howard. *Nature Perfected: Gardens Through History.* New York: Abbeville Press, 1991.

PARTHIAN KINGDOM

(247 B.C.E.–224 C.E.)

Ancient kingdom that occupied Parthia, an area to the southeast of the Caspian Sea, roughly corresponding to the province of Khroustan in present-day Iran. Parthia was originally a satrapy, or province, of the Persian Empire, and later a part of the empire of the Seleucid dynasty.

During the third century B.C.E., an Indo-European nomadic group known as the Parni made their way from Central Asia into Parthia, where they adopted the language of the inhabitants and became absorbed into the indigenous population. The Parni, who later became known as Parthians, were known for their extraordinary and distinctive military skill, which included the then unique ability to shoot arrows from horseback. They are best remembered for the "Parthian shot," a tactical deception in which a rider fired from horseback while appearing to be in retreat.

In cultural and governmental matters, the Parthians were adapters rather than creators. They took the administrative bureaucracy that their predecessors, the Seleucids, had inherited from the Hellenistic Empire of Alexander the Great (r. 336–323 B.C.E.), writing all official documents in Greek and borrowing laws from Babylonia, Persia, and Greece.

The traditional founder of the Parthian kingdom was Arsaces I (r. 247–211 B.C.E.), a provincial governor who revolted against his suzerain, Diodotus I (r. 256–248 B.C.E.), the king of Bactria, and established a new kingdom. In the second century B.C.E., Parthia emerged as a powerful military presence with the rise of the Parthian ruler Mithradates I (r. 171–138 B.C.E.), whose conquests during his reign stretched the boundaries of the kingdom from Bactria in the east to Babylonia in the west. The outlines of the Parthian Empire were pushed still further by Artabanus II (r. 128–123 B.C.E.) and Mithradates II (r. 123–87 B.C.E.), until Parthia encompassed all of the Iranian plateau and the Tigris-Euphrates Valley.

Parthia was well situated for trade, containing the main caravan route between Central Asia and China, which allowed the kingdom to control the flow of goods destined eventually for Greece and Rome. The resulting profits fueled an energetic building program throughout the kingdom. Unfortunately, Parthia's advantageous location also meant that the kingdom lay much of the time under the threat of Rome. Rome and Parthia clashed many times. After defeating the Romans in 53 B.C.E. at Carrhae, however, the Parthians remained, despite minor setbacks, able to limit Roman incursions in the kingdom.

Parthian rule was vested in an aristocracy that allowed the development of vassal kingdoms within the empire. But it was perhaps the lack of strong central rule that opened the door to the takeover of Parthia in 224 C.E. by one of these vassal rulers, Ardashir I (Artaxerxes) of Persia (r. 224–241). With his successful revolt against the Parthian king, Artabanus IV (r. 213–224), Ardashir I ended the Parthian kingdom and became the founder of the Sasanid dynasty of Persia.

See also: Hellenistic Dynasties; Persian Empire; Roman Empire; Sasanid Dynasty; Seleucid Dynasty.

Patent Letters, Royal

Written documents issued by a monarch that granted specific economic or political privileges, conferred royal favor on particular individuals, or enforced existing statutes.

In the kingdoms of the Western world, royal power usually included the right of legislation. Western rulers developed various forms of written legislation, each with a specialized function. These included proclamations, edicts, decrees, and patent letters.

Patent letters, or letters patent, first appeared in the Middle Ages and were "open" to the public so that anyone could read them. The letters were issued to grant certain privileges, usually economic but also political, and were frequently used to confer royal favor. This form of royal decree also was used as a means of enforcing existing laws or edicts.

Letters patent were used most commonly to grant economic privileges. Patent letters granted economic monopolies to one person or a firm, giving them the exclusive right to sell a product or manufacture. This was the origin of the modern concept of patents, which protect the ownership rights of individuals who create original inventions or works of art, literature, music, and so on.

In the sixteenth century, the Tudor monarchs of England used letters patent to grant foreign artisans the exclusive right to establish new forms of woolen manufacture. The letters gave the artisans the right to manufacture and sell the new textiles for a certain number of years. Patent letters also were issued to grant the exclusive right to collect some form of tax for the monarchy. The Bourbon monarchs of France, for example, used patent letters to grant the right to collect sales taxes and salt taxes to certain tax "farmers."

The greater function of letters patent, however, was to grant political privileges. Western monarchs used the documents for land grants, to confer titles of nobility, and to appoint government officials. For example, in the sixteenth century the Spanish Crown used letters patent to appoint the governors of their territories in the Americas. The letters could also be used to revoke privileges. For example, Francis I of France (r. 1515–1547) used letters patent in 1516 to prohibit the wearing of luxury clothes by his subjects.

Finally, letters patent were also issued to direct government officers to execute or enforce existing royal legislation. Some were issued to direct authorities to enforce prior laws that the Crown believed were not being enforced. In keeping with the traditional role of the letters patent, these issuances might direct specified officials to enforce specific royal statutes, hence giving them the "exclusive right" or authority to enforce the law. In France, for example, sumptuary laws, which restricted the ownership of luxury items, were the frequent subject of letters patent. The populace often ignored such antiluxury laws, forcing the monarch to grant individual officers of the Crown the privilege of enforcing them.

The development of letters patent conferring economic and political privileges reflected the European monarchs' increasing legislative power after the Middle Ages. The use of these documents signified the royal prerogative to grant privileges as the ruler saw fit.

See also: Monopolies, Royal.

Pedro I (1798–1832 c.e.)

First independent ruler (r. 1822–1831) of the empire of Brazil, who separated that former colony from Portugal.

Dom Pedro I was born in Lisbon in 1798, the son and heir of the king of Portugal, João (John) VI (r. 1816–1826). Alarmed at the expansionist aims of

Napoleon of France, João VI allied Portugal with England to defy the French. This incited Napoleon to march an invasionary force into Lisbon in 1808. The Portuguese king gathered his family together and fled to Brazil, then a Portuguese colony. Thus, Pedro spent his childhood not in the land of his ancestors but in the bustling Brazilian capital of Rio de Janeiro.

The royal family remained in exile in the New World until 1821, when João VI finally felt it was safe to return to Lisbon and reclaim his throne. He left Pedro, now twenty-three years old, to serve as regent of the Brazilian colony. Pedro, however, felt little personal connection to Portugal, a country he had not seen since he was an infant. He saw no reason for Brazil to be subordinate to a country so far away, and within a year of assuming the regency he declared Brazil an independent empire.

The United States, glad to encourage any trend that reduced European control in the Western Hemisphere, immediately recognized the new nation. In the face of U.S. support, and given the difficulties of attempting to assert his will on territories that lay so far away, Portugal had no choice but to follow suit. Brazil's independence was thus achieved without military confrontation. He followed up this success with an attempt to expand Brazil's control into Argentinean territory. In this effort, however, he failed.

Pedro I was Brazil's first emperor, but he did not rule long. Four years after assuming the imperial throne, João VI had died and Pedro inherited the throne of Portugal and bore the imperial name Pedro IV (r. 1826–1828). Pedro did not wish to have this responsibility, however, so he gave the Portuguese crown to his daughter, Maria II (r. 1834–1853), on the condition that she marry a kinsman, Dom Miguel, and establish a constitutional monarchy like the one he had instituted in Brazil.

Unfortunately, Dom Miguel, who was supposed to provide support for Maria, had grander ambitions. In 1828 he seized power and established an absolute monarchy in Portugal, ruling as Miguel I (r. 1828–1834). Pedro could not let this behavior stand unchallenged. He abdicated his throne in Brazil in 1831, turning over the reins of power to his son, Pedro II (r. 1831–1889), and set sail for Portugal to commence what came to be known as the Miguelist Wars. In the end, Pedro's faction won and Miguel was ousted from power. Maria was reinstated on the throne in 1832, and Dom Pedro died two years later, on September 24, 1834.

See also: BRAGANÇA DYNASTY; BRAZIL, PORTUGUESE MONARCHY OF; PEDRO II.

PEDRO II (1825–1891 C.E.)

Second and last emperor (r. 1831–1889) of an independent empire of Brazil, who is remembered as a modernizer.

Dom Pedro II was the son of Pedro I (r. 1822–1831), the first emperor of Brazil. Born in Rio de Janiero and heir to the Bragança dynasty that produced many Portuguese kings, Pedro II was only five years old when his father abdicated the Brazilian throne in 1831 to return to Portugal and fight the Miguelist Wars. The mantle of emperor fell to Pedro's young shoulders, but a regency handled the day-to-day affairs of the country while he was growing up. In 1840, at the age of fifteen, Pedro was deemed to be of suitable age to take full responsibility as emperor.

Pedro II was a modernizer who tried hard to bring economic prosperity to Brazil. Unfortunately, he was all too willing to allow himself to be drawn into the political squabbles among his neighbors—Argentina, Uruguay, and Paraguay—with the result that his military was frequently called to fight in other countries' wars. This earned him little love among his generals and the Brazilian populace. During his reign, he was also impelled to join the growing trend against the institution of slavery. In 1850 he acquiesced to the British-led movement to curtail the slave trade, and a few years later he instituted a policy of gradual emancipation. Since the Brazilian economy was based largely on plantation agriculture, these policies angered the wealthy landowners. When the institution of slavery was finally abolished in Brazil in 1888, the powerful landowners joined the military in their disaffection with the emperor.

This growing movement against Pedro's rule was further strengthened by his efforts at modernization. Rather than earning him the love of his subjects, these policies provided encouragement for an increasingly vocal group demanding that the monarchy be abolished and replaced with a republican government. Ultimately, even the powerful Catholic Church joined the chorus calling for the overthrow of the emperor. In 1889 the military staged a coup, led by Manuel Deodoro da Fonseca, and Pedro II was ousted. He opted for exile in Europe, where he remained until his death two years later.

See also: BRAGANÇA DYNASTY; BRAZIL, PORTUGUESE MONARCHY OF; PEDRO I.

PEGU KINGDOMS (1287–1757 C.E.)

Series of kingdoms centered on the city of Pegu in present-day Myanmar (Burma). Located on the Pegu River, the ancient city of Pegu is said to have been established in 573 by two princes of the Mon people, a Khmer group that occupied the Irrawaddy Delta region of Myanmar.

Pegu first rose to prominence with the collapse of the Pagan kingdom of the Burmese people at the hands of the Mongols in 1287. The Mon, having been defeated by Pagan in 1057, thus recovered their independence and captured the ports of Martaban and Pegu and the surrounding areas, giving them virtually the same territory they had held previously. In 1369, the Mon made Pegu the capital of their kingdom of Ramanadesa.

The next two centuries brought constant warfare between the Mon and Burmese peoples. The Mon were able to maintain their independence until 1539 when, under the reign of Takayupti (r. 1526–1539), they came under the control of the Burmese Toungoo dynasty. At this time, Pegu was an important seaport visited by many European traders, including the Portuguese, British, and Dutch. Pegu served as the capital of a united Burmese kingdom until 1599 and again from 1613 to 1634. During the sixteenth century, the port was used as a base for an invasion of neighboring Siam.

After the Burmese moved their capital to Ava in central Myanmar in 1635, Pegu was reduced in status to a provincial capital. But a Mon revolt in 1740 restored the city as the capital of a new, short-lived Mon kingdom. In 1757, the Burmese king, Alaungpaya (r. 1752–1760), invaded the Mon kingdom and swiftly incorporated its territory into a new, unified kingdom of Myanmar. Alaungpaya destroyed almost all of the city of Pegu, although he left its religious building intact. The destruction of the city effectively ended its role as a royal capital.

Of Pegu's many pagodas, the ancient Shwemawdaw ("Golden Shrine") is the oldest and most impressive. Legend says that it contains two hairs of Gautama Buddha. Originally built by the Mon, the temple was severely damaged by an earthquake in 1930 but restored in 1954. The Shwethalyaung, a colossal reclining statue of Buddha, is located to the west of modern Pegu and is reputedly one of the most lifelike of all the reclining Buddha figures. Believed to have been built in 994, it was lost when Pegu was destroyed in 1757 but rediscovered under a cover of jungle growth in 1881. From the nearby Kalyani Sima ("Hall of Ordination"), founded by the Mon king Dhammazedi (r. ca. 1472–1492), spread one of the greatest reform movements in Myanmar Buddhist history. Its story is related in ten stone inscriptions erected by the king close to the Sima. The Mahazedi, Shwegugale, and Kyaikpien are other notable pagodas in Pegu.

Pegu was rebuilt between 1782 and 1819 but no longer served as a seaport because the Pegu River changed course, leaving Pegu an inland town. The British annexed the Pegu area in 1852, and ten years later, they created the province of British Myanmar, establishing the colonial capital at Rangoon.

See also: ALAUNGPAYA DYNASTY; MON KINGDOM; SOUTHEAST ASIAN KINGDOMS; TOUNGOO DYNASTY.

PELAYO. *See* ASTURIAS KINGDOM

PENDA. *See* MERCIA, KINGDOM OF

PEPIN DYNASTY (613–741 C.E.)

Dynasty of Frankish "mayors of the palace," who were the predecessors to the Carolingian dynasty.

The Pepin dynasty was founded in the early 600s by Pepin of Landen, mayor of the palace for the Frankish kingdom of Austrasia. "Mayor of the palace" was a title given to a leading noble who held power behind the throne of the Merovingian dynasty of the Frankish kingdom. Pepin's grandson, Pepin II (ca. 680–714), and great-grandson, Charles Martel (714–741), both followed as mayors of the palace, progressively acquiring more power and territory

The Frankish king Pepin the Short, father of Charlemagne, is considered the founder of the Carolingian dynasty. He built a new sanctuary at Saint-Denis, the richest and most famous abbey in medieval France. Pepin and many other French monarchs are buried at Saint-Denis, and this sculpted head is from his tomb.

for the Pepin dynasty. In 751, Pepin the Short (Pepin III), the son of Charles Martel, became king of the Franks (r. 751–768); he is considered the founder of the Carolingian dynasty, whose most famous ruler was Charlemagne (r. 768–814).

The Merovingian kings after Dagobert I (r. 629–639) were weak and ineffective rulers. As a result, the mayor of the palace was the real power behind the throne, who acted as ruler while using the king as a figurehead to unite the kingdom. The wealthy and clever Pepin mayors of the palace used this situation to their advantage, so that their descendants eventually were able to claim the Crown of all France.

The first of the Pepin line to emerge as historically important was Pepin I, also called Pepin of Landen, who died in 640. A wealthy and powerful Austrasian, Pepin owned land in the Moselle Valley and in Liège (in present-day Belgium). In 613, he and a close ally, Bishop Arnulf of Metz, brought the Frankish king Chlothar II (r. 584–629) to rule Austrasia. Chlothar, perhaps to keep Pepin's power in check, appointed Pepin's rival, Rado, as mayor of the palace. It was not until Rado died around 617 that Pepin gained that position.

In 623, Chlothar's son Dagobert I (r. 623–639) became king of the East Frankish kingdom of Austrasia, and Pepin and Arnulf became his most powerful advisers. When Dagobert became king of all the Franks in 629, Pepin and Arnulf lost their influence to individuals from the newly incorporated kingdom of Neustria. However, after Dagobert's death in 639, Pepin rose in power, along with his ally Bishop Cunibert of Cologne. When Pepin died in 640, his power was inherited not by his young son Grimoald, but by a man named Otto, who, as the tutor of Prince Sigebert, the son of Dagobert, was strategically placed to take advantage of the situation.

For a number of tumultuous years, the fortunes of the Pepin dynasty waxed and waned. Finally, around 680, Pepin II (also called Pepin of Heristal or Pepin the Young), the grandson of Pepin I, gained power in Austrasia as mayor of the palace. He held that position from 679 until his death in 714. After the battle of Tertry in 687, in which Pepin II and his forces defeated the nobles of Neustria, Pepin also ruled as mayor of the palace over Neustria and all other Frankish kingdoms except Aquitaine.

Although Pepin II was the actual ruler, he kept the line of Merovingian kings as figureheads. Two of his sons preceded him in death, Drogo in 707 and Grimoald in 714. When Pepin died in 714, there was a legitimate infant son and an illegitimate adult son, Charles. His wife, Plectrude, tried to ensure that her infant son would inherit his father's powerful position. Within a short time, however, Charles had obtained the position of mayor of the palace for himself. He became known as Charles Martel (the "Hammer"), a name he earned because of his military victories over the Moors.

Like other mayors of the palace, Charles Martel was the true ruler of the Frankish kingdom. He used his tenure to expand the realm, primarily through military campaigns. He defeated King Chilperic II of Neustria, then challenged and won Burgundy, Aquitaine, and Provence. By uniting the Franks, Martel prepared the way for his son, Pepin the Short

(Pepin III), to usurp power from the Merovingian kings and become the first king of all Franks and founder of the Carolingian dynasty.

See also: AQUITAINE DUCHY; BURGUNDY KINGDOM; CAROLINGIAN DYNASTY; FRANKISH KINGDOM; MARTEL, CHARLES; MEROVINGIAN DYNASTY; MEROVINGIAN-FRANKISH KINGDOM; PEPIN THE SHORT (PEPIN III).

PEPIN THE SHORT (PEPIN III)

(ca. 714–768 C.E.)

Frankish king (r. 751–768), the son of Charles Martel (r. 714–741) and the father of Charlemagne as well as founder of the Carolingian dynasty. Pepin first served as mayor of the palace of the Frankish kingdom of Austrasia but became king of all the Franks when he deposed the Frankish king Childeric III (r. ca. 743–751).

When Charles Martel died in 741, his sons, Pepin and Carloman, inherited from him the position of mayor of the palace of the Frankish kingdom. The two brothers divided the regions so that Pepin controlled Neustria, Burgundy, and Provence, while Carloman had Austrasia, Alamania, and Thuringia. Although their roles as mayors of the palace made them very powerful, Pepin and Carloman decided it was to their advantage to allow Childeric III to be crowned the Frankish king in 743.

Childeric was a weak ruler; that, coupled with Carloman's decision to enter a monastery in 747, left Pepin sufficiently powerful to depose Childeric in 751. Before doing so, however, Pepin had the foresight to first request approval from Rome, which he received, perhaps in exchange for a promise to assist the pope with military force to restore order in Italy.

In 754, Pope Stephen II journeyed to France to anoint Pepin and his heirs as the rightful rulers of the Frankish kingdom, the first Frankish king to be crowned and anointed by the pope. Pepin repaid the pope for his support by helping defend Rome against the Lombards in 754. Also, in 756, he gave the pope a gift of land in Ravenna, Italy, which became known as the Donation of Pepin. The gift of this land laid the foundation for the later formation of the Papal States.

Pepin's reign was marked by various military campaigns, including a successful campaign against Aquitaine in southwestern France, and some domestic unrest fomented by rivals who sought to provoke revolts against his rule. Pepin's most important legacy, however, was to establish an anointed kingship that his son would inherit.

Pepin had two sons, Charlemagne, who became king of the Franks (r. 768–814) and emperor of the West (r. 800–814); and Carloman, who ruled briefly as king of Austrasia (r. 768–771). When Carloman died in 771, his brother Charlemagne seized the kingdom and incorporated it within his own domain.

See also: CAROLINGIAN DYNASTY; CHARLEMAGNE; FRANKISH KINGDOM; MARTEL, CHARLES; MEROVINGIAN DYNASTY; PEPIN DYNASTY.

PERAK KINGDOM

(1528 C.E.–PRESENT)

Islamic kingdom, situated on the west coast of Malaysia, that was founded by a dispossessed member of the Malacca (or Melaka) sultanate in the early sixteenth century. Perak briefly became a prominent kingdom after the discovery of rich tin deposits there during the nineteenth century.

In the late 1400s, Perak was part of a larger province ruled by a governor appointed by the sultan of Malacca, Mahmud Shah (r. 1488–1511). Mahmud had two sons, Muzaffar Shah and Alauddin Shah, Muzaffar was the sultan's heir, but he fell from favor after the birth of his younger brother, Alauddin, who was named the new heir when he was still an infant.

INDEPENDENCE AND EARLY HISTORY

Upon the death of Mahmud in 1511, Alauddin became the new sultan and Muzaffar was forced to flee. Muzaffar eventually made his way to the province of Perak, where he declared independence from Malacca and became the first sultan of Perak around 1529.

Sultan Muzaffar Shah I (r. 1529–1549) died in 1549 and was succeeded by his son, Mansur Shah I (r. 1549–1577). According to Perak legend, Mansur continued his father's work of organizing the country under a series of chieftains in order to exert greater control over the kingdom.

Shortly after Mansur's death in 1577, Perak was attacked and conquered by the kingdom of Acheh, which was centered on the island of Sumatra.

Mansur's widow and children were carried off to Acheh, but as guests rather than as prisoners. One of the queens of Acheh took Mansur's eldest son as a husband, and in 1579 he succeeded to the throne of Acheh. Meanwhile, Perak retained its autonomy.

By the reign of Mansur Shah II (r. 1619–1630), the population of Perak had grown from only a few hundred to over several thousand. Sometime between 1620 and 1627, Perak was attacked and conquered again by Acheh. This time, the conquerors despoiled the land and took many prisoners back to Acheh. Sultan Iskandar Muda (r. 1607–1636) of Acheh placed a captive prince, Mahmud Shah (r. 1619–1630), on the throne of Perak and kept the sultanate as a vassal state.

RELATIONS WITH THE DUTCH

One of Mahmud's successors, Muzaffar Shah II (r. 1635–1654), opened up Perak to the Dutch East India Company in 1639. In 1651, he had twenty-seven Dutchmen killed when it was rumored that a trading center being built by the Dutch company was being outfitted as a fort. Further violence against Dutch traders led to their temporary withdrawal from Perak in 1690.

Around 1720, Alauddin Ri'ayat Shah (r. ca. 1720–1728) acceded to the throne of Perak. Alauddin fought a series of wars against his brother Muzaffar, who was attempting to overthrow Alauddin. Alauddin retained power until his death in 1728, at which time his brother, with whom he had finally reconciled, took the throne as Muzaffar Shar III (r. 1728–1754).

Around 1743, Perak was invaded by the Bugis of Selangor, a rival sultanate in the region. The Bugis deposed Muzaffar, whose brother Muhammad Shah (r. ca. 1743–1750) took the throne. Muzaffar maintained control over part of the sultanate, however, and he moved his capital temporarily upstream. In 1746, Muzaffar negotiated the reunification of the kingdom under his control. That same year, Muzaffar allowed the Dutch East India Company to return to Perak. In return for trading rights, the Dutch agreed to provide defense for Perak against its regional rivals.

Muzaffar died around 1754 and was succeeded by Iskandar Dhu'l-Qarnain Shah (r. ca. 1754–1765). An energetic leader, Iskandar built a new royal capital, royal palace, and mosque during his reign. He also strengthened Perak's ties with the Dutch East India Company, which helped Perak's economy and continued to provide security. When Iskandar died in 1765, Perak was at the height of its wealth and influence. He is remembered as Perak's greatest leader.

THE BRITISH AND THE PRESENT

In 1795, the Dutch disbanded the Dutch East India Company and Perak was left without the defensive and economic benefits that the company had long provided. One result was that the kingdom again began to fade into obscurity. However, in 1848, during the reign of Sultan Shahabuddin Ri'ayat Shah (r. 1831–1851), a major deposit of tin was discovered in the area of Larut. The discovery of this important mineral resource helped to fuel economic recovery in Perak and expansion of the kingdom.

For a number of years before this, Great Britain had been showing interest in the burgeoning Malay states. In 1874, the Perak leader Abdullah Muhammad (r. 1874–1877) invited the British to support his installation as Perak's new sultan. In return, he would allow a British official to reside in the kingdom and act as an adviser on all matters except Islamic and Malay custom. Abdullah signed the Treaty of Pangkor with the British in 1874 and became the twenty-sixth sultan of Perak.

The Treaty of Pangkor effectively ended Perak's independence. The sultanate stayed under British control, with the brief exception of Japanese rule in World War II, until Malaysia gained independence from Great Britain in 1957. Today, Perak remains a sultanate and is part of the Malay Federation.

See also: ACHEH KINGDOM; POSTCOLONIAL STATES; SOUTHEAST ASIAN KINGDOMS.

FURTHER READING

Andaya, Barbara Watson. *Perak, the Abode of Grace: A Study of an Eighteenth-Century Malay State*. New York: Oxford University Press, 1979.

PERGAMUM KINGDOM

(ca. 300–129 B.C.E.)

Ancient Greek city and kingdom of western Asia Minor (present-day Turkey), also called Pergamus, Pergamon, and Pergamos, noted for its sculpture and its library. The city of Pergamum became the center of a large kingdom in the third century B.C.E., and it retained its status as a political and cultural leader into the Byzantine period.

The Hellenistic society that emerged following the conquests of Alexander the Great (r. 336–323 B.C.E.) in the fourth century B.C.E. was centered in cities. Pergamum was one of these cities, and it was deeply influenced by Greek urban culture. Like many ancient Greek cities, Pergamum had a ruling council and an assembly, but it was ruled by a king. This resulted directly from the influence of Alexander the Great, who established royal governors in each city in his empire, a practice that continued in different forms after his death.

During the second century B.C.E., King Eumenes II of Pergamum (r. 197–159 B.C.E.) followed a pro-Roman policy that allowed him to expand his power and wealth. In return for his help in the Roman victory over Antiochus III of Syria (r. 223–187 B.C.E.) in 190 B.C.E., Eumenes was granted all of Antiochus's possessions as far as Taurus in Asia Minor. However, Roman suspicions of Eumenes' disloyalty later put his kingdom on the brink of war with Rome, which was averted only by his death in 159 B.C.E. A vigorous ruler and an adept politician, Eumenes II helped make Pergamum an important cultural center, which contained a great library that was second only to that of Alexandria in Egypt. Pergamum's contained more than 200,000 volumes.

During the reign of King Eumenes II, most writing was done on papyrus that was cultivated in Egypt. As part of the competition between the two kingdoms, Egypt banned the export of papyrus to Pergamum. According to the Roman historian Pliny, as a result of this embargo, Pergamum began to produce a paper-like product from the skins of sheep and goats, called parchment. The thriving parchment industry, along with silver mining and textiles, assured Pergamum of a stable and varied economy.

When Eumenes II died in 159 B.C.E., his brother Attalus II (r. 159–138 B.C.E.) ruled until 138 B.C.E. when Eumenes's son took the throne as Attalus III (r. 138–133 B.C.E.). Attalus, however, bequeathed the kingdom of Pergamum to Rome. In 133 B.C.E., a second son of Eumenes, Aristonicus, tried to restore the monarchy, but he was captured by the Romans in 129 B.C.E., and Pergamum became part of the Roman Empire under the name of Asia Propria.

See also: ALEXANDER III, THE GREAT; ANTIOCHUS III, THE GREAT; ROMAN EMPIRE; SELEUCID DYNASTY.

PERLAK KINGDOM. *See* ACHEH KINGDOM

PERSIAN EMPIRE (ca. 550–330 B.C.E.)

Ancient empire centered in present-day Iran that was the most powerful state of its time, with a vast area under its control in the ancient Near East.

In the early 500s B.C.E., the area known as Persia (called Fars by the native peoples of the region and Persis by the ancient Greeks) was ruled by a king named Cambyses I, who was one of the earliest rulers of the Achaemenid dynasty. Upon his death around 559 B.C.E., the throne went to his son, Cyrus II, better known as Cyrus the Great (r. ca. 559–530 B.C.E.).

BUILDING THE EMPIRE

Although he was the leader of a royal family, Cyrus II of Anshan was under the dominion of the Median Empire in the mid-sixth century B.C.E. But the ambitious Cyrus wanted power returned to his family, the Achaeminids. He rebelled against the Median king, Astyages (r. 585–550 B.C.E.), in 550 B.C.E., took the Median capital city of Ecbatana, and began a great period of conquest. Cyrus is thus the true founder of the Persian Empire.

Over the next two decades, Cyrus expanded his empire throughout southwestern Asia. His first conquest was Lydia, to his west in Asia Minor (present-day Turkey). He next looked to Babylonia and, by 540 B.C.E., had conquered that empire. With the fall of Babylonia, Syria and Palestine easily succumbed to Cyrus as well. With these conquests, all of southwestern Asia to the border of Egypt was part of one empire for the first time in history. Cyrus was never content with the size of his empire, and he was attempting to expand it further to the east when he died in battle in 530 B.C.E.

Cyrus is called Cyrus the Great not only because of the powerful empire he created, but also because of his remarkable benevolence. A different kind of conqueror, he used a new weapon to gain control over those he defeated: respect. His style of rule was to be carried on by all subsequent Persian rulers and was a great tool in maintaining a peaceful regime.

Under Cyrus and his successors, the Persians

A ROYAL IMPOSTER

Cyrus the Great had two sons—Cambyses, who inherited the throne, and Bardiya, who was assassinated during the reign of Cambyses. While Cambyses was with his army conquering Egypt in 525 B.C.E., a Median priest named Gaumata claimed to be the dead Bardiya, whom he apparently resembled. Because of Cambyses's long absence from Persia, Gaumata had time to garner the loyalty of many prominent Persians and had himself declared king. Cambyses learned of this treachery on his way home from Egypt in 522 B.C.E. but did not survive the voyage to confront Gaumata. Darius I, a relative of Cambyses's who was traveling with him, led the army back home. Darius quickly overpowered Gaumata, killed him, and declared himself the new king of the Persian Empire.

showed great tolerance toward local religious traditions, and they did not interfere with the cultural life of the lands they conquered and ruled. They acted more as successors to the rulers they overthrew than as victors, and they allowed many areas to maintain some autonomy. Because of this more gentle approach, the Persians were able to gain territory in a less confrontational way and to manage their expanding empire far more easily than might have been possible using force alone.

GOVERNING A VAST EMPIRE

Cyrus the Great was succeeded by his son, Cambyses II (r. 529–522 B.C.E.). By the time that Cambyses took the throne, there was only one other great territory not under Persian control—Egypt. In 525 B.C.E., Cambyses and his army marched through the desert of the Sinai Peninsula and handily defeated Egyptian forces. With this conquest, the Persian Empire became the largest empire in history, stretching throughout all of southwestern Asia from the Mediterranean coast in the west to the border of India in the east. Moreover, this vast and powerful empire had no potentially threatening enemies. Cambyses died of unknown causes while on his way home from military campaigns in Egypt in 522 B.C.E.

Darius I (r. 521–486 B.C.E.), a relative from another branch of the Achaemenid family, declared himself king after the death of Cambyses. The first two years of Darius's reign were spent crushing rebellions throughout the empire and asserting his authority. His strength was as an administrator rather than as a conqueror, and he created a new organization that provided for local autonomy but also allowed unquestioned central control.

Although he ruled as an absolute "king of kings" (*shah an-shah*), Darius I, the third ruler of the Persian Empire, created an administration that allowed the vast empire to run smoothly. Darius established twenty separate regions called satrapies, each of which was governed by its own satrap, or governor, who reported directly to the king.

Darius built roads to tie all of his territories together. Along these roads he established a postal system that could convey messages quickly from one part of the empire to another. He was the first ruler to coin currency. And he had a waterway dug from the Nile River to the Red Sea to facilitate trade. Under Darius, the Persians also adopted cuneiform writing, and Aramaean became the principal language of the empire.

By adding a level of sophistication to the Persian Empire that had never been seen before, and by providing so many links to the disparate people of his far-flung empire, Darius established an administration that was to keep the empire intact for centuries.

TROUBLE WITH THE GREEKS

Near the end of Darius's life, some of the Greek cities on the coast of Asia Minor revolted with the assistance of Athens and other Greek city-states on

THE PERSIAN EMPIRE

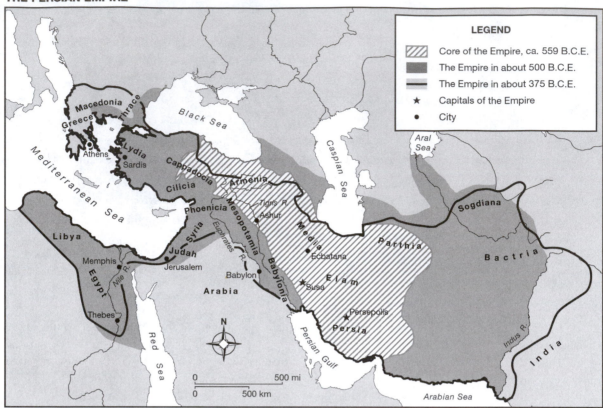

LEGEND

Core of the Empire, ca. 559 B.C.E.

The Empire in about 500 B.C.E.

The Empire in about 375 B.C.E.

★ Capitals of the Empire

• City

mainland Greece. Darius was able to stop the revolt, but when he sent his army to Greece in retribution for assisting the rebellious cities, the Persians lost to the Greeks at the battle of Marathon of 490 B.C.E. This was the first major loss that the Persian army had ever suffered.

After a nearly forty-year reign, Darius died in 486 B.C.E. and was succeeded by his son, Xerxes I (r. 485–465 B.C.E.). Xerxes faced two more battles with the Greeks, both of which he lost. These defeats marked a turning point for the Persian Empire.

However, it was the death of Darius II (r. 423–405 B.C.E.) some sixty years later in 405 B.C.E. that set off the real beginning of the end for the Persian Empire. Darius II had two sons, both of whom wanted to be king. The older of the brothers succeeded to the throne as Artaxerxes II (r. 404–359 B.C.E.). The younger brother, Cyrus, allied himself with some Greek soldiers and fought a civil war against his brother for rule of the empire. Cyrus was easily killed, but the war between the brothers caused a ripple effect, as others perceived the rift as a weakening in the royal family. Artaxerxes and the succeeding rulers of Persia faced repeated rebellions by the satraps.

It was Alexander III, the Great (r. 336–323 B.C.E.) of Greece who brought about the final end to the Persian Empire. After invading the Persian Empire in 334 B.C.E., Alexander won battle after battle with the weakened Persians on his way through their territory, finally conquering the last ruler of the Achaemenid dynasty, Darius III (r. 335–330 B.C.E.), in 330 B.C.E. With the establishment of his own empire, Alexander brought the Persian Empire to an end.

See also: ALEXANDER III, THE GREAT; ARTAXERXES I; CAMBYSES II; CYRUS THE GREAT; DARIUS I, THE GREAT; DARIUS III (CODOMMANUS); LYDIA, KINGDOM OF; MACEDONIAN EMPIRE; XERXES.

FURTHER READING

Asimov, Isaac. *The Near East: 10,000 Years of History.* Boston: Houghton Mifflin, 1968.

Hitti, Philip K. *The Near East in History: A 5000 Year Story.* Princeton, NJ: Van Nostrand, 1961.

Perry, Glenn E. *The Middle East: Fourteen Islamic Centuries.* Upper Saddle River, NJ: Prentice-Hall, 1997.

Sicker, Martin. *The Pre-Islamic Middle East*. Westport, CT: Praeger, 2000.

PETER I, THE GREAT (1672–1725 C.E.)

Tsar of Russia (r. 1682–1725) and first Russian emperor (r. 1721–1725), who was instrumental in turning Russia into a dominant political and military power, ultimately controlling nearly all of Northern Europe.

The grandson of the first Romanov tsar, Mikhail Fedorovich, Peter founded the city of St. Petersburg, introduced Russia to Western ideas and culture, and established the nation's first fully trained military. More interested in shipbuilding and military strategies than in the royal court, he nonetheless was a politically ruthless leader who ruled with an iron hand.

RISE TO POWER

From an early age, Peter was caught up in a power struggle between the families of the current and former wife of his father, Tsar Alexei Mikhailovich (r. 1645–1676). As the youngest son of Alexei's second wife, Natalia Kirillovna Naryshkina, Peter should not have been in line for the throne. But when Tsar Alexei's eldest son and successor, Feodor III (r. 1676–1672), died after ruling only four years, the Naryshkina family used its influence with the Russian Orthodox Church to have ten-year-old Peter succeed over Peter's sickly half-brother, fourteen-year-old Ivan.

Peter's elder half-sister Sofia, however, gained the support of the Kremlin Guard and launched a coup, resulting in Ivan V (r. 1682–1696) and Peter I being named joint tsars in 1682. Because both boys were too young to govern, Sofia was named regent of Russia, ruling the country for seven years. Upon Ivan's death in 1696, and with Sofia forever banished to a convent because of another attempted coup, the twenty-two-year-old Peter assumed sole reign.

INFLUENCES

Despite his chaotic childhood, Peter relished growing up in the Russian countryside, and he took an active interest in military strategy. He once discovered an abandoned British sailboat, which launched his lifelong passion for sailing and shipbuilding. Strong and more than six feet six inches tall, Peter greatly enjoyed physical labor, favoring the outdoors over court life in Moscow.

Prior to Peter's rule, Russia remained isolated from the rest of Europe, abiding the customs and dictates of the Russian Orthodox Church. Almost immediately after assuming the throne, Peter embarked on a two-year grand tour of Western Europe, learning as much as he could about Western European government, industry, and military techniques. He also indulged his love of ships, and there were reports that he hid his true identify to work briefly as a ship's carpenter in Holland.

ACCOMPLISHMENTS

Upon his return to Russia in 1698 to suppress yet another rebellion by the Kremlin Guard, Peter began re-creating Russia in the image of the West. He banned traditional Muscovite dress for all men, forced women out of seclusion, insisted Russian no-

Tsar Peter the Great devoted his rule to Westernizing and modernizing Russia. To promote closer contact with the West, he ordered the construction of a new capital city, St. Petersburg, on the shores of the Baltic Sea. In 1725, afer diving into the icy waters of the Baltic to save drowning sailors, he became ill and died a short time later.

bles be clean-shaven, placed the Orthodox Church under his authority, simplified the alphabet, and changed the calendar to coincide with the rest of Europe. He also brought in thousands of artisans, craftsmen, scientists, and other advisers from Western Europe to expose Russians to different ideas and concepts.

Most importantly, Peter created the strongest military Russia had ever known, expanding it from around 30,000 men in 1695 to nearly 300,000 men in 1725, including a newly formed Navy. He also authorized mass conscriptions of both peasants and nobles. To outfit the military, Peter created iron foundries and textile mills, which helped put Russia on the road to industrialization.

THE NORTHERN WAR AND FOUNDING OF ST. PETERSBURG

Determined to regain access to the Baltic Sea and Baltic trade, in 1700 Peter formed an alliance with Denmark, Poland, and Prussia to fight Sweden in the Northern War (1700–1721), which lasted more than two decades.

While the Russians suffered a huge early defeat at the battle of Narva, losing more than 9,000 men, it taught Peter a valuable lesson, and he worked to modernize his military even more. In 1703, he also established a fort in a desolate area of marshland to serve as a Baltic port for his supply ships. He named it St. Petersburg. To strengthen the fort, he ordered hundreds of Russians to move to St. Petersburg to build great houses, roads, and canals, ultimately relocating the capital there from Moscow.

Peter also implemented a policy in which any person under Russian control who gave or sold food to the enemy was to be hanged and the villages from which the food came were to be burned to the ground. As a result of this policy, Sweden's army faced starvation, weakening it considerably.

In 1721, Sweden finally made peace with Russia, recognizing Russia's hold on territory it had conquered, including Ingria, Estonia, Livonia, Vyborg (Viipuri), Kexholm (Piorzersk), and part of Karelia. Victorious, Peter proclaimed Russia an empire, declaring himself emperor of All Russia, Great Father of the Fatherland, from which the title Peter "The Great" evolved.

Although Peter had eleven children (the eldest of whom Peter imprisoned for suspected treason), he named no heir to the throne. Upon his death on Jan-

uary 28, 1725, his second wife Ekaterina Alexeevna succeeded him as Catherine I (r. 1725–1727).

See also: ROMANOV DYNASTY; RUSSIAN DYNASTIES.

FURTHER READING

Anderson, M. S. *Peter the Great.* 2nd edition. New York: Longman, 2000.

Lincoln, Bruce W. *Sunlight at Midnight: St. Petersburg and the Rise of Modern Russia.* New York: Basic Books, 2002.

Massie, Robert K. *Peter the Great: His Life and World.* New York: Wings Books, 1991.

PHILIP II (1527–1598 C.E.)

Spanish king who continued the policies of his father, Charles V, king of Spain and Holy Roman emperor (r. 1519–1556), in expanding Spanish power and control. Philip was born in Valladolid, Spain, on May 21, 1527, the only son of Charles V and Isabella of Portugal. Philip saw little of his father while he was growing up, and he lost his mother when he was twelve years old. His education was entrusted to a series of tutors who saw to it that he learned the sciences, mathematics, history, architecture, music, and several languages, including Latin and Greek. Charles V took charge of his son's political education through a series of letters.

At the age of sixteen, Philip's father appointed him regent of Spain, which he ruled with the help of a council. In the same year he wed his cousin, Maria of Portugal. On July 8, 1545, Philip's son and heir, Don Carlos, was born. Four days later Maria died.

In 1553 when Mary Tudor came to the throne of England, she had the intent of restoring her kingdom to Catholicism. Charles V saw this as an opportunity to unite the two countries by religion and marriage, and he proposed a union between Philip, now king of Naples and Sicily, and Mary. While Philip regarded the marriage as entirely political, Mary had high hopes of romance, particularly after she met her handsome suitor. The people of England were not enamored of the idea of England being ruled by a foreigner, and a revolt led by the radical Protestant Thomas Wyatt sought to replace Mary with her sister, Elizabeth. When the revolt was put down, Philip and Mary wed on July 25, 1554. He was twenty-six years old, she thirty-seven. Mary gave Philip the title of king of England. In 1555 Charles V ceded the Netherlands to his son, and in 1556 Philip was proclaimed king of Spain. To Mary's great sorrow, Philip spent very little time in England, particularly after it became clear that she would not be able to bear children. After Mary's death in 1558, Philip explored the possibility of marriage with Elizabeth, but she was determined not to marry.

Shortly after ascending the throne of Spain, Philip became embroiled in two wars. In Italy he fought to preserve Naples and Sicily as Spanish kingdoms, and at the same time he carried on his father's war with France for control of territories in the Netherlands. Philip was victorious on both fronts. His marriage in

A member of the illustrious Habsburg dynasty, King Philip II of Spain was a patron of the arts. The Venetian master Titian, painted this portrait of the king around 1550.

1559 to Elizabeth, daughter of Henry II of France, was another political union, designed to help keep the peace between the two nations. After Elizabeth's death, Philip married Anna, the daughter of Emperor Maximilian II. She bore him a son, Philip.

After his victory in the Netherlands, Philip returned to Spain and never left again. He alternated between Madrid and the Escorial, a compound not far from Madrid that included a palace, monastery, church, college, library, and art galleries that Philip constructed to fulfill a vow that he had made while battling the French in the Netherlands.

Determined to rid Spain of heretics, Philip used the apparatus of the Inquisition (an institution of judges established by the papacy responsible for seeking out, bringing to trial, and punishing those whose beliefs were opposed to those of the Catholic Church). He is said to have told a heretic about to be burned that if his own son were guilty, "I should lead him with my own hands to the stake." After doing away with Protestantism, Philip turned to the Moriscoes—Moors who had been forcibly converted to Catholicism after the defeat of Granada in 1492. Philip wanted them to alter how they dressed and to force them to speak Spanish, and in 1567 they rebelled. The conflict lasted three years until Don Juan, Philip's illegitimate half-brother, put it down. As a result of this defeat, many Moriscoes were sent away from the coasts into the interior of Spain.

In 1580 Philip took control of the Portuguese throne, uniting the Iberian Peninsula under one ruler, a situation that lasted until 1640. He fought many battles over the Netherlands, eventually losing the northern provinces to the French and ceding the southern provinces to his daughter Isabella and her husband, Archduke Albert of Austria in 1592. It was Elizabeth's attempt to send aid to the Protestants of the Netherlands that led Philip to send the great Armada to England. The fleet was almost completely destroyed by bad weather, thanks to an incompetent captain. This was a severe blow to the Spanish Navy and ultimately marked the end of Spain's role as a world power.

During his reign, Philip also fought with the Turks, who attempted to dominate the Mediterranean. He sent Spanish forces to join the fleet of the Holy League to oppose the Turkish fleet at the battle of Lepanto, roundly defeating the Turks in 1571. In 1578, Philip established a treaty with the Turks that continued until his death in 1598. He was succeeded by his son, Philip III.

While Catholics tended to regard Philip's legacy as a positive one, many Protestants called him a demon. During his reign, Spain conquered the Philippine Islands, which were named after him, and Portugal and Spain were united. He was a hardworking ruler, a good father, and a very devout Catholic. But he could also be cruel and unforgiving, and his methods of battling what he called heresy tend to overshadow his better qualities.

See also: CHARLES V; ELIZABETH I; MARY I, TUDOR.

FURTHER READING

Kamen, Henry Arthur Francis. *Philip of Spain.* New Haven, CT: Yale University Press, 1997.

Parker, Geoffrey. *Philip II: With a New Bibliographical Essay.* Chicago: Open Court, 2002.

PHILIP II OF MACEDON

(ca. 382–336 B.C.E.)

King of Macedon, father of Alexander the Great (r. 336–323 B.C.E.), and founder of the Macedonian Empire.

Philip II was born in the city of Pella in Macedonia around 382 B.C.E. The youngest son of King Amyntas III (r. 393–387, 386–369 B.C.E.), Philip did not stand directly in the line to inherit the throne. However, the early deaths of his older brothers in 368 and 359 B.C.E. left him the successor. Renowned for his military prowess, Philip trained a professional army with which he was able to expand dramatically the holdings of his kingdom. During Philip's rule, Macedon also made great cultural advancements, as well as tremendous economic strides.

TAKING CONTROL

When Philip came to power in 359 B.C.E., Macedonia had just suffered a defeat at the hands of the Illyrians, a neighboring peoples to the north and west. As a result, Macedonia was in political and military turmoil, and Philip immediately set about bringing the country and the people of Macedonia under his control.

After exacting revenge on the Illyrians by defeating them in 358 B.C.E., Philip sought to bring all of upper Macedonia under his control. His primary method of creating alliances and strengthening loyalties was through marriage. The most important marriage for Philip was his own marriage to Olympias, the daughter of King Neoptolemus of Epirus (r. dates unknown). Philip and Olympias were married by 357 B.C.E., and the new queen gave birth to their son Alexander the next year.

Philip achieved several innovations that helped make Macedonia a great power. First, he began providing education and training for the sons of nobles at the royal court, where they would develop loyalty for the king. This was also a way for Philip to hold the children hostage, in a sense, to keep their parents from interfering with his authority.

REFORMS OF THE MILITARY

Philip's military innovations created the great fighting power that his son, Alexander, would later inherit, giving Macedonia one of the most feared armies in the world. Philip introduced the *sarissa,* a wooden pike with metal tip, for use by his infantry. This weapon, when held upright by the rear rows of the infantry phalanx formation (there were usually eight rows), helped hide maneuvers behind the phalanx from enemy view. When held horizontally by the front rows of the phalanx, it was a rather brutal weapon. Enemy soldiers could be run through from twenty feet away, giving quite an advantage to the phalanx in hand-to-hand combat.

Philip also made the military a way of life for many Macedonian men. In the past, soldiering had only been a part-time job, something men would do

The father of Alexander the Great, Philip II of Macedon was himself a successful military leader and conqueror, and he laid the groundwork for the achievements of his son. Coins with his likeness were used as currency throughout his domain in Macedonia and Greece.

during the off-peak times of farming. When the fighting season ended at the start of the harvest, the men would return to the farms.

Philip, however, made the military an occupation that paid well enough that the soldiers could afford to do it year-round. By making the military a full-time occupation, Philip was able to drill his men regularly, building unity and cohesion within the army ranks. Largely because of the professionalism and training of the army, Alexander fought with the finest military machine ever seen in Greece or Asia.

Philip's greatest military success was against Greek forces at the battle at Chaeronea in August 338 B.C.E. Although Philip's army was greatly outnumbered by the armies of the Greek city-states of Athens and Thebes, his forces successfully overwhelmed them. Both cities were forced to become subjects of Philip and Macedonia, leaving Sparta as the only major Greek city-state not under Macedonian control.

DEALING WITH THE GREEKS AND PERSIANS

At the Council at Corinth in 337 B.C.E., Philip outlined his system for ruling the Greek city-states, creating the League of Corinth, also known as the Hellenic League. He gave freedom and autonomy to all the political parties in each state, yet established a network of bureaucracies that would be stable and loyal to Philip

Then, with the support of all Greece, Philip declared war on Persia to retaliate for the Persian invasion of Greece several generations before. In the spring of 336 B.C.E., Philip sent two of his generals, Attalus and Parmenion, with 10,000 troops into Asia Minor (present-day Turkey) to begin liberating Greek cities along the coast of that region. Just before Philip himself was to travel to Asia to begin the conquest, he was assassinated. Some Macedonians suspected that Philip's wife, Olympias, played a role in his murder, but this was probably not true. Upon his death, Philip was succeeded on the throne of Macedonia by his son, Alexander.

See also: ALEXANDER III, THE GREAT; GREEK KINGDOMS, ANCIENT; HELLENISTIC DYNASTIES; MACEDONIAN EMPIRE; MACEDONIAN KINGDOM.

FURTHER READING

Ashley, James R. *The Macedonian Empire: The Era of Warfare Under Philip II and Alexander the Great, 359–323 B.C.* Jefferson, NC: McFarland, 1998.

PHILIP II, AUGUSTUS (1165–1223 C.E.)

King of France (r. 1180–1223) of the Capetian dynasty, also known as Philip Augustus, who participated briefly in the Third Crusade (1190–1191), but spent most of his long reign recovering territories from the English kings of the Angevin dynasty and expanding his realm.

Born to the pious King Louis VII (r. 1137–1180), Philip Augustus took the throne in 1180, at age fourteen, upon the death of his father. Shortly after his accession, Philip engineered his own marriage to Isabella of Hainault, niece of the count of Flanders. By 1185, both the count and countess of Flanders had died, and, through his marriage to Isabella, Philip was able to extend his sphere of influence into Flanders.

With Flanders secure, Philip was free to concentrate on his struggle with the English kings of the Plantagenet dynasty: first King Henry II (r. 1154–1189), then King Richard I, the Lionheart (r. 1189–1199), and finally, King John (r. 1199–1216). Philip was single-minded in his desire to recover for France the Angevin holdings in Normandy, Brittany, Anjou, Maine, Tourmaine, and Poitou that were controlled by the English Crown.

Philip succeeded in this strategy, cleverly playing off the easily angered Richard the Lionheart against first one brother, then another—all of Henry II's four sons were at one time or another allied with Philip against their father. After spending little more than a year on the Third Crusade, Philip left an angry Richard the Lionheart in Palestine and returned to Europe to provoke Richard's regent, John, into open revolt. When Richard himself was captured by Leopold of Austria on his return journey from the Holy Land, Philip used every means available to prolong Richard's imprisonment.

Finally ransomed, Richard returned to England just long enough to raise funds and troops to attack Philip. Although Richard was the superior soldier, Philip fought tenaciously for five years until Richard was killed by a stray arrow in an unimportant skirmish in 1199. Faced now with Richard's less competent brother, King John, Philip took Normandy in 1204. By 1205, the English Angevin territories of Maine, Touraine, Anjou, and most of Poitou were all under French control.

Not all of Philip's gains were at the expense of the

English Angevins. He allowed his vassals to participate in Pope Innocent III's crusade against the Cathari (a non-Catholic Christian sect), a decision that opened the way for the eventual French annexation of Toulouse and the Languedoc. Philip's most important victory was the battle of Bouvines (1214) in which he defeated the combined forces of King John of England, the Holy Roman emperor Otto IV (r. 1198–1218), and the counts of Boulogne and Flanders. The outcome of this battle had far-reaching effects, putting Flanders under complete control of the French Crown and making France the strongest unified force in Europe.

Besides his conquests and broken treaties, Philip was notable for his patronage of individual municipalities and, particularly, of Paris. During his reign, Philip paved and walled the entire city of Paris. He also built the first Louvre palace there.

During Philip's forty-three-year reign, France tripled in size. At the same time, Philip weakened the feudal hold of French aristocrats on their subjects and increased the power of the French Crown at the expense of the nobility. When Philip died in 1223, he was succeeded by his son, Louis VIII (r. 1223–1226). Philip's successes laid the foundation for the powerful France that was eventually inherited by his grandson, Louis IX (1226–1270).

See also: ANGEVIN DYNASTIES; ANJOU KINGDOM; CAPETIAN DYNASTY; FLANDERS, COUNTY OF; FRENCH MONARCHIES; HENRY II; JOHN I; LOUIS VII; RICHARD I, LIONHEART.

FURTHER READING
Bradbury, Jim. *Philip Augustus: King of France, 1180–1223.* New York: Longman, 1998.

PHILIP IV, THE FAIR (1268–1314 C.E.)

King of France (r. 1285–1314), a member of the Capetian dynasty, who ruled as an absolute monarch with corrupt and extortionate administrators. Philip IV was called "The Fair" for his physical appearance, not for his methods of governing.

Philip IV was the son of Philip III (r. 1270–1285) and Isabel of Aragón. Philip became king of France upon the death of his father in 1285. He married Jeanne, the daughter of Henry I (r. 1270–1274), king of Navarre and count of Champagne and Brie. Philip

died in 1314 and was succeeded by his son, Louis X (r. 1314–1316). Because Louis X had no male heirs and died only two years after taking the throne, Philip's other two sons also ruled France in turn: Philip V (r. 1316–1322) and Charles IV (r. 1322–1328). Philip IV's only daughter, Isabel, became queen consort of Edward II (r. 1307–1327) of England.

An absolute monarch, Philip had a despotic reign that focused on strengthening the central government of France, in large part to increase his personal wealth. His rule relied on a new type of administrator, the *chevaliers de l'hotel,* which was not an inherited position, but one gained as a result of individual accomplishments and favor. These administrators were exceptionally loyal to the king, whose power made their position possible. They not only supported him in conflicts with the Church, but also aggressively and ruthlessly pursued their own interests. In 1302, a council of nobles, clergy, and commoners called the *états généraux* declared that the king was the highest power on earth, thereby justifying Philip's tyrannical actions as well as his claim of divine right.

Philip's power struggle with the Church was centered on wealth. In 1296, Philip fought with Pope Boniface VIII over a tax on the clergy. The French government claimed that since the Church had sometimes given money to help finance the crusades, there was a precedent that allowed the Church to be taxed for any military purpose. Boniface, underestimating the power of the French government, reacted belligerently to this claim rather than attempting to negotiate.

In 1302, Boniface issued a papal bull that proclaimed the ultimate sovereignty of the pope over kings, even to the point of deposing kings who refused to submit to papal authority. Philip eventually won Boniface's concession through a campaign of intimidation and harassment, including placing an embargo on precious metals so that no money could be exported, thus depriving the pope of necessary revenue.

After several years of power struggles between Philip and the pope, William de Nogaret, one of Philip's ministers, charged Boniface with being the enemy of both the Church and the French nation, accusing the pope of crimes ranging from heresy to murder. In 1303, French soldiers seized Pope Boniface VIII at his family's palace at Anagni. Although he escaped to Rome, Boniface died shortly thereafter in 1303.

The ongoing feud with the papacy was resolved

when Philip used his influence to get Clement V elected pope in 1305. Clement, a Frenchman, was unwilling to oppose the French king, and in a sign of subservience, he moved the papal residence and administrative center to Avignon in the French region of Provence.

Another source of conflict during Philip IV's reign involved the Knights Templar, who came under vicious attack from Philip and his ministers. The Templars were an order of knights that had been founded early in the twelfth century, whose mission was to protect pilgrims en route to Jerusalem. Despite their vows of poverty, the Templars were extremely successful in acquiring land, money, and influence.

By Philip's time, the Templars served as bankers for the Church and the European nobility. Philip, who envied their wealth and was unable to tolerate their competing power, destroyed them with the backing of Pope Clement V. The Knights were charged with heresy, and their trial, which lasted from 1307 to 1313, was marked by great cruelty. Torture was used to obtain confessions, and many of the knights were burned at the stake. In the end, the order was completely destroyed, its money and land confiscated by the Crown.

Philip also expanded French territory by marriage, stealth, and force. His marriage to Jeanne, the daughter of Henry I of Navarre, added a number of territories to France. In 1312, Philip captured the city of Lyon from the Holy Roman Empire during the absence of the emperor. Although the Hundred Years' War did not begin until 1337, the early stages began during Philip's reign when he tried, unsuccessfully, to expel the English from the duchy of Guienne. Philip was, however, able to obtain a settlement in which the son of Edward I ruled Guienne as Philip's vassal.

See also: CAPETIAN DYNASTY; CHARLES V; FRENCH MONARCHIES; NAVARRE, KINGDOM OF.

PHOENICIAN EMPIRE

(ca. 1300–322 B.C.E.)

Maritime power of the ancient world that spread its phonetic system of writing throughout the Mediterranean.

The core of ancient Phoenician culture stretched along the Mediterranean coast of modern-day Lebanon, centered on the cities of Tyre, Sidon, and Berut (modern-day Beirut). Although the origins of the Phoenicians are not clear, archaeological evidence suggests that they arrived in that region around 3000 B.C.E. Until the 1200s B.C.E., they were referred to by their biblical name, the Canaanites.

PHOENICIAN TRADE AND COLONIZATION

Like the Minoan civilization that preceded them in the eastern Mediterranean, the Phoenicians based their success on trade, trading primarily in timber, metalwork, wine, embroidery, salt, dried fish, glazed faience, textiles, and a luxurious purple dye that they refined from a type of snail. In their pursuit of trade routes to ever more distant locations, the Phoenicians established far-flung colonies to serve as waystations. Coastal settlements established by the Phoenicians along the Mediterranean extended as far as the Iberian Peninsula, and the Phoenicians may even have traveled as far as southwestern England in pursuit of tin.

As they traveled the known world, the Phoenicians spread their culture with their trading goods. Perhaps the most influential of Phoenician innovations was their system of writing, early samples of which date from the fifteenth century B.C.E. Phoenician writing, which was both phonetically based and standardized, proved to be more flexible than the cuneiform and hieroglyphic systems developed by the ancient Sumerians and Egyptians. The Phoenician system of writing was later adapted by the Greeks, the Etruscans, and the Romans, and it is the foundation for the alphabet used in the West today.

PHOENICIAN RULE

The various Phoenician settlements, such as Carthage and Utica in North Africa (established in the ninth century B.C.E.), functioned as largely independent states and city-states connected by a loose trade confederation and common cultural origins. Religion varied across the regions, and people worshiped a number of gods, including those from the Greek and Egyptian pantheons as well as local deities.

Phoenician cities were typically governed by hereditary kingships, although by the sixth century B.C.E., the monarchy of Tyre had been replaced by a republic, governed by "suffetes" or judges. By the fourth century B.C.E., Carthage also was governed by two elected suffetes.

The wealth of Phoenicia proved to be highly tempting to its neighbors and led to periodic foreign conquest. In the sixteenth century B.C.E., timber-poor Egypt attacked Phoenicia because of the forest resources of Phoenician Lebanon, and Egypt controlled the region for 200 years afterward. In the fourteenth century B.C.E., however, internal unrest weakened the Egyptian Empire, allowing the Phoenicians to regain their independence.

The Phoenician city-states enjoyed a period of successful autonomy from the twelfth to the ninth century B.C.E., during which time Phoenician fleets strengthened their hold on the Mediterranean trade routes. In the ninth century B.C.E., however, Phoenicia was once again threatened by foreign armies. Assyrian kings exacted tribute from Phoenician cities in Lebanon for a century until, under the rule of Tiglath-Pileser III (r. 744–727 B.C.E.), the Assyrian Empire was restructured and much of Phoenicia became Assyrian vassal states.

RELATIONS WITH PERSIA

The next period of Phoenician history was narrated by the ancient Greek historian Herodotus in his history of the Greek and Persian wars. By 539 B.C.E., Cyrus the Great of Persia (r. 559–530 B.C.E.) had conquered the remains of the Babylonian Empire, thereby becoming ruler of the Babylonian and former Assyrian provinces as well. The Phoenicians struck a deal with Cyrus's son and successor, Cambyses I (r. 529–522 B.C.E.): the Phoenician states would remain largely independent as long as they provided the Persians with the skilled fleet and crews needed to wage war successfully against the Greeks.

The Phoenicians thus enjoyed a special status in the Persian Empire while Persia dominated the ancient Near East (550–330 B.C.E.). This status was demonstrated when Cambyses planned to take Carthage a few years later, and the Phoenicians refused to sail against what they considered a Phoenician colony. Cambyses, highlighting the voluntary nature of the agreement the Phoenicians had made with Persia, agreed to back down.

Phoenician fleets played a crucial role in several Persian military successes against the Greeks, including the victory by Darius I (r. 521–486 B.C.E.) in 494 B.C.E. near the Aegean island of Lade. They were also involved in the crushing Persian defeat by the Greeks at the naval battle of Salamis in 480 B.C.E., in which many of the Phoenician manned ships fled the battle. The Phoenician retreat proved very damaging to Persian-Phoenician relations.

It was not until 465 B.C.E. that the Phoenicians again aided the Persians, this time in protecting the Phoenician colonies on Cyprus from the Athenians. The Phoenicians continued to defend Cyprus successfully for another seventy-five years. In 358 B.C.E., the Phoenicians and the people of Cyprus revolted against the Persians, then ruled by Artaxerxes III (r. 358–338 B.C.E.). But the revolt was put down by the treachery of King Tennes of Sidon (r. ca. 356–349 B.C.E.), who fled the city with most of his warriors and left the inhabitants to face the Persians. Tennes's betrayal of the Phoenicians led to the destruction of the city of Sidon and the mass suicides of thousands of its citizens, after which the rest of Phoenicia quickly capitulated to the Persians.

Persian control of Phoenicia lasted until the rise of Alexander the Great (r. 336–323 B.C.E.) of Macedonia. When Alexander led his army into Phoenicia, several Phoenician city-states, including Byblos and Aradus, surrendered without a fight. The city of Tyre, however, defended itself against the Greek forces during a hard siege that lasted from 333 to 332 B.C.E. This was the last significant military action by the Phoenicians; after Tyre was conquered, it and the rest of Phoenicia were largely subsumed into Hellenistic Greece. By Roman times, little of traditional Phoenician culture survived, although the Phoenician homeland was incorporated into Roman Syria in 64 B.C.E.

See also: ALEXANDER III, THE GREAT; CYRUS THE GREAT; DARIUS I, THE GREAT; MINOAN KINGDOMS; PERSIAN EMPIRE.

PHRYGIA KINGDOM (750–600 B.C.E.)

Kingdom in Anatolia (Asia Minor) established by tribes from the Balkan region, who migrated to Anatolia as early as the first part of the twelfth century B.C.E.

The first true Phrygian kingdom was not established until about 725 B.C.E, when King Midas (r. ca. late 700s–675 B.C.E.) declared himself to be the first king of Phrygia. Under his rule, Phrygia began to expand its boundaries, and by the time of his death in 675 B.C.E., the kingdom encompassed much of central and the southeastern Anatolia.

Soon after their arrival in Anatolia, the Phrygian people were influenced by both the existing Hellenistic and Hittite cultures of the region. As a result, they began to develop a rich and growing cultural heritage. The capital of the Phrygia kingdom was Gordion, which was strategically located directly on a main trade route through Anatolia. This location proved to be very beneficial both economically and culturally for the growth of the kingdom.

The kingdom of Phrygia reached the height of its prosperity between 725 and 675 B.C.E. Early in the seventh century B.C.E., attacks by Cimmerians from north and east of the Black Sea began to threaten the kingdom and left Phrygia weakened and vulnerable. In this weakened state, the kingdom was unprepared to deal with a subsequent invasion from Persia.

The Persian invasions of Anatolia in the sixth century B.C.E. left Phrygian settlements, including Gordion, impoverished and unable to maintain themselves. Left almost unnoticed, and lacking in social or political significance, Phrygia remained under Persian rule until 333 B.C.E., when Alexander the Great (r. 336–323 B.C.E.) reclaimed the region from the Persians. Alexander granted Phrygia its independence, but in the centuries that followed, the region began to adopt a more Hellenistic political and cultural tradition.

As a culture, the Phrygians are best known for their creativity and craftsmanship in metal and wood. They also created unique designs on woven materials, trading many of their arts and handicrafts with the Ionians, who lived in the coastal region of Anatolia and neighboring Aegean Islands. The Phrygians were also a highly literate people. Reading and writing, for instance, were not restricted to kings, but were readily available to the masses, a concept far different from that of many other ancient civilizations. A great majority of ordinary citizens were capable of reading and writing, and they used these skills often in their daily lives.

See also: ALEXANDER III, THE GREAT; HITTITE EMPIRE; PERSIAN EMPIRE.

FURTHER READING
Mazower, Mark. *The Balkans.* New York: Modern Library, 2000.

PIAST DYNASTY (ca. 850–1370 C.E.)

The first ruling dynasty of Poland, which supplied princes and kings for over five hundred years and es-

tablished the country as the eastern bastion of Latin Christianity.

From their emergence as regional tribal leaders in the early Middle Ages to their eventual coronation as kings in the late 900s, the Piasts were a source of continuity for the troubled and often ungovernable country of Poland. They therefore deserve credit for keeping Poland alive and maintaining its status as a major European state.

THE EARLY STATE
In the early Middle Ages, the lands that comprise present-day Poland were thinly populated by a number of Slavic tribes that relied on agriculture as the basis of their economies. The Polanian tribe, who lived around Gniezno in western Poland, gradually expanded their control over neighboring tribes under the leadership of a succession of hereditary dukes. The legendary Piast, the founder of the Piast dynasty, himself is variously said to have been a peasant or the chief steward at the court of the evil ruler Popiel, who eventually was overthrown, imprisoned, and eaten by mice in the dungeon of Kruszwica castle. Either Piast or his son Ziemowit was the first of his line to rule, sometime after 850.

The first Piast ruler to enter the contemporary historical record was Prince Mieszko I (r. ca. 963–992). Mieszko converted to Latin Christianity in 966, in order to win papal support against the German dukes to the west. By the time of his death, he had conquered the region of Pomerania on the Baltic Sea and Silesia to the south. His realm may have included Mazovia (the region around Warsaw) as well, thus reaching the borders of the Poland of today.

Mieszko's son, Boleslaw I, the Brave (r. 992–1025) was the first Piast to be crowned king of Poland. During his long reign, Boleslaw strengthened the country's civil, economic, and religious administration. The institutional structures he established served to keep Poland intact during the reigns of his weak successors, most of whom did not claim the royal title of king.

Boleslaw's descendant Boleslaw III (r. 1102–1138) was able to reconquer the lands that Poland had lost since the era of Mieszko I. But his decision to divide the realm among his four sons led to a 150-year struggle among the different branches of the family, a struggle that tended to increase the power of the country's nobles.

Not until 1290, with the accession of Przemysl I

(r. 1295–1296) did a Premysl ruler once again wear the Crown as king, although it cost him his life a year later, possibly at the hands of rival German princes. It was left to the last two Piast kings, Wladyslaw I (r. 1306–1333) and Casimir III (r. 1333–1370), to restore some of the glory of the Piast name, as well as the domestic and foreign strength of Poland.

When Wladislaw I was crowned king in Krakow in 1320, he had already spent some thirty years contending for leadership, yet he effectively controlled only a part of the country. He secured the support of Hungary and Lithuania by marrying two of his children into their ruling families.

HIGH POINT AND DECLINE

Casimir III, crowned at Wawel Cathedral in Krakow in 1333, ruled over a diminished territory of probably under a million inhabitants, substantial Polish lands having been lost in the west to Bohemia and the north to the Teutonic Knights. Casimir was able to compensate for these losses by conquests in the southeast, where he extended Polish rule into East Slavic territories.

Casimir's main achievements, those that won him the designation "Casimir the Great," were domestic. The Polish people consider his reign a golden age of justice and tolerance, in which law was respected and prosperity grew. Casimir established a university in Krakow in 1364 to support his codification of law and judicial procedure, and to ensure a steady supply of counselors and administrators for his government. A coinage reform in 1338 stabilized the Polish economy and promoted international trade. To encourage trade and crafts, Casimir actively sought Jewish merchants and artisans from Germany to settle in the many towns he had rebuilt, to which he granted advantageous legal status.

Casimir regained many old royal lands, settling dependent peasants on them. The income he derived, combined with receipts from the royal salt mines, financed the construction of about fifty forts to protect against Mongol incursions in the east, as well as other threats. According to tradition, under Casimir's rule peasants were protected against noble abuse, and grain stores were maintained for distribution when required.

Although Casimir revived Poland, he was unable to save the Piast dynasty. Four marriages failed to produce a male heir, and upon Casimir's death in 1370, the leading secular and religious magnates passed the Crown to Louis of Hungary (r. 1370–1382). The royal Piast era had finally come to its end, though the line continued for another two centuries among the dukes and princes of Mazovia, an ancient principality in eastern Poland.

See also: CASIMIR III; JAGIELLO DYNASTY; LITHUANIA, GRAND DUCHY OF; LOUIS I, THE GREAT.

FURTHER READING
Lukowski, Jerzy, and Hubert Zawadzki. *A Concise History of Poland.* New York: Cambridge University Press, 2001.

PICTS, KINGDOM OF THE

(ca. 80–839 C.E.)

Early kingdom in Scotland, from the fourth through early ninth century C.E., founded by the Picts, a Celtic people considered to be excellent warriors.

The Picts, or *Picti,* were probably a Celtic people who settled in northern and eastern Scotland in an area that became known as Pictland. Together with the Scots, the Picts invaded northern Britain in the first century C.E.; their first recorded battle against the Romans in Britain was that of Mons Graupius in 80. Hadrian's Wall in northern England, begun by the Romans in 122 to provide protection against the Picts, is a tribute to the fighting ability of the Pictish warriors.

Little is known of the tribal customs of the Picts. Except for king lists, no written Pictish records survive. Moreover, few classical references to the Picts are found. Based on those that do exist, historians long believed that the Picts were warriors who fought naked in battle and practiced body painting and polygamy. Current scholarship, however, suggests they wore leather jackets colored with natural dyes; from illustrations on Pictish stones we know they valued horses and played a triangular Celtic harp.

EARLY MEDIEVAL PERIOD

By the fifth century, Rome had withdrawn its troops from the northern frontier in Britain to fight the Goths and the Visigoths in continental Europe. With Roman authority weakened, Pictish raids on northern Britain intensified. Hadrian's Wall suffered serious damage in 367 and again following the withdrawal of frontier troops by Roman general Magnus Maximus in

383. By the early fifth century, the Britons were left to fight alone.

Much of what is known about the Pictish kings derives from their king-lists. The Picts apparently followed a complex matrilineal rule of succession; the king was succeeded by either his brother or by his sister's son, rather than his first-born son.

Bridei (r. ca. 550–586) inherited the throne from his father, Maelchon, around 550. His defeat of the Scots of Argyll (in present-day Scotland), which is listed in the Irish *Annals,* makes him the first king mentioned in any independent historical source and, therefore, the first historical king of the Picts. In the *Life of Columba* by the early Scottish Christian abbot, Adomnan, Bridei is described as a powerful king who gave Saint Columba (the missionary who converted the Picts to Christianity) permission to start a mission in Pictland and to establish a monastery on the Scottish island of Iona.

Bridei died in 586. With his death, the base of Pictish power seems to have moved from the northern to the southern part of Pictland. The era after Bridei's death saw increasing hostilities between the Scots and Picts.

THE PICTS AND NORTHUMBRIA

In the early seventh century, the Northumbrians of northern England conquered part of the Pictish and the Scottish kingdoms. For thirty years, the Picts paid tribute and perhaps did military service to the kings of Northumbria. Northumbrian hegemony ended under Bridei III (r. ca. 672–693), who successfully fought the Northumbrians in 684, trapping and massacring them at the battle of Nechtan's Mere, or Dunnichen. As a result, the Picts regained their independence. The victory was apparently significant, for it was recorded in all the histories of the period. Moreover, the kingdom of Northumbria never regained the conquered territories.

The Irish had introduced Christianity to the Picts in the late sixth or early seventh century. Hence, the Picts had followed the Celtic Rite, which included a number of differences from that of the Christian church in Rome. Among the differences was a different method of calculating the dates for celebrating Easter. For their part, the Northumbrians had introduced the Roman rite to the Picts, and Nechton (r. ca. 706–724), who inherited the throne upon the death of his father, Bridei IV (r. ca. 696–706), decided to follow Roman traditions. By asking the Northumbrian church for assistance in the matter, Nechton seems to have ended border conflicts with Northumbria.

Following Nechton's death, the early eighth century saw a series of wars for succession. Oengus (r. ca. 729–761), who won the throne in 729, proved to be the Picts' most skillful military leader. He conquered Scotland, then called Dalraida, and subsequently led an unsuccessful campaign against Strathclyde, then part of western Britain. By 756, his fortunes had declined, however, and his army was nearly wiped out in a battle against Strathclyde.

DECLINE OF THE PICTS

A number of factors seem to have contributed to the decline and fall of the Pictish kingdom. One of these factors was the Vikings. In 794, the Vikings began raiding the British Isles. For the next few decades, the Picts had to continually defend themselves against the Vikings, leaving them unable to concentrate on other dangers.

While the Picts focused on the threat posed by the Vikings, the Scots moved eastward for protection from Viking invasions of the Western Isles and west coast of Scotland. Some scholars speculate that the Picts, pressed on both sides, were subjugated by the Scots. Others believe that the Picts united with the Scots to fight the Vikings. Both the Pictish and the Scots kings died in 839. Their successor, Kenneth MacAlpin (r. 840–858), apparently inherited both the Scottish and the Pictish thrones, thus uniting the two peoples and their kingdoms.

See also: NORTHUMBRIA, KINGDOM OF; SCOTTISH KINGDOMS; STRATHCLYDE KINGDOM.

PIEDMONT KINGDOM (1720–1861 C.E.)

Kingdom in Italy formed in 1720 by the union of the duchy of Savoy and the island of Sardinia. The dukes of Savoy acquired Sardinia from Austria by the Treaty of London (1720). The kingdom lasted until it was incorporated into a unified Italy in 1861.

In 1720, the territory of the dukes of Savoy included Savoy, Piedmont, and Nice. The duke at that time, Victor Amadeus II (r. 1675–1730), became king of the new Piedmont kingdom. Victor Amadeus was an autocratic ruler but in the style of an enlightened despot. He instituted reforms in law, administration, finances, and education, but he also severely limited religious freedom. He was known as the "Piedmontese fox" because of his astute diplomatic maneuvers. Following an increasing mental decline, Victor Amnadeus II abdicated the throne in favor of his son, Charles Emmanuel III (r. 1730–1773) in 1730. The new ruler expanded the kingdom through the acquisition of Novara, Tortona, and Vigevaresco.

Napoleon took over Piedmont-Sardinia in 1798 and sent his stepson, Eugene de Beauharnais, to act as viceroy. At the Congress of Vienna in 1815, after Napoleon's final defeat, Piedmont-Sardinia regained its lost territories of Piedmont, Nice, and Savoy, and acquired the city of Genoa as well.

King Victor Emmanuel I (r. 1802–1821) of Piedmont-Sardinia was known for his repressive rule. After a popular uprising against him in 1821, he abdicated in favor of his brother, Charles-Felix (r. 1821–1831). But the ruling family, the house of Savoy, continued the same autocratic tradition.

King Charles-Albert (r. 1831–1849) encouraged free trade in the kingdom by eliminating export duties and lowering tariffs, which resulted in economic growth for Piedmont-Sardinia. He hoped to do this without giving up absolute power, but circumstances led to enormous changes in the kingdom.

The early nineteenth century saw the rise of the movement known as the *Risorgimento* (Resurgence), which sought modernization of government and the unification of Italy into a single nation. At that time, Italy consisted of the kingdom of Piedmont-Sardinia, the Papal States, the kingdom of the Two Sicilies, and a number of smaller states, as well as the territory occupied by Austria.

When Pope Pius IX took office in 1846, he initially gave encouragement to the liberal ideas of the *Risorgimento*. As a result, the rulers of several Italian states instituted liberal reforms, and Charles-Albert granted a *Statuto,* or constitution, to the people of his kingdom in January 1848.

But Pius IX soon retracted his liberal views. An uprising in the Papal States in 1848 gave rise to agitation throughout Italy. The nationalist movement was strongest in Piedmont-Sardinia, where widespread calls were made for a war to liberate northern Italy from Austrian control. A reluctant Charles-Albert went to war against Austria in 1848 but lost. In the face of this humiliating defeat, he abdicated the throne in favor of his son, Victor Emmanuel II (r. 1849–1878).

When he took the throne in 1849, Victor Emmanuel (known as "The Gentleman King") was a firm believer in absolute royal authority and was opposed to a constitutional monarchy. Nevertheless, he kept in place the *Statuto* his father had instituted. It was due to his prime minister, Camillo Cavour, that liberalization of the *Statuto* and other economic and political reforms were instituted in the kingdom. Under Victor Emmanuel II, Piedmont-Sardinia became the most progressive of the Italian states and the only one with a constitution. It became a haven for the liberals and nationalists fleeing reprisals in other parts of Italy.

On January 10, 1859, Victor Emmanuel II told his parliament that he could no longer ignore the pain of his fellow Italians under Austrian control. Piedmont-Sardinia thus joined with France in a war against Austria, and as a result, the kingdom was awarded the territory of Lombardy. Shortly afterward, the people of Parma, Modena, Romagna, and Tuscany voted to join the kingdom of Piedmont-Sardinia.

In 1860, Cavour sent troops to Sicily to aid the insurgents led by nationalist leader Giuseppe Garibaldi. After Garibaldi's victory over King Francis II (r. 1859–1860) of the Two Sicilies, that kingdom also joined Piedmont-Sardinia. Shortly afterward, most of the Papal States also voted to join the kingdom of Victor Emmanuel II.

At that point, all of Italy was united except for Venetia (which remained under Austrian control until 1866) and the core of the Papal States. Finally, on March 7, 1861, an all-Italian parliament voted Victor Emmanuel II the first king of a united Italy and Cavour the first prime minister. With this action, the kingdom of Piedmont-Sardinia ceased to exist as an independent state. Victor Emmanuel II continued to rule as king of Italy until his death in 1878.

See also: NAPOLEON I (BONAPARTE); PAPAL STATES; SAVOY DYNASTY; SICILY, KINGDOM OF; VICTOR EMMANUEL II.

FURTHER READING
Di Scala, Spencer M. *Italy: From Revolution to Republic: 1700 to the Present.* 3rd ed. Boulder, CO: Westview, 2004.

PLANTAGENET, HOUSE OF
(1154–1399 C.E.)

Name given to a royal house of England descended from Geoffrey of Anjou (r. 1113–1151), a French nobleman otherwise known as Geoffrey Plantagenet (whose name referred to a habit of wearing a sprig on his helmet). Ruling during a tumultuous time in English history, the Plantagenets witnessed the signing of the Magna Carta, the emergence of Parliament, the start of the Hundred Years' War (1337–1453), and numerous other social and political changes that pushed England towards the end of feudalism.

ORIGINS

In 1128, Geoffrey, the count of Anjou (a small but powerful province in western France), married Matilda, daughter and heir to King Henry I of England (r. 1100–1135). When Henry died without an heir in 1135, Matilda tried to claim the English throne but was unable to prevent her cousin Stephen from taking it. Geoffrey, meanwhile, was locked in a struggle with British forces for control of the French region of Normandy. Matilda, with few allies and an absent husband, left England in 1148, turning over the cause of contesting the throne to her and Geof-

frey's eldest son, Henry, who promptly invaded England in 1149. The struggle between Henry and Stephen came to an end when Stephen's heir died in 1153, thus making Henry the only legitimate successor to the throne of England. Henry took the Crown upon Stephen's death the following year, reigning as Henry II (r. 1154–1189), the first ruler of the Plantagenet dynasty.

STRUGGLES FOR THE CROWN

Henry's reign is mostly overshadowed by the events culminating in the murder of Thomas à Becket, the archbishop of Canterbury, in 1170. Henry, who had set about consolidating and increasing the power of the throne and the royal legal system, endeavored to limit the authority of the Church in England through a decree known as the Constitutions of Clarendon, which Becket fiercely opposed. Several years of quarreling ended in 1170, when Becket excommunicated Henry from the Church. In response, Henry caused Becket's murder by wishing aloud to be rid of the archbishop. Four of Henry's knights took this to

Fontrevault Abbey in Anjou, France, was the original home of the Plantagenet (Angevin) line of kings. It contains the tombs of the founder of that English dynasty, King Henry II, as well as his wife, Eleanor of Aquitaine, and his son, King Richard I.

be an order and murdered Becket in Canterbury Cathedral. Public consternation over the murder plagued Henry throughout his reign.

The final years of Henry's reign were marked by another English civil war, this time between the king and his sons, who felt that their authority was too limited. Henry's death in 1189 brought an end to the conflict, and his son Richard took the Crown as Richard I (r. 1189–1199). Also known as Lionheart, Richard is a prominent figure in English history, despite the fact that he spent less than a year of his reign in England. A talented warrior, Richard left England in 1190 to take part in the Third Crusade to recapture the Holy Lands from the Muslims. In Richard's absence, his younger brother John attempted to seize the throne. Although Richard spent much of his reign in battle or in the hands of Muslim captors, his subjects were loyal enough to put down John's rebellion. John eventually gained the throne anyway, after Richard was killed in 1199 battling Philip II of France (r. 1180–1223), who had conspired with John for Richard's overthrow.

John's reign (r. 1199–1216) was dominated by conflict. He had taken the throne over the seemingly more legitimate claims of his nephew Arthur, who was a child at the time of his father's death. Arthur's father, Geoffrey, was Johns' older brother, a fact that led many French nobles to support Arthur as the real successor to Richard. Philip of France and others immediately attacked English territories on the Continent, thus initiating a war that lasted the entirety of John's reign. Ultimately, John lost most of his lands in France and faced a French invasion near the end of his life.

John's historical significance rests largely in his signing of the Magna Carta, the first major step toward constitutional government in England. In 1215, a group of English nobles and barons, frustrated with John's attempts to rule autocratically, revolted and forced the king to sign the charter. Among other things, the Magna Carta stipulated that English subjects had rights that could not be violated by the king, thereby setting a basis for developing modern notions of civil rights.

STRIFE AT HOME

At John's death in 1216, the Crown went to his young son Henry, who reigned as King Henry III (r. 1216–1272). Henry's long reign was marked by a continuation of the conflict between the Crown and the barons, who wanted power to be more equally distributed and less Church influence in English governance. Henry's brother-in-law, Simon de Montfort, led the opposition, which in 1258 forced the king to observe the Provisions of Oxford, a document that created a council of nobles to serve as the king's advisers. When Henry overturned this in 1261, war began anew, and Montfort was able to take over most of England.

In 1265, Montfort called together, for the first time, a meeting of Parliament, which included

ROYAL RELATIVES

ISABELLA (1296–1358 C.E.)

Treated poorly by her husband Edward II, Isabella helped stage the invasion that removed Edward and put their son on the throne as Edward III. Always loyal to her family in France, Isabella had no intentions of returning to Edward when he sent her to meet with her brother, Charles IV, in 1325. She had grown to hate Edward's close companions, a family known as the Despensers, and when she was in France Isabella developed a close relationship with Roger Mortimer, an exiled baron who also despised Edward's influential advisers. Together Isabelle and Mortimer invaded in 1326 to popular approval and achieved the abdication and eventual murder of Edward in 1327. The pair haphazardly ran the country until Edward III, who had come of age, forced them out in 1330. Edward summarily had Mortimer executed and stripped his mother of her power, though he allowed her to live in peace.

wealthy nobles as well as local representatives. This new form of administration, which eventually became the foundation of British government, was unable to maintain solidarity, however, and the royal armies, led by Henry's son Edward, regained control of England. Montfort was killed in battle, and Edward came to the throne upon his father's death in 1272.

Like many of his predecessors, Edward I (r. 1272–1307), also known as Longshanks, reigned during a time of widespread and costly warfare. Most notably, Edward fought wars for control of the British Isles in both Wales and Scotland. Wales fell easily to the English in 1282, but Scotland proved to be an intractable foe. The Scottish opposition, led by William Wallace and Robert the Bruce, unexpectedly defeated the English at Stirling Castle in 1297 and never succumbed to Edward's forces, to the great frustration of the king.

Edward, like his father and grandfather before him, continually overstepped the bounds of his power and thus came into frequent conflict with the nobility. Edward also incurred the ire of the Church, whose authority he severely limited with his legal reforms. Upon his death in 1307, which occurred on a campaign against Scotland, Edward passed this domestic conflict on to his son, Edward II (r. 1307–1327).

Edward II struggled to maintain authority throughout his reign, beginning in 1311 when a council of nobles placed limits on his power with the Ordinances of 1311. A disastrous attempt to take Scotland in 1314 resulted in a political crisis, and a group of nobles led by Thomas of Lancaster, a member of the Plantagenet line, essentially controlled England for seven years. A series of minor domestic skirmishes throughout the early 1320s gave way in 1326 to an attack on Edward from France, which was led by Edward's wife Isabella, a French princess. The invading forces routed Edward, who had no supporters. The king was forced to abdicate in 1327 in favor of his son, who reigned as Edward III (r. 1327–1377).

TROUBLES WITH FRANCE AND DECLINE

The reign of Edward III saw more conflict, in particular the Hundred Years' War, which began in 1337. A variety of quarrels, both economic and political, had led to heightened tensions with France, which boiled over into war when Edward claimed rights to the French Crown by virtue of the royal holdings on the

Continent. The Hundred Years' War, which did not end until the 1450s, left the French countryside devastated and the English army seriously weakened, and resulted in very little gain for either country. An epidemic of the bubonic plague in both England and France in the mid-fourteenth century severely limited their abilities to wage war, and Edward became weary of fighting, especially since he was forced to share authority with a revitalized Parliament that included a powerful House of Commons. Parliament was able to capitalize on Edward's financial demands for the war to take charge of government spending. This proved to be a key development in the gradual dissolution of royal authority in England. Edward's death in 1377 brought his grandson to the throne as Richard II.

Under Richard II (r. 1377–1399), internal disagreements between the nobles and the Crown continued. Moreover, Richard's erratic behavior, likely caused by growing insanity, reached a peak when he banished his cousin Henry Bolingbroke to France in 1398 and took Henry's property, the duchy of Lancaster. The English people, frustrated by Richard's actions, welcomed Henry back when he invaded in 1399, and widespread support for Henry forced Richard to abdicate the throne. Richard's abdication marks the end of Plantagenet rule and the rise of the House of Lancaster. Although both the Lancastrians and their rivals in the House of York were actually related to the Plantagenets, historians see Henry's accession as King Henry IV (r. 1399–1413) as the beginning of a new line of rulers.

See also: EDWARD I; EDWARD II; EDWARD III; HENRY II; JOHN I; LANCASTER, HOUSE OF; RICHARD I, LIONHEART; RICHARD II; STEPHEN.

FURTHER READING
Costain, Thomas. *A History of the Plantagenets.* 4 vols. Cutchogue, NY: Buccaneer Books, 1994.

POLYGAMY, ROYAL

The practice of a man's having more than one wife. The reverse—the practice of a woman having more than one husband, known as polyandry—has been rare in human societies and has not played a role in monarchies.

Throughout the ages, kings have often chosen to

demonstrate their power by surrounding themselves with wives and concubines. Another motivation for polygamy is the crucial importance for most monarchs of having a son to ensure the succession. Certain religions, notably Christianity, Hinduism, and Shinto, have constrained the behavior of kings by heavily favoring monogamy. But the limitation to one official queen has not always prevented kings from displaying power by taking mistresses. When a queen fails to produce a male son, some kings, such as King Henry VIII of England (r. 1509–1547), have resorted to divorce to enable them to take a new queen.

THE OTTOMAN EMPIRE

Islam is alone among the monotheistic religions in allowing polygamy, though it puts strict limits on the practice: A good Muslim may have up to four wives, but only if he has the material and emotional resources to support them all and to treat them all equally.

Islamic rulers have tended to stretch the rules by having a harem of concubines in addition to the four wives the Koran allows. This was true among the Mamluk rulers of Egypt (1250–1517) and among the sultans of the Ottoman Empire (late 1200s–1918). The Ottoman harem was presided over by the *Valide Sultan*—the mother of the sultan—who wielded considerable power. The harem was guarded by eunuchs and was a private place, forbidden to strangers.

The women for the harem were selected from among prisoners of war and from slave markets, and they underwent a long period of training in the principles of Islam as well as learning skills such as embroidery, music, dancing, or story-telling. A woman from the harem whom the sultan chose to take to his bed was awarded the title of *haseki*. If a *haseki* became pregnant, she was granted special privileges and a private apartment; the first *haseki* to give birth to a son became a *kadin,* the most privileged of all.

The most famous of the powerful women of the Ottoman Empire is Kösem (1589–1631), wife of Sultan Ahmed I (r. 1603–1617). She had come into the harem as a slave, but because of her intelligence and wit quickly became Ahmed's favorite and bore him four sons. After Ahmed's early death, she and her sons had to retire from the palace for a time, but they returned in 1623 when her eldest son became Sultan Murat IV (1623–1640) and Kösem was installed as *Valide Sultan*. She exercised power not just in the harem but over government policies during the reigns of Murat IV and his successor, Ibrahim (1640–1648), another of Kösem's sons. Ibrahim was succeeded by his son Mehmed IV (1648–1687), whose mother, Türkhan, became the new *Valide Sultan*. But Kösem, determined not to give up her

ROYAL RELATIVES

KÖSEM

The most famous of the powerful women of the Ottoman Empire is Kösem (1589–1631), wife of Ahmed I (r. 1603–1617). She had come into the harem as a slave, but because of her intelligence and wit quickly became Ahmed's favorite, and bore him four sons. After Ahmed's early death she and her sons had to retire from the palace for a time, but they returned in 1623 when her eldest son became Murat IV (1623–1640) and Kösem herself was installed as *Valide Sultan*. She exercised power not just in the harem but over government policies during the reigns of Murat IV and his successor Ibrahim (1640–1648), another of Kösem's sons. Ibrahim was succeeded by his son Mehmed IV (1648–1687), whose mother, Türkhan, became the new *Valide Sultan*. Kösem, determined not to give up her power, plotted to kill both Mehmed and Türkhan, but the plan backfired and she was strangled on Türkhan's orders.

power, plotted to kill both Mehmed and Türkhan. The plan failed, and Kösem was strangled on the orders of Turkhan, the new Valide Sultan.

ANCIENT CHINA

In China, emperors for more than twenty-five hundred years maintained an elaborate system of primary wives, secondary wives, and concubines of several ranks. There are records showing that this system was in place in the spring and autumn period (770–453 B.C.E.).

The rules about whether a ruler could have more than one primary wife varied over the centuries, but secondary wives and concubines were never limited. Sometimes a favorite concubine might be promoted to primary wife, but the Chinese philosopher Mencius (c. 310–215 B.C.E.) records that this practice was frowned upon. Concubines were often of humble origin, and it was felt that their sons should not be allowed to inherit the throne because people would not be able to respect a ruler whose mother was of low birth.

Often when a ruler took a primary wife, usually from an aristocratic family he wished to make an alliance with, her younger sisters came with her as secondary wives. Promotion from the ranks of the secondary wives would then be quite natural if a primary wife died or failed to produce an heir, and a secondary wife's children would have the same relations on their mother's side as the primary wife's children would have. The primary wife's sons would be first in the line of succession, and those of the secondary wives next.

THE CH'ING DYNASTY

The Ch'ing dynasty (1644–1911) was a foreign power, from Manchuria, that took the Chinese imperial throne. Although the Ch'ing rulers courted the favor of their Chinese subjects by adopting many Chinese practices, they also introduced some changes. A rule that governed the choice of both wives and concubines for the members of the ruling family was that they had to belong to the families of the emperor's banner companies—the military organizations that, as an invading power, the Ch'ing employed to maintain their grip on power.

Han Chinese (members of the dominant ethnic group in China) could become bannermen and thus gain certain privileges. One of the duties of bannermen was to present their daughters in Beijing at the triennial imperial "draft." Every bannerman's daughter had to attend one of these drafts after she reached the age of thirteen, before she could be betrothed. The emperor and empress were given dossiers on the girls' family backgrounds and personally inspected the girls to select wives and concubines for members of the royal family. The Empress Dowager Tz'u Hsi entered the royal household in this way in 1852, as a sixth-rank concubine. (The concubine's rank was determined by her family's rank.)

An innovation of the Ch'ing dynasty was that the succession was no longer predetermined by the rank of the mothers of the emperor's sons. The emperor could choose any of his sons to succeed him, and his choice would be revealed by the opening of a sealed container after his death. He might choose the son of a concubine, and if he did, the new emperor was allowed to raise his own mother to rank of empress dowager, even if the deceased emperor's primary wife was still alive with that title. This is what happened with the Dowager Empress Tz'u Hsi (Cixi), who was able to manipulate her surroundings to dominate the government in the last years of the Ch'ing dynasty.

THE INCAN EMPIRE

In the Incan Empire of the Andes, the Inca—the supreme ruler—was the focus of the state religion and was regarded as holy. He was also seen as the potential spouse of every woman in his domains. Any woman whom he chose was his, and by virtue of having been chosen, those women participated in his holiness. It was a tremendous honor and cause for a family to celebrate if a daughter was chosen by the Inca.

In practice, the Incas do not seem to have maintained large personal harems. Instead, they maintained a kind of bank of virgins. Every time the territorially aggressive empire annexed a new village, a representative of the Inca would select from the village's young girls an *aclla*—an official wife for the Inca. She had to be very young because her virginity was considered important.

The *acllas* were taken back to Cuzco, the Incan capital, where they lived luxuriously in a special temple-palace and were treated with great respect. They might remain there, as vigilantly guarded virgins, performing the function of priestesses of the sun; they might be chosen to become actual wives of the Inca; or they might be given by the Inca to selected vassals or subordinates as secondary wives. Normally, only the Inca ruler was permitted to have more than one wife; for any other man to be granted another wife was a highly prized reward.

MODERN SWAZILAND

In many African cultures, it has been traditional for a man to have as many wives as he can support. Kings in particular have surrounded themselves with many wives. Only one hereditary monarch remains in sub-Saharan Africa today—Swaziland.

King Mswati of Swaziland, who was born in 1968, inherited the Crown in 1986 at age sixteen and took over from his mother's regency at age eighteen. Though educated in England, the king has favored traditional ways, including polygamy. Mswati has ten wives, as well as a current fiancée selected at the annual Reed Dance that took place in September 2003.

That year's Reed Dance ceremony, which involved young women dancing for the king for three hours wearing the traditional dance costume, attracted more participants than in any previous year. A seventeen-year-old interviewed by a reporter said, "I am tired of being poor. I want to be a queen." Yet this points out a current problem with the practice of polygamy there. Mswati has been criticized for exploiting the poverty of the young women in his kingdom and for setting a bad example of how to approach sexuality in a country that is ravaged by AIDS.

See also: Ch'ing (Qing) Dynasty; Concubines, Royal; Eunuchs, Royal; Henry VIII; Inca Empire; Mamluk Dynasty; Ottoman Empire; Swazi Kingdom.

FURTHER READING

Stafford, Pauline. *Queens, Concubines, and Dowagers: The King's Wife in the Early Middle Ages.* Washington, DC: University of Leicester Press, 1998.

Pomare IV (1813–1877 C.E.)

Last ruling queen of Tahiti (r. 1827–1877), who was unable to stave off France's intent to make her island nation a French protectorate.

Queen Aimatta Pomare IV was the illegitimate daughter of Pomare III (r. 1824–1827) and a member of the Pomare family, which had gained control of Tahiti in 1803 with the help of the Protestant Lon-

don Missionary Society. Pomare inherited the throne in 1827, while still only a teenager. Because of her youth and inexperience, she allowed herself to be guided by her Protestant allies. In 1836, when French Roman Catholic missionaries arrived on the island for the first time, the Protestants prevailed on the queen to expel them, and she promptly sent them back to France.

Six years later, in 1842, France responded by dispatching a warship to demand that the queen guarantee that future French visitors to Tahiti be recognized as "most favored foreigners." Queen Pomare, facing French guns, acceded gracefully to their request and then promptly wrote to Queen Victoria of England (r. 1837–1901) to request British protection against the French.

Queen Victoria, however, was uninterested in a conflict with France over a small Pacific island nation half a world away and refused to give Pomare assistance. The French, meanwhile, interested in securing a seaport in the South Pacific, tricked a local chieftain into signing a request that Tahiti be made a French protectorate.

When French troops, responding to this "request," surrounded the queen's palace at Papeete, the Tahitian capital, the Tahitians organized an armed defense, but Queen Pomare was finally forced to retreat to the island of Raiatea. Queen Pomare continued to resist the French for another five years, but after the last Tahitian stronghold fell in 1846, she agreed to return to Papeete.

Queen Pomare continued to rule as a figurehead monarch of Tahiti until her death in 1877, when the throne passed to her son, Teriitaria Ariiaue Pomare V (r. 1877–1880). When he abdicated three years later, in exchange for a generous French pension, Tahiti lost all independence and became a French colony.

See also: South Sea Island Kingdoms.

Postcolonial States

Independent states that exist as former colonies of other independent states. In its broadest definition, a postcolonial state can be any state formerly occupied by another; in its common use, however, the term postcolonial refers specifically to those states that received their independence following the European colonial expansion of the eighteenth, nineteenth, and twentieth centuries. By and large, these nations are located in Africa, Asia, Central and South America, and the Middle East.

INDEPENDENCE AND GOVERNANCE

Although a handful of colonies gained independence before World War II, it was not until after the war that the full reach of colonialism was dismantled and the modern system of postcolonial states came into being. Although it is true that the colonial powers—most notably Great Britain, but also France, Germany, and Belgium—came to see their colonies as no longer economically profitable, the major reason for widespread independence in the postwar era was native nationalism. Nearly every postcolonial state witnessed a widespread nationalist movement for independence, usually with charismatic and popular figures leading the way, such as India and Pakistan's Mahatma Gandhi and Jawaharlal Nehru and Sierra Leone's Milton Margai.

In several colonies, including Uganda, Nepal, and Bhutan, the old monarchy that had been displaced by the coming of colonialism became a nationalist symbol. The overwhelming majority of postcolonial states, however, attempted to change from colonies to democracies. In the few postcolonial states where monarchy survives, it is largely symbolic and lacks any real political power, as in the case of Uganda's King Ronald Muwenda Mutebi II (r. 1993–).

Many postcolonial states, especially those in Africa, have suffered extremely unstable political systems since gaining independence. Dictatorships and civil wars have been quite common in postcolonial states, with such nations as Algeria, Angola, Malaysia, Nigeria, Pakistan, Rwanda, Somalia, South Africa, Zaire, and Zambia all enduring political repression and severe bloodshed. Some postcolonial states that have achieved political stability, as in the case of India, have nevertheless undergone several humanitarian tragedies, such as massive refugee movements and widespread famines.

CHARACTERISTICS

Whether colonialism had any positive effects for postcolonial states is debatable. Great technological, administrative, and educational advances were grafted onto subject countries by their colonizers, but this process frequently had disastrous consequences, such as the eradication of local traditions and terrible environmental and social upheaval.

Many colonized people saw their established forms of government—frequently monarchy—either done away with entirely or, as in the case of India, put to work for their colonizers. Because modern colonial powers often attempted to justify their expansion on the basis of supposed cultural supremacy, racial and religious strife has gripped many postcolonial states. Native languages have also undergone significant change thanks to the imposition of colonial speech, especially English, French, and Spanish.

Postcolonial states have experienced a great deal of population movement, both within the country and to other countries. For example, large numbers of former colonial subjects and their descendants have migrated to European and North American cities in search of greater educational and economic opportunities. London, in particular, has become a global destination for many migrants from postcolonial states of the former British Empire, with nearly one-third of London residents having been born outside of Great Britain. Similarly, the significant presence of people of European descent throughout Africa and southern Asia is attributable to modern colonialism.

The economic consequences of colonialism for subject states have been almost universally negative. Many of the poorest nations in the world, especially in sub-Saharan Africa, are former colonies whose native economies were devastated by colonialism. The few former colonies that have achieved widespread economic success are those that had a high number of European settlers and a large degree of independence under colonial rule, such as Canada and Australia. As a consequence of these economic disparities, many former colonies have attempted to consolidate their power into larger political entities, such as the African Union of 2002.

See also: COLONIALISM AND KINGSHIP; EMPIRE; IMPERIAL RULE; NATIONALISM.

FURTHER READING

Young, Robert J. C. *Postcolonialism.* New York: Oxford University Press, 2003.

POWER, FORMS OF ROYAL

A variety of different forms that power can take in a monarchy, ranging from very limited power to titular monarchies to absolutism or despotism, in which all political power is consolidated in one person. Historians describe royal power in two broad categories: absolute monarchy and limited monarchy.

ABSOLUTE MONARCHY

Absolute monarchies are those in which ultimate political power is invested in the royal house and in the ruler of the kingdom. King Louis XIV of France (r. 1643–1715) famously described absolute monarchy by saying, *l'état c'est moi* ("I am the state").

Royal power and state power are one and the same in an absolute monarchy. Royal authority cannot be overruled, and the subjects of an absolute monarch are bound by law and tradition to obey the commands of their sovereign. Throughout history and around the world, absolute monarchies were the most prevalent form of royal power, though prefeudal forms of absolutism differed significantly from the forms of absolute rule that developed after the feudal period.

Prefeudal Absolute Monarchy

In many prefeudal monarchies, royal power was so great that monarchs were frequently considered to be divine. This was especially true in ancient Egypt, where the pharaohs were seen as manifestations of the god Horus. Such pharaohs as Ramses II (r. 1279–1212 B.C.E.) were considered virtually invincible, and they ruled Egypt with a strong hand.

Several other powerful monarchs of the prefeudal period were considered divine, including Alexander III, the Great of Macedon (r. 336–323 B.C.E.) and the possibly legendary first emperor of Japan, Jimmu (r. ca. 40–10 B.C.E.).

Divinity was not a requirement for prefeudal absolute monarchs, however. Several of the most powerful absolute monarchs of the ancient world, including the Roman emperor Augustus (r. 27 B.C.E.–14 C.E.) and Asoka of India (r. 268–232 B.C.E.), the ruler of the Maurya Empire, were openly hostile to the idea of being considered divine.

Absolute monarchies in the prefeudal period, however, tended to be similar in that monarchs could rule directly, with few intermediary channels of power that might limit royal authority. Prefeudal societies were by and large resistant to localized diffusions of power, and therefore the actions of monarchs had immediate effects throughout their domains.

Postfeudal Absolute Monarchies

The unilateral distribution of power from the royal house was the most prominent difference between pre- and postfeudal monarchies. The rise of feudalism put serious limits on royal authority, especially in Europe. Although monarchs were still theoretically the highest governing authority, local nobles and smaller political organizations and bureaucracies intervened between the royal house and the people.

This phenomenon happened differently in Asia. In China, for instance, a large bureaucracy of civil servants had been established under the T'ang dynasty (618–907), which limited the amount of authority the monarch could have, though the central government grew quite strong. In Japan, power was also consolidated in a central bureaucracy, rather than in one individual, especially under the very strict form of feudalism that was practiced during the Tokugawa shogunate (1603–1867).

In European feudalism, no monarch or centralized agency was able to hold absolute power. In the postfeudal era, however, several European monarchs attempted to rule absolutely, including King Louis XIV of France (r. 1643–1715), Henry VIII of England (r. 1509–1547), and Frederick II of Prussia (r. 1740–1786). Some European monarchs of this period, most notably Louis XIV, justified their rule according to the principle of divine right.

By and large, however, the most powerful monarchs of the postfeudal period were dependent on the newly emerging middle class, many of whom worked in government, for their ruling authority. Thus, the postfeudal era in both Europe and Asia saw a centralization of power toward governmental bureaucracies rather than toward individual monarchs.

LIMITED MONARCHY

Limited monarchy does not simply mean weak monarchy (as in European feudalism). Instead, it refers to monarchies that have had their authority legally restricted. As such, limited monarchy is a relatively recent phenomenon.

England was perhaps the first state to successfully place legal limitations on the power of the monarchy, which it did first with the signing of the Magna Carta by King John (r. 1199–1216) in 1215, and again with the Bill of Rights in 1689. These documents asserted that the English people had rights that could not be violated by the monarchy. The Bill of Rights carried this idea even further and made the monarchy subject to the authority of Parliament.

Limited monarchy—which is sometimes known as constitutional monarchy—became common in Europe in the nineteenth century, following the nationalist movements there. In China and Russia, the monarchy was eliminated entirely during revolutions in the early twentieth century. In Japan, the real power of the emperor had been limited for some time, but this fact was made legal after Japan's defeat in World War II.

Few monarchies remain in existence today, and the majority of these are limited monarchies, such as in Great Britain, Japan, Denmark, the Netherlands, and Thailand. A very small number of absolute monarchies still exist, including the monarchies of Saudi Arabia and Morocco.

See also: COUNCILS AND COUNSELORS, ROYAL; DIVINE RIGHT; DIVINITY OF KINGS; FEUDALISM AND KINGSHIP; NATIONALISM; RIGHTS, CIVIL; TYRANNY, ROYAL.

FURTHER READING
Spellman, W. M. *Monarchies, 1000–2000.* London: Reaktion Books, 2001.

POWYS KINGDOM (ca. 500s–1200s C.E.)

Medieval kingdom in east-central Wales that reached its peak of power in the 1100s. Powys began to play a dominant role in Wales at that time when its new king, Gruffydd ap Llywelyn (r. 1039–1063) claimed the Crown of the kingdom of Gwynedd to the north after Gwynedd's king was murdered by his own men in 1039.

After taking control of Gwynedd, Gruffydd spent fifteen years fighting to conquer the kingdoms of southern Wales. He gained enough power to offer military aid to an earl of Mercia in England who had been accused of treason. This led to war with Harold Godwinson of Wessex, who later became king of England (r. 1066) but was defeated by William the Conqueror in 1066. Gruffydd ap Llywelyn was killed by his own men in 1063. He was succeeded in Powys by Rhiwallon (d. 1070), who ruled with the approval of Edward the Confessor of England. Rhiwallon was followed by his brother Bleddyn (d. 1075).

The kingdom of Powys maintained a degree of independence into the twelfth century, although its

rulers, by this time styled "prince" rather than "king," had a nominal Norman overlord and various members of the Powys royal family were at times hostages of King Henry I (r. 1100–1135) of England. When Owain, son of Prince Cadwgan of Powys, carried off the wife of a Norman noble in 1109, Henry I retaliated by sending Cadwgan's nephews to take over the kingdom. In 1110 Henry replaced them with Cadwgan's brother Iorweth, who had been co-ruler of Powys with Cadwgan and three other brothers following their father's death in 1075. Iorweth had been Henry's prisoner since 1103. Iorweth was killed by his nephew Madog in 1111. Henry granted Powys to Cadwgan again, but Madog killed Cadwgan as well. Owain (d. 1115) followed his father as prince of Powys and acknowledged Henry I as his overlord. In 1113 Madog was finally killed by Owain and Maredudd, their only surviving uncle.

Powys was seriously weakened by these internal struggles. Following the rule of Prince Madog ap Maredudd (r. 1132–1160), Powys was divided into a series of small lordships. Like the other Welsh kingdoms, Powys lost any claim to independence after the death in 1282 of Llywelyn ap Gruffydd (r. 1246–1282), the prince of Gwynedd who united all Wales but was defeated by Edward I of England (r. 1272–1307).

See also: GWYNEDD KINGDOM; LLWELYN AP GRUFFYDD; WELSH KINGDOMS.

FURTHER READING
Holmes, George, ed. *Oxford Illustrated History of Medieval Europe.* New York: Oxford University Press, 1988.

Poole, A.L. *Domesday Book to Magna Carta: 1087–1216.* New York: Oxford University Press, 1993.

Stenton, Sir Frank. *Anglo-Saxon England.* New York: Oxford University Press, 2001.

Walker, David. *Medieval Wales.* New York: Cambridge University Press, 1990.

PREMYSL DYNASTY (870–1306 C.E.)

A strong family of rulers native to the territory of the present-day Czech Republic, who preserved their sovereignty despite their vassal-like ties to the Holy Roman Empire; also called the Premyslid dynasty. The head of the Premyslid house was usually designated a prince or duke until 1198, when Bohemia was declared a kingdom within the Holy Roman Empire. The first ruler of this kingdom was Ottocar I (r. 1197–1230).

The legendary origins of the Premysl dynasty date from the eighth century c.e. with the semilegendary founder Premysl, a peasant who married the Bohemian princess Libussa (Libue). The first historical Premysl ruler was Prince Borivoj I of Bohemia, (r. 870–895), who was converted to Christianity by Saint Methodius.

Borivoj's grandson, Prince Wenceslaus (Vaclav) (r. 921–929), following in his family's religious tradition, was noted for his zeal in spreading Christianity among his people. This prompted his pagan brother, Boleslav I (r. 929–972), to murder him around 929 and assume the throne. Vaclav, however, was viewed by Christians as a martyr and elevated to the status of patron saint of Bohemia and Czechoslovakia under the name of Saint Wenceslas.

Boleslav I extended the Bohemian realm to include Moravia and parts of Silesia. During the rule of his son and successor, Boleslav II (r. 972–999), the Christian church in Bohemia became officially organized with the founding of a bishopric in Prague. Following Boleslav II's death in 999, a struggle for power erupted between his sons, which ended in 1012 when the youngest son, Ulrich (r. 1012–1033), became prince of Bohemia. Ulrich was deposed in 1033 by his brother Jaromir (r. 1033–1034), who was deposed himself in 1034 and succeeded by his nephew Bretislav I (r. 1034–1055), the son of Ulrich.

Disputes and feuds over power within the Premysl family dominated the dynasty's reign for the next 150 years and hindered Bohemia's cultural and political development. These conflicts arose primarily because laws of succession to the throne were virtually nonexistent. During this period, Bohemia became increasingly dependent on the Holy Roman Empire to the west. Prince Vratislav II (r. 1061–1092) obtained the title of king of Bohemia from the Holy Roman emperor Henry IV (r. 1056–1105). However, it was not until the end of the twelfth century that the Holy Roman emperor raised Ottocar I (r. 1197–1230) to the hereditary rank of king of Bohemia, thus putting an end to the conflict by establishing a clear basis of succession.

During the reign of Ottocar I, Bohemia reached the height of its economic and political prosperity. He was succeeded by Wenceslaus I (r. 1230–1253), who invited many Germans to settle in Bohemia and Moravia and granted self-rule to many towns. Wenceslaus's successor, his son, Ottocar II (r. 1253–1278), became known as one of the greatest rulers of Bohemia. An ambitious expansionist, he built an empire that reached from Bohemia to the Adriatic Sea and included many lands that later became part of the vast realm ruled by the Habsburg dynasty.

Ottocar II died in battle in 1278 and was succeeded by his son Wenceslaus II (r. 1278–1305). Wenceslaus's political prowess and diplomacy earned him the Crown of Poland in 1300, but he died five years later in 1305. His only son, Wenceslaus III (r. 1305–1306), king of Hungary from 1301 to 1305, inherited Bohemia but was assassinated in 1306 while en route to Poland, thus ending the Premysl dynasty.

See also: Arpad Dynasty; Habsburg Dynasty; Holy Roman Empire.

FURTHER READING
Wolverton, Lisa. *Hastening Toward Prague: Power and Society in the Medieval Czech Lands.* Philadelphia: University of Pennsylvania Press, 2001.

Premysl Dynasty	
Borivoj I	870–894
Prince Wenceslaus	921–929
Ottocar I	1198–1230
Wenceslaus I	1230–1253
Ottocar II	1253–1278
Wenceslaus II	1278–1305
Wenceslaus III	1305–1306

Priests, Royal

Those who act as intermediaries between a deity and the people; persons who perform religious duties or rites on behalf of a royal household; individuals of noble birth who also hold religious office.

PRIESTLY RULERS

The ruling class and the priesthood emerged concurrently in many world cultures. For example, ancient Sumer, located in Mesopotamia and one of the earliest civilizations, was ruled by priests. Half a world away, and more than one thousand years after the fall of Sumer, the Mayan people of Mexico also had priest-kings.

In Europe, a class of priests and sages called Druids held ruling positions among the early Celtic populations as early as the third century B.C.E. Between the eleventh and fourteenth centuries C.E., priest-kings at Great Zimbabwe in Africa ruled an ancient stone city of about twenty thousand people.

In the small Asian kingdom of Bhutan, a monk named Ngawang Namgyal formed a theocratic government in 1616, and thereafter the kingdom was ruled by a dual monarchy consisting of a Dharma Raja, or spiritual leader, and a Deb Raja, or temporal ruler in charge of the civil government.

Because priests held the secret knowledge of the gods and performed rituals that appeased the gods and brought good fortune to the people, they maintained great power. The all-important sacrifices to ancient gods were the dominion of the priestly class in all societies. In fact, ancient Roman records refer to certain priests as *rex sacorum* (king of sacrifices).

Although priests have been members of all classes of society, in ancient Egypt they were usually of noble birth and among the most highly educated people in the kingdom. High priests in many other cultures also came from royal families. In India, for example, only those born into the high Brahmin caste were able to assume the duties of priesthood. Whether or not of noble blood, royal priests frequently resided within the official residence of the monarch and performed their duties only for members of the imperial household.

CHANGING ROLES FOR PRIESTS

Since priestly power rests on the beliefs shared by those whom the priest controls, this power does not extend to the followers of a different god. As a result, when groups of people conquered other lands and peoples, warrior rulers often replaced priestly rulers because their power was based on military strength and not religion.

The rise of secular rulers, however, did not mean that priests became powerless. Political rulers continued to recognize priestly influence and often courted the favor of religious leaders. For instance, when King Henry II of England (1154–1189) had the opportunity to appoint a new archbishop of Canterbury, he chose his good friend Thomas à Becket, in hopes that the Church would then support his policies to curb the growth of Church power.

With their perceived ability to manipulate the supernatural, priests acted as mediators between people and their gods. More importantly, royal priests often served as prophets or oracles for sovereigns, thereby exerting great influence over political affairs. The English monk Dunstan, who became archbishop of Canterbury in 960, prepared every detail of the coronation of England's King Edgar (r. 959–975). Dunstan rewrote the ceremony, emphasizing the anointing of the king and the link between God and king. The English coronation rite is still essentially the one written by Dunstan in the tenth century.

In some cases, priests could even determine who the ruler would be. When a Celtic king died, for example, his successor was identified through a dream ritual performed by Druid priests. Later rulers were well aware that their power could rest on winning or purchasing the approval of the chief religious leader in their kingdoms.

Royal priests sometimes became even more powerful than the monarch. For example, during the reign of King Louis XIII of France (r. 1610–1643), Cardinal Richelieu held a dual role as head of the Church and first minister and chief of state, leading to his virtual rule of the nation. During the early years of the reign of the young Louis XIV (r. 1643–1715), Richelieu's successor, Cardinal Mazarin, continued to wield great power.

One of the most notorious of the royal "priests" was the self-proclaimed Russian monk Rasputin. In spite of his reputation for scandal, Rasputin was able to endear himself to Tsar Nicholas II (r. 1894–1917) and his wife Alexandra when he eased their son's suffering from hemophilia. At a time of great civil unrest, the royal couple refused to accept criticism of Rasputin, who seemed to gain more and more power. When other royal family members finally acted to assassinate Rasputin, they were too late to stop the forces of the Bolshevik Revolution, which ended the reign of tsars in Russia.

Since relatively few monarchies remain in the world today, the office of royal priest is rarely found. One exception is Great Britain, where the Ecclesiastical Household of Her Majesty, the Queen, still includes clergy of St. George's Chapel, St. James's Palace, Hampton Court, and the Tower of London. Along with the customary duties of Anglican priests, these clergy have other specific responsibilities. The clergy at St. George's, for example, are charged with praying daily for the sovereign, the nation, and the Order of the Garter.

See also: CHRISTIANITY AND KINGSHIP; CLASS SYSTEMS AND ROYALTY; COUNCILS AND COUNSELORS, ROYAL; COURTS AND COURT OFFICIALS, ROYAL; DIVINATION AND DIVINERS, ROYAL; DIVINITY OF KINGS; RELIGIOUS DUTIES AND POWER.

PRIMOGENITURE

Principle of inheritance that determined the right of succession for the majority of the world's monarchies in all periods of history.

Primogeniture is a practice of inheritance common to many of the world's patrilineal royal and noble families. According to the principle of primogeniture, all property is passed to the eldest son, along with any royal or noble title associated with the land.

Primogeniture developed to keep estates intact and to provide for royal succession or the transfer of noble titles. The estate was inalienable, meaning that the heir could not sell or give away the property. In this sense, the property really belonged to the family or the lineage more than to any individual.

Under primogeniture, younger sons and daughters were excluded from inheritance so that the estate would not be divided. In cases where there were no surviving sons, the eldest daughter could inherit; this was the case in most European cultures. With land and titles kept within a family, primogeniture provided a power base for the monarch by ensuring the loyalty and stability of the landed nobility.

Primogeniture was part of the inheritance laws in a number of the world's monarchies. In addition to those in Europe, the royal and noble families of various Asian countries, including Korea and Japan, passed estates to the eldest son. In most of these areas, however, despite strict inheritance laws, the popularity if primogeniture was tied to economic conditions and to changing cultural considerations. In Japan, for example, legal primogeniture was derived from the old samurai code. In practice, how-

ever, primogeniture was often ignored in Japan, and was clearly more popular in some periods of Japanese history than in others.

Many of the world's monarchies did not practice primogeniture but opted instead for more flexible methods of determining inheritance. In the Middle East and India, where polygamy was commonly practiced, the reigning ruler was usually free to choose his heir and successor. These rulers often chose the sons of favorite wives, or they considered such factors as a child's talents when choosing an heir. During the era of British imperialism, the English often clashed with local rulers over the issue of primogeniture. In several cases, the British forced local rulers in India or other parts of the British Empire to conform with the European inheritance practice.

In reality, even throughout Europe, primogeniture was never strictly enforced, especially after the medieval period. The practice diminished further after the rise of the industrial classes and the advent of women's rights in the modern era. The principle of primogeniture still lingers, however, in the succession practices of some royal families, including those of Britain and Japan.

See also: DESCENT, ROYAL; INHERITANCE, ROYAL; LANDHOLDING PATTERNS; POLYGAMY, ROYAL; SUCCESSION, ROYAL.

PROPHETS, ROYAL

Seers, oracles, or spokespersons for a deity, who serve as messengers to proclaim the word of that deity to the ruling monarch and his or her household.

The word "prophecy" is often used to indicate a prediction of future events; however, this is only one of many types of prophetic proclamations. Prophets deliver messages of hope, warning, and condemnation that they receive through direct manifestations from a divinity, through "reading" physical portents and signs, through interpreting dreams, or through plotting the stars.

Ancient prophets generally claimed divine revelations and were concerned with how the people responded to their deity through worship, sacrifice, and daily life. Yet, they usually were not from the priestly class. They were often distinguished by having received the call to their personal mission directly from the deity, and they often accepted this call to a new life with great reluctance. Even when the seer's mission was to speak directly to the sovereign ruler, he or she was not generally a servant of the court and did not receive payment for his or her proclamations. The ancient Egyptian high priest was an exception to this; he was sometimes called the first prophet and served the pharaoh directly.

In biblical literature, many of the Hebrew prophets exhorted the people to return to the ways of God by encouraging social reforms that lessened the disparity between the rich and the poor. For example, both the prophets Isaiah and Amos chided the Hebrew leaders for their treatment of the poor. The prophet Ahijah's mission was to condemn King Jeroboam (931–910 B.C.E.), while Isaiah called upon the Hebrews to repent and foretold the coming of the Messiah.

Ancient Greek history and literature are full of references to the oracles of kings, the most famous of which is the oracle at Delphi. Here the Pythia, priestess to Apollo, would hear the questions of pilgrims and pronounce the god's reply, usually indefinite enough to prevent the god from being wrong. When the city of Thebes was suffering from plague, Oedipus consulted both the oracle at Delphi and the blind prophet Tiresias.

One of the most unusual stories of the relationship between king and oracles is that of Croesus, king of Lydia (r. 560–546 B.C.E.). When Croesus became fearful of the increasing power of Cyrus of Persia (r. 580–529 B.C.E.), he sent his messengers to consult different oracles and ask them if he should assemble an army and lead an attack on Cyrus. When he received an affirmative answer, he set about forming alliances and raising his forces. In the resulting battle, Cyrus unburdened his camels and sent them against the fierce cavalry of Croesus. The camels frightened the horses so much that the Lydians lost the battle and Croesus was captured. When Croesus and some of his men were about to be burned alive, Cyrus questioned the rival king and changed his mind about the pyre. Unfortunately, the fire had already been lit. According to legend, Croesus called on the gods, a storm arose, and the burning pyre was extinguished. After Cyrus learned that it was the oracle of the gods who had advised Croesus to mount an offensive against him, he made Croesus one of his principal advisers.

Prophecies might also be the result of revelations from the deity through dreams or visions. These visions might occur spontaneously or be induced by drugs or trances. Among the Celtic tribes in ancient Britain, for example, Druids utilized a dream ritual to identify a dead king's successor. Some African peoples, such as the Baule of the Ivory Coast region, also have traditions of divination that include trance dances. Individuals who have been chosen by a spirit or deity are instructed in rituals of the dance. While in a trance, the mystics are able to determine reasons for local troubles and make recommendations for dealing with problems.

One form of prophecy, astrology, remains particularly widespread in Asia today, with people of all classes consulting astrologers for advice about their lives. Nepalese astrologers are said to have predicted the deaths of several members of the royal family in 2001, killed by the then crown prince. Astrological predictions included the warning that the dynasty would not last more than ten generations. King Birendra of Nepal (r. 1972–2001) was the eleventh monarch in the family and had reached the age of fifty-five, also prophesied as the age at which he would die.

Sovereign rulers who can exert control over their present and those whose present is controlled by others still often desire to know the future as revealed by prophets, fortunetellers, and astrologers.

See also: CROESUS; CURSES, ROYAL; CYRUS THE GREAT; DIVINATION AND DIVINERS, ROYAL; WITCHCRAFT AND SORCERY.

PTOLEMAIC DYNASTY (305–30 B.C.E.)

Dynasty of Macedonians that ruled Egypt for more than two and a half centuries, blending Greek civilization with the traditions of the Egyptian pharaohs.

When Alexander the Great (r. 336–323 B.C.E.) died in 323 B.C.E., his empire was divided, and Egypt went to Ptolemy, one of Alexander's loyal generals. He ruled Egypt as Ptolemy I Soter (r. 323–283 B.C.E.) and started the Ptolemaic dynasty, which ruled until the death of Cleopatra VII (r. 51–30 B.C.E.).

Under the Ptolemaic dynasty, its capital city of Alexandria flourished as the economic and cultural center of the ancient world. The early Ptolemies were practical businessmen who wanted to increase the country's wealth. They expanded foreign trade and improved agriculture with irrigation and new crops such as cotton and grapes for wine.

The Ptolemies also supported many artistic and intellectual activities. Ptolemy I was not just a successful military officer, but also a scholar and historical writer. He wrote comprehensive descriptions of Alexander's battles and had a deep love of learning. His son and grandson were also passionate scholars. Ptolemy II Philadelphus (r. 285–246 B.C.E.) was very interested in science, and Ptolemy III Euergetes (r. 246–222 B.C.E.) was an avid book collector. The Ptolemies filled their royal court with renowned scholars, artists, poets, and scientists from all over the world, who also promoted scholarship in Egypt. Scholarly endeavors culminated in the famous Library in Alexandria, which had up to 50,000 books—an astounding number for ancient times. The librarians and kings who supported the Library made every effort to save and document all Greek knowledge and to get copies of all known works.

The Ptolemies were eager to spread knowledge and culture. Libraries were open to everyone who could read and who wanted to learn. Learning to read became easier because the Ptolemies supported use of the Greek alphabet, which had just thirty symbols rather than the many Egyptian hieroglyphs.

The Ptolemaic dynasty continued to rule Egypt with its Greek influence for nearly 300 years. During that time, Alexandria grew stronger and wealthier, and it became the core of a realm that extended up the coast of Syria and beyond. Gradually, however, internal conflicts arose, Roman influence grew, and the later Ptolemies were less skillful than their predecessors. Eventually, Greek dominance declined with the rise of the Roman Empire, which took control of Egypt after the death of Cleopatra, in 30 B.C.E.

See also: Alexander III, the Great; Cleopatra VII; Egyptian Dynasties, Persian, Hellenistic, and Roman; Ptolemy I.

The Ptolemaic dynasty of Egypt ruled for 275 years. It was founded by Ptolemy I Soter, a general of Alexander the Great. This cameo portrait, made in Alexandria in the third century C.E., shows the second ruler of the dynasty, Ptolemy II Philadelphus, and his wife, Arsinoe.

PTOLEMY I (ca. 367–282 B.C.E.)

Egyptian ruler (r. 323–283 B.C.E.) and founder of the Ptolemaic dynasty. Born in Macedonia, Ptolemy was a childhood friend and loyal general of Alexander the Great (r. 336–323 B.C.E.). Ptolemy's numerous military achievements included escorting Alexander on conquests of Asia Minor, Syria, and Persia, as well as Egypt. When Alexander died in 323 B.C.E., his empire was fought over and divided up among his generals. Ptolemy received Egypt and became its governor and eventually declared himself king in 306 B.C.E. Calling himself Ptolemy I "Soter" (the Savior), he was the founder of the Egyptian Ptolemaic dynasty.

While Ptolemy I ruled Egypt, he strove to strengthen his regime and enhance Egyptian civilization and culture. He also made every effort to preserve and achieve the idealistic and intellectual goals adopted by Alexander the Great.

Foremost among Ptolemy's achievements was the creation of a great library and mouseion (center of learning) in the city of Alexandria, which he made the Egyptian capital. Alexandria developed into one of the world's leading cities, and its library and mouseion became important centers of higher learning and of scientific and technological progress. Not unlike a modern teaching and research university (or a "think tank"), the mouseion became a gathering place for academic study. The king appointed a priest to direct it, and it was publicly funded. The library, which was probably part of the mouseion, grew to hold tens of thousands of books.

Toward the end of his reign, Ptolemy realized he needed to choose a successor. He chose his third son, Ptolemy II Philadelphus (r. 283–246 B.C.E.), whom he considered most likely to continue his ideas. He made Ptolemy II co-regent in 285 B.C.E. and upon the death of Ptolemy I in 283 B.C.E., his son took the throne.

See also: ALEXANDER III, THE GREAT; PTOLEMAIC DYNASTY.

in 1644. The Manchus, regarded as foreigners by ethnic Chinese, were strongly resented by the populace, and in 1911 a rebellion led by General Yuan Shih-kai swept them from power. Pu Yi was forced to abdicate his throne in 1912, when he was only six years old, but he was allowed to remain in the Forbidden City and was treated with extreme courtesy.

Courteous treatment, however, was no substitute for a normal childhood, and the young Pu Yi remained isolated in an elaborate world of ritual and formality. He received a limited education, studying Buddhism, poetry, and Chinese history. His every childish whim was indulged, and within the artificial confines of the Forbidden City, his power over his

PU YI (1906–1967 C.E.)

Last emperor (r. 1908–1912) of China, who ruled as a figurehead in service to a variety of masters in the contentious final years of the Chinese empire.

Pu Yi was born on February 2, 1906, in the Forbidden City of Beijing (so named because no commoners or foreigners were allowed to enter). His father, Prince Chun, was the brother of the nominal emperor of China, Kuang Hsu (r. 1875–1908), who had been imprisoned by Dowager Empress Tzu Hsi after she seized power in 1898. By the time of Pu Yi's birth, the empress was growing old. To ensure an orderly transition of power, she decided to name a successor. She chose Pu Yi, and to avoid controversy over his succession, it is rumored that she had Kuang Hsu poisoned in his prison cell. The empress died in 1908, and the infant Pu Yi became emperor. His father served as regent for the infant ruler.

Pu Yi spent his childhood in the lushly appointed Imperial Palace in the Forbidden City. In accordance with royal tradition, he was kept isolated from nearly everyone except his royal retainers for most of the time. His father was allowed to visit for two minutes every two months, and until he was twenty years old, Pu Yi never saw his mother at all. He rarely saw other children and was fully seven years old before his own brother and sister were permitted to visit.

Pu Yi's rule was interrupted several times during the course of his life, for this was a tumultuous period in China's history. His family was Manchu, a people who had come from the region of Manchuria in northeast China to found the Ch'ing (Qing) dynasty

The last emperor of China, Pu Yi ruled as a figurehead until the monarchy was abolished in 1912. Restored as a puppet emperor by the Japanese in 1934, he was forced to abdicate again in 1945. Under the Chinese Communists, Pu Yi was imprisoned, then stripped of all privileges and made to live like a commoner.

household was absolute; when angry or bored he commonly ordered one of his retainers to be flogged.

In 1917 a pro-Manchu faction led by General Chang Hsum attempted to restore the empire, seizing control of the Forbidden City and declaring Pu Yi emperor once again. This was a short-lived victory, however, and the now eleven-year-old ruler kept his throne for only six days before a bombing campaign was waged by the opposition, targeting the palace and forcing Pu Yi to abdicate once again. Meanwhile, the Manchus hoped to enlist foreign assistance to regain power. They enlisted an Englishman, Reginald Johnson, to serve as Pu Yi's tutor and to act as mediator with the British. Pu Yi learned fluent English from Johnson, and under his tutelage became fascinated with the Western world, even taking a Western name, Henry.

In his mid-teens, Pu Yi began to realize that the Forbidden City was simply a well-appointed prison, and he made futile efforts to escape. He was essentially docile, however, and when told that he had to marry at age sixteen, he accepted the woman chosen for him by his retainers: Wan Jung. Pu Yi's only rebellion was to insist on choosing a second wife, Wen Hsiu, who was more to his liking. In either case, it appears that he never consummated his marriages: he fled his bridal chamber in terror and never had any children with these or future wives.

In 1924, China was again convulsed by political unrest, this time by warring Communist and anti-Communist factions. General Geng Yu-hsiang of the Communists captured the Forbidden City and forced Pu Yi to leave—at the age of eighteen, it was the first time he saw what life was like among ordinary citizens. His English tutor helped him to enter the Japanese embassy, where he found asylum along with his wives and his entourage. The Japanese were willing to help because they thought Pu Yi would be useful in their plans to invade and conquer Manchuria.

In 1931, the Japanese did invade Manchuria, and they managed to smuggle Pu Yi in to act as the chief executive of the territory, which they renamed Manchukuo. In 1934, the Japanese gratified their young puppet ruler by giving him the title "emperor," but he was still completely under their control. Pu Yi's new stint as emperor, however, was not to last. The Russians invaded Manchuria in 1945, during World War II, and Pu Yi was forced once again

to abdicate his throne. He was promised safe passage to Japan but was permitted to take only a handful of people with him.

To make the journey, Pu Yi abandoned his wives (Wan Jung died in prison soon after). Instead of arriving in Japan, however, he found himself under house arrest in the Soviet Union. Again isolated, Pu Yi spent the next several years manipulated by his new masters, being trotted out for occasional public appearances and to testify against the Japanese for their actions in Manchuria. In 1950, the Russians apparently decided that he served no useful purpose, and Pu Yi was permitted to return to China.

Pu Yi's return to China was not triumphal. The Communist regime was fully entrenched by this time, and as a representative of the old imperial order, Pu Yi was forced into a prison camp. After nine years of menial labor and "re-education," Pu Yi was finally released, but he was stripped of all honors and privileges. In 1965, Chairman Mao Tse Tung, the ruler of Communist China, declared the Cultural Revolution, which was intended to sweep away China's pre-Communist past. Pu Yi died two years later, and many thought that Mao ordered his death as part of the effort to erase China's imperial history. It is more likely, however, that the officially recognized cause of Pu Yi's death, cancer, is correct, for by this time the lifelong puppet ruler presented no threat at all to the government.

See also: CH'ING (QING) DYNASTY.

FURTHER READING

Behr, Edward. *The Last Emperor.* New York: Bantam Books, 1987.

Power, Brian. *The Puppet Emperor: The Life of Pu Yi, Last Emperor of China.* New York: Universe Books, 1988.

PUNJAB PRINCELY STATES

(ca. 1700–1972 C.E.)

Muslim states located in the so-called Five Rivers region of northwestern India (now divided between India and Pakistan); home of the Sikh religion.

From the early sixteenth to mid-eighteenth century, the Muslim Mughal dynasty of India ruled most of northern India, including the Punjab region. However, the difficulties the Mughals encountered in trying to command and control such a vast area led to the rise of a series of independent princely states.

Under weak Mughal rule, local chieftains were able to hold land and raise small armies. Reliance on the personal support of relatives, lesser nobility, and their own peasants prevented these chieftains from becoming too powerful and threatening to the Mughals. Self-interests led to competition between the chieftains, who were always careful to defend their lands and prepared to expand their holdings and their wealth. By the mid-1700s there were about sixty separate chieftains in Punjab.

SIKHISM AND THE PUNJAB

In the language of the Punjab region, the word Sikh translates to "lion." In the fifteenth century, a wandering preacher, Guru Nanak, came to the city of Kartarpur in the Punjab. His teachings, a combination of devotional Hinduism and Sufi Islam, were included in the Adi Granth (First Book), the sacred scripture of the Sikh religion. The Sikh movement was not intended to be political, but as it grew, it came to be seen as a threat to the Mughal state.

In 1709, a Sikh leader named Banda Singh Bahadur set out to attack the Mughals and conquered a large portion of the eastern Punjab. The Mughal rulers waged an eight-month siege of the fortress town of Gurdas Nangal in 1715, during which they captured Banda Singh. The Mughals took Banda Singh to Delhi, where he was executed. Banda Singh Bahadur's death was followed by a long struggle between the Sikhs on one side and the Afghans and Mughals on the other.

By 1765, the Sikh chieftains of the Punjab united under another leader, Ranjit Singh (r. 1780–1839). With the help of foreign mercenaries, Ranjit Singh captured the city of Lahore in 1799 and gained control of the main trade routes from north India to Central Asia, Iran, and western Asia. With the increase in revenue gained from trade, Ranjit expanded his army to 40,000 cavalry and infantry. By 1809, Ranjit Singh was the master of the Punjab.

THE PUNJAB UNDER THE BRITISH

Following the death of Ranjit Singh in 1839, regional differences began to emerge within Punjab and social conflicts followed. It appeared that the state never made the transition from a conquering power to a stable system of alliances. Taking advantage of this weakness, the British annexed most of the Punjab for the British East India Company within ten years.

The British East India Company had arrived in India in 1600. Unable to win the spice trade from the Dutch and the Portuguese, British businessmen offered Indian ruling families sophisticated agreements that would permit them to live in grandeur while the British exploited their kingdoms and became wealthy. Annexation of Indian land, mistreatment of Indian people, and the growing westernization of the Indian culture and values led to the Sepoy mutiny of 1857, a rebellion of Indian soldiers against the British East India Company that grew into a widespread uprising against British rule in India

The Sepoy mutiny was not successful, but it led the British government to replace the East India Company with a viceroy. The British also stopped annexing Indian territories and came to agreements with most Indian states. The states would either be run as provinces, or Britain would allow ruling families to administer their kingdoms while remaining subject to British rule. The British would interfere in internal matters only if it was absolutely necessary. The rulers of these kingdoms were termed princes, and their realms were called princely states (because the British recognized only one king, the king of England). In 1877, over seven hundred Indian princely states entered into a treaty with the British Crown.

In the Punjab region the princely states, also known as *Riasats* during the British colonial era, included Kapurthala, Nabha, Patiala, Jind, Pataudi, Laharu, Dujana, Faridkotla, and Bahawalpur. The states of Nabha, Patiala, and Jind were collectively known as the Phulkian States because of their common ancestor named *Phul* (r. ca. 1618–1652.)

THE PUNJAB IN INDEPENDENT INDIA

The twentieth century witnessed a growing desire for independent rule in India. In 1935, the Government of India Act allowed for the voluntary accession of the princely states, either in union with adjacent existing provinces of British India or as separate self-governing units within the federation. The senior ruling prince within the union was usually appointed to the new position of *Rajpramukh,* an appointment designed to be for life. In return for surrendering the rule over their states, together with their revenues and military forces, the former ruling princes were guaranteed their hereditary titles, privileges of rank and honor, as well as living expenses for themselves and their families.

When India gained independence from Great Britain in 1947, Britain canceled all of its treaty relations with the princely states and encouraged the rulers to join the new federation. Some 730 princely states chose to join the Dominion of India at this time, while two states, Bhutan and Sikkim, became Indian protectorates. Three other states, Hyderabad, Junagadh, and Jammu, remained independent. India incorporated Hyderabad and Junagadh by force in 1948 and abolished the position of Rajpramukh throughout the new Indian nation.

Most of the state of Jammu, which had been part of the domain of Ranjit Singh in the nineteenth century, was incorporated into India in 1972 after the current Maharaja was forced to seek Indian military intervention. The other part of Jammu, which included parts of Kashmir, was incorporated within Pakistan.

See also: Colonialism and Kingship; Indian Kingdoms; Mughal Empire; South Asian Kingdoms.

FURTHER READING

Grewal, J.S. India. *The Sikhs of the Punjab.* New York: Cambridge University Press, 1991.

Pyu Kingdom (ca. 1000 b.c.e.–832 c.e.)

The first historically significant kingdom in Myanmar (Burma), which established city-states at Binnaka, Mongama, Shri Ksetra, and Halingyi, and governed each tribe within the kingdom by a democratic assembly.

As early as about 1000 b.c.e., Pyu peoples settled along the middle stretch of the Irrawwaddy River in Myanmar, but they did not establish settlements right along the river. This was in contrast to later periods, when the Pyu founded cities along the river itself. The emerging Pyu state provided an alternative to the overland trade route through Myanmar by establishing a route down the Irrawaddy to the Indian Ocean coast and then by sea to India and more remote parts of Southeast Asia.

The Pyu kingdom prospered from traveling merchants, who used the Irrawaddy trade route and enjoyed good relations with both India and the Mons people who settled in the Irrawaddy delta region. Early Chinese visitors to the Pyu kingdom reported that it had a surprisingly humane society. Prisons and chains were not part of the justice system, and the only punishment for criminals was often just a few lashes with a whip, except in cases of homicide, which received much more severe punishment.

The Pyu lived in wooden houses with roofing tiles of lead and tin. They used golden knives, and they surrounded themselves with various art objects made from gold, green glass, jade, and crystal. Both sexes dressed lavishly for the time, wearing bright blue clothing; the men wore gold ornaments in their hair. Parts of the city walls, the palaces, and the monasteries were built using glazed brick.

The Pyu rulers allowed their people considerable religious and political freedom. Some Pyu followed Hinduism, and others Theravada or Mahayana Buddhism. The Pyu rulers, however, officially emphasized Buddhist learning. Children, both boys and girls, had their heads completely shaved and were disciplined and educated in monasteries and convents as novices. Often the children would enter the monastery or convent at age seven and remain until they were twenty years old. By the seventh century c.e., the Theravada faith had become the dominant factor in the daily life of the Pyu kingdom.

One of the most significant periods in the history of the Pyu kingdom was the Vikrama era, which began in 638. Named after the Pyu Vikrama dynasty, the era saw a flowering of culture that spread to neighboring Thailand and Cambodia. During this period, the Pyu improved their system of irrigation and developed more advanced planning for their urban centers.

After moving the capital northward to Halingyi in the seventh century, leaving the city of Shri Ksetra to oversee trade in the south, the Pyu were defeated by the Mons people in the eighth century. Many of the Pyu fled north, but were captured by the Thai kingdom of Nan Chao. In 832, the Thais attacked the Pyu capital of Halingyi and destroyed it, ending the Pyu kingdom.

See also: Mon Kingdom; Southeast Asian Kingdoms.

QAJAR DYNASTY (1796–1925 C.E.)

A dynasty of shahs from the Qajar tribe that ruled Iran in the early modern era.

For about one hundred thirty years, from 1796 to 1925, the Qajar shahs exercised firm control over the entire territory of Iran, in roughly its present boundaries. Under pressure from the growing Russian and British empires, they made some attempts at social and governmental reforms, but their failure to modernize the country led to their overthrow in the early twentieth century.

ORIGINS AND EARLY RULE

The Qajars were a Turkmen tribe of northern Iran who rose to political prominence under the rulers of the Safavid dynasty and began to vie for power on their own in the eighteenth century. The founder of the dynasty, Agha Muhammad Khan (r. 1796–1797), was the son of a Qajar chief. Captured and castrated as a child by an enemy of his father, he spent many years as a hostage in Shiraz, the capital of Iran's then-ruling Zand dynasty.

Freed in 1779, Agha Muhammad quickly defeated rivals and assumed leadership of the Qajar tribes. By 1784 he controlled all of northern Iran, while the Zand dynasty was consumed by infighting among various pretenders to the throne. By 1796, he was master of the entire country, after brutally disposing of the final Zand shah, Lotf Ali Khan (r. 1789–1794), and a large number of his supporters. Agha Muhammad also restored Iranian control in the Caucasus, after Georgia, a Christian client state, tried to break free with the support of Russia.

During Agha's brief reign, he revived the Iranian concept of the shah as the shadow of God and absolute ruler. He also established the principle that the throne would pass from father to son, aiming to avoid a repetition of the succession struggles of the

previous century. Under Agha and his Qajar successors, the central government of Iran gradually came to overshadow the various tribal and provincial power centers.

The ruthless character that may explain Agha Muhammad's striking successes led to his own murder, in 1797, at the hands of two servants whom he had sentenced to death for quarreling. His nephew and successor, Fath Ali Shah (r. 1797–1834), was just as cruel to opponents, but he did not have his uncle's strength of purpose. Two border wars with the expanding Russian Empire, in 1804–1813 and in 1826–1828, resulted in huge territorial losses for Iran. Georgia, Armenia, and northern Azerbaijan were lost, leaving the northwest border of Iran fixed at approximately its present position.

CHALLENGES AND SUCCESSES

Fath Ali was succeeded by his grandson, Muhammad (r. 1834–1848), who had a relatively uneventful reign. Upon his death in 1848, his son, Naser al-Din (r. 1848–1896), became shah. Naser proved to be a relatively successful defender of his country's independence. But he was unable to defend Iran completely from foreign threats. He was also unable to hold back British incursions from India to the south and east; and by the 1850s, the British had established a series of protectorates on the Persian Gulf. In 1881, Russia conquered the regions of Turkmenistan and Uzbekistan in the northeast, severing Iran's historic ties to the cities of Bukhara and Samarkand.

Naser had greater success with domestic policy. In the first years of his reign, his prime minister, Mirza Taqi Khan, introduced major administrative and fiscal reforms; encouraged the introduction of Western education, science, and technology; and laid the groundwork for the first Western-style university in Iran, the Dar-ol-Fonun. Although Mirza was later forced out by powerful opponents who felt threatened by his reforms, many of his reforms took hold.

INCREASING FOREIGN INFLUENCE

Despite all efforts to maintain independence, Iran's modernizing economy fell increasingly under British influence. Western political values of freedom and democracy also made headway among many elements of the Iranian population.

These ideas bore fruit during the reign of Naser's son and successor, Muzaffar al-Din (r. 1896–1907), who was forced by pressure from the religious establishment, merchants, and protestors to grant a constitution in 1906. The constitution established an elected parliament, the *majlis,* with power to approve the cabinet. Civil and property rights were guaranteed in laws passed the following year. When Muzaffar's son and successor, Muhammad Ali (r. 1907–1909), tried to rescind the constitution, he was deposed in favor of his eleven-year-old son Ahmad (r. 1909–1925).

The century-long Qajar balancing act between the various European powers finally broke down in 1907, when Britain and Russia agreed to divide Iran into spheres of influence. When Russian, Ottoman Turkish, and British forces physically occupied the country during World War I, Ahmad's legitimacy was further undermined. A coup d'état in 1921, led by Reza Khan (who later became the first shah of the Pahlavi dynasty, r. 1925–1941), relegated Ahmad to figurehead status. The *majlis* formally deposed Ahmad four years later, bringing the Qajar dynasty to an end.

See also: Pahlavi Dynasty; Zand Dynasty.

FURTHER READING

Daniel, Elton L. *The History of Iran.* Westport, CT: Greenwood Press, 2001.

QIANLONG. *See* Ch'ien Lung

QIN DYNASTY. *See* Ch'in Dynasty

QING DYNASTY. *See* Ch'ing Dynasty

QUEENS AND QUEEN MOTHERS

The various female royal offices, including that of queen, queen mother, royal concubine, or royal sister. Because in monarchies the world over political authority has been the near-monopoly of males, female royal offices cannot properly be understood as equivalent to the office of king. Rules of inheritance, rights of succession, and access to resources have always favored men. Thus, whereas a male becomes king in his own right, most often a woman becomes queen by a more indirect route, by virtue of her association with a male, whether husband, brother, or father.

In a traditional monarchy, wherein the royal leader serves as something more than a symbolic figure, ultimate political authority rests in the hands of the titular (male) head of state. The linkage between the title and the office is relatively unambiguous, and the authority of an individual to serve in the office is generally validated by claims of divine right or descent from a founding ancestor. The claim of a female ruler to her throne, however, is less direct, generally mediated by marriage or motherhood. Generally speaking, then, the office of the queen does not exist without the presumption of a king at some point along the line.

A queen's primary function is to provide heirs, that is, sons who will be future kings. This does not mean that she does not exert political influence, however. As wife, mother, or sister of the ruling male, she may provide advice and counsel, she may embody a political alliance with the royal house and a powerful family (the family into which she was born), or she may serve in the capacity of a king's representative.

Much less frequently, a queen or queen mother may rule in her own right. This is usually the result of a failure in the male line of succession. For example, a queen may serve as regent if her husband, the king, dies before his heir, her son, is old enough to take the throne. When King Peter III of Russia was assassinated by a group of nobles, his German wife, Catherine, replaced him on the throne. This queen, Catherine the Great, was not only actively involved in the plot to kill her husband, but she also maintained her rule from 1762 to 1796.

Even in such situations, a queen's position is usually considered temporary, to be reliniquished to her son as soon as he is old enough to rule. It is also usually mitigated by the presence of (male) court officials. It is true but rare that some societies recognize the right of a royal daughter to inherit the king's office, if she has no male siblings. However, it is much more common that, in the absence of male heirs, the throne passes to the former king's brother or other close male relative.

When females do attain the highest rank of royalty and power, this is generally marked by ritual or linguistic markers that signify a transformation in her gender status, from female to gender-neutral, or for her to be accorded a kind of "honorary" maleness.

In many modern monarchies, the concept of royalty has become attenuated, as the political functions of the state have been taken over by elected officials such as prime ministers or other political representatives. In such cases, the power of the queen, or king, is tightly circumscribed. For example, Britain's reigning queen is an important symbol of national identity, but the actual work of governing is done by others. Even in some mostly symbolic monarchies, however, females may not be permitted to inherit the throne. This is true in Japan, where they are constitutionally prohibited from assuming the office of the emperor.

Sometimes a queen may use rationalizing myths to expand her claim to authority. For instance, among the Lovedu of the Transvaal, in southern Africa, the queen holds true power, based on the belief that the queen has a divine dispensation to rule. This is because she is believed to be able to control the rain, which is evidence of a supra-normal relationship with the land and the ancestors. The queens of societies that are heir to the Christian tradition provide a further example of this. Since the medieval period, Christianity has accommodated a cult of the Virgin Mary, according to which the mother of Jesus rules as the "Queen of Heaven." This provides a model and justification for queenly authority in the human realm as well.

See also: CATHERINE II, THE GREAT; CONCUBINES, ROYAL; COURTS AND COURT OFFICIALS, ROYAL; DESCENT, ROYAL; DIVINE RIGHT; ELIZABETH I; INHERITANCE, ROYAL; MARRIAGE OF KINGS; MYTH AND FOLKLORE; NATIONAL IDENTITY; PRIESTS, ROYAL; REGENCIES; SUCCESSION, ROYAL.

QUARAYSH. *See* HASHEMITE DYNASTY

QUTB SHAHI DYNASTY. *See*

GOLCONDA KINGDOM

RADAMA I (ca. 1793–1828 c.e.)

Ruler of Madagascar (r. 1810–1828), known as "Madagascar's Napoleon" because of his role in extending the rule of the Merina kingdom across the entire island.

Radama I was the son of Andrianampoinimerina (r. 1787–1810), the founder of the Merina kingdom on the island of Madagascar. It was Andrianampoinimerina who succeeded in uniting the various independent states that shared the central portion of the island. Radama, who was born around 1793, succeeded to the throne upon his father's death in 1810. He was only seventeen years old at the time.

When Radama came to the throne, the dominance of the Merina kingdom was well established in the territory around the capital city of Antananarivo. Like the other Madagascan kingdoms, Merina's wealth was based in large part on its involvement in the Indian Ocean slave trade. During Radama's rule, however, this changed dramatically as a direct result of his efforts to expand Merina's control outward to include the other kingdoms of the island.

To accomplish this objective, Radama I entered into an alliance with the British, who wished to establish a presence in the region. In an agreement reached in 1816, the British promised to supply modern training and firearms for Radama's military. Thus equipped, his army easily defeated the forces of his neighbors on Madagascar. This military superiority came at a price, however. In return for their assistance, the British demanded that Radama ban all slave trading from his kingdom.

Such an agreement would seem counterproductive for a ruler whose wealth was based almost wholly on the slave trade. However, the British promised to provide economic assistance and support for the development of manufacturing. At the same time, enforcement of the ban on slaving gave Radama an excuse to attack his neighbors while also undercutting their economies (which were also based on the slave trade). By the end of 1817, Radama controlled nearly the whole of Madagascar.

Radama I was strongly committed to a policy of Westernization. He welcomed the arrival of representatives of the London Missionary Society, who established schools and churches throughout the Merina kingdom. He encouraged his subjects to convert to Christianity. In addition, it was during the reign of Radama I that a written form of the local language (Malagasy) was developed. By the time of Radama I's death in 1828 (of an unknown disease), a small but rapidly growing literate class had developed in Merina, and the kingdom was producing its first local publications in Malagasy. Radama I was succeeded on the throne by his widow, Ranavalona I (r. 1828–1861).

See also: MADAGASCAR KINGDOMS; MERINA KINGDOM; RADAMA II; RANAVALONA I, MADA.

FURTHER READING

Kottak, Conrad P., ed. *Madagascar:* Society and History. Durham, NC: Carolina Academic Press, 1986.

Valette, Jean. *Etudes sur le regne de Radama I.* Antananarivo, Madagascar: Impr. nationale, 1962.

RADAMA II (1828–1830 C.E.)

Ruler (r. 1861–1863) of the Merina kingdom of Madagascar, who was most notable for his efforts to forge strong political and economic ties with Europe.

The son of Radama I (r. 1810–1828), Radama II was born to Queen Ranavalona shortly after her husband's death from an unknown disease in 1828. Ranavalona ruled the Merina kingdom after Radama I died, and she continued on the throne until her death in 1861, at which time rule passed to Radama II.

When Radama II came to the throne, the kingdom he inherited had turned its back on European ties and trade. Queen Ranavalona, nicknamed "the bloodthirsty," had been deeply distrustful of European influence and had attempted to eradicate it from Madagascar. The queen had severed all trade with the British and expelled or persecuted missionaries.

Radama II attempted to reverse these policies by making overtures to the French, whom he greatly admired. He made some progress in this regard, but his efforts ran afoul of powerful members of his royal court, most of whom shared the anti-Western attitudes of the late queen.

In 1863, Radama made a treaty of perpetual friendship with France, but his pro-French stance continued to alienate powerful members of his court. He was assassinated that same year, within two years of taking the throne, on the orders of his own ministers. His pro-Western stance was nonetheless continued during the rule of his widow and successor, Queen Rasoherina (r. 1863–1868).

See also: MADAGASCAR KINGDOMS; MERINA KINGDOM; RADAMA II; RANAVALONA I, MADA.

FURTHER READING

Kottak, Conrad P., ed. *Madagascar: Society and History.* Durham, NC: Carolina Academic Press, 1986.

Valette, Jean. *Etudes sur le regne de Radama I.* Antananarivo, Madagascar: Impr. nationale, 1962.

RAJASTHAN KINGDOM

(ca. 7–1947 C.E.)

Kingdom of the Rajputs, a mostly Hindu warrior caste in India that placed great value on military virtues and whose sworn duty was to defend the state and its people without regard to personal risk.

The modern Indian state of Rajasthan in northwestern India came into being in 1956. After India achieved independence in 1947, eighteen princely states, two chieftainships, and the British province of Ajmer-Merwara were merged in stages to form the new state of Rajasthan.

Prior to 1947, the region of Rajasthan was known as Rajputana, or "the country of the Rajputs." The term *Rajput* means "sons of the Rajas," and the Rajas were "princes." Thus, Rajasthan has often been called "the abode of the princes."

BEFORE THE RAJPUTS

The people of Rajputana originally came to the northern parts of India from many areas and ancient cultural traditions. Some declared that they had descended from the sun or moon or that they had been called forth from the great pit of the Hindu fire god

Agni by a Brahman priest. The location of settlements and the social, cultural, and economic life of the people was determined by geographical features, ranging from peaceful and productive valleys to mountain ranges, rivers, and deserts.

Ancient Indian inscriptions indicate that the emperor Asoka (r. 268–232 B.C.E.) of the Mauryan Empire controlled parts of Rajputana around 250 B.C.E. The Indo-Greeks from the region of Bactria (in present-day Afghanistan) ruled the region in the second century B.C.E., followed by the Sakas dynasty in the second to fourth centuries C.E. The Gupta dynasty controlled the southwestern part of Rajputana from the fourth to the sixth centuries, and there were invasions by the Huns in the sixth century.

THE RAJPUT PRINCES

The power of the Rajput princes began to arise in Rajputana between the seventh and thirteenth centuries. Most of the Rajputs were Hindu. The Rajputs became known for their valor and their devotion to Vaishnavism, the Hindu belief that a person must pursue the way of good works and spiritual knowledge. As a result, they gained the status of Kshattriyas—warriors, defenders of righteousness, and implementers of the law, whose solemn duty was to defend the state and its people without regard to personal risk. They enjoyed royal privileges and were called "princes of royal blood."

Of the many Rajput princely clans, a number stand out for their accomplishments and the size of their landholdings. These include the Guhilots of Mewar, Harsha, the Katchawaha Rajputs, the Bhati Rajputs, and the Rathors of Marwar.

THE GUHILOTS OF MEWAR AND HARSHA

The Guhilots of Mewar (ca. 568–1947), the oldest Rajput clan, outlived seven centuries of dominance by the Muslims of the Delhi sultanate. Although they experienced occasional defeats, the Guhilots never gave in easily, and, when defeated, they would wait to gather their strength and recover lost territory.

Separated from the rest of India by mountains and dense forests, the princely state of Mewar developed a spirit of iron discipline and stoic resolve. In the eighth century, the Hindu guru, Harit Rashi, laid down rules for the governance of the state. His tenets were based upon respect for humankind, service to the community, and, more importantly, adherence to and mainte-nance of the ancient Vedic culture. The Vedic religion, which originated in Iran, was the basis for Hindu beliefs. Eventually, Mewar was defeated by the Mughal emperor, Babur (r. 1526–1530) in 1527.

The Rajput prince, Harsha (r. ca. 606–674), ruled a large portion of northern India, including some of Rajputana in the early seventh century. A Hindu who converted to Buddhism, Harsha conquered many cities and kingdoms, but he generally left the rulers of these places on their thrones, expecting only tribute and homage. When Harsha died, his loose empire collapsed into anarchy.

THE KATCHAWAHA AND BHATI RAJPUTS

In the twelfth century, the Katchawaha Rajputs ruled in and around Jaipur, the present capital of Rajasthan, holding a large area bordering the kingdoms of Mewar and Marwar. Twenty-eight Rajput princes ruled Jaipur for six centuries and, in the past 250 years, only ten Maharajas have held the throne. The eleventh maharaja, Sawai Bhawani Singh (r. 1956–present), still leads the Katchawaha clan.

Also in the twelfth century, the Bhati Rajputs ruled in Jaisalmer, another region of Rajasthan. The Bhati were great camel riders and warriors; cattle theft and hunting were their major pastimes. Their kingdom was located along the Afghanistan–Delhi spice trade route, and they taxed passing caravans.

The Bhati Rajputs were brave and impetuous warriors who would fight a major battle with the slightest excuse. Since Jaisalmer was located deep in the desert, it escaped direct Muslim conquest when the Muslims began expanding into India. However, a raid on the royal baggage caravan of Muslim emperor Allaud-din Khilji (r. 1296–1316) resulted in a seven-year siege. Finally, facing certain defeat, the Bhatis killed their women and children, and then, clad in ceremonial saffron garments and intoxicated by opium, they opened the gates of the city and rushed out to meet their deaths at the hands of the Muslims.

THE RATHORS OF MARWAR

The Rathors of Marwar ruled the largest state in Rajasthan. The Pratihara dynasty held off invading Muslim forces for many years, but in 1192 the Muslim forces of Muhammad Ghuri defeated the Rajput army of Prithviraja III at the battle of Tarain. Kanauj, the Rathor capital for seven centuries, fell to the Afghan invaders in 1193, and within twenty years most of northern

India would be under control of the Muslim Mughal dynasty.

After their defeat, the Rathors reconsolidated, built an impregnable fort on a high ridge, and established their capital city of Jodhpur around it. Over the next 250 years they prospered from trade; they battled often and won.

RAJASTHAN AND THE MUGHALS

In 1459, Rao Ganga Singh of Jodhpur (r. 1516–1532) fought alongside the army of Mewar against the first Mughal emperor, Babur. It was from this time that the romantic view developed of the gallant Rajput warrior defending family, honor, and religion against the invading Muslims.

In 1567, Babur's grandson, Akbar (r. 1556–1605), captured the two great Rajput forts of Chitor and Ranthambhor in east Rajputana. The rulers of Jodhpur allied themselves with Akbar and were permitted to continue in power. Several became trusted lieutenants of the Mughals and were successful in battle, including Maharaja Jaswant Singh (r. 1638–1658).

With Mughal support, the Rajput court of Jodhpur flourished, and it became a center for the arts, culture, and trade. In 1657, however, Maharaja Jaswant Singh promised to support the Mughal prince, Dara Shikoh, in his struggle against his brother, Aurangzeb (r. 1658–1707), for the Mugal throne. At the last minute, Jaswant Singh reneged on his promise. Dara's army was defeated and Dara was executed.

Aurangzeb then sent Jaswant Singh to the frontier, as viceroy in Afghanistan, and attempted to seize his infant son, whom loyal retainers hid in a basket of sweets. The princely state of Jodhpur then formed an alliance with the states of Udaipur and Jaipur in order to counter Mughal oppression, but they faced years of turmoil as the Mughal Empire disintegrated and finally collapsed.

The Rajputs continued to rule until they accepted British sovereignty in 1818. After independence in 1947, the Rajput states in Rajasthan were merged to form the state of Rajasthan within the Indian nation.

See also: AKBAR THE GREAT; ASOKA; AURANGZEB; BABUR; HINDUISM AND KINGSHIP; INDIAN KINGDOMS; MAURYA EMPIRE; MUGHAL EMPIRE.

FURTHER READING

Duff, Mabel. *The Chronology of Indian History: From the Earliest Times to the 16th Century.* Delhi: Cosmo Publications, 1972.

RAMA IV. *See* MONGKUT

RAMA V. *See* CHULALONGKORN

RAMA DYNASTY. *See* BANGKOK KINGDOM

RAMA KHAMHENG (ca. 1239–1298 C.E.)

The third king (r. ca. 1279–1317) of the kingdom of Sukhothai in the north-central part of present-day Thailand, who is credited with creating the first Siamese state. His name means "Rama the Brave" or "Rama the Strong."

When Rama Khamheng inherited Sukhothai after the death of his older brother, Ban Muang (r. 1275–1279), in 1279, the kingdom was very small, just a few hundred square miles. During the course of the next twenty years—by using prudent diplomacy, wise alliances, and skillful military campaigns modeled on those of Mongol leader Kublai Khan (r. 1260–1294)—Rama Khamheng made many successful conquests and forced local rulers to become his allies or tributaries. In this way, Rama Khamheng extended Sukhothai's power over a region that extended into parts of Cambodia, Burma, Luang Prabang, and the Malay Peninsula. He united an area with a common new faith in Theravada Buddhism and an antagonism toward the Cambodian Angkor kingdom, which had previously controlled the area.

Sukhothai flourished because Rama Khamheng was a just king who was friendly to neighboring rulers and a patron of the arts. He apparently brought pottery workers from China and had kilns set up in Sukhothai. The ceramics produced by these potters and their apprentices became important items of international trade. Sukhothai artworks developed a distinctly Thai look, with especially significant advances made in bronze sculpture. Rama Khamheng also is thought to have invented the first Thai alphabet (still essentially in use today); a stone inscription dating from 1292, and praising the king's rule, is the earliest known example of Thai writing.

The foundation of Rama Khamheng's kingdom was his own exceptional abilities. When he died, many of his more remote vassals quickly separated from the kingdom. Nevertheless, the area retained a sense of unity and culture that were later built upon by the states that followed Sukhothai, especially the kingdom of Ayutthaya (Ayuthia or Ayudhya).

Rama Khamheng was all but forgotten for the next few centuries after his death. But King Mongkut of Thailand (r. 1851–1868) rediscovered the 1292 inscription about Rama Khamheng while traveling around as a Buddhist monk. After that, Rama Khamheng became a national hero in Thailand as the founder of the first true Siamese state.

See also: Ayutthaya Kingdom; Mongkut (Rama IV); Sukhothai Kingdom.

Ramses II, the Great

(d. ca. 1212 b.c.e.)

Powerful ancient Egyptian ruler (r. ca. 1279–1212 b.c.e.) of the Nineteenth dynasty, possibly the pharaoh of the Hebrew exodus from Egypt mentioned in the Bible, who spent most of his reign building monuments to himself along the Nile River, thus becoming a symbol of ancient Egyptian civilization.

The second longest ruling pharaoh of ancient Egypt, Usermare Ramses II was the son of Pharaoh Seti I (r. ca. 1294–1279 b.c.e.). Although he succeeded to the throne at about age twenty, Ramses II was well prepared for the task. While still in his teenage years, Ramses had been designated co-regent by his father, who took the young prince with him on military campaigns against Egypt's enemies.

Early in his reign, Ramses II built a new royal city in the Nile Delta, the home region of his family. He named the city Pi-Ramesse and adorned it with gardens, orchards, and canals. The city's name and location have led some scholars to identify it with Ramses, the city built by Hebrew slaves according to the biblical Book of Exodus.

In fact, Egyptian records show that the Apiru (usually identified with the Hebrews) were among Ramses II's brick makers and stone quarriers. Other information about Ramses II, including the fact that he outlived many of his heirs, also conforms to the account told in the Book of Exodus. But the Hebrew exodus is not mentioned in any Egyptian records.

EGYPT AND THE HITTITES

Pi-Ramesse served as an excellent starting point for Ramses's repeated forays into Syria, which were aimed at restoring Egyptian power in Asia. In the fifth year of his reign, he led his armies on a major campaign to dislodge the Hittites from Syria. The armies of the two empires met at Qadesh (Kadesh) on the Orantes River in western Syria, where a fierce and bloody battle ensued. Ramses II managed to extricate himself from an ambush only through great feats of personal courage and ferocity—at least according to his own accounts of the event.

The Egyptians eventually left the field at Qadesh without any gain. Historians call the battle, and the entire campaign against the Hittites, a standoff. But Ramses II described the battle as a great victory in his own records. He memorialized the battle of Qadesh in monumental stone depictions and inscriptions that he placed all over Egypt, and in three written papyrus accounts.

After several more campaigns against the Hittites, none of which changed the situation or gained any success, Ramses II signed a peace treaty around 1258 b.c.e. with the Hittite king Hattushili III (r. 1263–1245 b.c.e.), in part as protection against the rising power of Assyria. In removing the Hittite threat, the treaty allowed trade to revive between Egypt and other states of the ancient Near East, and it contributed to the increasing presence of foreigners in Egypt by ensuring safe passage along trade routes.

In later years, relations between the Egyptian and Hittite rulers and their families grew cordial, as can be testified to by dozens of letters from Ramses II to Hattushili III and his wife. The pharaoh later married two Hittite princesses. The first of these marriages was celebrated in Damascus in Syria by huge retinues from each side.

BUILDING PROJECTS

Apart from the Syrian campaigns and a few successful forays into Nubia and Libya to suppress rebellions, the long reign of Ramses II was blessed with peace. Revenues that might have been diverted to war were invested in massive construction programs instead. About half of the ancient Egyptian temples that survive today date from this era.

Ramses's vast new temples, especially those in the region of Nubia to the south, served to intimidate the population and reinforce the prestige and power

Among the many monuments built during the reign of Ramses II was the temple of Abu Simbel in southern Egypt. In the 1960s, the temple was cut from its rock base and moved to higher ground to escape the waters of Lake Nasser, rising behind the Aswan Dam. The facade of the temple is dominated by four seated statues of Ramses.

of the state. But most of the construction also seems to have been designed to glorify the pharaoh, a goal that was, in fact, achieved. Later Greek writers, impressed with the colossal statues and overpowering battle panoramas created during the reign of Ramses II, called him "the Great," an epithet that is still attached to his name today.

The building projects of Ramses II served to revive the ancient colossal style of construction used in earlier periods of Egyptian history. Among the most impressive buildings were the huge temples of Karnak and Abu Simbel. At the temple of Amun in the city of Tanis, Ramses gathered a collection of statues from various periods and locations around Egypt, forming a "museum" of Egyptian art.

THE SUCCESSION
Ramses II fathered more than 150 children by his many wives and concubines. Because Ramses lived to

be at least eighty-five years old, many of his prospective heirs died before he did. The fact that he had so many children, and his very long reign, made for a long and difficult succession crisis after Ramses's death in 1212 B.C.E. His immediate successors were his son Merenptah (r. 1212–1202 B.C.E.) and Amenmesses (r. 1201–1199 B.C.E.), who may have been another of his sons.

See also: Egyptian Dynasties, Ancient (Eighteenth to Twenty-sixth); Hittite Empire; Seti I.

FURTHER READING
Grimal, Nicolas-Christophe. *A History of Ancient Egypt.* Trans. Ian Shaw. Oxford: Basil Blackwell, 1992.

Hornung, Erik. *History of Ancient Egypt: An Introduction.* Trans. David Lorton. Ithaca, NY: Cornell University Press, 1999.

Johnson, Paul. *The Civilization of Ancient Egypt*. Updated ed. New York: HarperCollins, 1999.

RANAVALONA I, MADA

(ca. 1788–1861 C.E.)

Queen of the Merina kingdom (r. 1828–1861), who is remembered for the ruthlessness with which she fought the incursion of European colonial interests into her realm on the island of Madagascar.

A member of the royal family of the powerful Merina kingdom, Ranavalona was born around 1788. She became queen of Merina upon her marriage to Radama I (r. 1810–1828), who inherited the throne from his father, Andrianampoinimerina (r. 1787–1810). King Andrianampoinimerina was considered the founder of the Merina kingdom, having reestablished it after years of fragmentation and powerlessness.

Initially, Ranavalona's queenly status was due solely to her royal marriage. But Radama never designated a successor, and when he died in 1828, Ranavalona assumed rulership in her own right. (An infant son born soon after Radama's death was too young to take the throne.)

Ranavalona's claim to the throne was contested, but she eliminated her opposition by ordering the execution of any and all rival claimants, thus ensuring her reign. At the same time, she demonstrated political skills by cultivating the support of key members of the Merina royal court and army. Through her skill and ruthlessness, Ranavalona quickly managed to establish herself as absolute ruler of Merina.

Ranavalona was deeply distrustful of European influences. Among her first acts as queen was to withdraw from alliances with the British, who had held the island of Madagascar as a protectorate. When Ranavalona imposed severe restrictions on trade, the British—along with the French—attempted to force her to reverse her decision by launching a naval attack against her kingdom.

Displaying the same ruthlessness that she had employed against rivals to the throne, Ravanalona responded to this European assault with brutal effectiveness. She ordered that the corpses of her subjects who had been killed in the attack be decapitated and their heads placed on spikes along the beaches. This grisly sight broke the resolve of the European attackers, and the bombardments ceased soon after.

Ranavalona was not merely distrustful of European politicians and soldiers. She also recognized that Christian missionaries, who had been welcomed by her husband, constituted a threat to Merina traditional life. She therefore forbade her subjects from converting to Christianity, and she actively persecuted those Christian missionaries who continued to work in her kingdom.

Ranavalona's contempt and distrust for Europeans reached its highest point in the late 1850s, when she learned of a conspiracy between one of her sons and the French government. This son, Rakoto, had promised the formation of a French protectorate in exchange for financial support and assistance in the industrial development of Madagascar.

Outraged by this agreement, Ranavalona intensified her persecution of Europeans throughout the Merina kingdom. She even resorted to the use of torture and summary execution to rid her kingdom of European nationals. Nonetheless, she named her errant son, Prince Rakoto, as her successor. However, upon her death in 1861, another son, Radama II (r. 1861–1863), who was strongly pro-French, took the throne.

See also: MADAGASCAR KINGDOMS; MERINA KINGDOM; RADAMA I; RADAMA II.

RASTRAKUTA DYNASTY

(ca. 755–975 C.E.)

Indian dynasty of the Deccan region of central India, which, at the height of the its power, constituted one of the most important Indian ruling dynasties. During the dynasty's rule, Rastrakuta armies defeated all of the other powers of India.

The Rastrakuta dynasty was founded around 755 by Dantidurga (r. ca. 738–758), a feudatory chieftain of much debated origins. Some scholars claim that Dantidurga came from Karnataka, the city of Mysore in the southern Deccan region. Others say he came from the region of Lattalura, near Osmanabad in south-central India. Still others claim that Dantidurga was a descendant of the Rathor dynasty of northern India, while others say that he came from a line of farmers from Andhra, an area south of the central Indian mountain ranges. Despite such debate, most scholars have agreed that Dantidurga was a local official, because the word "Rastrakuta," the name of the dynasty he founded, indicates a person who is head of a "rashtra" or district.

A succession of conquests eventually brought Dantidurga into battle with King Kirtivarman II (r. 746–757) of the Chalukya dynasty, whom he defeated in 752. As a result of this victory, Dantidurga ruled the whole of the Maharashtra, which included most of the south-central and western Indian plain known as the Deccan plateau region. At the time, the Deccan region was the largest political entity in India.

Dantidurga was succeeded on the Rastrakuta throne by Krishna I (r. 758–773), who continued the momentum of conquest and expansion begun by his predecessor. Krishna I crushed what was left of the Chalukya dynasty and then conquered Mysore, Southern Koukan, and other regions. A great builder, Krishna I commissioned construction of the magnificent temple of Siva at Ellora, which was built into solid rock.

Govinda II (r. 773–780), the successor to Krishna I, preferred a life of pleasure and debauchery to military conquest. A younger brother, Dhruva, looked after the administration until Govinda II attempted to have him removed. The brothers took up arms against each other. Dhruva won and ascended to the throne in 780.

Dhruva (r. 780–793) continued to battle in successful campaigns against all who opposed him, and he eventually became ruler of the whole of the Deccan plateau region. Still ambitious, he decided to take control of all of northern India. Every kingdom he challenged fell before Dhruva's powerful armies. When he finally reached the Ganges and the Jumna rivers, no other powers in India could stop him. He returned home from his great conquests with enormous wealth.

When Dhruva's successor, Govinda II (r. 793–814), came to the Rastrakuta throne in 793, his first task was to stop a revolt led by his older brother, Stambha. He then made Stambha governor of the region of Gangavadi. Govinda II repeated Dhruva's march to the north with equally successful results. He then returned to put down a rebellion by a confederacy of the Ganga, Kerala, Pandya, and Pallava dynasties.

Between the late 700s and early 900s, the Rastrakuta dynasty maintained much of its power in India. In the early 900s, Indra I (r. 914–922)

marched north and conquered the kingdom of Kanauj, making him the ruler of more kingdoms than any other ruler in the history of India. His successors won further military victories, but also experienced increasing military losses and, many times, bad administration.

In 975, Khottiga Amoghavarsa IV (r. 968–975) failed to protect his capital city, Manyaketa, and it was sacked and destroyed by the Chalukya dynasty of Kalyana. The Chalukya ruler, Taila I (r. 975–997), took the throne, marking the end of the Rastrakuta dynasty. Until the Maratha confederacy in the eighteenth century C.E., no other dynasty from the Deccan region had such a powerful effect on the history of India.

See also: INDIAN KINGDOMS; MARATHA CONFEDERACY; MYSORE KINGDOM; PANDYA DYNASTY.

REALMS, TYPES OF

Various types of political structures, or domains, ruled by a monarch or other sovereign, such as an emperor. Realms include political entities such as empires, kingdoms, principalities, duchies, counties, and city-states. These various types of realms can also have different types of governmental structure, ranging from rule by absolute monarchs to theocracies to constitutional monarchies.

CITY-STATES
In the ancient world, beginning in Mesopotamia, one of the earliest types of political realms was established—the city-state. The formation of the city-state was due, in part, to such factors as agricultural specialization, the resulting population growth, the consolidation of tribal groups, and difficulties in travel and communication.

The city-state remained an important form of government in different parts of the world for many centuries. In Renaissance Italy, for example, city-states played an important role in the later development of the nation-state in Western Europe.

Most ancient city-states were ruled by monarchs, although some, such as the city-state of Athens in ancient Greece, saw the development of democracy. Overlords occasionally might rule more than one city-state, but by and large, the earliest were ruled independently.

IMPERIAL REALMS OF THE ANCIENT WORLD

Little is known about Sargon (r. ca. 2334–2279 B.C.E.), Mesopotamia's first known ruler. Thought to have founded the city-state of Akkad, Sargon used military conquest to greatly extend his realm, eventually establishing a great empire, called Sumeria, that included all of Mesopotamia and extended over Syria and other parts of the ancient Near East.

Empires, or imperial realms, continued to play a major role in world history for the next 4,000 years. Imperial realms varied a great deal in their organization and administration, depending on the particular emperor and the political, social, and cultural milieu in which the empire was formed. In organizing his ancient empire, Sargon of Akkad apparently left native rulers in place, even as he installed officials to represent him in the various regions he conquered. In this, he differed from the rulers of the ancient Egyptian and Persian empires, who appointed representatives to rule directly.

By about 1800 B.C.E., the dominance of Sargon's empire had faded, and a people known as the Amorites controlled much of Mesopotamia. They established their capital at Babylon, which eventually became the center of another great empire. Whereas Sumeria had allowed its subject states to be independent, the Amorite government was centralized and enjoyed far more power, including taxation and involuntary military service. The Hittites, who established an empire centered in Anatolia (present-day Turkey) that flourished from 1600 to 1200 B.C.E, further extended imperial power by making the king the owner of nearly all the property under his control and allowing only the military the right to control land.

One of the most important empires of the ancient Near East was that of Persia. Under Emperor Cyrus the Great (r. 559–530 B.C.E.), the Persian Empire was divided into twenty-one *satrapies,* or provinces, each ruled by a governor (satrap) who kept his capital under protection of a garrison. Each satrapy owed the king a certain amount of tribute, paid in gold and silver.

MEDIEVAL REALMS

A number of realms still seen today, such as duchies, date back to the medieval era. A duke would have recognized the overlordship of another lord, such as an earl, yet retained power of his own. Often, such a duke or earl might be the real power in a kingdom.

In fourteenth-century England, for example, during the minority of Richard II (r. 1377–1399), John of Gaunt, the duke of Lancaster, was the most powerful man in England.

Another type of medieval realm was the earldom, whose ruler was an earl. In medieval Scotland in the ninth century, the earldom of Orkney was part of a powerful Viking kingdom. In 1468, it was given to James III of Scotland (r. 1460–1488) by Christian I of Denmark (r. 1448–1481) as part of his daughter's dowry. Such transfers of property and realms were frequent in the Middle Ages. When realms changed hands, the populace would have to transfer their loyalty to the new overlord.

A few such realms, such the grand duchy of Luxembourg and the principality of Monaco, still exist and have remained independent. Until 1911, Monaco was an absolute monarchy, governed by a ruler who had absolute power. It then became a constitutional monarchy, in which the monarch's power is based on a body of laws. Currently, the prince of Monaco shares executive power with a minister of state and a council of government.

NATION-STATES

By the time of the Renaissance, some European rulers were powerful monarchs who had acquired complete control over their realms. This period saw the development of absolute monarchy, in which the ruler imposed total control over his or her country. England, France, and Spain all developed into powerful nation-states during this period. Many of these countries have today become figurehead monarchies, in which the monarch represents the country more as a symbol and performs ceremonial duties. In Great Britain, for example, Queen Elizabeth I (r. 1952–) presides over the opening of Parliament every year, but she has no say in its decisions. Today, figurehead monarchy is found in much of Western Europe as well as Japan.

See also: DYNASTY; EMPIRE; IMPERIAL RULE; KINGDOMS AND EMPIRES; REALMS, TYPES OF; ROYAL FAMILIES; TRIBUTE.

REBELLION

Means by which subjects oppose or limit the rule of a king.

The right of a monarch to rule absolutely was

rarely questioned in ancient cultures, although in democratic Athens, the great philosopher Aristotle suggested that citizens might be justified in rebelling in some circumstances. Early Christian texts also accepted the power of the king to rule.

Throughout the early medieval era, however, absolute monarchy, as practiced later in the eighteenth century, was not, politically or economically, an option. A king was to be obeyed in all matters—but it was to be assumed that the king would rule according to the law. In addition, Germanic custom assumed the king's will to be that of the people, and by the eleventh century, the first legislative bodies, usually representative of the nobility, were involved in advising the kings and even in choosing them. In England this body, known as the Witenagemot, elected Harold II (r. 1066) king in 1066 when Edward the Confessor (r. 1042–1066) died childless. A king was not required, automatically, to follow the decisions of the legislative body, but he was expected to follow custom and to consider the legislature's advice.

According to the medieval theologian, St. Thomas Aquinas, a group of people had the right to provide themselves with a king, so as to ensure order. It followed, therefore, that the same group of people had the right to depose the monarch if the monarch exercised tyranny. Aquinas defined a tyrant as one who makes a law that is contrary to God's law, and in such a case, Aquinas maintained, one is not bound to obey. In extreme situations, such as with the Roman emperor Domitian (r. 81–96), one might even justify tyrannicide, to rid the kingdom of a tyrannical ruler.

One of the most important early instances of rebellion against a monarch was the Magna Carta, or Great Charter, signed by John I of England (r. 1199–1216) in 1215. John imposed excessive taxation to finance his unsuccessful wars in France and ruthlessly penalized those who could not or would not pay. He arbitrarily imprisoned his opponents and seized lands belonging to church and nobleman alike. In 1215, a group of barons rebelled against him and seized London. On June 15, they gathered at Runnymede, a meadow outside London, and forced him to agree to their concessions, signing what became known as the Magna Carta.

The Magna Carta did not, as is sometimes assumed, create constitutional monarchy, but it was the first document that placed written limitations on a king's power. The most important of these limitations perhaps was the power it gave Parliament over the monarchy's spending, a right that proved particularly important in the seventeenth-century conflict between Parliament and the Stuart kings. Moreover, although many of the protections it provided were the feudal rights of the barons, it could also be assumed that the financial benefits it provided would be passed down to their subordinates.

Another example of opposition to a monarchy is usurpation, in which one nobleman, or prince, takes over the throne, in many cases killing the monarch as well. Such was the case with Richard II of England (r. 1377–1399), who had exiled Henry, earl of Bolingbroke, in 1398. When Henry's father, John of Gaunt, died in 1399, Richard made the mistake of seizing the Lancaster lands. Henry returned to claim his inheritance, and on his way to London, he gained a large number of supporters. Richard II, an unpopular figure whose policies were seen as tyrannical, was deposed, and Henry of Bolingbroke claimed the Crown as Henry IV (r. 1399–1413). In 1400, Richard II was murdered in Pontefract Castle.

In 1689, in the so-called Glorious Revolution, James II fled and was replaced by William III (r. 1689–1702) and Mary II (r. 1689–1695), who accepted the throne only after consenting to a list of conditions known as the Declaration of Right. This declaration is mostly known for its exclusion of all Catholics from the English throne. However, its other immediate restrictions on the monarchy were more important. The declaration denied the king's ability to dispense with or suspend laws that Parliament had passed as well as his ability to dissolve the Parliament once elected or to prosecute, in the King's Court, matters that were in Parliament's jurisdiction. These restrictions were important in limiting the powers of the king, and it is here, with the Declaration, that we see the real beginnings of a constitutional monarchy. Thus, a bloodless revolution had been effected, a new monarch brought to the throne, and the powers of the monarch strongly restricted.

See also: ABDICATION, ROYAL; DEACCESSION; DETHRONEMENT; ELECTION, ROYAL; JAMES II; JOHN I; KINGDOMS AND EMPIRES; LEGITIMACY; REGICIDE; TYRANNY, ROYAL.

FURTHER READING

Ashley, Maurice. *Great Britain to 1688.* Ed. Allan Nevins and Howard M. Ehrmann. Ann Arbor: University of Michigan Press, 1961.

"The Declaration of Right." (February 1689). In J. H. Robinson, ed. *Readings in European History*. Boston: Ginn, 1906.

RECCARED I (d. 601 C.E.)

King of the Visigothic kingdom of Spain from 586 to 601, whose conversion to Roman Catholicism brought the Visigoths closer to the other Christian kingdoms of early medieval Europe.

The son and successor of King Leovigild (r. 568–586), Reccared took the throne upon the death of his father. Unlike Leovigild, who pursued a policy of conquest, Reccared followed a much less aggressive foreign policy. Although he fought against the Basque peoples in northern Iberia and repelled several invasions by the Franks, he made peace with the Byzantine Empire and worked to improve relations with the Roman peoples who had occupied the Iberian Peninsula for centuries before the Visigoths.

Reccared's most significant accomplishment concerned religion. The Visigothic kings before Reccared, including Leovigild, had been Arian Christians since around the fourth century. Arian Christians denied the Catholic doctrine of the Trinity, claiming that Christ, the Son, was inferior to God, the Father. In 587, Reccared personally converted to the Roman form of Catholicism, and he extended this conversion to his kingdom at the Third Council of Toledo in 589. At this council, Reccared, his family, and other leaders of the kingdom formally renounced Arianism before the Catholic bishops of Iberia. The new regime became intolerant of Arians, and Reccared crushed a series of rebellions led by Arian clergy and believers.

The Council of Toledo marked the beginning of a close alliance between the Visigothic monarchs and the Catholic bishops that would extend beyond Reccared's own reign. Reccared adopted the religious rite of anointment and, like many kings of the time who were allies and benefactors of the Roman Church, he was hailed as a new Constantine (referring to the Roman emperor who established Christianity as the state religion of the Roman Empire). Upon Reccared's death in 601, he was succeeded on the Visigothic throne by his son, Liuva II (r. 601–603).

See also: CHRISTIANITY AND KINGSHIP; CONSTANTINE I, THE GREAT; VISIGOTH KINGDOM.

REGALIA AND INSIGNIA, ROYAL

The signs and symbols that identify a queen or king. Regalia are items that are worn or carried by the monarch, whereas insignia may be worn by or used by a monarch's subjects to indicate loyalty or connection.

In some kingdoms, regalia unique to the Crown are given to the monarch at the coronation ceremony. Regalia can include crowns, rings, seals, swords, banners, shields, and scepters. In medieval France, a crimson banner accompanied kings in battle. Use of the objects was central to the bestowing of royal power, and the symbolic nature of the royal objects was clearly understood by all. Royal ceremonies have a common purpose—to inspire and impress all who witness them—and regalia are an important part of their effect.

In the Western world, crowns have been the essential element of a monarch's regalia. They are often covered with precious stones and made of gold. In France, beginning in medieval times, coronation ceremonies could involve the use of several crowns. The archbishop conducting the ceremony would place the "official" crown—the crown associated with the office of monarch—on the head of the king or queen. Later in the rite, it would be replaced by the individual's personal crown. By the sixteenth century, the coronation ceremony had come to include yet another crown, after the official crown but before the personal one. Monarchs also had personal crowns that they specifically wore for certain occasions, such as for funerals.

In Russia during the coronation of a new tsar, the royal ceremonial objects were brought from the Winter Palace in St. Petersburg to the Moscow Armory, which served as the state treasury from the beginning of the eighteenth century. The ancient crown of the Russian tsars, the Cap of Monomach, was made in Central Asia in the thirteenth or fourteenth century. It is a gold dome topped with a knob and a cross, and is trimmed with a thick band of sable fur. This crown was replaced by a more Western-style crown in the late seventeenth century. Until 1762, a new crown was made for each monarch, but the elaborate diamond-encrusted creation designed for Catherine the Great (r. 1762–1796) by a well-known St. Petersburg jeweler was subsequently used for all succeeding monarchs, including the last tsar of the Romanov dynasty, Nicholas II (r. 1894–1917).

All monarchies have crowns and other regalia that serve as symbols of royal power and authority. The coronation regalia of Emperor Rudolph II of Austria, who ruled the Holy Roman Empire from 1576 to 1612, include a jeweled crown, an orb, and a scepter.

SEATS AND THRONES

A dramatic way to distinguish monarchs from the people around them was to give them special chairs to sit on. In some cultures these were thrones; in others, stools. The Asante people of Ghana have an elaborate tradition of decorated stools. The various designs have symbolic meanings, and some are reserved for particular kinds of people. Each clan of the Asante has its own king, who has his own stool design; several designs are reserved for the exclusive use of the Asantehene, the leader of all the kings, including the elephant stool, which symbolizes his strength, and the leopard stool, which symbolizes his power and influence.

The kings of Scotland had a special stool for use in coronation ceremonies: the Stone of Scone, or the Stone of Destiny. It was a rough-hewn block of granite, nothing special to look at, but legend had it that it was the very rock that the biblical Jacob had used as a pillow in the story told in Genesis, and that it had magical powers. It is unclear how many centuries the Stone of Scone had been used by the Scottish kings, but the last time was in 1292. When Edward I of England invaded Scotland in 1296, he stole the Stone, probably because it was an important symbol of the power of the Scottish kings. In 1301, he had a special coronation throne built with a space under the seat to house the Stone, and it was housed in Westminster

THE THAI CORONATION CEREMONY

Royal ceremonies have a common purpose—to inspire and impress all who witness them—and regalia are an important part of their effect. The symbolic nature of the royal objects is understood by all. The regalia used in the Thai coronation ceremony consist of five elements. The crown is made of gold, set with diamonds and enameled in red and green. It is in a distinctive Thai design with a tapering spire, and is 66 cm. high. The sword has a gold, jeweled hilt and scabbard, and symbolizes the king's duty to protect his people. The royal staff, made of cassia wood enclosed at the ends in gold, symbolizes the guiding of the king's steps on the path of justice. The royal fan and flywhisk represent the warding off of maleficent influences; the flywhisk is made from the tail of an albino elephant. There are also royal slippers, with upcurved toes, made completely of gold and lined in red velvet.

Abbey in London. English monarchs were seated in that throne for coronation for almost seven hundred years. It was not until 1996 that, under pressure from Scottish nationalists, the Stone was returned to Scotland. It now rests in Edinburgh Castle, along with the crown jewels of the Scottish throne.

See also: ACCESSION AND CROWNING OF KINGS; ENTHRONEMENT, RITES OF.

REGENCIES

Government in which the ruling monarch is deemed incompetent by virtue of youth, illness, or other special circumstance, and thus not legally qualified to govern. The usual situation involves a child, and the state is then ruled by one or more high-ranking members of the aristocracy, called regents, who stand in as ruler and make the government's decisions.

Regencies are particularly prone to strife and corruption as different nobles contend for power. During the fifteenth century, for example, Scotland under the Stewarts repeatedly had minority kings, beginning with James I (r. 1406–1437). Although the dynasty survived for 300 years, the country was weakened by quarrelsome nobility and the repeated threat of English invasion during the regencies of these monarchs.

"Cursed be the land that is ruled by a child!" was a common saying of the Middle Ages. American political theorist, Thomas Paine, in his book *The Rights of Man,* cites regencies and child kings as among his reasons for favoring democracy over monarchy: "A regency is a mock species of republic, and the whole of monarchy deserves no better description."

From earliest times through the late Middle Ages, a monarch was expected to have military as well as administrative aptitude. Therefore, a realm that was ruled by a regent often suffered militarily, as did England under Henry VI (r. 1422–1461, 1470–1471), when it lost the territories that Henry V (r. 1413–1422) had gained.

Some regents, either through circumstance or through skill, were able to regain power repeatedly. Catherine de Medici was regent for her husband, Henry II of France (r. 1547–1559), while he was campaigning at Metz, again during the minority of her eldest son, Francis II (r. 1559–1560), and a third time during the minority of her second son, Charles IX of France (r. 1560–1574).

Some regents were powerful and controlled their governments all too well. For example, the Chinese empress, Tz'u Hsi (1835–1908), was originally concubine to the emperor Hsien Feng (r. 1850–1861). She became regent for her young son, Tung Chih (Tongzhi) (r. 1861–1875), after Hsien Feng's death in 1861. Together with the dowager empress Tzu An, and with the help of Prince Kung, the emperor's brother, she seized control of the state and eliminated those who had opposed their regency, retaining power even after her son came of age.

Perhaps the most famous regency is that of King George III of England (1738–1820). George IV (1762–1830) was appointed regent for his father, George III, who suffered from porphyria, an illness with symptoms resembling madness. The last ten years of George III's reign is known as the Regency Era; architecture and fashions of the time were named for the period. During this time, England's government had evolved toward parliamentary democracy; however, final passage of parliamentary decisions still depended on the king's approval, and the monarchy still had a good deal of power.

See also: EMPERORS AND EMPRESSES; EMPIRE; IMPERIAL RULE; KINGDOMS AND EMPIRES; KINGS AND QUEENS; REALMS, TYPES OF; REGENCIES; ROYAL FAMILIES.

REGICIDE

Act of killing a king or the one who commits such an act; in English history, the name given to judges who ordered the execution of Charles I (r. 1625–1649).

Regicide is closely bound up with the idea of divine kingship, for it implies that to kill a king is to commit an offense somehow different from the killing of any other man. Equally, the term implies that the killing of a king is in some qualitative way distinct from any other political murder, for which the term *assassination* would be sufficient. Like *matricide* and *patricide*, the term used to denote the killing of a king marks its subject as something acutely troubling and particularly heinous.

According to the ideology of monarchical divinity accepted in many cultures, it would seem that a divine king could not be killed. He is, after all, not just godlike but in fact a god himself. An attempt to murder the king would seem as unthinkable as the attempt to assail God. Yet rulers throughout history have been killed with alarming frequency by their subjects, their court, or their own kin.

RITUAL REGICIDE
Noted anthropologist Sir James Frazer (*The Golden Bough*, 1940) has argued that regicide is a necessary adjunct to the concept of the divinity of the king. Although the king might proclaim himself the incarnation of God on earth, he cannot escape mortality. A king's stirring death on the battlefield could be celebrated, yet the same could not be said of a death in which the king lingered, ever-weakening or, worse, lost his wits. To avoid something so unthinkable, it could become necessary that the king be killed, clearing the way for a successor who could assume the divine status of the office.

The origins of the eight Ovambo kingdoms in modern Namibia are not clear, although myths trace the descent of their kings to ancient gods. By the time Europeans arrived in the Ovambo region in the mid-1800s, the traditions of matrilineal kingship were firmly established. When the ruling monarch was dying, elders and the queen deliberated to choose a new king from among the queen's relatives. The king-elect then had to undergo a series of tests to prove his fitness to rule, including killing his predecessor. When he accepted the throne, the king knew that he, too, would one day be killed by his successor.

THE POLITICS OF REGICIDE
In practice, ritual regicide is rare in the extreme. Rather than an act to perpetuate the idea of the god-king, regicide is nearly universally the ultimate in ambitious duplicity. Killing a king is done to clear the way for a new king to assume the throne and is more often than not done while the target of the killing is still quite intent on continuing to rule. A variation of regicide involves the killing of alternative heirs to the throne. In cultures that adhere to the concept of a divine king, the possession of the proper pedigree is enough to make one a potential claimant to the throne. In such societies, it is not uncommon that when there are several equally qualified claimants, the one who eventually emerges does so only after others have been eliminated by murder.

For example, when England's Edward IV (r. 1461–1483) died suddenly, his twelve-year-old son Edward should have inherited the throne. However, the young Edward, along with his younger brother Richard, quietly disappeared while the former king's brother, Richard of Gloucester (Richard III, r. 1483–1485), stepped forward to claim the kingdom.

REGICIDE AND THE GOOD OF THE PEOPLE
One aspect of the divine king is that he is fundamentally responsible for the well-being of his people, for

their fertility, for the bountiful harvest of their crops, and for their security. The divine king is able to provide these services through his special connection with God, because he enjoys the goodwill of a chain of ancestors that stretch directly from him to the divinity. How, then, can it be that, sometimes, the rains fail to come, the crops die on the vine, or the people suffer from the attacks of their neighbors? Clearly, God or the gods do not show him favor. Within the closed, circular logic of divine kingship, this can only be explained by asserting that this king is not the rightful ruler after all, for his incapacity must mean that his divinity has deserted him. At least, this is how those who would use the situation to install another ruler would justify such a king's assassination. No longer deserving of the office, he can—indeed, he must—be separated from it. Regicide in this sense is proclaimed as a therapeutic act designed to restore the body politic to health. A similar, if post-facto, rationalization can be made for the violent overthrow of a king by an ambitious usurper. If the king were truly fit to rule, he would survive any attempts to seize his office.

It is this circular reasoning that makes the idea of regicide so extraordinary. To kill a king is to strike not only at a ruler (and at God, in the case of divine kingship), but also at the very fabric of society, for which the king is the ultimate unifying symbol. Yet, to kill the king has been seen as the ultimate act of sacrifice when the king is perceived as being a danger to the society for which he is responsible. Therefore, simply by committing the act, the regicide puts himself beyond the bounds of society, becoming its most dangerous transgressor, even when he is also its savior.

EUROPE'S REGICIDES: THE DEATHS OF CHARLES I AND LOUIS XVI

The two most well-known regicides in European history are those of Charles I of England and Louis XVI of France. The first was performed at the order of the state, after a lengthy public trial, and culminated in the beheading of the king at Whitehall in 1649. The second arose from the winds of revolution, and the guillotining of Louis XVI marked not only the end of the person of the king, but of the institution of the French monarchy itself.

The reign of Charles I (1625–1649) was a time of great social upheaval, involving controversies in religion, internal political conflicts, and ultimately civil war. Charles attempted to deal with these problems autocratically, most notably by dissolving Parliament for long stretches of time and turning a deaf ear to the powerful contingents among his noble classes. His behavior became intolerable, and he was ultimately called to answer for his abuses of power in the court. But this was in direct contradiction to his belief in his divine right to rule. Charles's trial was marked by his initial refusal to acknowledge the court's right to try him. As king, he was above the jurisdiction of human courts. When it became clear that the court meant to sentence him to death, he sought to defend himself, but was caught in the contradiction inherent in his position. As king, he had asserted himself beyond the reach of the court. Thus, he had no right to a voice within the court. In executing Charles I, the regicides were killing not only the man, but also the particular approach to kingship that this man had come to represent.

Louis XVI (r. 1774–1792) was in a similar position in France. His rule, and the institution of the monarchy in general, was no longer acceptable to the French. With the rise of Republicanism in France, there was no safe place for a ruler, even if deposed. Were he allowed to live, he would provide a symbol around which those who wished for the return of the monarchy might rally. In his execution, the killing of the man was almost inconsequential, for what was being killed was the monarchy itself.

MODERN REGICIDE: RUSSIA AND NEPAL

In early twentieth-century Russia, revolutionary fervor brought down the House of Romanov. Here the regicide was breathtakingly complete, for not only was the reigning tsar Nicholas II (r. 1894–1917) killed, but his entire family, including the young heir to the throne, was also slaughtered. The rule of the tsars could just as easily have been ended by exiling the royal family, but it was not just the rule of a particular king that was being destroyed. The institution of monarchy itself was being killed, and the tsar, as both current ruler and symbol of all monarchic rule stood for, could not be allowed an ambiguous end.

A more recent example of regicide resulted in death for most of the royal family of Nepal. In 2001, King Birenda (r. 1972–2001); his wife Queen Aiswarya; their daughter, Princess Shruti; and another son, Prince Nirajan were all shot to death by Crown Prince Dipendra. Dipendra then also killed himself. This regicide was not for the good of the country, nor was it to gain the throne since the regicide himself was next in the line of succession. The killings and suicide resulted from a disagreement in the royal family about Dipendra's choice of bride.

LITERARY REGICIDE

For centuries, writers have made much of regicide. Sophocles wrote of Oedipus who unwittingly committed both regicide and patricide and then became king in his father's place. Shakespeare's *Macbeth, Hamlet*, and *Julius Caesar* all deal with the killings of rulers. These stories, whether fiction or fact, capture the imagination because the act of regicide is a crime not only against a man, but also against society, against the divine ruler, and in some cases, against God himself.

See also: CHARLES I; DIVINITY OF KINGS; LOUIS XVI; ROMANOV DYNASTY.

FURTHER READING

Frazer, Sir James George. *The Golden Bough: A Study in Magic and Religion.* Abridged ed. Mineola, NY: Dover Publications, 2002.

Poole, Steven. *The Politics of Regicide in England, 1760–1850: Troublesome Subjects.* Manchester: Manchester University Press, 2001.

Walzer, Michael, ed. *Regicide and Revolution: Speeches at the Trial of Louis XVI.* Trans. Marian Rothstein. New York: Columbia University Press, 1992.

REIGNS, LENGTH OF

Period of time that a monarch rules a realm. The number of years a monarch rules can affect the country in several ways—political, economic, and social. A long reign usually has a stabilizing effect on a country, while a short reign can create much turmoil, especially when several successive monarchs rule for short periods of time.

EFFECTS OF A LONG REIGN

A long reign, such as that of Elizabeth I of England (r. 1558–1603), can produce a stabilizing effect on a realm, for several reasons. In the case of Elizabeth I, she became a symbol of England, and she encouraged this symbolism with the image of a Virgin Queen. She also came to the throne during a period of religious upheaval, with England alternating between

Catholic and Protestant rulers. Initially, Elizabeth created more upheaval by changing the religion again, from Catholic to Protestant, but the length of her reign ensured the acceptance of the idea that England was a Protestant country.

One of Elizabeth's most important reforms was the complete recoinage of the currency. Elizabeth had inherited the economic problems, particularly inflation, that her father, Henry VIII (r. 1509–1547), had created by debasing the currency. Early in her reign, in 1560–1561, Elizabeth had the debased currency melted down and recast to slow inflation. Although she still had to cope with poor harvests and increased population, causing new inflation, her restoration of the currency meant renewed faith in the English economy as merchants in foreign countries no longer insisted on gold bullion in dealings with England.

Because a long reign can produce stability, it frequently produces a golden age of great literature, music, or art. For example, the Elizabethan era gave rise not only to the great Elizabethan playwrights, such as William Shakespeare and Christopher Marlowe, but also the music of William Byrd, the Renaissance composer, who became known as "The Father of English Music."

As rulers age, however, corruption and moral decay may set in; older rulers sometimes heed bad advice from friends, as did the Chinese emperor Xuanzong (r. 712–755). Xuanzong was an able emperor who reformed the T'ang bureaucracy and built roads; his reign saw the T'ang dynasty's greatest painting and poetry. But in his later years he became infatuated with his favorite concubine, Yang Guifei, and neglectful of his duties. Yang Guifei acquired too much power, naming her favorites as government officials. Among her favorites was the general An Lushan who rebelled against the emperor in 755. Consequently, Xuanzong's troops forced him to have Yang Guifei executed, and Xuanzong was compelled to abdicate.

A long-term ruler may fail in yet another respect: he or she may create hardships for the country by failing to see a need for technological, political, or economic reform. For example, the dowager empress Cixi (r. 1861–1908), by refusing to Westernize, created severe difficulties for China in the aftermath of her death. At a time when other governments, Eastern and Western, were becoming constitutional monarchies, Cixi maintained absolutist rule over China. She used the Boxers—secret anti-Western societies who opposed industrialization and modernization—to attack Westerners in 1898 in an uprising known as the Boxer Rebellion. Consequently, Western forces invaded Beijing and imposed reparations. At last, Cixi recognized the need for some reforms, but it was too little, too late.

EFFECTS OF A SHORT REIGN

In the case of a short-reigning monarch, the heir to the throne may be an infant, with the government consequently weakened by rule by a regent. In other cases, there will be no heir at all, which may lead to internal strife, and possibly civil war, as rival claimants to the throne struggle for power.

Embodying such problems was Henry V of England (r. 1413–1422), who in his nine years as king, both through military and diplomatic policy, tried to reestablish English superiority over France. Henry V died young, leaving an infant son, Henry VI (r. 1422–1461 and 1470–1471), too young to rule, and his regents opposed one another. These problems, combined with French victories over the English during the Hundred Years' War, weakened England's hold on France. By 1453, England held only Calais.

Similarly, a new ruler faces challenges if he or she tries to institute reforms. Changes are often resisted, and a ruler who reigns for a few years may not succeed in instituting new policies. Edward VI of England (r. 1547–1553), for example, ruled for only six years, and his reign had few long-term consequences. The policies of his regents were short-lived. His first regent, Edward Seymour, duke of Somerset, was concerned with the plight of the poor, but the revolt of the gentry and the collapse of his regency ensured that his reforms would be short-lived. Seymour was replaced by John Dudley, earl of Warwick, who made himself duke of Northumberland in 1551. Dudley controlled England for only four years. Although he went to great lengths to ingratiate himself with Edward, after Edward's death, Mary I (r. 1553–1558) overturned the Protestant policies he pursued.

At the same time, a short reign does not mean that a ruler will have no influence at all. Alexander III the Great (336–323 B.C.E.) ruled for only about twelve years, yet his conquests included all of Asia Minor, and he helped spread Greek culture as far as India. He also established new coinage to help trade. Because of Alexander's conquests, Greek became the common language and the common culture throughout much of Asia Minor.

See also: ALEXANDER III, THE GREAT; ELIZABETH I; EMPERORS AND EMPRESSES; IMPERIAL RULE; LEGITIMACY; REGENCIES; VICTORIA.

RELIGIOUS DUTIES AND POWERS

The responsibilities derived from religious beliefs that are required of a ruler.

Religious beliefs, practices, and ethical values often establish the kind of leadership and social institutions that make up a society. Moreover, a ruler often appoints the priests, or makes the decisions, for a society. During the Reformation in Europe, for example, monarchs—whether Catholic or Protestant—determined whether the state church of the country would be Catholic or Protestant. They also determined whether bishops or other church leaders were sufficiently orthodox, and they often found better choices with which to replace them.

Such religious duties have always been an essential part of kingship, but the rest of the population has had religious duties as well. In Islamic societies, all believers are expected to perform the *hajj,* or pilgrimage to Mecca. Similarly, all Muslim males are expected to pray five times a day facing Mecca. In earlier Catholic practices, religious duties would have included participating in the Lenten fast and abstaining from meat on Fridays. Although these devotions were demanded of everyone, a ruler who ignored such practices risked the loss of his authority with his subjects.

Religion also influences its adherents by giving them a sense of identity. People have fought wars to maintain their distinctiveness as defined by their religion—as in, for example, the Jewish war and resistance against Greco-Syrian influence on Judaism (168 B.C.E.), which came to be known as the Maccabean revolt, and the wars on religion in France in the 1500s and 1600s.

Religious power is sometimes merged with the political power of the leader of a tribe or kingdom. According to the biblical narrative, for example, Israel's first king, Saul (r. 1020–1010 B.C.E.), was chosen by name by God as was his successor, King David

(1010–970 B.C.E.). David's son, Solomon (970–931 B.C.E.), was rejected as Israel's king because of his sins, and Jeroboam (r. 931–910 B.C.E.) was ordained by God to be his successor. Because Jeroboam's kingship came from God and not man, it could not be challenged when he proved an ineffective ruler.

Muhammad, the founder of Islam, became a negotiator for the people of Medina and later rose to become the chief of their clan (r. 620–632 C.E.), due partly to their belief that he was a prophet of Allah. His victory over the Meccans in 624 was seen as God's vindication of his prophet. Those who converted to Islam shared in the administration of the growing Islamic state.

In the native Japanese religion, Shinto, the sun-goddess Amaterasu, a principal *kami* or sacred spirit, is credited with establishing the country's imperial line by sending her grandson, Ninigi, to rule Japan. Japan's subsequent rulers thus had an imperial authority that was divine in origin.

The sacred writings of a religion can also influence the governing of a nation. For ancient Israel, the Torah—the five books of Moses—provided the moral foundation on which government was based, in addition to setting a guide for everyday life. According to the Torah, the one chosen to be king was to write for himself a copy of the book of the Law (or Torah) and to keep it with him day and night. The prosperity of his reign and of the nation was linked to his obedience or disobedience to divine law as well as that of the people. Similarly, Muslim fundamentalists believe that all of Muslim life, including the political, is to be governed by the Qur'an, the sacred scripture of Islam.

In the same way as the Roman Empire fragmented and Christianity became the unifying force throughout Europe, a monarch's standing depended on the Church. Following his excommunication in 1077, the Holy Roman emperor Henry IV (r. 1056–1106) faced the threat of being deposed. To regain the Church's good favor, he stood barefoot in the snow for three days.

But a monarch was not without some control over the Church. On his second excommunication in 1080, Henry IV forced Pope Gregory VII into exile and elected Wilbert of Ravenna as Pope Clement III. Overall, however, the threats of excommunication and interdiction—banning all royal subjects from mass and the sacraments—became powerful forces for bringing a king back to the fold. Nevertheless, a

king was assumed to derive power from God. Although some theologians, including Saint Thomas Aquinas, acknowledged the right to disobey a monarch whose laws were contrary to those of God, the righteous monarch could expect absolute obedience from his subjects.

With the growth of Protestantism in the sixteenth century, the monarch no longer needed the Church's approval. On the other hand, the monarch was expected to defend his church and establish laws for its protection. Increasingly, a church's power became indistinguishable from that of the monarch's, as in Spain, where Ferdinand II of Aragón (r. 1479–1516) and Isabella I of Castile (r. 1474–1504) drove out the non-Christian population and strengthened the power of the Inquisition.

The concept of divine right was, in fact, a medieval one. But the upheavals of the Reformation and the Thirty Years' War (1618–1648) convinced people that a strong government was needed to protect society, and the doctrine of divine right was embraced in the seventeenth century. James I of England (r. 1603–1625) developed the theory in his writings; in his work *On the Divine Right of Kings,* he compared sedition to blasphemy.

With the coming of the Enlightenment in the eighteenth century, people questioned the doctrine of divine right. The Wars of Religion in Germany and France, and the religious persecutions of the era, made people question the monarch's right to establish the country's religion. Increasingly, the idea of government as a social contract, developed by French philosopher Jean Jacques Rousseau in the mid-1700s, became favored. Throughout Europe in the nineteenth century, the monarch's authority in all areas, including religion, went into decline.

See also: BUDDHISM AND KINGSHIP; CHRISTIANITY AND KINGSHIP; HINDUISM AND KINGSHIP; ISLAM AND KINGSHIP; JUDAISM AND KINGSHIP.

RICHARD I, LIONHEART

(1157–1199 C.E.)

Successor of Henry II (r. 1154–1189) as king of England (r. 1189–1199), duke of Normandy and Aquitaine, and count of Anjou. An accomplished soldier, Richard I fought the Muslim leader Saladin (r.

1175–1193) in Palestine on the Third Crusade, Philip II (r. 1180–1223) in France, his father and brothers at various times in England and France, and the local aristocracies of Cyprus and Sicily.

As son of Eleanor of Aquitaine and Henry II of England, Richard grew up in the shadow of his parents and in the contentious environment of his three ambitious brothers—Henry, Geoffrey, and John. As his mother's favorite, he was made duke of the wealthy and powerful duchy of Aquitaine at age eleven. This honor was followed by the patrimonies of Gascony and Poitiers in 1172.

Richard's first political moves were made under the direction of his mother and ended in an unsuccessful revolt in 1173–1174 against his father, who then pardoned him and his brothers. He subsequently directed his attention to his province of Gascony in France, which, aided by his brothers Henry and Geoffrey, eventually revolted against Richard's harsh feudal rule in 1183. Richard's father, however, moved to assist him. During these struggles, Richard's elder brother, Henry, died suddenly and the uprising collapsed. Henry's death also made Richard heir to the English throne.

Unwilling to wait for the Crown, and having learned guile from his previous rebellion, Richard submitted himself as a vassal to the young French king, Philip II, and together they attacked Henry II in

King Richard I of England was known for his chivalry, courage, and prowess in battle. He spent most of his reign fighting abroad and is especially remembered for his exploits fighting the Muslims in the Holy Land during the Third Crusade.

1189. Always a force to be reckoned with on the battlefield, Richard was successful in this war against his own father. The broken-hearted Henry II died shortly after signing a treaty ending the war, and Richard became king in 1189.

Soon after his coronation, Richard denied his pledge of vassalage to King Philip. War would have ensued, but both men took the cross and proceeded toward the Holy Land on the Third Crusade. On his way to Palestine, Richard became enmeshed in a complex affair in Sicily that involved his sister Joan, his nephew Arthur, Henry VI (r. 1190–1197) of Germany, and the Sicilian prince Tancred. Richard recovered his sister's dowry, declared Tancred king of Sicily and Arthur as Tancred's heir, and—having snubbed Henry VI's claims—angered the Germans. In a final stop before reaching Palestine, Richard conquered Cyprus, where he met and married Berengaria of Navarre in 1191.

When Richard landed in the Holy Land in 1191, he participated in the capture of Acre and Jaffa, but failed in two attempts to take Jerusalem because of victories by the brilliant Islamic leader, Saladin. Richard was thus unable to achieve the fundamental purpose of the Third Crusade, the taking of the Holy City of Jerusalem. Richard stayed in Palestine for a year, eventually signing a three-year truce with Saladin that ensured all Christian pilgrims safe passage to the holy sites of Palestine. During the struggles in the Holy Land, Richard angered Duke Leopold V of Austria and his sometime ally, Philip II of France. Philip left the Holy Land after only a few months and returned to Europe, where he plotted against Richard with Richard's regent and brother, John.

Forced on his return voyage to land in northern Italy, Richard was recognized and captured by agents of the angry Duke Leopold. He was imprisoned and then handed over to the Holy Roman emperor, Henry VI, whom Richard had antagonized previously in Sicily. After spending three years in prison, Richard was released upon payment of an enormous ransom, which was raised by his English subjects.

Richard returned to England in 1194. He quickly suppressed his brother John's rebellion, raised funds for a war against Philip II of France, and then crossed the English Channel to launch a war against the French king. For five years, Richard was successful whenever he met Philip in battle. In 1199, however, he was struck down in a minor skirmish and died at the early age of forty-two.

Richard spent most of his adult life in battle or preparing for battle. Richard the Lionheart was considered a chivalrous and worthy opponent, and the great Saladin claimed he would rather lose to Richard than to any other man. However, Richard's record as a son and as a ruler is one of impetuosity, ruthlessness, and treachery. Having spent a total of only six months of his reign in England itself, his memory in that country is untarnished by the opportunity of misrule.

See also: ANJOU KINGDOM; CRUSADER KINGDOMS; ELEANOR OF AQUITAINE; HENRY II; JOHN I; NORMAN KINGDOMS; PHILIP II, AUGUSTUS; PLANTAGENET, HOUSE OF; SALADIN.

FURTHER READING
Gillingham, John. *Richard I.* New Haven, CT: Yale University Press, 1989.

RICHARD II (1367–1399 C.E.)

The last Plantagenet king of England (r. 1377–1399), grandson of Edward III (r. 1327–1377), who showed great promise in his early life with an attempt to quell the Peasant Revolt of 1381 when he was only fourteen years old. Richard II met strong opposition during most of his reign, however, and was eventually deposed and murdered by the future Henry IV (r. 1399–1413).

The successive deaths within two years of Richard's father, Edward the Black Prince, and his grandfather, Edward III, placed the ten-year-old on the throne of England. His uncle, John of Gaunt, retained the power he had held during Edward's last days, but now John officially held the position of regent.

Though intelligent and powerful, John of Gaunt was not well loved by the people. In addition, he was not mindful of the social changes that the Black Death had wrought during the previous half-century. Labor was no longer cheap. There were few farmers left to till or sow or reap. The feudal system was under attack. Yeomanry and independence were on the rise.

These conditions led to the Peasant Revolt of 1381. In reaction to heavy taxes laid upon them by nonproductive barons, many English arose in a popular revolt that swept through southern England. In the spring of 1381, the leader of this revolt, a soldier named Wat Tyler, led his motley collection of farmers, craftsmen, and laborers through the streets of London, where they completely destroyed the palace of the hated John of Gaunt. During this dangerous episode, the fourteen-year-old Richard II stayed in Windsor Castle with his advisers, all of whom insisted that the best course of action was to wait out the rebellion.

Richard, however, rode out on June 14 to meet with Wat Tyler and his lieutenants to hear their demands. Richard granted all participants in the revolt royal amnesty and won the astonished respect of this rough group. He then retired to his castle, leaving London to Tyler's forces.

The next day, the young king met with Tyler again. This time he led Tyler outside of London to Smithfield. Richard brought with him the mayor of London, William Walworth, and several dozen knights and gentry, while Tyler, supremely confident, came to the parley alone. An argument and fight ensued, and the lord mayor of London struck Tyler down with the weapon he had concealed beneath his cloak. Tyler's army, trusting in the king's honor and amnesty, did not destroy the small band. The mayor of London rode back to town, mustered a sizable army, and summarily defeated the peasants. Richard returned to Windsor. Forced to renege on his general amnesty, he was a fallen hero to the peasants.

Early in his reign, Richard asserted his independence from the aristocracy, who had enjoyed their dominance of the government. However, the king soon became subject to the power plays of his own class. He placed lesser aristocracy in coveted court positions, angering many of the upper aristocracy. The anger of the barons reached its culmination in 1388 when Richard's uncle, the duke of Gloucester, convened the "Merciless Parliament," which stripped the king of many of his privileges, giving rights to the wealthy landowners.

Richard's most notable adversary was his cousin, the duke of Hereford, Henry of Bolingbroke. The son of the powerful John of Gaunt, Bolingbroke was also a grandson of King Edward III. In 1397, upon John of Gaunt's death, Richard was able to move forcefully against the factions lined against him. He arrested or banished many opponents, including Bolingbroke, confiscated John of Gaunt's vast holdings (primarily held as the duchy of Lancaster), and parceled out this inheritance to his own supporters.

Two years later, while Richard was campaigning in Ireland, Bolingbroke returned from exile to claim his divided inheritance. On his return to England, Bolingbroke was embraced by many of the barons. When Richard returned to England soon after, he was betrayed, forced to abdicate, and imprisoned in Pontefract Castle. Bolingbroke was crowned as King Henry IV. When popular uprisings in Richard's favor began erupting in different parts of England, Henry IV had him murdered.

See also: ABDICATION, ROYAL; DETHRONEMENT; EDWARD III; ENGLISH MONARCHIES; HENRY IV (ENGLAND); LANCASTER, HOUSE OF; PLANTAGENET, HOUSE OF; REGICIDE; SUCCESSION, ROYAL.

FURTHER READING
Cheetham, Anthony. *The Life and Times of Richard II.* New York: Welcome Rain Publishers, 1998.

RICHARD III (1452–1485 C.E.)

Last English king (r. 1483–1485) of the house of York, perhaps best known for the controversy surrounding his reign than for his accomplishments as king.

Richard was born in 1452, the youngest surviving child of Cecily Neville, duchess of York, and Richard Plantagenet, duke of York and the second-largest landowner in England. Richard's father was descended from King Edward III (r. 1327–1377) through both his parents. At the time of Richard's birth, the house of Lancaster held the throne through the usurpation of Henry IV (r. 1399–1413), who had supplanted Richard II (r. 1377–1399) as king in 1399. However, Henry VI (r. 1422–1461, 1470–1471) of the house of Lancaster was soon to be challenged by the house of York in what came to be called the War of the Roses (1455–1485).

RISE TO POWER
In 1460, during the War of the Roses, Richard's father, the duke of York, was killed in battle, but the Yorkist cause eventually defeated the Lancastrians and Richard's older brother was crowned King Edward IV (r. 1461–1470) the following year. In 1465, the young Richard was placed in the home of Richard Neville, earl of Warwick, for further education and military training.

In 1470, Richard's protector, the earl of Warwick, turned against the house of York and staged a rebellion. Warwick's rebellion was successful, and Richard followed his brother Edward into exile in Flanders, while Warwick proclaimed Henry VI the rightful monarch once again. This situation would not last long, however. Edward IV returned to reclaim the throne in 1471, imprisoning Henry in the Tower of London, where Henry died shortly after, possibly at the hands of Richard.

In 1472, Richard married Anne Neville, the daughter of the earl of Warwick. The king granted Richard large parcels of land in the north of England, making him the "Lord of the North." The following year, Anne gave birth to their only son, named Edward. In 1478, Richard's brother George, the duke of Clarence, was convicted of high treason and, according to legend, was drowned in a large barrel of wine.

King Richard III of the House of York had a reputation for treachery and murder, the view advanced by William Shakespeare in his drama, *Richard III*. Not all historians agree, however; some suggest he was falsely accused by the Tudors to justify their succession to the throne.

REIGN

King Edward IV died of a chill on April 9, 1483, and the Crown passed to his twelve-year-old son, Edward V (r. 1483), with Richard named as his Protector. Through Richard's instigation, the legitimacy of his nephew Edward and Edward's younger brother (also named Richard) was publicly called into question, probably with good reason. (There is evidence to suggest that the children really were illegitimate.) In a successful coup against Edward V's mother and family, the children were declared unfit to reign and were imprisoned in the Tower of London. The English asked the Crown Protector, Richard, the next in line of succession, to take the throne. He was crowned Richard III on July 6, 1483.

During his brief two-year reign, Richard held only one Parliament, in January 1484. The session produced a number of much-needed reforms that benefited the common people of England, but they were not popular with the aristocracy. At the same time, Richard also established the Council of the North to settle local disputes, one of his most important achievements.

Richard's son Edward, the prince of Wales, died in April 1484. By October of that year, the young sons of Edward IV had also disappeared from the Tower of London and were presumed dead, allegedly murdered on Richard's orders. In the spring of 1485, Anne Neville also died, and it was rumored that Richard had his wife murdered so he could marry his niece Elizabeth, a daughter of Edward IV.

On August 7, 1485, Henry Tudor, heir to the house of Lancaster, landed in England (from exile in France) with his troops to claim the throne. He and Richard met in battle at Bosworth Field on August 22, and Richard was killed. Richard III was the last English king to die in battle, and his death unofficially marks the end of the Middle Ages in England. Henry became King Henry VII (r. 1485–1509); his accession to the throne marked the end of the War of the Roses and the establishment of the house of Tudor, which ruled England until 1603.

Much of what is known about the life and reign of Richard III comes from the accounts of Tudor historians, who exaggerated Richard's defects (including his alleged hunched back) to justify the Tudor line. Shakespeare's famous drama, *Richard III*, was staged under the last of the Tudor monarchs, Elizabeth I (r. 1558–1603). The degree of Richard's guilt in the death of his young nephews will perhaps never be

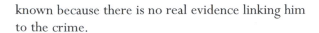

known because there is no real evidence linking him to the crime.

See also: ELIZABETH I; HENRY IV (ENGLAND); LANCASTER, HOUSE OF; PLANTAGENET, HOUSE OF; RICHARD II; TUDOR, HOUSE OF; YORK, HOUSE OF.

FURTHER READING

Cheetham, Anthony. *The Life and Times of Richard III.* New York: Welcome Rain Publishers, 1998.

Hammond, P.W., and Anne F. Sutton. *Richard III: The Road to Bosworth Field.* London: Constable, 1985.

Horrox, Rosemary. *Richard III: A Study of Service.* New York: Cambridge University Press, 1989.

RIGHTS TO ANIMALS

Privilege of kings and rulers with regard to hunting and ownership of valuable or unusual animals. In some societies, kingship itself has been derived from the hunting ritual, and in many monarchies, royalty has often controlled the rights to game.

HUNTING

Although hunting is primarily a recreation for modern man, it was of critical importance to the survival of the human race for hundreds of thousands of years. It is to be expected, then, that the protocols and customs surrounding the practice of hunting are complex and ancient.

Several thousand years ago, early humans in the ancient Near East improved upon the practice of hunting by domesticating animals, thus providing a more stable supply of meat and forestalling the uncertainty that accompanies even the surest of hunts.

The introduction of agriculture provided an even more reliable source of food. Yet, hunting retained its importance in both ancient and medieval societies. As the greatest hunters were often the greatest warriors, the greatest providers became leaders (eventually kings), and hunting rights became a royal or aristocratic privilege.

Special rights for the hunting of game, that is, rights reserved for aristocrats or royalty, began as early as the second millennium B.C.E. in Egypt, where oryx, gazelle, and even lions were hunted for sport from horseback or chariot. Similar hunting rights were reserved throughout the first millennium B.C.E. for the rulers of Babylon, Assyria, and other societies throughout the ancient Near East. For example, Ashurbanipal (r. 668–627 B.C.E.), the ruler of ancient Assyria, boasted that he had killed lions; he is known to posterity as "the Hunting King."

Another favorite sport of royalty, from as early as the eighth century B.C.E. until the late Middle Ages, was falconry—the use of birds of prey for hunting. In various times and places—from China to Scandinavia—the use of hunting birds was so highly regarded that its practice was frequently limited only to royalty. The Holy Roman emperor, Frederick II (r. 1212–1250), wrote a famous treatise on falconry in the thirteenth century.

DOMESTICATION OF ANIMALS

As leaders of their tribes or peoples, kings were able to express their physical superiority through the easily understood ritual of hunting. Yet, the royal connection to domestication was equally important.

Anthropologists generally agree that the domestication of animals (and plants) was the critical stage in the evolution of civilization, allowing for the development of cities and, later, states and nations. Without a concentration of population, humankind might well have remained in hunting and gathering tribes and never required the symbolic, administrative, and protective services of kings. Thus, the domestication of animals was an important step toward developing the monarchical system of government.

Efforts to domesticate the dog and the horse began over ten thousand years ago in the Middle East. By the time of Pharaonic Egypt (beginning around 4500 B.C.E), the dog, cat, cheetah, horse, and ox had been domesticated. Also, by this time, there were already particular types of animals which were considered "royal" or suitable to be owned only by royalty.

Royal animals were not just practical or for use in war, as were the horse and the elephant. The first pets were also royal animals. Rulers were the only members of early societies with the resources necessary to feed and take care of animals as pets, rather than providing for them because of their usefulness. Evidence of early royal pets may be found from China (the Pekingese dog) to Meso-America (the hummingbird) to rules about the ownership of certain hunting birds in the Middle East and Europe.

ANIMAL HUSBANDRY AND KINGSHIP

The Old Testament of the Bible frequently compares the relationship between kings and their peoples and the husbandry of domesticated animals. For instance, although historical evidence is unconvincing that King David (r. 1010–970 B.C.E.) was a shepherd before he became king, he is the foremost example of this relationship. David's legendary profession is not coincidental. As a seminal text for Western civilization, the Old Testament uses the metaphor of David's husbanding his flock, and then his people, to compare with Jehovah's husbanding of his flock—that is, the Hebrew people themselves.

This same analogy has frequently been used by royal personages (and their chroniclers) since that time. The importance of the shepherd maintaining the flock has been an activity easily related to by most peoples for almost ten thousand years. It is, however, a symbol that has become progressively less understandable to the modern mind and seems peculiarly suited to an openly hierarchical political structure like monarchy.

See also: BODIES, POLITIC AND NATURAL; HUNTING AND KINGSHIP.

RIGHTS, CIVIL

Those powers and privileges conferred upon all citizens by the governing authority, and which the governing authority is legally bound to observe.

Civil rights include the right to vote, the right to private property, and the right to freedom of expression. Such rights have increasingly come to be identified with natural or human rights; this identification is not entirely accurate, however, inasmuch as human rights are those held by all people in all societies, whereas civil rights can vary from nation to nation.

The development of civil rights over time has been controversial because the claim that the state has obligations to its citizens implies restriction of the state's powers. The process of inscribing civil rights in monarchical governments was particularly difficult for this very reason. Because of their numerous influential thinkers and documents on the subject, England and France have long been considered to be the birthplaces of modern civil rights.

ORIGINS

Several early legal codes, such as the Code of Hammurabi (ca. 1750 B.C.E.) in ancient Babylon and the Laws of Manu (ca. 200 B.C.E.) in ancient India, give

some indication that the rights of individuals were not subject to totally arbitrary action by the state. Similarly, several Chinese thinkers of the Chou dynasty (ca. 1027–256 B.C.E.), such as Confucius and Mencius, argued that rulers or monarchs had to respect the needs and desires of their individual subjects. These facts suggest that civil rights are not strictly a modern invention, but that they have ancient, though indirect, precursors.

The evolution of civil rights took a major leap forward with the classical civilizations of Greece and Rome. Both of these civilizations witnessed the development of a widespread belief in the notion of natural law, which is the idea that certain laws pertain to human beings whether or not the state observes them. The Romans, in particular, favored the idea of natural law, which the great orator Cicero advocated in the first century B.C.E. Natural law has been cited in many disputes between individuals and the state and is the basis for such documents as the Declaration of Independence of the United States.

THE MAGNA CARTA AND THE ENGLISH BILL OF RIGHTS

The period of the early Middle Ages saw little advancement in civil rights. However, one of the most important steps in the growth of individual sovereignty occurred in the thirteenth century: the signing of the Magna Carta by King John of England (r. 1199–1216) in 1215.

In 1215, the English barons, having grown angry over King John's misrule and oppressive financial policies, revolted and, through the intimidation of superior military strength, forced the king to sign the Magna Carta. This document stipulated, among other things, that English subjects possessed certain rights that the monarchy could not violate. The Magna Carta was the first document in history to guarantee constitutional protections for individuals against monarchial power, and as such, it became an important symbol of civil rights.

For all its later influence, the Magna Carta proved difficult to enforce, however, and many subsequent English monarchs virtually ignored it. For centuries the rights of individuals in England were not much better protected than they had been before 1215. The Glorious Revolution of 1688 changed that, as the English Parliament turned the Crown over to William III (r. 1689–1702) only on the condition that he observe the English Bill of Rights, which guaranteed numerous individual rights over the authority of the monarch. This document, much more than the Magna Carta, gave the people of England legal protection for their civil rights.

The English Bill of Rights was followed in the eighteenth century by important constitutional declarations of individual rights in the American colonies (and later the United States) and in France. People in both France and the United States followed the principle of civil rights to the point of discarding their monarchies. Several major thinkers of this period advocated the idea of individual rights, including John Locke in England, Jean Jacques Rousseau in France, and Thomas Jefferson and Thomas Paine in the United States.

Modern systems of civil rights spread far and rapidly in the nineteenth century and under military and economic pressure from Western nations, were even adopted in Japan during the Meiji Restoration, which began in 1868. In India, civil rights were guaranteed only after that country gained its independence from Great Britain in 1947. Efforts to introduce a modern system of civil rights in China and certain other countries around the world today still have not been successfully achieved.

The widespread growth of civil rights in the centuries after England's Glorious Revolution signaled the gradual demise of monarchical power and the rise of representative democracies as the major form of political organization around the world.

See also: JOHN I; MEIJI MONARCHY; POWER, FORMS OF ROYAL; WILLIAM AND MARY.

FURTHER READING

Hufton, Olwen, ed. *Historical Change and Human Rights.* New York: Basic Books, 1995.

Shapiro, Ian. *The Evolution of Rights in Liberal Theory.* New York: Cambridge University Press, 1986.

RIGHTS, LAND

The traditional foundation of wealth and power in human society. Whether in Asia, Europe, Africa, or the Americas, the goal of active monarchies has always been to acquire and control as much property as possible. In most early monarchies, all land was owned by the ruler. In some later monarchical societies, other groups were allowed the right to own and distribute land.

ORIGIN OF LAND RIGHTS

Anthropologists argue that kingship and monarchy did not exist before the concept of private property—and more specifically, the concept of land ownership—was widely accepted. Although there were probably leaders, perhaps even chieftains in premonarchical societies, the nomadic lifestyle imposed by hunting and gathering discouraged the need for a centralized ruler. Modern nomadic societies, such as the Lapps in northern Scandinavia and the horseherders on the Mongolian steppes, are current examples of such leaderless systems.

After the widespread development of agriculture and the resulting growth of populations and lifestyle changes, the security of land ownership—or, at least, land safeguarding—became critical for the survival of these larger populations. It was no longer a question of just moving on to winter hunting grounds. The first monarchs, therefore, probably based the power of their kingships on military prowess, which allowed them to defend their people and the land that provided for them, and therefore for their thrones.

As groups grew larger and learned the arts of farming, the rhythms of life changed; the cycle of cultivation and harvest created an entirely new lifestyle from the hunting and gathering system that had sustained human existence for hundreds of millennia. Hunters, used to the wild freedom of their vocation, were not well suited to the repetitive tedium and sedentary style of agricultural life. It was, however, apparent that more land would support more people, and so two problems were presented: the need for more land and the need for workers who would till, sow, and harvest.

Warfare offered new monarchs the answers to both of these problems. By defeating one's neighbors, a ruler gained not only land, but a new class of human labor, the slave, that could be forced to do anything—even the tedious, repetitive, and demeaning chores necessary for successful agriculture.

In the earliest of nations, land and property were frequently held in common among the free citizens of the group—another holdover of the pre-agricultural days when permanent secure ownership of property was not essential. However, most states began to adopt a system in which all the land belonged to either the sole monarch or to a select set of noble families (other warriors). This system continued with few modifications for thousands of years in most of Asia, North Africa, the Middle East, Mesoamerica, and those parts of Europe that were settled by postnomadic peoples.

In a majority of areas, monarchs became the "owners of record" of all lands. That is, they technically owned every field, every mountain, every river, and every plot on which every house stood. In practice, however, the use of these lands was typically "ceded" by custom to whoever occupied them; kings and queens only expected to receive revenue from whatever the current occupants produced on "their" land.

THE FEUDAL SYSTEM

A logical progression of this system was the feudalism that the Normans brought to most of Europe beginning in the eleventh century c.e. In this system, the king might, in effect, cede land to a noble who would, in turn, collect taxes from the produce of that land as if he were himself the king. The noble would also owe the king some portion of that which he gained from this bit of land. Thus, the noble was said to be "enfeoffed" to the king, and the peasants working the land were enfeoffed to the noble. This system sometimes became quite convoluted, as one noble could enfeoff another. As these complications grew, the direct control and benefit to the king grew increasingly less and less.

LAND REFORMS

Although most states and nations have conformed to the types of land ownership described here, there have also been many notable experiments and exceptions to these rules. The first great reformer in Western civilization was the Athenian archon Solon (d. 559 b.c.e.). His remarkably moderate and forward-looking laws, edicts, and constitution included a provision that forgave all mortgages on all lands. With this one act, Solon created a whole new class of freeholders in Athens, a class that would form the backbone of the Athenian democracy for centuries to come.

A few centuries later, in Rome, the tribune Tiberius Sempronius Gracchus attempted in 133 b.c.e. to redistribute the excess portions of the gigantic estates of the wealthiest Romans to the poorest Roman citizens. Four years of successive reforms culminated when Tiberius was murdered by Senate conservatives. With great public support, his brother, Gaius Gracchus, tried to implement Tiberius's land reforms and pass other measures aimed at creating a more egalitarian society, but he too was killed by the Senate conservatives in 121 b.c.e.

Not all early social land reforms occurred in Europe. In 1086 c.e., the Confucian scholar Wang An Shih won election as first minister for the Sung emperor T'ai Tsu. Wang was a determined and visionary reformer who ended state-mandated forced peasant labor and redistributed vast areas to humble Chinese farmers. Predictably, almost all conservative men of property opposed his reforms, and, after the unfortunate coincidence of several floods and an ill-omened comet, he was deposed from his position by the emperor, and his egalitarian reforms were undone by the aristocrats who succeeded him.

Not until the French Revolution, which began in 1787, and the Russian emancipation of the serfs in 1861 were such sweeping, democratic land reforms enacted with any lasting effect.

See also: CLASS SYSTEMS AND ROYALTY; CONQUEST AND KINGSHIPS; FEUDALISM AND KINGSHIP; LAND-HOLDING PATTERNS; PARKS, ROYAL; TAXATION; TRIBUTE.

RITUAL, ROYAL

Ceremonies and rites performed at various times during a monarch's life and reign. Much of the public and private lives of most monarchs is defined by ritual. Royal rituals accompany a host of events: birth of a monarch, religious initiations such as baptism or circumcision, accession to the throne, royal marriages, state occasions, (such as the opening of Parliament by the British monarch), reception of ambassadors and delegations, issuance of proclamations, birthdays and holidays, declarations of war or peace, approval of laws and treaties, designation of heirs, meetings with other monarchs, and deathbed and funeral rites. The carrying out of prescribed rituals, such as the Chinese emperor's sacrifice to Heaven, is central to a monarch's duties in many cultures.

Royal ritual is seldom merely a matter of rote but is intended to carry meaning. The Roman emperor Diocletian (r. 284–305) imposed a requirement that those who approached him prostrate themselves (lie face downward on the floor before him), emphasizing the emperor's exalted position, in order to stabilize the empire after a period when numerous generals and politicians had claimed the imperial title.

Planned disruptions in ritual also carry meaning. A famous example is the disruption of the coronation of Napoleon I (r. 1804–1815) as emperor. As Pope Pius VII (r. 1800–1823) was about to crown Napoleon, the French leader removed the crown from the pope's hands and placed it on his own head. Aware of precedents drawn from the pope's crowning of Charlemagne (r. 768–814) as emperor in 800, Napoleon did not want it to seem as if the pope was granting him power. Unplanned disruptions in ritual, by contrast, can weaken a monarch's position if they are viewed as bad omens.

Modern communications media have considerably broadened the audience for royal ritual. Among the pioneers in this area was the British monarchy, which, in the twentieth century, gained a reputation for the best rituals and ritual specialists. King George V (r. 1910–1936) introduced the custom of the monarch's Christmas radio broadcast in 1932, for both the monarch and radio listeners. The ritualistic aspects of this practice include its annual recurrence on a religious holiday. The televising of the coronation of Elizabeth II (r. 1953–) in 1953 was considered a great popular success, with broad viewership and expressions of broad-based affection for the new queen and, by extension, the British monarchy. With the loss of political power that most monarchies have experienced in the twentieth century, ritual often comprises an even larger proportion of royal public activity, stressing the symbolic role of the monarch.

See also: ACCESSION AND CROWNING OF KINGS; ENTHRONEMENT, RITES OF; ETIQUETTE, ROYAL; FUNERALS AND MORTUARY RITUALS; OATHS AND OATHTAKING; WEDDINGS, ROYAL.

RIURIKID DYNASTY (ca. 862–1598 C.E.)

Family founded by the Rus prince Rurik (r. ca. 862–878), branches of which ruled Novgorod, Kiev, other Rus principalities, and Russia until 1598.

Tradition asserts that Rurik assumed the leadership of some Slavic tribes in the area around Novgorod (in present-day Ukraine) around the year 862. The Rus were Scandinavians, also known as Varangians, who came into the Slavic regions between the Dnieper and Volga rivers to raid, trade, and eventually settle.

Upon Rurik's death in 879, the Rus principality was ruled by Oleg (r. ca. 879–924), a kinsman of Rurik. It is possible, however, the Oleg only served as regent while waiting for Rurik's son to reach his majority. Oleg established a capital at Kiev. He also united the eastern Slavs and signed a commercial treaty with the Byzantine Empire.

When Oleg died in 924, rule passed to Igor (r. 924–945), who may have been Rurik's son. He ruled until 945, when he was killed by members of a tributary tribe. Igor's wife Olga then took over as regent for their son, Sviatoslav, until he was able to take command himself in 962. Under Sviatoslav (r. 945–972), the Kievan Rus reached the height of its power.

Following Sviatoslav's death in 972, his sons Iaropolk (r. 972–978) and Vladimir (r. 978–1015) ruled Kiev and Novgorod, respectively. After war broke out between Iaropolk and another brother, Vladimir defeated Iaropolk with a Scandinavian army and became Prince Vladimir I of Kiev, subjecting the other Slavic tribes in the region to his rule. Vladimir made Greek Orthodox Christianity the state religion.

Under Vladimir's Riurikid descendants, the Kievan Rus continued to expand in a network of towns and territories ruled by related princes. Conflicts between the princes over dynastic and territorial interests prevented Kiev from ever becoming a strong, united power, although Prince Vladimir II Monomakh (r. 1113–1125) briefly united the territories during his reign.

The conquest of Kiev and destruction of that town by the Mongols in 1237–1240, and the long Mongol suzerainty over the region, lasting until 1480, did not end Riurikid rule. During this period, the city of Moscow and the grand duchy of Muscovy rose to preeminence under members of the Riurikid dynasty, who ruled as vassals of the Mongol khans until the collapse of the Mongol Golden Horde in 1395.

During the reigns of grand princes Vasili II (r. 1425–1462) and his son Ivan III (r. 1462–1505), most of the eastern Slavic lands were brought under the rule of the Riurikid grand princes of Moscow. In 1547, Ivan III's grandson Ivan IV (Ivan the Terrible, r. 1533–1584) became the first ruler of Russia to adopt the title of tsar. The last member of the Riurikid dynasty to rule Russia was Ivan's son, Tsar Feodor (Theodore) I (r. 1584–1598). With Feodor's death in 1598, the Riurikid dynasty came to an end.

During the seven centuries that branches of the

Riurikid dynasty ruled Russia, the region went from an assemblage of warring tribes to an empire with an autocratic ruler and a strong central government. Riurikid rule laid the foundations on which the Romanov dynasty would make Russia one of the largest (and most autocratic) empires of Europe and a significant player in nineteenth-century politics.

See also: IVAN III, THE GREAT; IVAN IV, THE TERRIBLE; KIEV, PRINCEDOM OF; MONGOL EMPIRE; RURIK; RUS PRINCEDOMS; RUSSIAN DYNASTIES.

ROBERT I (ROBERT THE BRUCE) (1274–1329 C.E.)

One of Scotland's best-known monarchs (r. 1306–1329), who rose above a checkered early history to become a powerful and popular ruler.

A member of Scotland's illustrious Bruce family, Robert Bruce was born at Turnberry Castle on the Firth of Clyde in 1274. Robert lived during a tumultuous period in Scottish history. Since the death of Margaret, the Maid of Norway, the kingdom had been without an independent ruler from 1290–1292 and 1296–1306 and a brief rule by an ineffectual king, John Balliol (r. 1292–1296). During this period, Edward I of England (r. 1272–1307) sought to conquer the kingdom, taking advantage of the lack of a legitimate Scottish king.

The Bruce family was often Edward's ally in this struggle. Robert himself switched sides five times, allying on one occasion with the Scottish hero William Wallace in a fight for Scottish independence, while at other times preferring English patronage and swearing fealty to Edward.

In 1292, Robert became earl of Carrick, and in 1304 he inherited his father's lordship of Annandale, with its English lands. His rise to leadership was also marked by treachery. At Greyfriars Kirk in 1306, Robert met John Comyn, a rival leader of the Scots, and in the midst of a heated argument, he apparently stabbed Comyn to death.

Robert was excommunicated from the Catholic Church for his crime, but he made a bid for the empty throne and declared himself king in 1306.

Under Robert's leadership, Scotland fought the English armies and eventually won a resounding victory against Edward II at the battle of Bannockburn

One of the national heroes of Scotland, King Robert I—known as Robert the Bruce—achieved military and diplomatic success. His victory at the Battle of Bannockburn in 1314 secured Scottish independence from England.

in 1314. The Scottish victory, against a much larger English force, turned the tide of the war. In the Treaty of Edinburgh-Northampton (1328), Edward promised to honor Scotland's independence and Bruce's claim to the throne.

Robert Bruce thus gained fame for securing Scottish independence, and he became known as "Good King Robert" for the innovative rule that left his son David II (r. 1329–1371) with a well-ordered and peaceful kingdom. Robert the Bruce died in 1329, declaring remorse for the deeds of his youth. Following his wishes, his heart was cut out and taken to the Middle East on a crusade as a gesture of atonement, though according to legend it was later returned to Scotland for burial in Melrose Abbey.

See also: EDWARD I; SCOTTISH KINGDOMS.

ROBERT GUISCARD. *See* NAPLES,
KINGDOM OF; NORMAN KINGDOMS

RODERIC (d. ca. 711 C.E.)

Last Visigoth king of Iberia (present-day Spain) (r. 710–711), after whose death much of the Iberian Peninsula was overrrun by the Moors, who invaded from North Africa.

Information on the life and career of Roderic is sketchy, although he may have been the son of Theodefred, a noble of the Germanic Visigoths. When the weak ruler of the Visigoths in Iberia, King Wittiza (r. 702–710), died in 710, Visigothic nobles chose Roderic as king over Wittiza's own sons. Civil war ensued, and Wittiza's heirs went to Africa to seek aid from Moorish forces there. After some exploratory raids, the Moors, under the leadership of Tariq bin Ziyad, launched a full-scale invasion against the unguarded Iberian Peninsula in 711.

At the time, Roderic was in northern Iberia subduing Basque and Frankish rebels. In July 711, Roderic met Tariq at the Guadalete, in the southernmost part of Spain. Influenced by Wittiza's supporters, many of Roderic's troops deserted, leaving the Visigoth king with a greatly reduced and weakened force. The Moors defeated the remaining Visigoth troops, and Roderic was probably killed in the battle. According to some legends and sources, however, Roderic continued fighting the Moors until 713, when he was slain.

In either case, the Moorish invaders continued their conquest of Iberia, taking the cities of Córdoba and then Toledo, the Visigothic capital. In 712, Musa bin Nusayr, Tariq's superior, invaded the Iberian Peninsula with an even greater force. Within a few years, most of the Iberian Peninsula had been conquered by the Moors.

See also: IBERIAN KINGDOMS; VISIGOTH KINGDOM.

ROMAN EMPIRE (27 B.C.E.–476 C.E.)

The empire founded by Augustus Caesar in 27 B.C.E., which underwent many changes and metamorphoses in its long life. The initial structure of the empire was not imposed on Roman society from the outside, but rather drew on Roman and Mediterranean political tradition. Emperors inherited many aspects of their role from Roman generals and politicians of the late Republic. They sponsored races and gladiatorial con-

tests, and had power over the creation of cities. They also bestowed Roman citizenship on individuals and groups. Other aspects came from Hellenistic monarchies, which were particularly influential when emperors faced the Greek-speaking population of the Eastern, more economically developed portion of the empire. Imperial autocracy was less concealed in the East. One aspect can be seen in the words used to define their role. The Roman emperors always avoided the title "rex," meaning king, as Roman tradition emphasized the freedom of the Republic after the overthrow of the ancient kings of the Tarquin dynasty. The word "imperator"—meaning commander—originally referred only to a military leader. However, Greek speakers in the Empire routinely referred to the emperor as "basileus," or king. The imperial office tended to move away from its republican origins toward explicit autocracy. The emperor also lived in an increasingly monarchical manner. In Rome, the main imperial residence from the days of Augustus was on the Palatine Hill. Eventually, any place the emperor lived was referred to as "palatium," from which came the word "palace."

One accompaniment of the imperial office was a divine cult. The cult of the emperor dates back to the initial reign of Augustus (although elements can be seen in the earlier rule of his uncle Julius Caesar.) Augustus's reign saw the foundation of temples of "Rome and Augustus" throughout the Empire. The cult that arose around the living Augustus was more like that of heroes and benefactors than that of the actual gods. This changed after his death in 14 C.E., when the Roman Senate enrolled "divus Augustus," divine Augustus, among the gods of the Roman state. His successor, Tiberius, encouraged the worship of Augustus and sponsored an official priesthood. (He and all subsequent emperors also took the names "Caesar Augustus.") The emperors also judged legal cases, made laws, and issued coinage. Much of what we know about the emperor's cultural, religious, and economic programs comes from surviving coinage.

Although the imperial office had a strong military component from the beginning—the title "imperator" was originally given to successful Roman generals—it became even more so. The original dynasty founded by Augustus—the "Julio-Claudians"—kept the succession within an extended family, although succession was not purely hereditary. When the Julio-Claudian dynasty ended ignominiously with Nero in 68 C.E., the succession was not settled by

ROMAN EMPIRE

Roman Emperors

The Julio-Claudians

AUGUSTUS*	27 B.C.E.—14 C.E.
TIBERIUS*	14–37
GAIUS (CALIGULA)	37–41
CLAUDIUS*	41–54
NERO*	54–68
GALBA	68–69
OTHO	69
VITELLIUS	69

The Flavians

VESPASIAN	69–79
TITUS*	79–81
DOMITIAN	81–96

The Five Good Emperors

NERVA	96–98
TRAJAN*	98–117
HADRIAN*	117–138
ANTONINUS PIUS	138–161
MARCUS AURELIUS*	161–180
LUCIUS VERUS	161–169
COMMODUS	180–192
PERTINAX	193
DIDIUS JULIANUS	193

The Severi

SEPTIMUS SEVERUS	193–211
GETA	211
CARACALLA	211–217
MACRINUS	217–218
ELAGABALUS	218–222
SEVERUS ALEXANDER	222–235

The Soldier Emperors

MAXIMINUS (THRAX)	235–238
GORDIAN I	238
GORDIAN II	238
PUPIENUS	238
BALBINUS	238
GORDIAN III	238–244
PHILIP I, THE ARAB	244–249
PHILIP II	247–249
DECIUS	249–251
HERENNIUS ETRUSCUS	251
HOSTILIAN	251
TREBONIANUS GALLUS	251–253
VOLUSIAN	251–253
AEMILIAN	253
VALERIAN	253–260
GALLIENUS	253–268
SALONINUS	260
CLAUDIUS II, GOTHICUS	268–270
MARIUS	269

The Soldier Emperors (continued)

Quintillus	270
Aurelian	270–275
Tacitus	275–276
Florian	276
Probus	276–282
Carus	282–283
Numerian	283–284
Carinus	283–285

Diocletian and the Tetrarchy

Diocletian*	284–305
Maximian	285–305 and 307–308
Constantius I, Chlorus	305–306
Galerius	305–311
Severus	306–307
Maxentius	307–312

Dynasty of Constantine

Constantine I, the Great*	307–337
Licinius	308–324
Maximinus II	310–313
Valerius Valens	316–317
Martinian	324
Constantine II	337–340
Constans	337–350
Constantius II	337–361
Magnentius	350–353

Julian the Apostate*	360–363
Jovian	363–364

Dynasty of Valentinian

Valentinian	364–375
Valens	364–378
Gratian	375–383
Valentinian II	375–392

Dynasty of Theodosius

Theodosius I, the Great*	379–395
Maximus	383–388
Victor	387–388
Eugenius	392–394

Western Roman Emperors

Honorius	395–423
Constantius III	421
John	423–425
Valentinian III	425–455
Petronius Maximus	455
Avitus	455–456
Majorian	457–461
Libius Severus	461–465
Anthemius	467–472
Olybrius	472
Glycerius	473–474
Julius Nepos	474–475
Romulus Augustus	475–476

*Indicates a separate alphabetical entry.

THE GAMES AND SHOWS OF AUGUSTUS CAESAR

The Roman historian Suetonius, author of a collection of biographies of the rulers of Rome from Julius Caesar to Domitian, described how the first emperor provided entertainment for Rome. He claimed Augustus showed games, usually combats and chariot races, twenty-four times in his own name and twenty-three times in the names of others. He also exhibited strange animals, such as a rhinoceros, a tiger, and a huge snake. The games and shows displayed the emperor's power and wealth, fulfilling a role expected of a Roman leader but on a scale that was unprecedented.

family intrigues but by military maneuverings and battles between top generals, with provincial armies playing a central role. The Roman historian Tacitus referred to 69 as the year when it was discovered that emperors could be made elsewhere than at Rome. The winner, Vespasian (r. 69–79), founded the short-lived Flavian dynasty of himself and his two sons, Titus and Domitian. Vespasian, who ruled from 69 to 79, provided stable, if tight-fisted, government after the turmoil of Nero's reign and the disruptions of the civil wars. Titus also ruled effectively, though for only two years. Domitian (r. 81–96) was a hard-working ruler and a great builder, but also harsh and tyrannical. He was assassinated, and his memory was condemned by the Senate, in contrast to his deified father and brother.

Domitian was followed by five rulers known as the "adoptive emperors," because each selected his heir outside his own family, or the "five good emperors." These emperors, whose rule stretched from 96 to 180, were stark contrasts in personality—the warlike Trajan, the peaceful Hadrian who traveled incessantly throughout the Empire, the sedentary Antoninus Pius who seldom left Rome—but all benefited from relative peace on the frontiers and a system whereby emperors adopted their successors. This period ended when the last of the five, Marcus Aurelius, was succeeded by his dissolute and egomaniacal son Commodus (r. 180–192). Commodus's assassination was followed by another period of competition like the one that followed Nero's. The eventual winner was Septimius Severus (r. 193–211), a grim but effective ruler known for his advice to his

successor that the only thing necessary was to keep the soldiers happy. Severan rulers, first Severus's sons and then the children of his wife's sister, ruled with interruption until 235, when mutinous troops killed Alexander Severus. The next emperor, Maximinus Thrax (r. 235–238), was the first emperor to have begun his career as a common soldier and only the second to come from outside the Senate. Senatorial opposition helped make his reign a short one, as were most of the rest for the next fifty years. The empire suffered from frequent civil wars, multiple claimants to the throne, plagues, the temporary breakaway of large portions of the empire, barbarian invasions, and wars with Persia. (Persia inflicted the greatest humiliation in imperial history, when Valerian (r. 253–260) was captured alive and forced to be the stepping-stool for the Persian king to mount his horse.) In these circumstances, the emperors who emerged were mostly soldiers, many from the Illyrian and Danubian provinces, who spent less and less time in the city of Rome. The greatest of these was Diocletian (r. 284–305), who realized that the empire was too big to be effectively run by one man, and instituted an administrative division between eastern and western emperors that eventually became permanent.

The most important emperor since Augustus was Constantine (r. 307–337). His founding of a new capital, Constantinople, and his adoption and aggressive promotion of Christianity wrought a revolution in imperial affairs that reached its eventual flowering in the Byzantine Empire. The emperor abandoned his pagan religious role and took on a

THE ROMAN EMPIRE

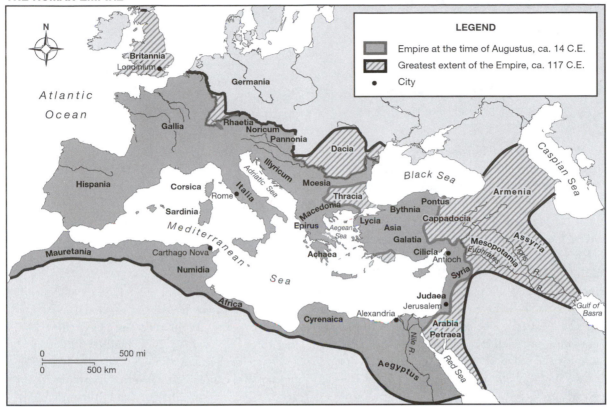

new one as protector and arbiter of the Christian church, although being dragged into the church's doctrinal disputes was as much a liability as an advantage. (Exceptions were Julian the Apostate and the nominally Christian pretender emperor Eugenius (r. 392–394), who promoted paganism against Christianity.) The last emperor of the whole Roman Empire, Theodosius the Great (r. 379–395), was forced by the bishop of Milan, Ambrose, to publicly repent for his sins.

Following Theodosius, the Western empire with its capital at Rome declined rapidly. This was matched by a decline in the power of its emperors, many of whom were puppets of the supreme military commanders. These men, some of Roman and some of barbarian descent, usually controlled the foreign and military policy of the Western empire. The eastern emperors, by contrast, kept control of the government of the richer and more powerful half of the empire from their capital at Constantinople. In 476, the last Western emperor, the young Romulus Augustulus, was overthrown by the barbarian military commander Odoacer, who took the title king of Italy while continuing to acknowledge

the authority of the Roman emperor at Constantinople.

The legacy of the Roman Empire was profound and long-lasting. The Byzantine Empire was a direct continuation of the Eastern Roman Empire, and even its Ottoman conquerors referred to themselves as rulers of "Rum," meaning Rome. Medieval Europe's Holy Roman Empire drew on Roman tradition and imagery, as did the medieval papacy. Even the tsars of Russia, Orthodox Christian rulers who saw themselves as Byzantium's heirs, had a title ultimately derived from "Caesar."

See also: Augustus; Byzantine Empire; Caesars; Caligula; Christianity and Kingship; Claudius; Constantine I, the Great; Diocletian; Emperors and Empresses; Hadrian; Holy Roman Empire; Julian the Apostate; Julio-Claudians; Julius Caesar; Marcus Aurelius; Nero; Palaces; Theodosius I, the Great; Tiberius; Titus; Trajan.

FURTHER READING

Millar, Fergus. *The Emperor in the Roman World, 31 BC–AD 337.* Ithaca, NY: Cornell University Press, 1992.

ROMAN EMPIRE, HOLY. *See* HOLY ROMAN EMPIRE

ROMANIAN MONARCHY

(1859–1947 C.E.)

Kingdom in Eastern Europe that emerged in the nineteenth century from two principalities of the Ottoman Empire—Wallachia and Moldavia.

By the mid-1800s, the bonds between the Ottoman Empire and some of its territories in southeastern Europe were fraying, and Russian influence in that region was becoming stronger. In 1859, in the aftermath of the Crimean War (1853–1856), the principalities of Wallachia and Moldavia elected the same person as their prince, Alexander Cuza (r. 1859–1866). Cuza, who was from a family of Moldavian nobles, obtained recognition from the Ottoman sultan for the union of the two principalities during his own lifetime. The European powers and Russia, however, preferred a foreign prince rather than a Romanian noble to sit on the throne, and they forced Cuza to abdicate on February 23, 1866.

Cuza's successor was Karl (r. 1866–1914) of the house of Hohenzollern-Sigmaringen, a branch of the Hohenzollern dynasty that occupied the throne of Prussia. Unlike the Prussian Hohenzollerns, Karl was Catholic rather than Protestant. When Karl was proclaimed king by the Romanian national assembly on May 22, 1866, he took the Romanian version of his name, Carol I. A few months later, in October, he received recognition from the Ottoman sultan.

Carol I was a constitutional monarch, taking his oath on the Romanian constitution and respecting the authority of its representative institutions. During his reign, he focused primarily on foreign affairs, attempting to avoid the factionalism that affected domestic policies. In fact, the monarch and heirs to the throne were forbidden to marry Romanians in order to limit the influence of factions upon their decisions.

Taking advantage of the Russian defeat of the Ottoman Turks in 1877, Carol threw off the last vestiges of Ottoman suzerainty and proclaimed Romania a fully independent country. On June 22, 1884, the Romanian parliament granted Carol and his successors a large royal estate, making the king the biggest landowner in the country.

Carol and his wife Elizabeth had only one child, a daughter who died at the age of four. After Carol's death in 1914, the throne passed to his nephew, Ferdinand I (r. 1914–1927). Ferdinand faced the difficult challenge of guiding Romania through World War I. Despite the crushing defeat of Romania's army by the Germans early in the war, Romania ended up gaining territory from the Allied victory in 1918, adding Transylvania, a Romanian-inhabited part of the Austro-Hungarian Empire, to his realm.

The wife of Ferdinand I, Marie of Romania, a granddaughter of Queen Victoria of England, became a leading figure in her own right. During World War I, she served as a war nurse, and in the aftermath of the war she attended the peace conference at Versailles in an effort to negotiate a better deal for Romania.

Ferdinand's son Carol was forced to renounce his right of succession because of a scandal involving a mistress. As a result, upon Ferdinand's death in 1927, the throne passed to his grandson, Michael (r. 1927–1930). Because Michael was still only a child, a regency was appointed to govern the country. The regency faced many challenges due to the unstable political situation in the country. Supported by those who urged stronger leadership, Michael's father Carol retracted his renunciation of the succession and took the throne as Carol II (r. 1930–1940) in 1930.

Carol II attempted to rule Romania more directly than did previous rulers, and he had some initial successes. But on April 16, 1938. he decreed all political parties and associations dissolved and set up a "royal dictatorship." Two years later, on September 6, 1940, Ion Antonescu, a member of the fascist Iron Guard, and his supporters forced Carol to abdicate again and leave the country for good.

Carol's son Michael returned to the throne, but the young king had little real power, as Antonescu and the fascists maintained control. At the start of World War II, Antonescu led Romania into the war as an ally of Germany. After the war, Michael attempted to resist the takeover of the country by communists and Soviets, but he was forced to abdicate and leave the country with the declaration of a "People's Republic" on December 30, 1947.

Since the fall of communism in Romania in 1989, Michael has visited his former kingdom a number of times. A small but active royalist movement exists there, hoping that one day the monarchy might be restored.

See also: DACIA KINGDOM; HOHENZOLLERN DYNASTY; OTTOMAN EMPIRE; VLACH PRINCIPALITY.

ROMANOV DYNASTY (1613–1917 C.E.)

Royal family that ruled Russia for more than three centuries, until the Russian Revolution overthrew the tsarist monarchy in 1917.

The earliest recorded progenitor of the Romanov family is Andrei Kobyla, an adviser to the princes of Moscow in the fourteenth century. His descendants served the Muscovite court for more than two centuries and changed the family name to Zakhar'in. In the sixteenth century, the family entered the highest circles of influence when Anastasia Zakhar'in married Tsar Ivan IV (r. 1533–1584).

Anastasia's brother, Nikita Romanovich, served as regent to Ivan's son and successor, Tsar Feodor I (r. 1584–1598). Feodor's death ended the Riurikid dynasty because there was no immediate heir. During the ensuing turmoil, known as the Time of Troubles, the Russian regent, Boris Godunov, banished the Romanov family. But in 1613, a national assembly, searching for a ruler who had legitimate ties to the Riurikids, elected Nikita Romanovich's grandson, Michael Romanov, to the Russian throne. Significantly, the assembly declared Michael to be a hereditary ruler endowed with divine right. This assertion ensured that the Romanovs would hold the throne as long as an heir existed.

When Michael Romanov (r. 1613–1645) assumed the throne, Russia's economy was severely depressed because Godunov had mismanaged the agricultural economy. To raise revenue, Michael replaced land taxes with taxes on the workers who farmed the land. This new system of taxation established the foundation of Russian serfdom, an insti-

The Romanov dynasty ruled Russia from 1613 until 1917, when Tsar Nicholas II was forced to abdicate in the face of the Bolshevik Revolution. Nicholas, his wife Alexandra, his four daughters, and his son Alexei were murdered by revolutionaries in July 1918.

tution that would repeatedly hamper the Romanovs and eventually lead to their demise.

Michael Romanov also attempted to establish Russia's power abroad. He envisioned a greatly expanded Russian territory defended by a formidable military force. This vision, like serfdom, became a legacy for the Romanov rulers. Because of Russia's depleted resources, however, Michael did not fulfill his vision, and he also failed to dislodge Poland, Sweden, and Turkey from lands he coveted.

It was Michael's grandson, Peter I, the Great (r. 1682–1725), who transformed Russia into an international force. Peter enacted reforms designed to augment Russia's military strength. He authorized compulsory military service for all male citizens, created numerous taxes to finance the military, and built a massive bureaucracy to collect them. Most importantly, Peter ensured that serfdom became an integral feature of Russian society. Originally, peasants had been hired employees, but under Peter, their labor became obligatory, and they became bound to the land.

These measures helped Peter successfully increase Russia's power. He defeated Sweden and established a Russian presence on the Baltic Sea. He also consolidated his power within Russia by subjugating the peasant Cossacks of the Ukraine and other rebellious groups. Yet Peter's oppressive social measures created a social discord that repeatedly plagued his successors.

His grandson, Peter III (r. 1762), was the first to suffer the repercussions of these reforms. Faced with a violent insurrection, Peter III ended mandatory military service for the nobility. The act did not earn him a reprieve, however, because he was deposed and executed the same year he took the throne. His wife, a German princess, then assumed the throne as Catherine II (r. 1762–1796), also known as Catherine the Great.

Catherine recognized that serfdom stunted Russian society; landowners lost the impetus to improve their land, and the serfs relied upon increasingly outdated farming methods. Furthermore, the economy's dependence upon agriculture contrasted sharply with Europe's developing industrialism. Catherine, however, did not believe she had the power to defy the landowners and eliminate serfdom. Instead, she strengthened Russia's cultural institutions to reflect advancements in other European countries.

During the reign of Catherine's grandson Alexander I (r. 1801–1825), Russia finally fulfilled the vision of Michael Romanov and Peter the Great. In 1814, Alexander oversaw the defeat of Napoleon, and this victory established Russia as Europe's most prominent military power. However, public animosity engendered by serfdom and the sprawling governmental bureaucracy also exploded during Alexander's reign. In 1825, a radical group, the Decembrists, staged a dangerous rebellion that proved the viability of a popular revolution.

For the next century, Alexander's successors adopted alternate methods to eradicate the revolutionary threat. Nicholas I (r. 1825–1855) created a police state and severely restricted personal liberties. However, his son, Alexander II (r. 1855–1881), in an act of appeasement, allowed the emancipation of the serfs. Ultimately, even emancipation did not satisfy the growing revolutionary movement, which demanded the creation of a representative government.

Finally, in 1917, Nicholas II (r. 1894–1917), plagued by a crippled economy, humiliating losses to the Germans in World War I, and the developing Russian Revolution, abdicated the throne. He and his family were assassinated the following year, thereby ending Romanov rule in Russia. Serfdom and strict authoritarian rule, the tools that Michael Romanov and his descendents used to develop their power, ultimately subverted their dynasty.

See also: CATHERINE II, THE GREAT; NICHOLAS I; NICHOLAS II; PETER I, THE GREAT; RIURIKID DYNASTY; ROMANOV, MICHAEL.

FURTHER READING

Cowles, Virginia. *The Romanovs.* New York: Harper & Row, 1971.

Raleigh, Donald J., ed. *The Emperors and Empresses of Russia.* Armonk, NY: M.E. Sharpe, 1996.

ROMANOV, MICHAEL (1596–1645 C.E.)

Founder of the Romanov dynasty (which ruled Russia until 1917), under whose rule serfdom increased and some Western military and industrial techniques were introduced.

Mikhail Fedorovich Romanov reluctantly accepted election as tsar of Russia in 1613, after several false pretenders struggled for power. The grandnephew of Anastasia, the wife of Ivan IV, the Terrible (r. 1533–1584), the young new tsar was the sixteen-year-old son of Fyodor Romanov and Ksenia

Ivanovna Shestovaia, both of whom had been forced to take religious vows during the reign of Boris Godunov (r. 1598–1605). Michael's mother accompanied him, along with the agents of the *zemski sobor* (the Russian ruling council who had chosen Michael), to Moscow in 1613 so he could take the throne. For the next five years, the young tsar's policies were directed by opportunistic members of his mother's family and by the experienced members of the *zemski sobor* who surrounded him in the Kremlin, the citadel in Moscow that contained the palaces and administrative buildings of the tsarist realm.

In 1619, Michael's father, Fyodor, was named grand patriarch of the Russian church and also assumed the regency for his son. Between the progress that had already been made under the direction of *zemski sobor* and the able leadership of Fyodor, Russia recovered from the tumultuous "Time of Troubles" that had preceded Michael's accession.

In the twelve years between the death of Michael's father Fyodor in 1633 and Michael's own death, the family of the tsar's mother once more took control of Russian policy. Michael seems not to have resented these usurpations of his power, perhaps because he realized that his abilities were modest.

When Michael died in 1645, he was succeeded on the throne by his sixteen-year-old son, Alexis (r. 1645–1676). The Romanov line that Michael had founded continued to rule Russia until the death of Tsar Nicholas II (r. 1894–1917) in 1917 during the Russian Revolution.

See also: IVAN IV, THE TERRIBLE; ROMANOV DYNASTY; RUSSIAN DYNASTIES.

FURTHER READING
Smith, David. *Russia of the Tsars.* London: Ernest Benn, 1971.

ROTSE KINGDOM. *See* LOZI KINGDOM

ROYAL FAMILIES

The monarch's family, including parents, spouse, children, and, in most cases, siblings, some if not all of whom are in the line of succession.

Royal families differ in size and in kind for a number of reasons. In some cultures, families engage in polygamy or concubinage, and the immediate royal family can be enormously large. This practice of having multiple wives or concubines was common to older Middle Eastern and Asian societies. In modern European cultures, royal families are usually comparatively small. In earlier centuries, however, families were large to ensure a number of surviving children. In addition, if the wife died in childbirth, a monarch might marry two or three times, thus ensuring a large family.

Even today, extended royal families can be fairly large. For example, the British royal family includes not only the four children and six grandchildren of Queen Elizabeth II (r. 1952–), but many royal cousins and other relatives of the monarch.

MARRIAGES
Most monarchs choose their consorts, or spouses, from a relatively narrow group among the nobility. Often, rulers who cannot marry another individual of highest royal blood choose to marry someone who is in line to inherit another throne or who is able to influence that country's decisions. Sometimes, as with Isabella I of Castile (r. 1474–1504) and Ferdinand II of Aragón (r. 1479–1516), such a marriage results in the joining of two kingdoms or two groups at war with each other. At the end of the Wars of the Roses (1455–1485), Henry Tudor, of the house of Lancaster, declared himself heir to the throne after the death of Richard III (r. 1483–1485). As Henry VII (r. 1485–1509), he took for his queen Elizabeth of York, the oldest daughter of Edward IV (r. 1461–1483), from the house of York. Henry's choice of a bride was conciliatory; through the marriage, he joined the two warring parties and ended the Wars of the Roses.

Although an extended series of marriages in a family is intended to create beneficial alliances and strengthen a country's international status, it can, in the long run, weaken it. For example, in 1700, when King Charles II of Spain (r. 1665–1700) died childless, the royal families of France, England, and Portugal all had contenders for the succession, and each fought for his claim to the throne. The Wars of the Spanish Succession followed, and in the aftermath, Philip V (r. 1700–1746), the grandson of Louis XIV of France (r. 1643–1715), held the throne. As a result, the Habsburg dynasty ended in Spain, and the kingdom became a vassal of France under the Bourbon dynasty.

ROYAL RELATIVES

ILLEGITIMATE CHILDREN

In Northern Europe, illegitimate children of monarchs were cared for by giving them gifts such as land or money; rarely, if ever, could they hope to inherit the title. In much of Southern Europe, on the other hand, particularly Italy, the attitude was much different. When Alfonso I of Aragón (r. 1435–1458) occupied the city of Naples in 1444, he arranged for his illegitimate son, Ferrante, to succeed him there as Ferdinand I (r. 1458–1494). Similarly, when Emperor Conrad IV (r. 1250–1254) assumed power in southern Italy and Sicily, he named his illegitimate half-brother Manfred to rule as his substitute. When Conrad IV died in 1254, Manfred (r. 1254–1266) assumed power in his own right. Such widespread acceptance of illegitimate children as successors in the Italian states astonished Northern Europeans, who regarded Italy as both a scandalous and fascinating place.

An issue that sometimes arises in royal marriage is intermarriage among dynasties or families. Repeated intermarriage among royalty can sometimes result in physical problems. One such example is found in Charles II of Spain (r. 1665–1700), known as Charles the Mad, who inherited traits of mental instability as a result of continued intermarriage within the Habsburg dynasty. Charles inherited the throne at age four; even by then it was obvious that he was so severely handicapped that he could neither speak nor eat properly.

CONCUBINES AND MISTRESSES

The preferred form of producing an heir for a ruler in the Ottoman Empire was through slave concubinage. A wife of an Ottoman sultan was held to have a vested interest in government affairs and so was considered more of a liability than was a concubine. Children born to a concubine were legitimate and could inherit the Ottoman throne.

One weakness of the Ottoman monarchy, however, was its lack of a law of succession. As a result, the death of a sultan frequently was followed by lengthy struggles for power. In the fifteenth century, Sultan Mehmet II Fatih (r. 1451–1481) decreed after inheriting the throne that all his siblings be put to death. This practice continued until the seventeenth century, when the right to inherit was given, by law, to the eldest son, and the rest of the family was imprisoned in part of the harem. As a result, potential

rulers often came to the throne without any training or experience. These practices eventually contributed to the Ottoman decline.

Far Eastern monarchs were permitted any number of concubines, many of whom might be from the lower classes. Frequently, as in the Ottoman Empire, these women were slaves, and they remained in the harem after the emperor lost interest in them.

In China, there were differing grades of concubines; a woman who pleased the emperor might be moved up to a higher grade. The empress T'zu Hsi (Cixi), admitted to the harem as a third-grade concubine, became a first-grade concubine after her son's birth. In these situations, a woman might have influence over the emperor; on rare occasions, she might even become regent, as Tzu Hsi did after the death of emperor Hsien Feng in 1861, when she became regent for her son, T'ung Chih (r. 1861–1875). Technically, the empress's son was the heir, but, in practice, instead emperors frequently named a son born to a favored concubine as the next heir.

European monarchs sometimes had mistresses as well, but the children born to these women were considered illegitimate and could not inherit the throne. Officially, they often were not even considered part of the royal family. Although the mistress of a European king might exert considerable influence over his decisions, she rarely had any status after his death. Unless legitimized, her children could not inherit lands or titles. In many cases, a European mon-

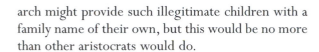

arch might provide such illegitimate children with a family name of their own, but this would be no more than other aristocrats would do.

See also: EMPERORS AND EMPRESSES; KINGS AND QUEENS; LEGITIMACY; REGENCIES; ROYAL LINE; SUCCESSION, ROYAL.

ROYAL IMPOSTERS

False claimants to royalty have often taken the identity of a charismatic royal who died or was assassinated at a young age and who was surrounded by an aura of mystery or glamour. Many people believe in these false claimants because of the hope they arouse. Perhaps the most famous such royal pretenders have been those claiming descent from the last Romanov tsar of Russia, Nicholas II (r. 1894–1917), and his family, who were murdered in 1918 by the Bolsheviks, and whose bodies long remained undiscovered.

The most notorious Romanov pretender was a woman named Anna Anderson, who, from 1921 until her death in 1984, claimed to be the tsar's youngest daughter Anastasia. In 1991, the bodies of the tsar's family were discovered and unearthed near Ekaterinburg, the place in Russia where they had been killed. DNA analysis finally proved that Anna Anderson was not a Romanov.

After Louis-Charles, the son of Louis XVI (r. 1774–1792) and Marie Antoinette, apparently died in prison at the age of ten in 1795, some French monarchists claimed that the young prince had escaped and that another boy had been substituted for him. In 1814, a German man named Karl Wilhelm Naundorff claimed to be Louis, and debate over who was the real prince continued for almost two centuries. In 1998, Naundorff's remains were compared by DNA analysis to those of Bourbon descendants, and his claim was disproved. Further DNA tests performed in 1999 on tissue from the boy who died in prison indicated he was the real Louis-Charles.

Pretenders sometimes have a real throne to gain if their claims prove true. Often, however, they make their claims to the Crown because of an attachment to the idea of a royal past and the glamour and splendor associated with it, a feeling that is shared by many of those who believe in these pretenders.

See also: BLOOD, ROYAL; CONSORTS, ROYAL; DESCENT, ROYAL; GENEALOGY, ROYAL; LEGITIMACY.

FURTHER READING
Cheesman, Clive, and Jonathan Williams. *Rebels, Pretenders and Impostors.* New York: St. Martin's Press, 2000.
Hindley, Geoffrey. *The Royal Families of Europe.* New York: Carroll & Graf, 2000.

ROYAL LINE

Those individuals who are in the line of succession to inherit a throne; a succession of rulers from the same royal line is known as a dynasty.

The concept of the royal line has much in common with that of the succession, and at times they may seem identical. There are some differences, however: the monarch's extended family, including the children of his or her brothers and sisters, and in many cases their children, are usually considered part of the royal family; they too have a place, although distant, in the line of succession.

There may be legal differences between the royal line and the succession. Great Britain, for example, still follows the law of succession as established by the Bill of Rights in 1688 and the Act of Settlement in 1701. Those individuals claiming descent from James II (r. 1685–1688), or any branch of the Stuart family, are no longer in the royal line; the heir must come through the Hanover line. Moreover, the English monarch must be in communion with the Church of England; Catholics are not allowed to inherit the throne. Although a bill to repeal the Act of Settlement has been brought before Parliament, the law remained in force as of mid-2003.

A Catholic in the Hanover line, though unable to succeed to the throne, remains technically in the royal line. For example, George Windsor, earl of St. Andrews (b. 1962), is barred from the succession because he married a Roman Catholic. Nevertheless, Windsor's place in the royal line is often found in unofficial listings—although it is acknowledged that he may not inherit the throne for religious reasons. It remains possible for Windsor to inherit, however, provided his wife converts to the Anglican Church.

An interesting example of the relationship between the royal line and succession involves John of

Gaunt, the duke of Lancaster and third son of King Edward III (r. 1313–1377) of England, who was thus in the royal line of succession. John of Gaunt's children by his wife, Katherine Swynford, were distant members of the royal line. Despite the fact that their heirs were, at the time, barred from the succession, their descendant, Henry Tudor, was able to lay claim to the throne as Henry VII (r. 1485–1509) at the end of the Wars of the Roses (1455–1485), so depleted was the aristocracy.

Various difficulties have occurred over the royal line and succession. In the Ottoman Empire, for example, frequent difficulties arose regarding succession because the Ottomans did not follow primogeniture (inheritance by the oldest son), and there was no specific royal line. Consequently, the death of an Ottoman sultan was frequently followed by a political struggle among his sons. Such a struggle erupted following the death of Sultan Bayezid I (r. 1389–1402).

When Sultan Mehmed II (r. 1451–1481) took the throne, he had his siblings put to death and enacted a decree establishing the practice that was followed into the early seventeenth century. From this time on, the sultans followed the law of primogeniture, and other surviving males of the family, instead of being killed, were locked up in a part of the imperial harem that was known as "The Cage." Consequently, the Ottoman Empire was sometimes ruled by a series of mad or incompetent sultans who had spent too much time imprisoned and isolated, lacking contact with the outside world. Most historians agree that this practice of imprisoning potential heirs contributed to the decline of the Ottoman Empire.

See also: EMPERORS AND EMPRESSES; EMPIRE; IMPERIAL RULE; KINGDOMS AND EMPIRES; KINGS AND QUEENS; ROYAL FAMILIES; SUCCESSION, ROYAL.

ROYAL PRETENDERS

Descendants of a royal house who are not in the direct line of inheritance but who claim the throne; or the heirs to a deposed king who hope to regain power; or people who falsely claim to be royal descendants. Even after the decline of monarchy in modern times, there have been many royal pretenders.

Royal descendants not in direct line to the throne have used various methods to legitimize their claims.

After his victory at the battle of Agincourt in 1415, Henry V of England (r. 1413–1422) claimed the throne of France by right of his descent from Edward III (r. 1327–1377), the grandson of a king of France. Henry also claimed that the dauphin, the future Charles VII (r. 1422–1461), was illegitimate and therefore had no right to be king. In 1420, the French Parlement and the University of Paris accepted Henry's claim.

When Henry IV (r. 1399–1413) usurped the English throne from Richard II (r. 1377–1399) in 1399, at first he tried to alter his genealogy to legitimize his rule. He was actually descended from a junior line of the house of Lancaster, through Edmund Crouchback, the younger brother of Edward I (r. 1272–1307). Henry and his father, John of Gaunt, insisted that Edmund was really the older brother of Edward I, but had been forced to give up his royal rights because he was a hunchback.

Claims of illegitimate birth have also been used against pretenders. After James II (r. 1685–1688) fled England in 1688, Protestant supporters of the new king, William III (r. 1689–1702), alarmed at the prospect of a Catholic heir to the throne, disputed the legitimacy of the young prince James, born to the deposed monarch and his staunchly Catholic wife, Mary of Modena. They claimed that the infant James was really the son of a woman named Mary Grey.

Modern pretenders to defunct thrones include the various descendants of the Bourbon line, who claim to be the rightful king of France, a country where surprisingly strong royalist sentiments remain. In addition, there have been a number of twentieth-century claimants to the throne of the last Byzantine emperor, Constantine XI (r. 1448–1453), who died in 1453.

Some modern claims to the throne rest on untraditional arguments. In 1993, for example, Brazil was about to hold a plebiscite to decide whether the monarchy should be reinstated. Neninho de Obaluaye, president of the Center for Black Resistance in Sao Paulo, argued that the Crown should not go to the former ruling dynasty, the Orleans-Braganza family, which had been deposed by a republican movement in 1889. Instead, he maintained, the Crown of a reestablished monarchy should go to the descendants of African slaves, whose labor actually built Brazil during the colonial era.

See also: ROYAL IMPOSTERS.

FURTHER READING

Cheesman, Clive, and Jonathan Williams. *Rebels, Pretenders and Impostors.* New York: St. Martin's Press, 2000

Hindley, Geoffrey. *The Royal Families of Europe.* New York: Carroll & Graf, 2000.

RUDOLF I (1218–1291 C.E.)

Elected king of medieval Germany (r. 1273–1291) and first monarch of the powerful and long-lasting Habsburg dynasty. Rudolf's reign, though not especially noteworthy in terms of German history, is important in the history of Europe, as he began the accumulation of land and resources that enabled the Habsburg line to rise to great prominence in later years.

Rudolf was born in 1218 to Albert, the count of Habsburg, and Hedwig of Kyburg. Both families held small estates in Germany. Rudolf furthered his political prospects by marrying Gertrude of Hohenberg in 1245, and he then took quick advantage of the collapse of the powerful German Hohenstaufen dynasty by seizing a variety of unclaimed estates. By the time Pope Gregory X (r. 1271–1276) forced an election for the German throne in 1273, Rudolf was one of the most powerful figures in Germany. He won the Crown over the opposition of Bohemian king Ottocar II (r. 1253–1278).

Ottocar refused to recognize Rudolf as king, and tensions quickly mounted across Central Europe as the two monarchs vied for power. A series of diplomatic efforts failed to appease either side, and Rudolf went to war against Ottocar in 1278, defeating and killing his rival in the fierce battle of Marchfeld. With his throne intact, Rudolf focused his efforts on securing landed legacies for his descendants, especially in Austria. These lands, taken from Ottocar, became the basis for much of the Habsburg family's future power.

Although the princes of Germany ostensibly supported Rudolf, the king's efforts to quell local rivalries through peace agreements were unsuccessful, largely because he lacked the manpower to enforce them. Rudolf was similarly unsuccessful in his efforts to push his kingdom southward into Italy and in his attempts to centralize political power through a series of taxes and economic controls. Despite these setbacks, Rudolf acquired significant political power for the Habsburgs.

In hopes of gaining papal approval for his coronation as Holy Roman emperor, Rudolf followed a conciliatory polity toward Pope Nicholas II (r. 1277–1280) in the late 1270s by renouncing sovereignty over the Papal States and seeking the withdrawal of the house of Anjou from central Italy. These efforts failed, however, and Rudolf never received papal recognition as emperor.

After Rudolf's death in 1291, German princely electors, nervous about the growing power of the Habsburgs, refused to elect his son Albert as king. Albert was able to restore the Habsburgs to power, however, by deposing his chief rival, Adolf of Nassau, in 1298, and taking the German throne as Albert I (r. 1298–1308).

See also: ALBERT I; ELECTION, ROYAL; HABSBURG DYNASTY; HOHENSTAUFEN DYNASTY; HOLY ROMAN EMPIRE.

RURIK (d. 879 C.E.)

Semilegendary founder (r. ca. 862–879) of the princely Riurikid dynasty of medieval Russia. which ruled until 1598.

In the ninth century, bands of Scandinavian Vikings known as the Varangians raided and eventually settled between the Dnieper and the Volga rivers (roughly the area of present-day Ukraine). As they had done in the duchy of Normandy in France, the Vikings formed an aristocracy that ruled and intermixed with the Slavs who were already living there.

Rurik (also spelled Riurik or Ryurik) is described in early sources as a warrior prince of the Varangians, who came to be called the Rus (the origin of the word "Russia"). Around 862, Rurik established himself at Novgorod, where he built fortifications and created an orderly government. A legend from the eleventh or twelfth century says that he and his brothers were mercenaries invited by warring Slavic tribes to rule over them and establish peace. But this myth may be merely justification of past conquest or evidence of factional strife within the tribal leadership.

Rurik's kinsmen and descendants enlarged the Rus territory, first dominating the region around the Dnieper River, an important trade route. After Rurik's death, his kinsman Oleg (r. ca. 879–912) assumed leadership of Novgorod and seized the city of Kiev, where he laid the foundations for the powerful

Kievan Rus. Oleg's successor, Igor (who may have been Rurik's son), ruled as duke of Kiev (r. 912–945) and is considered the true founder of the Riurikid dynasty. Later Riurikids also came to rule the grand duchy of Muscovy. As the Riurikids expanded their territory, they came into conflict with Mongol and Turkic tribes, such as the Khazars, and with the Byzantine Empire.

In 1547, the Riurikid ruler Ivan IV (Ivan the Terrible, r. 1533–1584) adopted the title tsar and ruled over all the Russian states. However, the Riurikids ruled Russia as tsars only until the death of Ivan's son and successor, Feodor I (Theodore I) in 1598.

See also: Ivan IV, the Terrible; Kiev, Princedom of; Riurikid Dynasty; Russian Dynasties.

Rus Princedoms (ca. 850–1236 c.e.)

Medieval princedoms in present-day Russia, Ukraine, and Belarus that were the early foundations for the Russian state and empire.

In the sixth and seventh centuries, members of various East Slavic tribes migrated into a forested region of present-day Russia and Ukraine, which stretched from Novgorod in the north to Kiev in the south. These tribes, whose descendants became the modern Russians, Ukrainians, and Belorussians, were the first inhabitants of what later came to be known as Kievan Rus. As their population grew, these peoples occupied additional land from the Polish and Hungarian borders in the west to the upper Volga River region in the east.

During the ninth century, the loosely affiliated Rus settlers faced increasing attacks from various Scandinavian tribes known collectively as the Varangians. Slavic tribal leaders responded to this threat by inviting Rurik, a powerful Varangian leader, to occupy Novgorod and protect the East Slavs from further attack. While Rurik assumed control of Novgorod, two of his followers, Askold and Dir, inhabited Kiev and transformed it into a major metropolitan area. After Rurik's death, around 879, his kinsman Oleg attacked Kiev, killed Askold and Dir, and established the city as the center of the Kievan Rus, one of the major Rus kingdoms. Over the next century, Oleg (r. 879–912) and his successors subjugated the East Slavic tribes, often by executing tribal leaders and razing tribal villages, and expanded their realm.

Under Oleg and his immediate successors, the Rus population consisted mainly of farmers and foresters. Agricultural methods were very crude; unaware of the benefits of crop rotation, the farmers tilled the land until the soil was depleted, then moved to open land. Forestry practices were similar. After an area had been deforested, workers simply relocated. Therefore, the early Rus population was largely nomadic.

When Grand Prince Vladimir I (r. 978–1015) assumed control of Kiev in 978, he fundamentally altered these practices. First, he recruited Varangian mercenaries to patrol the Rus kingdoms and stabilize their borders. Second, he adopted Orthodox Christianity as the official Rus religion. Although it was impossible to quickly convert the Slavic tribes from their pagan practices, the introduction of a single religion provided another element around which the Rus kingdoms could develop.

Vladimir also encouraged the growth of cities, which not only served as refuges from foreign attacks, but also became centers for early industry as artisans such as glassmakers, jewelers, and ironworkers congregated there and developed their trades. Finally, Vladimir introduced the concept of land ownership. To reward his supporters, Vladimir would grant them vast amounts of land. These grants sharply curtailed nomadic agricultural practices; farmers became attached to a specific parcel of land, cultivating it for the newly appointed landowner. In turn, these landowners assumed an authoritative position over the farmers. The most powerful landowners became governors, and they consequently replaced the tribal leaders whose powers had greatly diminished.

Vladimir's son, Yaroslav the Wise (r. 1019–1054), further developed the Kievan Rus society. During his reign, foreign raids were virtually eliminated. Benefiting from this increased safety and the growing artisan population, Yaroslav developed the region's fledgling cultural institutions. He oversaw the construction of cathedrals, libraries, and other civic buildings and encouraged the immigration of Byzantine artists, historians, and teachers. Yaroslav also wrote the first major Russian law code. Under his reign, the Rus kingdoms experienced their greatest period of unity and affluence.

After Yaroslav's death in 1054, the Rus kingdoms became increasingly fragmented. Unable to cooperate with one another, the individual states faced increasing attacks from the Polovtsian tribes who inhabited the region's southern borders, and the Rus princes watched their powers steadily deteriorate. By 1150, the Kievan Rus had divided into several separate autonomous principalities. Among these, Kiev retained the most political influence, but Suzdalia became the region's cultural leader and Novgorod the most prosperous commercial center.

The emergence of the Rus principalities was violently stifled in 1223, when a Mongol scouting party defeated a Rus army in a battle at the Kalka River. Yet, even the Mongols' ferocious victory failed to alleviate the bitter rivalries that had developed among the Rus principalities. As the number of Mongol invasions increased over the next decade, the Rus princes refused to consolidate their forces and offer a united opposition. Consequently, when the Mongols launched a major invasion in 1236, they successfully conquered the Rus principalities one by one, leading to more than two centuries of Mongol dominance.

See also: KIEV, PRINCEDOM OF; MONGOL EMPIRE; RURIK; VLADIMIR PRINCEDOM; YAROSLAV I, THE WISE.

FURTHER READING

Martin, Janet. *Medieval Russia: 980–1054.* New York: Cambridge University Press, 1995.

Pelenski, Jaroslaw. *The Contest for the Legacy of Kievan Rus'.* New York: Columbia University Press, 1998.

RUSSIAN DYNASTIES (800s–1917 C.E.)

Two ruling dynasties of Russia, the Riurikids and Romanovs, who led the country from its founding in the ninth century until the Russian Revolution of 1917.

In the ninth century, a group of Scandinavian traders and warriors, the Varangians, became established in the region that is now western Russia. The name of their country became known as Rus, perhaps a term that designated the Varangians. One of the Rus princes—Rurik (r. ca. 862–879)—became ruler of Novgorod (r. ca. 862–879) and is considered the traditional founder of Russia. Rurik was the ancestor of the many family branches of the Riurikid dynasty, which ruled until 1598. His son and succes-

sor, Igor (r. 913–945), made the city of Kiev the capital of the region.

GROWTH OF THE RUS KINGDOMS

Under Igor's son and successor, Sviatoslav (r. 945–972), the princedom of Kiev reached its peak of power. Upon his death, however, a struggle for power broke out between his sons, with Vladimir (r. 978–1015) eventually gaining power.

Vladimir carried on the work of previous generations by subjecting most of the eastern Slavic region to his rule. He was the first Russian ruler to convert to Christianity. Vladimir's descendants made Kiev the center of a confederation of territories ruled by related princes. Collateral succession between brothers or cousins was the usual pattern of inheritance; the senior prince of the senior generation ruled Kiev as

Built between 1499 and 1508 by the grand princes of Moscow, the Terem Palace was the imperial residence until 1712, when Peter the Great moved the Russian capital from Moscow to St. Petersburg. Located in the Kremlin, the ornate palace was refurbished in the early 1600s by Tsar Michael and Tsar Alexei, the first two Romanov rulers.

Riurikid Dynasty (862–1598)

RURIK*   862–879

GREAT PRINCES OF KIEV

OLEG I   879–913,
                         REGENT AND CO-RULER

IGOR I   913–945

OLGA   945–962,
                         REGENT

SVIATOSLAV I   962–972

IAROPOLK I   972–980

VLADIMIR I   980–1015

SVIATOPOLK I   1015–1019

YAROSLAV I THE WISE*   1019–1054

IZYASLAV I   1054–1078

VSESLAV I   1068–1069

SVIATOSLAV II   1073–1076

VSEVOLOD I   1093–1113

VLADIMIR II   1113–1125

MSTISLAV I   1125–1132

IAROPOLK II   1132–1139

VYACHESLAV I   1139–1146

IZYASLAV II   1146–1154

ROSTISLAV I   1154–1164

YURI I   1149–1157

GREAT PRINCES OF VLADIMIR

ANDREI I   1157–1174

VSEVOLOD III   1176–1212

YURI II   1212–1237

YAROSLAV II   1237–1246

SVIATOSLAV III   1247

ANDREI II   1247–1252

ALEXANDER I NEVSKY*   1252–1263

YAROSLAV III   1264–1271

VASSILY II   1271–1276

DMITRI I   1277–1294

ANDREI III   1294–1304

MIKHAIL III   1304–1319

YURI III   1319–1322

DMITRI II   1322–1325

ALEXANDER II   1326–1328

IVAN I   1328–1341

SIMEON I   1341–1353

IVAN II   1353–1359

DMITRI III   1360–1362

GREAT PRINCES OF MOSCOW

DMITRI IV*   1359–1389

VASSILY I   1389–1425

VASSILY II   1425–1462

IVAN III THE GREAT*   1462–1505

VASSILY III   1505–1533

TSARS OF RUSSIA

IVAN IV THE TERRIBLE*   1533–1584

FEODOR I   1584–1598

BORIS GODONOV   1598–1605

FEODOR II   1605

PSEUDO-DMITRI   1605–1606

VASSILY IV   1606–1610

(POLISH INTERREGNUM 1610–1613)

Romanov Dynasty (1613–1917)

MIKHAIL ROMANOV*	1613–1645	ELIZABETH	1741–1762
ALEXEI	1645–1676	PETER III	1762
FEODOR IV	1676–1682	CATHERINE II, THE GREAT*	1762–1796
IVAN V	1682–1696, CO-RULER	PAUL I	1796–1801
PETER I THE GREAT*	1682–1725, CO-RULER TO 1696	ALEXANDER I*	1801–1825
		NICHOLAS I*	1825–1855
CATHERINE I	1725–1727	ALEXANDER II*	1855–1881
PETER II	1727–1730	ALEXANDER III	1881–1894
ANNA	1730–1740	NICHOLAS II*	1894–1917 (EXECUTED 1918)
IVAN VI	1740–1741		

*Indicates a separate alphabetical entry.

the "Great Prince" or "Grand Duke," the overlord to whom the other princes owed allegiance.

The Great Princes of Kiev ruled over a prosperous network of commercial towns, maintaining political and trade relationships with the Byzantine Empire. However, Kievan Russia suffered continual internal conflicts. In 1169, Prince Andrew I of Vladimir (r. 1157–1174), a Riurikid ruler of another princedom, sacked Kiev as punishment for a revolt and moved the capital to Vladimir. From the reign of Vsevolod III (r. 1176–1212) until the predominance of the princedom of Moscow in the 1360s, the Great Princes of Vladimir were the preeminent rulers among the many Russian princes.

INTERNAL CONFLICT AND EXTERNAL THREAT

During the late twelfth century, the history of Russia became a succession of wars between brothers, cousins, uncles, and nephews. This chaotic situation was the result of the collateral transmission of power, in which the succession passed not from the son but from the most senior member of the elder generation to the next eldest of that generation. Izyaslav II of Kiev (r. 1146–1154) attempted, unsuccessfully, to change the principle of collateral succession to a system in which the prince designated his own successor. Thus, continuing internal conflicts weakened the young Russian state.

Late in 1237 the Mongols began their conquest of

Russia. After Kiev was taken by the Mongols of the Golden Horde in 1240, the Kievan Rus became part of the Mongol Empire, which dominated all of Eurasia. In Russia, the Mongols extracted tribute and levied taxes but left cooperative native rulers in place as vassals of the Mongol khan.

During the period of Mongol dominance, the princes of the Russian territories continued to come from families of the Riurikid dynasty. The center of power, however, shifted from Vladimir to Moscow, a process that began with Ivan I Kalita of Vladimir (r. 1328–1341). Ivan Kalita also changed the custom of succession so that the direct heir would receive the greatest portion of power and territory, decreasing the tendency for the territories to become subdivided among many heirs.

The princes of Moscow were given the right to collect tribute from the other Russian princes for the Mongols; this naturally added to the power, prestige, and wealth of Moscow. Dmitri IV (r. 1362–1389) established the principle of direct hereditary succession by which a single son should follow his father. He also enlarged Moscow's territory and began to establish it as an autocratic power that dominated the other Russian principalities.

THE TSARDOM AND IVAN THE TERRIBLE

Mongol suzerainty over Russia ended through a combination of continued Russian opposition from the

ROYAL RELATIVES

CHILDREN OF THE LAST TSAR

The children of Tsar Nicholas II and his wife Alexandra were the Grand Duchesses Olga, Tatiana, Marie, and Anastasia, and the heir to the throne, the Tsarevitch Alexei, who suffered from hemophilia.

The family of the tsar lived a life insulated from the poverty suffered by the majority of the Russian populace. Unlike most upper-class children of the time, however, they were not kept remote from their parents. Family was the center of their lives.

In 1917, the Russian Revolution forced Nicholas II to abdicate and he and his family were imprisoned. In the spring of 1918, the imperial family was exiled to Ekaterinburg in the Ural Mountains, far to the east of Moscow. At first, the Bolsheviks planned to put the tsar on trial. But believing that White Russian and Czech forces would capture Ekaterinburg and liberate the family, the revolutionaries decided to execute them. On the night of July 16 the royal family were shot and bayoneted. Accounts of the disposal of the bodies differ. Some or all were burned in a kerosene-fueled bonfire, before or after being damaged with sulphuric acid and dumped in a mineshaft with a grenade, to be reburied shortly after.

After World War I, tsarist pretenders began to surface. Most claimed to be surviving members of the family, usually Anastasia or Alexei. The most famous of these pretenders was Anna Anderson, a Polish woman who claimed to be Anastasia Romanov. DNA testing proved this claim false in 1994, and every similar case has likewise been discredited by DNA analysis. Recent forensic examinations have failed to identify Alexei and either Marie or Anastasia among the nine skeletons exhumed in 1991, but given the attempt to destroy even the bones, this can hardly be considered proof of their survival. All evidence so far indicates that the last tsar's five children died with him.

---

fourteenth century onward, and internal conflicts among the Mongols. Grand Prince Ivan III of Moscow-Vladimir (r. 1462–1505), called Ivan the Great, formally declared independence from the Mongols in 1480. Ivan married the niece of the last ruler of the Byzantine Empire, thus identifying the rulers of Moscow with the heritage of Byzantium and the Eastern Roman Empire. Ivan III sometimes used the title "tsar" (derived from the Roman title "caesar") although it was his grandson, Ivan IV, the Terrible (r. 1533–1584), who would adopt it officially.

During his reign, Ivan IV greatly increased the territory controlled by Moscow and worked to centralize the Russian government, limiting the power of the Russian nobility, the boyars, at the same time. Ivan conquered the Tatar khanates of Astrakhan and Kazan and fought a long and unsuccessful war against Livonia (now Estonia and Latvia), Lithuania, Poland, and Sweden. At the end of his reign, Russia annexed western Siberia. Laws prohibiting peasants from moving also were passed for the first time during Ivan's reign, beginning the institution of Russian serfdom.

Ivan IV was the first tsar to summon the *zemsky sobor,* an assembly that included not only boyars and clergy, but also representatives of all the free classes of Russian society (which did not include serfs and slaves). Previous Russian princes had been advised by assemblies of noblemen called *duma.* Ivan IV also established a secret police, and, fearing conspiracy, he ordered the massacre of thousands of people in Novgorod in 1570. In a fit of rage, Ivan also killed his eldest son. His second son, Feodor I (r. 1584–1598), was the last ruler of the Riurikid dynasty. He died without an heir.

TIME OF TROUBLES, ROMANOVS, AND REVOLUTION

Boris Godunov, the brother-in-law of Feodor I and the real ruler during Feodor's reign, succeeded him as tsar (r. 1598–1605). The patriarch of the Russian Church offered Godunov the Crown, and the *zemsky sobor* elected him tsar. Godunov's enemies, however, accused him of killing Feodor's younger half-brother Dmitri, and his claim to the throne was contested by many of the boyars as well as by a Polish-supported pretender known as the Pseudo-Dmitri, who claimed to be the youngest son of Ivan IV. Boris Godunov died in 1605, his son Feodor II was murdered the same year, and the pretender Dmitri (r. 1605–1606) became tsar. Following Dmitri's murder, Vasily IV (r. 1606–1610), who was related to the Riurikids, became tsar with the support of the boyars.

The early seventeenth century was truly a time of troubles for Russia: famine from 1601 to 1603, lawlessness, foreign invasion, violent revolts, and equally violent suppressions of revolts. Another pretender to the throne, Dmitri II, appeared in 1608 and ruled as a rival tsar to Vasily until 1610. Dmitri led an armed resistance until his capture and execution in 1614. Poland invaded Russia in 1609 and Vasily V was deposed. A Polish prince, Vladislav, was elected by the *zemsky sobor* in his place in 1610.

A New Dynasty

In 1613, Poland was driven out of Russia by a unified national effort, and the *zemsky sobor* elected a new tsar. The individual chosen was sixteen-year-old Mikhail (Michael) Romanov (r. 1613–1645), a member of a boyar family called the Romanovs. Ivan IV's first wife, Anastasia, had been a member of the Romanov family, so part of the family's prestige was due to its connection with the Riurikid dynasty.

Mikhail Romanov restored order in Russia, assuming the title "autocrat" in 1625. He made peace with Poland and Sweden and continued to extend Russian control eastward into Siberia. Mikhail also increased the restrictions on Russian peasants and serfs. The tsars who followed Mikhail faced revolts and controversies within the Russian Church, but the Romanovs remained securely in power, eventually adding the Ukraine to the lands ruled by Moscow.

Peter I, the Great (r. 1682–1725) of the Romanov dynasty changed Russia forever. Succeeding to the throne as a boy, he was co-ruler with his half-brother Ivan V (r. 1682–1696) under the regency of Ivan's older sister Sophia. Once Peter began ruling on his own in 1696, he instituted a number of military and administrative reforms. He brought the Russian Orthodox Church under a greater degree of state control and founded a new capital at St. Petersburg. He visited Europe and promoted Western culture in Russia.

In 1721 Russia defeated Sweden in war, thereby giving Russia access to the Baltic Sea, which it had sought for generations. Sweden ceded the regions of Estonia, Latvia, and Ingria. (Ingria is still part of Russia today.) During his reign, Peter also founded the Russian senate as a nonrepresentative legislative council to carry out his will. The senate remained the main legislative body in Russia under the tsars until 1802. Although Peter changed the rules governing inheritance so that the tsar could designate his own successor, he himself failed to designate a successor. Upon his death, his widow, Catherine I (r. 1725–1727), ruled for two years before the throne went to Peter's grandson, Peter II (r. 1727–1730) in 1727.

Powerful Women on the Throne

During the reign of the tsarina Elizabeth (r. 1741–1762), the daughter of Peter I and Catherine I, Russia became more involved in European affairs, allying with Austria against Sweden and taking part in the War of the Austrian Succession (1740–1748) and the Seven Years' War (1756–1763) against Prussia. Elizabeth designated her nephew Peter as her heir. But when Peter III (r. 1762) took the throne in 1762 he was very unpopular because of his pro-Prussian stance. With the support of the army, his wife, German princess Sophia of Anhalt, deposed him and became Tsarina Catherine II; she would become known as Catherine, the Great (r. 1762–1796). Her adoption of the Russian Orthodox faith and her attempts to become more "Russian" made her popular despite her German heritage.

Under Catherine the Great, Russia warred with Turkey and with Poland, gaining access to the Black Sea and annexing the Crimea and Lithuania. She also continued the attempts begun by Peter I to make Russia more European in outlook. During her rule, however, the institution of serfdom became more entrenched and the powers of landowners over their serfs more severe, resulting in several violent and widespread revolts.

A Changing Monarchy

Catherine's son and successor, Paul I (r. 1796–1801), changed the rules of inheritance again, forbidding females from succeeding to the Russian throne. Under Paul I, Russia and its former enemy, Turkey, joined England, Austria, and Naples against Napoleon and France in 1798. Paul was assassinated by a conspiracy of military officers and courtiers in 1801.

Paul's son and successor, Alexander I (1801–1825), reformed the Russian government, making the senate insignificant and instead installed the State Council as the main legislative body in 1810. Alexander abolished serfdom in some territories, but not in Russia itself, fearing the reaction of the landowning nobles.

Russian serfs were essentially the property of landowners, and they constituted a large, unhappy, and potentially dangerous part of the population. Freed serfs, who had no land of their own and thus no means of supporting themselves, also presented a potential problem. The issue of serfdom would trouble Russia throughout most of the nineteenth century.

Under Alexander I, Russia played an important role in the final defeat of Napoleon and was rewarded with much of Poland by the terms of the Congress of Vienna (1815). The reigns of his successors vacillated between reactionary and liberal. Alexander I's brother and successor, Nicholas I (r. 1825–1855), downgraded the State Council, increasing the autocratic powers of the tsar. However, he also passed laws limiting serfdom and issued a new law code.

Alexander II (r. 1855–1881), the son of Nicholas I, was a liberal reformer who ended serfdom in 1861, made great legal and administrative reforms, and championed the Orthodox Christian countries of the Balkans against the Ottoman Empire. However, under his rule, discontent increased greatly; liberals demanded more reform, and so revolutionary groups formed to try to force change. Alexander was assassinated in 1881—ironically on the same day he signed a document that could have been the basis for a constitution and representative assembly.

His son and successor, Alexander III (r. 1881–1894), reacted to his father's assassination and attempts at reform by suppressing liberals and revolutionaries, increasing censorship, imposing government control on universities, and strengthening the role of the nobles again.

Nicholas II (r. 1894–1917), the son of Alexander III, failed to make any significant changes in policy. The Russo-Japanese War of 1904–1905 and Russian involvement in World War I brought the Russian people's dissatisfaction with their government to a head. In 1905, Russia experienced the first of the revolutionary uprisings, strikes, and mutinies that would later culminate in the Bolshevik Revolution of 1917. Forced to abdicate by revolutionaries in 1917, Nicholas II, his wife, and his children were killed in July 1918, ending the Romanov dynasty and more than a millennium of Russian monarchy.

From the time of the legendary Rurik to the last Romanov, Russian's monarchy consistently tended toward autocracy. Russian assemblies—the *duma, zemsky sobors*, senates, and state councils—never became established as a voice for the people. Russia never effected the balance between monarch, church, and nobles that the Western European countries managed to achieve. Some Western European countries worked to moderate the power of all three, which led them to look to the common people as a potential power base with which to negotiate. In the end, this failure contributed to the violent end of the Russian monarchy. However, the pattern of strong centralized power established by the Riurikid and Romanov dynasties continued even under the Soviet political system in the twentieth century.

See also: ALEXANDER I; ALEXANDER II; ALEXANDRA; CATHERINE II, THE GREAT; IVAN III, THE GREAT; IVAN IV, THE TERRIBLE; KIEV, PRINCEDOM OF; NICHOLAS I; NICHOLAS II; PETER I, THE GREAT; RIURIKID DYNASTY; ROMANOV DYNASTY; RURIK; RUS PRINCEDOMS; YAROSLAV I, THE WISE.

FURTHER READING

Freeze, Gregory L., ed. *Russia: A History*. New York: Oxford University Press, 1997.

Grey, Ian. *The Romanovs: The Rise and Fall of a Russian Dynasty*. New York: Doubleday, 1970.

Massie, Robert K. *The Romanovs: The Final Chapter*. New York: Random House, 1995.

Vernadsky, George. *Kievan Russia*. New Haven, CT: Yale University Press, 1973.

———. *A History of Russia*. New Haven, CT: Yale University Press, 1987.

SABAEAN KINGDOM

(ca. 1000 B.C.E.–300 C.E.)

One of the principal empires in the southwestern part of the Arabian Peninsula (in present-day Yemen) that was famous primarily for its legendary ruler Bilqis, the queen of Sheba (r. ca. 1005–965 B.C.E.).

The Sabaeans were one of the three main peoples in ancient South Arabia (the others were the Minaeans and the Himyarites), and their city of Saba was the most powerful of a number of city-states in that region. Although the Sabaeans were never united politically or ethnically, Saba gradually increased its political control to embrace all the main kingdoms of southern Arabia.

Saba was very wealthy, and with the most rainfall anywhere in Arabia, the area was lush and fertile. The Sabaeans were able to export valuable exotic plants, spices, and luxury products all over the Mediterranean and Asia. Its commercial success was boosted by its strategic position on ocean-trade routes to India and Africa and at the south end of land-based routes along the coast of the Arabian Peninsula.

From about 1000 B.C.E. to 200 C.E., the Sabaeans totally dominated international trade on the Red Sea and the Indian Ocean, as well as the land trade that took spices and other products through Arabia into the Mediterranean. Items such as myrrh and frankincense were especially profitable, for they were highly valued by the ancient Egyptians, Greeks, and Romans for a variety of native rituals. At the peak of their power, the Sabaeans had trading posts or colonies from one end of North Arabia to the other, and it is likely that the queen of Sheba came from one of those.

By about the middle of the eighth century B.C.E., the Sabaeans had created their own kingdom, which became the leading power in southern Arabia under the kings Yathiamar (flourished ca. 725–700 B.C.E.) and Karibil Watar (flourished ca. 700–650 B.C.E.). The Sabaean capital, Marib, flourished more than any other city in ancient Arabia. This was partly because of its strategic location for trade and partly because of a remarkable dam that supplied water for the people and for agriculture.

Marib's dam lasted more than one thousand years, demonstrating the highly developed technical capability of Sabaean society. The ancient Sabaeans also used an alphabet similar to that of the Phoenicians. Inscriptions and other writings, as well as excavations at Marib, corroborate the Sabaeans' high level of civilization and affluence based on agriculture and trade.

Marib was fortified by a wall that successfully protected it from various enemies, including the Romans, who attacked in 25 B.C.E. However, by the first century C.E., the Sabaean kingdom began to decline in power. The Himyarites, in particular, weakened Saba with persistent attacks and finally overcame the Sabaeans in the second century.

See also: SHEBA, QUEEN OF.

SACRAL BIRTH AND DEATH

The sacred rites, beliefs, and events associated with the birth and death of rulers. In many societies, the birth or death of monarchs has been treated as an event of great religious significance, assigned meanings and accompanied by rites that have differed from those commemorating the life passages of the rulers' subjects.

SIGNS OF DIVINITY OR GREATNESS
Egyptian pharaohs, including Hatshepsut (r. 1503–1483 B.C.E.), had their own births portrayed in their temples, with their mothers serving as vessels into which the divine essence was conveyed. Alexander the Great (r. 336–323 B.C.E.) made a similar claim of divine status, claiming to have been begotten on his mother by the god Zeus Ammon in the form of a snake.

Whether or not a ruler claimed divine parentage, the birth of a future monarch often was claimed to be accompanied by providential signs marking the infant for greatness. The Roman historian Suetonius recounts a plethora of signs (some modeled on legends associated with Alexander the Great) that accompanied the conception, development, and birth of the first Roman emperor, Augustus (r. 27 B.C.E.–14 C.E.). This included a dream his mother had while she was pregnant with him in which her bowels stretched to the stars. In the case of the Dalai Lamas who ruled Tibet before the Chinese conquest in 1950, divine signs were crucial to the identification of the new ruler, who, as with all previous Dalai Lamas, was conceived as a new incarnation of the same deity.

SACRED CONCEPTIONS OF DEATH

In many societies, the death of a king was portrayed as an apotheosis, or the raising of the dead ruler to the rank of a god. Some rulers even claimed this themselves. The Roman historian Suetonius, for example, alleged that the Emperor Vespasian (r. 69–79) remarked, "I think I am becoming a god" when Vespasian was first seized by the distemper that later killed him.

Monotheistic religions, including Judaism, Christianity, and Islam, have denied the possibility of apotheosis. But adherents to these faiths have provided alternative religious conceptions of royal death, particularly death by violence. The first medieval king to be recognized as a saint, Sigismund of Burgundy (r. 516–523), owed his saintly reputation, in part, to having been murdered by the Franks in 523. The Anglo-Saxon kingdoms, which produced many royal saints in the early Middle Ages, had several rulers who died fighting pagans. Both Christianity and Islam, in particular, have often praised death on the battlefield against a religious foe. Even the death of Ottoman sultan Suleyman I (r. 1520–1556), who died in his tent rather than in battle while campaigning against the Christians, earned him the title of "Martyr."

Death by murder, as well as battle, has also been treated as sacred. The death by execution of Charles I (r. 1625–1649) of England was portrayed by his admirers as a martyrdom, paralleling the Passion and death of Jesus. Handkerchiefs dipped in the blood that Charles shed on the scaffold were treated as sacred relics and were even credited with healing powers. Tsar Nicolas II (r. 1894–1917) of Russia, murdered by the Bolsheviks in 1918, was canonized by the Russian Orthodox Church in 2000 as a "passion bearer," for the humility with which he bore captivity and death. Like the British royalists who venerated Charles I, many Russian supporters of Nicholas's canonization compared him to Christ and looked to a restoration of the monarchy.

See also: FUNERALS AND MORTUARY RITUALS; KINGLY BODY; SACRED KINGSHIPS.

SACRED KINGSHIPS

Monarchies claiming a particular relationship to the gods or the divine.

The most extreme form of sacred kingship is divine kingship, the worship of the monarch as a god. The earliest developed society known to follow this practice was that of ancient Egypt, whose pharaohs were considered to be gods. Contact with Egypt may have influenced the decision of Alexander the Great (356–323 B.C.E.) to proclaim himself divine and the son of a god. Many Hellenistic monarchs followed his example. God-kings are also found in Africa and in pre-Columbian America. Kings could also be ritually married to goddesses, as was a common custom in pre-Christian Ireland.

RULERS AS INTERMEDIARIES BETWEEN HUMAN AND DIVINE

Even when not conceived as gods or consorts of goddesses, monarchs are frequently ascribed as having a direct relationship with the divine not granted to ordinary people. This was often expressed through ritual activity. Chinese emperors, for example, carried on a complex cycle of annual sacrifices, culminating in the sacrifice to Heaven on the winter solstice and the sacrifice to earth on the summer solstice. These sacrifices emphasized the role of the emperor, the "Son of Heaven," in binding together the different realms of Heaven and Earth. The kings of the ancient city-states of Sumeria in Mesopotamia also were seen as intermediaries between the earthly and divine.

Some monarchs devoted themselves to ritual religious activity to the exclusion of political responsibilities. The classic example of this kind of monarchy is the Japanese emperor, who is viewed as a descendant of the sun-goddess Amaterasu. Japanese emperors have been politically powerless (with rare exceptions) for nearly a millennium, but so important was their ritual function that the institution was never threatened until Japan's defeat at the end of World War II. A sacralized version of Japanese monarchism—state

Shinto or emperor worship—became the official ideology of the Japanese state following the Meiji Restoration in 1868 but was abolished by Americans in the postwar occupation after World War II.

State Shinto was based on ethnic nationalism and emphasized the particular virtues and destiny of the Japanese "race." By contrast, emperor worship in the pagan Roman Empire provided a focus of loyalty that transcended ethnicity in a multiethnic, multicultural empire. It was because emperor worship was so closely related to loyalty to the Roman Empire that Christian refusal to worship the emperor aroused such hostility from the Roman state (as it also did from the Japanese).

SACRED MONARCHY IN MONOTHEISTIC SOCIETIES

Kings being worshiped as gods was not a possibility in the traditions of the great monotheistic religions of Zoroastrianism, Judaism, Christianity, and Islam. Nonetheless, kings continued to assert a particularly close relation to God.

King David (r. 1010–970 B.C.E.) became the archetypal king in both Jewish and Christian tradition. The Byzantine emperors held the title of *isapostolos,* or equal of the apostles. In Western Europe, claims to be the successor of the apostles were monopolized by the pope, and kings made different claims to sacred status.

The Holy Roman emperors and the kings of France, who were called the "Most Christian" kings, were particularly likely to present themselves as sacred monarchs. A central element of the coronation ritual of the French king was anointment with oil from the "ampule," a vial supposedly brought down from Heaven by the Holy Spirit in the form of a dove at the coronation of the first king of the Franks, Clovis (r. ca. 482–511). Consecration with holy oil, modeled on the anointment of King David of Israel, was part of the coronation ritual of many monarchs and gave kings a particularly holy status.

One check on the development of the fully sacralized monarchy in Europe was the presence of a rival group of religious professionals, the priesthood or clergy. The popes, in particular, opposed the ascription of supernatural powers to kings, especially the Holy Roman emperors, preferring to keep a monopoly for the church.

The shrinking of papal political power in the sixteenth century, caused by the Protestant Reformation and the increased power of the Catholic monarchs, saw a resurgence of sacred monarchy. Political and theological writers of the time frequently referred to a biblical passage in Proverbs—"A Divine Sentence is in the lips of the King"—to ascribe to kings a direct connection with the divine that bypassed the Catholic or Protestant priesthood. This was the height of the theory of the "divine right of kings," which emphasized the divine origins of a monarch's rule. Sacralization of a monarch not only established the king's independence of ecclesiastical authority, but it also helped exalt kings above their nobility.

A central element of the great judicial regicides of the early modern period—the executions of English king Charles I (r. 1625–1649) and French king Louis XVI (r. 1774–1792)—was aggressive desacralization, a process by which the sacred aspects of kingship were removed. Desacralization was only partially successful in the case of Charles's beheading; handkerchiefs dipped in the sacred blood of the martyred king were widely believed to have healing powers. Louis XVI's execution had more wide-ranging consequences, resulting in the secularization of the European monarchy after the French Revolution.

The earliest Muslim leaders after the Prophet Muhammed (ca. 570–632), the caliphs, were believed to have a special relationship with God, although not as close as that of Muhammed himself. The caliph's position as the religious leader of the community of Muslims persisted after the decay of his political and military power. Eventually, after the end of the Abbasid caliphate in 1256, powerful Sunni Muslim rulers, such as the Ottoman sultans, began adding caliph to their other titles in order to emphasize their role as protectors of Islam in their territories. The last powerful Ottoman Sultan, Abd al-Hamid II (r. 1876–1909), used the title of caliph to claim leadership over Muslims everywhere, in addition to his direct rule over the Ottoman Empire.

The Shi'ite sect of Islam has been more likely to see monarchs as semidivine figures than has the Sunni sect. The Shi'ite concept of the Imam, a man sent from heaven to lead the community of true Muslims, has been the basis of the legitimacy of many monarchical dynasties. The Fatimid dynasty of caliphs—founded in North Africa in 910 by the Imam Al-Mahdi (r. 910–934), who claimed descent from Muhammed's daughter Fatima—lasted more than two and a half centuries.

See also: BUDDHISM AND KINGSHIP; CALIPHATES; CHRISTIANITY AND KINGSHIP; DIVINE RIGHT; DIVINITY OF KINGS; EARTH AND SKY, SEPARATION OF; HEALING POWERS OF KINGS; HINDUISM AND KINGSHIP; ISLAM AND KINGSHIP; JUDAISM AND KINGSHIP; RELIGIOUS DUTIES AND POWER; SACRAL BIRTH AND DEATH.

FURTHER READING

Finer, S.E. *The History of Government from the Earliest Times.* New York: Oxford University Press, 1997.

Monod, Paul. *The Power of Kings: Monarchy and Religion in Europe, 1589–1715.* New Haven, CT: Yale University Press, 1999.

SACRED TEXTS

Writings based on religion, theology, or philosophy; books considered holy by followers of a particular faith.

Egyptian pharaohs, Chinese and Japanese emperors, Roman kings, and other world sovereigns have often considered themselves gods or descendants of gods. Many of these rulers have concerned themselves with the writing and preservation of sacred texts, especially those that legitimize their rule.

Monarchs frequently dictated the religion their people would follow and determined both the preservation and destruction of sacred writings. The extant sacred texts of ancient Egypt, including *The Book of the Dead* and *The Book of the Opening of the Mouth,* are available primarily because they were found in the tombs of the pharaohs. The most ancient of the principal sacred texts of Hinduism are the four Vedas. The Indian ruler Rajendra Chola (r. 1012–1044) helped preserve the Vedas by establishing a Vedic school where the texts were taught.

On the other hand, Chinese emperor Ch'in Shih Huang (r. 221–210 B.C.E.) was responsible for the loss of many of the ancient Confucian texts when he ordered them burned in 213 B.C.E. When later philosophers and emperors wanted to reestablish the teachings of Confucius, the works had to be retrieved, restored, and sometimes reinvented. It is therefore difficult for scholars to know how much of the four principal books in the Confucian canon—*The Analects, Mencius, Great Learning,* and *The Doctrine of the Mean*—is actually the teaching of Confucius and how much has been added by others.

THE BIBLE AND MONARCHS

In medieval Europe, sovereigns not only supported the study of the Christian Bible, but they built monasteries as centers of learning that produced books and amassed libraries concentrated on religious writings. Most of the medieval manuscripts were written in the Latin used by the Catholic Church. Because both the Church and the monarchs felt their authority would be challenged if people had free access to the Bible, translations into the vernacular were often violently opposed. English reformer John Wycliffe and English translator William Tyndale, who made English translations of the Bible around 1380 and 1525, respectively, were considered heretics because they created vernacular texts that could be read by laypersons.

Yet, monarchs have been known to modify sacred texts to further their own political purposes. When Henry VIII (r. 1509–1547) established the Anglican Church, he supported the creation of an English version of scripture as a further break with Catholicism. However, it was a later English king who is responsible for the most widely known translation of the Christian Bible. King James I (r. 1603–1625) gathered more than fifty scholars and authorized them to complete the King James Bible, printed in 1611. This work set the standard for English prose for centuries and is still used in many Protestant churches. James's reason for sponsoring the work had less to do with furthering religion, however, than it did with countering the popular Geneva Bible (1599), which included copious marginal notes making it possible for the less educated to read with understanding, and which James saw as a threat to his divine authority.

ISLAMIC AND BUDDHIST AUTHORITY

Other sacred texts have been used to support the rule of governments. The Qur'an, the sacred text of the Islamic faith, makes no distinction between secular and religious rule; a Muslim nation is one founded on principles of faith. The Qur'an is viewed as the word of Allah given voice through the Prophet Muhammad. For the Muslim, since the revelations of the Qur'an were spoken in Arabic, a translation is an interpretation, not the true word of Allah. Rulers in Islamic nations continue to use the Qur'an as a guide for their personal and political decisions.

In the sixteenth-century, the sacred texts of Buddhism became the foundations of government in Tibet when the head of the Gelukpa sect took control and became the first Dalai Lama. The line of ruler priests has continued unbroken until today, although the present and fourteenth incarnation of the Dalai Lama has lived in exile since 1959, when a Tibetan uprising against Chinese control was ruthlessly crushed.

Sacred texts have also played an important role in the oath-taking ceremonies of monarchs. On taking the throne, monarchs usually swear to fulfill their responsibilities on a holy book, emphasizing their divine imperative to rule.

See also: DIVINE RIGHT; HENRY VIII; JAMES I OF ENGLAND (JAMES VI OF SCOTLAND); OATHS AND OATH-TAKING; SACRAL BIRTH AND DEATH; SACRED KINGSHIPS; SHIH HUANG TI (SHIHUANGDI); TIBETAN KINGDOM.

SAFAVID DYNASTY (1502–1736 C.E.)

Iranian dynasty that unified the many different ethnic and linguistic populations of Iran and established Shi'ite Islam as the state religion. The Safavids were descendants of Sheykh Safi ad Din (1253–1334) of Ardabil, head of the Safaviyeh (or Safawiyah) Sufi order. Around 1399, however, the Safavids changed their religious preference from Sufism to Shi'ism.

The Safavid dynasty was founded by Ismail I (1502–1524), who became shah of Iran in 1502, uniting all of Persia under Iranian control following about 900 years of interrupted or foreign rule. During the ensuing decade, Ismail overpowered most of Iran and took possession of the neighboring Iraqi provinces of Baghdad and Mosul. Even though that area was mainly Sunni, Ismail I declared Shi'ism the state religion.

In 1514, Ismail's power declined when the Ottoman sultan, Selim I (r. 1512–1520), defeated him in battle. Thereafter, the ongoing conflict with the Sunnis, including both the Ottomans in the west and the Uzbeks in the northeast, caused the Safavids to lose parts of their territory, including the provinces of Kurdistan, Diyarbakir, and Baghdad.

Iran grew considerably weaker under the rule of Ismail's oldest son, Shah Tahmasp I (r. 1524–1576), and his successors Ismail II (r. 1576–1577) and Muhammad Khudabanda (r. 1577–1587), who were unable to withstand continual Ottoman assaults on the country. When Abbas I, (r. 1587–1629) came to power, he reversed the course of the Safavid dynasty, establishing a

standing army and driving out the Ottoman and Uzbek forces. Abbas also reclaimed the territory the Turks had seized and recaptured Baghdad.

The reign of Abbas I (known as Abbas the Great), with its important military victories and well-organized administration, greatly elevated the status and prosperity of Iran. Industry and trade with the West increased, and the capital, Isfahan, became a showcase of Safavid architectural accomplishments. Abbas I promoted science and the arts, and some of Iran's greatest philosophers lived during his reign.

The Safavid dynasty lasted about 100 years after the death of Abbas I in 1629. However, that century was an era of decline except for a period under Shah Abbas II (r. 1642–1666). Abbas II acceded to the throne when he was only ten years old. He had a very strict early upbringing but later embraced a more liberal attitude. Apparently broadminded in religious matters, he was also kind to his subjects. Numerous renowned monuments were built in Isfahan during the rule of Abbas II, including the Khajou Bridge and the Mosque of Hakim.

Other successors of Abbas I, including Safi I (r. 1629–1642), Safi II (r. 1666–1694), and Sultan Husayn (r. 1694–1722), were weak rulers, easily influenced by religious leaders to whom the Safavids had given significant power in their effort to make Shi'ism the state religion. During the reign of Sultan Husayn, opposition forces gained strength in neighboring Afghanistan and began to threaten Iran.

In 1722, the Afghans of Qandahar seized Isfahan and forced Husayn to abdicate, effectively ending Safavid rule. Husayn's son, Tahmasp II (r. 1729–1732) was able to recapture Isfahan in 1729, but he was deposed by his lieutenant, Nadir Qoli Beg, a member of the Afshar tribe, who became Nadir Shah (r. 1736–1747) in 1736 and founded the Afsharid dynasty.

See also: ABBAS THE GREAT; NADIR SHAH; SELIM I, THE GRIM.

SAFFARID DYNASTY

(flourished 800s C.E.)

Muslim dynasty that ruled a large part of eastern Iran from Sistan (or Seistan), the native province of the dynasty's founder, Yaqub ibn Layth al-Saffar (r.

867–879). The dynasty's name means "coppersmith," which was Yaqub's occupation.

Yaqub ibn Layth al-Saffar was the first ruler to unite Persians as Shi'ites (followers of the Shi'a branch of Islam, which considers the Prophet Muhammad's cousin Ali and his descendants to be Muhammad's true successors). A popular hero in Iranian history, Yaqub is credited with starting a great resurgence of Iranian culture. He is also celebrated for establishing an empire, minting his own coin, creating an army that was loyal to its leader rather than to religious beliefs, and requiring that verses praising him be translated from Arabic into Persian.

After forming his army during a time of considerable turbulence and instability, Yaqub occupied much of the area of present-day Afghanistan in 861 and then took control of Sistan in eastern Iran and southwestern Afghanistan in 867. He then expanded his power into northeastern India.

The Saffarid Empire reached its height of power in 873, after the defeat of the Tahirid dynasty of Khurasan and the conquest of that kingdom in northeastern Iran. With this conquest, the Saffarid Empire stretched, on the north, from the Oxus River west to the Caspian Sea; and on the south, from the edge of the central Iranian deserts east to the mountains of central Afghanistan, possibly even to the Indian border. Worried by Yaqub's growing power, the caliphate at Baghdad—on which the Saffarids were nominally dependent—attempted to appease Yaqub by making him amir, or governor, of the areas he had conquered. Unsatisfied by this offer, Yaqub attacked Baghdad in 876 but was beaten back by the forces of Caliph al-Mutamid (r. 870–892).

After Yaqub's death in 879, the caliph recognized Yaqub's brother and successor, Amr ibn Layth (r. 879–902), as governor of Khurasan, Isfahan, Fars, Sistan, and Sind. But when Amr tried to seize the region of Transoxania (in present-day Uzbekistan, Turkmenistan, and Kazakhstan) from the Samanid dynasty in 900, he was overpowered by Ismail ibn Ahmad (r. 982–907), one of the Samanids' best-known rulers. Amr was put to death in Baghdad in 902. His death led to the eclipse of the Saffarid dynasty, although members of the dynasty retained power in some areas until the late fifteenth or early sixteenth century C.E. Nevertheless, by the early years of the tenth century, the Saffarids had become subordinate to the Samanids, who were one of the first purely indigenous Persian dynasties to rule Iran

since the Arabs conquered the region in the 700s and 800s.

See also: SAMANID DYNASTY.

SA'ID, SAYYID IBN (1791–1856 C.E.)

Sultan of Oman and Zanzibar (r. 1806–1856) who helped reassert Oman's traditional claims in East Africa and established the island of Zanzibar as the principal commercial center of that region.

Born a member of the Omani ruling dynasty, Sayyid ibn Sa'id was the son of Sultan ibn Ahmed (r. 1792–1804), who ruled the port city of Muscat. Orphaned at thirteen years of age by his father's death, Ibn Sa'id could have expected to assume his father's position, but he was too young to ward off the challenge of an older and stronger cousin, Badr ibn Saif (r. 1804–1806), who took control of the country.

Saif, however, was a proponent of Wahhabism, a form of Islam that was particularly unpopular in Oman. As a result, he lost the support of the people he hoped to rule. This gave Sa'id an opportunity to create a base of support in Muscat, and in 1806, he successfully led a coup that unseated his cousin and left him in control of the port city. He was only fifteen years old at the time.

Though young, Sa'id was a gifted diplomat. To make his rule secure, he gained the support of potential rivals and enemies by making an alliance with his powerful neighbors, the Saudis, and also with the British, who had strategic interests in the region. In return for helping the British protect their access routes to India, Sa'id gained preferential trading agreements with Great Britain. Equally important, he obtained British assistance in eliminating the pirates that had long plagued Omani coastal territories.

Having secured his position in Muscat, Sa'id turned his attention to expanding his territory. The best opportunities for expansion were along the eastern coast of Africa, where prosperous Swahili trading centers had long been established. In 1822, Sa'id captured the island of Pemba off the East African coast. He continued his campaign of expansion over the next fifteen years, acquiring more and more of the East African coast until, in 1837, he crowned his efforts by capturing the city of Mombasa.

In 1840, Sa'id moved his capital from Muscat to the island of Zanzibar, allowing him a better overview of his newest campaign. This campaign involved creating a great trading enterprise that encompassed all of his territory, which now stretched from Oman to Mozambique. Initially, Sa'id specialized in the choicest of trade goods at the time—slaves—which were in high demand throughout the lands surrounding the Indian Ocean. This activity greatly displeased his British allies, however, who had long worked to halt the slave trade.

In 1847, Sa'id finally found himself bound by a British prohibition against continuing in the slave trade. Looking for a replacement trade good, Sa'id chose cloves, a spice that was in great demand locally as well as in Europe. The clove trade became hugely successful, in large part because Sa'id kept costs down by using the slaves he could not sell as laborers on his clove plantations.

Sa'id continued to rule until his death in 1856. With his death, the united sultanate that he had ruled was divided between his two sons, Thuwaini (r. 1856–1866) and Majid (r. 1856–1870). Thuwaini was granted Oman, while Majid took control of the island of Zanzibar.

See also: SULTANATES; ZANZIBAR SULTANATE.

SAILENDRA DYNASTY

(flourished ca. 750–850 C.E.)

Buddhist dynasty of Javanese origin that later ruled the Srivijaya Empire in Sumatra. The dynasty arose after the collapse of the Funan kingdom on the mainland of Southeast Asia. The Sailendra rulers claimed to be descended from the rulers of Funan, and they probably took the dynastic name Sailendra ("king of the mountain") from the title of the Funan kings.

The Sailendra dynasty may have been related to the Chandella dynasty of India, which flourished in the seventh and eighth centuries. According to some traditional accounts, a rift developed within the Chandella family between members still faithful to Hinduism, who retained the name Chandella and stayed in India, and those who converted to Buddhism, the Sailendras, who departed to Indonesia as early as the fourth century.

Under the Sailendras, a remarkable cultural renaissance occurred that was related to the emergence of the Mahayana sect of Buddhism. The dynasty also reached an advanced level of artistic achievement, evident in the many temples and monuments built under its kings. The most famous was the *stupa* (dome-shaped temple) of Borobudur in Sumatra, constructed between 778 and 824. This enormous monument, the earliest great Buddhist structure in Southeast Asia, had an influence on the construction of subsequent monuments, including the great Angkor Wat in Cambodia.

The Sailendra dynasty appears to have originated in the farming lowlands of interior Java sometime prior to the eight century, but it quickly expanded its influence to the northwestern coast of Java, where it facilitated trade with and raids against the Malay Peninsula and Indochina.

At its height, around the first quarter of the ninth century, the Sailendra kingdom reigned over more than half of eastern Java as well as Bali, Lombok, the coastal regions of Kalimantan, southern Sulawesi, and areas of current-day Cambodia. In the middle of the ninth century, however, the Sailendra kingdom of Java ended, and the Sailendra line was driven to Sumatra (Palembang) when Prince Patapan (r. ca. 832–850?) of the neighboring Sanjaya dynasty captured the Javan throne.

The Sailendra dynasty of the Srivijaya state in Sumatra suffered a terrible blow in the early eleventh century, when a great naval raid from the Chola Empire in India raided Sumatra and plundered many of its most important cities. Greatly weakened by this invasion, the Sailendra kingdom began to disintegrate into a number of smaller states.

These remnants of the Srivijaya state were eventually absorbed into the Majapahit Empire in the thirteenth century. The Sailendra dynasty disappeared, although the founder of the Malacca sultanate, which dominated the Straits of Malacca between Sumatra and the Malay Peninsula, may have been a member of the Sailendra royal house.

See also: ANGKOR KINGDOM; CHANDELLA DYNASTY; FUNAN KINGDOM; JAVAN KINGDOMS; SOUTHEAST ASIAN KINGDOMS; SRIVIJAYA-PALEMBANG EMPIRE.

SAKALAVA KINGDOM

(ca. 1400–1800 C.E.)

One of the eighteen recognized indigenous kingdoms on the island of Madagascar.

During the 1700s, the Sakalava ("people of the long valley") dominated the western half of the island of Madagascar and forced even the powerful and more numerous Merina peoples to pay tribute to them. The Sakalava, who still exist as an ethnic group on Madagascar, like most of the island's peoples, are the product of several intermarrying groups who came to the island in a series of migrations, from Indonesia and India (prior to the ninth century) and from the Persian Gulf countries and the east coast of Africa (ninth through fifteenth centuries). These peoples spread out to inhabit most of the island. From the ninth century on, different kingdoms, defined largely by reckonings of lineage rather than discrete ethnic differences, came to be dominant. Among groups such as the Merina and Sakalava, powerful leaders sometimes arose who had the force of will and personality to unite the people of surrounding settlements and forge larger political units.

The Sakalava kingdom's rise to power began around 1400 when King Andrianmisara I (dates unknown) built the city of Andakabe (now Morondava) as the capital for his powerful tribe inhabiting the southwestern part of the island. In 1610, King Andriandahifotsy (1600–1680?), aided by weapons he obtained from slave traders, began expansion of the Sakalava kingdom to the north. In 1690, a powerful king, Tsimanatona, also known as Andriamandisoarivo (r. 1690–1720), succeeded in forging a number of Sakalava settlements into a unified state called Iboina (Boina). Within ten years, he had led his forces on a campaign of expansion that resulted in the conquest of all the peoples of western Madagascar, and had penetrated well into the central portion of the island, where the Merina peoples predominated. Another Sakalava territory, Menab, also gained more power during the late 1700s. The Sakalava reached their peak in the early 1750s, when the greatest of the Sakalava kings, Andrianinevenarivo (r. 1730–1760), controlled the largest kingdom yet known on Madagascar.

The Sakalava buried their dead in cemeteries near their villages, and the influential *dady* sect preserved the remains of deceased rulers in sacred places where they were worshiped. The religion emphasized the worship of royal ancestors, a practice that helped legitimize the ruler's power. Spiritual mediums, in a ceremony known as *tromba,* would deliver the dead ancestors' words to the tribe.

The Sakalava attained dominance by virtue of their fierce warriors, but they retained dominance by monopolizing trade, initially with the Swahili and Omani, and during the late 1700s with the Portuguese, British, and French. They raided neighboring, non-Sakalava settlements on Madagascar and the Comoros Islands, and served as brokers for slaves brought over from the African mainland. The capital cities of Toliara in Menabe and Mahajanga in Iboina became centers of the slave trade.

The latter half of the eighteenth century saw a decline in Sakalava fortunes. The ruler at the time was Queen Ravahiny (1767–1808). During her reign, Islam was on the rise in Madagascar, especially in the Iboina kingdom. Some adherents of Islam were even making claims to the throne. At the same time, in the central region of the island, a powerful Merina leader named Andrianampoinimerina (r. 1787–1810) had begun consolidating the local settlements, forging the Imerina kingdom. As the Merina gained power, they refused to continue paying tribute to the Sakalava, further contributing to the kingdom's decline. By the start of the 1800s, the Merina had fully eclipsed the Sakalava.

The Sakalava unsuccessfully attempted an uprising in 1828, and thereafter were never able to regain their dominance on the island. After the Merina conquest, some Sakalava migrated to the nearby islands of Mahoré and Mwali, but many of the tribe remained in Madagascar where their descendants represent about 6 percent of the island's present population.

See also: MADAGASCAR KINGDOMS; MERINA KINGDOM.

FURTHER READING

Kottak, Conrad P., ed. *Madagascar: Society and History.* Durham, NC: Carolina Academic Press, 1986.

Lambek, Michael. *The Weight of the Past: Living with History in Mahajanga, Madagascar.* New York: Palgrave Macmillan, 2003.

SALADIN (ca. 1137–1193 C.E.)

Emir of Egypt, Syria, and Palestine (r. 1175–1193) who founded the Ayyubid dynasty, recovered Jerusalem and most of Palestine and Syria from the Christian Crusaders, and was renowned for his modesty, generosity, and chivalry.

Born Salah ad-din Yusuf Ibn Ayyub in Mesopotamia

of Kurdish stock, Saladin was the son of Najm ad-din Ayyub, the governor of Baalbek and later of Damascus. During his youth, Saladin lived for ten years at the court of Syrian ruler Nur ad-din (r. 1146–1174), in Damascus, where he became interested in Islamic theology. Later, he assisted his uncle, Shirkuh, in military campaigns against the Fatimid dynasty in Egypt. Saladin proved so fine a soldier that he was given command over the Egyptian city of Alexandria. Not long afterward, he was made vizier of Egypt, which was a high government office. While vizier, Saladin quietly deposed the incompetent Fatimid caliph and named himself governor.

Saladin's overriding interest was to recapture the virtue, vigor, and vitality of the early Muslim culture. In this spirit, he went to the relief of Syria, a nation suffering from petty civil wars and from the barbarism and misrule of the Frankish Christians. Saladin succeeded quickly in his limited goals in Syria and then returned to Egypt and named himself Malik, or king, in 1175. Nur ad-Din had died the year before, in 1174, and Saladin advanced into and took control of Syria and Damascus, thus founding the Ayyubid dynasty there.

In 1186, Reginald of Chatillon (r. 1153–1160), a former Christian ruler of the Principality of Antioch, attacked a Muslim caravan, capturing Saladin's sister. With the uneasy peace with the Christians now broken, Saladin responded, and on July 4, 1187, the most decisive battle of the early Crusades was fought at Hattin, near Tiberias in Palestine. Saladin's army took advantage of the midsummer heat, while the Christians failed to secure an adequate water supply. The result was a crushing defeat for the Christian Crusaders. Reciprocating a pledge made by the militant Christian orders against Muslims, the normally merciful Saladin uncharacteristically killed all the combatant Christian knights.

Moving on to Jerusalem, Saladin acted with more typical clemency. He presented the inhabitants of the city with generous terms and, after its surrender, dealt with them honorably—providing a sharp contrast to the slaughter that had occurred eighty-eight years before upon the Christian conquest of the city during the First Crusade.

The fall of Jerusalem resounded mightily throughout Europe, precipitating the Third Crusade, the primary aim of which was to recapture the Holy City. This massive new Christian incursion reached the Holy Land in force in 1191, led by Philip II of France (r.

1180–1223) and Richard I, Lionheart of England (r. 1189–1199). Saladin met the army of Crusaders with patience and ingenuity. The two warriors, Richard and Saladin, met personally and on the field several times. They were well matched in military prowess and soon came to respect each other's abilities.

Skirmishes and battles between Muslims and Christians ensued periodically for almost two years, but none was decisive. Richard succeeded in capturing the important Mediterranean port of Acre but scored no other meaningful victories. Finally, the two warriors signed a peace agreement on September 2, 1192, whereupon Richard returned to Europe and Saladin resumed his duties as the effective conqueror and ruler of Syria, Palestine, and Egypt. The Christians would not return again to Palestine as a serious threat.

Saladin's clemency, justice, and moderation were widely acclaimed by his contemporary enemies as well as by Muslim chroniclers. Wherever he traveled, he built schools and hospitals, and he personally dealt with all injustices brought to his attention; his reputation was one of kindness to the weak and generosity to the vanquished. Saladin is generally regarded as one of Islam's greatest heroes. When he died in 1193, he was succeeded as emir of Egypt and Syria by his son, Al-Aziz Uthman (r. 1193–1198).

See also: AYYUBID DYNASTY; CRUSADER KINGDOMS; FATIMID DYNASTY; RELIGIOUS DUTIES AND POWER; RICHARD I, LIONHEART.

SALIAN DYNASTY (1024–1125 C.E.)

Dynasty that ruled Germany and the Holy Roman Empire, during the period of the Investiture controversy, which involved imperial claims to the right to appoint bishops. The Salian dynasty oversaw one of the most chaotic times in medieval German history.

When the last emperor of the Ottonian dynasty, Henry II (r. 1002–1024), died without an heir in 1024, there were two claimants to the Crown of Germany, both descendants of Otto I (r. 936–973) through his daughter. One of these was a Franconian noble named Conrad, a member of the Salian dynasty. Conrad was chosen to rule by Henry's widow and was duly elected as Conrad II (r. 1024–1039) of Germany in 1024. He was crowned emperor in 1027. During his reign, the kingdom of Burgundy was added to the empire and German rule over Italy was made more secure. Conrad II even exerted control over the papacy.

In 1039, Conrad II died and was succeeded by his son, Henry III (r. 1039–1056). Henry III continued to dominate papal affairs and maintain the imperial right to appoint bishops. He made himself overlord of the kings of Bohemia and Hungary, but faced opposition within Germany from nobles opposed to a strong central government, particularly Duke Conrad of Bavaria, who rebelled in 1052. Henry deposed the duke, who fled to Hungary and renewed opposition to German rule there, resulting in the empire's loss of Hungary.

When Henry III died in 1056 he was succeeded by his six-year-old son, Henry IV (r. 1056–1106). During the reign of Henry IV, the Investiture controversy reached its height. Pope Gregory VII (r. 1073–1085) opposed imperial involvement in Church affairs, while Henry regarded the Church as a tool of the Crown. In 1076 Gregory excommunicated Henry and declared him deposed.

In January of 1077, Henry met the pope at Canossa in Italy, appearing before the pope as a barefoot penitent. This symbolic submission was accompanied by negotiations that resulted in Henry's restoration to the throne. However, a group of German nobles opposed to Henry elected a Swabian nobleman, Rudolf II (r. 1077–1080), as king instead. Hermann of Luxembourg (r. 1081–1088) and Conrad of Franconia (r. 1087–1098) were also elected as anti-kings (as such rival claimants are often termed), during Henry IV's reign, resulting in internal military campaigns against the rebels.

Gregory deposed and excommunicated Henry IV again in 1080. This time, however, Henry had the support of many German and some Italian archbishops and bishops, who elected a rival anti-pope, Clement III (r. 1080–1100), as an alternative to Gregory. Henry besieged Rome four times between 1081 and 1084, eventually forcing Gregory from the city. Conflict between the emperor and papacy was renewed under Pope Urban II (r. 1088–1099).

Throughout his reign, Henry IV faced rebellion from his nobles. He lost the region of Lombardy in a rebellion by his son Conrad (d. 1101). In 1105, the emperor's second son, Henry, also revolted against his father. The two Henrys were still at war when Emperor Henry IV died in 1106. During his trou-

bled reign, Henry IV had been forced to allow the nobility greater power and independence, but he had also increased the importance of the *ministeriales* (unfree administrators and knights) and the embryonic middle class of townsmen, and he upheld the imperial right to appoint bishops.

Henry V (r. 1106–1125) succeeded his father and continued to uphold the right of lay investiture of bishops. Henry V won a concession to the right of investiture from Pope Pascal II (r. 1099–1118) by imprisoning him, and he was crowned emperor by Pascal in 1111. During his reign, Henry V retook imperial lands in Italy that had been lost during his father's time. However, revolts among German nobles led to the loss of effective imperial control over much of northern Germany. Henry V continued his father's policy of seeking support from the *ministeriales,* minor nobility, and townsfolk, against the greater nobles.

In 1122, Henry V's continued conflict with the papacy, which had resulted in his twice being excommunicated and in the election of two anti-popes, was resolved in an agreement called the Concordat of Worms. It was agreed that the pope would appoint the higher Church officials but that the emperor would have the right of veto over them. Although this settled the Investiture controversy in the Holy Roman Empire at that time, the debate reoccurred throughout the Middle Ages. Henry V died without an heir in 1125, the last of the Salian dynasty to rule. German nobles elected Lothar II of Saxony (r. 1125–1137) as his successor.

During the rule of the Salian dynasty, Germany and the Holy Roman Empire suffered near-constant internal conflict. Germany lost control of much of Italy, the papacy gained power within Europe, and the German nobility became strong at the expense of the Crown. The German Crown failed to curb the independence of its duchies at a time when centralized royal government was increasing in strength in France and England. As a result of this disunifying trend, Germany lost its place as a significant power in Europe.

See also: CONRAD II; HENRY IV (HRE).

FURTHER READING

Holmes, George, ed. *The Oxford Illustrated History of Medieval Europe.* New York: Oxford University Press, 1988.

SAMANID DYNASTY (819–999 C.E.)

The first indigenous Muslim-Persian dynasty that arose in Iran after the Arab conquest of the 700s. Gathering together a variety of Muslim and Persian artists and learned men, the Samanids contributed significantly to the development of an Iranian national identity and culture.

The Samanid dynasty was named after its founder, Saman-Khuda, a member of the Persian aristocracy who claimed to be a descendant of the Sasanid general Bahram Chubin. Saman converted to Islam in the 720s, and in the early 800s his four grandsons were given provinces by the Abassid caliph, al-Mamun (r. 813–833), as reward for their loyalty to Islam. Saman's grandson Nuh received Samarkand, Ahmad got Fergana; Shash was given Yahya, and Elyas was given to Herat. With these affluent cities, the Samanids were able to benefit greatly from trade all across Asia.

By the rule of Saman's great-grandson Nasr (the son of Ahmad)(r. 864–892), the Samanids reigned over a burgeoning realm. In 875, Nasr became governor of Transoxania, a region in the northern part of the Iranian province of Khurasan, adding yet another territory to Samanid control. Nasr's brother, Ismail I (r. 892–907), defeated the Saffarids in Khurasan and the Azydites of Tabaristan in 900 and set up semiautonomous rule over both Transoxania and Khurasan, establishing a Samanid capital at Bukhara.

The area under Samanid rule prospered, with major increases in industry and trade, as evidenced by the use of Samanid silver coins throughout northern Asia by the 900s. The cities of Bukhara and Samarkand developed into important cultural centers, where Persian art and literature flourished.

Under the Samanids, the renowned poet Rudaki, regarded by many as the father of Persian poetry, became the first major poet to write in New Persian, which used the Arabic alphabet. The Saminids also encouraged scholarship in history, philosophy, and other forms of learning, which became the basis of Iranian Islamic culture.

Samanid architecture was noteworthy, too. One of the most impressive examples is Ismail's mausoleum, which is still standing in present-day Bukhara. Its originality resides in the perfect symmetry of the building, which is made entirely of brick, including ornamental patterns in brick bas-relief.

After about 950, Samanid power gradually began to wane, largely because of interruptions of commerce along northern trade routes and intense military pressure from the Turks in the north and the Ghaznavids in the east. Although Samanid power was revitalized briefly under Nuh II (r. 976–997), the increasing movement of Muslim Turks into the Abbasid Empire (in present-day Iraq) eventually led to further weakening of the Samanid state.

With the overthrow of Abdul-Malik II (r. 999) by the Turkish Ghaznavids and Qarakhanids in 999, the capital of Bukhara fell and the Samanid dynasty faced imminent collapse. The last ruler of the dynasty, Ismail II (r. 1000–1005), struggled to keep Samanid territory, but his assassination in 1005 brought the Samanid dynasty to an end.

See also: BANU KHURUSAN; GHAZNAVID DYNASTY; SAFFARID DYNASTY; SASANID DYNASTY.

SAMOAN KINGDOMS (200–1877 C.E.)

Kingdoms located in the Polynesian archipelago of Samoa and populated by a series of chieftainships that vied for control of the islands before being colonized by Europeans.

The Samoan Islands were first settled around 1000 B.C.E., probably by immigrants from the islands of Tonga. By 200 C.E., the Samoan Islands were themselves centers of population and cultural dispersement in eastern Polynesia, with trade routes set up with Fiji and Tonga.

The historical Samoans were part of a maritime culture steeped in the Polynesian traditions of sailing, fishing, and navigation, but they also utilized the lush landscape of Samoa to cultivate various domestic crops, including yams, taro, and sugarcane. Perhaps unsurprisingly, most Samoan settlements were located along the coast of the islands, where the Samoan people had easier access to the resources of the sea.

Samoan life was centered around communal extended families, and kinship ties were important in political as well as daily life. Oral traditions suggest that each Samoan family group elected a *matai*, or chief, from among their numbers. Theoretically, the *matai* in a village worked together in council to control village affairs. Disputes between villages often led to warfare, but the island terrain of Samoa made conquest difficult.

Sighted by the Dutch in 1722, the Samoan Islands had, by the 1770s, become a relatively common stopover point for European traders along the Pacific spice route. Victimized by European diseases and the brutality of encounters with profit-seeking traders, the Samoans were unwelcoming to many of the early European settlers who began arriving afterward, and they soon developed a reputation in Europe as a bloodthirsty and aggressive people.

Using weapons brought by the Europeans, the Samoan chieftain Malietoa Vainu'upo managed to wrest control of the islands during the late 1820s and 1830s. When he converted to Christianity at the promptings of the missionary John Williams, most of the islands found it politically expedient to follow suit, and mass conversions ensued. The conversions were further facilitated by a traditional Samoan prediction of the coming of a new, more powerful religion and by the general compatibility of native Samoan and Christian religious beliefs.

As the nineteenth century progressed, Germany, England, and the United States began to jockey for power in Samoa. A series of foreign political machinations led to the islands changing hands several times, and it was not until 1962 that a portion of Samoa regained independence. The eastern Samoan Islands remain under U.S. control.

See also: SOUTH SEA ISLAND KINGDOMS.

SAMSU-ILUNA (d. ca. 1712 B.C.E.)

Ruler of Babylon (r. ca. 1749–1712 B.C.E.) in ancient Mesopotamia, the son and successor of Hammurabi (r. ca. 1792–1750 B.C.E.), who spent much of his reign suppressing rebellions by city-states on the northern and southern frontiers of his kingdom.

During the reign of Samsu-iluna, the Babylonian Empire was gradually whittled down by war and revolt. The city-states of Larsa and Eshnunna broke away from Babylon around 1739 B.C.E., but they were reconquered around 1730 B.C.E. At that time, the walls of the cities of Larsa, Ur, and Uruk were razed by Samsu-iluna's forces. The state of Elam, which Ham-

murabi had conquered in 1764 B.C.E., revolted successfully in the 1730s as well, resulting in a resounding defeat for Babylon. In addition, the area known as the Sealand, a portion of southern Babylonia bordering the Persian Gulf, became independent as well.

Samsu-iluna, like his father Hammurabi, kept a series of administrative and legal texts recording his activities. In one such text, written around 1749 B.C.E., Samsu-iluna made the first known reference to the Kassites, whose incursions were successfully repelled by the Babylonian Empire. However, it was the Kassites who later conquered Babylon, around 1595 B.C.E., and proceeded to rule it for more than four centuries.

By the end of Samsu-iluna's reign, Babylon had lost the entire southern portion of its empire, and other frontier areas of the kingdom were under constant threat from groups wishing to break away or invade. Upon Samsu-Iluna's death around 1712 B.C.E., he was succeeded on the throne by his son, Abieshuh (r. ca. 1711–1684 B.C.E.)

See also: HAMMURABI; KASSITES.

SAMUDERA-PASAI (1200s–1500s C.E.)

Islamic kingdom founded in the thirteenth century on the north coast of Sumatra that is regarded as the earliest Islamic kingdom in Southeast Asia

The name *Samudera* derives from the Sanskrit word for "ocean." A seaport of that name, located on the north coast of Sumatra, may have given rise to the name Sumatra for the entire island. The port of Samudera and its twin capital of Pasai lie on opposite sides of the Pasangan River. Samudera, the older site, was visited by Marco Polo in 1292. Polo was especially impressed by the palm wine of Samudera, "better than any wine or any other drink that was ever drunk."

Samudera-Pasai was probably the first Southeast Asian kingdom to be ruled by a Muslim. When Marco Polo visited, Sultan Malik al-Salih (r. ?–1297) was ruler of the kingdom. His tombstone, (which dates from 1297), still stands in Pasai. In the fourteenth century, the well-known Arab traveler, Ibn Battuta, visited Samudera twice, in 1345 and 1346, on trips to and from China. Ibn Battuta reported that he saw a ship belonging to the Pasai ruler in China, suggesting that Samudera-Pasai might have had close economic relations with the Chinese.

The conversion of Samudera-Pasai to Islam is

recorded in a fourteenth-century local historical romance, the *Hikayat Raja-Raja Pasai.* In the text, the pre-Muslim name of the ruler at the time is given as Merah Silu, and he is identified with Malik al-Salih. The kingdom swiftly became an important center of dissemination for Islam through Southeast Asia. The first ruler of the Malay state of Malacca, Parameswara (r. ca. 1400–1424), became Muslim after marrying the daughter of a Pasai ruler. Sunan Gunung Jati, one of the nine *wali* or Sufi missionary teachers credited in folklore with having converted Java to Islam, came from Pasai.

In the fourteenth century, Samudera-Pasai became a vassal of Majapahit, a powerful kingdom in Java. Samudera is listed among Majapahit's territories in the *Nagarakrtagama,* a courtly text composed in Majapahit in 1365. According to other texts from the period, the Majapahit rulers had a monopoly over the trade that passed through Samudera and Pasai. They also had commercial connections from Gujarat and Bengal in India to Pegu and Tenasserim in Burma, as well as with Java and China.

Despite Majapahit's overlordship, the kingdom of Samudera-Pasai was perhaps the busiest commercial center in the Straits of Malacca during the fourteenth century. Pasai was a major pepper producer and also provided gold and benzoin (a resinous natural product used as incense). Pasai is also reported to have made silk, as well as importing large quantities of it, providing further evidence of the kingdom's close connection with China.

Samudera-Pasai managed to remain independent of Malacca's control when that kingdom replaced Majapahit as the dominant state in the Straits of Malacca in the fifteenth century. The kingdom also maintained tributary relations with China during this period. The last record about Samudera-Pasai makes reference to a Diogo Lopes de Sequeira, a Portuguese traveler who visited in 1509.

See also: JAVAN KINGDOMS; SOUTHEAST ASIAN KINGDOMS.

FURTHER READING

Loeb, Edwin. *Sumatra: Its History and People.* Singapore: Oxford University Press, 1989.

Miksic, John, ed. *Indonesian Heritage: Ancient History.* Vol. 1. Singapore: Archipelago Press, 1996.

Reid, Tony, ed. *Indonesian Heritage: Early Modern History.* Vol. 3. Singapore: Archipelago Press, 1996.

Ricklefs, M.C. *A History of Indonesia Since c. 1200.* Stanford, CA: Stanford University Press, 2001.

SANCHO III, THE GREAT

(970–1035 C.E.)

Also known as Sancho III Garcés (r. 1004–1035), king of Navarre (frequently called Pamplona until the twelfth century), whose realm was the largest kingdom on the Iberian Peninsula during his reign.

The son of García II (r. 994–1004) of Navarre, Sancho inherited the kingdom, which included Aragón, upon the death of his father in 1004. During his reign, Sancho annexed most of the rest of Christian Iberia, primarily through marriage, subterfuge, and implicit threat rather than open conquest.

Between 1015 and 1019, Sancho seized the Frankish territories of Sobrarbe and Ribagorza from the Moors. He later became overlord of the county of Barcelona after forcing Count Berenguer Ramon I (r. 1017–1035) to become his vassal. Sancho gained control of Castile and the provinces of Vizcaya and Alava, through the inheritance of his wife, who was the sister of Count Garcia II (r. 1017–1029) of Castile. In 1017, Sancho became the young Garcia's protector, and when the count was assassinated in 1029, Sancho took full control of that realm.

Sancho also pressed Castile's dynastic claims in the eastern part of Léon, the neighboring kingdom to the west. In 1034, he was crowned "emperor" of Léon in the Leonese capital of Valladolid, assuming the title as legitimate heir to the kingdom according to ancient Visigothic and Asturian traditions. All of these territorial gains took place in an era of civil strife among the Muslim rulers on the Iberian Peninsula, which helped to ease the Islamic threat to both Sancho and other Christian kings of Iberia.

During Sancho's reign, communication with Christians on the northern side of the Pyrenees Mountains increased, and French influence in his kingdom grew. Sancho encouraged the growth of monasteries modeled after the monastery of Cluny in France. His kingdom also benefited greatly from the increased traffic of Catholic pilgrims on their way to Santiago de Compostela in the northwestern corner of Iberia, the site of a shrine dedicated to the apostle of Christ, Saint James, and one of the most important pilgrimage sites in Europe.

In his will, Sancho redivided his lands among his four sons, provoking years of dynastic conflicts among their descendants in both Spain and Portugal. The idea of dividing the king's domain after his death was rooted in the concept of feudal vassalage. Upon Sancho's death in 1035, his son Garcia became King Garcia III of Navarre (r. 1035–1054); Ferdinand I was king of Castile (r. 1029–1065); Ramiro I ruled as king of Aragón (r. 1035–1069); and Gonzalo (r. 1035–1043) ruled the combined kingdom of Sobrarbe and Ribagorza.

In the dynastic struggles that later ensued, Sancho's son Ferdinand I reestablished control of Léon, and by 1064 he had successfully led the reconquest of Moorish lands as far south as present-day Coimbra in Portugal, thus extending Castilian influence into the northern areas of that neighboring state. Yet, like his father, Ferdinand also divided his lands among his heirs, igniting twelfth-century conflicts between Portuguese and Spanish cousins.

See also: ARAGÓN, KINGDOM OF; BASQUE KINGDOM; CASTILE, KINGDOM OF; IBERIAN KINGDOMS; LÓN, KINGDOM OF; NAVARRE, KINGDOM OF.

SANUSI DYNASTY (1837–1969 C.E.)

Members of a Muslim religious movement in North Africa, which also became a ruling dynasty that held considerable political power, especially in opposing Italian rule in Libya in the early 1900s.

The Sanusi dynasty was founded originally as a Sufi Islamic mystical order in the Arabian holy city of Mecca by an Algerian, Sayyid Muhammad al-Sanusi al-Idrisi (r. 1837–1859). Al-Sanusi, who claimed descent from the ancient Idrisid dynasty of Morocco, established the religious movement because he wanted to restore the simple and pure life of early Islam.

After successfully advancing his faith among the Bedouin of the Hejaz region in western Arabia, al-Sanusi moved to the desert in Cyrenaica (the easternmost part of Libya) in 1843 and set up his first *zawiyah,* or monastery. Under al-Sanusi and his son and successor, Sayyid Muhammad al-Mahdi (r. 1859–1902), the movement spread quickly in Libya as a militant theocracy that asserted the Islamic principles of peace, equality, and brotherhood. By 1884, the Sanusi movement had thousands of followers and more than one hundred monasteries spread throughout North Africa and beyond, and its political importance grew as well.

In 1902, al-Mahdi was succeeded by his nephew, Ahmad al-Sharif (r. 1902–1916), who mainly had to deal with threats from other countries during his rule. Al-Sharif directed the Sanusi resistance against the French in the Sahara and against the Italians who invaded Libya in 1911. During World War I, the Sanusis sided with the Central Powers (Germany, the Austro-Hungarian Empire, and the Ottoman Empire), and they unsuccessfully attacked British-occupied Egypt.

Following the war, the Allied powers (France, Britain, and Russia) made al-Sharif give up his command, whereupon his cousin, Muhammad Idris (r. 1916–1969), took the reins of power. Idris ceded control of Libya's coastal areas to Italy, but he set himself up as emir (prince) of the interior of Cyrenaica. The rise of fascism in Italy led to more conflict between the Sanusi and that country, and Libya became an Italian colony in 1931.

During World War II, the Sanusis helped the Allies (Britain, France, and the United States) beat the Axis forces of Germany and Italy. After the war, in 1951, Libya became independent under Sanusi rule, with Idris taking the title of king. Called the Federal United Kingdom of Libya, the country was the only modern state established by a Sufi religious order. Elections and parliamentary sessions were held in 1952, and in 1953, Libya joined the Arab League. The kingdom became a member of the United Nations in 1955.

In the mid-1950s, the oil industry in Libya began to develop rapidly, greatly enriching the country. In 1956, King Idris granted a 14-million-acre concession to American oil companies. Several years later, in 1961, he opened a 104-mile pipeline linking important interior oil fields to the Mediterranean Sea—enabling Libya to export oil for the first time. Later that year, the king decreed that Libya's share of profits from agreements with oil companies would rise from 50 to 70 percent.

In the early 1960s, internal tensions arose between the three semiautonomous provinces of Libya (Cyrenaica, Tripolitania, and Fazzan) and also among individual politicians in the kingdom. In order to improve the administration of the country, King Idris transformed Libya from a federation to a unitary state by abolishing the three provinces and their separate parliaments and establishing ten administrative divisions within the state. A council of ministers appointed by the king, and answerable to a single parliament, became responsible for overall administration of the state.

Despite the great wealth brought in by oil, many of the Libyan people did not benefit from oil industry profits. Economic disparity in the country led to plots to overthrow the monarchy and to establish a more fundamentalist Islamic state. The plots finally succeeded in 1969, when a group of army officers led by Colonel Muammar Gaddafi, a devout Muslim, deposed King Idris, overthrew the Sanusi monarchy, and established the Libyan Arab Republic.

The Gaddafi government put almost all of Libya's economic activity under state control, including its oil industry. It also tried to constrain and dishonor the Sanusis by prohibiting members of the religious order from creating more meeting places and by implying that they encouraged corruption and distorted Islam. Despite actions to suppress the Sanusis, the Sanusi religious movement still exists and is a major source of opposition to the Gaddafi regime.

See also: ISLAM AND KINGSHIP.

FURTHER READING

Iliffe, John. *Africans: The History of a Continent.* New York: Cambridge University Press, 1995.

SARGON II (d. 705 B.C.E.)

King of the Assyrians (r. 721–705 B.C.E.) who strengthened the northern and eastern borders of Assyria and prevented the invading Cimmerians from conquering the empire.

Sargon II, the founder of the last great Assyrian dynasty, may have been a usurper to the throne who gave himself the name Sargon, meaning "True King." When Sargon II succeeded Shalmaneser V (r. 726–722 B.C.E.), who may have been his brother, on the throne in 722 B.C.E., he found himself ruler of a restless empire. Many of the territories conquered by Tiglath-Pileser III (r. 744–727 B.C.E.), were growing restive, and Shalmaneser had left Sargon with several unfinished sieges. During Sargon's reign, the kingdom of Assyria was reorganized into twenty-provinces, and the capital was moved from Kalah to Dur Sharrukin shortly before his death in 705 B.C.E.

Early in his reign, Sargon faced difficulties on multiple fronts: the Chaldeans and Aramaeans in the south, the kingdom of Urartu in the north, and Syria and Palestine in the west were all growing restless under Assyrian hegemony. Sargon had no sooner gained the throne before a rebellious Chaldean leader, Merodach-Baladan (also known as Marduk-apal-iddina II, r. 722–710 B.C.E.), seized control of southern Babylonia. Although the details of Merodach's revolt are somewhat unclear, it is evident that Sargon was unable to focus on this Babylonian revolt for another twelve years, during which time Merodach-Baladan continued to rule over Babylon.

During Sargon's early reign, it seems that he was first occupied with finishing the siege of the northern Israelite kingdom of Samaria, which Shalmaneser V had begun three years before. After taking Samaria and deporting and separating its Israelite tribes, Sargon proceeded to lay siege to and capture the Phoenician cities of Tyre and Carchemish. He also conquered the cities of Hamath, Ekron, and Gaza, collected tribute from King Ahaz of Judah (r. 730–715 B.C.E.), and defeated the Egyptians at Rafia, burning the city and deporting nearly 10,000 of its inhabitants. Sargon also defeated the armies of Assyria's traditional enemy, the kingdom of Urartu, which was located to the north in the Caucasus region.

With Urartu and other enemies subdued, Sargon finally turned his attention toward Babylon. In 709 B.C.E., he successfully reconquered the region, but he allowed Merodach-Baladan to go into exile in Elam, a decision that plagued his son and successor, Sennacherib (r. 704–681 B.C.E.), decades later.

By the time he conquered Babylon, Sargon had also become concerned with the hordes of Cimmerians moving in from the north and massing along the Assyrian borders. Alarmed by the threat they posed, Sargon rode to meet them in 705 B.C.E. Sargon was killed in the ensuing battle, but his Assyrian forces defeated the Cimmerians, saving Assyria and most of western Asia from invasion. Upon Sargon's death, he was succeeded by his son, Sennacherib.

See also: ARAMAEN KINGDOMS; ASSYRIAN EMPIRE; PALESTINE, KINGDOMS OF; SENNACHERIB; SHALMANESER V; TIGLATH-PILESER III; URARTU KINGDOM.

FURTHER READING

Dijkstra, Henk, ed. *History of the Ancient & Medieval World: Egypt and Mesopotamia.* New York: Marshall Cavendish Corporation, 1996.

Edwards, I.E.S., C.J. Gadd, and N.G.L. Hammond. *The Cambridge Ancient History.* New York: Cambridge University Press, 1977.

Sargon of Akkad (d. ca. 2279 B.C.E.)

Great conqueror and the first ruler (r. ca. 2334–2279 B.C.E.) of the ancient kingdom of Akkad, who created the first large, organized state in Mesopotamia and who spread Sumerian and Semitic civilization over a large empire. Sargon's empire extended from the area between the Tigris and Euphrates rivers to parts of present-day Turkey.

Records from the time of Sargon's reign are extremely rare, in part because his capital city of Akkad was eventually destroyed and has never been located. What is known of Sargon's reign has been gleaned from rare contemporary texts, later copies of these texts, and Sumerian king lists, which are inscribed on various ancient stones and which do not always agree with one another.

According to one ancient Akkadian text, Sargon was born to a priestess and a nameless wanderer. Supposedly, when Sargon was an infant, his mother placed him in a basket sealed by pitch and set it in the Euphrates River. Miraculously, the baby was saved from drowning by a gardener named Aqqi who adopted Sargon and raised him as his son. When Sargon grew up, he became cup-bearer to Ur-Zababa (r. ca. 2356–2350 B.C.E.), the king of Kish. This was a position of great influence and trust, as it was the cup-bearer's responsibility to prevent the king from being poisoned.

Around 2350 B.C.E., Ur-Zababa was killed or dethroned by King Lugalzaggisi of Uruk (r. ca. 2340–2316 B.C.E.), who had conquered and united the city-states of Sumer. Seizing this opportunity, Sargon raised an army and attacked Uruk around 2334 B.C.E. Soon after, he took the throne of Kish as *lugal* (king). Sargon's move against Uruk proved to be the first step toward a life of conquest, and it was probably at this time that he adopted the name Sargon or Sharru-kin ("True King").

After Sargon became ruler of Sumer by taking control of Uruk, he proceeded to expand his empire, conquering most of Syria and Anatolia (present-day Turkey), as well as the kingdom of Elam and the two city-states of Mari and Ebla. With these conquests, Sargon secured trade routes that stretched, according to one of Sargon's surviving records, "as far as the Forest of Cedars [Lebanon] and the [Taurus] Mountains of Silver."

Sargon adopted a number of policies to deal with conquered lands. He allowed local officials to continue ruling if they swore allegiance to him. To maintain military control, he established the world's first permanent army. He rewarded his troops by giving them large tracts of land, a policy that also helped to ensure their loyalty. Sargon also established a great trade network that brought merchants to Akkad from as far away as India.

According to the Sumerian king list, Sargon's rule lasted fifty-six years, the latter portion of which was troubled by rebellion, as some conquered lands began to chafe under Akkadian control. Nevertheless, when Sargon died around 2279 B.C.E., he passed to his successors, including his grandson Naram-Sin (r. 2254–2218 B.C.E.), one of the first empires in history.

See also: Akkad, Kingdom of; Naram-Sin.

Sasanid Dynasty (224–651 C.E.)

Ancient Persian dynasty that prospered for more than four centuries until it was destroyed by the Arabs between 637 and 651. The dynasty was named after Sasan, one of the ancestors (probably the grandfather) of its first ruler.

The founder of the Sasanid dynasty was Ardashir I (r. 224–241), who overthrew the last king of Parthia, Artabanus V (r. 213–224), in 224. Persia had been ruled by the Parthian Empire for nearly five hundred years. The Sasanids established an empire whose size kept shifting as it responded to attacks from Rome and Byzantium in the west and various groups in the east. Ardashir I was clearly an able king and soldier, who also is credited with creating or rebuilding many cities, digging canals, and erecting bridges.

Ardashir's son and successor, Shapur I (r. 241–272), continued the struggle against the various groups that threatened the Sasanid Empire. He even defeated, captured, and imprisoned the Roman emperor Valerian (r. 253–260) in 260. The expanded Sasanid Empire eventually reached from Sogdiana and Iberia (Georgia) in the north to the Mazun region of Arabia in the south, and from the Indus River in the east to the upper Tigris and Euphrates River Valleys of Mesopotamia in the west.

Persian nationalism flourished under the Sasanid dynasty, and many of the traditions of the ancient Achaemenid dynasty (ca. 550–330 B.C.E.) were revived. Under the Sasanids, the government of the empire was centralized, and provincial officers reported to the Sasanid ruler. The state financed agriculture as well as the construction of roads and urban buildings.

The Sasanids revived the ancient Zoroastrian religion and made it the official state religion, while sometimes persecuting those who practiced other faiths. Ardashir I used Zoroastrianism to centralize Sasanid authority and secure political stability. He worked hand in hand with Zoroastrian priests, and he even claimed to be God's agent on earth, associating himself with signs of divine authority.

Social classes became rigidly stratified under the Sasanids. Just below the Sasanid rulers and nobles was the clergy, which included priests, judges, temple guardians, teachers, and ascetics. Next in the social hierarchy was the military, followed by a class that included scribes and others who wrote official communications and historical records, plus physicians, astronomers, poets, and accountants. The lowest social class consisted of artisans, farmers, herdsmen, and merchants. This class system perhaps reflected a Sasanian obsession with control—rulers were always worried about maintaining stability.

Although obsessed with control, the authority of early Sasanid rulers was curbed by a Zoroastrian principle that obliged the ruler to adhere to social justice and tolerance. The later Sasanid kings often neglected the notion of tolerance, however, supporting a religion that paid increasing attention to rites and practices rather than to beliefs and that desired power more than justice.

The Sasanid period witnessed a flowering of art and culture, which was particularly noticeable in monumental architecture, striking sculptures, and intricate metalwork and gem engraving. The dome and vault construction typically associated with Persian architecture was of Sasanid origin, and the first recognized Persian carpet was from a Sasanid royal palace. The Sasanids also promoted learning and had books from both East and West translated into Pahlavi, the indigenous language of the Sasanids.

The long reign of Shapur II (r. 309–379), one of the best-known rulers of the Sasanid dynasty, was very successful militarily. Shapur was able to defeat Central Asian tribes and annex much of the area that they had taken back earlier. Then Shapur renewed warfare against the Romans and won control of the Roman province of Armenia in the Caucasus region.

The Sasanid Empire reached its peak under Khusrau I (r. 531–579). Although Khusrau's power was rooted in absolute monarchy, he was known as Khusrau the Just because his exercise of justice was based on political pragmatism as much as philosophy. He embellished his palace lavishly and worked closely with Zoroastrian priests, who certified his authority, thereby assuring their own favor in the political and social hierarchy.

Khusrau I boosted Persia's military might, which helped his successors expand Sasanid territory in Byzantium, reaching all the way to Constantinople by 620. However, a revived Byzantium retaliated several years later, in 626, during the rule of Khosru II (r. 590–628). The Byzantines attacked the capital city of Ctesiphon, forcing the king to flee. This loss greatly weakened the Sasanid dynasty, which collapsed when its last ruler, Yazdgard III (r. 632–652), died in 652 following the Arab conquest of Persia.

See also: ACHAEMENID DYNASTY; PARTHIAN KINGDOM.

SATAVAHANA DYNASTY

(ca. 235 B.C.E.–225 C.E.)

Also called the Andhras dynasty, early ruling dynasty in the Deccan region of India, known for its currency, social reform, and religious tolerance.

The Satavahana dynasty has been identified as originating in Andhradesa in northwestern India, but it may have begun in Maharashtra, a province in the northwestern part of the Deccan plateau. At some point, the Satavahanas lost their territories in the northwest and emerged as rulers of the Deccan in south-central India.

HISTORICAL OVERVIEW

Sources of information about the Satavahanas are scarce and ambiguous. Some scholars claim that there were 19 kings in the dynasty, which ruled for 300 years, whereas others believe that there were 30 kings who ruled for 456 years.

Andhradesa was part of the Maurya Empire under

Asoka (r. 268–232 B.C.E.), but it became independent after Asoka's death, under the leadership of the Satavahana ruler, Simuka (r. ca. 235–212 B.C.E.). According to tradition, Simuka was a capable leader who built Jain and Buddhist temples, but who later became wicked, was dethroned, and finally killed.

Kanha, also known as Krishna (r. ca. 212–195 B.C.E.), succeeded Simuka as ruler of Maharashtra and continued to expand the Satavahana empire westward as far as the city of Nasik, famous for its temples and steps that go down to the sacred Godavari River.

Satakarni I (r. ca. 195–193 B.C.E.), the son of either Kanha or Simuka, accomplished a great deal in his short reign. He performed a large number of sacrifices and two Asvamedha (horse) sacrifices. Taking advantage of the Greek invasions in the north, Satakarni I conquered the western part of the kingdom of Malwa and the territories now known as the Narmada Valley and Berar. He probably died on the battlefield.

Vedisiri and Satisiri, Satakarni's two young sons, succeeded Satakarni at his death in 193 B.C.E. But because they were minors, control of the kingdom fell to their mother, Nayanika, who ruled as regent with the help of her father, Maharathi Tranakayiro. Vedisiri died while still a youth, and Satisiri probably took over as king. Little is known of his reign, however.

Satakarni II (r. 166–111 B.C.E.) continued the policy of conquest, taking eastern Malwa during his reign. The most important peacetime king of the Satavahana dynasty was Hala (r. 20–24 C.E.). Called the "poet king" and the "king of peace," Hala married Lilavati, the daughter of the king of Ceylon.

The most famous king of the Satavahana dynasty was the warrior Gautamiputra Satakarni (r. 70–95), who defeated the Sakas (Scythians) and Yavannas (Greeks) as well as the Pallava dynasty of southern India, bringing a vast territory under the control of the Satavahana dynasty. Gautamiputra's kingdom stretched from the Bay of Bengal in the east to the Arabian Sea and Indian Ocean in the west. A social reformer, he took an interest in the welfare of his subjects and only taxed when it was justified.

The reign of Gautamiputra's son and successor, Pulumayi II (r. 96–119), marked the high point of the Satavahana dynasty. Pulumayi was able to maintain the full extent of his father's empire, and his rule was a time of great economic prosperity.

From this point forward, however, the empire of the Satavahana began to fail. Pulumayi IV (r. ca. 215–225) was the last ruler of the main lineage of the Satavahana dynasty. During his reign, the empire, worn out by time and wars, broke up into a number of small states ruled by the Abhira, Chutu, Ikashvaku, and Pallava dynasties.

POLITICAL SYSTEM AND COMMERCE

The Satavahana monarchy was hereditary through the male line. Kings controlled everything in the kingdom, and they led their soldiers in battle, but they did not claim divine power. They ruled under the traditional customs of the kingdom and were guided by a code of laws known as the Dharmasastras.

The Dharmasastras divided the empire into Janapadas, or small states, and then into Aharas, or districts. Each Ahara was administered by an appointed governor. Taxes were not excessive. Women had prominent roles in society and could own property.

Foreign trade flourished under the Satavahanas. The ancient Romans sought Indian silk and spices, and those goods moved through Satavahana ports. The Satavahana system of currency, which consisted of silver, copper, and gold coins, spread throughout India. The material prosperity that developed under the Satavahanas paid for the army and encouraged religious tolerance, social reform, and the arts.

CULTURE

The Satavahana rulers were Hindus of the Brahman, or priestly, class. They worshiped the Hindu gods Indra, Krishna, Siva, Vishnu, and others. However, Buddhism also flourished in the Satavahana kingdom. Skilled artisans carved many Buddhist chaityas (worship halls) and Viharas (monasteries) out of rock. The most famous chaitya is at Karle, in the province of Maharashtra.

The Satavahana period is famous for its art, especially for its truly Indian style of art. During this period, craft and trade guilds were established that far outlasted the dynasty; many sculptures and stupas (dome-shaped shrines) from the Satavahana period survived for centuries, and some still exist today.

See also: ANDHRA KINGDOM; ASOKA; COINAGE, ROYAL; INDIAN KINGDOMS; MALWA KINGDOM; MAURYA EMPIRE.

FURTHER READING
StrongJouveau-Dubreuil, G. *Ancient History of the Deccan.* Trans. V.S. Swaminadha Dikshitar. New Delhi: Classical Publications, 1978.

SAURASHTRA KINGDOM. *See*

KATHIAWAR KINGDOM

SAVOY DYNASTY (1032–1946 C.E.)

European dynasty that ruled the region of Savoy in southeastern France and the Piedmont region of northwestern Italy, as well as the kingdoms of Sardinia, Sicily, and Italy.

Savoy, located in the eastern French Alps south of Lake Geneva, was part of Burgundy in the fifth century. A territory of the kingdom of Arles by the tenth century, and then part of the Holy Roman Empire, Savoy was part of the territorial holdings of Humbert I "White Hands," a feudal lord of Arles. In 1032, Humbert (r. 1000–1048), founded the house of Savoy when he gained the title count of Savoy.

EXPANSION OF SAVOY POWER

Through marriage, diplomacy, and conquest, Humbert gradually expanded his holdings to include a number of areas in France, Switzerland, and Italy, including Bresse, Bugey, Chablais, Lower Valais, Gex, Ivrea, Pinerolo, Nice, parts of Vaud, and Geneva.

Humbert's son and successor, Count Odo of Savoy (r. 1051–1059), married Adelaide, the marchioness of Segusium (in the Italian province of Turin). Through her, the house of Savoy inherited the Piedmont region of Italy in 1091. The Piedmont had developed from Turin and Ibrea, the western provinces of the Lombard kingdom of Italy. When Prince Thomas I of Savoy (r. 1189–1233) died in 1233, Piedmont went to his younger son, Thomas II (r. 1233–1259). His son, Amadeus V (r. 1285–1323), united Piedmont with Savoy in 1285.

LOSSES AND DECLINE

The title of count of Piedmont, along with Piedmontese territory, then went to the counts of Savoy. In 1434 the duke of Savoy, Amadeus VIII (r. 1391–1440), appointed his son Felix regent and retreated to Ripaille, on Lake Geneva, where he formed the Order of Saint Maurice. Five years later, the Council of Basel, which had broken with the main body of the Roman Catholic Church, elected him anti-pope, and he was crowned as Pope Felix VI in Basel the following year. In 1449, Amadeus VIII ended the papal schism by recognizing Nicholas V as pope.

Amadeus's son and successor, Louis (r. 1440–1465), married Anne de Lusignan, heir to the Crusader kingdoms of Jerusalem, Cyprus, and Armenia. As a result of this marriage, future dukes of Savoy bore the titles king of Jerusalem, Cyprus, and Armenia.

By the late 1400s, the power of the Savoyard dukes was in decline and their territory was threatened by both the French and Swiss. From ancient times, the Piedmont had been a key prize for conquerors because of its Alpine passes, which provided access between Italy and France.

As the Swiss expanded their territory and as wars with Italy raged (1494–1559), the Savoy duchy fell apart. Between 1475 and 1536, the Swiss succeeded in capturing lower Valis and the Vaud in Switzerland, and they declared Geneva independent. Meanwhile, King Francis I of France (r. 1515–1547) claimed what was left of the regions of Savoy and Piedmont.

During the rule of Duke Emmanuel Philibert (r. 1553–1580), the house of Savoy regained most of its territory under the 1559 Treaty of Cateau–Cambrésis with France. That same year, Emmanuel Philibert married Margaret of Valois, the sister of King Henry II of France (r. 1547–1559).

In 1563, the capital of the Savoy duchy shifted from Chambéry, which had been the seat of the counts of Savoy since 1232, to Turin. Although now linked geographically to Italy, the court of the Savoy duchy remained predominantly French in language and culture until the late 1700s.

NEW POWER IN ITALY

Under the Peace of Utrecht (1713–1714), a series of treaties that concluded the War of the Spanish Succession (1701–1714), the house of Savoy was granted rule over Sicily. Victor Amadeus II of Savoy (r. 1713–1720) ruled the island until 1720, when he was ousted and Sicily was returned to Austrian rule. As compensation, the house of Savoy received Sardinia, which Victor Amadeus ruled from 1720 to 1730.

During the reign of Charles Emanuel IV (r. 1796–1802), the house of Savoy lost all its territory except Sardinia to Napoleon Bonaparte. In 1802,

Charles Emanuel IV abdicated as king of Sardinia and his brother, Victor Emmanuel I (r. 1802–1821), assumed the throne. Savoy and the Piedmont were recovered before Victor Emmanuel also abdicated in 1821 following a rebellion in the Piedmont. His brother Charles Felix (r. 1821–1831) succeeded him as king.

Charles Felix died without heirs and was succeeded by Charles Albert (r. 1831–1849) of Savoy-Carignan, who introduced a constitution in Sardinia in 1848. During his reign, the Savoy and Piedmont regions emerged as the center of the Risorgimento, a movement that eventually led to the unification of Italy. The efforts of the Italian nationalists eventually led Charles Albert to abdicate in favor of his son Victor Emmanuel II (r. 1849–1861).

In 1860, Savoy and Nice were ceded to France, and in compensation, Victor Emmanuel II was given the Italian regions of Tuscany and Emilia. That same year, an Italian parliament opened in Turin, and in 1861, Victor Emmanuel II (r. 1861–1878) assumed the title of king of Italy.

Victor Emmanuel was succeeded as king of Italy by his son, Umberto I (r. 1878–1900). His grandson, Victor Emmanuel III (1900–1946), abdicated the throne in 1946, after the end of World War II, and was succeeded by his own son, Umberto II (r. 1946). After only a few months, however, Umberto II abdicated and Italy became a republic. Umberto II was the last member of the house of Savoy to rule.

See also: SICILY, KINGDOM OF.

FURTHER READING

Koenigsberger, H.G. *Medieval Europe, 400–1500.* New York: Longman, 1987.

Sauvigny, G. de Bertier de, and David H. Pinkney. *History of France.* Arlington Heights, IL: Forum Press, 1983.

Tierney, Brian, and Sidney Painter. *Western Europe in the Middle Ages 300–1475.* 6th ed. New York: McGraw-Hill, 1999.

SAXE-COBURG-GOTHA DYNASTY (ca. 1800s–2000s C.E.)

Politically powerful ducal family, based originally in Germany, which has placed rulers on the thrones of Belgium, Bulgaria, Great Britain, Italy, Mexico, Portugal, and Romania. The family has only been successful as rulers in Great Britain, where the Saxe-Coburg-Gotha line is still in power under the name of the house of Windsor, and in Belgium, where they have ruled from the 1800s to the present.

ORIGINS AND SPREAD

The German branches of Saxe, Coburg, and Gotha—all part of the house of Wettin—had been powerful for centuries. But it was not until 1826 that the lines were united when Ernest III (r. 1806–1826), duke of Coburg and Saalfeld, inherited Gotha in central Germany upon the death of Frederick, its last duke. Ernest then became known as Ernest I of Saxe-Coburg-Gotha (r. 1826–1844).

Ferdinand, Ernest's younger brother, had a son who became Ferdinand II of Portugal (r. 1837–1853) upon marrying Portugal's Queen Maria II (r. 1834–1853) in 1837. Another Ferdinand, the nephew of Ferdinand II, was elected prince of Bulgaria in 1887 and then czar Ferdinand I of Bulgaria in 1908.

Meanwhile, Ernest's youngest brother Leopold, a military leader and government worker in Britain, France, and Russia, was elected king of an independent Belgium in 1831 and crowned Leopold I (r. 1831–1865). Ernest's only sister, Victoria, married Edward, duke of Kent, who was the son of King George III of Great Britain (r. 1760–1820). The couple's only child, Victoria (r. 1837–1901), later ruled as the longest-reigning monarch of Great Britain.

THE BELGIAN LINE

The Saxe-Coburg-Gotha dynasty lasted longest in Belgium. During his thirty-four-year reign, Leopold I instituted a series of administrative and financial reforms that set Belgium on the way to becoming a major player in European politics. His daughter Carlotta became empress of Mexico in 1864 when her husband, Maximilian of Austria, was named emperor of Mexico (r. 1864–1867). However, a rebellion in Mexico led to the execution of Maximilian, and Carlotta was forced to flee the country.

Leopold's son, who took the Crown of Belgium as Leopold II (r. 1865–1909) upon his father's death in 1865, was highly respected for his efforts to promote economic growth. But his imperialist zeal ensnared Belgium in a century-long struggle in the central African region of the Congo.

Albert I (r. 1909–1934), the nephew of Leopold II, came to the Belgian throne in 1909. His personal leadership of the Belgian resistance against Germany during World War I earned Albert international respect, as did his liberal social policies. His daughter Marie married Umberto II (r. 1946), the last king of Italy, who was forced out almost immediately after taking the throne as the Italian people initiated a republican government.

The son and successor of Albert I, Leopold III (r. 1934–1951), was forced to abdicate because many Belgians believed that he had colluded with the Nazis during the war. He was succeeded by his popular and well-respected son, Baudouin (r. 1951–1993). Upon Baudouin's death in 1993, the Crown passed to his younger brother, Albert II (r. 1993–), the current reigning constitutional monarch of Belgium.

THE BRITISH LINE

In Great Britain, the Saxe-Coburg-Gotha dynasty entered the royal line through Victoria, the niece of King William IV (r. 1830–1837), who married her cousin, Albert of Saxe-Coburg-Gotha. Albert, who eventually earned the respect of the British people after a period of initial distrust, was intensely close to Victoria, and the couple saw Britain become the dominant world power of the nineteenth century.

Their eldest son became King Edward VII (r. 1901–1910) upon Victoria's death in 1901. While not as popular as his mother, Edward was still widely respected, especially for his efforts to forge a stronger relationship between Britain and France. His son, George V (1910–1936), came to the throne at a time when Europe was mobilizing and moving toward World War I. In order to dispel the perception that the royal family was tainted by its German origins, George changed the family's dynastic name from Saxe-Coburg-Gotha to Windsor.

The house of Windsor continues to occupy the throne of Great Britain. The present monarch is Queen Elizabeth II (r. 1952–). The British monarchy no longer has any political power, however, and its rulers function primarily as symbols of British national identity.

DECLINE ELSEWHERE IN EUROPE

In other parts of Europe, the Saxe-Coburg-Gotha dynasty has waned and disappeared as a ruling family. Marie, the granddaughter of Queen Victoria of Great Britain, married King Ferdinand I (r. 1914–1927) of Romania in 1893. Their son, Carol II (r. 1930–1940), attempted to create a dictatorship but was overthrown. His son and successor, Michael II (r. 1940–1947) was ousted in the communist revolution of 1947.

Another line of the Saxe-Coburg-Gotha dynasty, in Portugal, came to an end with King Manuel II (r. 1908–1910), the great-grandson of Maria II and Ferdinand of Saxe-Coburg-Gotha. Manuel was driven from the throne in the republican revolution of 1910.

The house of Saxe-Coburg-Gotha survived in Bulgaria until 1946, when the Communist Party took control of the country and abolished the monarchy. Bulgaria's ruling monarch, Simeon II (r. 1943–1946), the grandson of Ferdinand I of Saxe-Coburg-Gotha, was driven into exile, ending the dynasty's rule.

See also: BELGIAN KINGDOM; BULGARIAN MONARCHY; ENGLISH MONARCHIES; ROMANIAN MONARCHY; VICTORIA; WINDSOR, HOUSE OF.

FURTHER READING

Hibbert, Christopher. *Queen Victoria: A Personal History.* New York: Basic Books, 2000.

SAXON DYNASTY (919–1024 C.E.)

German dynasty that ruled various duchies and principalities in Central Europe and that held the Imperial Crown of the Holy Roman Empire in the tenth and eleventh centuries.

Around 900, the East Frankish state, one remnant of the Frankish empire of Charlemagne (r. 768–814), contained five districts: Saxony, Franconia, Lorraine, Swabia, and Bavaria. Previously under the sway of Charlemagne's descendants, by 900 each of these districts was headed by separate local leaders. With the end of the Carolingian dynasty, which had united the region, these dukes found it expedient to elect a single leader to try to regain some of the unity they had known under the Carolingians. They chose the weakest of their number, Conrad I, duke of Franconia, who ruled as German king (r. 911–918).

Conrad's election marked the earliest beginnings of Germany, but he was a weak king. Under his rule, Germany lost significant territory to France. In addition, Conrad was unable to hold back the Magyars of Hungary, who had swept out of Asia and were steadily expanding westward into Europe. Deciding that a stronger king was needed to deal with such threats, the East Frankish dukes selected Duke Henry I of Saxony (known as Henry the Fowler) to be king (r. 919–936). Henry's election marks the beginning of the Saxon dynasty's rule of Germany.

Henry I defeated the Magyars and expanded German territory eastward. He also gained the region of Lotharingia, which had been allied with France. As a result of his successes, Henry gained enough power to have his son, Otto I, designated as successor. As German king, Otto I the Great (r. 936–973) further consolidated the power of the house of Saxony and founded the Holy Roman Empire in the process.

Otto deliberately set about to create an image of himself as the successor to the great Charlemagne, first by having himself elected at Aachen, Charlemagne's capital. Otto successfully quashed internal rebellions in 939 and 953. In addition, he ended Magyar incursion into Western Europe once and for all in 955, at the battle of Lechfeld in southern Germany. In 962, Otto was crowned Western emperor by the pope, John XII, a title that later evolved into that of Holy Roman emperor.

Otto established a policy of working closely with the higher clergy within his realm, and he granted considerable secular power to the Church. Initially, this policy proved sound. Because the clergy derived their power from the king, they were more likely to support him rather than powerful German dukes. Moreover, since the higher clergy were expected to be celibate, their titles could not be passed on to descendants.

To ensure that his power would pass to his own descendants, Otto had his son and namesake crowned co-emperor in 967. Otto II (r. 973–983) had a brief and troubled reign, spending the first seven years suppressing rebellions. Upon his death in 983, Otto's son and successor, Otto III (r. 983–1002), was only an infant. But the power of the Saxon dynasty was such that Otto II's widow, the Byzantine princess Theophanu, was able to serve effectively as regent for her son. When she died in 991, her mother-in-law, Adelaide, took over as regent.

Otto III began ruling in his own right in 994 at age fourteen. Continuing the family policy of working closely with the clergy, Otto appointed two popes—his cousin, Gregory V, who crowned Otto emperor, and his tutor, Gerbert, who took the name Sylvester II.

Otto III died in 1002 without an heir and was succeeded by his cousin, Henry II of Bavaria (r. 1002–1024). As king and emperor, Henry II gained control of Italy as well as Germany. Yet, he struggled to maintain his power throughout his reign. Following his death in 1024, the Crown passed to Conrad II (r. 1024–1039), a Franconian noble of the Salian dynasty who was descended from a daughter of Otto I. With the accession of Conrad, the Saxon dynasty came to an end on the German and imperial thrones.

The close association between the clergy and the popes was beneficial for the Saxon dynasty during the tenth century C.E. However, as the eleventh century progressed and the power of the popes increased, this relationship became problematic because the papacy increasingly challenged German hegemony. In addition, the early Holy Roman emperors were, of necessity, deeply involved in Italian affairs. As a result, the nobles of Germany were left to pursue their own interests, a situation that, some historians have argued, delayed the unification of Germany for centuries.

See also: HOLY ROMAN EMPIRE; OTTO I, THE GREAT.

FURTHER READING
Koenigsberger, H.G. *Medieval Europe, 400–1500.* New York: Longman, 1987.
Stenton, F.M. *Anglo-Saxon England.* 3rd ed. New York: Oxford University Press, 2001.

SAXON KINGDOMS (ca. 100–1918 C.E.)

Small territories in northern Germany that, like those of most Germanic tribes of late Roman and post-Roman Europe, were governed by a combination of forces—shared religion, a tribal assembly of free men, kings whose function may have been primarily religious, and war-leaders whom Roman writers often termed *rex* (king). The Saxon lands were regions ruled by a tribe, rather than a clearly delimited state ruled by a king, and in this sense, they were not true kingdoms.

EARLY SAXON RULE
The Saxons first appear in classical writings in the second century. According to these early sources, the

Saxons inhabited an area in northern Germany below Denmark, near the mouth of the Elbe River. By the fourth century, they were raiding Britain and northern Gaul, and in the following centuries, invasions by war-bands of Angles, Saxons, Jutes, and Frisians led to the establishment of permanent territories and eventually to Anglo-Saxon kingdoms in Britain. The Saxons who established kingdoms in Britain probably had not ruled as kings in the regions they had come from, but were leaders of war-bands held together by bonds of loyalty and promises of lands and plunder.

Little is known about the tribal organization of the continental Saxons; they appear to have had no real central authority. Most pagan Germanic tribes had some form of assembly of free men that gave or withheld assent to decisions taken by their leaders. Some historians, particularly in the 1800s, saw in these assemblies the roots from which the concepts of elective and constitutional monarchy developed. Among these tribes, kings were chosen from within a royal family and were often separate from the leaders chosen in times of war. However, late Roman writers often identified the chieftains with whom they had contact as *rex* (king), or *dux* (duke or commander).

THE SAXONS AND FRANKS

By the eighth century, there were three main divisions of Saxons in Germany: the central Angarians along the Weser River, the Eastphalians along the Elbe River, and the Westphalians along the Rhine River. All three peoples were pagan, which was one factor that brought them into conflict with the Christian Franks under Charlemagne (r. 768–814). Another factor was continued Saxon raiding into Frankish lands and the Frankish desire to create in the Saxon region a buffer state against tribes farther north and east.

During Charlemagne's first campaign against the Saxons in 772, he not only seized fortresses and hostages, but destroyed Irminsul, the Saxon sacred tree. Charlemagne finally conquered the Saxons between 772 and 804. For Charlemagne, political and religious domination of the Saxons went together. In 785 he made death the penalty for any Saxon refusing to be baptized, or for any who insulted Christianity deliberately or by failing to conform to its laws.

Saxon revolts against Frankish rule and Frankish reprisals continued for many years, but Frankish and Anglo-Saxon missionaries, with the backing of Frankish military might, eventually converted the Saxons to Christianity. Although the Saxons became part of the Carolingian Empire, they maintained their identity as a separate people within that empire as well as within the German kingdom and Holy Roman Empire that followed.

MEDIEVAL TO MODERN SAXONY

From the tenth to the twelfth century, the duchy of Saxony was an important power within Germany. King Henry I of Germany (r. 919–936), known as Henry the Fowler, was the son of the first duke of Saxony, Otto (r. 880–912).

In 1180, Saxony was divided among other duchies and archbishoprics following Duke Henry the Lion's conflict with Emperor Frederick I Barbarossa (r. 1152–1190) of the Holy Roman Empire. Only two small areas, Saxe-Lauenburg near Holstein and Saxe-Wittenberg near Leipzig, retained the name. Much of the old Saxon duchy was reunited in the German state of Lower Saxony (Niedersachsen) following World War II.

In the fifteenth century, the margravate (territory ruled by a margrave) of Meissen in eastern Germany also became known as Saxony, when its ruler, Frederick I the Warlike, became duke and elector of Saxony in 1422. Saxony (the area around the city of Dresden), under Frederick Augustus III (r. 1763–1827), sided with France during the Napoleonic Wars. In appreciation, Napoleon granted Saxony conquered Prussian territory and made Frederick king of Saxony in 1806.

A significant portion of Saxony's territory was ceded to Prussia by the Congress of Vienna in 1815, becoming the Prussian province of Saxony, though the kingdom of Saxony continued to exist. Defeated by Prussia in 1866, the kingdom became a part of the North German Confederation in 1867 and then part of the German Empire in 1871. Saxony still retained its own king, however. The last king of Saxony, Frederick Augustus III (r. 1904–1918), abdicated in November 1918, after Germany's defeat in World War I. With the abdication of its king, the former Saxon kingdom became a state in the newly formed German Weimar Republic.

See also: CHARLEMAGNE; FRANKISH KINGDOM; FREDERICK I, BARBAROSSA; HOLY ROMAN EMPIRE.

FURTHER READING

Holmes, George, ed. *Oxford Illustrated History of Medieval Europe.* New York: Oxford University Press, 1988.

SCOTTISH KINGDOMS

The various kingdoms that have existed in Scotland from prehistoric times until the Act of Union, or Union of Crowns, with England in 1707.

ANCIENT SCOTLAND

Scotland was originally ruled by a collection of scattered tribes and small kingdoms. By the beginning of the first centuries C.E., these tribes were of British Celtic origin, speaking a language related to modern Welsh and Cornish.

The most prominent pre-Gaelic Scottish kingdoms were those of the Picts, who governed a large area of northern Scotland from the third century. Their fierceness in battle impressed the Roman occupiers of southern Britain, who gave them the name Picts (from the Latin word for "painted") because of the blue patterns they drew on their skin. The Pictish kingdom of Fortriu was the dominant political power in Scotland until the ninth century. Like most other early Celtic kingdoms in Europe, the Picts practiced a pagan religion. During this same period, a British Celtic kingdom of Strathclyde, and an Anglo-Saxon kingdom of the Angles, known as Northumbria, also ruled over some parts of present-day southern Scotland.

GAELIC KINGDOMS

Around 500, the Scots, who were Gaelic-speaking Celts from northern Ireland, followed their king Fergus Mor to the west coast of Scotland and established the kingdom of Dalriada (named after an Irish kingdom of the same name). The Scots traced their heritage through a legendary genealogy back to Scota, who was supposedly the daughter of an Egyptian pharoah.

The Scots practiced a pagan Celtic religion in which kingship had strong religious ties, especially to the physical land of the kingdom. Scottish Dalriada was less a centralized kingdom than a collection of petty tribal or clan-based kinship groups, the most prominent of which were the Cenel Loairn, Cenel nOengusa, and Cenel nGabrain.

In the sixth century, Dalriada embraced Christianity under the guidance of Saint Columba, an Irish missionary who came to evangelize Scotland in 563. In time, a form of Celtic Christianity, with strong ties to the religious community on the isle of Iona off the west coast of Scotland, became an important component of Scottish kingship.

Around 840, a tribal chief named Kenneth macAlpin became king of the Scots (r. ca. 840–858). Two years later he took control of the Pictish kingdom through conquest and possibly matrilineal inheritance. Kenneth macAlpin was therefore the first ruler of a Scottish kingdom that encompassed most of modern mainland Scotland. MacAlpin apparently started the tradition by which kings were crowned on the symbolic Stone of Scone to cement their attachment to the land. The dynasty he established ruled Scotland until Duncan I (r. 1034–1040) became king in 1034.

Duncan I, whose line was the house of Dunkeld, already ruled the small kingdom of Strathclyde, which he merged with the larger Scottish kingdom. Duncan was killed in 1040, probably by his cousin Macbeth, whose legend inspired the play of that name by William Shakespeare. Macbeth ruled Scotland until his death in 1057,

Scotland's King Malcolm III, also known as Malcolm Canmore, established the House of Canmore in the eleventh century. His life and reign are commemorated on this heraldic windowpane from Charlecote Park, a manor house in Warwickshire in England.

when the throne passed to his distant relative Lulach. However, Lulach was deposed a year later by Duncan I's son Malcolm III (r. 1057–1093), also known as Malcom Canmore ("big head" in Gaelic), who established the house of Canmore.

Malcolm III's Anglo-Saxon wife, Queen Margaret (Saint Margaret), helped change the nature of the Scottish kingdom by spreading Anglo-Saxon and Norman influence at the expense of traditional Gaelic heritage. The Anglo-Scots dialect replaced Gaelic in the lowland regions of Scotland, and older Celtic concepts of kingship and social structure faded. Because of Margaret's religious devotion and influence, the Iona-based Celtic Christianity that had been so important to the Scottish kingdoms was superseded by strong ties to the mainstream Catholic Church.

During the twelfth and thirteenth centuries, the Scottish kingdom expanded north and west at the expense of the small quasi-independent Viking kingdoms in the northern isles of Scotland, such as those ruled by the earls of Orkney and Shetland. Three Canmore kings named Alexander all fought to establish control over these regional Viking lords. The victory of Alexander III (r. 1249–1286) over Norway resulted in the Treaty of Perth (1266), in which Norway ceded most of its lands in Scotland. The Canmore dynasty continued to rule Scotland until the death of the Maid of Norway, Alexander III's heir, in 1290.

MEDIEVAL AND RENAISSANCE KINGDOMS

Throughout the medieval and early Renaissance periods, the Scottish kingdom, based in Edinburgh and Stirling, faced continual challenges from England and from fringe kingdoms in the northern and western isles. A two-year interregnum followed the end of the House of Dunkeld/Canmore in 1290, as potential Scottish heirs struggled among themselves and with Edward I of England (r. 1272–1307) over the throne.

The coronation in 1306 of Robert I (Robert the Bruce, r. 1306–1329) ended this period of civil strife and English dominance. The house of Bruce was short-lived, however. After Robert's son David II (r. 1329–1371) died in 1371, the throne passed to the Stewart dynasty through the marriage of Marjory Bruce, daughter of Robert the Bruce, to Walter Stewart, the sixth high steward of Scotland.

The Stewarts were the last Scottish dynasty to rule an independent Scotland. Throughout much of their rule, they struggled with challenges from English monarchs as well as other Scottish quasi-kingdoms, such as the Gaelic remnant kingdom of the Lords of the Isles. When James VI of Scotland (r. 1567–1625) became James I of England (r. 1603–1625) in 1603, the Stuart dynasty, as it was called thereafter, became rulers of both Scotland and England. In 1707, Queen Anne of England (r. 1702–1714) signed the Act of Union, which merged the kingdom of the Scots with that of England and Wales, creating Great Britain. That act marked the end of a separate Scottish kingdom.

See also: DAVID I; DAVID II; JAMES I OF ENGLAND (JAMES VI OF SCOTLAND); KENNETH I (KENNETH MACALPIN); LORDS OF THE ISLES; MARY, QUEEN OF SCOTS; PICTS, KINGDOM OF THE; ROBERT I (ROBERT THE BRUCE); STEWART DYNASTY.

FURTHER READING

Lynch, Michael. *Scotland: A New History.* London: Pimlico, 1992.

Mackie, J.D. *A History of Scotland.* New York: Penguin Books, 1984.

Roberts, John L. *Lost Kingdoms: Celtic Scotland and the Middle Ages.* Edinburgh: Edinburgh University Press, 1997.

Ross, Stewart. *Monarchs of Scotland.* New York: Facts on File, 1990.

SCYTHIAN EMPIRE

(flourished 700s–300s B.C.E.)

Wealthy and powerful empire that stretched from the Danube River of Europe in the west to the borders of China in the east. The empire was established by the Scythians, a nomadic people, probably of Iranian origin, who migrated from western Siberia in Central Asia to southeastern Russia during the eighth and seventh centuries B.C.E.

The ancient Scythians spoke an Iranian language related to Old Persian. Centered around the present-day region of Crimea and the Black Sea in southern Russia, their empire lasted hundreds of years before it was forced to surrender to the Sarmatians, another nomadic people related to the Scythians, between the fourth and second centuries B.C.E.

FORMATION OF THE EMPIRE

The Scythians were great warriors, who were especially skilled in horsemanship and who were perhaps the first horse-riding people in southern Russia. Their skill with horses made them a formidable foe militarily and also gave them great mobility, allowing them to travel swiftly across great distances.

As the Scythians migrated into southern Russia in the ninth century B.C.E., they eventually arrived in the land of the Cimmerians, who ruled the Caucasus region and the vast plains north of the Black Sea. The Scythians fought against the Cimmerians for thirty years, finally defeating them and driving them southwestward into Anatolia (present-day Turkey).

After the defeat of the Cimmerians, a group of Scythian people known as the Royal Scyths founded a kingdom in the Crimean region. The Royal Scyths served as the ruling class of this kingdom, while the native inhabitants of the region worked primarily as farmers.

As Scythian power grew, their empire and power expanded southward into the ancient Near East, where they encountered opposition from a number of groups, including the Assyrians. In the late 600s B.C.E., taking advantage of a decline in Assyrian power, the Scythians launched devastating invasions into Syria, Palestine, and Egypt. Allying with the Medes of Persia and the Babylonians, the Scythians contributed to the eventual collapse of the Assyrian Empire.

After the collapse of Assyria, the Scythians began to encounter problems with their former allies, the Medes, who launched attacks in the early 500s B.C.E. that forced the Scythians back to the Caucasus region and Scythia, which was the core of the Scythian Empire. At this point, the empire extended from the northern border of Persia into southern Russia. Blocked from further expansion to the south, the Scythians invaded Eastern Europe, eventually extending their raids as far as present-day Poland and Austria.

SCYTHIAN CIVILIZATION

The Scythians developed an extraordinary civilization, with highly developed skills in metalworking and superb metalwork featuring animal designs and motifs. Their decorative art embellished everyday objects, such as saddles, rugs, swords, and vases, many with depictions of solitary animals and battle scenes between animals. Both mythical and real creatures were portrayed in a style that was uniquely Scythian. Since the Scythians remained a largely nomadic people, most of the objects they produced were not very large. Yet, they often contained precious materials and demonstrated excellent workmanship.

Scythian society was headed by a wealthy class of aristocrats and chieftains, the Royal Scyths, who were buried in ornate graves containing elaborate gold items and other valuable objects. Around the third century B.C.E., these Scythian rulers intermarried with the Greeks, and Greek influence on Scythian society increased.

Although they were nomads, the Scythians established a variety of permanent settlements. The huge fortified settlement of Kamenka on the Dnieper River, established in the late fifth century B.C.E., became the heart of the Scythian kingdom under the ruler Ateas (r. ?–339 B.C.E.), who was killed in a battle against Philip II of Macedon (r. 359–336 B.C.E.) in 339 B.C.E.)

DECLINE AND FALL

The Scythians' power began a slow decline in the late 500s B.C.E., but they remained strong enough to stop an invasion by Darius I of Persia (r. 521–486 B.C.E.) in 512 B.C.E. In the 300s B.C.E., Scythia regained some of its power, enough to resist attacks by the Macedonians under Philip II of Macedon.

This resurgence of power was brief, however. By the late 300s, Scythian power began to decline dramatically, and in the 200s B.C.E., Scythia lost most of its territory in Russia to the Sarmatians, who invaded from their territory east of the Don River. With the loss of this territory, the Scythian Empire was reduced to part of the Crimean Peninsula and a narrow coastal strip along the Black Sea.

The Scythian Empire was finally destroyed in the second century B.C.E., during the reign of king Palakus (r. ca. 100s B.C.E.), by the Sarmatians. Although the Scythians ceased to exist as a single nation, some Scythian tribes remained in the area in the Balkans and the Asian part of the Russian steppes.

See also: ASSYRIAN EMPIRE; MEDES KINGDOM; PHILIP II OF MACEDON.

FURTHER READING

Gorelik, M. V., E. N. Cernenko, and E. V. Gerneko. *Scythians, 700–300 B.C.* London: Osprey, 1983.

SECLUSION OF MONARCH

Instances in which a monarch is separated from the court and society and remains secluded for a period of time.

Monarchs may seclude themselves for many reasons, some personal and some institutional. Frederick II of Prussia (r. 1740–1786) chose moderate seclusion in the latter part of his reign because of his personal desire to live apart from society. Dwelling at Potsdam outside his capital of Berlin, Frederick had no royal court, saw his ministers only when he commanded, and communicated with his government by writing rather than in person. Undistracted by society, Frederick devoted his waking hours to work.

Queen Victoria of England (r. 1837–1901) adopted a secluded existence because of the tremendous grief she experienced after the death of her husband, Prince Albert, in 1861. Victoria's refusal to show herself publicly greatly inconvenienced the ministers who dealt with her and led to a decline in the monarchy's popularity.

Seclusion is a relative state. Monarchs have often tried to control zones of space with varying degrees of public access. Early modern English monarchs, for instance, established the Privy Chamber, a zone of the court where only the monarch and selected courtiers, servants, and family members were allowed. The Privy Chamber eventually became so crowded that a new secluded zone, the Bedchamber, was established where the monarch could have some privacy.

Certain types of monarchical leadership make complete or even extended seclusion impossible. For example, monarchs with active military, social, or judicial roles cannot isolate themselves from their soldiers or subjects and expect to rule efficiently and effectively. Moves to institutionalize seclusion are often associated with the removal of a monarch from day-to-day government and have a particularly isolating effect in restricting the monarch's access to information. Monarchs, such as the emperors of Japan, whose main role is carrying out ritual activities, are better able to function in seclusion than rulers who have policy and other responsibilities.

Monarchical seclusion reached its height in China during the late Ming dynasty (1368–1644), when an entire district of Beijing, known as the "Forbidden City," was given over to the imperial residence. Late Ming emperors had face-to-face interactions with few people other than courtiers, eunuchs, concubines, and servants. Even major government ministers rarely saw the emperor. It is said that the last Ming emperor, Ch'ung Chen (r. 1627–1644), only learned of the rebellion against him when the rebels were actually climbing the walls of the Forbidden City.

See also: BEHAVIOR, CONVENTIONS OF ROYAL; COURTS AND COURT OFFICIALS, ROYAL; ETIQUETTE, ROYAL; EUNUCHS, ROYAL; HAREMS; SERVANTS AND AIDES, ROYAL.

SECOND EMPIRE (1852–1870 C.E.)

Period in France during the reign of Louis Napoleon, president of the Second Republic (r. 1848–1852), after he staged a military coup and became Emperor Napoleon III (r. 1852–1870). Great economic success early on, followed by imperial growth and moves toward liberalization, were all hallmarks of the short-lived Second Empire. Having begun in a violent coup, the empire ended with the crushing defeat of France in the Franco-Prussian War (1870–1871).

ORIGINS

After his election to the presidency of the restored Republic in 1848, Louis Napoleon, the nephew of Emperor Napoleon I (r. 1804–1815), began a complex and deliberate process of securing and consolidating his power, with an eye to the eventual overthrow of the elected government. Popular with both the powerful clergy and the working classes, Louis, a consummate politician, played the many different political groups of republican France against one another. In 1851, he forced a constitutional crisis when he pushed for an amendment to remove the term limit for the presidency. When the amendment was rejected by the National Assembly, the stage was set for a military takeover.

As president, Louis had filled key positions in government with men loyal to his ambitions. This helped ensure rapid victory, which came near the end of 1851 when the French army, in accordance with the plans of Louis and his half-brother Charles de Moray, took over the offices of the government. Louis immediately called for a popular vote on the proposed revisions to the constitution. Violent scare tactics and threats to deport his opponents allowed Louis to easily win the concessions regarding term limits that he sought. By the autumn of 1852, another public referendum resulted in Louis being crowned as Emperor Napoleon III, an event that marked the establishment of the Second Empire.

SUCCESS AT HOME, TENSIONS ABROAD

Emperor Napoleon III immediately went to work securing his power by promoting widespread economic growth. Although there was initially some internal resistance to the Second Empire, large public works projects, such as the redesign of Paris's streets by civic planner Baron Haussmann, and easily available lines of credit for business and industrial leaders drowned concerns in a tide of new wealth. The lower classes were placated not only by the jobs created under the Second Empire, but by its esta-

The nephew of Napoleon Bonaparte, Emperor Napoleon III first served as president of France's Second Republic. A man of ambition, he assumed dictatorial power and the title of emperor of the Second Empire in 1852. His reign lasted only until his deposition in a bloodless revolution in 1870.

blishment of many charitable organizations as well. Many French citizens felt as if the glorious days of Napoleon I had been restored, a feeling Napoleon enhanced with his decorous court.

In the spirit of extending the glory of the Second Empire, France challenged Russian supremacy in the eastern Mediterranean Sea and the decaying Ottoman Empire. The resulting conflict, the Crimean War (1854–1856), restored France as one of the major powers of Europe and allowed for the French construction of the Suez Canal through northeastern Egypt. After victory in the Crimean War, the Second Empire supported the Italian movement for national unity, thus pitting France against the Austrian Empire, which controlled northern Italy. But Napoleon betrayed the Italians and made peace with Austria in 1859, greatly damaging future relations between France and Italy, as well as causing the emperor's popularity to sink at home.

Fearful of overthrow, Napoleon conceded to numerous liberal demands and rescinded some of the onerous restrictions on individual freedom against which many in France had agitated. In an attempt to appease commercial interests, Napoleon also eliminated trade barriers between France and England in 1860. In an effort to further the imperial ambitions of France, the Second Empire took over part of Indochina in Southeast Asia, thus embroiling itself in a century-long colonial endeavor in that region. A similar experiment in Mexico from 1861 to 1867 proved disastrous; the French not only failed in their attempt to protect the rule of Emperor Maximilian (r. 1864–1867), but they seriously weakened their military as well by overcommitting forces to a far away region in a losing cause. This would prove fatal in the coming conflict with Prussia.

DECLINE AND DEFEAT

By the late 1860s, it was becoming clear that Prussia, led by William I (r. 1861–1888) and Chancellor Otto von Bismarck, was at the helm of a unifying Germany. Napoleon and his foreign minister, the duc de Gramont, concerned that French power would be threatened by a stronger Prussia, began to agitate for war in the late 1860s. An attempt by the French to block the accession of a Prussian prince to the throne of Spain in 1870 was met with hostility by Bismarck and William I, leading to heightened tensions. Bismarck, as desirous of German unification and glory as Napoleon was of French supremacy, effectively maneuvered the French into declaring war in the summer of 1870 through the careful editing and publication of a secret Prussian document known as the Ems dispatch.

Unprepared for war, the French were crushed by the Prussian military in just six months. Napoleon, captured while commanding his troops in September 1870, was subsequently deposed by a provisional French government established in his absence. Adolphe Thiers, the leader of the interim administration, negotiated a peace settlement with Prussia and became the first president of France's Third Republic in the spring of 1871. The monumental collapse of the Second Empire after its early successes left a deep wound in French national pride and created a French-German rivalry that helped ignite the fires of World War I.

See also: NAPOLEON I (BONAPARTE); NAPOLEON III.

FURTHER READING

Smith, William. *Napoleon III: The Pursuit of Prestige.* London: Collins and Brown, 1991.

SELEUCID DYNASTY (312–63 B.C.E.)

Ruling dynasty centered in Asia Minor (present-day Turkey) and present-day Syria that emerged from the conquests of Alexander the Great (r. 336–323 B.C.E.)

The Seleucid dynasty was founded in 312 B.C.E. by Seleucus I (312–281 B.C.E.), one of the generals and close friends of Alexander the Great. At Alexander's death in 323 B.C.E., Seleucus took over Babylonia, and in later years, he greatly expanded the kingdom.

Seleucus did not take the title of king until after Alexander's death. Also known by the title Nicator ("victor"), he became the most successful participant in the endless wars among the Diadochi, the successors to Alexander. By the end of Seleucus I's reign, he controlled an empire that stretched from Asia Minor to the region of Bactria in Central Asia.

The dynasty founded by Seleucus I drew from both Greek, Macedonian, and Near Eastern traditions of rule. The Seleucid monarch was theoretically not identified with a particular people. In practice, however, he identified strongly with Greek culture. Greeks and Macedonians comprised the vast majority of the kingdom's governing elite, which were known as the "King's Friends."

The Seleucids claimed a particularly strong relationship with the Greek god Apollo. The Seleucid seal incorporated an anchor, an item traditionally associated with Apollo, and it was claimed that Seleucus I had a birthmark in the shape of an anchor. The Seleucids also patronized the traditional religion of Babylon, however, and presented themselves as rulers in the Mesopotamian and Persian traditions by adopting their monarchical customs.

The original capital of the Seleucid dynasty was Seleucia on the Tigris River in Mesopotamia. For a brief period it was moved to Seleucia in Pieria in Macedonia, but then was finally settled at Antioch in Syria. The vast size of the Seleucid Empire made centralized authority virtually impossible. Drawing from the Persian political tradition of the Achaemenid dynasty, the early Seleucids divided the empire into large administrative districts ruled mostly by members of the royal family.

The successors of Seleucus I lost much of their direct control over Iran and Bactria, where new Greek (Bactria) and non-Greek (Parthia) kingdoms arose. In the late third century B.C.E., Antiochus III (r. 223–187 B.C.E.), known as "Megas" ("the Great"), reasserted Seleucid overlordship over many of the lost territories in the east. He also advanced Seleucid power over Palestine and Phoenicia, areas that had long been contested by the Ptolemaic dynasty of Egypt. However, Antiochus III also suffered the first defeats at the hands of the power that would eventually cause the downfall of the Seleucids—Rome.

While the Romans put pressure on the Seleucids from the west in the second century B.C.E., the rise of Parthia did so from the east. Even the acquisition of Palestine by Antiochus III proved more of a headache than an overall gain because of the volatile political situation there. Antiochus IV (r. 175–164 B.C.E.) was an avid promoter of Greek culture and the cult of the divine ruler. These policies provoked a revolt by the Jews in Palestine, led by the Maccabees, who eventually succeeded in splitting off Judea as an independent kingdom. Antiochus IV also was forced into a humiliating withdrawal from Egypt in 168 B.C.E. Just as he was on the verge of conquering that kingdom, the Roman Senate sent an emissary demanding that Antiochus withdraw. Faced with the growing threat of Roman power, he reluctantly agreed.

Antiochus IV died in 164 B.C.E. while attempting to restore Seleucid power in the East. His death was followed by more Seleucid defeats as well as turmoil within the Seleucid house itself between the descendants of Antiochus IV and his brother and predecessor, Seleucus IV (r. 187–175 B.C.E.). In 140 B.C.E., Mithridates I (r. 171–138 B.C.E.) of Parthia captured the Seleucid ruler Demetrius II (r. 145–139 B.C.E.), and two years later he took Babylon. The Seleucids made a partial recovery under Antiochus VII (r. 139–129 B.C.E.), who advanced far into Parthian territory until he was killed in battle in 129 B.C.E.

While the last Seleucids fought bitterly among themselves for control of the empire, the dynasty's power dwindled in Syria. The late Seleucid state was briefly conquered by Tigranes (r. 96–55 B.C.E.) of Armenia, and Syria finally was reduced to a Roman province by the Roman general Pompey in 64 B.C.E. The last ruler of the Seleucid dynasty, Antiochus XIII (r. 69–64 B.C.E.) was murdered shortly after the Roman takeover of Syria.

See also: Alexander III, the Great; Antiochus III, the Great; Hellenistic Dynasties; Macedonian Empire; Parthian Kingdom; Ptolemaic Dynasty.

Selim I, the Grim (1467–1520 c.e.)

Ottoman ruler (r. 1512–1520) who was known as Yavuz, or "the Grim," for his cruel, if pragmatic, policies and his military prowess.

Selim I was born in Amasya, a provincial town in northern Anatolia (present-day Turkey), where Ottoman princes were often raised and sent to practice the tools of rule in case of their eventual succession to the throne. Selim's father, Beyezid II (r. 1481–1512), named Selim heir to the throne in order to resolve a disruptive and destabilizing conflict between the young prince and his brother Ahmed over who would eventually rule.

Under the Ottoman law of fratricide, sultans often executed their brothers and nephews to prevent such power struggles, as primogeniture (which gave firstborn sons the right of inheritance) was not used as a method of succession in the Turkic tribes that gave birth to the Osmanli dynasty. When Selim came to the throne in 1512, he made sure to rid the empire of all possible rivals for the throne, save for his favorite son Suleyman.

Selim's short reign was marked by great military conquests. Instead of marching further into Europe, however, he turned south and eastward. In 1514 he won a major battle against the Safavid sultan of Persia, Ismail I (r. 1501–1524), settling a conflict over where the eastern borders of the Ottoman Empire would lie. He also brought several southeastern Anatolian provinces under Ottoman rule, bringing many Kurdish subjects into the empire.

Soon Selim found himself at war with the Mamluk Empire of Egypt, which resented his southward expansion into their sphere of influence. In 1516, the Ottomans handed the Mamluks a major defeat near Aleppo (in present-day Syria), and proceeded to march rapidly across the desert to conquer Cairo. Selim's military campaigns brought Egypt, Iraq, Syria, Palestine, and much of the Arabian Peninsula under Ottoman rule. He thus became ruler over the three holiest cities of Islam: Mecca, Medina, and Jerusalem, thus winning the title "Protector of the Holy Places."

After these conquests, Selim returned to Anatolia, the center of the Ottoman Empire, and prepared to march from the city of Edirne on a new campaign against the island of Rhodes. On the way, he died of an infected boil in 1520, leaving the much-expanded empire to his son Suleyman I (r. 1520–1566), also known as Suleyman the Magnificent.

See also: Beyezid II; Mamluk Dynasty; Ottoman Empire; Suleyman I, the Magnificent.

Selim III, the Great
(1761–1808 c.e.)

Ottoman sultan (r. 1789–1807) who devoted his rule to attempts at reforming the institutions of the Ottoman Empire.

The son of Sultan Mustafa III (r. 1757–1774), Selim grew up in the *kafes*, or "cage," the part of the royal harem where Ottoman princes were imprisoned and raised in seclusion after the law of fratricide was abandoned. Such imprisonment and seclusion prevented the widespread killing of potential heirs, but it often impaired their leadership abilities by denying them the experience gained by earlier Ottoman princes, who often served as provincial governors and military leaders to test their mettle and prepare them for rule. Instead of gaining that type of experience, Selim composed music and studied with tutors in the confinement of the palace walls.

Selim became sultan in 1789 upon the death of his uncle, Abdulhamid I (r. 1774–1789), who had ruled after the death of Selim's father, Mustafa. Selim immediately began efforts to revitalize the decaying Ottoman Empire, which had lost much of its military strength and bureaucratic efficiency. The Ottomans also had become increasingly subject to challenges from European imperialism.

Selim set out to reform the army, rebuild the navy on European models, and rid the empire of the overpowerful, elite corps of Janissaries, which had dominated the Ottoman military since the 1600s. During his reign, the Ottomans forced the armies of Napoleon Bonaparte to withdraw from Egypt in 1801, but at the price of seeing Egypt become almost independent under the pasha Muhammad Ali (r. 1805–1848). The Ottomans also suffered a serious defeat in the second Russo-Turkish War, although the Treaty of Jassy in 1792 resulted in little territorial loss.

Angered by Selim's Westernizing reforms and military defeats, the Janissaries and conservative religious factions deposed him in 1807 and placed his mentally ill cousin, Mustafa IV (r. 1807–1808), on the throne. The Janissaries reimprisoned Selim in the harem where he had spent his youth.

When army supporters stormed Constantinople in 1808 in an attempt to restore Selim to the throne, Mustafa ordered the execution of the former ruler. Despite Selim's death, his supporters soon triumphed over Mustafa and executed him. They then installed Mustafa's brother, Mahmut II (r. 1808–1839), as the new sultan. Selim's reforms were well intentioned, but they came too late to stop the continuing decline of the Ottoman Empire.

See also: MUHAMMAD ALI; OTTOMAN EMPIRE

SELJUQ DYNASTY (900s–1308 C.E.)

A Turkic dynasty that ruled a large swath of Central Asia and the Near East in the eleventh and twelfth centuries.

The Seljuq (or Seljuk) dynasty emerged from Central Asia in the tenth century. Its founder was Seljuq, the chieftain of a nomadic Turkic tribe that originated in the steppes of Central Asia near the Oxus River. Seljuq's descendants, Muslim Turkic tribes led by his grandson Tughril Beg (r. 1038–1063), moved westward and swiftly conquered much of present-day Iran. Tughril and his followers took the city of Isfahan in 1043 before marching on to Mesopotamia.

In 1038, the Abbasid caliph in Baghdad, al-Qaim (r. 1031–1075), granted Tughril the title of sultan, and the Seljuqs became the first Islamic dynasty ruled by a leader with this title. Although the Seljuqs supported the declining Abbasid caliphate in order to gain religious legitimacy, they regarded the caliphate as a religious authority with little political importance.

The Seljuqs under Tughril Beg conquered Baghdad, the seat of the caliphs, in 1055 and drove out the Shia Buyid dynasty, which had ruled the city since 946. During the remainder of his reign, Tughril battled the Egypt-based Fatimid dynasty for its lands in Syria, often ruling from his base camps rather than from his capitals of Nishapur and Isfahan in Iran. Tughril died in 1063 and was succeeded by his nephew, Alp Arslan (r. 1063–1072).

Alp Arslan's reign was a high point for the Seljuqs, who experienced continued military victories against the Fatimids in the south and the Armenians in the north. In 1064, Alp Arslan's Seljuq army conquered the Armenian capital of Ani. After that victory, the Byzantine emperor, Romanus IV Diogenes (r. 1068–1071), who had become increasingly frustrated by raids against his Anatolian territory from various Turkic tribes that had followed the Seljuqs westward, decided to attack the Seljuq kingdom.

In 1071, Byzantine forces attacked the Seljuq army at Manzikert, near Lake Van in southeastern Anatolia. The Seljuqs defeated the Byzantine army resoundingly, and Anatolia was thereafter open to settlement by various Turkic tribes and kingdoms. This Islamic advance into Christian Byzantine territory troubled European leaders and was one of the factors that led them to launch the First Crusade.

Alp Arslan had little interest in conquering the rest of Anatolia, and other Turkic kingdoms sprouted up in the conquered lands. A separate Seljuq kingdom, known as the Seljuq sultanate of Rum (Anatolia), was established at this time and was led by Sulayman ibn Qutalmish (r. 1077–1086).

After Alp Arslan's death in 1072, his son Malik Shah I (r. 1072–1092) became the Seljuq ruler. Malik developed the primary Seljuq sultanate of Hamadan, based in Baghdad, and became a patron of artists and writers, including the famous Persian poet Omar Khayyam. The Seljuq dynasty proved fruitful for the arts, and distinctive Seljuq architecture still graces many Turkish and Iranian cities today.

After Malik Shah's death, the Seljuq Empire continued to fragment into a series of small principalities and kingdoms. One reason for this dissolution was that primogeniture (inheritance by first-born son) was alien to the Turkic tribal traditions that underlay Seljuq rule. Therefore, multiple sons would inherit from a ruling father, splitting the land. Thus with each generation, the territory became more fragmented. The Christian Crusades were also a destabilizing force. Between the efforts of the Crusaders and the Khwarazm-shahs, a Seljuq successor state, the original empire was largely conquered and dismantled by 1157.

The Seljuqs of Rum continued to rule in Anatolia, intermittently battling the Byzantine Empire and the rival Turkic kingdom of the Danishmends. In 1176, the Seljuqs handed the Byzantines a devastating defeat and were able to expand northward towards the Black Sea. However, the rule of the Seljuqs of Rum was short-lived. In 1243, the Mongols under Jenghiz Khan (Genghis Khan) decisively defeated the Seljuq army and made the Seljuq realm a vassal state, although Seljuq sultans continued to rule small remnants of Anatolian territory until 1308.

See also: BUYID (BUWAYHID) DYNASTY; BYZANTINE EMPIRE; FATIMID DYNASTY; OTTOMAN EMPIRE; TURKIC EMPIRE.

SENNACHERIB (d. ca. 681 B.C.E.)

Assyrian monarch (r. 704–681 B.C.E.) who destroyed Babylon and rebuilt the city of Nineveh.

The son of Sargon II (r. 721–705 B.C.E.), Sennacherib came to the Assyrian throne after his father's death as an experienced military leader and soldier. The first two years of his reign were peaceful, and he concentrated his energies on rebuilding ancient city of Nineveh—an enormous task that required redirecting the Tebiltu River and doubling the size of the city. He constructed a new and vast palace called "the Incomparable," which featured colossal metal statuary and an elaborate orchard and park.

Annals of Sennacherib's reign indicate that this period of peaceful construction ended in 703 B.C.E.,

when the rebel leader Marduk-apla-iddina II (the Hebrew Bible's Merodach-Baladan)—whom Sargon II had battled some eighteen years before—seized control of Babylon. Despite an alliance between the Babylonians and the Elamites, Sennacherib quelled the rebellion, but Merodach escaped.

Leaving a governor to manage Babylon, Sennacherib set out with his armies to conquer the kingdom of Judah in Palestine, a campaign described in the Hebrew Bible. After seizing the Judean countryside in 700 B.C.E., Sennacherib laid siege to Jerusalem. But he retreated without finishing the siege, possibly as a result of a deadly pestilence that killed a significant number of his troops.

In 689 B.C.E., Babylon revolted once again under the leadership of Merodach-Baladan II, assisted by the Elamites. This time, Sennacherib did not stop at quelling the uprising; he sacked the city of Babylon, burned it to the ground, and diverted the Euphrates River so that its waters would flood the ruins.

Sennacherib was no longer troubled by Babylonian rebellion, but that was not his last experience with revolt. In 681 B.C.E., after he named his youngest son, Esarhaddon (r. 680–669 B.C.E.), as his heir, Sennacherib's older sons Adrammelech and Sharezer revolted and assassinated their father. Upon Sennacherib's death, Esarhaddon took the throne and his brothers fled the kingdom.

See also: ASSYRIAN EMPIRE; ESARHADDON; SARGON II.

SERBIAN KINGDOM (1167–1459 C.E.)

Powerful kingdom that ruled in the Balkan region prior to the domination of that area by the Ottoman Turks in the fourteenth century.

The history of Serbia dates back to the sixth century, when the first Serbian state blossomed. From then until the end of the twelfth century, Serbian history was marked by a brief period of stability followed by a series of internal crises that culminated in the mid-1100s with the establishment of the first kingdom of Serbia.

In 1159, Stefan Nemanja (r. 1167–1196), whom the Byzantine emperor recognized as leader of Serbia, fought his brothers for control of the region. Nemanja emerged victorious and went on to establish the first kingdom of Serbia, founding a dynasty that ruled for nearly two hundred years. During his rule, sometimes aided by Byzantine allies, Nemanja expanded Serbian territories while building monasteries and other cultural institutions. Nemanja gave his eldest son, Vukan, rule of the Zeta region, which later became known as Montenegro.

Nemanja's second son, also named Stefan (r. 1196–1228), succeeded his father as leader of Serbia in 1196. The younger Stefan received much support from his younger brother, Sava, a well-respected monk who campaigned for social justice. Sava's influence helped Stefan obtain a Crown and title from the pope in 1217, thus making Stefan Serbia's first king. Two years later, in 1219, Sava became the first archbishop of Serbia, thus earning the kingdom both political and religious independence.

After an initial period of rapid cultural and political growth, the Serbian kingdom grew stagnant under future generations of rulers. The reigns of Stefan's sons—Radoslav (r. 1228–1234), Vladislav (r. 1234–1243), and Uros I (r. 1243–1276)—were marked by Serbian dependence on the stronger neighboring states of Byzantium, Hungary, and Bulgaria. As a result of Hungarian influence, Uros I was succeeded in 1276 by his son Dragutin (r. 1276–1282), who had married a Hungarian princess.

Dragutin abdicated the throne in 1282, passing control to his younger brother Milutin (Uros II) (r. 1282–1321). King Ladislaus IV of Hungary (r. 1272–1290) offered Milutin territory in northeastern Bosnia in order to maintain and strengthen the alliance between the two powers.

Milutin proved to be a strong ruler and able diplomat, who continued his family tradition of building churches and promoting cultural growth, despite the fact that he was also engaged in multiple wars during his reign. Under his son, and successor, Stefan Decanski (r. 1321–1331), Serbia expanded its territory dramatically through the acquisition of Nis to the east and several sections of Macedonia to the south. Decanski continued his father's architectural legacy with the construction of the Visoki Decani Monastery, one of the prime surviving monuments of medieval Serbian architecture.

Serbia reached the height of cultural and political advancement in the fourteenth century under the rule of Stefan Dusan, who ruled first as king (r. 1331–1346) and then as tsar (r. 1346–1355). During his reign, the *Dusanov Zakonic,* a unique legal code granting judicial powers uncommon among feudal states, was devised and implemented. Serbian art and architecture also flourished during Dusan's reign, and territorial expansion led to a doubling of the size of the Serbian kingdom. Serbia, at this time, became the most powerful kingdom on the Balkan Peninsula.

Upon his death in 1355, Dusan was succeeded by his son, Uros IV (r. 1355–1371), often called Uros the Weak. This name was apt, for Uros allowed the kingdom to become stagnant and dependent politically, socially, and economically. Ultimately, a state of anarchy developed, opening the door to aggression from the Ottoman Turks in Anatolia (present-day Turkey), who were hungry for territorial expansion. Succeeding rulers were unable to prevent Serbia's further decline, and by 1459, the Ottoman Turks had completed their conquest of Serbia, and the kingdom became a part of the Ottoman Empire.

Serbia remained fully under Turkish control for more than 350 years. In 1811, a Serbian patriot named Karadjordje led an uprising against the Turks. Though successful for a time, the rebellion faltered when the Turks returned to the Serbian city of Belgrade in 1813, forcing Karadjordje to flee to Austria. At the conclusion of the Russo-Turkish War (1828–1829) Serbia became an autonomous principality of the Ottoman Empire.

As an autonomous principality, Serbia was ruled by a series of princes who ruled as vassals of the Ottoman state. For a short period between 1842 and 1858, however, Serbia regained greater independence when Karadjordje's son, Prince Aleksander (r. 1842–1858, returned and took control. However, Aleksander was eventually deposed by the Turks in 1858.

In 1903, disturbed by political insurgencies, the Serbian parliament requested that Prince Peter Karadjordjevic, the son of Prince Aleksander, be allowed to assume the throne of Serbia as Peter I (r. 1903–1921). Peter I was committed to establishing autonomy for the kingdom of Serbia, and during the Balkan Wars (1912–1913), Serbia defeated Turkey and expanded its territory.

Shortly before the Balkan War, in 1908, the Serbs and their neighbors, the Croatians, enraged by Austria's annexation of Bosnia-Herzegovina, experienced an upsurge of nationalist sentiment that would have monumental consequences. This nationalism led to the assassination of Austrian Archduke Franz Ferdinand by a Serbian, Gavrilo Princip, in 1914, which marked the beginning of World War I.

After World War I, Serbia and other Balkan kingdoms combined as the kingdom of the Serbs, Croats, and Slovenes under the rule of Peter I. However, threats from neighboring kingdoms, as well as internal disputes over religious, cultural, and political differences among the various nationalities, ultimately caused tensions within the kingdom.

In 1919, Peter I imposed a dictatorship, hoping to keep his rule in place long enough to reestablish democracy in the newly renamed kingdom of Yugoslavia. He was unable to accomplish his goal, however, and after his death in 1921 the kingdom was ruled by a series of appointed regents. In 1945, at the end of World War II, the new communist leaders of Yugoslavia abolished the monarchy, ending centuries of royal rule in Serbia and the other Balkan kingdoms.

See also: AUSTRO-HUNGARIAN EMPIRE; MONTENEGRO KINGDOM; OTTOMAN EMPIRE.

FURTHER READING

Stavrinos, Leften Stavros. *The Balkans Since 1453.* New York: New York University Press, 2000.
Temperly, Harold W. *History of Serbia.* New York: AMS Press,

SERVANTS AND AIDES, ROYAL

Those who perform domestic, personal, or official duties for the ruler.

Royal households need a wide variety of servants and aides to perform duties for monarchs and other members of the royal family and court. Their tasks range from preparing and serving meals, cleaning, or helping with the wardrobe to taking care of correspondence and advising the monarch on affairs of state. A social hierarchy within the royal household generally determined the duties and rank of servants. Individuals from the nobility might hold positions such as secretary, while working-class individuals may perform household cleaning and other menial tasks.

Royal households can become quite large, with a multitude of servants assigned very specific duties. In the kitchens of King Charles VI of France (r. 1380–1422), for example, specific servants were responsible for turning the spits on which meat was roasted, peeling vegetables and cleaning fish and poultry, keeping the fires going and water boiling, carving roasts and cooking poultry, and assisting the Strong Queux, or Head Cook (a hereditary position).

An elaborate title could add to a servant's prestige. Among the many servants and aides in the court of Elizabeth I of England (r. 1558–1603) were four Gentleman Ushers, a Keeper of the Gardens, a Keeper of the Wardrobe, a Royal Barge Master, a Master of the Horse, and a Clerk of Her Majesty's Green Cloth. In Great Britain today, the Lord Chamberlain directs the members of the queen's household. Even though the specific duties in the royal household have evolved to meet modern needs, many of the servants and aides keep traditional titles, such as ladies-in-waiting. The Master of the Household, a position created in 1539 during the reign of Henry VIII (r. 1509–1547), oversees cleaning, upkeep of palace grounds, dining arrangements, and other domestic matters.

Whereas the titles of royal servants in some royal courts may be lofty or complex, in other cases, the titles of aides are simple. For example, the Lovedu tribe of Africa is ruled by a queen who, according to tradition, does not marry. To insure a female heir, the royal council approves consorts for the queen. Chief among her servants are maidens, called wives, who manage the household.

Although some servants and aides serve only the monarch, others perform duties for many members of the royal household. For instance, nursemaids, governesses, and tutors have often assumed the major responsibility for care of royal children. A wet-nurse was often employed to breastfeed infants. When Queen Victoria of England (r. 1837–1901) learned that her daughter Alice had breastfed one of her newborn children, the queen expressed her disapproval by naming a cow in the royal dairy "Princess Alice." Children of monarchs often lived in separate apartments or wings of royal residences and would seldom see their parents, being cared for instead by a host of servants and aides.

Travel for a ruler often meant that an entire retinue of servants would accompany the monarch on the trip. Kaiser Wilhelm II of Germany (r. 1888–1918) bought a retreat on an island in Greece so that his family could experience the simple life. Their life was not so simple, however, that a retinue of servants was not required. The Greeks were astounded by the size of the kaiser's household, although the number of servants and aides he brought was far fewer than the approximately 3,500 that made up his court at home.

Perhaps the most unusual, and sometimes powerful, servant in the employ of rulers in the past was the royal eunuch, found primarily in Middle Eastern and Asian cultures. Traditionally, eunuchs guarded the concubines in the king's harem. It is said that some Chinese emperors had as many as 3,000 eunuchs in the royal household. Royal eunuchs sometimes had great status and power. Chinese parents would sometimes castrate their own sons, hoping that these boys could enter the royal household and achieve a position of power and status within it.

Royal servants and aides have always been necessary in royal households and at the royal court. Without them, it would be almost impossible to keep the household and court functioning effectively, allowing sovereigns to attend to the important affairs of government.

See also: COOKS, ROYAL; COURTS AND COURT OFFICIALS, ROYAL; EDUCATION OF KINGS; EUNUCHS, ROYAL; GROOMS OF THE STOOL; HAREMS.

SETI I (ca. 1333–1279 B.C.E.)

Second king (r. ca. 1291–1279 B.C.E.) of Egypt's Nineteenth dynasty (during the so-called New Kingdom period), who was renowned for his military triumphs and elaborate building projects.

Seti I was the son and successor of Ramses I (r. 1293–1291 B.C.E.). Apparently inheriting his father's military prowess, Seti I wasted no time leading his troops into battle. As soon as he became king, he led military campaigns into Sinai, Syria, and Palestine to reclaim territory from the Hittites and various nomadic tribes. Signing a peace treaty with the Hittites, Seti succeeded in strengthening Egyptian power to the east. As a result of his victories, Seti restored much of the territory and prestige that Egypt had lost during the Eighteenth dynasty.

The military accomplishments of Seti I are depicted on the walls of the famous Temple of Karnak, an immense complex of temples built and expanded over a thirteen-year period that overlapped Seti's reign. Seti added to Karnak the vast Hypostyle Hall, which, with its massive decorated columns, is regarded as one of the greatest architectural works in the world. Seti enlarged temples and built new ones throughout Egypt, especially in important religious centers such as Thebes, Abydos, and Karnak.

Seti's temple of Abydos has many magnificent bas-reliefs (sculpted designs raised slightly from a flat

Pharaoh Seti I of Egypt's Nineteenth dynasty was renowned for his military victories and building projects. This painting from his tomb in the Valley of the Kings shows the goddess Hathor placing a magic collar on the pharaoh. According to Egyptian mythology, this made Seti the goddess's mystical consort and connected him to her energy.

surface) that are considered among the finest examples of ancient Egyptian art. He also used this art form to adorn his tomb, which was the largest in the Valley of the Kings at Thebes.

Seti I had four children, two boys and two girls; but his first son died unexpectedly at a very young age. Toward the end of Seti's rule, he shared the throne with his second son, Ramses II (r. 1279–1212 B.C.E.), who went on to become perhaps the greatest pharaoh of Ancient Egypt.

See also: EGYPTIAN DYNASTIES, ANCIENT (EIGHTEENTH TO TWENTY-SIXTH); RAMSES II, THE GREAT; THEBES KINGDOM.

SHAH DYNASTY (1769 C.E.–Present)

Nepalese dynasty from the Gurkha region that conquered the Kathmandu Valley in 1768 and unified Nepal under King Prithvi Narayan Shah (r. 1769–1775).

The Shah dynasty is perhaps best known for two spectacular massacres. In September 1846, during a period of palace intrigues, clan rivalries, and assassinations, Queen Lakshmidevi called for the military and administrative elite of Kathmandu to gather in the courtyard of the palace armory, or *kot*. In a turnabout that remains mysterious to this day, the troops of a military commander named Jang Bahadur attacked and decimated the assembled elite. Jang Bahadur proclaimed himself prime minister for life, taking the title *Rana*, and made the office hereditary. For good measure, he arranged marriages between his own children and the children of the royal family. For the next century the Ranas would rule autocratically and live lavishly, all the while assiduously courting British favor.

The Ranas' corrupt rule came to an end when British withdrawal from India deprived their unpopular regime of its prop. In 1951, under Indian protection, the Shah dynasty was restored by King Tribhuvan, who had become a rallying point for the anti-Rana forces. But the hopes raised by the restoration were not fulfilled under Tribhuvan or his son and successor King Mahendra (r. 1955–1974). Despite sporadic efforts at democratic reform, during the rule of King Birendra (r. 1974–2001) political factionalism frustrated real progress and popular discontent fed a Maoist insurgency, which established a base of strength in western Nepal.

In June 2001, under circumstances that remain unexplained, virtually the entire royal family, including King Birendra, was gunned down in the palace—reportedly by Crown Prince Dipendra, who himself died of a bullet to the temple. The only surviving members of the family were the Queen Mother, her younger son, the king's brother Gyanendra, out of the country when the massacre occurred, and his son Paras. Gyanendra, considered much more of a hardliner than Birendra, succeeded to the throne. Summoning international support for Nepal's war on terrorism, he escalated the battle against the insurgency, which by early 2005 controlled nearly all of the country outside Kathmandu.

SHAKA ZULU (d. 1828)

Founder and paramount chief (r. 1816–1828) of the Zulu kingdom, who subjugated many states in southern Africa and made enemy peoples his vassals.

Shaka was the illegitimate son of a Zulu chief, Senzangakona (r. 1781–1816), who controlled a clan in the area of modern Natal in South Africa. At the time of Shaka's birth, the Zulu were a minor clan who lived within, and paid tribute to, the Nguni kingdom, then ruled by King Dingiswayo (r. ?–1816). Rejected by his father, and made to feel like an outsider because of his illegitimacy, Shaka left his clan when he was still quite young and went to the court of King Dingiswayo, to whom he offered his services.

A natural warrior who had extraordinary strategic and tactical abilities, Shaka quickly distinguished himself in Dingiswayo's army, helping to forge it into the most powerful military force in the region. This newfound military might was important because southern Africa at the time was in a state of extreme upheaval, as the Nguni and other Bantu peoples fought violently over ever-decreasing supplies of land for settlement and pasturage for their cattle herds.

Shaka made use of his military regiments in an innovative way that rendered Nguni forces virtually unstoppable. He created a battle formation inspired by the horns of a bull, with two long extensions that could flank the enemy on either side, trapping them between, while a third rank marched forward to attack the enemy at the center. Coupled with this military tactic was Shaka's own fierce appetite for violence. When he raided a village, the buildings were razed to the ground; the children, old men, and most of the women were slaughtered; and the survivors were forcibly impressed into Shaka's troops.

For as long as Dingiswayo lived, Shaka was content to serve as commander of the Nguni army. However, when Dingiswayo died in 1816, Shaka had no intention of remaining a subordinate. He used the support of his deadly warriors to seize the whole of Dingiswayo's realm, and by 1818 he had made good on his claim to rule, subduing all rivals and creating the Zulu kingdom.

Shaka's rise to kingship did little to change the focus of his life. Before becoming king he had been consumed by warfare, and he remained so afterward. As king of the Zulu, Shaka expanded his territories ever further, requiring conquered peoples to pay tribute, which enriched the kingdom and made the Zulu increasingly powerful. Shaka also pressed southward against the European settlers who were encroaching on the best lands in southern Africa.

Under Shaka, the Zulu kingdom had no capital or formal administration. It was held together by the sheer terror that his military inspired in others. However, this did not stop the defection of several of his military commanders who, after making successful raids on his behalf, decided to keep the spoils of war and move elsewhere to establish their own kingdoms. One such commander, Mzilikazi (r. 1837–1868), left and founded the Ndebele kingdom.

As his armies seemed to lose ground in the late 1820s, Shaka became increasingly unstable, and some of his people even thought he was going mad. Shaka died as he had lived, by violence. He was assassinated in 1828 by his half brothers, other sons of his father. One of these brothers, Dingane (r. 1828–1840), claimed the kingship and become ruler of the Zulu kingdom that Shaka had created.

See also: AFRICAN KINGDOMS; MZILIKAZI; NDEBELE KINGDOM; ZULU KINGDOM.

FURTHER READING

Gump, James Oliver. *The Formation of the Zulu Kingdom in South Africa: 1750–1840.* San Francisco: E. Mellen Press, 1990.

Oliver, Roland, and Anthony Atmore. *Africa Since 1800.* 5th ed. New York: Cambridge University Press, 2004.

SHALMANESER III (d. ca. 824 B.C.E.)

Assyrian monarch (ca. 858–824 B.C.E.) and builder who had only mixed success in his military campaigns.

The son of Ashurnasirpal II (r. ca. 883–859 B.C.E.), Shalmaneser III succeeded to the Assyrian throne upon the death of his father in 859 B.C.E. Like his father, Shalmaneser pursued an expansionistic military policy. Unlike Ashurnasirpal II, however, Shalmaneser conducted military campaigns that only rarely were completely successful.

Attempts by Shalmaneser III to overcome Syria around 853 B.C.E. resulted in only partial success. While he succeeded in subjugating northern Syria, repeated attempts to take the south and the city of Damascus all failed. Shalmaneser also failed to completely subjugate the kingdom of Urartu in the Caucasus region, although he returned from this area with much needed raw building materials.

In 841 B.C.E., Shalmaneser marched his troops to the Mediterranean coast and managed to make King Jehu of Israel (r. 841–814 B.C.E.) his tributary. He also forced the Phoenician city-states of Sidon and Tyre to pay tribute to Assyria. By 832 B.C.E., Shalmaneser had invaded and conquered Cilicia in Anatolia (present-day Turkey) and made that region a province of Assyria.

One of the best-known artifacts from Shalmaneser's reign, the Black Obelisk, details his policy of collecting tribute. Indeed, a number of Shalmaneser's undertakings are represented not only in written records but also in Assyrian artworks, such as steles (stone pillars) and statues. Hammered bronze doors from the city of Imgur-Enlil depict many of Shalmaneser's military campaigns.

Shalmaneser's reign was also notable for the construction of temples, canals, fortifications, and palaces. His palace at Kalah was of particular historical interest, for it was there that Shalmaneser erected the black marble obelisk detailing the accomplishments of his reign as well as an enormous ziggurat.

The annals on the black obelisk at Kalah give some information regarding the events of 825 B.C.E., when several cities, including the ancient Assyrian capital of Nineveh, revolted against Shalmaneser under the leadership of one of his sons, Assur-danin-pal. With the help of another son, Shamshi-Adad, Shalmaneser III put down the revolt. Shalmaneser III died soon afterward, in 824 B.C.E., and was succeeded by his son, Shamshi-Adad V (r. 823–811 B.C.E.).

See also: ASSYRIAN EMPIRE; ISRAEL, KINGDOMS OF; SHALMANESER V; URARTU KINGDOM.

SHALMANESER V (d. 722 B.C.E.)

Assyrian monarch (r. 726–722 B.C.E.) remembered chiefly for his siege of Palestinian Samaria in the 700s B.C.E.

No Assyrian records from the reign of Shalmaneser V have survived because his successor, Sargon II (r. 721–705 B.C.E.), had them all destroyed after condemning Shalmaneser for blasphemous acts. Knowledge of his reign is thus largely dependent on outside sources, all of which pose some chronological confusion.

The Bible gives an account of a campaign by Shalmaneser V against Samaria, to which he laid siege because of an Egyptian-backed revolt against Assyrian rule. After taking the city, the Assyrians deported the Israelites to foreign regions, a strategy commonly used to weaken the cohesiveness of a rebellious group. It is unclear whether this deportation was carried out by Shalmaneser or by his successor, Sargon II; the biblical source seems to conflate the two reigns, and ancient Assyrian texts suggest that it was, in fact, Sargon who transplanted the Israelite tribes.

An account of Shalmaneser's reign by the ancient historian Josephus reiterates the biblical version of the siege of Samaria and the deportation of the Israelites, and also seems to follow the Bible's example in combining the reigns of Shalmaneser V and Sargon II under Shalmaneser's name. Josephus refers to several campaigns as having been executed by Shalmaneser—including the successful subjugation of the Phoenician city-state of Tyre—that are clearly attributed to Sargon in ancient Assyrian texts.

Although Shalmaneser V did not apparently participate in the siege against Samaria that resulted in the deportation of the Israelites, biblical texts may have ascribed some of Sargon II's campaigns to him as well. Because Sargon II was so meticulous in erasing the records of Shalmaneser V after the latter's death, we may never know definitively which actions belonged to which ruler.

See also: ASSYRIAN EMPIRE; SARGON II.

SHAMSHI-ADAD I (d. 1776 B.C.E.)

Early Assyrian monarch (r. 1808–1776 B.C.E.) who united several independent Assyrian city-states and whose kingdom has been called the first Assyrian Empire.

Shamshi-Adad's father was king of the small city-state of Ekallatum. When King Naram-Sin (r. ca. 1830–1815 B.C.E.) of Eshnunna conquered Assyria around 1836 B.C.E., he also captured Ekallatum. Shamshi-Adad fled to Babylon, but he later returned to retake the city after Naram-Sin's death. Around 1808 B.C.E., Shamshi-Adad invaded and conquered the city-state of Ashur, the ancient capital of Assyria.

Shamshi-Adad continued to expand his kingdom by seizing land from Mari and Babylon and by taking control of important trade routes in Syria and Anatolia (present-day Turkey). At the height of his power, he controlled most of northern Mesopotamia. Although Shamshi-Adad united numerous city-states under Assyrian control, he allowed them to maintain local traditions and limited autonomy.

Shamshi-Adad was a capable administrator who monitored all aspects of his kingdom. Like many ancient Mesopotamian kings, he engaged in an extensive building program, and his reign is especially known for the construction of canal and irrigation systems. He moved the Assyrian capital from Ashur to the city of Shubat-Enlil in the far northern part of Mesopotamia, leaving his sons to rule as viceroys of the city-states of Mari and Ekallatum on the Tigris River.

Upon the death of Shamshi-Adad in 1776 B.C.E., his elder son, Ishme-Dagan (r. 1775-1736 B.C.E.), assumed the throne of Assyria. Shamshi-Adad's successors, however, were not as capable rulers. The kingdom eventually collapsed, and the various city-states regained independence.

See also: ASSYRIAN EMPIRE; MIDDLE EASTERN DYNASTIES.

SHAN KINGDOMS (1228–1555 C.E.)

Kingdoms that dominated much of Myanmar (Burma) from the thirteenth to sixteenth centuries. The Shan were a Buddhist people who inhabited mainly the hilly plateau regions bordering China in the north, Laos in the east, and Thailand in the south.

The Shan people began to expand from their homelands in the twelfth century, with the extension of their rule to the lowland regions of Myanmar. The Shan population in these areas continued to grow with the influx of refugees fleeing the Mongol conquest of Nan Chao in 1253.

By the thirteenth century, Shan power had grown substantially, and they set out to conquer Myanmar. After defeating the Mongols in the late thirteenth century and the Pagans in 1325, the Shan became kings of the states of Myinsaing, Pinya, and Sagaing. They also gained control of the Ahom kingdom in the region of Assam in India.

The Burmans and other peoples of the lowland regions of Myanmar expelled the Shan from the Irrawaddy Delta in the fifteenth century, eventually retaking most of northern Myanmar. By 1555, the Shan, forced back to their homelands, had formed more than thirty small states ruled by hereditary chiefs, or *sabwas.*

In 1766, the Shan repelled a Chinese invasion, but the attack left them exhausted and a declining power. By the nineteenth century, the *sabwas* had become tributaries to the Burman kings, to whom they paid tribute. Attacked by the Chinese again in 1873, the eastern Shan states were defeated in a gruesome campaign. The Shan had pleaded for military assistance from the Burman kings, but they were ignored, and the Chinese were able to hold onto their conquests in the region.

The *sabwas* renounced their allegiance to the Burman state in the 1870s, creating chaos in northern Myanmar. The resulting confusion gave the British the opportunity they had been looking for to intervene in Burman affairs. The British annexed the Shan states in 1886 and left the Shan princes to rule under British supervision. The succession of the princes was also left to the approval of British colonial authorities. Not a part of the British colony of Burma, each Shan state maintained direct and independent treaty relations with the British.

In 1922, the Shan principalities were united into the Federated Shan States within the British protectorate of Burma. A single Shan state was established by the Burman constitution of 1947, which promised Shan secession after ten years, if desired. Within months of Burma's independence from Great Britain in January 1948, the new government declared the 1947 constitution null and attempted to impose direct rule of the Shan Federation. When the Shan states continued trying to secede under the terms of that constitution, the Burman government retaliated and stripped the princes of their weapons and privileges. The insult to their national dignity united the

Shans in a war against the Myanmar government in 1960. Although the autonomy of the Shan states has continued to be eroded by the government of Myanmar, the Shan people continue struggling to preserve their distinct ethnic heritage.

See also: BURMESE KINGDOMS; MON KINGDOM; PAGAN KINGDOM; PYU KINGDOM; SOUTHEAST ASIAN KINGDOMS.

FURTHER READING

Harrison, Brian. *South-East Asia: A Short History.* 3rd ed. New York: St. Martin's Press, 1966.

Minahan, James. *Nations without States: A Historical Dictionary of Contemporary National Movements.* Westport, CT: Greenwood Press, 1996.

SHAN STATES. *See* ALAUNGPAYA DYNASTY

SHANG (YIN) DYNASTY

(ca. 1766–1122 B.C.E.)

The first Chinese dynasty from which artifacts and written documents have been recovered.

The Shang dynasty was founded around 1766 B.C.E. when T'ang the Victorious (r. ca. 1766–1753 B.C.E.) of the Shang clan defeated the despotic ruler of the Hsia (Xia) dynasty, King Jie (r. ca. 1818–1766 B.C.E). At the time, the Hsia state consisted of numerous tribes. Instead of physically conquering these tribes, T'ang solicited their allegiance by convincing tribal leaders that the Hsia monarchs were tyrannical. After earning tribal support, Tang captured the Hsia capital near Zhengzhou, a major urban center, and exiled the last members of the Hsia dynasty.

The Shang populace was originally nomadic. But after T'ang erected a capital at Xibo on the Luo River, he created an agricultural economy based mainly upon wheat, millet, and rice production. The Shang monarchs eventually relocated the capital in Zhengzhou, but around the fourteenth century B.C.E. they constructed a new capital called Anyang in Henan province. To solidify their power overly a widely dispersed populace, the Shang monarchs maintained a large standing army and frequently compelled peasants to complete public construction projects such as palaces, temples, and massive tombs.

Shang (Yin) Dynasty

T'ANG	1766 B.C.E.– 1753 B.C.E.
T'AI CHIA	1753–1720
WU TING	1720–1691
TA KENG	1691–1666
HSAIO CHIA	1666–1649
YUNG CHI	1649–1637
T'AI WU	1637–1562
CHUNG TING	1562–1549
WAI JEN	1549–1534
HO T'AN CHIA	1534–1525
TSU I	1525–1506
TSU HSIN	1506–1490
WU CHIA	1490–1465
TSU TING	1465–1433
NAN KENG	1433–1408
YANG CHIA	1408–1401
P'AN KENG	1401–1373
HSIAO HSIN	1373–1352
HSIAO I	1352–1324
WU TING	1324–1265
TSU KENG	1265–1258
TSU CHIA	1258–1225
LIN HSIN	1225–1219
KENG TING	1219–1198
WU I	1198–1194
T'AI TING	1194–1191
TI I	1191–1154
CHOU HSIN	1154–1122

After the capital of Anyang was completed, Shang society became more sedentary, and many historians believe this period marks the beginning of modern Chinese civilization. Shang scholars developed a written language and a precise calendar. Priests in the Shang society created a cohesive religion. The most revered religious figure was Di, a supreme deity who ultimately decided the outcome of crucial events such as battles. Other gods who controlled such natural elements as the rivers and mountains stood below Di. The ancestors of the Shang monarchs occupied the lowest supernatural tier. Royal priests used the bones of deceased oracles to invoke the spirits of previous monarchs. These spirits, unlike the living Shang monarch, had access to Di and could serve as intermediaries between Di and the current monarch.

During the fourteenth century B.C.E., trade with Mesopotamia and other parts of southwestern Asia brought three crucial acquisitions to the Shang dynasty: wheat, goats, and knowledge of bronze metallurgy. The introduction of wheat and goats further transformed the Shang tribes into an agricultural society. Success in farming these two products also created a new, abundant wealth that helped to develop Shang society. The introduction of bronze greatly strengthened the Shang monarchy. Shang metallurgists crafted bronze chariots, daggers, axes, and spears. These objects made the Shang military even more formidable and elevated military leaders to a social position beneath only that of the royal family.

Consequently, a new social order emerged in China. Prominent military leaders were granted large tracts of farmland as rewards for their military service. These leaders also were given peasants to work the farms. Although not technically enslaved, these peasants endured living conditions similar to those of peasants who had lived centuries earlier. The new landowners enjoyed an immense affluence. After paying the monarch a set tribute, they were allowed to keep the remainder of their profits, which were often spent on items such as jade statues, silk gowns, elaborately decorated pottery, and large bronze vessels for food and wine known as *ding*.

The Shang dynasty crumbled in the eleventh century B.C.E. when the Chou (Zhou) tribe rebelled against the monarchy. The Chous were originally one of the nomadic tribes that had pledged fealty to the Shang dynasty. In return, the Shang monarchs had granted the Chous a large territory in the western portion of the empire and charged them with repelling any invaders. But two Chou kings, Wen and Wu, rejected this agreement and attacked the Shang capital at Anyang. Aided by a large number of Shang slaves and peasants, the Chou invaders successfully overthrew King Chou Hsin (Dixin) (r. ca. 1154–1122 B.C.E.), the final Shang monarch, bringing an end to the Shang dynasty.

To convince the other tribes to honor the new Chou dynasty, king Wen's son proclaimed that Chou Hsin was an immoral king who had tortured his subjects and engaged in licentious behavior. These actions had egregiously defied the god Di. Therefore, overthrowing Chou Hsin was an example of divine retribution. This proclamation came to be known as the Mandate of Heaven and was subsequently used to justify the insurgency of each new dynasty. As Valerie Hansen claims in *The Open Empire* (2000), "Heaven would show that it had withdrawn support for the dynasty by sending natural disasters in the form of earthquakes, unusual celestial events, excessive rain, or drought, and/or man-made disasters."

See also: CHOU (ZHOU) DYNASTY; HSIA DYNASTY.

FURTHER READING

Chang, Kwang-chih. *Shang Civilization.* New Haven, CT: Yale University Press, 1980.
Hansen, Valerie. *The Open Empire: A History of China to 1600.* New York: W. W. Norton, 2000.

SHARQI DYNASTY. *See* JAUNPUR KINGDOM

SHEBA, QUEEN OF (ca. 900s B.C.E.)

Legendary queen mentioned in the sacred texts of Judaism, Christianity, and Islam. Although the story of the Queen of Sheba and King Solomon varies according to cultural tradition, in each tale she is beautiful, wealthy, and powerful. The exact location of the kingdom of Sheba is unknown, but it is probably an ancient name for a kingdom near present-day Yemen.

BIBLICAL VERSIONS

The Christian and Jewish biblical account of the Queen of Sheba is found in the Old Testament. According to the biblical story, the queen met with King Solomon of Israel because she had heard of his great wisdom and wanted to test it by asking him several riddles. Solomon answered each riddle, and the two monarchs bestowed lavish gifts on each other before she returned home. The Queen of Sheba is also mentioned in the New Testament, where Jesus refers to her as Queen of the South and praises her for seeking the wisdom of King Solomon. Her visit to Israel may also have been a trade mission to ensure her kingdom's profitable commerce in frankincense and myrrh.

KORANIC AND RELATED VERSIONS

The Koran contains another version of the story of the Queen of Sheba, also reflected in a number of later Arabic and Persian folk tales. In these sources, it is Solomon who goes to meet the queen, traveling south to her capital in Marib (Yemen). These tales call the queen "Bilqis" and portray her as a fair and caring ruler who worships the sun and the moon.

Bilqis was the focus of several other versions of the

The visit of the Queen of Sheba to King Solomon of ancient Israel has been celebrated in art and literature throughout the ages. In Renaissance Italy, the master sculptor Lorenzo Ghiberti depicted the meeting of the two monarchs on his bronze doors for the Baptistery of the Duomo in Florence.

legend as well. In one, Solomon hears that Bilqis and her subjects are sun worshippers and asks her to worship God instead. When she comes to his court, demons—who fear Solomon will be tempted to marry her—warn him that she has hairy legs and hooves. The tale does not make clear whether or not she marries Solomon, but she does become a believer in his God.

ETHIOPIAN VERSION

Among various other versions, the most compelling is an Ethiopian story featuring a queen called Makeda. The queen learns about the wisdom and riches of King Solomon and is so impressed that she decides to go to Jerusalem to meet him. He welcomes her royally, and she stays for six months. The queen learns much from Solomon and even converts to his religion, Judaism. King Solomon falls in love with her, but she tells him she has to return home. However, she agrees to stay a little longer and becomes pregnant with his child.

In some of the Ethiopian accounts, Solomon gives Makeda a banquet with particularly spicy food before she leaves, and then he invites her to stay overnight with him. She consents but first makes him promise that they will have separate beds and that he will not force himself on her. Solomon agrees, provided Makeda promises not to take anything in his palace. Their beds are on opposite sides of his chamber, and he places some water near her. Soon the seasoned food makes her unbearably thirsty, and she drinks some of the water. Solomon sees and stops her, saying that she has broken her promise by taking the water. She objects that water is too trivial and plentiful to count, but he argues that nothing is more precious than water since nothing can live without it. Makeda has to agree, so Solomon lets her drink and then takes her to bed. That night, Solomon dreams that a dazzling light, which he interprets as the divine presence, departs Israel and soars over Ethiopia. He tells Makeda of this dream before she leaves and says that her country might be blessed because of her.

Soon after Makeda gets home, she gives birth to a son, whom she names Ebna Hakim ("son of the wise man"). When Ebna is twenty-two years old, Makeda sends him to visit his father, Solomon, who is delighted and wants him to stay and become his heir. Ebna is adamant about going back home, however, so Solomon sends the sons of his counselors with him because they can help convert Ebna's people to Judaism. It is said that these young men stole the Ark of the Covenant from Jerusalem and took it with them. Many people were indeed converted, establishing a community of Falasha (Black Jews) of Ethiopia, who still exist there in large numbers.

According to this legend, the queen ruled until 955 B.C.E., after which Ebna Hakim succeeded to the throne as Menelik I, founding the first (Solomonic) of the great Ethiopian dynasties.

See also: SABAEAN KINGDOM; SOLOMON.

FURTHER READING

Madden, Annette. *In Her Footsteps: 101 Remarkable Black Women from the Queen of Sheba to Queen Latifah.* New York: Gramercy Books, 2001.

SHIH HUANG TI (SHIHUANGDI) (259–210 B.C.E.)

Founder of the Ch'in (Qin) dynasty and ruler (r. 221–210 B.C.E.) of the first unified China, whose system of administration became the blueprint for all future Chinese dynasties.

Shih Huang Ti (Shihuangdi) was born "Cheng the Upright" to King Chuang Hsiang (Zhuang Xiang) (r. 246 B.C.E.) in the western state of Ch'in (Qin). Although his real father may have been Lu Pu Wei (Lu Buwei), a wealthy merchant who bestowed his favorite concubine, Cheng's mother, upon the king, Cheng was accepted as the Ch'in heir and demonstrated the same shrewdness and military skills that distinguished earlier Ch'in rulers.

Cheng ascended to the throne of the Ch'in dynasty in 246 B.C.E. Under his rule, the Ch'in eliminated all rival feudal states by 221 B.C.E. King Cheng then declared himself Ch'in Shih Huang Ti, the "First August Emperor of the Ch'in." As the title indicates, Shih Huang Ti envisioned a dynasty that would stretch far into China's future.

Together with his adviser, Li Ssu (Li Si), Shih Huang Ti implemented reforms that consolidated the former Warring States into a unified and centrally administered empire. He standardized weights, measures, currency, and the writing system; built roads, canals, and fortifications, and organized an effective bureaucracy to govern the empire. He expanded walled portions of Ch'in, which later became known as the Great Wall. His imposition of harsh laws and his repression of all dissent allowed him to maintain absolute control, acts that condemned him in the eyes of some later historians.

Over time, the superstitious side of Shih Huang Ti's nature emerged. After three assassination attempts, he became obsessed with the pursuit of immortality. He searched for magical herbs and sent expeditions to find the mythical Isles of Penglai, where the immortals resided, so that he could learn their secret. When informed that these excursions had failed because of the interference of a large fish, he prowled the coastline himself until he spotted what he thought was the fish and killed it. Ironically, he died soon after this act.

After Shih Huang Ti's death in 210 B.C.E., Li Ssu secretly transported his body back to the capital of Xianyang; the smell of the decaying corpse on the six-week trip was disguised by the presence of several fish carts that surrounded the carriage. By not disclosing Shih Huang Ti's death, Li Ssu was able to manipulate the succession to the throne. Despite his machinations, without the leadership of Shih Huang Ti, the Ch'in dynasty quickly toppled, coming to an end in 207 B.C.E. when Emperor Erh Shih was deposed by the Wei dynasty.

Shih Huang Ti, the first emperor of imperial China, was buried in a magnificent tomb that he had been preparing since 247 B.C.E. He was guarded in death by a vast terra-cotta army, which archaeologists discovered in the mid-1900s.

See also: CH'IN (QIN) DYNASTY; EAST ASIAN KINGDOMS.

SHILLUK KINGDOM

(1500s C.E.–Present)

A tribal state on the west bank of the White Nile River in southern Sudan. Traditionally, the Shilluk have been primarily settled farmers and herdsmen. Most of their communities comprise a number of villages with a headman elected by a council consisting of members of the major families of the area.

Historically, the Shilluk peoples have been unified under a *reth,* or divine king, selected from the sons of preceding kings. The hierarchical social structure of the kingdom consists of commoners, royal servants and slaves, and members of the royalty. The Shilluk royalty can be traced back to their first king, the legendary Nyikang.

According to legend, Nyikang was the son of the god Juok (believed to be creator of the world) and the mythical river creature Nyakaya. Nyikang's birth had a specific purpose: to start a line of mortal kings. Although Nyikang is considered a divine king, all succeeding Shilluk kings are human and are regarded as his descendants. Initiation ceremonies for new Shilluk kings include a mock fight with Nyikang, after which his immortal spirit goes to inhabit them.

Traditionally, the health and state of mind of Shilluk kings have been thought to predict good or bad luck for the kingdom. A healthy, brave, responsible, and capable king signified a flourishing kingdom, while an ailing, angry, weak, or depressed ruler was indicative of a suffering kingdom. If a king failed in his responsibilities to the kingdom, his wives had a duty to suffocate him so that Nyikang could come to dwell in a more dependable member of the royal family.

Although the royal families were responsible for matters of state, the local headmen had a priestly function and watched over the day-to-day life of the Shilluk society. The men of the kingdom mainly took care of the animals, while the women worked in the fields and took care of domestic matters. Cattle were used as payment rather than food, and the size of herds was a measure of personal wealth.

Before battles or rain-making rituals, the Shilluk sacrificed various animals to Juok and Nyikang, believing that Nyikang had created their nation and brought the rain to revitalize them after a long dry spell. In fact, Nyikang represented to the Shilluk the three major elements of their world: earth, sky, and water. The headmen of the tribes also prayed to ancestral spirits, believing that those spirits could bring harm or good.

Shilluk life changed little over the centuries. For many years, the remoteness of the kingdom gave it some protection from invaders. However, during the period of European exploration and colonization, although the Shilluk suffered less than some of the other Nilotic tribes, it soon became clear that a new era had begun. As the world around them changed under European colonialism, the Shilluk became more of a tribe than a kingdom.

FURTHER READING

Levy, Patricia. *Sudan.* New York: Marshall Cavendish, 1997.

SHOGUNATE

A regime in medieval and early modern Japan, in which the government was headed by a hereditary ruler known as the *seii tai-shogun,* or "barbarian-subduing general."

Shogunal rule in Japan was military, and the shogun's government was known as the *bakufu,* or "tent" government, after the tents that housed military commanders in the field. The position of shogun, like that of the Japanese emperor, was not necessarily held for life—many shoguns retired officially, while maintaining control over the government behind the scenes. (Retirement was one way of avoiding ritual duties that could take up much of a shogun's time.) There was no fixed rule of succession, but like many military-based hereditary offices, the shogunate was held only by men (in contrast to the imperial office).

Shoguns theoretically respected the position of the emperor at Kyoto, usually locating their own capitals elsewhere. In practice, however, strong shoguns controlled the imperial house, often determining the succession to the imperial throne. As shogunal dynasties continued, however, shoguns themselves often lost effective power. Lacking the divine aura possessed by the emperors, shoguns could also be challenged by leaders of rival noble dynasties.

The shogunate emerged from the civil wars fought by houses of Japanese noble warriors in the twelfth century C.E. The first shogun was Yoritomo (r. 1192–1195) of the Minamoto family, who established the first shogunal capital at Kamakura. Yoritomo held power from 1185, but he did not receive the title of shogun from the emperor until 1192. Under Yoritomo, the shogun's rule was essentially feudal, based on a network of personal loyalties. After Yoritomo's death, much of the actual power of the shoguns passed into the hands of his widow, Masako, and her family, the Hojo. A succession of Hojos ruled as regents while the shogunal office was held by children or other puppets. The Hojos weathered several challenges, but their regime fell apart during the early fourteenth century in a series of civil wars launched by the emperor Go-Daigo (r. 1318–1339), who wanted to reassert imperial rule.

The second major shogunal dynasty was the Ashikaga shogunate, founded by General Ashikaga Takauji (r. 1338–1358), who received the title of

In 1393, the Japanese shogun Yoshimitsu Ashikaga built the Kinkaku-ji, or Golden Pavilion, in the imperial capital of Kyoto as a symbol of his prestige and power. Originally intended as the shogun's retirement villa, the Kinkaku-ji was converted into a temple after his death. After a fire in the 1950s, the temple was rebuilt according to the original design.

shogun from a puppet emperor in 1338. The Ashikaga established their headquarters in the imperial capital of Kyoto. The most successful of the Ashikaga shoguns was Yoshimitsu (r. 1369–1395), who abdicated in 1395. However, upon his death in 1408, the Ashikaga line lost its direct power, and much of the country fell into civil war. By the late sixteenth century, the title of shogun had fallen out of use.

The most enduring shogunal dynasty was the last, the Tokugawa shogunate. It was founded by Tokugawa Ieyasu (r. 1603–1605) in 1603 after his victory over rival nobles at the battle of Sekigahara in 1600. Ieyasu retired after only two years as shogun, but he retained power until his death in 1616. The Tokugawa capital was Edo (present-day Tokyo), and the Tokugawa period of Japanese history is also referred to as the Edo period. Under the Tokugawa, the shogun directly controlled about one-quarter of Japan, including the major cities. The rest of the country was controlled indirectly, under the rule of local *daimyo* (nobles), some related to the Tokugawa family and some not.

The Tokugawa family retained a measure of government control until the death of the last strong Tokugawa shogun, Yoshimune (r. 1716–1745) in

1751. Subsequent shoguns were, in effect, puppets of their ministers. The Tokugawa regime came under increasing foreign pressure in the early nineteenth century, and a growing movement of "imperial loyalism" attacked the shoguns as illegitimate usurpers of imperial power. Many of the leaders of the opposition to the shogunate came from *daimyo* families with a long tradition of independence from the Tokugawa. The last Tokugawa shogun, Yoshinobu (r. 1867–1868), abdicated under pressure from the daimyo in 1868, and the office of shogun was abolished.

See also: ASHIKAGA SHOGUNATE; KAMAKURA SHOGUNATE; MINAMOTO RULERS; TOKUGAWA SHOGUNATE; YORITOMO.

FURTHER READING

Shinoda, Minoru. *The Founding of the Kamakura Shogunate, 1180–1185.* New York: Columbia University Press, 1960.

Totman, Conrad D. *Tokugawa Ieyasu, Shogun: A Biography.* San Francisco: Heian, 1983.

SHOGUNS

A reference to the title *seii taishogun* ("barbarian-subduing generalissimo"), designating samurai warrior rulers of Japan appointed by the emperor to subdue imperial enemies, keep peace in the realm, and manage the affairs of the country. Shoguns were military dictators whose succession became hereditary by virtue of their control over and influence with the imperial court of the Japanese emperors.

ESTABLISHMENT OF SHOGUNAL RULE

During the eighth and ninth centuries C.E., the term *shogun* appeared from time to time in Japan as a title awarded by the emperor, usually as a reward for leading a successful military expedition against disloyal factions or against "barbarians," such as the Emishi tribes in northern Japan. The shoguns gained great power beginning in the eleventh century, and between then and 1868, three great shogunates, or governments ruled by shoguns, were the real power in Japan, while the emperors ruled merely in name.

The first great shogunal government was the Kamakura shogunate (1192–1333), established by the warrior lord Minamoto no Yoritomo (r. 1192–1195) in 1192 and named after the section of Kyoto where he established his headquarters. The second was the Ashikaga shogunate (1338–1573), founded by Ashikaga Takauji (r. 1338–1358) in 1338. This was also known as the Muromachi period, since the shogunal headquarters was moved to the Muromachi section of Kyoto in 1378. The third great shogunal government was the Tokugawa shogunate, dating from the appointment of the warlord Tokugawa Ieyasu (r. 1603–1605) as shogun in 1603. Ieyasu moved the capital to Edo (present-day Tokyo), so the Tokugawa era is also known as the Edo period. This last great shogunate lasted until 1868, when the imperial powers of the Japanese emperors were restored under the Meiji rulers.

IN THE NAME OF THE EMPEROR

Centralized power in Japan was always vested in the emperor, but until the end of the twelfth century, it was largely imperial councilors and regents who wielded power at court and who controlled the bureaucracy that collected taxes and administered law. At the same time, local lords who either administered or owned lands in the provinces represented an ever present counterforce, which sometimes threatened and sometimes supported the central government. Within this context, Japanese history is marked by nearly constant conflict between different aristocratic families for influence and power.

The military leaders who became shoguns by exploiting these conflicts were dynamic, militarily competent, and politically shrewd leaders. They instituted sound government reforms, and if they did not end open conflict, they at least brought other military leaders temporarily under their control.

Typically, however, after a generation or two, the shoguns who followed the founder of a shogunal dynasty became increasingly indolent, corrupt, or incompetent. At that point, a new line of hereditary regents and councilors would establish control over the hereditary shoguns, and they would rule in the name of the shoguns over a series of puppet emperors.

This separation of title and power in Japanese history is referred to as "dyarchy," for instead of overthrowing the emperor, the shoguns and their regents would legitimize their role though a complex chain of appointment that led back to the higher authority of the sovereign emperor of divine descent.

THE BAKUFU

Under Yoritomo no Minamoto and thereafter, the shogunal government became known as the *bakufu*, a word designating the field headquarters of a military commander and a description suggesting the idea of a temporary government called upon in times of stress and danger. While consistent with Zen Buddhist ideas of simplicity and discipline, the *bakufu* centers were more often seated in luxurious castles and surrounded with great wealth and culture.

The Kamakura *bakufu* marked the rise to power of the samurai warrior class. Yoritomo rewarded his supporters with estates and offices and established the personalized lord-vassal relationship that characterized Japanese government for almost seven hundred years. His administrative reforms relied on personal loyalty and were developed to control conflicts between the military lords and the court aristocrats, as well as to contain overzealous policies of the powerful temples and shrines.

The fiefs granted by Yoritomo were located strategically around the country and became the basis of the growing power of the *daimyo,* the local feudal landlords. Following the Kamakura period, the 250-year span under the Ashikaga shoguns (from 1338 to 1573) was a period of constant civil war at all levels of government, further accelerating a process of decentralization and fragmented administrative control.

The *daimyo* were finally brought under control during the last quarter of the sixteenth century through the military victories of Japan's three most famous warlords—Oda Nobunaga (1534–1582), Toyotomi Hideyoshi (1536–1598), and Tokugawa Ieyasu (1543–1616), the only one to claim the title of shogun.

The Tokugawa shoguns and their regents held the warrior classes in check for more than two hundred fifty years with a rigidly enforced status quo. The *daimyo* owed fealty, or loyalty, to the shogun and were required to administer government and taxation according to rigid shogunal guidelines for every level from province to village. Punishment for infractions was severe. *Daimyos* risked losing their domains if they displeased the shogun, who forced their families to live in Edo, the Tokugawa capital, and who managed their lives down to what they could wear and whom they could marry.

See also: ASHIKAGA SHOGUNATE; BUDDHISM AND KINGSHIP; KAMAKURA SHOGUNATE; MINAMOTO RULERS; ODA NOBUNAGA; SHOGUNATE; TOKUGAWA IEYASU; TOKUGAWA SHOGUNATE; TOYOTOMI HYDEYOSHI; YORITOMO.

SHULGI (ca. 2000s B.C.E.)

Most important ruler of the Third dynasty of Ur, an ancient city-state in the region of Sumeria in Mesopotamia. Shulgi (r. ca. 2094–2047 B.C.E.) was a skilled soldier, diplomat, administrator, and writer.

Shulgi inherited the throne from his father, Ur-Nammu (r. 2112–2095), the founder of the Third dynasty of Ur. The first twenty-one years of Shulgi's forty-eight-year reign seemed to have been largely uneventful. In 2073 B.C.E., however, Shulgi began to reorganize his empire. First, he divided the kingdom into provinces and placed each province under the control of an appointed military commander. He also issued an order to organize state recordkeeping, resulting in numerous clear and precise records of Shulgi's reign.

Shulgi was not only a proponent of careful recordkeeping, he was also a skilled poet as well as a self-described linguist, musician, and wise arbitrator concerned with providing justice to his people. A strong proponent of education, he built new schools throughout Ur during his reign. He also instituted a uniform system of weights and measures, along with a bureau of standards to oversee their use, which remained standard until the fall of Babylon thousands of years later. Shulgi also restructured the Sumerian calendar and worked to preserve ancient texts from earlier periods of Sumerian history.

Shulgi was a successful military leader as well. After building a large standing army, he conquered the province of Karakhar (in present-day Turkey and Iraq) in 2070 B.C.E. He proved victorious in later campaigns as well, especially against the hill-tribes of the north and east. During his reign, Ur became the dominant power in Mesopotamia.

Shulgi died in 2047 B.C.E. and was succeeded by his sons, Amar Suena (r. 2046–2038 B.C.E.) and Shu Suen (r. 2037–2029 B.C.E.). But neither Shulgi's tomb at Ur nor his dynasty survived long afterward. The same northern and eastern hill-tribes whom Shulgi had fought successfully during his reign swept down, captured Ur, and sacked it around 2004 B.C.E. Ur was never again to rise as a major power in the ancient Near East.

See also: UR-NAMMU.

SHUPPILULIUMA I

(flourished 1300s B.C.E.)

Hittite ruler (r. ca. 1344–1323 B.C.E.) and conqueror who forged an empire centered in Anatolia (present-day Turkey) that rivaled the empires of Egypt and Assyria.

The son of the Hittite king Tudkhaliya III (r. ca. 1355–1344 B.C.E.), Shuppiluliuma served as a general in his father's army, gaining several victories that earned him a reputation as a capable leader. He succeeded to the throne upon the death of his father.

Shuppiluliuma began his reign by consolidating Hittite lands and strengthening the defenses of the Hittite capital of Hattusas. He then turned his attention to the borders of his empire. To the east lay the kingdom of Mitanni—a powerful ally of Egypt and the principal enemy of his predecessors. Shuppiluliuma successfully attacked and sacked the Mitanni capital of Wassukkani. When Egypt did not come to its ally's aid, Shuppiluliuma's army pushed further southward and conquered much of the Levant—in what is now present-day Syria and Lebanon.

After these conquests, Shuppiluliuma returned to his capital at Hattusas to perform his religious duties, leaving his son Telipinus to defend Syria. During Shuppiluliuma's absence, however, Telipinus was unable to prevent a new king, Artatama, from gaining control of a battered Mittani and forging a new alliance against the Hittites with the newly arisen Assyrian state.

Shuppiluliuma traveled back to Syria, retook the territory that had been lost, and installed the son of Artatama's predecessor on the Mittani throne. He was thus able to maintain Mittani as a buffer state between Assyria and the Hittite Empire, which was also known as Hatti.

The annals of Shuppiluliuma, told by his son Mursili II (r. ca. 1321–1297 B.C.E.), give some insight into Shuppiluliuma's growing influence in this period. While besieging the Mittani city of Karkamish (Carchemish), Shuppiluliuma had received a personal letter from the queen of Egypt, whom most scholars believe was Ankhesanemun, the widow of Tutankhamen (r. 1334–1325 B.C.E.), requesting one of Shuppiluliuma's sons as a husband. Distrustful of the offer, Shuppiluliuma sent a messenger to determine her sincerity. Reassured by a second personal letter from the queen, he complied with the request and sent his son Zannanza to Egypt.

On the way to Egypt, Zannanza was assassinated. An angry Shuppiluliuma wrote to the Egyptian queen demanding an explanation and discovered that Egypt had a new pharaoh, Ay (r. ca. 1325–1321 B.C.E.). Hatti and Egypt returned to a state of war, but Shuppiluliuma did not live to see its conclusion. He died of a plague brought by Egyptian prisoners of war, sometime around 1323 B.C.E.

Shuppiluliuma was succeeded by his son Arnuwanda II (r. 1322), who died soon after taking the throne, probably of the same plague that had killed his father. The Hittite throne then passed to Arnuwanda's young and inexperienced brother, Mursili II.

See also: HITTITE EMPIRE.

SIAM, KINGDOMS OF

(1200s C.E.–Present)

Series of kingdoms located in the Southeast Asian region of Siam, renamed Thailand in 1939. The monarchy has been at the core of Siam's history, from the first kingdom in Siam in the 1200s to the present day. The Thai people today continue to revere their kings, and they celebrate the fact that their national identity has remained intact for centuries, despite the many colonial efforts of other countries.

EARLY INFLUENCES

Between 600 and 900, the Mon people of Burma moved east into Siam and formed new kingdoms there, building cities and quickly developing a civilized culture. Over the next few centuries, the Mon were confonted by other groups from the north, and as the region filled with people, local kingdoms emerged and vied for supremacy.

Siam's earliest kingdoms were the Davaravati kingdom, located in the central region of the country, and the Srivijaya Empire, whose realm stretched from the island of Sumatra and along the Malay Peninsula to the south. Over the course of 400 years, the power of these empires was gradually usurped by relatives of the Mon, the Khmer of Cambodia, whose

Siam modernized rapidly during the reign of King Chulalongkorn from 1868 to 1910. This picture, from *The Illustrated London News* of June 17, 1882, shows the king, also known as Rama V, and his wife, Queen Saowabha.

Khmer kingdom covered Siam. While no longer the rulers of their land, the Mon retained influence through religion, introducing the Khmer and Thais to Buddhism.

Kingdom of Sukhothai (1238–1438)

In 1238, Thai military leaders overthrew their Khmer rulers and established the first united Thai state, the independent kingdom of Sukhothai. During the Sukhothai period, called the "dawn of happiness," Siam became known as a land of abundance with fatherly, compassionate rulers, including King Ramkhamhaeng the Great (r. 1279–1317), who is credited with creating the Thai alphabet.

At its peak, the Sukhothai kingdom had 80,000 inhabitants and covered more land than modern-day Thailand. By 1350, however, a new state, the kingdom of Ayutthaya, began to emerge as a new power in the region. In the fourteenth century C.E., Sukhothai was conquered and incorporated into the Ayutthaya kingdom, and by 1438, Sukhothai ceased to exist.

Ayutthaya Kingdom (1350–1767)

Founded in 1350, the kingdom of Ayutthaya claimed sovereignty over all of Siam and parts of neighboring Burma, Cambodia, and Laos. This kingdom, which lasted for more than four hundred years, would have a lasting influence on all future kingdoms of Siam.

The king of Ayutthaya both represented and sought the harmony of earthly and cosmic forces. He was sometimes referred to as a future Buddha or god-king. Symbolism was evident in the construction of great palaces, which had three concentric moats representing the three seas surrounding Mount Meru, the throne of the Hindu god Indra.

On special occasions, the king had above him nine tiers of umbrellas as a "crown," a symbol still found in Thailand's royal regalia. The king's princes and officials also were given symbols denoting their rank. Under Ayutthaya, the Thai culture flourished, especially in architecture, art, and literature.

Europeans began to explore the Ayutthaya kingdom in the 1500s, beginning with the Portuguese and followed by the Dutch and the British, who declared the city of Ayutthaya as "big and impressive as London." For most of the 1600s, Thais and Europeans traded goods freely. Late in the 1600s, however, Thai leaders became suspicious of European colonial ambitions, and they abruptly ended all trade, an embargo that lasted until the late 1800s.

Thonburi Era (1767–1782)

In 1767, a Burmese army conquered and burned the city of Ayutthaya, killing many of its inhabitants. The Burmese, however, did not control Siam for long. That same year, a young Thai general named P'ya Taksin (r. 1767–1782) rallied his troops and drove out the Burmese, establishing a new Thai kingdom with a new capital at Thonburi, near the site of modern Bangkok.

Thonburi's location near the sea was strategic, providing for ease of trade and the import of arms, as well as a speedy withdrawal in the event of future Burmese attacks. A new capital was not enough to unite the people of Siam, however, and Taksin spent most of his brief fifteen-year reign trying to resolve political discord among the citizens.

CHAKRI DYNASTY (1782–Present)

After King Taksin died in 1782, Rama I (r. 1782–1809) became the first king of the Chakri dynasty. His descendants have reigned in an unbroken succession to the present day.

Rama I transferred the capital of the Thai kingdom to Bangkok and began construction of a Grand Palace, which was finished by his successor, Rama II (r. 1809–1824). Rama III (r. 1824–1851) reopened the kingdom's relationship with European countries and developed new trade opportunities with China.

King Mongkut Rama IV (r. 1851–1868) was responsible for establishing the boundaries of modern Thailand. (He was also the subject of *The King and I,* a musical based on the memoirs of a British governess whom he employed to educate some of his eighty-two children.) During a period of commerce and expansion, Siam never lost its identity or its core land to Europeans eager to extend their empires. Its economy, however, became dependent on people from other countries, primarily the British, who purchased great quantities of rice.

Mongkut's son and successor, King Chulalongkorn, Rama V (r. 1868–1910), modernized Siam rapidly, abolishing slavery and establishing schools, rail lines, and roads. Under King Vajiravudh, Rama VI (r. 1910–1925), education became mandatory for all Thai children. During the reign of King Prajadhipok, Rama VII (r. 1925–1935), a group of civil servants and army officers staged a bloodless coup, overthrowing the current ruler and bringing an end to the era of absolute monarchy. In its place, a constitutional monarchy was established.

DEMOCRATIC CONSTITUTIONAL MONARCHY

Beginning with the rule of King Bhumibol Adulyadej, Rama IX (r. 1946–present), Thai kings have been elected by a majority vote of the citizens of the country. In 1939, Siam was renamed Thailand, and, not long after, the Thai army overthrew the monarchy and ruled for the next few decades. However, student demonstrations in the 1970s brought military rule to an end and the monarchy was restored. King Rama IX is the longest reigning monarch in Thai history.

See also: AYUTTHAYA KINGDOM; CHAKRI DYNASTY; CHULALONGKORN; KHMER EMPIRE; MON KINGDOM; MONGKUT (RAMA IV); SUKHOTHAI KINGDOM.

FURTHER READING

Library of Nations: South-east Asia. Amsterdam: Time-Life Books, 1987.

Williams, Lea E. *Southeast Asia: A History.* New York: Oxford University Press, 1976.

SIBLINGS, ROYAL

Members of a royal house including brothers, sisters, brothers-in-laws, and sisters-in-laws. Royal siblings have played several roles in royal courts, ranging from close advisers to bitter enemies.

Rules of succession by primogeniture, or hereditary succession of the first-born son, often resulted in disputes within royal families over the order in which heirs would have rights to the throne. In several instances throughout history, one sibling has murdered another in an effort to guarantee a claim to the throne.

Caracalla and Geta, sons of the Roman emperor Septimius Severus (r. 193–211 C.E.), were rivals for the throne throughout their lives. Their intense rivalry began when the older boy, Caracalla, was raised to be the heir, while Geta was often neglected. The rivalry between the two brothers was so bitter that on his deathbed, the emperor begged them to cooperate and reach some kind of agreement. The two came up with a plan to divide Rome so that each could rule half the empire. But less than a year after his father's death in 211, Caracalla, dissatisfied with this plan, murdered Geta in front of their mother. Caracalla (r. 211–217) ruled all of Rome for a short time but was very unpopular, being perceived as a ruthless and vicious murderer.

An even more extreme case of sibling rivalry is that of Sultan Mehmed II of the Ottoman Empire (r. 1444–1446, 1451–1481) who implemented a "law of fratricide," which allowed a new sultan to execute all of his siblings in order to prevent disputes over the throne. Upon ascending the throne, Mehmed II had his young brother murdered to ensure that his place as sultan was secure. One of his successors, Mehmed III (r. 1595–1603), utilized the law, killing off nineteen brothers and twenty sisters to avoid threats to his rule. While intended to make the rules of succession secure, the law of fratricide actually incited dynastic revolt since rebellion was the only alternative to being executed.

In the Tudor dynasty of England, Lady Mary, daughter of King Henry VIII (r. 1509–1547) and his first wife Catherine of Aragón, was responsible for raising her younger half-sister Lady Elizabeth. After her father remarried and declared Mary illegitimate, she became intensely jealous of her younger sister. Having previously been the heir to the throne, Mary resented the fact that she was now required to serve Elizabeth as a lady in waiting. The rivalry between the two continued for years. After the early death of their young brother, King Edward VI (r. 1537–1553) in 1553, Mary seized the throne with the help of her supporters and ruled as Mary I (r. 1553–1558). Soon afterward, she had Elizabeth imprisoned in the Tower, believing that her younger sister had conspired in a rebellion against her.

Not all royal sibling relationships were characterized by intense rivalry. Loyal siblings were often appointed to powerful posts within the Church or military or were sent to rule over regional territories. In the Angkor kingdom of Southeast Asia, for example, members of the royal family were ranked in order of their genealogical proximity to the monarch, and then they were appointed to different royal offices according to rank. The king's brothers ruled various territories that fell under the control of the empire. Queens were ranked below princes and appointed to lesser positions that corresponded to their rank.

In royal families that followed strict rules of male primogeniture, female siblings generally served a different role from the males. Since women were less frequently considered as eligible for succession, competition for the throne was less of a problem for female siblings. Older female siblings were frequently responsible for raising their younger siblings.

The female siblings of their male counterparts often were married to other royal families for strategic political gain. Hieroglyphic records of ancient Maya civilization, for example, show that high-ranking women were married off to foreign nobility as a way to cement ties between major Mayan centers and their vassal cities.

In the 1200s and 1300s, the Mongol rulers of China were able to use this strategy to control the kingdom of Koryo (in present-day Korea). Princesses of the Yuan (Mongol) dynasty were sent to Koryo to marry their kings. The sons of these marriages had rights of succession to the Koryo throne but also had loyalty to the Mongols, thus making Koryo an appendage of the Yuan dynasty.

In ancient Egypt, marriage between brothers and sisters was considered acceptable within the royal family. This practice was carried out as a way of guaranteeing that succession of the throne stayed within the family; it was also believed to have strengthened the king's right to the throne. This practice may have

also been carried out in order to keep property within the royal family, as this type of marriage would not include a dowry. Ancient records indicate that the pharaoh Tutankhamen (r. 1334–1325 B.C.E.) married his sister Ankhesenamun when he was just nine years old.

The ancient Yamato state of Japan (ca. 40 B.C.E.–710 C.E.) collected taxes from regions it had conquered in the form of tributary siblings. The siblings of local leadership would be sent as servants to Yamato rulers, with the dual effect of garnering regional loyalty for the Yamato state as well as providing necessary labor to the court.

See also: BLOOD, ROYAL; COMPETITION, FRATERNAL; DESCENT, ROYAL; DYNASTY; GENEALOGY, ROYAL; INCEST, ROYAL; INHERITANCE, ROYAL; LEGITIMACY; MARRIAGE OF KINGS; PRIMOGENITURE; ROYAL FAMILIES; ROYAL LINE; ROYAL PRETENDERS; SISTERS, ROYAL; SUCCESSION, ROYAL.

FURTHER READING

Davidoff, Leonore. *Worlds Between: Historical Perspectives on Gender and Class.* New York: Routledge, 1995.

SICILY, KINGDOM OF

(1139–1861 C.E.)

Former monarchical state established on the island of Sicily, in the Mediterranean Sea off the southern coast of the Italian Peninsula. Occupied for centuries by the Greeks, Romans, Carthaginians, and Byzantines, Sicily did not emerge as a proper kingdom until the twelfth century. From that point forward, it was near the center of some of the major political struggles in the history of southern Europe.

ORIGINS

The history of the kingdom of Sicily is closely connected with that of the nearby Naples kingdom, as the two frequently shared the same rulers. The kingdoms came into existence in the twelfth century, under the rule of Roger II (r. 1105–1154), the nephew of Norman nobleman Robert Guiscard.

Roger's uncle had helped drive the Byzantines out of Sicily and southern Italy in the eleventh century, and in 1139 Pope Innocent II granted him the lands that he captured. Although the reign of Roger II was a prosperous one, Norman rule over Italy and Sicily was lost eventually to the Hohenstaufen dynasty in 1194, under the powerful Holy Roman emperor, Henry VI (r. 1190–1197).

The history of the kingdoms of Sicily and Naples began to diverge at the end of the Hohenstaufen reign in the mid-thirteenth century. In 1266, Pope Clement IV named Charles of Anjou head of the two kingdoms, largely in reaction to the Hohenstaufens' refusal to grant papal supremacy throughout the Italian Peninsula. The reign of Charles of Anjou, who ruled as Charles I (r. 1266–1285), brought the Angevin dynasty to power in Naples and Sicily.

Charles was thoroughly despised in Sicily, and resistance against his rule began to build. The situation on the island worsened until 1282, when Sicilian pro-independence leaders, supported by forces from the Byzantine Empire and the kingdom of Aragón in Iberia, staged an uprising known as the Sicilian Vespers Revolution.

A CENTURY OF STRUGGLE

This led to nearly a century of intermittent warfare. The Sicilians named Peter I of Aragón their new king (r. 1282–1285), thus putting Aragonese forces on the island of Sicily in direct competition with the French Angevin rulers on the Italian Peninsula at Naples. The conflict was not resolved until 1373, when Joanna of Naples gave up her claims to Sicily, leaving the Aragón rulers firmly in control of the island.

Aragónese rule in Sicily was decidedly different from the later Spanish domination over the kingdom of Naples, which was brutal and oppressive and granted little power to the people of Naples. Under Aragón supervision, Sicilian political bodies, especially the parliaments, were granted much autonomy, and the Sicilian people had, for a time, more sovereignty than almost any other group in Europe.

Although the later years of Spanish rule saw rising political and economic tensions, these tensions never played themselves out fully in Sicily, overshadowed as they were by the War of the Spanish Succession (1701–1714) and the War of the Polish Succession (1733–1735). These conflicts caused Sicily to change hands repeatedly, ultimately returning to an altered form of Spanish rule in the presence of the Spanish Bourbon king, Charles III (r. 1734–1759). Charles's rule was progressive and enlightened, and he was widely respected by the people of Sicily.

FINAL YEARS

The marriage of Charles's son and successor, Ferdinand IV (r. 1759–1816), to Marie Caroline, the daughter of Maria Theresa of Austria and sister of Marie Antoinette of France, set the stage for more conflict in Sicily. Marie Caroline helped guide the Bourbon monarchy in Naples and Sicily into war with the French Republican government in the wake of the French Revolution of 1789.

The ensuing battles between France and Spain ultimately led to Ferdinand's declaration of rule over a unified Naples and Sicily, known as the kingdom of the Two Sicilies, in 1816. Ferdinand, henceforth known as Ferdinand I, was a brutal ruler and was widely despised by the Sicilian people, as were his successors.

The kingdom of the Two Sicilies lasted until 1860, when it was conquered by Victor Emmanuel II of Italy (r. 1849–1878) and Giuseppe Garibaldi, who led the movement for Italian unification known as the *Risorgimento*. Although Sicily officially became part of Italy, it has maintained an uneasy relationship with the Italian mainland government ever since.

See also: ANGEVIN DYNASTIES; ARAGÓN, HOUSE OF; ARAGÓN, KINGDOM OF; CHARLES III; FERDINAND I; FERDINAND II; MARIA THERESA; MARIE ANTOINETTE; NAPOLEON I (BONAPARTE); SICILY, KINGDOM OF; VICTOR EMMANUEL II.

FURTHER READING

Smith, Denis Mack. *A History of Sicily.* New York: Dorset, 1988.

SIGISMUND (1368–1437 C.E.)

Margrave of Brandenburg (r. 1378–1415); king of Bohemia (r. 1419–1437), Germany (r. 1410–1437), and Hungary (r. 1387–1437); the last German-born Holy Roman emperor (r. 1433–1437); and the last emperor of the Luxembourg dynasty.

The second son of Holy Roman Emperor Charles IV (r. 1347–1378), Sigismund married Princess Marie of Hungary and Poland, a member of one branch of the Anjou dynasty. Marie became queen of Hungary (r. 1382–1385) upon the death of her father, Louis I (r. 1342–1382), in 1382, but she was deposed three years later because of dynastic conflicts with a branch of the Anjou line in Naples.

Charles III of Naples (r. 1381–1386) took the Hungarian throne as Charles II (r. 1385–1386) but ruled only briefly until his murder in 1386. Marie was then restored (r. 1386–1395), and her husband Sigismund was crowned king of Hungary in 1387. Sigismund consolidated his control over the country with the help of his brother, the emperor Wenceslas (r. 1378–1400).

In 1395, Sigismund led a European crusade against the Ottoman Turks, who were advancing into Hungary from the south. But Ottoman sultan Beyazid I (r. 1389–1402) defeated the Europeans soundly at the battle of Nikopol in 1396. Meanwhile, Sigismund's absence from Hungary, together with the death of Queen Marie in 1395, weakened his hold on that country, and Sigismund was forced to put down a revolt there in 1403.

After the death of German king Rupert of the Palatinate (r. 1400–1410) in 1410, both Sigismund and his cousin, Jobst of Moravia, claimed victory in the imperial elections, as did the previously deposed Wenceslas, Sigismund's brother. However, Jobst died, Wenceslas withdrew, and Sigismund became German king and Holy Roman emperor-elect.

Upon taking the imperial throne, Sigismund persuaded the anti-pope, John XXIII (r. 1410–1415), to summon a Church council at Constance. The schism between the various contenders for the papacy ended in 1417, after two years of discussions, but not until the council had condemned the Czech religious reformer, John Hus, and burned him at the stake. Sigismund, who had guaranteed Hus safe conduct to the council, signed the death warrant, earning him the lasting hatred of the Czechs.

Sigismund became king of Bohemia upon the death of his brother Wenceslas in 1419, but rebellious Bohemians opposed his accession to the throne. He convinced Pope Martin V (r. 1417–1431) to proclaim a crusade against the followers of Hus, but the Hussites defeated Sigismund and forced him to withdraw from the region. In 1421, a Czech assembly declared Sigismund deposed. Meanwhile, renewed attacks by Ottoman Turks occupied Sigismund in Hungary, while the Hussites began a series of successful incursions into Germany.

Eventually, the Hussite rebellions ended with a religious agreement at the Council of Basel (1431–1449) and led to Sigismund's acceptance as king of the Bohemians in 1437.

Shortly after gaining recognition as king of Bo-hemia, Sigismund died. The last Holy Roman emperor of the Luxembourg dynasty, he arranged to be succeeded by his son-in-law, Albert of Austria, a member of the Habsburg dynasty, whose reign as King Albert II (r. 1438–1439) began a long period of Habsburg rule for the Holy Roman Empire.

See also: CHARLES IV; HOLY ROMAN EMPIRE; LUXEM-BOURG DYNASTY; WENCESLAS IV.

FURTHER READING
Heer, Friedrich. *The Holy Roman Empire.* New York: Praeger, 1968.

SIHANOUK. *See* NORODOM SIHANOUK

SIKKIM KINGDOM (700s–1975 C.E.)

Asian kingdom known for its spiritual and religious contributions to the world's intellectual history. Sequestered by the Himalayan mountain ranges in the northern regions of India, Sikkim is often depicted in literary texts as a symbolical heaven, a "Shangri-la." In addition to its idealization, its small size has been influential in determining its political history.

Not much is known about Sikkim until the arrival of the Lepcha people in 700, migrants from upper Myanmar (Burma). The name Lepcha means the "ravine folk," or Rong. The two other predominant ethnic groups in Sikkim are the Bhutias (from Tibet) and the Nepalese (from Nepal). Nestled between Bhutan and Nepal, Sikkim has always been exposed to invasions between these warring nations.

The Bhutias first introduced Mahayana Buddhism to the Lepchas, who gradually converted from their original Shamanist beliefs, which included witchcraft and the worship of natural elements and seasons. The Lepchas were migrant farmers who lived in loosely bound, self-sufficient agrarian communities. The practice of distributing land for a farmer's personal profit was lost by the seventeenth century, when the undisputed rule of monarchy was simultaneously established.

Sikkim was ruled by monarchs for three centuries. The royal family of Sikkim has no political power, however. Traditionally, a king was not merely a political figure, but a great philosopher who had succeeded to the highest spiritual realm of Buddhist teachings. The aura of spirituality attached to kingship was a result of the control that the Lamas, or Buddhist priests, had over Sikkim's political and religious infrastructure.

In the 1600s, the Lamas chose the first king, or Chogyal, of Sikkim. By that time, priests had been elevated to positions of political power, and they orchestrated the succession of kings and defined the rules of kingship. The most influential Lamas, the Red Lamas, had the responsibility of finding and anointing the ruler of Sikkim. According to custom, the Red Lamas followed the ambiguous clues of a current ruler's dreams or visions, and then wandered in search of his reincarnation.

In 1642, the search for a new ruler resulted in Sikkim's first official king, a Tibetan named Phuntshog Namgyal (r. 1642–1670) (later known as Denjong Gyalpo). The Lamas made their choice on the basis of not only divinely inspired premonitions, but also of Namgyal's royal lineage. Since the inception of the kingship in 1642, it can be said that the presence of a kingly figurehead synthesized the spiritual and political powers of Sikkim.

The first Chogyal was a descendant of the legendary Tibetan prince, Khye-bum-sar. The political marriage of Sikkim and Tibet was sealed in 1268, when Khye-bum-sar adopted Sikkim as his home after a pilgrimage. He won the trust of the chief of the Lepchas, Thekongtek, who named Khye-bum-sar's son as his successor.

Khye-bum-sar's substantial influence on Sikkim's future signaled a change in the role of the ruler of the state. The combination of Khye-bum-sar's rise to power and his noble birth foreshadowed the beginning of sovereign rule in Sikkim, which began officially with Phuntshog Namgyal. Indeed, since the seventeenth century, every ruler of Sikkim has been a direct descendant of the legendary prince Khye-bum-sar.

During the eighteenth century, Sikkim was under constant threat of invasion by the Bhutanese in the east and the Gurkhas from Nepal in the west. In 1700, the bitter fight for the throne between Phuntshog Namgyal's grandchildren, Chador Namgyal (b. 1686), and his sister, Pende Ongmu, drove the princess to form an alliance with the Bhutanese against her brother. Ironically, both brother and sister were brutally assassinated in the same year, 1717, by loyal factions from opposing sides. This family feud initiated tremendous territorial losses for Sikkim. Not until the British came to its aid in 1815 was Sikkim able to stave off invasions from Bhutan and Nepal.

Foreign powers continued to infiltrate and agitate Sikkim's stability in the mid-1800s. Great Britain offered to help, but its offer actually implemented British control over Sikkim's borders with India and a trading route to Tibet. Eventually, in 1861, Sikkim became a protected territory of the British Empire.

When Sir Tashi Namgyal (r. 1914–1963) became Sikkim's Chogyal in 1914, he inherited a kingdom without national unity. Hoping to modernize and unite his country, Chogyal Tashi Namgyal established land reforms that allowed the people a share of the land. He also introduced democratic electoral reform, allowing representatives appointed by the people to represent each of Sikkim's diverse ethnic groups. His son, Palden Thondup Namgyal (r. 1963-1975), became the king of Sikkim in 1963.

Following India's freedom from British rule in 1947, India became the new protector of Sikkim's borders. A new treaty was signed with India in 1950, recognizing Sikkim's independent sovereignty but allowing India to control Sikkim's defense and external relations.

By 1974, a number of different political factions in Sikkim merged to form the Sikkim Congress. These political factions began to agitate for independence and called for the end of the monarchy. Unable to resist their attempts to dethrone him, Chogyal Palden Thondup Namgyal urged the Indian government to intervene on his behalf. However, India responded by preparing a constitution for Sikkim in 1975, which established India's annexation of Sikkim and abolished the monarchy. Sikkim is now a part of the Indian Union and one of the eight states in northeast India.

See also: INDIAN KINGDOMS.

FURTHER READING

Kandell, Alice S. *Mountaintop Kingdom: Sikkim.* New York: Norton, 1971.

SILLA KINGDOM (ca. 57 B.C.E.–935 C.E.)

One of Korea's so-called Three Kingdoms, along with Koguryo and Paechke, that occupied the Korean Peninsula from about 75 B.C.E to 934 C.E. Silla was the last of these Three Kingdoms to develop, and it outlived both of the others.

The Silla kingdom began as a loose confederation of cities in the southeastern portion of the Korean Peninsula during the first century B.C.E. The kingdom was not unified as a single entity until the reign of King Naemul (r. 356–402 C.E.). Initially, the Silla throne had alternated among the region's three leading families, but Naemul gained control of the throne for the Kim family and established a permanent hereditary monarchy.

During its early years, Silla possessed a weak army and faced attacks from the neighboring kingdom of Paekche and overseas raids from Japan. To protect itself, the kingdom at first allied itself with

Kings of Silla

HYOK-KO-SE	57 B.C.E.—04 C.E.		SONG-DOK	702–737
NAM-HAE	04–24		HYO-SONG	737–742
YU-RI	24–57		KYONG-DOK	742–765
T'AL-HAE	57–80		HYE-GONG	765–780
PA-SA	80–112		SON-DOK	780–785
CHI-MA	112–134		WON-SONG	785–799
IL-SONG	134–154		SO-SONG	799–800
A-DAL-LA	154–184		AE-JANG	800–809
POR-HYU	184–196		HON-DOK	809–826
NAE-HAE	196–230		HUNG-DOK	826–836
CHO-BUN	230–247		HI-GANG	836–838
CHOM-HAE	247–262		MIN-AE	838–839
MI-CH'U	262–284		SIN-MU	839
YU-RYE	284–298		MUN-SONG	839–857
KI-RIM	298–310		HON-AN	857–861
KOR-HAE	540–576		KYONG-MUN	861–875
CHIN-JI	576–579		HON-GANG	875–886
CHIN-P'YONG	579–632		CHONG-GANG	886–888
SON-DOK	632–647		CHIN-SONG	888–898
CHIN-DOK	647–654		HYO-GONG	898–913
MU-YOL	654–661		SIN-DOK	913–917
MUN-MU	661–681		KYONG-MYONG	917–924
SIN-MUN	681–692		KYONG-AE	924–927
HYO-SO	692–702		KYONG-SUN	927–935

the third Korean kingdom, Koguryo. As Silla's power increased, however, Koguryo recognized the growing threat and invaded the fledgling kingdom. Silla responded by joining forces with Paekche in an alliance to deter Koguryo and allow itself to develop.

Silla society was extremely hierarchical. In 520, King Pophung (r. 514–540) instituted the "bone-rank" system. Under this social hierarchy, potential heirs to the throne were designated as "hallowed-bone" individuals, while other royal relatives were given "true-bone" status. Only true-bone members could hold high government and military positions. Six other bone-ranks also were established. Only members of the top three ranks could hold government office, own land, or receive military promotion. The three lower ranks consisted of peasants, artisans, farmers, and slaves. Bone-rank was used not only to establish position in society, but also to determine where individuals could live, what clothing they could wear, and what possessions they could own.

Other aspects of Silla civilization mirrored this social stratification. Military posts, located throughout the kingdom, were occupied by groups of *hwarang*—young soldiers dedicated to the king, devoted to Buddhism, and ferocious in battle. The monarchy also implemented uniform and highly modern farming techniques, and Silla experienced a rapidly increasing affluence. This abundant wealth strengthened the monarchy and made Silla a powerful kingdom.

Under the bone-rank system, Silla initially flourished. In 551, King Chinhung (r. 540–576) invaded Koguryo and captured a large portion of the Han River basin. He then renounced Silla's alliance with Paekche and conquered its portion of the Han region as well. These two victories greatly increased Silla's available farmland and provided access to the Yellow Sea, opening direct access to China.

Silla's relationship with China was pivotal over the next century. Enraged by their earlier defeats, Koguryo and Paekche joined forces and repeatedly attacked Silla during the six and seventh centuries. In response, Silla enlisted China's support, and in 660 the two nations crushed the Paekche army, ending Paekche's autonomy. Seven years later, Silla and China again united to overcome Koguryo.

After these conquests, China energetically pursued control of the entire Korean Peninsula and established *commanderies,* or military outposts, in Paekche and Koguryo. Even more brazenly, China also located a commandery in Silla. Although Silla's

King Munmu (r. 661–680) was the titular governor of the commandery, he was expected to obey the edicts of the Chinese protectorate in Pyongyang, where the Chinese colonial government was located. Silla, however, soon attacked the invading forces. In 671, Silla gained control of Paekche, and in 676, it reconquered the Han River territory it had previously annexed from Koguryo. With these victories, the unified Silla kingdom emerged.

Unified Silla occupies a critical position in Korean history because it prevented the Chinese from obtaining complete control of the Korean Peninsula. Moreover, the military successes of the kingdom allowed the growth of an independent, unique culture characterized by historical writings, beautiful pottery, and its own architectural style.

However, the kingdom's rigid social hierarchy eventually destabilized Silla. After the expulsion of Chinese forces in 668, Silla monarchs possessed complete authority, and only a select number of "hallowed-bone" aristocrats living in the capital at Kyongju were granted any power. When this centralized authority alienated "true-bone" families living in outlying areas, Silla monarchs bequeathed large amounts of land to them in an effort to appease them. Because the land was granted in perpetuity and was tax exempt, lower class landowners were forced to pay unbearable tax levies instead. Some were reduced to slavery because of their debt, while others abandoned their land and joined groups of bandits that raided larger farms.

Even though Silla's "true-bone" families enjoyed the wealth created by their untaxed lands, they still resented their lack of political power. Their restlessness, coupled with the rapidly increasing number of dispossessed bandits, quickly undermined the monarchy. When King Kyongdok (r. 826–837) died in 837, the Silla monarchy crumbled and several prominent families battled for control. In 934, the kingdom of Koryo, which had developed in the former Koguryo region, conquered Silla and integrated it into its domain. The demise of Silla marked the end of Korea's Three Kingdoms.

See also: KOGURYO KINGDOM; KORYO KINGDOM; PAEKCHE KINGDOM.

FURTHER READING
Eckert, Carter J., et al. *Korea Old and New.* Cambridge, MA: Harvard University Press, 1990.

SISTERS, ROYAL

Roles that sisters have played in monarchies at different periods and in different cultures.

Royal sisters have occupied a variety of roles in relation to their brother rulers, from being heirs or rivals for power to serving as wives in order to secure succession or maintain the royal bloodline. In ancient Egypt, for example, it was customary for pharaohs to marry their sisters. By blocking the possibility of a pharaoh marrying into a nonnoble house, brother-sister marriages kept the royal bloodline pure and kept the pharaoh's family separated from nonroyal Egyptians.

If royal sisters had legitimate nonincestuous offspring, they could hope to compete with a male ruler's own children. For this reason, royal sisters were sometimes prevented from marrying or were even forced into convents so that they would not bear children. Louis the Pious (r. 814–840), the sole surviving legitimate son of Charlemagne (r. 768–814), forced his sisters into convents immediately after succeeding to the throne.

Royal sisters, like royal children, could also be diplomatic assets, however, to be married to individuals (or into realms) with whom a royal brother wished to form an alliance. King Charles II of England (r. 1660–1685), for example, married off his sister Henrietta to the duke of Orleans, brother of King Louis XIV of France (r. 1643–1715). Henrietta's position at the French court made her an invaluable informant and diplomatic go-between for her brother. Relations between a ruling brother and a sister at another royal court did not always go smoothly, however. While they were children, Frederick II of Prussia (r. 1740–1786) and his sister Wilhelmina were close, but conflict between Frederick and her husband, Margrave Frederick William of Bayreuth, led to a period of estrangement.

Royal sisters could be influential political actors and patrons in their brothers' courts, as was Marguerite of Navarre, the sister of King Francis I of France (r. 1515–1547). Marguerite was the author of the *Heptameron,* an important work of sixteenth-century French literature, as well as a protector of several of the more Protestant-leaning preachers and theologians of the time.

In those European kingdoms that allowed female succession to the throne, the eldest sister came after the youngest brother in the line of succession. One of the best known examples of sisterly succession was that of the three legitimate children of Henry VIII of England (r. 1509–1547), whose only legitimate son, Edward VI (1547–1553), died a few years after his coronation and was succeeded by his eldest half-sister, Mary I (r. 1553–1558). When Mary died childless, she was succeeded by her half-sister Elizabeth I (r. 1558–1603).

While the childless Mary I was alive, her sister Elizabeth was a focus for opposition, enmeshed in a struggle very similar to those that took place between childless kings and their brothers. In states where succession was less settled, brothers and sisters openly contended for power. In the twelfth century C.E., the Byzantine royal sister, Anna Comnena, led a revolt shortly after the accession of her hated brother, Emperor John Comnenus (r. 1118–1143). John spared her life but sent her into exile. Peter the Great of Russia (r. 1682–1725) faced a fierce struggle for power with his sister Sophia, who ruled Russia as regent until Peter overthrew and imprisoned her in 1689.

See also: BLOOD, ROYAL; GENDER AND KINGSHIP; INCEST, ROYAL; INHERITANCE, ROYAL; QUEENS AND QUEEN MOTHERS; ROYAL FAMILIES; SIBLINGS, ROYAL; SUCCESSION, ROYAL.

SLAVE DYNASTY. *See* MU'IZZI DYNASTY

SLAVERY, ROYAL

Royal slaves are human beings considered to be property of kings and other royalty. Holding varying social positions from submissive and ill-treated laborers to powerful state officials, such slaves have been found over most of the world and attached to all religious faiths that considered slavery legitimate, including Christianity and Islam.

The institution of slavery has existed since the earliest known kingdoms or state societies. Slavery formed a crucial part of the labor force and often of the military manpower and internal administration of kingdoms.

There have been many forms of servitude, from full chattel slaves (bought and sold like animals) to the indentured servitude of family members working to pay off family debts. Although not all forms of slavery have been tied directly to enslavement and possession by royal rulers, there are relatively few kingdoms in history in which slavery has not existed.

Slaves were acquired in three common ways: by capture, by purchase, and by breeding. In ancient times, the losers of battles were often captured by the victors and forced into slavery. As far back as early Rome, slaves were taken as spoils of war.

Slaves greatly increased a society's ability to produce goods and provide services to the kingdom and to the royal court. The reverse holds true for the land from which the slaves were taken. Through sheer volume, the practice of capturing the defeated in battles had the potential of weakening the social structure of a region. With his victories in northern Greece, the Roman general Aemilius Paullus captured and then sold 150,000 people into slavery, thus decimating the region's population and providing further inoculation against future reprisals.

Beginning in the seventh century, Muslim conquests and conversions added to this process, since the Islamic faith provided for the enslavement of infidels. In the fifteenth century, thousands of Javanese slaves of merchants living in the spice trade port of Malacca were converted to Islam, and, through their numbers, helped to improve relations between religiously conflicting Southeast Asian states. Religious differences between slave and master are also seen in the Saharan kingdom of Songhai, where the Muslim king Askiya Dawud (r. 1549–1583) enslaved non-Muslims to work on large plantations.

During the fifteenth and sixteenth centuries in the countries that comprised the Ottoman Empire, slavery was legal and considered part of the social fabric in line with the natural order. Slaves in the Ottoman region belonged to distinct categories, including agricultural, domestic, and military slaves.

An important category comprised eunuchs—castrated males. Because they could not produce children and could not become founders of competitive royal lines, they were given many important political positions (although many established their own petty states independent of the rulers at Constantinople). Eunuchs also were placed in charge of the royal harems, which likely included a number of female slaves. Slavery continued in the Ottoman region until World War I.

At royal palaces, slaves served in various capacities, providing manual labor, attending to a royal, and, on a rare occasions, serving as a king's advisor. Slave women were often used for breeding either by their owners or by male slaves to produce slave offspring. Some female slaves, like those of Aztec King Axayacatl (r. 1469–1481), were concubines and lived at the palace in Tenochititlan. The concubines were likely local women from a lower class; their numbers could run into the hundreds.

Slaves in royal courts were often physically different from the monarch they served. In the Mayan courts, people who were deformed either by birth or by being deliberately injured as children by breaking and disjointing back bones as a means to enhance their value, served as slaves. The most common deformities of these slaves were hunchbacks and/or diminutive statures; many of them served in bathhouses to bathe kings and queens.

As well as being acquired as war captives, slaves were purchased from professional slave traders. Slavery in Africa existed for hundreds of years before the advent of the slave trade with Europe. By 1075, the African Saifawa dynasty of Kanem north of Lake Chad specialized in exporting slaves to the north.

Europeans involved in the Atlantic slave trade and Arabs involved in the trade across the Indian Ocean (which lasted centuries longer than the Atlantic trade and involved far greater numbers) generally did not themselves capture slaves. Instead, they purchased the slaves from indigenous African kings, who captured them for sale to outsiders. The slave trade exploded after Europeans became involved in the early seventeenth century.

Royal slavery has virtually vanished today with the fading importance of independent kingdoms. Still, forms of slavery persist in the disguised servitude of indentured laborers, indebted farmers, and palace servants.

SOBHUZA I (ca. 1780–1839 c.e.)

Founder of the Swazi kingdom (r. ca. 1815–1839) in southwestern Africa. A powerful leader of the Nguni people, Sobhuza I united various Nguni-speaking peoples in the late 1700s to create a new kingdom for himself.

Instead of relying primarily on military means to achieve his goal, Sobhuza created a powerful network of personal loyalties between his clan and others in the region. He accomplished this, in part, by arranging marriages between members of his clan and individuals from the households of neighboring chiefs. In this way, Sobhuza created kinship ties that did not exist previously. As leader of his own clan, he had the authority to allocate rights to use land, and he used this power to buy the favor of others among the Nguni.

Once Sobhuza had gathered the independent Nguni chiefs under this authority, he advanced his ambitions militarily, calling upon his followers to join in a campaign of conquest throughout the region. In time, he succeeded in carving out an extensive territory, which became the Swazi kingdom. Sobhuza managed to hold this kingdom even in the face of challenges from the formidable Zulu peoples.

By the late 1830s, Sobhuza's authority was relatively secure, but he sought to secure his power by negotiating with the European forces that were growing stronger in the region. However, Sobhuza died in 1839, without completing the task of gaining British protection and assurances of autonomy.

See also: AFRICAN KINGDOMS; SOBHUZA II.

SOBHUZA II (1899–1982 C.E.)

Modern ruler of the Swazi kingdom (r. 1921–1982) whose skillful diplomacy helped to restore the kingdom's power in the face of powerful European colonial forces.

A descendant of Sobhuza I (r. 1815–1839), Sobhuza II was born sixty years after the death of his ancestor and namesake, who was the founder of the Swazi kingdom. His eventual rule over Swaziland was determined at the time of his birth in 1899, when he was named heir to the throne. However, the Swaziland that Sobhuza II inherited when he took the throne in 1921 was much reduced in power and influence. European dominance in the region at that time meant that true autonomy was impossible, and any ruler would need extraordinary diplomatic skills to avoid becoming a mere puppet of the colonial powers.

Sobhuza II proved exceptionally skilled and talented in that respect. Through skilled diplomacy, and by playing off European settlers, colonial officials, and local rivals against each other, he succeeded in keeping the settlers and the colonial government at bay, while retaining the respect and admiration of his people.

The king of Swaziland from 1921, Sobhuza II was a benevolent leader who helped negotiate his country's independence from Great Britain in 1968. At the time of his death in 1982, he was the longest-reigning monarch in the world.

When Great Britain granted Swaziland independence in 1968, Sobhuza II remained on the throne as king. However, the legislation that established independence transformed his rule from an absolute monarchy to a constitutional one. An extremely popular ruler, Sobhuza II remained on the throne until his death in 1982. He was succeeded by his son, Mswati III (r. 1986–).

See also: AFRICAN KINGDOMS; SOBHUZA I.

SOBIESKI, JOHN. *See* JOHN III

SOGDIAN KINGDOM. *See* CENTRAL ASIAN DYNASTIES

SOKOTO CALIPHATE (1808–1903 C.E.)

State forged from the conquest of the Hausa states of northern Nigeria during the *jihad* (holy war) of Uthman dan Fodio (r. 1804–1808), which became the largest independent state in all of western Africa in the nineteenth century.

Prior to 1804, northern Nigeria was dominated by a collection of autonomous Muslim Hausa states. One of these states was Gobir, in which a young Fulani (Fulbe) man named Uthman dan Fodio grew up in the tradition of Islamic scholarship and eventually became a teacher of Islam of great renown.

Uthman dan Fodio brought his personal vision of Islam to groups usually overlooked by most of his fellow Muslim teachers: women, the urban poor, and rural pastoralists who were looked down upon by the Hausa elites. He became so popular with the common people that the ruler of Gobir ordered his assassination. Escaping from Gobir, the young Muslim teacher organized an army that he led in a holy war against all the Hausa states of the region. Uthman dan Fodio declared that the aim of this *jihad* was to establish an ideal Muslim society in Africa.

The *jihad* lasted four years, ending with Uthman dan Fodio's conquest of Gobir. The Muslim caliphate he created consisted of the old Hausa states, now sworn to accept the religious authority emanating from the newly established capital city of Sokoto. Uthman dan Fodio, however, did not remain long at the apex of this new state. Instead, he retired to the quiet life of a scholar, leaving control of the caliphate in the hands of his brother, Abdullahi (r. 1808–1817), and his son, Muhammad Bello (r. 1817–1837).

The conquest of the Hausa states was facilitated, in part, by Uthman dan Fodio's sequential campaigns, attacking the states one at a time, and also by the failure of the ruling elites of those states to garner the support of their citizens. Had the Hausa states banded together to present a united opposition to Uthman's *jihad*, he might have been stopped.

However, the states were far more accustomed to internal rivalries than to cooperation, and they thus fell quickly under Uthman's attacks.

During Uthman's lifetime, the Sokoto caliphate was divided into two sections, with Abdullahi and Muhammad each administering one of them. Upon Uthman's death in 1817, Muhammad assumed overall control of the caliphate, and Abdullahi served as his vizier. In each individual state within the empire, emirs (princes or commanders) were charged with handling local administrative issues under the close supervision of the Sokoto court.

The Sokoto caliphate remained very powerful throughout the nineteenth century. In 1903, however, it was overthrown by the Hausa, who had allied themselves with British forces. The decisive battle of Sokoto, which overthrew the current regime, took place on March 15, 1903. After that time, the caliphs of Sokoto were appointed by the British, who claimed the region as part of their colony of Nigeria.

See also: AFRICAN KINGDOMS; CALIPHATES; ISLAM AND KINGSHIP; UTHMAN DAN FODIO.

SOLOMON (d. ca. 931 B.C.E.)

King of Israel (r. ca. 970–931 B.C.E.) who was renowned for his wisdom and the splendor of his kingdom; reputed to be the author of the books of Ecclesiastes, Proverbs, the Song of Solomon, and the Wisdom of Solomon in the Hebrew Bible. Solomon's wisdom is described many times in the Bible; perhaps the best-known example is the story in which he proposes to slash a baby in two in order to find out which of two women claiming to be the baby's real mother was telling the truth.

The son of King David of Israel (r. 1010–970 B.C.E.) and Bathsheba, Solomon inherited a healthy kingdom upon his father's death that included the regions of Israel and Judah as well as a number of vassal states and conquered realms. The kingdom of Israel at that time reached from the Red Sea to the Euphrates River. During the early years of his reign, Solomon lost Damascus in Syria and Edom near the Dead Sea, but he kept his kingdom strong by concentrating on the security of Israel and Judah.

Solomon used diplomatic ties rather than military force to preserve and increase his control and maintain Israel's security. He made many alliances, including important ones with Phoenicia and Egypt. He had a large harem and took many of his wives in order to maintain alliances with other countries. He even kept Egypt from threatening Israel by marrying a pharaoh's daughter.

As a result of his many alliances, Solomon received many gifts and assistance from other lands. The Phoenicians helped him send trading ships to Ophir (a land renowned for its gold) and many other ports, and treasures such as gold, silver, ivory, horses, and linen poured into Solomon's kingdom.

Because of Solomon's legendary wisdom, rulers from far-off lands, as well as his own subjects, came to the king for consultation. One of these rulers, the Queen of Sheba, brought Solomon gifts of gold, spices, and precious gems and was astonished by the magnificence of his court and his ability to answer her riddles.

With his kingdom at peace, Solomon executed a major construction program designed to glorify the realm. Most remarkable was the growth of Jerusalem north of the old City of David. There Solomon built a magnificent palace and a great temple, with an entirely gold-covered interior, dedicated to Jehovah, the god of the Israelites. Jerusalem thus became the religious center of Israel as well as an important commercial and political center.

The new buildings may have served as testaments to Solomon's greatness, but they also contributed to Israel's financial ruin because Solomon depleted treasury funds to maintain his luxurious court. Eventually, the people paid for Solomon's extravagance when he imposed new taxes and forced labor in order to support the lavish splendor.

Solomon also permitted his many foreign wives and concubines to build altars to their own foreign gods, thereby compromising the religious unity that had been one of Israel's main strengths. He apparently even participated in pagan rituals and neglected the Israelite god.

The apparent weakening of Solomon's character was accompanied by his weakened hold over his people. Under his son Rehoboam (r. 930–914 B.C.E.), who succeeded Solomon after his death in 931 B.C.E., the kingdom was divided in two (the northern kingdom of Israel and the southern kingdom of Judah), and Solomon's great temple was destroyed.

See also: DAVID; HEBREW KINGS; ISRAEL, KINGDOMS OF; SABAEAN KINGDOM.

SONG DYNASTY. *See* SUNG DYNASTY

SONGHAI KINGDOM (900s–1600s C.E.)

A powerful African empire that arose on the middle Niger River sometime during the ninth century, and became one of the greatest states of West Africa.

The middle Niger region of West Africa was the home of a variety of peoples, primarily the Sorko, who fished the Niger River; the Do, who were primarily hunters; and the Gow, who were farmers. Each of these peoples maintained independent communities but traded with one another. Around the eighth century, however, the Sorko found that their mastery of the waterways gave them the opportunity to control this trade, for goods were mostly transported by boat. The Sorko grew wealthy by demanding payment for goods carried along the Niger River. They then began to conquer their neighbors, bringing the formerly independent communities under one rule. This was the beginning of the Songhai state.

EARLY YEARS

By the ninth century, Songhai's traders established contact with the Muslim trading center at Gao, one of the southernmost outposts of the trans-Saharan trade route. Muslim merchants exchanged salt from the north in return for food goods from Songhai. In addition, these merchants brought the teachings of Islam to the region. By the eleventh century, Songhai's rulers had adopted the new religion.

During Songhai's first few centuries, the dominant power in western Africa was the empire of Ghana, which lay to the west. By the eleventh century, however, Ghana's power was waning, and as it grew weaker, it was replaced by a new rising power, the kingdom of Mali. From the earliest days of Mali, its rulers desired to control the entire Niger River basin. This brought Songhai into Mali's sphere of influence, and by the thirteenth century, Songhai was forced to pay tribute to Mali's kings. In the fifteenth century, however, Mali was in decline as a result of internal strife, and Songhai began to assert its independence.

RISE TO DOMINANCE

Songhai's rise to regional dominance can be traced to the reign of Sunni Ali (r. 1464–1492). In the early 1400s, Songhai had suffered attacks by Tuareg raiders who swept down from the Sahara to disrupt the trade caravans. These raiders had even captured one of Songhai's great trading cities, Timbuktu. Sunni Ali raised a powerful army and set out to recapture Timbuktu. His army won back the city and then went on to conquer lands that lay even further to the north. Sunni Ali eventually extended Songhai control far to the north and west, even claiming much land that once belonged to Mali.

Ali's son was the last of his lineage to rule Songhai. He was succeeded on the Songhai throne by Muhammad Ture (r. 1493–1528), who founded a new dynasty, the Askiyas. Ture used Islam to justify further wars of conquest. His devotion to Islam won him the support of powerful figures in the Muslim world, including the caliph of Egypt. Ture established Timbuktu as a center of Islamic scholarship and promoted the faith throughout his realm. He did not, however, force his subjects to convert to Islam.

Ture is credited with greatly enhancing the trans-Saharan trade by subduing the Tuareg raiders, thus ensuring the security of the trade caravans. Ture promoted stability within the Songhai Empire as well. For instance, as new territories were brought under Songhai control, he replaced their traditional rulers with appointed officials who had earned his trust, and he charged each with creating a local army that could maintain order and collect tribute.

Although Songhai enjoyed relative domestic peace, it was not immune to political turmoil. In 1528, Ture's son, Musa (r. 1528–1531), growing impatient awaiting his turn on the throne, gathered a following and deposed Muhammad Ture. The next several decades were marred by further dynastic squabbles and, in the 1580s, a devastating drought. Life within the empire, however, was relatively peaceful, and over time the great Songhai army grew weak. Nonetheless, the empire continued to grow in wealth through its participation in the trans-Saharan trade.

DECLINE AND FALL

In the late 1500s, Songhai's wealth drew the attention of the sultan of Morocco, Ahmad II al-Mansur (r. 1578–1603). Al-Mansur equipped a force of some four thousand soldiers with the latest European firearms and sent them south across the desert to take Songhai by surprise. The Moroccan forces attacked near the city of Gao in 1591, and their superior weaponry earned them victory in the battle.

Although the Moroccans were never able to wholly subdue Songhai, they did force the once pre-eminent empire to pay tribute. In addition, the empire was broken up into several smaller states, each administered by governors appointed by al-Mansur. The court of the Moroccan sultan was too far away for him to easily control his new client state, and by 1660 the remnants of Songhai had ceased to acknowledge Moroccan rule. However, the Songhai Empire never regained territorial unity, and out of its remnants new kingdoms arose. Notable among these kingdoms was the Bambara state of Segu.

See also: AFRICAN KINGDOMS; BAMBARA KINGDOM; GHANA KINGDOM, ANCIENT; MALI, ANCIENT KINGDOM OF; SUNNI ALI.

FURTHER READING

Robinson, Calvin R., Redman Battle, and Edward W. Robinson. *The Journey of the Songhai People.* Philadelphia, PA: Pan-African Federation Organization, 1987.

SONINKE KINGDOM (ca. 100–400 C.E.)

Precursor to the ancient kingdom of Ghana, which was among the first of the trade-based kingdoms to arise in Western Africa, spurred by the growth of the trans-Saharan trade.

The Soninke kingdom is named for its founders, Mande-speaking migrants who originally came from the region just south of the Sahara Desert. The reason for the migration of the Soninke people is unknown. Their early settlements were well situated to enable them to participate in the growing trans-Saharan trade, which was expanding southward as traders sought out sources of goods for growing markets.

Initially, Soninke trade was based on locally grown grain, which they traded for salt. Soon, however, the Soninke learned that they could gain even greater wealth by controlling the trade in more highly prized products and goods, particularly gold, which was being produced in the forests of present-day Ghana.

Some time around 100, a Soninke leader named Dinga Cisse (r. dates unknown) gained the support of several Soninke settlements, uniting them with the aim of conquering the gold-producing peoples of the region. According to Soninke legend, Dinga Cisse proved his worth to the people by killing a goblin (a spirit generally considered to be malevolent) and marrying the goblin's three daughters. More likely, Dinga Cisse defeated another local leader in battle and took that leader's daughters as wives. These marriages created ties between Cisse's followers and the clan that he had just conquered.

However he came to power, Dinga Cisse established a settlement called Kumbi Saleh, which was located on the southern edge of the Sahara Desert, in what is today the country of Mauritania. From there, he was able to send out warriors to conquer neighboring groups, gradually extending his control into the gold-rich forests of Ghana and creating a monopoly on the flow of trade. As his wealth from trade increased, Dinga Cisse was able to build a powerful army and further strengthen his control over the region. The Soninke kingdom that he created soon became the dominant political and military power of the area.

The kings that followed Dinga Cisse built upon these early successes, and by about 400, the Soninke kingdom had become the preeminent power of western Africa. By the fifth century, the line of Soninke kings was well established. These rulers took the royal title *ghana,* and it is by this term that the kingdom became known to the wider world. From a relatively small, local state, the Soninke kingdom eventually grew to become the great Ghana Empire, which dominated the region until it was supplanted by the kingdom of Mali, which was founded around 1210.

See also: GHANA KINGDOM, ANCIENT; MALI, ANCIENT KINGDOM OF; SUNDJSATA KEITA.

FURTHER READING
Shillington, Kevin. *History of Africa.* New York: St. Martin's Press, 1989.

SOTHO (SUTO) KINGDOM

(1830 C.E.–Present)

Kingdom in southern Africa established in the early nineteenth century by Moshoeshoe I (r. 1828–1870), which is today a constitutional monarchy.

The Sotho (also called Suto) are a Bantu-speaking people of the highveldt (grassland) region of southern Africa. Until the 1800s, the Sotho lived in small communities ruled by hereditary chiefs. Like other Bantu peoples, their economy centered on cattle-keeping, and neighboring communities frequently raided one another to increase their own herds of cattle. Such raids were not particularly violent, and this state of affairs could conceivably have continued with little change were it not for the arrival of outsiders from the northeast, who invaded the highveldt territory of the Sotho in 1821.

The newcomers were Hlubi and Ngwane peoples, displaced from their homelands by the violent military campaigns of Zulu leader, Shaka Zulu (r. 1816–1828). The Hlubi and Ngwane attacked the Sotho settlements with raiding parties, but unlike the traditional cattle raids that had been common occurrences, these attacks were devastating in their violence. Not content with stealing cattle, the foreigners burned villages to the ground, setting off wave after wave of starving refugees. This period is known as the *mfecane,* which means "the scattering."

Many thousands of Sotho died during the *mfecane,* but some found safety by fleeing into the hills. Among these survivors was a man named Moshoeshoe, the son of a minor clan chief. He organized the refugees into a military force, and by 1823 his following numbered in the thousands. Moshoeshoe led his people to Thaba-Bosiu, an easily defensible mountain stronghold, where he established the Sotho kingdom.

Under Moshoeshoe I, the Sotho kingdom comprised a confederation of chieftaincies under his supreme rulership. To strengthen the bonds of loyalty between himself and the chiefs, Moshoeshoe took numerous wives from the chiefly families, using the kinship bonds thus formed to create a sense of unity among the kingdom's different clans.

Moshoeshoe ensured the survival of his kingdom by avoiding conflict with his powerful neighbors, the Zulus, Ndebele, and Ngwane. He paid tribute to their leaders in return for the promise that his lands would remain unmolested. Moshoeshoe further attempted an alliance with the white European settlers, the Boers (of Dutch ancestry), of the Cape Colony. He invited Christian missionaries from the Cape to settle in his kingdom, and he began to trade with the colony for modern firearms and horses.

With a now formidable military, Moshoshoe was able to assert the independence of his kingdom and drive off would-be invaders. By 1840, the Sotho kingdom was one of the most powerful in southern Africa. Nonetheless, Moshoshoe could not stop the increasing encroachment of Boer settlers onto his lands, and he was forced to turn to the British for help.

In 1868, the Sotho kingdom became a British protectorate and was called Basutoland. Upon Moshoeshoe's death in 1870, the kingdom was annexed by the Cape Colony, which was then under British control. Although the Sotho kingship continued under British rule, the office of king was relegated to a primarily symbolic and ritual function.

In 1966, Basutoland gained independence from British colonial rule and became a constitutional monarchy, known today as the kingdom of Lesotho. The government, then as now, was modeled on the British system: a prime minister acted as head of state, and the king served primarily as a figurehead. However, the king at that time, Moshoeshoe II (r. 1960–1990, 1994–1996), seeking to take a more direct role in governing the country, attempted to gain the support of the people by calling a rally at Thaba Bosiu, the stronghold that had formed the heart of the original Sotho kingdom. The prime minister, Chief Leabua Jonathan, placed the king under house arrest and ultimately forced him into exile.

Moshoeshoe II was allowed to return to Lesotho in 1970 but had no significant role in government. In 1986, a military coup led by Major General Justin Metsing Lekhanya overthrew Chief Jonathan's administration, and Lekhanya turned to Moshoeshoe II for support of the new regime. In return for that support, Lekhanya offered the king a more substantial role in the government.

In 1990, when Moshoeshoe II opposed Lekhanya's policies, he was once again forced into exile, replaced on the throne by his son, King Letsie III (r. 1990–1995, 1996–present). Another military coup, this time led by Colonel Elias Phisoane Ramaema, overthrew Lekhanya's regime in 1991, and for a time the political situation in Lesotho was chaotic.

In 1994, King Letsie came forward and dissolved the Ramaema government. In an effort to restore some sense of stability, he recalled Moshoeshoe II from exile and restored him to the throne. When Moshoeshoe II died in a car crash in 1996, Letsie III became king once again.

See also: AFRICAN KINGDOMS; MOSHOESHOE I; MZILIKAZI; NDEBELE KINGDOM; SHAKA ZULU; ZULU KINGDOM.

FURTHER READING

Stevens, Richard P. *Lesotho, Botswana, and Swaziland: The Former High Commission Territories in Southern Africa.* London: 1967.

Thompson, Leonard M. *Survival in Two Worlds: Moshoeshoe of Lesotho, 1786–1870.* Oxford: Clarendon Press, 1975.

SOULOUQUE, FAUSTIN ELIE

(1785–1867 C.E.)

Illiterate ex-slave who became the self-proclaimed emperor of Haiti (r. 1849–1859).

Faustin Elie Soulouque was born into slavery in the village of Petit Goave, Haiti, in 1785. His parents were of Mandingo descent, having been brought to Haiti as slaves from West Africa. His early childhood was spent in slavery, but on August 29, 1793, when he was eight years old, his owners granted him his freedom.

In 1802, the black and mulatto population of Haiti revolted against French colonial rule and the institution of slavery. Soulouque joined the insurrection, which was led by Toussaint l'Ouverture, Jean-Jaques Dessalines (r. 1804–1806), Henri Christophe, Alexandre Petion, and Jean-Pierre Boyer. Although Toussaint was captured by French forces and died in prison, his revolution succeeded, and Dessalines became emperor of Haiti in 1804. As reward for his service in the revolution, Soulouque received the first of many promotions.

Dessalines was assassinated in 1806, and the republic was split in two, with Henri Christophe controlling the north and Alexandre Petion the south. Soulouque served with Petion and once again distinguished himself enough to earn promotions and the trust of the president. When Petion died in 1820, Jean-Pierre Boyer succeeded him in office and reunited the northern and southern portions of Haiti. Soulouque transferred his allegiance to Boyer and continued to rise in the ranks of the army. However, when a rival to Boyer appeared on the horizon, Soulouque joined the newcomer to the political scene.

This change in loyalty served Soulouque well, for the rival, Riviere Herard, became the next president of Haiti, and he rewarded Soulouque with more promotions. Herard's successors did the same. In 1847, however, the extreme volatility of Haitian politics left the island with no clearly designated ruler, and several political leaders put Soulouque's name forward. Other candidates were also suggested, but Soulouque won the election, in part because he skillfully played to the (majority) black population, as opposed to the wealthier and more privileged mulatto faction.

President Soulouque's nation occupied one-third of the island of Hispaniola, the remainder of which comprised the Spanish colony of Santo Domingo. Soulouque saw no reason why his rule should not extend over the entire island, and in March 1849 he ordered 4,000 troops to invade Santo Domingo. The invasion failed, but this did not harm Soulouque's popularity among the Haitian people. In August of that same year, he declared himself emperor to widespread popular support and with the blessing of the Haitian senate.

Soulouque did not give up his dream of uniting the island under his rule, but for a time he postponed his imperial plans and addressed himself to domestic issues, both personal and political. In December 1849 he married a woman named Adelina. He presented Haiti with a new constitution but reserved the right to amend it whenever and however he chose. Soulouque's rule was frequently brutal; he was not shy about ordering the execution of his rivals or using extreme force to put down localized rebellions. In 1852, three years after his imperial proclamation, he held an elaborate ceremony in Port-au-Prince during which he was formally crowned emperor.

In 1855, Soulouque once again mounted an invasion of Santo Domingo, this time with twice as many troops. Once again he was forced to withdraw. In 1856, he tried and failed again. This time his military failure was exacerbated by an economic crisis at home, and the people of Haiti lost all patience with him. The minor insurrections that had plagued his rule over the years blossomed into a full-scale revolt, and in 1859 Soulouque was deposed. He fled to the French consulate for protection, and from there he arranged safe passage to Jamaica for himself and his family. He carried with him a great deal of wealth, much of which he had extorted from the government coffers.

In the early months of 1867, the Haitian government granted Soulouque permission to return to his hometown of Petit Goave. Soulouque was now an old man and was growing increasingly frail. He died on August 6, 1867, less than a year after coming home to Haiti.

SOUTH AMERICAN MONARCHIES

Civilizations that developed in South America between the thirteenth and sixteenth centuries. The distinctive qualities of these societies were political centralization, agricultural economies, large territories, and relatively developed bureaucracies. Their autonomous development was interrupted by the arrival of the Spanish conquerors in the early 1500s.

THE CHIBCHAS (1200–1539 C.E.)
The Chibchas, or Muiscas, were a civilization that developed in the Andean Mountains of western Colombia. According to recent studies, they originated in southern Central America and shared cultural patterns with the native peoples of Honduras, Costa Rica, and Panama.

Historical Periods
Scholars have divided Chibcha history into two periods. In the early period (800–1200) the Chibchas lived in numerous independent communities. The size of settlements varied, but the typical one had less than two hundred inhabitants. The main economic activity was agriculture, complemented by fishing, hunting, and gathering.

During the early period, the Chibchas may have practiced long-distance trade to obtain gold artifacts related to status and religion. They may have also developed some craft specialization. By the end of the period, there was a significant population increase, possibly stimulated by climatic changes that made more agricultural land available. Some villages in the Cauca Valley and the area around present-day Bogotá had populations of about one thousand inhabitants.

In the late-Chibcha period (1200–1539), a number of autonomous chiefdoms emerged. Among the largest of these were Bacatá (Bogotá), Hunza (Tunja), Iraca, Guatavitá, and Tundama. The most powerful chiefdoms were Bacatá and Hunza, which were constantly striving for hegemony over the others. The ruler of Bacatá was called *zipa*, while the ruler of Hunza was called *zaque*.

The title of *zipa* was hereditary, and succession

was matrilineal (through the female line). The ruler was aided by *uzaques,* who performed administrative and military functions. Chibcha shamans were called *xeques,* and they had both political and religious authority. The elite of the society included *gueches* (warriors), artisans, and traders. At the bottom of the social hierarchy were commoners and slaves.

Mythical Origins and Political Conflicts

According to a Chibcha myth, a divine couple came from the east to the Colombian Andes. The husband, named Bochica, was associated with the sun; his wife, Chia, was related to the moon. Bochica had a positive influence on the natives, teaching them basic cultural practices such as agriculture, pottery, and architecture. Chia, on the other hand, had a negative influence, practicing witchcraft and causing cataclysms. At the end of his life, Bochica left the chief of Iraca in charge of his religious powers.

The chief of Iraca arranged peace among the different Chibcha chiefdoms and gained the acceptance of Hunzahúa, the *zaque* of Hunza, as the main leader. After conquering Fugasugá and Tibacuy, the *zipa* of Bacatá, Saguanmachica, threatened the authority of Hunzahúa. Both Saguanmachica and Hunzahúa died fighting each other.

The next *zipa,* Nemequene, took over Guatavitá, Ubaque, Ubaté, Susa, and Fúquene. The conquest of Guatavitá was particularly significant because this chiefdom had an important ceremonial center. Nemequene died fighting against the *zaque* Quemuenchatocha. His successor, Tisquesusa, continued warring against Hunza.

Around 1539, during a truce between Bacatá and Hunza, the Spanish conquistadors arrived in the Chibcha region. The Spaniards took over the Chibcha territory and killed the *zipa.* By then, the total Chibcha population is estimated to have been between 500,000 and 2.5 million.

THE AYMARAS (1200–1500 C.E.)

The Aymaras were a pre-Columbian people who developed a state in the *altiplano,* a high-plateau region located in southeastern Peru and northwestern Bolivia, around Lake Titicaca. The Aymaras originated around 1200, but very little is known about them until they were conquered by the Incas in the fifteenth century.

In the early fifteenth century, there were twelve Aymara kingdoms: Canchi, Cana, Caranga, Charca,

Bacatá Rulers

SAGUANMACHICA	1470–1490
NEMEQUENE	1490–1514
TISQUESUSA	1514–1538
SAGIPA	1538–1539

Hunza Rulers

HUNZAHÚA	?
MICHUA	1470–1490
QUEMUENCHATOCHA	1490–1538
AQUIMINZAQUE	1537–1540

Inca Emperors

MANCO CÁPAC	CA. 1200?
SINCHI ROCA	?
LLOQUE YUPANQUI	?
MAYTA CÁPAC	?
CÁPAC YUPANQUI	?
INCA ROCA	?
YAHUAR HUACAC	?
VIRACOCHA*	?
PACHACUTI*	1438–1471
TOPA INCA*	1471–1493
HUAYNA CÁPAC*	1493–1524
HUASCAR*	1524–1532
ATAHUALPA*	1532

Vilcabamba State Rulers

TÚPAC HUALPA	1533
MANCO INCA	1533–1545
SAYRI TÚPAC	1545–1560
TITU CUSI YUPANQUI	1560–1571
TÚPAC AMARU	1571–1572

*Indicates a separate alphabetical entry.

Colla, Collagua, Collahuaya, Lupaca, Omasuyu, Pacasa, Quillaca, and Ubina. The Inca conquest of the *altiplano* began around 1430, and the last kingdoms to be subdued were Collas and Lupacas.

As part of the Inca Empire, the Aymara region was called Collasuyu. Although the native Aymara dynasties were allowed to remain in power, they were subject to the Incas. In the late 1400s, the Aymaras launched a series of revolts against Inca rule, but the Incas put down these rebellions.

THE INCAS (1400–1532 C.E.)

Inca civilization originated in the southern Andes of Peru. Over a short period of time, the Incas conquered most of the Peruvian coastal and highland regions, southern Colombia, Ecuador, northern Chile. and northwestern Argentina. The gradual conquest of the Inca realm by the Spanish began in 1532 and ended around 1570.

Historical Periods

The Incas were originally an ethnic group located northwest of Lake Titicaca. Around the tenth century, they migrated north to the Urubamba Valley of Peru, founding the city of Cuzco. In the fourteenth century, the Inca began a rapid expansion through military conquests and political alliances. The Incas called their empire Tawantinsuyu ("Kingdom of the Four Quarters"). These quarters were Collasuyu (in the southern Andes), Chinchaysuyu (in the northern Andes), Contisuyu (along the southern coast), and Antisuyu (in the eastern Andean foothills).

Mythical Origins

According to one Inca myth, the sun ordered his children, Manco Cápac and Mama Ocllo, to establish a kingdom on earth. The couple emerged from Lake Titicaca and headed north, looking for a place where Manco Cápac could thrust his magic staff. They found a place on a hill called Huanacauri, and the divine couple proceeded to establish a city nearby and called it Qosqo or Cuzco.

According to another myth, four brothers and four sisters emerged together from a cave at the hill of Tambotoco, located south of Cuzco. The brothers were Ayar Uchu, Ayar Cachi, Ayar Mango, and Ayar Auca; the sisters were Mama Ocllo, Mama Huaco, Mama Ipacura, and Mama Raua. The eight siblings headed north, looking for a place to settle.

On the way, they decided to trap Ayar Cachi inside the cave at Tambotoco because they feared his magical powers. After a while, they converted Ayar Uchu into a sacred rock and left him at the foot of a hill. Finally, Ayar Auca tried to settle at Guayanaypata, a place that seemed suitable, and he turned into another sacred rock. He ordered Ayar Mango to found a kingdom at this site and to switch his name to Manco Cápac. Manco kept the four sisters as his wives.

Inca Rulers

When a new Inca ruler came to power, he formed his own *ayllu,* or community, with his wives and children. Some scholars believe that the Incas had both a primary and a secondary ruler. There is debate on the mechanisms of succession, but it is possible that after the death of each ruler, his real and symbolic sons competed for power.

Different historical accounts agree that Pachacuti (or Pachacútec) (r. 1438–1471), the ninth Inca ruler, began a great expansion of the empire. His son and successor, Túpac Inca Yupanqui, also known as Topa Inca (r. 1471–1493), conquered the Chimú Empire, located on the northern coast of Peru. He also extended the Inca Empire up to Ecuador and founded the city of Quito.

Topa Inca was succeeded as ruler by his son, Huayna Cápac (r. 1493–1524), who died suddenly without a clear successor. Some scholars believe that Huayna Cápac died of smallpox, a disease that was introduced by the Spaniards in the Caribbean and that reached the Andes before the Europeans.

After Huayna Capac's death, two of his sons, Huáscar (r. 1524–1532) and his half-brother Atahualpa (r. 1532), began warring against each other for power. Spanish conquistador Francisco Pizarro arrived in Peru in 1532 during this civil war and captured Atahualpa. While Atahualpa was in captivity, his troops defeated and killed Huáscar.

Pizarro decided to kill Atahualpa in order to reduce the possibility of Inca resistance. He then captured the Inca city of Cuzco and appointed a puppet ruler, Manco Inca (r. 1533–1545). Abused and mistreated, Manco Inca rebelled against the Spaniards in 1536. Failing to take Cuzco, he withdrew to Vilcabamba, a remote area in the Andes, and established an independent kingdom that resisted conquest until 1572, when the Spaniards defeated and killed the last Vilcabamba ruler, Tupac Amaru (r. 1571–1572).

See also: ATAHUALPA; HUASCAR; HUAYNA CAPAC; INCA EMPIRE; MAYA EMPIRE; PACHACUTI; VIRACHOCHA.

FURTHER READING

Murra, John V. *Economic Organization of the Inca State.* Greenwich, CT: JAI Press, 1980.

Rostworowski de Diez Canseco, María. *History of the Inca Realm.* New York: Cambridge University Press, 1999.

SOUTH ASIAN KINGDOMS

Numerous and varied kingdoms established throughout South Asia from ancient times to the early twentieth century.

During the third millennium B.C.E., the first unified South Asian civilization formed in the Indus River basin. This civilization stretched from the northernmost and largest city, Harappa, to Mohenjo-daro, located 400 miles south along the Indus. The Harappan civilization included nearly forty cities.

The Harappans developed an agricultural economy that featured sophisticated irrigation systems. They became the first civilization in the world to convert cotton into cloth, and their cities were laid out in efficient block patterns with functional sewage systems. The earliest incarnation of the Hindu god Shiva emerged during the Harappan period; artifacts depict him as both a fertility and war god.

Around 1750 B.C.E., an unidentified disaster, possibly a major flooding of the Indus River, severely weakened the Harappans. Many of their cities were destroyed, while less developed nomads from the civilization's outlying regions assumed control of the remaining communities. Consequently, the Harappans were unable to resist the encroachment of the Aryans, the first major invaders of South Asia. The Aryans had originated in Central Asia, but early Mongol raiders forced them from that region. As they splintered into tribes, the Aryans migrated as far west as Europe and southeastward to South Asia, crossing the Hindu Kush Mountains through the Khyber Pass and entering the Indus plain.

THE AGE OF THE ARYANS

Although the Aryans referred to the Harappans as *dasas,* or dark-skinned slaves, they were in many ways less advanced than the native Harappans. The Aryans lived in small migrant tribes, had not learned to carve or build with stone, lacked a written language, and left no evidence of art. However, they introduced three elements that permanently transformed South Asian civilization.

First, they had mastered the use of iron, allowing them to fashion both weapons and farm implements. The weaponry, coupled with the endurance derived from their long migration, facilitated their defeat of the Harappans. Iron plows helped the Aryans convert the dense forests that separated the plains of the Indus and Ganges rivers, opening vast tracts of land to settlement and development.

Second, the Aryans introduced the Vedas, the "Books of Knowledge." The Vedas contained hymns, poems, and stories that detailed Aryan customs and traditions and became the basis of South Asian culture. They described the Aryan gods Indra, Varuna, Agni, and Soma, who later occupied important positions in Hinduism. Because the Aryans initially lacked a written language, the Vedas were orally preserved. Their language, Sanskrit, eventually became the dominant language of northern India.

Finally, the Aryans instituted a social hierarchy that has come to be known as the caste system. The *brahmans,* consisting of priests and scholars, formed the highest class and were the most revered. Tribal leaders and warriors occupied the next class, the *kshatriyas.* All other Aryans belonged to the next class, the *vaishyas.* Eventually, the *vaishyas* class was divided into separate *jati.* Each *jati* consisted of a specific profession, such as blacksmiths or weavers. Finally, the *shudra* class consisted of slaves and conquered people, such as the Harappans. Eventually, a fifth-class designation, *panchamas* or "untouchables," was applied to non-Harappan natives who succumbed to Aryan rule.

During the next five centuries, between 1300 and 800 B.C.E., the Aryans became fully assimilated with their Harappan predecessors as they expanded across the northern reaches of the Indian subcontinent. As their populations and territories increased, the Aryan tribes' ruling rajas (princes), advised by brahmanic councils, gained more power. The tribes also became less mobile and adopted the Harappans' agricultural economy, while professions such as blacksmiths, weavers, and herders were developed. Aryan scholars created the Brahmanas, a second series of Vedas that stipulated a dual universe consisting of truth and falsehood. Strict, extensive sacrifices

Maurya Dynasty

CHANDRAGUPTA MAURYA*	321–297 B.C.E.
BINDUSARA	297–272
ASOKA*	273–232
DASARATHA	232–224
SAMPRATI	224–215
SATADHANVA	215–209
BRIHADRATHA	209–187

Gupta Dynasty

CHANDRAGUPTA I	320–330
SAMUDRAGUPTA	335–375
CHANDRAGUPTA II	375–415
KUMARAGUPTA I	415–455
SKANDAGUPTA	455–470
KUMARAGUPTA II	470–475
BUDHAGUPTA	475–495
NARASIMHAGUPTA	495–510
KUMARAGUPTA II	510–525
VISHNUGUPTA	525–550

DELHI SULTANATE (1206–1526)

Mu'izzi Dynasty

AYBAK	1206–1210
ARAM SHAH	1210–1211
ILTUTMISH	1211–1236
FIRUZ I	1236
RADIYYA	1236–1240

BAHRAM	1240–1242
MAS'UD	1242–1246
MAHMUD I	1246–1266
BALBAN	1266–1287
KAYQUBADH	1287–1290
KAYUMARTH	1290

Khalji Dynasty

FIRUZ II	1290–1296
IBRAHIM I	1296
MUHAMMAD I	1296–1316
UMAR	1316
MUBARAK I	1316–1320
KHUSRAU	1320

Tughluqid Dynasty

GHIYASUDDIN TUGHLUQ SHAH I	1320–1324
MUHAMMAD BIN TUGHLUQ II	1324–1351
FIRUZ SHAH III	1351–1387
MUHAMMAD SHAH III	1387–1388
TUGHLUQ SHAH II	1388–1389
ABU BAKR*	1389–1390
ALAUDDIN SIKANDAR I	1390–1394
NASIRUDDIN MAHMUD II	1394–1413
DAULAT KHAN LODI	1413–1414

Sayyid Dynasty

KHIDR KHAN	1414–1421
MUBARAK II	1421–1434

Sayyid Dynasty *(continued)*

MUHAMMAD IV	1434–1445
ALAM SHAH	1445–1451

Lodi Dynasty

BAHLUL LODI	1451–1489
SIKANDAR II	1489–1517
IBRAHIM II	1517–1526

Suri Dynasty

SHIR SHAH SUR	1540–1545
ISLAM SHAH	1545–1553
MUHAMMAD ADIL	1553–1555
IBRAHIM III	1555
SIKANDAR III	1555

*Indicates a separate alphabetical entry.

and rituals, performed by brahman priests, were required to help the Aryans discover truth and placate their gods.

THE FIRST INDIAN KINGDOMS

By approximately 800 B.C.E., the Aryan tribes had consolidated into sixteen groups loosely resembling kingdoms, although they were still led by tribal councils. Among these, the kingdoms of Kosala and Magadha emerged as the two most powerful. Kosala, located in the northern reaches of modern India, relied upon the natural resources of the Himalayas for its wealth, and it became a dominant provider of furs and mineral ores. Magadha encompassed the Ganges plain and traded its agricultural products to enrich itself. During this period, trade with other regions as distant as Greece and China began, roads were constructed to increase this trade, and enormous cities, such as the Magadhan capital of Pataliputra, were built.

Kosala and Magadha also incubated the growth of Buddhism. Over the centuries, dissent with the rigid brahmanic rituals had steadily intensified. A third series of Vedas, the Upanishads, emphasized the individual's role in achieving enlightenment, or *moksha*. The Upanishads stated a belief in *karma*, that an individual's actions would affect the quality of the following life. During the sixth century B.C.E., Siddhartha Gautama, the Buddha, refined these ideas. Gautama advocated virtue, pacifism, and poverty as the means to overcome the suffering and ignorance that was an inherent part of life. His teachings, the basis of Buddhism, rapidly gained popularity and were quickly disseminated.

THE RISE OF INDIAN EMPIRES

During the reigns of Bimbisara (r. ca. 540–491 B.C.E.) and his son, Ajatasatru (r. ca. 491–159 B.C.E.), their kingdom of Magadha subdued the Kosala kingdom, making Magadha the first significant empire in South Asia, stretching from modern Bengal in the east to Pakistan in the west.

Although two subsequent dynasties replaced Bimbisara's line, Magadha flourished until 326 B.C.E., when Alexander the Great of Macedonia (r. 336–323 B.C.E.) launched the second great invasion of South Asia. The Macedonians rapidly conquered Magadha's western territories, but Alexander retreated when his weary troops threatened to rebel. Before he left the region, Alexander encountered Chandragupta Maurya, an outcast from the Magadhan royal family.

Alexander's victories inspired Chandragupta Maurya (r. 321–297 B.C.E.) to create his own empire. In 323 B.C.E., Chandragupta arranged the slaughter of the Magadhan monarchy, seized the capital at Pataliputra, and initiated the Maurya Empire, one of the largest and most powerful in South Asian history. To maintain this empire, Chandragupta assembled a massive army and created South Asia's first bureaucracy. Different government agencies oversaw such functions as taxation, public projects, trade, and the census. The government employed all artisans and consequently controlled industries such as cotton weaving, metallurgy, and masonry. The Maurya emperor owned all land and natural resources, such as mines, but leases were provided to farmers. In return, the farmers were taxed one-fourth of their crops.

Built between 1638 and 1648 during the Mughal dynasty, the Red Fort in Delhi, India, is named for the red stone used in its construction. The magnificent building served as a palace, and the Delhi Gate, shown here, was originally the main entrance.

Chandragupta constantly sought to expand his empire. He eventually gained control over the northern portion of the Indian subcontinent, a territory that extended from present-day Afghanistan to Bangladesh. Chandragupta was also the first Indian ruler to make a concerted push over the Vindhya mountain range into southern India.

A group of people known as the Dravidians, contemporaries of the Harappans, originally inhabited the southern portion of the Indian subcontinent. The Dravidians had possibly migrated from East Africa, riding rafts pushed by the monsoon winds across the Arabian Sea. The Aryans had occasionally clashed with the northern Dravidians, but the Deccan plateau served as a natural barrier between the two races. By about 300 B.C.E., the Dravidians had sepa-

rated into three main kingdoms: Kerala, Chola (Cola), and Pandya.

These Dravidian kingdoms were fairly wealthy. They traded onyx, cotton, silks, and spices with the Southeast Asian kingdoms, with the Greeks, and with the Romans. Roman financial records contain complaints of the inordinate trade balance with these kingdoms. More importantly, however, these kingdoms oversaw the genesis of modern Hinduism. The conception of Vishnu and all his avatars (incarnations of forms) emerged from southern India, as did the figure of Krishna, a new incarnation of Shiva, and the pantheon of lesser Hindu gods. The Vedic brahmans throughout India gradually assimilated these deities, incorporating them into their brahmanic rituals.

Chandragupta Maurya failed to conquer the Dra-

ROYAL PLACES

DELHI

Delhi holds special significance for Hindus because it shares its location in northern India with Indraprashtha, the mystical capital in the Hindu epic, the *Mahabharata*. During the eleventh century C.E., the Tomara dynasty constructed the modern city of Delhi. In 1193, the Ghur dynasty conquered the city, and it remained under Muslim control until the Mughal Empire ended in 1857. Muslim rulers constantly rebuilt the city, renovating it as many as seven times over the centuries. The Mughals constructed buildings such as the Old Fort and the Jumma Masjid, which today stand as the most significant structures in the city. The city survived three major plunderings in 1398, 1739, and 1757, and continued to thrive when the British moved their colonial capital to Calcutta. But in 1912, the British constructed New Delhi, located six miles from the original city. It now serves as India's capital, a visible symbol of the many transformations the India has endured.

vidian kingdoms, but he did subdue the rest of the Indian subcontinent. His grandson, Asoka (r. 268–232 B.C.E.), first sought to further Mauryan dominance. But after a bloody battle at Kalinga against the kingdom of Kalinga (Orissa) in 268 B.C.E., Asoka converted to Buddhism and adopted a pacifist philosophy. After his conversion, Asoka raised pillars inscribed with Buddhist beliefs throughout his empire. During his reign, Buddhism attained its greatest prominence in South Asia.

When Asoka died in 232 B.C.E., the Maurya Empire quickly crumbled, although the dynasty retained control of Pataliputra for several centuries. For nearly five hundred years, no single empire unified the Indian subcontinent. The Indo-Greeks of Bactria (in present-day Afghanistan), descendants of the Macedonian invaders, briefly controlled the northwest portion of the subcontinent, but Scythian and Parthian invaders from Central Asia drove them further into India during the first century C.E. Although the Scythians and Parthians initially raided the region, they ultimately settled in it and assimilated with the native inhabitants.

By the second century, the Shuga dynasty had replaced the Mauryas as the dominant force in the plains of the Ganges River. A series of lesser dynasties, such as the Kanvas and Satavahana, ruled the Deccan plateau, while the three Dravidian kingdoms remained intact in southern India until the Pallavas

dynasty defeated them in the tenth century. But despite the absence of a central power, South Asian civilization flourished. Trade was highly profitable, distinct forms of art and literature developed, and Hinduism continued its rapid growth.

In 320, the Gupta dynasty attained control of the Gangetic plain and the abundant commerce that passed through it. Using this economic advantage, the Guptas reunited much of northern India under the Gupta Empire. During the reign of Chandra Gupta II (r. 375–415), the Guptas conquered western India as far as the Arabian Sea, and they signed treaties with various powers in the Deccan region.

The ascendancy of the Guptas marked India's Classical Age. The Guptas lavishly patronized the arts, encouraged the open practice of all religions, and built magnificent temples and other public structures. Emulating their Mauryan predecessors, the Guptas controlled all industries and land, renting it to farmers for a fixed rate. They also expanded trade with China and Southeast Asia. However, constant Hun raids from Central Asia drained the empire of its resources, and by 515, the Guptas lost control of their empire.

THE MUSLIM INVASION OF INDIA

The Hun raids were a harbinger of the next major shift in South Asian power. In 622, the prophet Muhammad introduced Islam in Mecca on the Arabian Peninsula. The spread of Islam was unprecedented, and Muhammad's followers eagerly accepted his edict to wage *jihad,* or holy war, against members of opposing faiths. When Muslim leaders witnessed the treasures that traders brought from India, their desire for such goods increased enthusiasm for *jihad.*

By the tenth century, eastern sultans had broken away from the main caliphate in Baghdad. One of these sultans, Mahmud of Ghazni (r. 998–1030), became the first Muslim leader to invade India. He launched numerous raids into northern India and ultimately conquered the Punjab region in the tenth century. When the Ghur dynasty replaced the Ghaznis in 1175, they expanded Muslim control over northern India and established a sultanate at Delhi, which became known as the Delhi sultanate.

During the fourteenth century, the Tughluqs became the third Muslim dynasty to rule northern India. While the Tughluqs expanded Muslim control across northern India into Bengal and southward into the Deccan, they harshly persecuted the Hindu natives. In response, Hindu warriors retreated south and founded the Vijayanagar kingdom. The most prominent Tughluq sultan of Delhi, Muhammad Shah I (r. 1325–1351), also alienated his Muslim subjects. He forced many of them to occupy the harsh Deccan plateau, and he instituted disastrous economic policies.

When a seven-year drought began in 1335, Muhammad Shah made little effort to provide relief to either Muslims or Hindus. Consequently, he faced widespread rebellion. Both the Bengal and Deccan governors founded their own sultanates, while Hindus in Rajputana frequently attacked Delhi. As a result, Muslim power in India temporarily shifted from Delhi to the newly established Bahmani sultanate in the Deccan. For two centuries, the Bahmanis and their successors repeatedly fought Hindu rivals in Vijayanagar, while two weak dynasties—the Sayyids and Lodis—struggled to maintain power in the Delhi sultanate.

In 1526, Babur, the king of Kabul and a descendant of both Genghis Khan (r. 1206–1227) and Tamerlane (r. 1370–1405), led the last significant invasion through the Khyber Pass into India. Babur (r. 1526–1530) deposed the Lodi dynasty from Delhi and established the Mughal Empire, the last major empire to rule India.

The Mughal Empire reached its peak of power during the reign of Babur's grandson Akbar the Great (r. 1556–1605). Akbar greatly expanded the empire's territory, developed its economy, and instituted a universal educational system. Although he heavily taxed Hindus and barred them from serving in his government, he refused to persecute them and allowed them to own property and businesses. Akbar also built countless public buildings that served both Muslims and Hindus. Consequently, Hindus were largely supportive of Akbar's monarchy, and the Rajput rajas (princes) of Rajasthan even became his loyal allies.

Unfortunately, Akbar's successors squandered his wealth. When his great-grandson, Aurangzeb (r. 1658–1707), assumed the Mughal throne in 1658, he pushed the empire's control deeper into the Indian subcontinent. But he also eliminated Akbar's policy of religious toleration and brutally suppressed the Hindus. The economic and military strains of Aurangzeb's campaigns of conquest, coupled with increasingly prevalent Hindu rebellions, rapidly undermined the Mughal Empire.

After Aurangzeb died in 1707, the Mughal Empire steadily declined. Although Mughal emperors remained in power until 1858, they increasingly served as puppets for the British East India Company. During the sixteenth century, the British, Portuguese, Dutch, and French battled for control of the enormously lucrative Indian trade. The British ultimately expelled the other Europeans from the region, and after Aurangzeb's death, they gained control of the regions of Bengal, Orissa, and Bihar.

In 1857, Indian troops (known as sepoys) serving under the British revolted in a massive uprising. When the Sepoy Mutiny erupted, the British accused the last Mughal emperor, Bahadur Shah II (r. 1837–1858), of abetting it. The British deposed him, and Britain formally took control of the subcontinent as a colony.

British control of India lasted until 1947. After World War II drained Great Britain of much of its resources, the British abandoned most of their colonies. As their last act, the British united Bengal and Pakistan, the predominantly Muslim regions of the Indian subcontinent, as East and West Pakistan. The remaining area was designated as India.

A rebellion in 1971 severed the two Pakistans, and an independent Bangladesh replaced the former East Pakistan. Despite this change, and the division between Muslim Pakistan and Bangladesh and Hindu

India, the tensions originally initiated by Mahmud of Ghazni's first Muslim invasion of the subcontinent still remain. This is most evident in the Indian and Pakistani dispute over the region of Kashmir.

See also: AKBAR THE GREAT; ASOKA; AURANGZEB; BABUR; BAHMANI DYNASTY; CHANDRAGUPTA MAURYA; COLA KINGDOM; DELHI KINGDOM; GHAZNAVID DYNASTY; GHUR DYNASTY; GUPTA EMPIRE; INDIAN KINGDOMS; KALINGA KINGDOM; KANVA DYNASTY; KOSALA KINGDOM; MAGADHA KINGDOM; MAHMUD OF GHAZNA; MAURYA EMPIRE; MUGHAL EMPIRE; PANDYA DYNASTY; RAJASTHAN KINGDOM; SATAVAHANA DYNASTY; TUGHLUQ DYNASTY; VIJAYANAGAR EMPIRE.

FURTHER READING

Keay, John. *India: A History.* New York: Atlantic Monthly Press, 2000.

Stein, Burton. *A History of India.* Oxford: Basil Blackwell, 1998.

Watson, Francis. *India: A Concise History.* Rev. ed. New York: Thames & Hudson, 2002.

SOUTH SEA ISLAND KINGDOMS

(ca. 1000 B.C.E.–Present)

Kingdoms located on volcanic or coral islands scattered throughout the southern part of the Pacific Ocean. The South Sea Islands, often referred to as Oceania, comprise about twenty-five thousand islands and atolls. Ethnographically, the area is frequently divided into Polynesia, Micronesia, and Melanesia.

Because of the great distances between settlements in Oceania, the islanders developed diverse customs, religious rites, and languages. Each island or small group of neighboring islands also developed its own system of government. The South Sea Island kingdoms included such places as French Polynesia, Tonga, Samoa, the Marquesas, the Cook Islands, Tuvalu, and Hawaii.

MIGRATING TO NEW LANDS

Polynesia was one of the last regions of the world to be populated, with evidence indicating that the earliest inhabitants arrived around 1000 B.C.E. A number of archaeologists believe that these initial settlers migrated from Southeast Asia. However, some linguists and geneticists question this theory and suggest other possibilities for the origin of the islands' populations.

The early South Sea islanders were skilled navigators and traveled the vast area of the Pacific Ocean, settling on the most promising islands over several centuries. The Hawaiian Islands, north of the equator, were the last to be inhabited, sometime between 900 and 1300 C.E. According to a history of the Hawaiian Islands by King Kalakaua (r. 1874–1891), the first chief to bring his tribe to Hawaii was Nanaula, probably from the Samoan Islands. Later, chief Nanamaoa led his tribe to conquests of the big island of Hawaii and of Maui and Oahu.

TRIBAL ORGANIZATION

Some South Sea islanders, such as the Maori of New Zealand and the early Hawaiians, lived in various villages, each led by a local tribal chief. Political power was decentralized because there was no ruling king. In other cultures, such as that on the island of Rotuma northwest of the Fiji Islands, the local chiefs selected a high king from among themselves. The king's term of office was for varying periods of time but not usually for life.

Among the tribes on Easter Island (Rapa Nui), the Miru were the highest ranking group, for they claimed to be direct descendants of the island's first settler, Hotu-matua. The high chief of the island, who also served in a priestly role, came from the Miru tribe. In contrast, civil and religious powers were separated on the island of Mangala (part of the Cook Islands), where hereditary kings were entrusted with spiritual duties, and a victorious warrior was chosen as the head of government.

Disputes inevitably arose among the various chieftains, and war was common in some areas. The mythology of Easter Island, for example, contains the story of wars between two tribes called the Long-ears and the Short-ears. With the arrival of European explorers in the South Sea Islands beginning in the sixteenth century, native ways of life were disrupted and displaced. Guns and gunpowder—supplied by white men in return for goods, women, or sometimes slaves—gave power-hungry chieftains an advantage over their rivals.

In the Hawaiian Islands, King Kamehameha I (r.

The only remaining South Sea island kingdom is Tonga. Its current ruler, King Tupou IV, took the throne in 1965, and he rules as a constitutional monarch.

1795–1819) used guns to defeat rival kings and unite Hawaii under his rule, establishing a dynasty that lasted more than one hundred years. The Maori king Hongi Hika (r. ca. ?–1828) traveled to England in 1820 hoping to gain possession of double-barreled guns to use in his intertribal warfare. This intertribal fighting, coupled with diseases introduced by white men, greatly reduced the Maori native population of New Zealand.

KINGDOMS BECOME COLONIES

European contact with the islands of the Pacific soon changed from an interest in commerce with native peoples to the desire to possess the islands themselves. During the nineteenth century, many Pacific Islands and island groups, such as Hawaii, New Zealand, and the Marquesas, underwent an explosion of European and American settlers. These foreign settlers claimed ownership of much of the native land and put in place their own forms of colonial government, usurping the rights of hereditary rulers.

Christian missionaries from Europe and the United States also descended on the South Sea Islands and changed native beliefs and customs. Nevertheless, the island populations formed strong ties with the homelands of the white settlers. For example, Tuvalu (formerly the Ellice Islands) became part of the Gilbert Islands, a British protectorate, in 1892. In 1916, the Gilbert and Ellice Islands became a British colony. Today, Tuvalu remains part of the British Commonwealth, with Elizabeth II of England (r. 1952–) the titular ruler.

On the Hawaiian Islands, European and American companies developed sugarcane and pineapple plantations and imported workers from Asia and the Pacific. In 1887, white settlers forced King Kalakaua to accept the so-called Bayonet Constitution, which took away much of his power and the land of many Hawaiian royals.

The United States gained preeminence in Hawaii when Kalakaua granted the nation sole rights to the use of Pearl Harbor. Kalakaua's successor, Queen Liliuokalani (r. 1891–1893), was deposed in 1893 by a group of American businessmen aided by United States Marines. Despite attempts by Hawaiians to restore her throne, President William McKinley formally annexed the Hawaiian Islands in 1898. In 1959, Hawaii became the fiftieth state, giving its people full U.S. citizenship.

Since World War II, many changes have taken place in the way the islands of the Pacific are governed. Although some of the islands remain territories of foreign nations, such as the French Marquesas, others have reclaimed their autonomy.

The island archipelago of Tonga is the only remaining monarchy in the Pacific. The hereditary king, Taufa'ahau Tupou IV (r. 1965–present) rules Tonga today with the help of a prime minister and deputy minister appointed for the life of the monarch. The thirty-seat legislative assembly of Tonga has only nine elected positions.

See also: HAWAIIAN KINGDOMS; KAMEHAMEHA I, THE GREAT; LILIUOKALANI; MAORI KINGDOMS; MARQUESAS KINGDOMS; SAMOAN KINGDOMS; TAHITIAN KINGDOM; TONGA, KINGDOM OF.

FURTHER READING

Fornander, Abraham. *An Account of the Polynesian Race: Its Origins and Migrations, and the Ancient History of the Hawaiian People to the Times of Kamehameha I.* Boston: Charles E. Tuttle, 1981.

Scarr, Deryck. *A History of the Pacific Islands: Passages through Tropical Time.* London: Routledge Curzon, 2001.

SOUTHEAST ASIAN KINGDOMS

Southeast Asia's political development had already begun in the prehistoric period, but without written documents it is difficult to describe the process or processes responsible for the evolution of principalities throughout the region. Ancient Southeast Asian kingdoms were highly diverse and evolved in different directions. It is difficult at this point to form any general explanations for their paths of development, their rises, or their falls.

EARLY KINGDOMS

During the late centuries B.C.E., certain parts of Southeast Asia were already showing signs of making the transition from village-level society to the formation of kingdoms. Evidence of trade with South Asia during the late prehistoric period has been found in central Thailand, west Java, and Bali. So-called circular sites, consisting of large artificial mounds ringed by one or more concentric ditches or moats and embankments, have been found in northeast Thailand and in the "Terres Rouges" or Red Earth region along the border between Cambodia and Vietnam. These earthworks strongly suggest that local rulers had the ability to mobilize labor from more than just one settlement.

In the late second century B.C.E., the kingdom of Nan-yueh, in what is now northern Vietnam, was conquered by the Han Chinese and absorbed into the empire. During this period, the area south of China's Yangtze River was in the early stages of Chinese imperial influence, and Nan-yueh (or Nam-Viet) partook of this process. After a period during which Nan-yueh was governed by military commanders, the region around Hanoi was made a regular province of China.

The Chinese were mainly interested in the commercial contacts that this conquest provided. The south was associated in the Chinese mind with rare and precious objects, such as perfumed woods and exotic birds' feathers used for jewelry. The people of northern Vietnam embraced numerous features of Chinese culture but did not abandon their sense of their own nationhood. In the tenth century C.E., the Vietnamese finally threw off Chinese rule and reasserted their independence.

It is not known how highly organized the preconquest kingdoms of Southeast Asia were. They seem to have possessed a two- or possibly three-stage hierarchy of settlements, and the ceremonial bronze objects such as the enormous Dongson drums made in the north Vietnam area were circulated as far as New Guinea. This evidence suggests that the political organization of these kingdoms may also have been elaborate. Because they did not possess written documents, however, the system of administration they practiced may never be known.

THE HISTORIC ERA

Southeast Asia enters the historic era around 200 C.E., when the first inscription was set up in the region at a site called Vocanh in southern Vietnam. The inscription, written in a script derived from South Asia, contains no date, but the style of the letters indicates that it was erected in the late second or early third century. Unfortunately, the inscription does not contain the name of any king or kingdom, and since the language used is Sanskrit, the ethnicity of the ruler who was probably responsible for its carving cannot be determined.

Writing did not spread quickly through Southeast Asia, at least not on permanent materials such as stone. Nor did the first kingdoms form near the border with India, despite the fact that the early historic rulers of Southeast Asia adopted a great deal from South Asian culture. In the fourth century, the kingdom of Champa in southern Vietnam appears in inscriptions in the region. The Cham people, who were closely related to the Indonesians, Malays, and Filipinos, established several kingdoms, including Vijaya and Panduranga along the coast of southern Vietnam, which produced important works of architecture and art. They were also involved in maritime trade until they were defeated first by the Khmer people in the late twelfth century, and later by the Vietnamese, who encroached from the north and gradually infiltrated all their lands.

One of the most prominent early kingdoms in Southeast Asia is known almost entirely from Chinese sources. From the third until the seventh centuries, Chinese records contain numerous references to the Funan kingdom. No inscriptions with a name corresponding to this Chinese transcription have been discovered, but numerous sites in the lower Mekong River area seem to correspond to the general area where Funan should have been located. Archaeological remains indicative from that area reveal a densely populated site with active trading relations

BURMA

Tagaung Dynasty

PYUSAWHTI	167–242
THINLIKYAUNG	344–387

Pagan Kingdom

ANAWRAHTA	1044–1077
SAWLU 1077–	1084
KYANZITTHA	1084–1113
ALAUNGSITHU	1113–1167
NARATHU	1167–1170
NARATHEINKHA	1170–1173
NARAPATISITHU	1173–1210
NANTAUNGMYA	1210–1234
KYASWA	1234–1250
UZANA	1250–1254
NARATHIHAPATE	1254–1287

Ava Kingdom

THADOMINYA	1364–1368
NGA NU	1368
MINKYISWASAWKE	1368–1401
MINHKAUNG	1401–1422
THIHATHU	1422–1426
MINHLANGE	1426
KALEKYETAUNGNYO	1426–1427
MOHNYINTHADO	1427–1440
MINREKYAWSWA	1440–1443
NARAPATI	1443–1469
THIHATHURA	1469–1481
MINHKAUNG	1481–1502
SHWENANKYAWSHIN	1502–1527
THOHANBWA	1527–1543
HKONMAING	1543–1546
SITHUKYAWHTIN	1546–1552

Toungoo Dynasty

MINKYINYO	1486–1531
TABINSHWEHTI	1531–1551
BAYINNAUNG	1551–1581
NANDABAYIN	1581–1599
NYAUNG TAN	1599–1606
ANAUKPETLUN	1606–1628

MINREDEIPPA	1628–1629
THALUN	1629–1648
PINDALE	1648–1661
PYE	1661–1672
NAYAWAYA	1672–1673
MINREKYAWDIN	1673–1698
SANE	1698–1714
TANINGANWE	1714–1733
MAHADAMMAYAZA DIPATI	1733–1752

Konbaung Dynasty

ALAUNGPAYA	1752–1760
NAUNGDAWGYI	1760–1763
HSINBYUSHIN	1763–1776
SINGU MIN	1776–1782
MAUNG MAUNG	1782
BODAWPAYA	1782–1819
BAGYIDAW	1819–1837
THARRAWADDY	1837–1846
PAGAN MIN	1846–1853
MINDON MIN	1853–1878
THIBAW	1878–1885

CAMBODIA
Funan Kingdom

KAUNDINYA	LATE FIRST CENTURY C.E.
FAN SHIH-MAN	202–225
KAUNDINYA II	DIED BEFORE 434
RUDRAVARMAN	514–539

Chenla Empire

BHAVAVARMAN I	550–600
MAHENDRAVARMAN	600–611
ISANAVARMAN I	611–635
BHAVAVARMAN II	635–650
JAYAVARMAN I	650–713
JAYADEVI	713–?

Angkor Kingdom

JAYAVARMAN II	802–834
JAYAVARMAN III	834–877
INDRAVARMAN I	877–889

Angkor Kingdom (continued)

Yasovarman I	889–900
Harshavarman I	900–922
Isanavarman II	922–928
Jayavarman IV	928–942
Harshavarman II	942–944
Rajendravarman II	944–968
Jayavarman V	968–1001
Udayadityavarman I	1001–1002
Suryavarman I	1002–1050
Udayadityavarman II	1050–1066
Harshavarman III	1066–1080
Jayavarman VI	1080–1107
Dharanindravarman I	1107–1113
Suryavarman II	1113–1150
Dharanindravarman II	1150–1160
Yasovarman II	1160–1165
Tribhuvanadityavarman	1165–1177
Interregnum	**1177–1181**
Jayavarman VII	1181–1219
Indravarman II	1219–1243
Jayavarman VIII	1243–1295
Indravarman III	1295–1308
Indrajayavarman	1308–1327
Jayavarman Paramesvara	1327–1353

THAILAND

Sukhothai Kingdom

Rama Khamhaeng	1275–1317
Lo Tai	1317–1347

Ayudhya

Rama Tibodi	1350–1369
Ramesuen	1369–1370
Boromoraja I	1370–1388
Tong Lan	1388
Ramesuen	1388–1395
Ram Raja	1395–1408
Intaraja	1408–1424
Boromoraja II	1424–1448
Boromo Trailokanat	1448–1488
Boromoraja III	1488–1491
Rama Tibodi II	1491–1529
Boromaja IV	1529–1534
Ratsada	1534
Prajai	1534–1546
Keo Fa	1546–1548
Khun Worawongsa	1548–1549
Maha Chakrapat	1549–1569
Mahin	1569
Maha Tammaraja	1569–1590
Naresuen	1590–1605
Ekatotsarot	1605–1610
Intaraja II	1610–1628
Jetta	1628–1630
Atityawong	1630
Prasat Tong	1630–1656
Chao Fa Jai	1656
Sri Sutammaraja	1656–1657
Narai	1657–1688
Pra Petraja	1688–1703
Prachao Sua	1703–1709
Tai Sra	1709–1733
Maha Tammaraja II	1733–1758
Utumpon	1758
Boromoraja V	1758–1767

Bangkok

Pya Taksin	1767–1782
Rama I	1782–1809
Rama II	1809–1824
Rama III	1824–1851
Rama IV*	1851–1868
Rama V*	1868–1910
Rama VI	1910–1925
Prajadhipok (Rama VII)	1925–1935
Ananda Mahidol (Rama VIII)	1935–1946
Bumipol Adulet (Rama IX)	1946–

Lang Chang

Fa Ngum	1353–1373
Sam Sene Tai	1373–1416
Lan Kham Deng	1416–1428
Pommatat	1428–1429

Lang Chang (continued)

PAK HOUEI LUONG	1429–1430
TAO SAI	1430
PAYA KHAI	1430–1433
CHIENG SAI	1433–1434
KAM KHEUT	1434–1435
SAI TIAKAPAT	1435–1438
TENE KHAM	1438–1479
LA SENE TAI	1479–1486
SOM POU	1486–1496
VISOUN	1496–1501
POTISARAT	1501–1520
SETTATIRAT	1520–1548
SENE SOULINTA	1548–1571
MAHA OUPAHAT	1571–1575
SENE SOULINTA	1575–1580
NAKHONE NOI	1582–1583
INTERREGNUM	**1583–1591**
NOKEO KOUMANE	1591–1596
TAMMIKARAT	1596–1622
OUPAGNOUVARAT	1622–1623
POTISARAT II	1623–1627
OUPAGNAOVARAT	1627–1637
SOULIGNA VONGSA	1637–1694
TIAN TALA	1694–1700
NAN TARAT	1700
SAI ONG HUE	1700–1735

Vien Chang (Ventiane)

ONG LONG	1735–1760
ONG BOUN	1760–1778
INTERREGNUM	**1778–1782**
CHAO NAN	1782–1792
CHAO IN	1792–1805
CHAO ANOU	1805–1828

Luang Prabang

KINGKITSARAT	1707–1713
KHAMONE NOI	1713–1723
INTHASOM	1723–1749
SOTIKAKUMAN	1776–1781
SURIYAVONG	1781–1787

INTERREGNUM	**1787–1791**
ANURUTTHA	1791–1816
MANGTHATURAT	1816–1837
SUKSOEM	1837–1850
CHANTHARAT	1850–1870
OUN KHAM	1870–1891
SAKARIN	1891–1904
SISAVANG VONG	1904–?

VIETNAM

The Tran Dynasty

TRAN THAI-TON	1225–1258
TRAN THANH-TON	1258–1278
TRAN NHON-TON	1278–1293
TRAN ANH-TON	1293–1314
TRAN MINH-TON	1314–1329
TRAN HIEN-TON	1329–1341
TRAN DU-TON	1341–1369
DUONG NHUT-LE	1369–1370
TRAN NGHE-TON	1370–1372
TRAN DUE-TON	1372–1377
TRAN DE-HIEN	1377–1388
TRAN THUAN-TON	1388–1398
TRAN THIEU-DE	1398–1400

Later Le Dynasty

LE LOI	1418–1420
LE NGA	1420–1426
TRAN CAO	1426–1428
LE THAI-TO	1428–1433
LE THAI-TON	1433–1442
LE NHON-TON	1442–1459
LE NGHI-DAN	1459–1460
LE THANH-TON	1460–1497
LE HIEN-TON	1497–1504
LE TUC-TON	1504
LE UI-MUC DE	1504–1509
LE TUONG-DUC DE	1509–1516
LE CHIEU-TON	1516–1522

Later Le Dynasty
(continued)

Le Hoang-De-Xuan	1522–1527
Le Trang-Ton	1533–1548
Le Trung-Ton	1548–1556
Le Anh-Ton	1556–1573
Le The-Ton	1573–1597
Nguyen Duong-Minh	1597
Nguyen Minh-Tri	1597–1599
Le Kinh-Ton	1599–1619
Le Thanh-Ton	1619–1643
Le Chan-Ton	1643–1649
Le Thanh-Ton	1649–1662
Le Huyen-Ton	1662–1671
Le Gia-Ton	1671
Le Hi-Ton	1671–1705
Le Du-Ton	1705–1729
Le De Duy-Phuong	1729–1732
Le Thuan-Ton	1732–1735
Le I-Thon	1735–1740
Le Hien-Ton	1740–1786
Le Man Hoang-De	1786–1804

The Mac Dynasty

Mac Dang-Dung	1527–1530
Mac Dang-Doanh	1530–1540
Mac Phuc-Hai	1540–1546
Mac Phuc-Nguyen	1546–1562
Mac Mau-Hop	1562–1592
Mac Toan	1592
Mac Kinh-Chi	1592–1593
Mac Kinh-Cung	1593–1623
Mac Kinh-Khoan	1623–1638
Mac Kinh-Hoan	1638–1677

The Trinh Dynasty of Tongking

Trinh Kiem	1539–1569
Trinh Coi	1569–1570
Trinh Tong	1570–1623
Trinh Trang	1623–1657
Trinh Tac	1657–1682
Trinh Con	1682–1709
Trinh Cuong	1709–1729
Trinh Giang	1729–1740
Trinh Dinh	1740–1767
Trinh Sam	1767–1782
Trinh Can	1782
Trinh Khai	1782–1786
Trinh Phung	1786–1787

Tay Son Dynasty

Nguyen Van Nhac	1778–1793
Nguyen Van-Hue	1788–1792
Nguyen Quang-Toan	1792–1802

Nguyen Dynasty of Hue

Nguyen Hoang	1558–1613
Nguyen Phu-Nguyen	1613–1635
Nguyen Phuc-Lan	1635–1648
Nguyen Phuc-Tan	1648–1687
Nguyen Phuc-Tran	1687–1691
Nguyen Phuc-Chu	1691–1725
Nguyen Phuc-Chu	1725–1738
Nguyen Phuc-Khoat	1738–1765
Nguyen Phuc-Thuan	1765–1778
Nguyen Phuc-Anh	1778–1802
Gia-Long	1802–1820
Minh-Mang	1820–1841
Thieu-Tri	1841–1848
Tu-Duc	1848–1883
Nguyen Duc Duc	1883
Nguyen Hiep-Hoa	1883
Kien-Phuc	1883–1884
Ham-Nghi	1884–1885
Dong-Khanh	1885–1889
Thanh-Khai	1889–1907
Duy-Tan	1907–1916
Khai-Dinh	1916–1925
Bao Dai	1926–1945

*Indicates a separate alphabetical entry.

as far west as India and indirectly with the Mediterranean Sea. Raw materials, especially metals such as tin, gold, and iron ore, were imported and processed here. The earliest writing in Southeast Asia has been discovered on this site, but it is in the form of short inscriptions in Hindu script and does not provide any true historical information.

Further up the Mekong River, the site of Angkor Borei provides various pieces of evidence suggesting the possible location of a political capital for the Funan kingdom. In the seventh century, Chinese sources suggest that Funan broke into two kingdoms, Land and Water Zhenla, and that Land Zhenla defeated Water Zhenla, which subsequently disappeared. As a result, the center of political power in what is now Cambodia shifted from the lower Mekong to the Tonle Sap area. Historians have noted that this account poses numerous problems and may not be entirely accurate. The fact is that the lower Mekong was no longer an important locus of political or economic power after the early seventh century, whereas northwestern Cambodia became the center of one of the most powerful Southeast Asian kingdoms in history, subsequently known as Angkor.

Another Southeast Asian kingdom (the name of which is unknown) enters history in the fourth century. A set of inscriptions commemorating sacrifices to Hindu gods erected in the Kutai region of east Borneo seem to suggest a kingdom that flourished briefly in this region but that quickly lapsed back into comparative obscurity.

The first known kingdom in Java appeared in the fifth century. Several inscriptions in the area of Jakarta and Bogor commemorate the existence of Tarumanegara (r. ca. 400s), a king who appears to have been interested in the Hindu god Vishnu. Chinese records from around the same period report the arrival of the first known diplomatic embassies from Java. The kingdom's center was located in the hinterland, perhaps in the environs of modern Bogor, but it also controlled a stretch of coast that enabled it to maintain maritime contact with distant countries.

On the Malay Peninsula, no names of early kings are recorded, but the oldest inscriptions, from the fifth century, mention a "Red Earth Land" from which Buddhist sea captains set out to sail to South Asia. These inscriptions come from Kedah, northwest Malaysia, but the location of Red Earth Land and its political status are unknown.

The first inscription in the Mon language appeared around 600. The name of one early Mon kingdom in the region of central Thailand was Dvaravati. Little is known of the nature or extent of this state, however. There were probably several kingdoms in the Chao Phraya valley during the late first millennium.

In the late seventh century, the kingdom of Srivijaya appeared in southern Sumatra. Srivijaya's capital was located in the environs of modern Palembang, and the kingdom is sometimes known as Srivijaya-Palembang. Srivijaya left several inscriptions dating from 682 to 686, both around Palembang and in other places in central and southern Sumatra.

Srivijaya's inscriptions are written in Old Malay, mixed with numerous terms in Sanskrit. The religion of the kingdom's rulers was Buddhism of a type that has been termed Mahayana, Northern, or Esoteric Buddhism. Statues of Buddhist *bodhisattvas* have been discovered at Palembang, along with images of Buddha and deities such as Shiva and Ganesha. A Vishnu statue found on the island of Bangka just off southern Sumatra suggests that this deity was also popular there before the emergence of Srivijaya.

AUTHORITY IN EARLY SOUTHEAST ASIAN STATES

The kingdom termed itself Srivijaya *mandala* (literally "circle"; figuratively a magical diagram describing the disposition of deities in patterns with mystical significance). The concept of the *mandala* was extremely influential in early Southeast Asian states. It seems that the rulers sought to portray themselves as the *cakravartin*, the supreme ruler analogous to the deity occupying the central place in a *mandala*. Subordinate rulers surrounded him, autonomous in many respects but whose glory was dimmed by the radiance of the figure at the center. By replicating the structure of the macrocosm implied by the *mandala* pattern, the ruler would ensure harmony and prosperity in his own domain.

Thus, the practical authority of the central ruler was generally confined to the domain around his capital. More distant subordinate rulers may have been forced or threatened to declare vassalage to him, but their subjugation mainly required them to attend court on certain occasions to perform ceremonial obeisance, and to pay certain taxes and services to the central power. Otherwise, they governed their own domains more or less in the same manner as the supreme ruler governed his.

In Cambodia, the early rulers seem to have derived their authority from the ability to mobilize labor for constructing water retention systems or ponds. These early chiefs, called *poñ,* were replaced during the seventh and eighth centuries by rulers with different titles and probably different functions and attributes. Water symbolism no doubt remained significant to the continued dominance of the elite, however, as evidenced by the huge *baray* (large earthen structure built to retain water) built at Angkor and other satellite sites.

GENDER AND CULT IN SOUTHEAST ASIAN KINGDOMS

Females were important in the calculation of rights to the throne in many Southeast Asian kingdoms. Rival claimants often used their maternal lineage to strengthen their legitimacy. In some cases, females became supreme rulers, both in Cambodia and later in Java and Sumatra. This was not common, however. Rather, the role of women was to provide a line of descent to which claimants to the throne could appeal in the case of disputed successions. Matrilineal connections were at least as pertinent as, if not more so than, patrilineal relatives. In Cambodia, certain priestly offices also descended in the female line, that is, from uncle to nephew.

The so-called *devaraja* ("god-king") cult of Southeast Asia has aroused much controversy. This phenomenon is mainly known through the Sdok Kak Thom inscription of 1052. Many scholars have assumed that this inscription describes a situation in which the founder of Angkor, Jayavarman II (r. ca. 802–850), claimed to be deified, but later scholars have shown that this is not accurate. By the tenth century, a Khmer ruler did claim to be divine, but this was apparently an innovation, not a continuation of a previous practice. Similarly, rulers in Java did not claim divinity until well after 1000.

Southeast Asian rulers sought to embody several roles—as devotees of certain gods, ascetic adepts, distributors of wealth, and champions in warfare. South Asian martial epics, such as the *Ramayana* and *Mahabharata* of India, were popular in Southeast Asia at an early period, and kings seem to have sought to emulate or embody the qualities of the heroes of these texts.

MARITIME TRADE AND SOUTHEAST ASIAN KINGDOMS

Southeast Asian kingdoms of the ninth through fourteenth centuries shared certain fundamental characteristics, but in other respects, they were quite distinct. The kingdom of Srivijaya and later Sumatran kingdoms, such as Melayu, relied mainly on maritime trade for prosperity and as a means of attracting followers in a landscape where the population was always sparse. In agrarian societies. where the population was less mobile, rulers could be more authoritarian. In early Burma and Cambodia, coinage, which had existed from the fifth century, was eventually abolished. The economies of these kingdoms seem to have been run strictly by royal command, whereby basic commodities were collected and redistributed by the administration. This made it possible to erect large monumental complexes. In Java, by contrast, though intensive agriculture was practiced, a maritime orientation also existed, and coinage of gold and silver evolved. In the thirteenth and fourteenth centuries, the local coinage was replaced by imported Chinese copper coins, which was more efficient in small-scale transactions.

By the eighth century, Southeast Asian kingdoms attained a general form that they would retain for the next 500 years, marking the so-called Classical period. Then, in the fourteenth century, new religions began to gain adherents in the region—Theravada Buddhism on the mainland and Islam on the islands. At this time, the traditional kingdoms of Southeast Asia entered a period of flux that continued until the first Europeans arrived in the region in 1509.

See also: BANGKOK KINGDOM; CAMBODIAN KINGDOMS; CHAMPASSAK KINGDOM; CHIANGMAI; JANGGALA KINGDOM; JAVAN KINGDOMS; MAJAPAHIT EMPIRE; MINANGKABAU KINGDOM; NANCHAO KINGDOM; PANJALU KINGDOM; SAMUDERA-PASAI; SUKHOTHAI KINGDOM.

FURTHER READING

Coedés, George. *The Indianized States of Southeast Asia.* Ed. Walter F. Vella; trans. Susan Brown Cowing. Canberra: Australian National University Press, 1975.

Hall, D.G.E. *A History of South-East Asia.* 3rd ed. New York: St. Martin's Press, 1981.

Reid, Anthony. *Charting the Shape of Modern Southeast Asia*. Singapore: Institute of Southeast Asian Studies, 2000.

SPANISH MONARCHIES

(1516 C.E.–Present)

Kingdoms and dynasties in Spain since the unification of the various Iberian kingdoms in the early sixteenth century.

The marriage of Isabella I of Castile (r. 1474–1504) and Ferdinand of Aragón (r. 1479–1516) in 1474 laid the foundations for the unification of the various kingdoms that existed in the Spanish portion of the Iberian Peninsula. The future of a unified kingdom of Spain was assured when their grandson, Charles, assumed the throne in 1516 as Charles I (r. 1516–1556). A member of the Habsburg dynasty through his paternal grandfather, Emperor Maximilian I (r. 1493–1519), Charles also inherited the Imperial Crown of the Holy Roman Empire, becoming Emperor Charles V (r. 1519–1558) in 1519.

HOUSE OF HABSBURG

Charles V was the first Habsburg monarch of the kingdom of Spain, which included the kingdoms of Castile, Aragón, and Navarre. In 1556, Charles gave the throne to his son, Philip, and later retired to a monastery, though he continued to take an active interest in politics. During Charles's reign, the Spanish kingdom greatly expanded as a result of its discoveries and colonizing activities in the Americas.

Philip II ruled not only Spain but also Naples and Sicily (r. 1554–1598) and Portugal (r. 1580–1598), as well as the Low Countries (present-day Belgium and the Netherlands). Philip's rule was notable for many things, including the Spanish Inquisition, the defeat of the great Spanish Armada while attempting to invade England, and the revolt of the Netherlands, which led to that country's independence. His greatest military success was in Portugal. As grandson of King Manuel I of Portugal (r. 1495–1521), Philip was recognized as the new Portuguese ruler when King Henry of Portugal (r. 1578–1580) died without an heir in 1580.

Upon the death of Philip II in 1598, Spain and Portugal were passed to his son and grandson, Philip III (r. 1598–1621). During his reign, Spain became

SPANISH MONARCHS

House of Habsburg

CHARLES I	1516–1556
PHILIP II*	1556–1598
PHILIP III	1598–1621
PHILIP IV	1621–1665
CHARLES II	1665–1700

House of Bourbon

PHILIP V	1700–1724
LOUIS I	1724
PHILIP V (AGAIN)	1724–1746
FERDINAND VI	1746–1759
CHARLES III	1759–1788
CHARLES IV	1788–1808
FERDINAND VII	1808

House of Bonaparte

JOSEPH NAPOLEON	1808–1814

House of Bourbon

FERDINAND VI	1814–1833
ISABELLA II	1833–1868
INTERREGNUM	**1868–1870**

House of Savoy

AMADEUS I	1870–1873
(FIRST REPUBLIC	1873–1874)

House of Bourbon

ALFONSO XII	1874–1886
ALFONSO XIII	1886–1931
(SECOND REPUBLIC	1931–1939)
(SPANISH STATE	1939–1975, DICTATORSHIP)
JUAN CARLOS	1975–PRESENT

*Indicates a separate alphabetical entry.

The palace and monastery complex of San Lorenzo de El Escorial near Madrid was built in the 1500s by King Philip II of Spain. This masterpiece of austere classical Spanish Renaissance architecture contains a church, royal apartments, monastery, library, and crypt for Spanish kings.

involved in the Thirty Years War (1618–1648). His son and successor, Philip IV (r. 1621–1665), preferred to leave the affairs of state to others, as his father had done before him. During his reign, Spain continued its involvement in the Thirty Years War, and the monarchy also faced further unrest in the Netherlands and had to deal with the revolt of Portugal and Catalonia.

The last Habsburg ruler of Spain was Charles II (r. 1665–1700), who was both physically and mentally disabled. His mother, Mariana of Austria, served as regent, but her sympathy to Austria was very unpopular in Spain. Charles, who was childless, designated Philip of Anjou as his heir, an action that precipitated the War of the Spanish Succession (1701–1714) as various claimants all vied for the throne of Spain. The war ended with the Peace of Utrecht in 1714, and Philip of Anjou retained the Spanish throne as King Philip V (r. 1700–1724).

HOUSE OF BOURBON

The Peace of Utrecht confirmed the House of Bourbon as the ruling family of Spain. However, Philip V's kingdom had been severely contracted as a result of the war. The Spanish Netherlands, Sardinia, Milan, Naples, and Sicily had all been lost, while Spain's supremacy as a colonial power was in decline. Nevertheless, Philip V waged successful dynastic wars that won back Naples and Sicily for his son Don Carlos and gained Parma and Piacenza in Italy for another son, Philip.

Don Carlos of Bourbon ascended the throne as Charles III (r. 1759–1788) in 1759, following the death of his half-brother, Ferdinand VI (r. 1746–1759). Regarded as one of the greatest Bourbon kings of Spain, Charles instituted a variety of economic and administrative reforms in the kingdom.

Charles IV (r. 1788–1808), the son and successor of Charles III, was forced to abdicate the throne by the European conquests of Napoleon Bonaparte. Napoleon also forced Charles's heir, Ferdinand VII (r. 1808, 1814–1833) into abdicating. Both monarchs were imprisoned in France while Napoleon's brother Joseph Napoleon ruled on his behalf. In 1814, Ferdinand VII was restored to the throne after Napoleon abdicated his rule in France and fled to exile to the island of Elba.

ROYAL PLACES

EL ESCORIAL

In 1557, Philip II won a victory over the French at Saint-Quentin on August 10, the feast of St. Lawrence. To thank the saint for his victory, Philip vowed to build a magnificent palace and monastery complex. Work was begun in 1563 under the supervision of architect Juan Bautista de Toledo. The church was consecrated in 1586, and the pantheon, or royal crypt, was completed in 1654. Located northeast of Madrid, El Escorial is both an architectural gem and a treasure house of Spanish history and art reflecting the power and wealth of Spain's Habsburg monarchs.

In 1812, during the Napoleonic invasions, the Spanish Cortes, or parliament, had introduced a liberal constitution. One of Ferdinand VII's first actions after being restored to the throne in 1814 was to rescind this constitution, greatly angering many people in Spain. Numerous uprisings followed, and in 1820, Ferdinand restored the constitution. However, in 1823, with the assistance of France, Ferdinand again quashed the constitution in favor of more conservative rule.

Disregarding the tradition of male inheritance, Ferdinand designated his only child, Isabella, as his heir, instead of his brother, Don Carlos. The accession of Isabella II (r. 1833–1868) sparked the so-called Carlist Wars, a civil war pitting the supporters of Don Carlos against those of Isabella.

Deposed in 1868, Isabella II went into exile in France, and two years later, in 1870, she abdicated in favor of her son, Alfonso. In the meantime, however, the Cortes had established a constitutional monarchy and chose Duke Amadeus of Savoy as king. Amadeus I (r. 1870–1873) ruled for only three years before being replaced by the rightful Bourbon heir, Alfonso XII (r. 1874–1886) the son of Isabella II.

A popular king, Alfonso XII ruled eleven years before dying in a cholera epidemic. His pregnant wife, Maria Christina, served as regent during the minority of their son, Alfonso XIII (r. 1886–1931). Alfonso came to the throne at the age of eighteen. Although he was personally popular, by this time the monarchy had become the target of social agitators and several attempts were made to assassinate the king.

Unhappy with Spain's parliamentary government, Alfonso XIII supported General Miguel Primo de Rivera in establishing a military dictatorship in 1923. In 1931, a year after Rivera lost power, Alfonso went into exile in Italy after realizing that a majority of Spaniards favored a republic rather than a monarchy. Yet, shortly before Alfonso died in 1941, he designated his son, Don Juan de Bourbón, as his successor.

The Spanish republic, which lasted from 1931 to 1939, was ultimately ended by the Spanish Civil War (1936–1939), which was followed by the long dictatorship of General Francisco Franco. From his exile in Italy, Don Juan, along with monarchist supporters, arranged for his son, Prince Juan Carlos, to be placed under Franco's supervision in the hopes that the monarchy would eventually be restored.

Juan Carlos thus went to live in Spain and was educated at Spanish military academies and the University of Madrid. In 1969, Franco named the prince to be his successor, and after Franco's death in 1975, Juan Carlos took the throne. His accession restored the Bourbon dynasty to the Spanish throne, and he presided over a peaceful transition in Spain from dictatorship to a democratic, constitutional monarchy.

See also: ARAGÓN, KINGDOM OF; BOURBON DYNASTY; CASTILE, KINGDOM OF; CHARLES V; FERDINAND II AND ISABELLA I; HABSBURG DYNASTY; JUAN CARLOS; PHILIP II.

FURTHER READING

Carr, Raymond, *Spain, 1808–1975*. Oxford: Clarendon Press, 1982.

Sparta, Kingdom of

(ca. 900–100 b.c.e.)

Ancient city-state centered in Sparta in the Peloponnesian region of Greece that was known for its militaristic discipline and rigid social structure. Throughout much of its history, Sparta was a rival of Athens.

FOUNDING OF SPARTA

Sometime around 900 b.c.e., several villages in Laconia, a region in the southern part of the Peloponnesus, united to form the city of Sparta. By 730 b.c.e., the Spartans had conquered the remaining Laconians, whom they called *Perioikoi. Perioikoi* could serve in the Spartan army, but they did not have the full privileges of Spartan citizenship, such as a voice in assemblies.

After control of Laconia was complete, Sparta, under the leadership of King Theopompus (r. ca. 720–675 b.c.e.), began the First Messenian War, which resulted in the conquest of the neighboring territory of Messenia. Theopompus allotted Messenian land among the Spartans, who then used profits from the land for their support, giving them time to pursue their military training more fully. The Messenians were enslaved to work the land. There were so many slaves, called helots, that they formed the majority of the population of Sparta.

SPARTAN LAW AND GOVERNMENT

According to tradition, about the time Sparta completed its conquest of Messenia, a legendary king called Lycurgus set out to reform the Spartan government with a new constitution. Under the new laws, each citizen of Sparta was equal, but citizenship applied only to those individuals of Spartan descent who were capable of bearing arms.

The laws of Lycurgus also regimented every aspect of Spartan life. Lifelong military training was required, with boys being placed in military camps at the age of seven. Men and women lived virtually separate lives; the men resided in barracks, where their simple meals were eaten at common messes. All citizens, male and female, were required to abide by a code of absolute obedience to the laws.

Spartan women were expected to produce healthy children in order to perpetuate the state. Babies thought too frail were left exposed on a mountaintop to die. Weakness of any sort was not tolerated in Spartan society. Sparta also forbade foreign travel and was suspicious of visitors, fearing the possible corruption of Spartan values.

Spartan government consisted of a dual monarchy (two kings at the same time), a council of aristocrats, and an assembly of citizens. After Lycurgus's reforms were put in place, a council of five officials called *ephors* was elected each year. Citizens elected as *ephors* had judicial powers that included bringing other officials to trial and imposing the death sentence on non-Spartans; they served only once on the council. The assembly of citizens, all male Spartans over the age of thirty, elected all council members and the *ephors* and had the responsibility for declaring war and approving royal decisions.

SPARTANS AT WAR

Spartan society centered around military life, and wars were frequent in its history. The Messenian helots revolted in the Second Messenian War (ca. 650–630 b.c.e.), winning a significant victory at the battle of Senyclarus. Even though the Spartans were superior soldiers to the Messenians, it took Sparta nineteen years to defeat their opponents and enslave them again. Another lengthy conflict, the Tegean War (ca. 575–555 b.c.e.), resulted in the city-state of Tegea becoming a Spartan vassal, required to supply troops to Sparta and to follow Spartan policy, but remaining a sovereign kingdom.

Throughout the sixth century b.c.e., Sparta developed alliances that became known as the Peloponnesian League, an organization of Greek city-states that contributed up to two-thirds of the troops under Spartan leadership. The League played a major role in Greek affairs, especially when the city-states were faced with invasions by the Persians in the Greco-Persian Wars (ca. 490–479 b.c.e.).

During the wars with Persia, Sparta's reputation as a military power earned it the command of the land defense of Greece. Perhaps its most famous action was the defense of Thermopylae, a coastal pass that the Persians had to traverse to reach southern Greece. In 480 b.c.e., a group of about three hundred Spartans, along with other Greek forces, defended Thermopylae against a huge Persian force numbering in the thousands. The Spartans held off the Persians for days before they were routed, giving other Greek forces time to prepare for war and eventually defeat the Persians.

Although Sparta and Athens were allies in the Persian Wars, there was a long history of divisions between the two city-states. This division eventually resurfaced in open conflict between them. In 431 B.C.E., the long and debilitating Peloponnesian War began, pitting Sparta against Athens and its allies. Although Sparta was victorious, both it and Athens were irreparably damaged, and for the next century, Greece remained divided and at war with itself.

During the fourth century B.C.E., Sparta, and all of Greece, faced another threat from outside forces: the Macedonian armies of Philip II (r. 359–336 B.C.E.) and of his son Alexander III, the Great (r. 336–323 B.C.E.). By the time of Alexander's death in 323 B.C.E., the Greek city-states were so weakened that they never regained their dominance. During the next few centuries, Sparta attempted but failed to regain its former glory, existing as just a minor Greek city-state. In the second century C.E., Sparta and the rest of Greece was absorbed by the Roman Empire, and the Visigoths destroyed the city of Sparta itself in 396.

See also: ATHENS, KINGDOM OF; MYCENAEAN MONARCHIES; PERSIAN EMPIRE; ROMAN EMPIRE; TROJAN KINGDOM.

FURTHER READING
Cartledge, Paul. *Sparta and Lakonia: A Regional History, 1300–362 B.C.* New York: Routledge, 2001.

SRIVIJAYA-PALEMBANG EMPIRE

(600s–1200s C.E.)

Buddhist kingdom located in what is present-day Palembang and Jambi in southeast Sumatra, which during its height of power, controlled most of Sumatra, part of Java, and parts of the Malay Peninsula, and dominated the Malacca Straits, an important maritime trading route.

First mentioned by early Chinese sources, Srivijaya was identified as a kingdom on the southeastern coast of Sumatra. By the seventh century, it was already active in trade between the Indian Ocean, China, and the Spice Islands in the Indonesian Archipelago. The kingdom probably came to dominate various harbors along the Sumatran coast, as well as the Straits of Malacca, which are located between Sumatra and the Malay Peninsula.

RISE TO POWER
Srivijaya came to dominate the area for two main reasons. First, the southeastern coast of Sumatra had natural harbors, safe anchorage, and elaborate river systems that gave access to the interior. The swamps lining these rivers also offered protection against attack from the coast. The port of Palembang became a major transit center for various trade goods, including local forest products that were sold or exchanged for products from China and India. The southeastern coast of Sumatra also provided the easiest navigational access to China.

Srivijaya-Palembang also rose to prominence because it was able to draw on networks of labor, mainly coastal Malay peoples. These networks were extremely effective in securing strategic sites for maritime settlements as well as in bringing ships to Palembang. Srivijaya-Palembang's success in establishing its status depended largely on its naval supremacy and its ability to subdue potential rivals.

EARLY SRIVIJAYA AND ITS RULERS
In 671, a Chinese monk named I-Ching visited Srivijaya-Palembang while on voyage from China to India. He referred to the capital as a center for Buddhist learning, where a large community of monks resided. While staying at a monastery in Palembang, I-Ching copied and translated various Buddhist texts into Chinese. His account of Srivijaya showed that it was already a center for Buddhist learning comparable to universities in India.

According to an Old Malay inscription, in April 682, a king began a *siddhayatra* (expedition and search for spiritual power) that eventually brought victory, power. and wealth to Srivijaya. The king who commissioned the inscription was probably Jayanasa (r. ca. 680s), who founded a public park near Palembang in 684.

There is little information about Srivijaya-Palembang from this point until 775, when, according to another ancient source, a Srivijayan king sponsored Buddhist sanctuaries on the Malay Peninsula. This king may have been the father of a Sumatran princess who married a Javanese noble of the Sailendra dynasty and bore a son named Balaputra. Balaputra probably fled from Java in the ninth century to become the ruler of Srivijaya. Through him, the Sailendra dynasty came to the throne of Srivijaya-Palembang.

Srivijaya-Palembang probably reached its pinnacle

of power and prosperity during the late eighth and early ninth centuries. Archaeological excavations in the Palembang region have unearthed evidence that economic activities flourished from the eighth through eleventh centuries. Scholars believe that Srivijaya's influence during this period extended from southeastern Sumatra as far as southern Thailand. It is uncertain whether Srivijaya-Palembang remained a cohesive unit throughout these three centuries. Chinese records suggest that Srivijaya's power began to fade in the early ninth century.

DECLINE OF THE SRIVIJAYAN EMPIRE

In the early eleventh century, the Srivijaya-Palembang Empire declined following attacks by the Cola (Chola) kingdom of southern India. The invaders succeeded in capturing the then Srivijayan ruler, Sangramavijayottungavarman of Kadaram (r. ca. 1020s).

Although some scholars suggest that these attacks directly caused the downfall of Srivijaya-Palembang, the invasion might have been only one factor in the kingdom's decline. Other factors may have included the expansion of Javanese power and the spread of Chinese shipping and settlement at rival ports during China's Sung (Song) dynasty. In any event, by the 1200s, Srivijaya-Palembang was no longer a great imperial power. The center of power in the region had shifted to eastern Java.

See also: COLA KINGDOM; JAVAN KINGDOMS; SOUTHEAST ASIAN KINGDOMS.

STANISLAS I (1677–1766 C.E.)

King of Poland for two brief periods (r. 1704–1709, 1736), who was a celebrated advocate for Polish reform and independence during a fifty-year exile in France.

In the 1700s Poland, though technically an independent kingdom, was dominated by its powerful neighbors, Sweden and Russia. The two powers vied for control by supporting rival candidates for the throne. In 1704, the invading Swedish monarch, Charles XII (r. 1697–1718), ordered an assembly of nobles to elect Stanislaw Leszczynski, a member of a prominent family of Protestant Polish aristocrats, as King Stanislas I. Five years later, the superior forces of Russia's tsar, Peter I, the Great (r. 1682–1725), deposed the young ruler in favor of the man he had

replaced, Augustus II (r. 1697–1704, 1709–1733), of the German house of Saxony.

After his deposition, Stanislas settled into a comfortable exile in France, Sweden's ally. In 1726, he married his daughter Marie to King Louis V of France (r. 1715–1774) in order to ensure continued French support for his claim to the Polish throne.

At the death of Augustus II in 1733, Stanislas returned to Poland, buoyed by a wave of antiforeign sentiment. Some 13,000 nobles elected him king by acclamation. But once again, and this time more promptly, the popular monarch was overthrown by force of Russian arms, as a rival assembly of 4,000 nobles met a few months later to choose Augustus III (r. 1733–1763), the son of Augustus II, to be king.

Stanislas now fled to the Baltic port city of Danzig to await French support, but a successful Russian siege of the city forced him to flee from there as well. According to the terms of the peace settlement of 1735, the Treaty of Vienna, Augustus III remained the effective ruler of Poland. However, Stanislas was made duke of Lorraine, which was ceded by Austria to French control, and he was allowed to keep his honorary title of king of Poland.

The exiled ruler set up a small but distinguished court in Luneville, the capital of the Lorraine duchy, surrounding himself with refined courtiers and philosophers. An humane and enlightened ruler, he proved to be a capable duke. Stanislas also maintained steady contact with his native Poland and educated many of his countrymen in local academies. Through his thought and writings, including the book, *A Free Voice Insuring Freedom* (1749), he continued to influence Polish politics and was widely admired for his calls for social and political reform. When Stanislas died in 1766, the duchy of Lorraine passed to the French Crown.

See also: LOUIS XV; PETER I, THE GREAT; SAXON DYNASTY.

STANISLAUS II (1732–1798 C.E.)

Last king of Poland (r. 1764–1795), who was the first fully constitutional monarch in Europe.

Born Stanislaus Augustus Poniatowski, Stanislaus II was a member of a minor noble family related to the powerful Czartoryski family, a relationship that helped him further his career. In 1756, Stanislaus became Polish ambassador to Russia. He was sent to the Russian capital of St. Petersburg, where he became the lover of Russian Grand Duchess Catherine, who later became Tsarina Catherine II, the Great.

When King Augustus III of Poland (r. 1733–1763) died in 1763, Catherine, now the ruler of Russia, used her power to secure the election of Stanislaus as successor to the Polish throne. As a result, Russian influence in Poland grew substantially, and Russia's ambassador to Poland played a significant role in ruling the country.

Stanislaus revealed reformist tendencies in the choice of his coronation name, August, which was a reference to ancient Rome, whose civic devotion had become a model for enlightened Europeans of the time. Most of his reign, however, was marred by squabbling between rival reformist factions, and his attempts to forge an effective constitutional state were hampered by the repeated intervention of both Russia and Prussia.

Stanislaus nonetheless managed to enact some reforms in economic, financial, military, and educational matters. He strengthened the kingdom's central administration, opened public offices to the middle class, reorganized the educational system, and improved the lot of Polish peasants, although he did not abolish serfdom. Stanislaus also was a generous patron of the arts, science, and literature.

In 1768, anti-Russian members of the Polish nobility, angered by Russian influence in the country, united and formed the Confederation of Bar. Two years later, in 1770, these nobles revolted and declared Stanislaus deposed. However, the Russians crushed the revolt, and, in 1772, Poland was partitioned between Russia, Prussia, and Austria, each of which took vast territories from the kingdom.

Between 1788 and 1792, while Russia was distracted by a long war with the Ottoman Turks, the Polish *Sejm* (parliament) passed a series of dramatic reforms supported by Stanislaus. The high point of the reform movement was the adoption in 1791 of a written constitution, the May Constitution, which provided for a parliamentary monarchy.

Russia, viewing a parliamentary monarchy as a threat to its influence in Poland, sought to restore the old system of government. Joined by Prussia, Russia invaded Poland in 1792. This resulted in a second partition of the kingdom in 1793 and left Stanislaus a vassal of Russia.

Two years later, in 1795, the rest of Poland was carved up among Russia, Prussia, and Austria, whose rulers agreed to end the Polish monarchy and retire the Crown. With no power to maintain the throne, Stanislaus had no choice but to abdicate that same year, becoming the last king of Poland. He retired to St. Petersburg, where he died in 1798.

See also: CATHERINE II, THE GREAT.

STEPHEN (ca. 1097–1154 C.E.)

King of England (r. 1135–1154), grandson of William the Conqueror (r. 1066–1087), whose reign witnessed a period of instability and civil war. Although Stephen managed to retain the throne—except for a brief period when his cousin Matilda held it—the repeated challenges to his rule and resulting civil war greatly weakened his power. Many Norman nobles were able to take advantage of this to greatly increase their own power. Stephen's reign is more noted for the disruption of civil life than for any accomplishments.

The son of Count Stephen of Blois and Chartres, and Adela, the daughter of William the Conqueror, Stephen was raised not in Normandy or France, but in the household of King Henry I of England (r. 1100–1135), his mother's brother. Stephen was thus well placed, when Henry I died without a male heir in 1135, to claim the throne of England for himself. However, Henry had a daughter, Matilda, who disputed her cousin Stephen's claim. Although many nobles, including Stephen, had earlier sworn fealty to Matilda as Henry's successor, Stephen was proclaimed king by England's nobles after he arrived in London shortly after Henry's death.

Despite support from the English and Norman nobles, Stephen had difficulty governing, and in 1139, Matilda took advantage of the instability to invade England from France. She had support from King David I of Scotland (r. 1124–1153), who invaded England from the north but was soon defeated by Stephen's forces. Matilda's forces eventually captured Stephen at the battle of Lincoln in 1141. She reigned for a brief time but later was forced to exchange Stephen in order to free her ally and half-brother, Robert of Gloucester, who had renounced his allegiance to Stephen and had been captured soon after Matilda's success at Lincoln. Unable to maintain the throne, Matilda withdrew in 1148 and went to Normandy, leaving Stephen as king.

Stephen's rule was challenged again in 1152 by Henry of Anjou, the son of Matilda and heir of Geoffrey of Anjou. Geoffrey had taken control of Normandy in 1144, giving his son Henry a powerful base from which to challenge Stephen. Henry was unsuccessful in his attempt to defeat Stephen. But under the Treaty of Westminster (1153), Stephen agreed that succession to the English throne would pass to Henry, who became Henry II (r. 1154–1189) when Stephen died in 1154.

See also: ENGLISH MONARCHIES; HENRY II; WILLIAM I, THE CONQUEROR.

STEPHEN I (St. Stephen) (ca. 970–1038 C.E.)

Hungarian duke (r. 997–1001) and first ruler of Hungary to bear the title of king (r. 1001–1038). He is now regarded as the patron saint of the nation.

Stephen was the son of Geza (r. ca. 970–997), duke or prince of the Magyars (Hungarians) of the house of Arpad. At his birth, Stephen was given the pagan name Vajk, but in 985 he was baptized a Christian, together with his father, and given the name Stephen.

In 996, Stephen married Gisela, daughter of German duke Henry II of Bavaria (r. 955–976, 985–995). Upon the death of his father, Geza, the following year, Stephen assumed rulership of the Magyars. However, because the hereditary principle was not yet firmly recognized, he had to fight rival pretenders. To strengthen his rule, Stephen persuaded Pope Sylvester II (r. 999–1003) to have him crowned king in a religious ceremony, probably in early 1001. The actual crown sent by the pope was eventually lost; the existing "St. Stephen's Crown," treasured by Hungarians as a priceless relic, was probably made after Stephen's death.

After consolidating his hold on the Magyar tribes, Stephen settled into a long peaceful reign, which he used to reorganize and centralize his realm. He divided the country into forty counties centered on royal forts, appointing a governor over each. All land not held by freeholders or the Church became Crown property. With two-thirds of tax revenue accruing to the king, Stephen guaranteed royal power for another hundred years, though a rudimentary Senate and Council were already in place.

Stephen I of Hungary was the first ruler of that country to bear the title of king. He united the Magyar people into a single nation and played a major role in Christianizing the country. The patron saint of Hungary, Stephen was canonized in 1083.

During Stephen's reign, the population of Hungary became more stratified. Traditional chieftains and new landowners benefited from strict laws protecting property rights, and most peasants working on their lands became serfs. The inhabitants of royal towns and estates were generally assigned hereditary roles, such as artisan, soldier, farmer, hunter, or vineyard tender. Trade and agriculture expanded.

Stephen invited Western clergy to staff two new archbishoprics, ten bishoprics, and many monasteries (where Latin religious and legal texts were compiled and a Latin alphabet was created for the Hungarian language). Several thousand churches were built at royal command, and most of the population was converted from paganism to Christianity. Stephen's role in Christianizing Hungary led to his canonization as a saint in 1083. Stephen died in 1038 and was succeeded by his nephew, Peter (r. 1038–1041).

See also: ARPAD DYNASTY.

STEWART DYNASTY (1371–1625 C.E.)

Scottish dynasty that began as a family of hereditary courtiers and eventually won possession of the thrones of both Scotland and England. From their medieval origins in the 1100s, the Stewarts guided Scotland through wars, alliances, revolts, the Renaissance and Reformation, and finally union with England.

ORIGINS
The long-lived Stewart dynasty originated in Normandy and came to Scotland by way of medieval England. Around 1136, King David I (r. 1124–1153) of Scotland (of the house of Dunkeld) made Walter Fitz-Alan, an Anglo-Norman knight, his Royal Steward. The Royal Steward was responsible for managing the royal household and was thus among the courtiers closest to the king.

Walter and his descendants took the name of their hereditary office as a surname, and Steward was later changed to Stewart. The Stewart family's prominence rose steadily within the kingdom. In the early 1300s, Scottish monarch Robert the Bruce (r. 1306–1329) rewarded Walter Steward, the sixth member of the family to hold the office, with the hand of his daughter Marjory. Their son Robert, born in 1316, eventually became Robert II (r. 1371–1390), the first Stewart king of Scotland.

THE SCOTTISH THRONE
When David II (r. 1329–1371) of the house of Bruce died childless in 1371, the throne passed to Robert Stewart, who, though his mother Marjory, was the closest male relative to the Bruce line. Despite a promising youth, Robert II ruled ineffectively, and in 1390, shortly before his death, he handed the throne over to his eldest son John, who chose to be crowned under the name Robert III (r. 1390–1406).

Melancholy and left crippled by a horse, Robert III fared little better than his father. In 1406, as relations with England deteriorated, he sent his son James to France for safety. Robert III died in despair shortly after the English captured his son and heir.

James I (r. 1406–1437) began his rule inauspiciously as a prisoner of the English. While in England, he fell in love with and married Lady Joan Beaufort in 1424, after which he was released under the terms of the Treaty of London, which provided for James's release in return for a large ransom.

An accomplished poet and author of *The Kingis Quair* (a story of his captivity in England and romance with Lady Joan), James I ruled competently but made a number of enemies. Assassinated by a group of Scottish nobles in 1437, he was succeeded by his six-year-old son, James II (r. 1437–1460), who was called "the Fiery Face" for his red birthmark.

James II's early life was marked by political turmoil, and he spent much of his reign subduing the powerful and ambitious Black Douglas family. He also reformed the courts of justice and regulated Scottish coinage. James II was killed in 1460 when one of his own cannons exploded at Roxburgh, leaving the throne to his eight-year-old son, James III (r. 1460–1488).

James III had a taste for fine living, to the dismay of some of his countrymen. Yet, his marriage to Margaret of Denmark in 1469 brought both the Orkney and Shetland Isles under the Scottish Crown. James's attempts to make peace with England failed, however, leading to a tumultuous period that ended in an uprising in 1488 supported by his eldest son, in which James was defeated and murdered.

Unlike his father, James IV (r. 1488–1513) possessed a talent for connecting with his subjects. The cosmopolitan monarch (known as "James of the Iron Belt" for the chain he wore around his waist as penance for his role in the uprising that led to James III's murder) was fluent in several languages and was also a skilled administrator who improved judicial procedures in Scotland and encouraged the growth of manufacture. In 1503, James IV married Margaret Tudor, the daughter of King Henry VII of England (r. 1485–1509). This marriage would eventually have great consequences for the Stewart line.

During yet another war with England, James IV died at the battle of Flodden in 1513 and was succeeded by his infant son, James V (r. 1513–1542). Like his grandfather, James III, the child king was subjected to a power struggle among his advisers. However, he ruled Scotland in his own right from the age of sixteen.

James V did much to strengthen the ties of the so-called Auld Alliance, the special relationship between

Scotland and France that was far more than a defensive pact against England, their mutual enemy. The Stewart dynasty stood at the heart of the Auld Alliance. One branch of the family, the Stewarts of d'Aubingy, was influential in the French court and often supplied captains of the Garde Ecossaise (Scots Guard) that protected the French kings. It was the Auld Alliance that led James V to successive marriages to Madeleine of France and Mary de Guise, the daughter of an extremely influential French noble family.

Mary de Guise bore James his only surviving child, a daughter who became Mary, Queen of Scots (r. 1542–1567). When James lay ill and despairing over news of the Scottish defeat by the English at the battle of Solway Moss in 1542, he was heard to say of his dynasty: "It came with a lass and it will pass with a lass," referring to Marjory Bruce and his baby daughter, Mary.

Mary, Queen of Scots was not the last of the Stewart dynasty, however, although she was the last Stewart monarch to rule just Scotland. Mary's life was as eventful and ill-fated as those of her Stewart forebears—from an early marriage to the French crown prince, which brought the Auld Alliance to the brink of union to her execution in England in 1587 on the grounds of conspiring in plots to murder the English queen, Elizabeth I (r. 1558–1603).

Years before her execution, however, Mary had given up the Scottish throne because of religious conflicts in the country and scandal in her court. Faced with a loss of public support, she abdicated the throne in 1567 in favor of her infant son, who became James VI (r. 1567–1625)

THE ENGLISH THRONE

It was through Mary, Queen of Scots that the Stewarts rose to the throne of England. When Queen Elizabeth I of England died in 1603, Mary's son, James VI of Scotland, claimed the English throne on the basis of his descent from Margaret Tudor of England, his great-grandmother and the daughter of Henry VII. The so-called Union of Crowns in 1603 brought the Stewart king to the throne of England. From that point forward, the dynasty was known by the French spelling favored by both James and his mother: Stuart.

See also: DAVID I; ELIZABETH I; JAMES I OF ENGLAND (JAMES VI OF SCOTLAND); MARY, QUEEN OF SCOTS; ROBERT I (ROBERT THE BRUCE); SCOTTISH KINGDOMS.

FURTHER READING

Lynch, Michael. *Scotland: A New History.* London: Pimlico, 1992.

Mackie, John Duncan. *A History of Scotland.* New York: Penguin, 1984.

Ross, Stewart. *Monarchs of Scotland.* New York: Facts on File, 1990.

STRATHCLYDE KINGDOM

(CA. 400–870 C.E.)

Ancient kingdom that developed in southern Scotland and northern England following the departure of Roman forces from Britain in 368. At its height, the kingdom of Strathclyde covered territory from the capital Ail-Cluathe (Dumbarton) to Wales.

The origins of the Strathclyde kingdom began in the fourth century with the merger of two tribes, the Damnonii and the Votadini. These people were Britons whose language was an early form of Welsh. One of the first kings of the kingdom was Coel Hen (the Old King Cole of nursery rhymes), who ruled around 412. His successor, Ceretic Gulectic (ca. 420), moved the capital from the area of York (or possibly Trepain Law in Lothian) to the northwest. As his people were known as North Britons, the capital was called Dun Breatann, or "fortress of the Britons." Cerectic Gulectic established the royal house of Strathclyde.

The history of Strathclyde is very sketchy, and little is known of its rulers. One of the first mentions of the kingdom appears in early Irish literature, which tells of the battle of Muchramha, in which the Britons of Strathclyde fought against invading Irish forces in the third century C.E. Wars against the Scots, who came from Ireland, and the Picts, the native people of northern Britain, continued through Coel Hen's reign.

The kingdom of Strathclyde lasted until 870, when it was destroyed by Dublin-based Vikings. After the Viking victory, many Straythclyde nobles fled to northern Wales. In 1034, the remnants of these people merged with Alba (the early name for Scotland) to form the beginnings of the later kingdom of Scotland.

See also: SCOTTISH KINGDOMS; VIKING EMPIRE.

STUART DYNASTY (1603–1714 C.E.)

Royal family originating in Scotland that ruled England throughout much of the 1600s, through the English civil war, the restoration of the monarchy, and the eventual deposition of the last Stuart monarch in the so-called Glorious Revolution.

The house of Stuart produced four kings of England—James I (r. 1603–1625), Charles I (r. 1625–1649), Charles II (r. 1660–1685), and James II (r. 1685–1688)—and one queen—Anne (r. 1702–1714). Originally the Scottish house of Stewart, the dynasty held the throne of Scotland from 1371 to 1625. In the sixteenth century, the spelling of the family name was changed to Stuart, reflecting French influences on the Scottish royal court.

FROM SCOTLAND TO ENGLAND

The Stewarts, whose name derives from their hereditary post as stewards or overseers of the royal household, came to England from Brittany in the 1100s. Walter Stewart entered the service of King David I of Scotland (r. 1124–1153) and was thereafter appointed his official steward. In 1371, the Stewarts assumed the throne of Scotland with the coronation of Robert II (r. 1371–1390).

The first Stuart king of England was James I, the son of Mary, Queen of Scots (r. 1542–1567), and Henry Stuart, Lord Darnley. When Mary remarried just two months after the suspicious murder of Lord Darnley in February 1567, she outraged Protestant preachers and many Scots and also alienated many nobles who had supported her. Forced to step down from the throne later that same year, she was succeeded by her infant son James, who became King James VI of Scotland (r. 1567–1625).

The Stuarts came to the throne in England by way of succession problems in that kingdom and blood ties between James and the English Tudor dynasty. The last Tudor monarch of England, Elizabeth I (r. 1558–1603), had no direct heirs. As she approached old age, her choice of a successor became a subject of much speculation.

Eventually, through a fortuitous set of circumstances, Elizabeth chose James, whose great-grandmother was Margaret Tudor, the daughter of King Henry VII of England (r. 1485–1509), as her successor. Although Elizabeth had imprisoned and executed her rival for the throne—James's Catholic mother Mary, Queen of Scots—James was a staunch Protestant and an ally of Elizabeth. Upon the death of Elizabeth in 1603, James VI of Scotland became James I of England. His succession united the Crowns of England and Scotland, a unification that has lasted to the present day.

TROUBLES ARISE

Upon the death of James I in 1625, his son Charles became the second Stuart monarch of England (and ruler of Scotland). Soon after he assumed the throne, Charles I came into conflict with Parliament over a number of issues, including the power and authority of the king. These conflicts grew into the English civil war, which resulted in Charles being beheaded by the Parliamentary Party in 1649. For the next nine years, England was ruled by Oliver Cromwell, a Parliamentarian leader who assumed the title Lord Protector. When Cromwell's son Richard failed to live up to the office left open by his father's death in 1658, the English eventually invited the Stuarts back to England.

Charles and James Stuart, the two sons of Charles

The Stuart Dynasty ruled England during a turbulent period of the nation's history, including struggles between king and Parliament and the clash between Catholicism and Protestantism. Charles II, shown in this portrait, was restored to the throne in 1660 after the 11-year Interregnum, during which England was without a monarch.

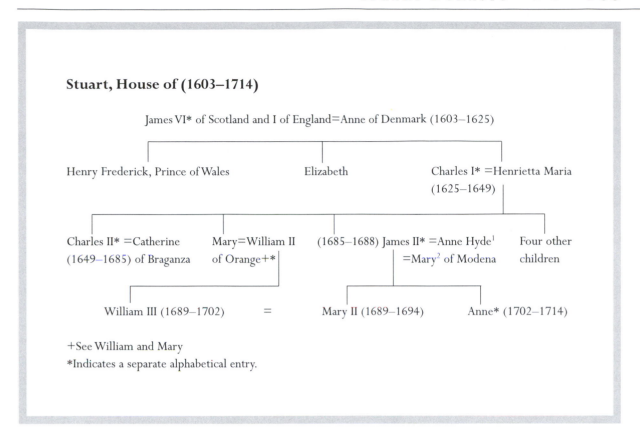

Stuart, House of (1603–1714)

James VI* of Scotland and I of England=Anne of Denmark (1603–1625)

Henry Frederick, Prince of Wales   Elizabeth   Charles I* =Henrietta Maria
(1625–1649)

Charles II* =Catherine   Mary=William II   (1685–1688) James II* =Anne Hyde[1]   Four other
(1649–1685) of Braganza   of Orange+*   =Mary[2] of Modena   children

William III (1689–1702)   =   Mary II (1689–1694)   Anne* (1702–1714)

+See William and Mary
*Indicates a separate alphabetical entry.

I, had been living in France during the so-called Interregnum, the period of Parliamentary rule under the Cromwells. When they were recalled to England in 1660, the oldest son, Charles, took the throne as King Charles II. His reign, known as the Restoration because the monarchy had been restored, was a period of moral laxity and general prosperity. Charles II left no legitimate heirs, so at his death his younger brother James became James II. James was the last of the direct male line of Stuart kings.

James II had converted to Catholicism years earlier. But as king, he promoted religious toleration in England, a necessary policy to appease English Protestants. However, when his staunchly Catholic wife, Mary of Modena, gave birth to a son who might rule as a Catholic, Protestant leaders forced James from the throne in favor of his Protestant son-in-law, William of Orange, the husband of James's Protestant daughter Mary. This bloodless transfer of power is known as the Glorious Revolution.

LAST STUART MONARCHS

William III (r. 1689–1702) and Mary II (r. 1689–1694) held the throne jointly and were succeeded by James's other Protestant daughter, Anne (1702–1714). Anne left no heir, and her death in 1714 marked the end of Stuart rule in England. The next dynasty to occupy the English throne was the house of Hanover. Sophia of Hanover, the wife of German Elector Ernest Augustus (r. 1679–1698), was a granddaughter of King James I of England. Her son, George Louis of Hanover, became King George I of England (1714–1727), the first ruler of the Hanoverian dynasty.

Although direct male descendants of the Stuart line were still alive and holding court in France, they were excluded from the English throne because of their Catholic faith. James II's son, James Francis Edward Stuart, also known as the Old Pretender, attempted but failed to regain the throne for the Stuarts after the death of Queen Anne. His son, Charles Edward Stuart, also known as Bonnie Prince Charlie and the Young Pretender, likewise staged an invasion of Britain in 1745 on behalf of the Jacobites, or supporters of the Stuart line. Although the Jacobite armies made some initial advances, the attempt to regain England failed, destroying the last hopes of a Stuart restoration.

See also: ANNE; CHARLES I; CHARLES II; ELIZABETH I; ENGLISH MONARCHIES; HANOVER, HOUSE OF; JAMES I OF ENGLAND (JAMES VI OF SCOTLAND); JAMES II; MARY, QUEEN OF SCOTS; STEWART DYNASTY; TUDOR, HOUSE OF; WILLIAM AND MARY.

FURTHER READING

Ashley, Maurice. *The House of Stuart: A Study in English Kingship.* London: J.M. Dent, 1958.

Kenyon, J.P. *The Stuarts: A Study in English Kingship.* London: Severn House, 1977.

Lockyer, Roger. *The Early Stuarts: A Political History of England, 1603–1642.* 2nd ed. New York: Longman, 1999.

SUBJECTS, ROYAL

Those individuals under the authority of the ruling monarch or government. In the past, it was generally assumed that subjects owed loyalty to their monarchs in exchange for certain protections and services provided by the Crown. Over time, however, royal subjects began to demand more rights and political powers, which ultimately led to the decline of monarchical forms of government and the formation of democratic ones in their place.

EARLY RELATIONSHIPS BETWEEN MONARCHS AND SUBJECTS

Most historians agree that early forms of monarchical power were largely based on military prowess, wherein those individuals who could maintain the greatest military might became rulers. The earliest societies of which there are written records bear this out. Ancient Egyptian pharaohs, such as Menes (ca. 3100 B.C.E.), the founder of Egypt's First dynasty, were great military leaders, as was Tang (ca. 1520 B.C.E.), the founder of the Shang dynasty in China.

The Ancient Period

The fact that most early monarchs were military leaders suggests that royal subjects were generally indebted to their monarchs for protection and defense. Although subjects in both the Egyptian and Chinese civilizations had many freedoms, their ultimate loyalty was to the monarchy. The fact that many early monarchs such as these also served as religious figures helped to guarantee additional allegiance from their subjects.

Although the tradition of monarchs as military leaders would continue for some time, the widespread allegiance of royal subjects gradually diminished, especially with the democratic and republican ideals of the emerging Greek and Roman civilizations, which prospered until the fifth century C.E. Although several Roman emperors, including Caligula (r. 37–41) and Nero (r. 54–68), notoriously demanded total allegiance from their subjects, none were able to meet the needs of their people, and consequently they had largely unsuccessful reigns.

Feudal Subjects

The obligations of monarchs to their subjects decreased drastically during the feudal era following the collapse of the Roman Empire in the fifth century. As feudal systems invested local lords with considerable power and responsibility, including military defense, royal subjects tended to be more immediately loyal to their local lord than to the monarch. The fact that local nobles were said to be representative of the king guaranteed the allegiance of subjects to the Crown in theory, but in practice this was rarely the case. In twelfth-century Japan, for instance, a feudal lord (or *daimyo*) named Minamoto Yoritomo (r. 1192–1195) grew so powerful that he led his local subjects in an armed overthrow of the imperial government and established the Kamakura shogunate, becoming the first shogun of Japan.

GROWING ALIENATION

The end of the feudal era saw the return of "divine right" philosophies of monarchical power, which supposedly inspired total allegiance from royal subjects. How those subjects actually perceived their obligations to the Crown is a matter of debate. It is true, however, that none of the absolute monarchs of this period, such as King Louis XIV of France (r. 1643–1715), were able to fulfill their obligations to their people in such a way that the Crown did in fact hold total power.

The beginning of the Enlightenment in the eighteenth century saw notions of natural and civil rights gain in popularity, which resulted in diminished feelings of allegiance on the part of royal subjects. The growing political power of the middle class at this time furthered this alienation from the monarchy, as powerful local governments supported by the bourgeoisie (middle class) were now performing many of the services formerly provided by monarchs, such as military protection and public works.

SUBJECTS IN REVOLT

Two major revolutions, the nonviolent Glorious Revolution in England in 1688 and the French Revolution that began in 1789, served to further change the definition of royal subjects. Both of these events stripped considerable political power from the monarchy and transferred it to more democratic bodies, thereby changing the object of subjects' allegiance. In England, for instance, subjects were still said to have obligations to the Crown; however, "Crown" was no longer taken to mean the royal personage, but rather the government and nation as a whole.

As monarchal power waned in the face of emerging democratic forms of government, subjects became less tied to specific monarchs and more committed to the nation as a whole. This led to the formation of modern constitutional monarchies, in which subjects have no real relationship to their monarchs beyond the strictly symbolic level. In most countries with this type of political organization, monarchs have little more actual political power than other individuals in the society.

See also: DIVINE RIGHT; FEUDALISM AND KINGSHIP; MILITARY ROLES, ROYAL; POWER, FORMS OF ROYAL; RIGHTS, CIVIL; TYRANNY, ROYAL.

SUCCESSION, ROYAL

Method by which the Crown passes from one monarch to the next. Most succession is hereditary. Generally, it passes to the eldest son, or, if there is no son, to the eldest female relative, with the male heirs almost always having preference over the females. This practice is called *primogeniture,* and it is still the guiding principle of a number of surviving monarchies today.

LAWS OF SUCCESSION

Beginning in the early Middle Ages, France followed Salic Law, a Germanic Frankish law that did not allow for the possibility of a female succession. The Salic Law came from a code of law written about the time of Clovis (r. 481–511), king of the Salic Franks in northern Gaul. According to Salic Law, a daughter could not inherit property; moreover, no title could be passed through her. Hence, her sons could not inherit. If there were no surviving sons, the Crown would then go to the king's nearest male relative. This practice followed ancient Roman law, in which

women were considered the property of their husbands and fathers.

Some countries follow what is sometimes referred to as Semi-Salic Law, in which all male descendants from all branches of a dynasty have precedence over the female descendants. A female may inherit only if there are no male descendants in any of the dynastic lines. Russia, Austria, and a number of German states observed this practice, and it is still followed in the monarchies of both Liechtenstein and Luxembourg.

Other countries follow what is called cognatic succession, or absolute primogeniture. In this form of succession, the eldest child of the monarch, either male or female, may inherit the throne. The system is still practiced in Norway, Sweden, and the Netherlands.

MATRILINEAL SUCCESSION

Most succession is patrilineal; that is, inheritance passes from the father to the son. Occasionally, however, succession can be matrilineal, in which the Crown passes through the female line, and a king may be succeeded by his brother or his sister's son. Such succession is rare, although the Picts of early Britain are thought to have practiced it in the first through fourth centuries. There is no record of a Pictish son succeeding his father until the last years of the kingdom, at which point the Picts had joined with the Scottish kingdom to fight the Vikings. The change in the rules of Pictish succession may thus have been influenced by Scottish procedures.

Finally, in some societies, such as Poland and some medieval German states, the ruler or monarch can be elected, usually by a representative body. In the case of Poland, members of the ruling dynasty were *domini naturales* (natural lords) from among whom the monarch was chosen. However, this method of selection, by election, is also rare. Poland is one country that practiced it through much of its history. From 1572 onward, candidates for the throne did not have to be from any particular dynasty, and all of the nobility were allowed to participate in electing the ruler. In the seventeenth and eighteenth centuries, however, Poland encountered difficulties with this process, when its legislative body began to vote for foreign monarchs.

REGENCY OR WEAK MONARCHS

The lack of an adult successor can be of particular concern to a monarchy. In such cases, high-ranking nobles are apt to struggle among themselves to serve as regent, or acting ruler, giving them control of the throne until the monarch is old enough or capable enough to rule. Regents may also be chosen to rule while an adult king is absent from the throne because of illness, to participate in military campaigns in foreign lands, or any other reason that leaves the throne temporarily vacant.

Similarly, weak monarchs can also produce chaos in a kingdom, as different factions fight to dominate the ruler. Long-ruling monarchs who are weak may create such serious problems for the kingdom that they may be deposed. Moreover, when a monarch is ousted, problems regarding the succession to the throne are likely to follow, often resulting in civil strife or warfare.

See also: ACCESSION AND CROWNING OF KINGS; BLOOD, ROYAL; DESCENT; INHERITANCE, ROYAL; KINGDOMS AND EMPIRES; KINGS AND QUEENS; REGENCIES; REIGNS, LENGTH OF; ROYAL FAMILIES.

SUDANIC EMPIRES. *See* AFRICAN

KINGDOMS

SUI DYNASTY (581–618 C.E.)

Chinese dynasty that reunited China in the sixth century after more than three hundred years of political upheaval.

The Sui dynasty succeeded the Northern Chou (Zhou) dynasty in the late 500s. For the preceding three centuries, China had endured the so-called Period of Disunion in which no single power controlled the country. In 581, however, a distant relative of the reigning Chou family, northern nobleman named Yang Chien (Jian), deposed the last Northern Zhou ruler, Hou Chu (Zhu), and executed the majority of Chou loyalists. Yang Chien assumed the royal appellation Wendi and founded the Sui dynasty.

At first, Wendi (Wen Ti) (r. 581–604) forcefully consolidated the fragmented Chinese kingdom. In 587 he defeated the armies of the Later Liang dynasty in the Hubei province. Then, in 589, he easily conquered the Ch'en dynasty and captured its capital at Nanjing. Wendi next ensured his control by eliminating all of

the hereditary privileges of the aristocracy, including their claims to land and government positions.

Wendi used an "equal field" system to redistribute his newly acquired land. All land was classified as either personal share land or perpetual holdings. Each household, depending on its size, was given an amount of personal share land to farm. In turn, individual families paid taxes based on the size of their share. Also, to show their gratitude for the land grants, adults were required to work on public construction projects. Each farm was reassessed every three years and could be expanded or decreased. Perpetual holding land was designated for the sole purpose of silk production.

To staff the government, Wendi relied solely on civil service examinations and insisted that promotions be based only upon merit. Three departments, the *sansheng,* oversaw all governmental functions. Under previous dynasties, each province had maintained its own militia, but Wendi organized the national *fubing,* a unified army controlled by the monarchy.

Wendi next initiated several massive public projects, beginning with the erection of a new capital, Daxingcheng. Designed to be the world's largest city, it was not completed during the Sui dynasty. In 584, Wendi began constructing a large canal that would unite western Daxingcheng with eastern China. Finally, he rebuilt the Great Wall to diminish the constant threat of raids from the north and west by the Eastern Turks.

Wendi died from a sudden illness in 604 and was succeeded by one of his younger sons, Yang Kuang (Guang) (r. 604–617). Yang Guang originally had not been named crown prince, but he skillfully denigrated his older brother until Wendi reduced the crown prince to commoner status. Subsequently, Yang Guang ascended the throne in 604 and assumed the royal title Yangdi (Yang Ti).

Sui Dynasty	
WEN TI (WENDI)	581–604
YANG TI (YANGDI)	604–617
KUNG TI (GONGDI)	617–618

Yangdi immediately introduced a number of ambitious policies. He added a new level to the civil service examinations, the *jinshi* degree, which became the most prestigious degree in China for many centuries. He also extended the Sui territory by gaining control over much of the Silk Road, occupying the western Xinjiang province, and conquering northern Vietnam. To help protect his enlarged empire, Yangdi ordered a major expansion of the Great Wall in 607.

Like his father, Yangdi also commissioned huge public projects. Even though the capital of Daxingcheng was far from completion, Yangdi constructed a second, eastern capital at Luoyang. He also erected numerous opulent pleasure palaces. Yangdi then reconstructed the original Grand Canal so that it stretched from Luoyang to Beijing, and he oversaw an enormous development in road building. These improvements established a highly effective infrastructure throughout the sprawling country.

These projects, however, also bankrupted the Sui dynasty both financially and physically. To fund them, Yangdi raised taxes to unprecedented levels. Farmers struggled to pay these burdensome taxes, however, because several seasons of devastating flooding in the Yellow River basin had ruined much of the richest Chinese farmland. Conscription also depleted the population. Over one million peasants died during the expansion of the Great Wall and the construction of Daxingcheng and Luoyang.

Finally, between 611 and 614, Yangdi launched three disastrous expeditions against the Korean kingdom of Koguryo. As a result, a huge revolution erupted in the Sui state and Yangdi was forced to flee to Jiangdu. He was deposed in 617 and assassinated the next year. For two years, Gongdi (Kung Ti) (r. 617–618), a child-emperor, served as the figurehead of the Sui dynasty. The country was ruled by the emperor's regent, Li Yuan, who had been one of the leaders of the revolution against Yangdi. In 618, Li Yuan deposed the emperor, took the imperial name Kao Tsu (Gaozu) (r. 618–626), and established the T'ang dynasty.

Despite the Sui dynasty's brief existence, its accomplishments, such as the new civil service organization and greatly expanded canal system, provided a substantial foundation for the T'ang dynasty and benefited China for centuries. But these accomplishments came at a heavy cost for the Sui emperors. Their young dynasty could not withstand the upheaval caused by such rapid changes.

See also: T'ANG DYNASTY.

FURTHER READING

Bingham, Woodbridge. *The Founding of the Tang Dynasty: The Fall of Sui and the Rise of Tang.* New York: Octagon Books, 1970.

Hansen, Valerie. *The Open Empire: A History of China to 1600.* New York: W.W. Norton, 2000.

SUKHOTHAI KINGDOM

(ca. 1200s–1300s C.E.)

Buddhist kingdom in central Thailand, centered on the city of Sukhothai, which was one of the most powerful kingdoms in the region during its zenith but then quickly declined.

The Sukhothai kingdom rose to prominence with the overthrow of Khmer (Cambodian) control during the early decades of the thirteenth century. Two Thai chiefs brought about its independence by forming an alliance and defeating the Khmer governor of Sukhothai. One of these chiefs, Bang Klang Thao, was crowned king of Sukhothai and ruled as Sri Indraditya (r. 1238–1275).

Indraditya's third son and successor, Rama Khamheng (r. 1279–1317), became one of Thailand's most prominent historical figures. In 1287, Rama Khamheng took a blood oath of sworn brotherhood with Mangrai of Chiangrai and Ngam Muang of Muang Phayao. This marked both the beginning of an alliance among the three subregions of Thailand and the first instance of Thai shared ethnic identity.

Information on the geneology of Rama Khamheng is inscribed on a stele, or stone pillar, dated to 1292. The stele also includes other information pertinent to Rama Khamheng's reign, such as a description of the capital city of Sukhothai. It also describes the establishment, in 1285, of a *stupa* (a Buddhist monument shaped like an earthen mound) in Sawankhalok and the construction of a stone throne at Sukhothai in 1292. Rama Khamheng conquered many towns during his long reign, including Saraluang in the east, Phetchaburi and Si Thammarat in the south, a number of towns along the coast of the Martaban Gulf, and Luang Prabang in Laos.

Chinese court records, *The History of the Yuan*, reveal two diplomatic missions to China during Rama Khamheng's reign—one in 1295, at which Sukhothai presented the Chinese with a gold tablet and white horses with saddles and bridles, and another in 1299. These Chinese records suggest that Rama Khamheng died before 1299, but modern scholars believe his reign ended later.

Unlike Rama Khamheng, his successors, Lo Thai (r. 1317–1354) and Li Thai (r. 1354–1376), were more interested in promoting Buddhism than in conquest. In 1349, the newly created kingdom of Ayuthia launched an expedition against Sukhothai and brought about the submission of Lo Thai. By 1350, Sukhothai had become a vassal of Ayuthia.

In the fourteenth century, Sukhothai attempted to regain its independence. But it failed when the king of Ayuthia, Boromoraja I (r. 1370–1388), led a series of invasions to Sukhothai, culminating in the cession of Sukhothai's western districts to Ayuthia in 1378. By 1438, Sukhothai had ceased to exist as a separate kingdom, having become merely a province of Ayuthia.

See also: AYUTTHAYA KINGDOM; BANGKOK KINGDOM; SIAM, KINGDOMS OF; SOUTHEAST ASIAN KINGDOMS.

FURTHER READING

Gosling, Betty. *Sukhothai: Its History, Culture, and Art.* New York: Oxford University Press, 1991.

Hall, D.G.E. *A History of South-East Asia.* 3rd ed. New York: St. Martin's Press, 1981.

Wyatt, David. *Thailand: A Short History.* New Haven, CT: Yale University Press, 1984.

SULEYMAN I, THE MAGNIFICENT (1494–1566 C.E.)

The most renowned of all the Ottoman sultans, known to his countrymen as Suleyman Kanuni, or Suleyman the Lawgiver, and to the rest of the world as Suleyman the Magnificent (r. 1520–1566).

Suleyman was born in 1494, the son of Sultan Selim I (r. 1512–1520), and became Selim's favorite child and carefully groomed successor. Suleyman inherited the throne in 1520 at age twenty-six, when Selim died en route to a new military campaign. Suleyman upheld the martial tradition of the early Ottoman sultans: thirty of his forty-seven years of rule were spent on military campaigns.

Suleyman was feared and admired not only in his own empire, but throughout Europe and Asia. He captured Belgrade in 1521 and Rhodes in 1522. Suleyman's forces crushed the Hungarian army at Mohacs in 1526, and his territorial gains in Hungary and Austria brought his armies to the gates in Vienna in 1529. The siege of Vienna was unsuccessful, but Suleyman's conquests in Europe, Mesopotamia, and Persia brought the Ottoman Empire to the peak of its geographical expansion. He also expanded the dominance of the Ottoman navy, defeating the combined Venetian and Spanish fleets at the battle of Preveza in 1538. Under the leadership of the admiral Barbarossa, Suleyman's vassal, the Ottoman navy dominated the Red Sea and Mediterranean, attacking the coast of North Africa and the territory of the Holy Roman Empire in Italy.

Suleyman's territorial gains were matched by his domestic achievements. He commissioned a comprehensive codification of Qur'anic and Ottoman law, the likes of which had never previously been undertaken in Islamic history, and therefore earned the name Kanuni, or Lawgiver. He wrote poetry and was a patron of arts, sponsoring the works of the great Ottoman architect Sinan. Suleyman fell in love with Hurrem, also called Roxelana, a Russian girl in his harem. In defiance of tradition and expectation, he married her and remained faithful throughout his lifetime.

Suleyman was ruthless in the preservation of his empire. When some of his advisers, allied with Roxelana, convinced him that his beloved son and heir Mustafa was plotting a coup, Suleyman had Mustafa strangled, as he watched from behind a curtain. Suleyman died on campaign in Europe in 1566, and was succeeded by his son with Roxelana, Selim II (r. 1566–1574). With Suleyman's death, the Ottoman dynasty's height of splendor passed as well.

See also: OTTOMAN EMPIRE; SELIM I, THE GRIM.

During the reign of Suleyman the Magnificent, the Ottoman Empire ranked at the forefront of world powers—militarily, politically, and culturally. A great conqueror feared by Europeans, Suleyman laid siege to the city of Vienna in 1529, an event depicted in this sixteenth-century painting by an Islamic artist.

SULTANATES

Territories ruled by a "sultan," a term that derives from an Arabic root meaning "power." In the Qur'an, the holy book of Islam, the word "sultan" is used to describe spiritual or moral authority over people, but it also came to refer to all forms of governance. Although "sultan" had religious connotations, it denoted temporal as well as spiritual authority, and over time it became essentially a political title. Most Islamic sultans have been Sunni Muslims, members of the majority Islamic denomination. Monarchs of the rival Shi'a, or Shi'ite, branch of Islam, which denies the legitimacy of all but the first four caliphs

after the Prophet Muhammad, generally preferred other titles. A famous *hadith,* or Islamic oral tradition, says that the sultan is "the shadow of God on earth." In Arabic literature, the word "sultan" still carries the meaning of power or government.

Although various early Arab Islamic officials and governors were occasionally referred to as sultans, the Turkic Seljuk dynasty of the eleventh century was the first to regularly use the title for its rulers. The Seljuk sultan Tughril Beg (r. 1038–1063) of Persia was the first to issue coins bearing the word "sultan." Traditionally, only the caliph, the spiritual leader of the Muslim community, was supposed to have the authority to grant kings and princes the right to use the title of sultan. The Abbasid caliph in Baghdad granted that right to Tughril, and after the rise of the Seljuks, "sultan" became a popular title for Muslim rulers. The Seljuks of Rum in Anatolia (present-day Turkey) also used the title, and Saladin (r. 1175–1193), the famous Ayyubid ruler of Egypt, was sometimes referred to as a sultan in literature, although he did not use the title on his coinage.

After the fall of the Abbasid caliphate in 1258, a number of Muslim rulers began to style themselves "sultans." Most notably, the leaders of the powerful Mamluk dynasty of Egypt were called sultans, increasing the status of the title. The most famous sultans, however, were those of the Ottoman Empire. The first three Ottoman rulers were called beys, but the caliph in Cairo named Beyezid I (r. 1389–1402) a sultan, and all of his successors bore the title also. The Ottoman sultans, who used various other titles such as "padishah," eventually claimed the title "caliph" as well, explicitly linking religious authority to the vast political power exercised by the sultans.

In the Ottoman Empire, when the word "sultan" was placed after a name it also meant princess or queen. For example, the mother of the reigning sultan was known by the title of "valide sultan." The powerful example of the Ottomans later led other rulers to adopt the title. It was used by the rulers of Morocco from 1666 to 1957, when they became kings, and also by some minor West African Islamic rulers. Ahmad Mirza (r. 1909–1925), the last shah of Persia, also called himself a sultan. Fuad I of Egypt (r. 1917–1936) called himself a sultan before switching to the title of king.

A parallel usage of the title "sultan" arose among Southeast Asian Muslim princes. Rulers in Sumatra, Java, Malacca, and parts of Malaya and Indonesia governed over sultanates during the seventeenth and eighteenth centuries. Some, such as Sultan Agung (r. 1613–1645), the ruler of Mataram in Java, apparently appealed to religious authorities in Mecca for the right to use the title, in accordance with the tradition of the caliph's authority to define who was and was not a sultan. Others simply assumed the title sultan when they converted to Islam. The most famous remaining sultan is the last of these Southeast Asian sultans, the sultan of Brunei, Hassanal Bolkiah Mu'izzaddin Waddaulah (r. 1967–). The country of Oman on the Arabian Peninsula, ruled by Sultan Qaboos ibn Said since 1970, is the only other country that is still considered a sultanate.

See also: ISLAM AND KINGSHIP; MAMLUK DYNASTY; OTTOMAN EMPIRE; SELJUQ DYNASTY.

FURTHER READING

Goodwin, Jason. *Lords of the Horizons: A History of the Ottoman Empire.* New York: Picador, 2003.
Robinson, Francis, ed. *The Cambridge Illustrated History of the Islamic World.* New York: Cambridge University Press, 1998.

SUMATRAN KINGDOMS. *See* ACHEH KINGDOM; SAILENDRA DYNASTY

SUMER. *See* AKKAD, KINGDOM OF

SUNDJATA KEITA (ca. 1210–1255 C.E.)

Founder and first ruler (r. 1235–1255) of the ancient empire of Mali, which was located in the Sahel region of western Africa. Born of royalty, Sundjata Keita was the son of the king of the Mandinka, a state that paid tribute to the ancient kingdom of Ghana. Sundjata was not assured of the Mandinka throne, however, for his father had several sons, many of whom had greater claim, or greater opportunity to claim the throne.

When Sundjata was only seven years old, his father died and an elder brother became king. This placed Sundjata's life at risk, for his newly crowned brother viewed any male siblings as potential rivals to the throne. To protect her son, Sundjata's mother took him and her other children into exile, spending time in several of the small kingdoms that dotted the landscape of western Africa at that time. They eventually settled in the kingdom of Mema, where Sundjata rose to some prominence in the royal court.

Sundjata's brother, as king of the Mandinka, faced many threats to his sovereignty, for neighboring states envied his wealth and sought to take it for their own. The kingdom of Ghana, to which the Mandinka often turned for assistance, was of little help because it was in decline and struggling with civil war. Sundjata's brother was forced to flee his domain when one of his neighbors, the Soso, conquered the kingdom of Ghana and installed a new ruler, Sumanguru Kante

(r. dates unknown) upon the Ghana throne. Kante claimed Ghana's former subject states as well, including the Mandinka kingdom, and his brutality inspired several unsuccessful revolts by the Mandinka people and other groups.

Seeking a strong leader, the people of the Mandinka kingdom sent emissaries to Mema to beg Sundjata for help. Sundjata assembled an army and traveled back to the land of his birth. In 1235, his forces defeated Kante's army in an epic battle near Krina, on the banks of the Niger River. The victorious Sundjata was then acclaimed king of the Mandinka.

With the defeat of Kante, Sundjata became the most powerful king in the region, and his army was the greatest in western Africa. He invited the leaders of neighboring states to a council, at which he asserted his rule over all, establishing his own state as the successor to the once-great kingdom of Ghana. Thus, Sundjata founded the Mali Empire, which grew to become the largest, most powerful African empire of the time. At its greatest extent, Mali's territory stretched from the fabled trading city of Timbuktu all the way to the Atlantic Coast and from the edges of the Sahara Desert southward to the forests of Ghana.

Sources disagree on the length of Sundjata's rule, but all accounts suggest that it lasted at least twenty years. He established his capital at Niani, the town of his birth. One reason for the success of Sundjata's reign was the wisdom with which he administered conquered peoples. Sundjata allowed his subject states a great deal of autonomy, and he did not attempt to interfere in their customary rituals and practices. His military ensured the peace and guaranteed safe passage along the roads and trails used by traders, thus guaranteeing the free flow of goods to the trans-Saharan caravans from all parts of the empire.

Sundjata converted to Islam during his reign, possibly as a concession to the Muslim traders who dominated the trans-Saharan trade from which Mali gained its great wealth. The manner and exact date of his death are unknown. He was succeeded on the throne by his son, Uli (r. 1255–1270).

See also: GHANA KINGDOM, ANCIENT; MALI, ANCIENT KINGDOM OF.

FURTHER READING

McKissack, Fredrick, and Patricia McKissack. *The Royal Kingdoms of Ghana, Mali, and Songhay: Life in Medieval Africa.* New York: Henry Holt, 1995.

Niane, D. T. *Sundiata: An Epic of Old Mali.* Trans. G. D. Pickett. London: Longman, 1965.

SUNG (SONG) DYNASTY

(960–1279 C.E.)

Chinese dynasty famous for its advances in technology, painting, philosophy, and expansion of the examination system. China reached new heights under the Sung dynasty, leading the world in nearly every category. Advances in Chinese technology were unsurpassed. The flourishing economy introduced the world's first paper currency. Cities blossomed into centers of culture and pleasure where the arts reached new heights. The printing of books created a more educated population, sparking a cultural renaissance and the birth of a new class, the scholar-gentry.

THE NORTHERN SUNG (960–1126)

Five different dynasties rose and fell in northern China in the fifty years following the collapse of the T'ang dynasty (618–907). This time of chaos ended in 960 when Zhao Kuangyin (r. 960–976), a general under the last of these dynasties, the Later Zhou, proclaimed the Sung dynasty, in response to his officers' request that he take control.

This first period of Sung rule, with its capital at the city of Kaifeng, is known as the Northern Sung. Taking the reign name of Taizu, the new emperor reconquered much of China, including the feuding regional kingdoms that had ruled the south since the fall of the T'ang. To prevent further coup attempts, Taizu gave generous pensions to his generals and encouraged them to retire.

Taizu instituted a highly centralized government, giving himself direct control over all areas of the administration. He promoted Confucianism and extended the examination system, which brought more educated men into his bureaucracy. His ministers debated policy openly, the prime minister held real power, and Taizu often deferred to the opinions of his advisers. Taizu was succeeded by his capable brother, Taizong (T'ai Tsung) (r. 976–997).

The first five emperors of the Northern Sung dynasty were all intelligent, conscientious rulers who lived modestly and ruled humanely over a peaceful, prosperous realm. Although their empire enjoyed rel-

Emperor Hui Tsung, the last ruler of China's Northern Sung dynasty, was a patron of the arts. This painting on silk, painted several centuries after his reign, shows Hui Tsung taking part in a festival.

ative domestic peace, it faced constant threats from hostile border states. Militarily weak, the Northern Sung were forced to rely heavily on diplomacy to keep their empire intact. This policy included the paying of tributes to border states to prevent invasion.

Military issues contributed to the Northern Sung's financial difficulties. Defending the empire from its hostile neighbors was expensive, requiring tax increases that sparked public unrest. Hoping to revive the struggling empire, the famous reformer Wang Anshi, chief councilor to Emperor Renzong (r. 1022–1063), introduced a series of controversial economic and military reforms, including compulsory military service and the extension of credit to peasants.

The last emperor of the Northern Sung, Huizong (Hui Tsung) (r. 1100–1126), was a famous patron of the arts whose reign ushered in a great era in Chinese painting. But Huizong spent extravagantly and was uninterested in politics. Financial troubles led him to raise taxes, which led to a rebellion in 1120. In 1127, Jurchen tribes from Manchuria attacked the Northern Sung empire, taking the capital of Kaifeng in 1126 and establishing the Jin dynasty (1127–1234).

Huizong abdicated in favor of his son, but both were soon imprisoned by the Jin.

THE SOUTHERN SUNG (1127–1279)

A Sung prince, Gaozong, eluded the Jin and escaped south to found the Southern Sung dynasty. Gaozong (r. 1127–1162) established a new capital at the city of Hangzhou in the lower Yangtze River Valley. With a weak military, Gaozong opted for conciliation with the Jin, agreeing to pay them a large annual tribute to keep the peace.

Centered on the great city of Hangzhou, the Southern Sung enjoyed a thriving economy. Tariffs on the growing foreign trade, encouraged by the government, filled government coffers. Chinese civilization flourished, surpassing that of the Northern Sung. but the military remained weak. Factionalism at court also plagued the dynasty, as did excessive bureaucracy. The number of regulations and cumbersome rituals mushroomed. In one famous instance, rules concerning the reception of Korean emissaries totaled 1,500 volumes. Moreover, surrounded by hostile states, the Sung were forced to expend large amounts on defense.

Although Chinese civilization blossomed under the Southern Sung, a threat rose in the north as Genghis Khan expanded his Mongolian Empire. In 1234, the Mongols, led by Genghis Khan's grandson Kublai Khan, captured north China from the Jin dynasty. The mighty Mongolian army then swept south, capturing the Southern Sung capital of Hangzhou in 1276. Three years later, the last of the Sung forces were destroyed in a sea battle in which the last Sung emperor, six-year-old Bing Di, was drowned.

A GOLDEN AGE

The period of the Northern and Southern Sung dynasties was an era of unprecedented prosperity, technological advancement, and cultural renaissance in China. Trade flourished, printing spread, and the Chinese enjoyed a high standard of living in the world's largest cities. Patronized by the emperors, Chinese painting reached new heights. As the examination system grew, a new class emerged that would dominate China for centuries.

Trade, Commerce, and Technology

Under the Sung, the introduction of new strains of rice dramatically increased the rice crop, fueling a population surge that contributed to a rapid expansion of cities. Both Sung capitals, at Kaifeng and Hangzhou, grew into thriving centers of culture and trade. Hangzhou, with a population of more than one million, became the largest city in the world at that time. City dwellers enjoyed bustling markets and entertainment quarters with numerous tea shops, restaurants, and theaters.

Throughout China, the standard of living rose. But a dark side of the new prosperity was the spread of foot binding. Made possible by the new ease of living, this practice became very popular during the Sung as a mark of prestige. Young girls' feet were bound tightly with cloth, forcing them to grow deformed into a small, curved shape that was considered feminine.

As Sung cities swelled in size, demand increased for luxuries from abroad. Foreign trade, encouraged by the government, expanded dramatically. Chinese merchants sailed as far as the East Indies, trading Chinese silks, porcelain, copper, paper, and other manufactures for Indian spices and other foreign goods. Taxes on the bustling trade created large revenues for the government, surpassing land revenue for the first time. Domestic commerce also flourished under the Sung dynasty. Rivers and canals were filled with boats carrying goods within the thriving empire. This increase in commerce fueled the demand for currency, prompting the introduction of the world's first paper money.

Sung technology was the most advanced in the world. The Sung dominated the seas with ships that carried up to 500 people and boasted four decks and six masts. The abacus and the compass came into use at this time. Numerous advances in military technology included the catapult and the cannon, and the first military use of gunpowder. Technical advancement extended to industry, with refinements in the production of silks, porcelain, and paper. Advances in metallurgy led to a dramatic increase in iron production.

Scholarship and the Arts

The Sung emperors expanded the Confucian-based examination system, making it a central institution in Chinese life for the first time. The examinations tested knowledge of classical texts and were used to select the most talented scholars for the government bureaucracy. Efforts were made to avoid favoritism to the sons of wealthy families. The increased importance of the examinations in Chinese life led to the rise of a scholar-gentry class that replaced the old hereditary aristocracy as China's elite.

Led by the scholar-gentry, the Sung era was a

ROYAL RITUALS

SUNG LANDSCAPE PAINTING

The art of landscape painting in China reached its pinnacle during the Sung dynasty (960–1279). Patronized by the Sung emperors, painting became a prestigious occupation for the first time. The era's great painters studied at the imperial academy of painting, founded by Sung emperor Huizong (r. 1100–1126). Under Huizong's son, Gaozong (r. 1127–1162), landscape painting reached its height.

Paintings were done on paper and silk scrolls, oriented both vertically and horizontally. The silk scrolls later were unrolled slowly from right to left, allowing viewers to appreciate the unfolding scene in segments. Smaller pieces were painted to decorate fans or for collection into albums.

Sung landscape paintings possess a dreamy, impressionistic quality and often feature mountains, which the Chinese considered sacred. Many of the paintings are quite large, depicting vast landscapes representing nature's magnificence and power. Human figures appear small in these paintings, reflecting the Daoist belief in humanity's insignificance in the cosmos. This attitude contrasted sharply with Western painting, where landscapes were considered mere background until centuries later.

Sung Dynasty

T'AI TSU* (TAIZU)	960–976
T'AI TSUNG	976–997
CHEN TSUNG	997–1022
JEN TSUNG	1022–1063
YING TSUNG	1063–1067
SHEN TSUNG	1067–1085
CHE TSUNG	1085–1100
HUI TSUNG (HUIZONG)	1100–1126
CH'IN TSUNG	1126–1127
KAO TSUNG* (GAOZONG)	1127–1162
HSIAO TSUNG	1162–1189
KUANG TSUNG	1189–1194
NING TSUNG	1194–1224
LI TSUNG	1224–1264
KU TSUNG	1264–1274
KUNG TI	1274–1276
TUAN TSUNG	1276–1278
TI PING	1278–1279

*Indicates a separate alphabetical entry.

time of intellectual curiosity and experimentation. Sung scholars were prolific intellectuals, producing numerous encyclopedias and charting new frontiers in the arts, philosophy, and technology. A cultural renaissance occurred as Sung scholars began to reexamine their own past, studying Chinese history and classical texts.

The study of ancient texts sparked the birth of Neo-Confucianism, a system of thought that would dominate Chinese thought until the twentieth century. Espoused by the scholar Zhu Xi (1130–1200), Neo-Confucianism revived and reformulated ancient Confucian ideas. Zhu Xi's ideas emphasized humane behavior and empirical investigation and became China's central political and ethical philosophy.

Although paper had been developed in China centuries previously, the Northern Sung were the first to print books. As printing spread, books became more widely available. The educated class grew, and more women learned to read and write.

Chinese arts flourished under the Sung. Many Sung emperors patronized the arts, but the most enthusiastic was Emperor Huizong. A skilled painter in his own right, he founded an academy of the arts where artists developed new styles of painting. His massive collection of fine Chinese paintings numbered in the thousands. Under Huizong's son, Gaozong, Chinese landscape painting reached its height. The Sung period is also notable for its beautiful porcelain and for the poetry of Su Dongpo (1037–1101), one of China's greatest writers.

See also: FIVE DYNASTIES AND TEN KINGDOMS; GENGHIS KHAN; KAO TSUNG (GAOZONG); KUBLAI KHAN; T'AI TSU (TAIZU); T'AI TSUNG (TAIZONG); T'ANG DYNASTY; YUAN DYNASTY.

FURTHER READING

Chaffee, John W. *Branches of Heaven: A History of the Imperial Clan of Sung China.* Cambridge, MA: Harvard University Press, 1999.

SUNGA DYNASTY (184–73 B.C.E.)

A short-lived dynasty of the kingdom of Magadha in Central India that was able to stop Greek incursions from Bactria into northern India.

The Sunga dynasty was founded in 184 B.C.E. by a military leader named Pusyamitra of the Maurya Empire of India. Angered that the Mauryan emperor, Brihadratha (r. ca. 194–187 B.C.E.), had failed to stop an invading Greek army under Demetrius I of Bactria (r. ca. 200–185 B.C.E.), Pusyamitra murdered the emperor in 187 B.C.E.

When Demetrius withdrew his forces from northern India soon after because of wars at home, Pusyamitra (r. ca. 187–151 B.C.E.) seized the throne, establishing the Sunga dynasty. The fall of Brihadratha marked the end of the Maurya Empire. India lost the political unity it had enjoyed under the Mauryas and split up into a number of kingdoms.

A militant Hindu, Pusyamitra is alleged to have planned to destroy the teachings of Buddha and to have offered money for the heads of monks of the

Jain religion. However, given the record of religious tolerance in ancient India, it is unlikely that these allegations are true. Moreover, Buddhism flourished during Pusyamitra's rule.

A period of peace and prosperity in the Magadha kingdom allowed Pusyamitra to conduct two *asvamedha,* or horse sacrifices, in which a horse was consecrated and allowed to wander freely for a year. The king would follow with his army, and if the horse crossed into another territory, that territory would have to fight or submit. If the liberation succeeded, the king would return as a hero and be entitled to add the term *cakravartin* ("universal monarch") to his title. If the king failed, he would face ridicule. After one year, the horse would be returned amidst a great festival and would be sacrificed.

Before one such *asvamedha,* the horse was captured by a squadron of Greek cavalry along the banks of the Indus River. After a battle, the Greeks were defeated. It has been speculated that the Greeks were the advance forces of Menander (r. 155–130 B.C.E.), ruler of Bactria (in present-day Afghanistan), who is thought to have led a large foray into central India but was repulsed by Pusyamitra.

According to one ancient historian, Pusyamitra waged war against a Greek ruler for the sake of a beautiful woman and died fighting the Greeks around 151 B.C.E. He was succeeded by his son, Agnimitra (r. ca. 151–143 B.C.E.), who is portrayed as a great hero in the *Kalidasa,* a famous ancient Indian epic.

According to tradition, there were ten Sunga rulers, but scholars know little about those who followed Pusyamitra. The last Sunga king, Devabhumi (r. ca. 85–75 B.C.E.), was murdered by the daughter of a female attendant when she posed as the queen. The mastermind behind the plot, Vasudeva (r. ca. 75–66 B.C.E.), ascended the throne and established the short-lived Kanvas dynasty (ca. 75–30 B.C.E.).

See also: INDIAN KINGDOMS; INDO-GREEK KINGDOMS; KANVA DYNASTY; MAURYA EMPIRE.

SUNNI ALI (d. 1492 C.E.)

Ruler of the Songhai Empire (r. 1464–1492), known for his great energy and leadership skills, who greatly expanded the borders of his empire.

Sunni Ali was born into a powerful Muslim family of the Sunni dynasty, which had ruled the great West African empire of Songhai since the 1300s. By the start of his reign, however, the empire had declined markedly in power and influence, as upstart kingdoms in the region challenged its supremacy. Worse yet, the centerpiece of Songhai, the great trading city of Timbuktu, had been conquered by fierce Tuareg raiders who swept down from the Sahara Desert.

Sunni Ali, believing it his duty to restore Songhai to its previous glory, amassed an army and set forth to conquer the peoples who lived along the Niger River. In time, he succeeded in restoring Songhai rule over a vastly expanded territory. He achieved his greatest triumph in 1468, when he finally reclaimed Timbuktu and ousted the Tuaregs.

Sunni Ali was not welcomed as a hero by the scholars and merchants of Timbuktu, however. Although he was Muslim, the leaders of the city doubted his devoutness. Moreover, Sunni Ali was brutal in his treatment of all those whom he believed were insufficiently respectful of his authority. In a city renowned for its tolerance of the free exchange of ideas, Sunni Ali came to be viewed as a tyrant.

Sunni Ali exceeded even his own initial hopes for restoring the power of the Songhai Empire. Soon the state he created through conquest gathered a greater influence than it had ever known before. But his worldly glory was evanescent. In 1492 (some sources say 1493), Sunni Ali is said to have been riding his horse along the Koni River when his mount missed its footing. Horse and rider fell into the river and both drowned.

See also: ISLAM AND KINGSHIP; MALI, ANCIENT KINGDOM OF; SONGHAI KINGDOM.

SUSENYOS (ca. 1580–1632 C.E.)

Emperor of Ethiopia (r. 1607–1632), who is remembered as a modernizer but whose efforts to break with Ethiopia's traditional religion (Coptic Christianity) eventually led to his downfall.

Born to the ruling family of Ethiopia, Susenyos was the nephew of Sarsa Dengel, who ruled the empire from 1563 to 1597. When Susenyos was still in his teens, Emperor Sarsa Dengel died and the throne passed to Dengel's son, Ya'iqob (r. 1597–1603). At that time, succession to power in Ethiopia was a highly contentious issue, marked by bloody civil wars. When Ya'iqob died in 1607 and Susenyos inherited the throne, the new emperor was determined to institute a more orderly process for Ethiopian royal succession.

Missionaries from the Roman Catholic Church had long sought to bring Ethiopia under the Vatican's influence, and so in 1622 they convinced Susenyos that his conversion to Catholicism offered a greater chance of modernization and political stability for the Ethiopian Empire. Susenyos obligingly officially converted to Catholicism declaring that henceforth Catholicism would become the state religion.

This decision constituted an important breach of tradition, however, because Ethiopia had long been affiliated with the Coptic Church and the patriarch of Alexandria. The Ethiopian people greatly resented this change, but Susenyos ignored them and approved an aggressive policy of Romanizing the church hierarchy and liturgy. Predictably, the people rebelled against such disrespect to the Coptic Church, the faith of their ancestors. The Ethiopian people were further outraged by the brutality with which Susenyos attempted to enforce religious reforms.

Because he was so closely associated with the changes to the Ethiopian Church, Susenyos soon found that his rule had become hopelessly compromised by opposition and dissent. He sought to heal the divisions in his country by abdicating the throne in 1632, handing over the Crown to his son, Fasiladas (r. 1632–1667), who promptly reversed his father's religious reforms and restored the Ethiopian Orthodox (Coptic) Church.

See also: Aksum Kingdom; Amhara Kingdom; Haile Selassie I; Menelik II; Tewodros II; Zara Ya'iqob.

Sussex, Kingdom of

(ca. 477–825 C.E.)

One of several early medieval Anglo-Saxon kingdoms of England, located in what is now the modern county of Sussex in southern England. The name "Sussex" derives from the Anglo-Saxon word for South Saxons, one of a group of Germanic tribes that invaded England in the period following the retreat of the Roman Empire from Britain in the fifth century. The Anglo-Saxons established several small kingdoms that began in Southern England and eventually spread northward.

According to legend, an Anglo-Saxon leader named Aelle landed in England in 477 and defeated the Britons, the Celtic group that inhabited the country. Aelle established the kingdom of Sussex in the south of England and became its first king. No records exist for Sussex from the reign of Aelle until 607. In that year, Ceolwulf (597–611), king of Wessex, is recorded to have waged war against the kingdom of Sussex. Toward the end of the seventh century, the peoples of Sussex were converted to Christianity by Wilfred of York, after his explusion from the kingdom of Northumbria in northern England.

Sussex was one of the least powerful of the Anglo-Saxon kingdoms. In the seventh and eighth centuries, dominion over this region was often not held by a single monarch but was divided among several rulers. In the late seventh century, Prince Caedwalla of Wessex (r. 685–688) invaded the kingdom. Caedwalla was later overthrown by Berhthun and Andhun, two Sussex nobles, who ruled Sussex jointly. In 825, Sussex was conquered by Egbert (802–839), ruler of the more powerful kingdom of Wessex, and was incorporated into that realm. Sussex never reestablished itself as an independent kingdom.

See also: Anglo-Saxon Rulers; Kent, Kingdom of; Mercia, Kingdom of; Wessex, Kindgom of.

Swahili Kingdoms

(flourished ca. 970–1600 C.E.)

A series of primarily coastal settlements along the eastern length of the African continent, founded as outposts to service the Indian Ocean trade routes. Forty towns in all dotted the coastline for a thousand miles from Mogadishu in the north to Sofala in the south, and included settlements on the islands of Zanzibar, Pemba, and the Comoros. In these port cities, gold, exotic woods, iron, ivory, and slaves from Africa were traded for pottery, porcelain, and fabrics from the East.

The name *Swahili* means "peoples of the coast." Swahili settlements share a linguistic tradition (kiSwahili), a religion (predominantly Sunni Mus-

lim), and a founding motive as trade entrepôts, but through most of their history they have maintained independence from one another, never forming anything that could be called a true confederation.

The Swahili people are predominantly ethnic Africans, but these indigenous people intermarried with the traders from Arabia who came in search of ivory, gold, and slaves between the years 970 and 1050. The first settlements to be founded were the more northerly, including settlements on the island of Lamu, off the Kenyan coast. The language is believed to have originated from the Bantu dialect spoken on these islands, with words added as the result of the cross-cultural trade. Around 1100, the Swahili language was recorded using Arabic letters.

Between 1050 and 1200, the established Swahili towns received a new wave of Muslim immigrants who came from the Persian city of Shiraz and called themselves Shirazi. It was during this period that some of the most influential of the settlements located on Pemba, Kilwa, and Zanzibar developed and were ruled by members of the Shirazi dynasty. The Shirazi intermarried with the Swahili and soon families who aspired to high status began to assert claims to Arabic descent, giving rise to a ruling Afro-Arab class and classes of commoners and slaves who were primarily African.

The mainland Swahili city of Mogadishu monopolized the trade in gold for about two centuries. Around 1200, however, Kilwa, which was located much closer to the gold-producing regions near the ports of Oman, appropriated the trade, eclipsing Mogadishu in importance and in wealth.

The Swahili city-states reached the height of their power and influence between the thirteenth and fifteenth centuries. During these centuries, buildings were constructed in the unique Swahili architecture that used elaborate coral and stonework. Portuguese traders arrived in Africa during the sixteenth century and soon began conquering the Swahili trade centers. In the seventeenth century, the Omani sultanate captured the coastal cities of Africa and ruled there for the next two centuries.

See also: Z ANZIBAR S ULTANATE.

FURTHER READING

Middleton, John. *The World of the Swahili: An African Mercantile Civilization.* New Haven, CT: Yale University Press, 1992.

S WAZI K INGDOM

(ca. 1815 C.E.–Present)

Established in the early nineteenth century, the longest enduring kingdom still in existence in the sub-Saharan region of Africa.

The kingdom of Swaziland, located between the Union of South Africa and Mozambique, still retains its monarch, called the *ngwenyama* in the Swazi language. All the kingdom's rulers have come from the Nkosi Dlamini clan, a subgroup of the Nguni people.

The kingdom of Swaziland was founded in the early 1800s during a time of great demographic upheaval in southern Africa. At the time, European settlers from Cape Town in South Africa were moving northward in ever increasing numbers, displacing the indigenous peoples of the region. This migration of European settlers had a devastating impact on the cattle-keeping people of the region, because the lands where their cattle grazed were being taken to create farms for the European settlers.

In response to the encroachment of European settlers, a powerful leader named Shaka Zulu (r. 1816–1828) created a militaristic kingdom, the Zulu kingdom, and led his warriors in raids against his neighbors, both African and European. Zulu warfare, in turn, touched off a series of massive population movements, as people fled from Shaka's violence or formed their own warrior states.

The Dlamini clan of the Nguni, which originated somewhere around Maputo in present-day Mozambique, felt threatened by the violence of the times. Around 1815, the clan's leader, Sobhuza (r. ?–1839), led his people into the mountains in hope of finding greater safety there. Sobhuza then set about creating alliances with the predominantly Sotho peoples who lived in the region. To do this, he arranged marriages between important Nguni and Sotho families. Within a few years, Sobhuza had gained a large enough following to begin waging his own campaigns of conquest. His army became powerful enough to withstand challenges from even the powerful Zulu nation.

Sobhuza died in 1839 and was succeeded on the throne the following year by his son, Mswati II (r. 1839–1865). Because the new king was too young to rule alone, his mother acted as regent until he came of age in 1846. Mswati secured the territorial gains achieved during Sobhuza's rule, and he entered into a cooperative relationship with the British, who were

ROYAL RITUALS

THE POWER OF ANCESTORS

Although Swaziland is nominally a Christian nation, royal rituals invoke elements of Swazi traditional religion, which was powerfully influenced by ancestral cults. Nkosi Dlamini ancestors are believed to be the most powerful of all the ancestral spirits, to whom the ruler may appeal for help in ending drought or to guarantee a bountiful harvest. One of the Swazi king's most important ritual performances occurs annually in December or January. This is called the inKwala (Festival of the First Fruits), during which the king performs a dance of renewal. By this dance, the king draws strength from the ancestors, and through his ritual renewal as an individual, the strength and good fortune of the Swazi people are also renewed.

interested in acquiring the region as a colonial possession. In 1863, Mswati demonstrated his loyalty to the British by attacking an outpost held by the Portuguese, who were Britain's rivals in the region. The British rewarded Mswati by formally acknowledging his sovereignty.

Mswati II died in 1865. The next three Swazi rulers—Ludvonga II (r. 1865–1874), Mbandzeni (r. 1874–1889), and Bhunu (r. 1889–1899)—continued the policy of cooperating with the British, who by this time had became the main colonial power in southern Africa. In return, Swaziland was granted limited autonomy, although it was subordinated to colonial rule.

By the time Sobhuza II (r. 1921–1982) took the throne in 1921, the office of the king had become primarily ceremonial and symbolic. Nonetheless, Sobhuza II was successful in preventing the takeover of more land to colonial settlers, due largely to his skill in diplomacy and negotiations with the British.

In the 1960s, Swaziland joined many other African colonial possessions in demanding independence, achieving it in 1968. Sobhuza II acknowledged the will of his people by creating a constitutional monarchy, patterned on the British system. Upon Sobhuza's death in 1982, his son and successor, Mswati III (r. 1982–present), came to the Swazi throne.

See also: AFRICAN KINGDOMS; SHAKA ZULU; SOBHUZA I; SOBHUZA II; ZULU KINGDOM.

FURTHER READING

Hamilton, Carolyn, ed. *In Pursuit of Swaziland's Precolonial Past.* Manzini, Swaziland: Macmillan Boleswa, 1990.

Kuper, Hilda. *The Swazi: A South African Kingdom.* New York: Holt, Rinehart & Winston, 1986.

SWEDISH MONARCHY

(900s C.E.–Present)

Scandinavian kingdom that has existed from the Viking era to the present day.

The kingdom of Sweden came into being in the tenth century when several small regional kingdoms were gradually consolidated under the rule of stronger leaders. Little is known of this early period. One significant early Swedish king was Olaf Skötkonung or Olaf III (r. 995–1022). In 1000, Olaf became the first Swedish king to convert to Christianity, although the kingdom as a whole was not converted to the Christian faith until the twelfth century.

Through much of the early Middle Ages, the history of the Swedish monarchy was marked by a continual struggle between the Crown and regional interests under nobles with dynastic ambitions of their own. The Swedish monarchy was elective: the people, assembled in a parliament-type body known

King Carl XVI, shown with his wife, Queen Silvia, has ruled Sweden since 1973. The Swedish monarchy, like others in Scandinavia, is constitutional. The king is primarily a ceremonial head of state.

as the *Thing,* had to approve the king, who was usually a member of the royal family. In practice, it was the nobles who elected or deposed kings, and the kings themselves generally attempted to make the Crown hereditary by designating successors within their lifetime and even sharing rule with them. Gustavus I Vasa (r. 1523–1560) was the first ruler who attempted to make hereditary succession the norm.

The three most important dynasties in the history of the Swedish monarchy are the Folkung, the Vasa, and the Bernadotte. The Folkung dynasty (1250–1364), which began with Waldemar I (r. 1250–1275), oversaw a period of increasing centralization in government and Swedish territorial expansion. The last ruler of the Folkung dynasty was King Magnus II (r. 1319–1364), who was briefly deposed by

his son, Erik XII (r. 1356–1359), and then lost Sweden to Albert of Mecklenburg (r. 1364–1389) in 1364. In 1389 Albert was defeated by the forces of Queen Margaret I of Denmark (r. 1387–1396), whose great-nephew Erik XIII became king of Sweden in 1396 with her as regent. In 1397 Sweden became part of the Kalmar Union, of which Erik became sole ruler upon Margaret's death in 1412.

The Vasa dynasty (1523–1654), founded by Gustavus I Vasa, ruled Sweden after the kingdom revolted against the Danes and ended the Kalmar Union. His son Erik XIV (r. 1560–1568) attempted, unsuccessfully, to gain control over the Baltic region, and fought Denmark, Poland, and the Hanseatic League from 1563 to 1570 without making any gains for the kingdom. Erik was deposed by his brother

Johan III (r. 1568–1592) in 1568. Gustavus II Adolphus (r. 1611–1632) of the Vasa dynasty made Sweden into a great military power and was one of the foremost generals during the Thirty Years War in Europe. His daughter, Queen Christina (r. 1632–1654), was the last of the Vasa line, abdicating after secretly becoming a Roman Catholic in an overwhelmingly Protestant country.

During the Napoleonic Wars (1803–1815) Sweden sided with England against French emperor Napoleon Buonaparte. Because of his disastrous domestic and foreign policies at this time, King Gustav IV (r. 1792–1809) was deposed in 1809 and replaced by his uncle, Carl XIII (r. 1809–1818). Sweden also was at war with Russia during this period and, forced to make peace on that front, it ceded Finland, which Sweden had controlled.

In 1810, the childless Carl XIII adopted one of Napoleon's marshals, Jean Baptiste Bernadotte, as his successor. Bernadotte assumed the name Carl Johan and took over the practical leadership of the country from the by-then senile king. Carl Johan broke with Napoleon, made an alliance with Russia, and acquired Norway from Denmark after invading that country. In 1818, he succeeded to the throne as Carl XIV of Sweden and Carl II of Norway (r. 1818–1844). His accession to the throne marked the founding of the Bernadotte dynasty, which ruled both Sweden and Norway until Norway gained independence in 1905. The dynasty continues today as the royal family of Sweden.

Today, Sweden has a hereditary constitutional monarchy. Throughout the 1800s, the Swedish parliament gained power as the political function of the monarchy declined. Between 1917 and 1919, the monarchy officially became a constitutional one, which meant that the king could no longer oppose the decisions of parliament. A constitution confirming the symbolic role of the monarch as head of state came into effect on January 1, 1975.

Another recent change to the Swedish monarchy is the Act of Succession of 1979, which altered the law of primogeniture (inheritance by the oldest son) by allowing the oldest child rather than just the oldest son to succeed to the throne. Crown Princess Victoria, who was born in 1977 to King Carl XVI (r. 1973–   ) and Queen Silvia, is the first Swedish princess to be affected by this change. Victoria, rather than her younger brother Carl, is heir to the throne of Sweden.

See also: CHRISTINA; DANISH KINGDOM; FOLKUNG DYNASTY; GUSTAVUS I (VASA); GUSTAVUS II (ADOLPHUS); KALMAR UNION; NORWEGIAN MONARCHY; VASA DYNASTY.

FURTHER READING

Anderson, Ingvar. *A History of Sweden.* Trans. Carolyn Hannay. London: Weidenfeld and Nicolson, 1956.

Nordstrom, Bryan J. *Scandinavia Since 1500.* Minneapolis: University of Minnesota Press, 2000.

SYRIAN KINGDOMS

(2000s B.C.E.–Present)

Diverse series of kingdoms that have ruled in the area around present-day Syria from ancient times to the twentieth century. Syria is a land of great antiquity, and the history of its kingdoms stretches from the earliest Mesopotamian empires to the aftermath of World War I. Greater Syria—an area that includes modern Syria and Lebanon, as well as parts of Anatolia (present-day Turkey), Jordan, and Palestine—was the birthplace or center of many great Middle Eastern dynasties, but it has also frequently been dominated by external powers.

ANCIENT KINGDOMS

Inhabited from very early times by Semitic peoples, ancient Syria experienced successive waves of invasions during the third millennium B.C.E., including invasion by the Canaanites, Phoenicians, Aramaeans, and others.

Among the earliest Semitic peoples to settle the region of Greater Syria were the Amorites, who came from the Arabian Peninsula around 2100 B.C.E. and established a number of small states. In the second millennium B.C.E., the Amorites ruled a powerful kingdom called Amurru, based at the ancient Syrian city of Mari.

Another kingdom established in the region in the third millennium B.C.E. was that of Ebla in northern Syria. Ebla flourished from about 2400 to 2250 B.C.E. but was then nearly destroyed by Naram-Sin (r. 2254–2218), the king of Akkad in Mesopotamia. Ebla flourished again between about 2000 and 1800 B.C.E., although it was never able to regain the power and greatness it had achieved centuries before.

From about the 1400s to 1200s B.C.E., the region of Greater Syria was dominated by the Hittite and

Egyptian empires, which competed for control of much of the ancient Near East. Rule over the region changed hands a number of times as Hittites and Egyptians struggled for hegemony.

By about 1250 B.C.E., a seafaring people known as the Phoenicians had established several city-states along the Syrian coast, mostly in present-day Lebanon. The most important of these city-states were Tyre, Sidon, and Byblos. Skilled navigators and traders, the Phoenicians traveled around the Mediterranean, establishing a commercial empire based on independent city-states located along the coast of North Africa and Southern Europe as far as present-day Spain. The Phoenician city-states along the Syrian coast lasted for centuries, until they were finally absorbed by Persian and Greek civilizations beginning in the 300s B.C.E.

Beginning in the thirteenth century B.C.E., parts of Greater Syria were also ruled by the Israelites and the Aramaeans. The wealthy and powerful Aramaean kingdom, also known as the biblical kingdom of Aram, was based in the capital city of Damascus (in present-day Syria), while the Israelite kingdom was centered in Palestine. From the 1000s to 500s B.C.E., Syria suffered from periodic invasions and domination by the Assyrians. The Assyrian Empire eventually eclipsed the Aramaean kingdom, and then the Babylonian king Nebuchadrezzer (r. 605–562 B.C.E.) conquered much of Syria in 606 B.C.E. and destroyed the Israelite capital of Jerusalem in 586 B.C.E. The Persian Empire took Syria from the Babylonians in the sixth century B.C.E.

HELLENISTIC AND ROMAN KINGDOMS

The Greek Macedonian leader, Alexander the Great (r. 336–323 B.C.E.), conquered the Persian Empire in the 330s, starting a period of Hellenic domination of Greater Syria. One of Alexander's leading generals, Seleucus Nicator, inherited Syria upon Alexander's death in 323 B.C.E. and founded the Seleucid dynasty. The resulting kingdom of Syria ruled from its capital of Damascus from 301 to 64 B.C.E., despite competition from the Nabataean kingdom based at Petra (in present-day Jordan).

The Roman occupation of Syria began in 64 B.C.E., and Syria was ruled as a Roman province for several centuries. After the division of Rome into Eastern and Western empires in the fourth century C.E., Syria became an important part of the Byzantine Empire. Under the Byzantines, a local Christian

Arab dynasty called the Ghassanids ruled Syria. Ghassanid rule lasted until 611, when the Sassanid rulers of Persia invaded Syria and took control. Although the Byzantine Empire retook Syria soon thereafter, its weak support of the Ghassanids left the kingdom vulnerable to a new empire rising in the Middle East—that of Islam.

ISLAMIC AND CHRISTIAN CRUSADER KINGDOMS

In 635, Syria was invaded again, this time by Muslim armies that conquered Damascus and made Greater Syria part of an Islamic caliphate ruled from Arabia. Muawiya I (r. 661–680), leader of the Banu Umayya tribal dynasty, proclaimed himself caliph in 661 and moved his capital to Damascus, making Syria the center of a new Islamic kingdom ruled by the Ummayad dynasty.

In 750, the Umayyads were conquered by another Arab dynasty, the Abbasids, who moved the caliphate to Baghdad. Abbasid rule over Greater Syria was incomplete, however: the Hamdani dynasty ruled much of northern Syria from their capital city of Aleppo before falling to the Seljuk Turks in 1049, and the Egypt-based Fatimid dynasty encroached on parts of Syria as well.

In the eleventh century, the Crusades brought waves of European invasions to Greater Syria, which resulted in the establishment of several small Crusader states, namely, Edessa, Antioch, and Tripoli, and the Latin kingdom of Jerusalem. Nur al-Din, an Islamic prince from Iraq, retook much of Greater Syria from the Seljuks and Crusaders in the mid-1100s. His lieutenant, Saladin (r. 1175–1195), then completed the task, reconquering Jerusalem in 1187 C.E. and founding the Ayyubid dynasty. The Ayyubids and their fragmented successor states ruled Egypt and Syria until the Mamluk dynasty took power in 1250.

Syria continued to suffer invasions and partial domination by Seljuk and Mongol kingdoms in the following years. However, it remained under superficial Mamluk control until 1517, when the Ottoman sultan Selim I (r. 1512–1520) conquered Greater Syria and made it part of the Ottoman Empire. Syria remained under Ottoman control until World War I and the Arab Revolt of 1916.

The Hashemite-led Arab revolt against the beleaguered Ottoman Empire in 1916 resulted in the establishment in 1920 of a kingdom of Greater Syria under King Faisal I (r. 1921–1923). But Faisal was soon removed by the French, and the League of Nations made Syria part of the French Mandate, never again to be ruled by a formal monarchy.

See also: ABBASID DYNASTY; ARAMEAN KINGDOMS; AYYUBID DYNASTY; CRUSADER KINGDOMS; FAISAL I; HASHEMITE DYNASTY; MAMLUK DYNASTY; OTTOMAN EMPIRE; PALESTINE, KINGDOMS OF; PHOENICIAN EMPIRE; SALADIN; SELJUQ DYNASTY.

FURTHER READING

Mansfield, Peter. *A History of the Middle East.* New York: Penguin, 1992.

Sicker, Martin. *The Pre-Islamic Middle East.* Westport, CT: Praeger, 2000.

Queen Pomare IV, who ruled from 1827 to 1877, was the last monarch of the Tahitian kingdom. Unable to prevent France from making Tahiti a protectorate, she was essentially a figurehead for the last thirty-one years of her reign.

TAHITIAN KINGDOM (1789–1880)

Protestant Polynesian island kingdom founded by Pomare II (r. 1803–1808) with the help of European mercenaries, incorporated into the French Empire in 1880.

The Tahitian Islands were settled by Polynesian immigrants from the Society Islands. These immigrants soon built a culture and political system that, like most Polynesian states, was organized around the extended family.

Tahitian family structures were intricate in their balance of authority, and each family was tied to a temple. Prominent families, led by *arii nui*—high chieftains—maintained their prominence only with the help of the religious priesthood. Archaeological evidence suggests that, before European contact, this priesthood practiced ritual human sacrifice.

Europeans, primarily the French and the English, began to explore the islands in the 1700s. Awed by the natural beauty of the islands, they returned home with tales of the islanders as "noble savages" and of

the Tahitians' alleged liberal sexual practices. In 1789, the famous mutiny on the ship *Bounty* left Fletcher Christian and his fellow mutineers available for hire as mercenaries by the Pomare family who, with the aid of European weapons and Protestant missionaries, came to control the islands, unifying them for the first time under King Pomare II. The king promptly established a Christian kingdom based on a scriptural code of laws.

As European interest in the islands' reputation as a paradise increased—helped by the works of Herman Melville, Paul Gauguin, and Robert Louis Stevenson—prostitution, foreign disease, and Christianity were introduced. Without natural immunity to the foreign diseases, the Tahitian population plummeted. Missionaries, insisting that many of the traditional Tahitian practices were shameful, had many of the native Tahitian temples destroyed. As Christianity—particularly Protestantism—became the ruling religion, much of traditional Tahitian religion was lost.

Queen Pomare IV (r. 1827–1877), faced with

squabbling missionaries, made a fateful wrong decision when she deported two French Roman Catholic missionaries in response to a Catholic-Protestant missionary dispute. The French, already eyeing the lush island as a potential colony, seized the pretext to wrest control of the islands from her, setting her up to rule as a figurehead. In 1880, King Pomare V abdicated under French pressure, accepting a generous pension in exchange for his Crown, and Tahiti became a French colony.

See also: POMARE IV.

T'AI TSU (TAIZU) (928–976 C.E.)

Chinese general who founded the Sung (Song) dynasty and ruled from 970 to 976.

T'ai Tsu, meaning "Grand Progenitor," was the posthumous title given to Chao K'uang-yin (Zhao Kuangyin), the founder of the Sung (Song) dynasty. T'ai Tsu served in the military of the Later Chou (Zhou) dynasty, the last of China's so-called Five Dynasties, and was eventually appointed commander of the Palace Corps by Emperor Shih Tsung (Shizong) (r. 954–959). When Shih Tsung died in 959, his seven-year-old son, Kung Ti, succeeded him. Seizing this opportunity, a group of generals immediately staged a coup, deposed the child, and placed T'ai Tsu on the throne.

T'ai Tsu recognized that military insurgencies had plagued the Five Dynasties. He therefore offered generous pensions and land allotments to most of the military leaders in return for their peaceful resignations. T'ai Tsu replaced these leaders with individuals he knew he could trust, and he insisted on commanding the military himself when it engaged in combat. He also dismissed many of the lower ranking military officials who had come to dominate the bureaucracy during the Five Dynasties period.

To staff his new government, T'ai Tsu reintroduced the T'ang civil service examinations. Although nominally open to all citizens, the examinations required a high level of education that was available mainly to the upper classes. T'ai Tsu actively courted the support of the social elite. He developed the *yin,* a particular privilege that allowed male relatives of existing bureaucrats to take an easier exam and gain access to the government. During T'ai Tsu's reign, the government bureaucracy consisted of members of about one hundred families who successfully manipulated the *yin.* These individuals formed a new literati class that replaced the military's influence upon the central government.

After stabilizing the military and the bureaucracy, T'ai Tsu next sought to rebuild the entire T'ang Empire. Between 963 and 975, he defeated the lesser dynasties that controlled the Yangzi, Sichuan, Guangdong, Anhui, Jiangxi, and Hunan provinces. However, after two attempts, he failed to defeat the Khitans, who had gained a foothold in northern China during the Later Chin (Jin) dynasty. To prevent any Khitan raids, T'ai Tsu agreed to pay them a large annual tribute of silver and silk. The government struggled to make these payments, but the Khitans actually used much of the tribute to purchase other goods from Sung merchants.

With the country relatively secure, the threat of military insurrection diminished, and the government run by the new literati, T'ai Tsu sought to develop a new Sung culture. T'ai Tsu portrayed himself as a benevolent ruler who abided by the Confucian virtues, and he expected these virtues to be reflected in Sung society. He actively patronized writers, philosophers, and other artists. T'ai Tsu also strongly emphasized familial relationships. He commissioned writers and poets to construct detailed genealogies of the most famous families in China. He also supported the Qingming festival, a ceremonial funeral rite that involved the entire family of a deceased individual.

By the time T'ai Tsu died in 976, he had already created a strong foundation for the Sung dynasty. His policies of limiting the power of military commanders and expanding the role of the literati in the government provided his brother and successor, T'ai Tsung (Taizong) (r. 976–997), with the tools necessary to expand Sung control over the remnants of the T'ang Empire. Therefore, he had ably earned his royal appellation, T'ai Tsu, the "Grand Progenitor."

See also: FIVE DYNASTIES AND TEN KINGDOMS; SUNG (SONG) DYNASTY.

FURTHER READING
Hansen, Valerie. *The Open Empire: A History of China to 1600.* New York: W.W. Norton, 2000.
Mote, F.W. *Imperial China.* Cambridge, MA: Harvard University Press, 1999.

T'AI TSUNG (TAIZONG)

(600–649 C.E.)

The second emperor (r. 626–649) of the T'ang dynasty and one of the greatest of China's early emperors.

T'ai Tsung, meaning "Grand Ancestor," was the posthumous title of Li Shimin. In 618 T'ai Tsung helped his father, Kao-Tsu (Gaozu) (r. 618–626), overthrow the Sui dynasty and establish the T'ang dynasty. After Kao Tsu ascended the throne, T'ai Tsung became a general in the imperial army and successfully subdued rebellious forces throughout the new empire. His victories gained him a widespread popularity among the T'ang populace.

Alarmed by this popularity, Kao Tsu plotted with T'ai Tsung's two older brothers to demote or even assassinate him. After discovering their scheme, T'ai Tsung killed his oldest brother and ordered one of his officers to kill the other brother. Then, in 626, T'ai Tsung forced his father to abdicate the throne, and he assumed control of China.

Although his succession had been achieved violently, T'ai Tsung oversaw a great period of prosperity for the T'ang dynasty. In 630, he ensured China's national security by subduing the eastern Turks, whose raids had plagued China for centuries. With the Turkish threat removed, China regained control of the Silk Road and the immense wealth its trade generated. T'ai Tsung eschewed China's traditional distrust of foreigners and allowed Arab, Jewish, and Persian merchants to work in Changan, the T'ang capital. These merchants introduced cultural and religious influences never before experienced in China.

Chief among these influences was Buddhism. T'ai Tsung personally practiced Confucianism, and he built Confucian temples in every county. But he also recognized the importance of Buddhism to the Chinese public. During his reign, Zen Buddhism emerged in China. Traditional Buddhism maintained that enlightenment could be obtained only through arduous study and meditation, but Zen Buddhism argued that it could be suddenly achieved through intuition. When the famous Zen Buddhist scholar Xuanzang returned from India, T'ai Tsung built the Wild Goose Pagoda, which still stands, to house and honor him.

T'ai Tsung also improved the bureaucracy of the T'ang Empire. He expanded the civil service examinations that his father had reintroduced. Kao Tsu had largely relied on officials from his native region in northwestern China to staff the government. But T'ai Tsung actively recruited qualified officials from across the country in order to make the bureaucracy more representative. He embraced the Confucian principle that a ruler should be manifestly beneficent, and he relied upon his ministers to guide him and shape public policy.

As one of his most significant acts, T'ai Tsung reshaped the T'ang law code that his father had introduced. He divided it into two sections. The first listed the general principles of T'ang law; the second described specific crimes and their corresponding punishments. Local magistrates prosecuted most crimes and passed judgments dictated by the code, but provincial governors handled more serious cases. Only the emperor could approve the death penalty.

The law code also recognized three social classes: the privileged, commoners, and inferiors. Members of the lower classes generally received harsher punishments. But the code also made exceptions for certain individuals. For example, children, pregnant women, and seniors older than ninety could not be executed. Individuals with disabilities such as blindness, deafness, or amputated limbs also generally received light sentences. Finally, T'ai Tsung commanded that the law code be reformed every fifteen years so that it would not become outdated. Because of its efficiency, the T'ang law code was widely copied throughout Asia.

As T'ai Tsung aged, he struggled to ensure his succession. T'ai Tsung's first heir, his eldest son, was mentally ill, disdained the T'ang court, and refused to speak Chinese. When T'ai Tsung learned that the heir had plotted to kill his brothers and potential rivals, he executed his oldest son and named his ninth son, Kao Tsung (Gaozong) (r. 649–683), to succeed him. When T'ai Tsung died in 649, Kao Tsung and his wife, Empress Wu, initiated a period in which the T'ang bureaucracy became increasingly corrupt. Despite this growing corruption, T'ai Tsung had solidified the rule of the T'ang dynasty and positioned it to be one of the strongest in Chinese history.

See also: T'ANG DYNASTY.

FURTHER READING

Embree, Ainslie, ed. *Encyclopedia of Asian History.* New York: Scribner, 1988.

Hansen, Valerie. *The Open Empire: A History of China to 1600.* New York: W. W. Norton, 2000.

Macgowan, J. *The Imperial History of China.* 2nd ed. New York: Barnes & Noble, 1973.

Perkins, Dorothy. *Encyclopedia of China.* New York: Facts on File, 1999.

TAIFA RULERS (ca. 1009–1091 C.E.)

Petty Muslim rulers, known as the "party (or faction) kings" (*Muluk al-Tawa'if* in Arabic), who created independent kingdoms in the Islamic areas of the Iberian Peninsula that had previously been combined under the Cordoban court of the Umayyad caliphate.

The Taifa appeared in the early eleventh century at a time of extreme political disintegration after the dissolution of the Cordoban Umayyad caliphate in Iberia. Following the rule of the Umayyad caliph, Hisham II (r. 976–1009), and the ensuing civil war, the caliphate was no more than a puppet government. As a result, the various Taifas were able to establish independent kingdoms through the area.

At least twenty-three Taifa states were created between 1009 and 1091, when the Almoravids of North Africa conquered the last of them. The Berber Taifa states included the Aftasids of Badajoz, the Dhu al-Nunids of Toledo, and the Hammudids of Malaga. The Andalusian Taifas, or Hispano-Arabs, consisted of the Abbadids of Sevilla, the Jahwarids of Córdoba, and the Hudids of Zaragoza. The Saqalibah (Slav mercenaries) had no dynasties but formed taifa kingdoms such as Tortosa, Denia, and Valencia.

There were many wars between the Taifa states, which did not hesitate to seek both Christian assistance against enemy Muslim kings and North African support against Christian princes. Because they were not unified, the Taifa kingdoms became easy targets of the Christian *reconquista* (reconquest) of Iberia. Before long, the Taifa kingdoms of Toledo, Badajoz, Zaragoza, and even Sevilla were paying tribute to the Christian king, Alfonso V, the Brave of León (r. 999–1028).

Although they proved politically inept, the Taifa kings did succeed in promoting a great Islamic cultural resurgence in Iberia. Taifa courts, set up in principal cities such as Córdoba, Toledo, Sevilla, and Zaragoza, developed into Islamic centers that competed with each other for artists and intellectuals. As in the courts of the Islamic caliphates, they supported poets and encouraged the study of philosophy, mathematics, and natural science. Out of the Taifa era emerged such notables as the poet-king al-Mutamid of Sevilla (r. 1069–1091) and the poet-philosopher-scholar Ibn Hazm.

See also: ALMORAVID DYNASTY; CALIPHATES; CÓRDOBA, CALIPHATE OF; UMAYYAD DYNASTY.

TAIZONG. *See* T'AI TSUNG

TAIZU. *See* T'AI TSU

TAKAUJI ASHIKAGA. *See* ASHIKAGA SHOGUNATE

TAMERLANE (TIMUR LENG)
(1336–1405 C.E.)

Mongol conqueror (r. 1370–1405), self-proclaimed restorer of the Mongol Empire, and founder of the Timurid dynasty (1370–1507), who, by reviving the military techniques of Genghis Khan (r. 1206–1227), subdued a territory that stretched from Mongolia to the Mediterranean Sea.

By the time of Tamerlane's birth in 1336, the Mongol Empire had deteriorated into a series of squabbling smaller states, called khanates. Tamerlane, born Timur and later contemptuously dubbed Timur Leng (Timur the Lame) by his Persian enemies, was a member of the Islamic Barlas tribe, who were vassals of the Chagatai khanate in Transoxania (modern-day Uzbekistan).

When the leader of the Chagatai khanate, Amir Kazgan (r. ?–1357), died in 1357, Timur declared his allegiance to a rival khan, Tughluq Temur, who occupied Chagatai's chief city, Samarkand, in 1361. Tughluq named Timur minister of the khanate and adviser to the khan's son, Ilyas Khoja. Soon afterward, however, Timur defected to join his brother-in-law, Amir Husayn, in a coup to gain possession of the region. By 1366 they had done so, and Tamerlane then promptly turned on Husayn, besieging him and his forces in Balkh and proclaiming himself khan of Chagatai when Husayn was assassinated.

Over the next three decades, through treachery,

The Mongol leader Tamerlane, or Timur, conquered and controlled a vast territory that stretched from Mongolia to the Mediterranean Sea. As depicted in this painting of the Persian School, Tamerlane besieged the city of Herat in 1381 and made it the capital of his empire.

the Byzantine Empire. As a ruler he was ruthless. While occupied with defeating the Golden Horde, he was troubled by revolts in Persia. He responded by ordering entire cities in Persia utterly razed, their populations massacred, and towers built of the skulls. When Tamerlane died in 1405, he was preparing to invade China.

Although not a direct descendant of Genghis Khan, Tamerlane saw himself as the spiritual successor of that great conqueror. He also considered himself a devout Muslim—although, in the Mongol warrior tradition, he both drank and gambled to excess. He often referred to himself as the "Scourge of God," detailing the punishment of sinners as his destined duty. Yet, addicted to debate and chess, he was also a great patron of the arts, and throughout his reign he took great care to protect the artisans and educators of the cities he ravaged, often having them escorted safely to Samarkand even as their home cities were being demolished.

Scornful of the growing Turkish influences upon his increasingly settled people, Tamerlane encouraged a revival of the nomadic principles of traditional Mongol life, even as he rebuilt Samarkand into the most magnificent city in Asia. The Gur-e Amir, his mausoleum in Samarkand, is regarded as a masterpiece of Islamic architecture, and the mosaic-encrusted structures of the city remain as a bizarre but beautiful monument to the destroyer of so many great capitals, who never established a permanent residence.

After Tamerlane's death in 1405, the empire he ruled was divided, as he had indicated it should be, between his two sons and his grandsons. The result, perhaps inevitably, was civil war, after which the territory was reunified by Tamerlane's youngest son, Shagh Rokh (r. 1405–1447). This reunification ensured the continuance of the Timurid dynasty, which ruled the empire until the beginning of the sixteenth century.

See also: GENGHIS KHAN; MONGOL EMPIRE.

deceit, and the utilization of the highly effective techniques of mobile warfare developed by Genghis Khan, the charismatic Tamerlane led his army in bloody conquest throughout central and southwestern Asia, establishing an empire that stretched from the Russian steppes to the Hindu Kush Mountains to the Mediterranean Sea. He defeated the empire of the Golden Horde in Russia, sacked Baghdad and Damascus, and accepted the surrender of Egypt and

T'ANG DYNASTY (618–907 C.E.)

Chinese dynasty that attained power when an outbreak of peasant revolutions weakened the Sui dynasty.

Li Yuan, the founder of the T'ang dynasty, was originally a Sui military commander in the Gansu and Shanxi provinces, where he suppressed serious rebellions. In 617, however, he recognized the impending collapse of the Sui dynasty. Seizing the opportunity, he joined rebel forces and attacked the Sui capital at Daxingcheng. In 618, he deposed the last Sui monarch, Kung Ti (Gongdi) (r. 617–618), and changed the capital's name to Changan.

Li, known by his posthumous title Kao Tsu (Gaozu) (r. 618–626), realized that most Sui social institutions were still fundamentally sound. Therefore, he retained the *sansheng,* the three departments that comprised the bureaucracy, the Sui civil service examinations, and the "equal field" land distribution system. However, he reformed the two areas that had crippled the Sui dynasty: overtaxation and unreasonably long military service. Kao Tsu created the *zuyongdiao,* a fixed tax levied on grain and cloth, and he limited the length of military obligation. Most notably, in 624, he codified the Sui laws, creating uniform legal standards throughout the country.

In 626, Kao Tsu's second son, T'ai Tsung (Taizong), killed his older brother and deposed his father. T'ai Tsung (r. 626–649) significantly increased the T'ang dynasty's control over the country. He divided China into ten *dao,* or administrative units, and decreased corruption by rotating his ministers among them. He also greatly expanded the army and defeated the Eastern Turks, China's most dangerous enemy. Under T'ai Tsung, the T'ang dynasty experienced its first great period of prosperity.

When T'ai Tsung died in 649, his son Kao Tsung (Gaozong) (r. 649–683) assumed the throne. After suffering several strokes, Kao Tsung increasingly relied upon his wife, Empress Wu, to rule. The empress, Kao Tsung's former concubine, had convinced the emperor to divorce his first wife and marry her after she produced two sons. Wu brazenly filled the bureaucracy with her supporters and dismissed her opposition. However, she initially balanced this favoritism with qualified candidates who had passed the *jinshi* examination. Wu also oversaw two major military victories. In the west, China gained control

The T'ang Dynasty ruled China during one of the greatest periods in that nation's long history. For three centuries, the T'ang witnessed a flourishing of literature, art, trade, Buddhism, and Confucian education and administration. This painting on silk, titled *The Thirteen Emperors,* portrays the T'ang rulers of the seventh century.

T'ang Dynasty

Kao Tsu	618–626
T'ai Tsung* (Taizong)	626–649
Kao Tsung* (Gaozong)	649–683
Chung Tsung	684
Jui Tsung	684–690
Wu Tse-T'ien* (Wu Zetian)	690–705
Chung Tsung	705–710
Jui Tsung	710–712
Hsuan Tsung	712–756
Su Tsung	756–762
Tai Tsung	762–779
Te Tsung	779–805
Shun Tsung	805
Hsien Tsung	805–820
Mu Tsung	820–824
Ching Tsung	824–827
Wen Tsung	827–840
Wu Tsung	840–846
Hsiuan Tsung	846–859
I Tsung	859–873
Hsi Tsung	873–888
Chao Tsung	888–904
Chao Hsuan T'i	904–907

*Indicates a separate alphabetical entry.

tually deposed her two sons, Chung Tsung (Zhong-zong) (r. 684) and Jui Tsung (Ruizong) (r. 684–690), and executed the majority of the T'ang royal family.

Wu's constant scheming eventually imploded. She died in 705 after reinstating Chung Tsung as her successor. But Chung Tsung's wife, Empress Wei, poisoned him. The brief reign of the empress was extremely corrupt because her retainers ignored the country's problems. But in 712, Chung Tsung's nephew, Hsuan Tsung (Xuanzong), deposed the empress and instituted a new government.

Hsuan Tsung (r. 712–756) removed Wei's corrupt ministers, increased the number of dao from ten to fifteen, and assigned new governors to each one. He divided the military into ten units and enlisted qualified commanders to lead them. By improving the granary and canal systems, he improved over 800,000 farms and enjoyed a corresponding increase in tax collections. As a result of such policies, the first decades of Hsuan Tsung's rule saw the Tang dynasty regain its former prosperity.

As Hsuan Tsung aged, however, he became enchanted with mystical Daoism and allowed his chief minister Li Linfu to run the government. When Li died in 752, a power struggle ensued. In 755, a powerful military governor named An Lushan attacked and occupied the T'ang capital at Luoyang. Hsuan Tsung was then deposed in favor of his son, Su Tsung (Suzong) (r. 756–762).

Although An Lushan was assassinated in 757, his rebellion had significantly weakened the T'ang dynasty, and other military leaders assumed virtual control over their districts. Consequently, the T'ang monarchy lost a large portion of the taxes collected in those areas. To replace this revenue, the emperor Te Tsung (Dezong) (r. 779–805) initiated a new tax in 780. He solicited the support of the aristocracy by ending the "equal land" system and allowing them to amass large estates. The new taxes and increased land values forced many peasants to become tenant farmers.

Through these maneuvers, Te Tsung and his successor, Hsien Tsung (Xianzong) (r. 805–820), regained the monarchy's power. But the T'ang society was still weak. When harsh weather ruined several harvests in the 830s, peasant rebellions erupted and lasted for three decades. Finally, in 875, an outlaw named Huang Chao organized a massive revolt that irreparably crippled the T'ang dynasty and instigated a bloody struggle for control of China.

In 903, Zhu Wen, a former military commander,

of all land as far as the border of Persia. In the east, the Tang temporarily subdued their ancient nemesis, the Korean kingdom of Koguryo.

These successes, however, sapped the monarchy's resources. Wu increasingly raised taxes to fund the augmented empire and struggled with rising civil dissension. After her husband died in 683, she even-

captured Changan and killed almost all government officials. Four years later, he deposed the last T'ang monarch, Chao Hsuan T'i (Zhaoxuan) (r. 904–907), and founded the Later Liang dynasty. The T'ang dynasty, one of the most powerful in China's history, ultimately could not maintain its vast empire.

See also: HSUAN TSUNG (XUANZONG); KAO TSUNG (GAOZONG); SUI DYNASTY; T'AI TSUNG (TAIZONG); WU TSE-T'IAN (WU ZETIAN) (WU ZHAO).

FURTHER READING

Benn, Charles D. *Daily Life in Traditional China: The Tang Dynasty.* Westport, CT: Greenwood Press, 2002.

TARA HIGH KINGSHIP. *See* IRISH KINGS

TARQUIN DYNASTY

(ca. 616–510 B.C.E.)

Last Etruscan dynasty of early Rome that included three rulers: Lucius Tarquinius Priscus (r. ca. 616–579 B.C.E.), Servius Tullius (r. ca. 578–535 B.C.E.), and Lucius Tarquinius Superbus (r. ca. 534–510 B.C.E.). These three rulers expanded the boundaries of Rome and built much of the infrastructure that would serve the city for centuries.

Roman legend attributes the ancestry of Romulus, the mythical founder of Rome, to the gods rather than to the Etruscans. Moreover, there are no records or hints that Numa Pompilius, the mythic king of Rome, was from the region of Etruria (home of the Etruscans) either. However, both the third and fourth monarchs of Rome, Tullus Hostilius (r. ca. 673–642 B.C.E.) and Ancus Marcius (r. ca. 642–617 B.C.E.), have Etruscan names and seem much more likely to have been historical personages than their two predecessors.

Legendary sources agree, however, that the Roman ruler Lucius Tarquinius Priscus came from Etruria. According to legend, when he entered Rome, his future wife, Tanaquil, witnessed an eagle snatch the cap from his head and return it. She interpreted this as a sign that Priscus would soon rule in Rome. He did, beginning his rule around 616 B.C.E. as the first ruler of the Tarquin dynasty.

During his reign, Lucius Tarquinius Priscus drained the land that became the Forum Romanum, built the great arena known as the Circus Maximus, and captured a number of neighboring towns, incorporating them into Greater Rome. Disinheriting and exiling his sons because of yet another omen, Tarquinius Priscus adopted a young slave, Mastarna, and made him heir to the throne.

The sons of Rome's previous king, Ancus Marcius, returned to Rome around 579 B.C.E. and hired two farmers to kill Priscus. They succeeded but were unable to claim the throne. Instead, Mastarna, now called Servius Tullius, inherited the kingship. Tullius reorganized and retrained the Roman army into heavily armored infantry (probably patterned on the successful Greek infantry troops known as hoplites). He also emulated the closely packed Greek phalanx (a troop formation) for his new legions. Having incorporated the Quirinal, Viminal, and Esquiline hills into Rome, Servius Tullius also built the first wall around the city.

Meanwhile, Tanaquil, the widow of Tarquinius Priscus, raised her son Tarquinius Superbus in exile, but they returned to Rome in 534 B.C.E. to claim the throne. Tullius appealed to the people of Rome, but the aristocrats backed Tarquinius Superbus. They felt that Tullius had been far too even-handed with the lower classes, and Superbus subsequently had Tullius assassinated.

Lucius Tarquinius Superbus, also known as Tarquin the Proud, made important contributions to Rome. He built the great temple of Jupiter Capitolinus, the Cloaca Maxima (the enormous sewage drain that made the Forum habitable), and extended Roman territory in several directions. However, Superbus proved to be a cruel and intolerant autocrat. He was deposed by the Roman Senate in 510 B.C.E., bringing an end to the Tarquin dynasty and to the Roman monarchy. From this point until the reign of the Emperor Augustus, Rome was a republic without a king.

Gladiatorial combat; public sanitation; reliance on and reverence for omens, augurs, and soothsayers; a military based on discipline and training; and a hatred of tyrants and autocrats (due especially to Tarquinius Superbus): these were the emblems and principles created during the reign of the Tarquin dynasty. These practices and ideas shaped Rome throughout the period of the Roman Republic, and they remained strong even after Rome became an empire.

See also: ETRUSCAN KINGDOMS; ROMAN EMPIRE; TARQUIN THE PROUD.

TARQUIN THE PROUD

(555–496 B.C.E.)

Third and last of the ancient Roman kings (r. ca. 534–510 B.C.E.) of the Tarquin dynasty, known to have been of Etruscan ancestry. The son of Lucius Tarquinius Priscus (r. ca. 616–578 B.C.E.), Tarquin the Proud ruled Rome mercilessly from about 534 until 509 B.C.E., but he was eventually deposed by the Roman Senate, thus precipitating the creation of the Roman Republic.

In 578 B.C.E., Tarquinius Priscus was murdered by the sons of his kingly predecessor, Ancus Marcius (r. 642–617 B.C.E.). Priscus's son, Lucius Tarquinius Superbus, was raised in exile by his mother, Tanaquil. In the meantime, another Etruscan, Servius Tullius (r. 578–534 B.C.E.), stepped in and became a popular ruler in Rome.

After Tarquin reached maturity, he returned to Rome in 534 B.C.E. and challenged Tullius's legitimacy to rule. Servius submitted his popularity to a plebiscite and won the vote. However, receiving the support of many of the Roman aristocracy, Tarquin had Servius assassinated.

The wealthy families who had supported Tarquin's challenge to Servius soon found that they had substituted an autocrat for a strong, fair-minded ruler. Tarquin wasted no time in asserting his power. Much to the horror of the aristocracy, he sentenced free men to forced labor, crucified citizens in the Roman Forum, and made it very clear to all that his power was absolute. [It should be noted that all sources of information for this are Roman; no Etruscan records are available, so it is possible that these sources present a one-sided view of Tarquin.]

Experiencing growing unrest among his subjects, Tarquin declared what he hoped would be popular wars against the neighboring Volscians and Rutuli. This tactic seemed to be working until one of his family returned from the front and raped Lucrece, the wife of a leading Roman citizen.

Lucius Junius Brutus was both the nephew of Tarquin and the best friend of Lucrece's husband. In 508 B.C.E., he exhorted the Roman Senate to depose Tarquin and expel all his family from Rome. The Senate agreed and deposed Tarquin. They then formed a new type of government, a *res publica* (or commonwealth) that would be headed by two equal officials called consuls, each elected for a period of only one year. This marked the end of the Roman monarchy and the beginning of the Roman Republic.

Tarquin fled to Etruria, the land of the Etruscans, and persuaded his distant kinsman, Lars Porsena, to attack and reclaim Rome for the Etruscans. Porsena agreed and prevailed against the Romans. However, Porsena did not replace Tarquin on the throne, and within a decade, Rome had ended Etruscan rule for good. The Roman Republic that emerged would thrive for over four hundred years.

See also: DETHRONEMENT; ETRUSCAN KINGDOMS; ROMAN EMPIRE; TARQUIN DYNASTY.

TAUFA'AHAU TUPOU IV (1918–)

King of Tonga (r. 1965–present) who was responsible for ending Tonga's status as a British protectorate but whose long rule has been plagued by financial scandal and the Tongan democratic movement.

King Taufa'ahau Tupou IV inherited the Tongan throne from his mother, Queen Salote Tupou III (r. 1918–1965), upon her death in 1965. Almost immediately after taking the throne, the new king—already in his forties and an alumnus of the Sydney University law school in Australia—set about modernizing his country and encouraging tourism.

After organizing the construction of Tonga's first modern hotel and an airport that could handle jet aircraft, King Taufa'ahau turned his attention to the seventy-year-old agreement with Great Britain that made Tonga a British protectorate. A new treaty was negotiated in 1968, and in 1970 the British granted emancipation from protectorate status, making Tonga an independent nation. Since then, the king of Tonga has been responsible for the kingdom's foreign affairs and defense.

As Taufa'ahau encouraged foreign contact, more and more of his subjects spent time abroad, studying or working in democratic countries. In the late 1980s, Tonga's first independent newspaper, *Kele'a,* was founded. Since that time, Taufa'ahau's administration has been rocked again and again by financial scandal, often connected to the king's management of foreign affairs.

When the Tongan parliament met in a special session in 1991 to amend the Tongan constitution to permit the sale of Tongan passports to foreign nationals—a practice declared unconstitutional by the Tongan High Court—hundreds of Tongans participated in the island's first protest. When Taufa'ahau disregarded public opinion and continued the sale of the documents, a pro-democracy conference was organized, resulting in elections being held in 1993. Taufa'ahau was able to ignore calls for reform, however, since the Tongan constitution guarantees twenty-one of the thirty seats in parliament to hereditary nobles.

Since the first elections in 1993, King Taufa'ahau Tupou IV has continued to refuse to recognize the Tonga Human Rights Democracy Movement, and most experts expect the Tongan monarchy to stay in place as long as Taufa'ahau lives.

See also: SOUTH SEA ISLAND KINGDOMS.

TAXATION

Any process whereby the government of a state raises income through direct and compulsory contributions from its citizens.

Taxation is the primary means through which states, including monarchies, obtain the funds necessary to operate and provide their inhabitants with services such as education and national defense. Taxation is also used to protect the domestic economy by placing high tariffs on imported goods.

Taxes have been in place throughout recorded history and have frequently been a source of intense political disputes, sometimes leading even to warfare. Historically, monarchs have been especially vulnerable to popular unrest over taxation, as their subjects generally have had little or no influence over how their taxes are spent.

EARLY FORMS OF TAXATION

Taxation can be traced at least as far back as the dynasties of ancient Egypt, all of which operated rudimentary tax systems. One of the earliest forms of taxation was the extraction of physical labor from the pharaoh's subjects, generally to build civic projects such as temples or mausoleums. Many durable goods, especially those relating to agricultural production, were taxed, including livestock, grains, and cooking oils. Like modern states, the Egyptian kingdoms exempted certain people from paying taxes, as is evident from inscriptions on the Rosetta Stone, which describes the rescinding of specific taxes by Pharaoh Ptolemy VI (r. 180–145 B.C.E.).

Taxation continued throughout the Greek and Roman periods, with the Greeks raising taxes explicitly for the purpose of funding the military. The Greeks also issued the first tax refunds, sending excess money back to the populace. The Roman Empire is well-known for its advanced monetary and taxation system, especially as it developed under the reigns of Julius Caesar (r. 49–44 B.C.E.) and the emperor Augustus (r. 27 B.C.E.–14 C.E.) Both rulers promoted a comprehensive system of personal, sales, trade, poll, inheritance, and property taxes that helped fuel the rapid expansion of the Roman Empire. Massive civic projects such as welfare, aqueduct systems, and a network of roads that stretched throughout Africa, Asia, and Europe were funded with Roman tax revenues. Some historians have argued that the Roman tax system became so excessive that it actually stifled the economy and contributed to the downfall of the empire.

Beginning in the third century B.C.E., the Ch'in (Qin) dynasty in China initiated the most spectacular public works project in history, the building of the Great Wall of China. Construction of the Great Wall was funded almost entirely by a system of heavy personal and agricultural taxes, and it was built using tens of thousands of forced laborers. Construction of the Great Wall was such a massive project that neither the wall nor the tax system that funded it came to an end until the Ming dynasty.

THE FEUDAL AND MODERN ERAS

Throughout the Middle Ages, taxes continued to be levied worldwide, most notably through the feudal economic systems of Western and Eastern Europe, China, Japan, India, and Russia. Although significant distinctions can be drawn between the feudal systems of these areas, they all had one thing in common: a structure in which the monarchy and its local representatives (the nobility) held absolute ownership of all arable land, and extracted labor and payment from the peasants who farmed the land in exchange for military protection and the right of subsistence. Although the collapse of the feudal system in Europe in the fifteenth through seventeenth centuries did much to liberate peasants and the working classes from exploitation, it did not result in the remission of taxes, which were levied on things ranging from land and crops to tea and paper.

It was taxes on tea and paper that galvanized the most famous tax revolt in history, the American Revolution against Britain's King George III (r. 1760–1820). Because the British colonists in America had no influence over how their tax money was spent, they deeply resented taxes and pushed to force the British government to guarantee the rights of political representation along with the obligations of taxation. The British Crown would not agree, however, and its refusal led directly to the American Revolution.

Today, taxation occurs in almost every nation on the globe, including the surviving kingdoms scattered around the world. These taxation systems range from simple tithing (giving a percentage of income or goods) to immensely complex systems that employ entire industries of specialists.

See also: COMMMERCE AND KINGSHIP; TRIBUTE.

FURTHER READING

Webber, Carolyn, and Aaron Wildavsky. *A History of Taxation and Expenditure in the Western World.* New York: Simon & Schuster, 1986.

TEMUCHIN. *See* GENGHIS KHAN

TEWODROS II (1816–1868 C.E.)

Emperor of Ethiopia (r. 1855–1868), who was called the "King of Kings" for his efforts to reunify Ethiopia and restore it to the glory of its earlier days.

The man who became known to history as Tewodros was named Kasa at the time of his birth, in 1816, to parents of noble descent. A child of status and privilege, Kasa was educated by monks of the Ethiopian Orthodox (Coptic) Church. By the early 1800s, Ethiopia had suffered nearly a hundred years of internal conflict, having become fragmented into dozens of small, independent groups that waged constant warfare with their neighbors. The unity of Ethiopia's earlier days, which had contributed to the greatness of the kingdom, seemed irrecoverable.

As a young man, Kasa became convinced that he was destined to reunify his country. He became an outlaw, making a dubious living through armed robbery in the countryside. His exploits gained him notoriety, however, and attracted many followers. By 1852, Kasa had amassed a large army and began his mission in earnest, aiming to seize the throne of Ethiopia and establish himself as ruler. Within three years he had succeeded in his goal, and at his coronation he took the Christian name of Tewodros (Theodore).

Tewodros found it difficult to create unity from the fractious collection of strongmen and warlords who constituted the only real authority throughout much of Ethiopia. Thus, in the mid-1860s, he turned to the British for help in restoring order to Ethiopia and in modernizing the nation. The British ignored his requests for assistance, however. Angered by their unwillingness to help, Tewodros made a diplomatic error of major proportions: he ordered the British consul and other foreigners to be seized and thrown into prison. The British ignored Tewodros no longer, but their attentions were not what he had originally hoped to receive. In 1868, the British retaliated by attacking Tewodros's fortress in Magdala, forcing him to release his prisoners. In April 1868, Tewodros acknowledged his failure as ruler by committing suicide.

See also: AKSUM KINGDOM; AMHARA KINGDOM; HAILE SELASSIE I; MENELIK II; TEWODROS II; ZARA YA'IQOB.

FURTHER READING

Rubenson, Sven. *King of Kings: Tewodros of Ethiopia.* Addis Ababa: Haile Sellassie I University, 1966.

THEATER, ROYAL

Dramatic presentations sponsored by monarchs and often performed at the royal court.

The principal involvement of monarchs in the theater has been as patrons and founders of theaters or acting companies. One of the few rulers known to have actually written plays is the tyrant of Syracuse, Dionysius the Elder (ca. 430–367 B.C.E), whose now lost work he submitted to the competition at Athens. The Roman emperor Augustus (r. 27 B.C.E.–14 C.E.), also began but then abandoned work on a tragedy about the ancient Greek hero Ajax. The most prolific playwright among sovereigns was Catherine II the Great of Russia (r. 1762–1796), who wrote several plays and opera libretti in Russian that were later performed. Catherine's plays served her cultural agenda by attacking Russian backwardness and Freemasonry.

Many monarchs have founded theaters or acting companies, or otherwise promoted the theater. Catherine II of Russia founded an Opera House in the Winter Palace in 1763 and the Hermitage Theater in St. Petersburg in 1785. The royal and theatrical worlds were deeply connected during the reigns of kings James I (r. 1603–1625) and Charles I (r. 1625–1649) of England.

James I's predecessor on the English throne, Elizabeth I (r. 1558–1603), had generally limited plays before the court to groups of six or eight at certain holidays such as Christmas. James I increased the number of plays and dramatic performances presented before the court on these occasions, and he also had plays presented at other times of the year as well.

James I took over a leading company of players, the Lord Chamberlain's Men, and re-styled it as the King's Servants. Other leading companies were sponsored by other members of the royal family. James I also fostered the career of the playwright Ben Jonson.

The British monarchy's involvement in the theater continued under James's son and successor, Charles I. Charles's wife, Henrietta Maria, actually appeared on stage with her ladies in some court theatricals, attracting unfavorable notice from Puritans who condemned actresses as prostitutes. The Puritans, after their victory in the English Civil War of the 1640s, abolished both the monarchy and the theater.

Although both came back with the Restoration of Charles II (r. 1660–1685) in 1660, the close connection of the English royal court and the theater was never restored. Charles did participate in the theater in one way that was common among kings, however—he took an actress, Nell Gwyn, as his mistress. Of the many actors or actresses who became the sexual partners of monarchs, the best known is Theodora, who became the wife and empress of the Emperor Justinian I (r. 527–565 C.E.) of the Byzantine Empire.

See also: ARENAS, ROYAL; CATHERINE II, THE GREAT; CHARLES I; JAMES I OF ENGLAND (JAMES VI OF SCOTLAND); LITERATURE AND KINGSHIP; MUSIC AND SONG; RITUAL, ROYAL; THEODORA.

THEBES KINGDOM

(ca. 1570–1085 B.C.E.)

Kingdom that flourished in Egypt during a period known as the New Kingdom (ca. 1550–332 B.C.E.).

Located on the Nile River in the southern part of Egypt, the ancient city of Thebes became the capital of Egypt during the Twelfth dynasty (1991–1775 B.C.E) but reached its height of importance during the Eighteenth to Twentieth dynasties (ca. 1570–1070 B.C.E.). Thereafter it began to decline as the center of Egyptian rule shifted further north. For a time in the tenth century B.C.E., Thebes was also a separate kingdom under sacerdotal, or priestly, rule.

Although Thebes developed very early from a number of small villages, it remained a relatively obscure site until about 2100 B.C.E., when one of its leading families established Egypt's Eleventh dynasty (2134–1991 B.C.E.). The city quickly gained prominence as both a royal residence and as the seat of worship of the god Amun. Thebes also became the burial place of many Egyptian kings and nobles, who were buried in great splendor in the nearby Valley of the Tombs.

Thebes is particularly well known for these tombs and its magnificent temples, many of which are well-preserved because of the dry climate. The famous temples of Karnak and Luxor were built on the east bank of the Nile, while the well-known funerary temples and royal burial places—including that of King Tutankhamen in the Valley of the Kings—were erected on the west bank of the river.

TEMPLE OF KARNAK

Ancient Egyptians called the Temple of Karnak "Ipetisut," which means "the most select of places." It is actually a complex of temples dedicated mainly to the gods Amun, Mut, and Khonsu. Nearly all the New Kingdom kings added on to the complex, which grew to be Egypt's greatest religious gathering place.

The Temple of Amun, the principal god of Thebes in the New Kingdom, was built by Rameses III (r. 1182–1151 B.C.E.) during the Twentieth dynasty. The Temple of Montu, the war god, dates from the Eighteenth dynasty under Amenhotep III (r. 1386–1349 B.C.E.). Ancient warriors asked the god Montu to look after Thebes when they went off to battle. The Temple of Mut (Amun's wife) also was built by Amenhotep III. The temple complex at Karnak in-

The Thebes Kingdom prospered under several of the best-known and most powerful pharaohs in Egyptian history. One of these was Tutankhamen, whose tomb in the Valley of the Kings contained many beautiful artifacts and murals, including this painting of the king's funeral cortege.

cluded a number of smaller temples and Sacred Lakes where the priests bathed and cleaned implements for divine rites.

TEMPLE OF LUXOR

South of Karnak, the Temple of Luxor—considered the dwelling place of Amun—was known to the ancient Egyptians as "Ipt rsyt" or the "southern sanctuary." The temple was the center of the most important festival in Thebes, the festival of Opet, which fused the current ruler's human aspect and his divine office.

The festival of Opet was basically a procession of images of the royal family and the gods carried on barges along the Nile from the Temple of Karnak to the Temple of Luxor. Many soldiers, dancers, musicians, and important officials walked alongside the barges on the riverbanks. The festival was a time for people to ask favors of the kings' or gods' images.

After the king arrived at the temple with his priests, he and his *ka* (divine essence, created at birth) were merged, thereby transforming the king into a god. This festival and the Temple of Luxor served as the power base of the pharaoh's government.

FUNERARY TEMPLES

As part of the funerary cult of the kings, numerous temples were built on the plain between the Nile River and the valleys where kings were buried because there was no room for the temples to be placed next to the royal tombs. Like the temples connected to the pyramids, they were the site of rituals to ensure the king's immortality and passage to the next world as a god. The most important and best-preserved examples of these are the temples of Eighteenth dynasty rulers Hatshepsut (r. 1503–1483 B.C.E.) and Tuthmosis III (r. 1504–1450 B.C.E.), Nineteenth dynasty pharoahs Seti I (r. 1291–1279

B.C.E.), and Ramses II (r. 1279–1212 B.C.E.), and Ramses III of the Twentieth dynasty.

THE VALLEY OF THE KINGS

The Valley of the Kings on the west side of the Nile contains many of the tombs of New Kingdom rulers. The area was chosen because it was near Thebes and had a mountain peak perhaps reminiscent of the Pyramids. More than sixty royal tombs have been discovered there, most with rock-cut corridors, burial chambers, halls, and pillars. The walls and ceilings were adorned with representations of the king's journey from the present to the afterlife, with illustrations and inscriptions from a variety of funerary texts.

The earliest royal tomb in the area is that of Tuthmosis I (r. 1524–1518 B.C.E.) of the Eighteenth dynasty, and the latest is the tomb of Ramses XI (r. 1098–1070 B.C.E.) of the Twentieth dynasty. The most famous and well-preserved tomb, however, is that of the young pharaoh Tutankhamen (r. 1334–1325) of the Eighteenth dynasty. His burial site—complete with the ruler's mummy and a large amount of treasure—was discovered by English archaeologist Howard Carter in 1922 and is considered one of the greatest archaeological discoveries ever made.

Tutankhamen was buried in three nesting coffins. The outer two were covered with gold leaf, and the inner one was solid gold encrusted with gemstones. A mass of jewelry and amulets were found with the mummy, as well as a splendid gold portrait mask. Four shrines of hammered gold over wood surrounded the coffins; and furniture, statues, clothing, a chariot, weapons, and many more items filled the other rooms of the burial place. Much of this treasure is now on display at the Egyptian Museum in Cairo.

See also: HATSHEPSUT; RAMSES II, THE GREAT; SETI I; TUTANKHAMEN.

THEODORA (d. 548 C.E.)

Byzantine empress, the wife of Emperor Justinian I the Great (r. 527–565), whose skill and intelligence helped to advance the Byzantine Empire.

Theodora's birthplace is the subject of debate: she was born either on the Greek island of Crete or in Syria. The daughter of a bear trainer, Theodora worked during her youth as a mime and an actress, an occupation likened to prostitution at that time. A daring entertainer, she frequently performed at the Hippodrome (a public stadium) in Constantinople, the capital city of the Byzantine Empire, where she was known for her acrobatics.

At age sixteen, Theodora traveled widely in northern Africa, where she remained for four years before returning to Constantinople. During these journeys, she went to the city of Alexandria in Egypt, where she learned about Monophysitism, a form of Christianity that viewed Christ as wholly divine. This view of Christ was contrary to Orthodox Christian belief, which viewed Christ as both human and divine.

Theodora's support for Monophysitism put her in opposition to the Orthodox Christian church that was the accepted faith of the Byzantine Empire. Yet, through her influence, Justinian attempted to reconcile these competing Christian beliefs.

When Theodora returned to Constantinople in 522, she became a wool spinner near the palace of Emperor Justin I (r. 518–527), where she drew the attention of the emperor's nephew Justinian, who was a high government official. Theodora was both beautiful and intelligent, qualities that caused Justinian to fall in love with her and to campaign against an old Roman law that forbade government officials from marrying actresses. Justinian and Theodora were married in 525. Two years later, in 527, Justinian succeeded to the throne at the death of his uncle. He and Theodora ruled as emperor and empress, unofficial joint monarchs.

In some ways, Theodora was a much stronger individual than her husband. During the Nika revolt of 532—when two rival political groups started a riot and proclaimed a new emperor—Justinian was prepared to flee Constantinople. But Theodora gave a moving public speech about the greater significance of the life of someone who died as a ruler over that of someone who lived but was nothing. She convinced Justinian and his officials to attack the rebels, and the resulting victory saved Justinian's throne.

A pioneer advocate for the rights of women, Theodora passed laws that prohibited forced prostitution and established homes for prostitutes. She also enacted laws that granted women more rights in divorce, allowed women to inherit property, and established the death penalty for rape.

See also: BYZANTINE EMPIRE; JUSTINIAN I.

FURTHER READING

Browning, Robert. *The Byzantine Empire*. Rev. ed. Washington, DC: Catholic University of America Press, 1992.

Browning, Robert. *Justinian and Theodora*. New York: Thames and Hudson, 1987.

Vasiliev, Alexander A. *History of the Byzantine Empire, 324–1453*. Madison: University of Wisconsin Press, 1952.

THEODERIC THE GREAT

(ca. 454–526 C.E.)

King of the Ostrogoths (r. 474–526) and conqueror of Italy, who adopted many Roman ideas and policies while remaking the land into a Goth kingdom.

The son of King Thiudimir (r. ca. 469–474) of the Ostrogoths by a concubine, Theoderic was born around 454 in the Roman province of Pannonia (in central Europe in present-day Hungary). His given name was Dietrich, a common Germanic name that translated in Latin to Theodericus.

Theoderic's father, along with his brothers, Valamer and Videmer, led the Ostrogoths as part of an alliance of nations fighting the Romans and Visigoths on behalf of the Huns. After losing the war, Thiudimir was forced to sign a peace treaty with the Romans around 464, stipulating that the young Theoderic be sent as a slave to Constantinople, the capital of the Eastern Roman Empire.

Theoderic stayed in Constantinople for about ten years, absorbing Greco-Roman culture and values more than any previous barbarian ruler had. Even so, Theoderic remained true to the nature of his Ostrogothic people by being well versed in the ways of war and never learning to read or write.

Theoderic returned to Pannonia at the death of his father in 474. Elected king, he took control of the eastern portion of the Ostrogothic lands and began to establish himself as a military ruler by defeating the Samartians, a people in central-eastern Europe that had plagued the Romans for years. Theoderic's ambitions on the battlefield enabled the Ostrogoths to take control of new lands along the lower Danube River, and he also earned for them the status of Roman federates.

Theoderic's relationship with the Byzantine Emperor Zeno (r. 474–491) was inconsistent, swinging constantly between deepest friendship and outright hostility. Between his successful campaigns against Macedonia in 479 and Thessaly in 482, Theoderic helped Zeno put down two major rebellions within the Byzantine Empire.

Theoderic's attention to his own rule took precedence after the death of his chief rival, Theoderic Strabo. With Strabo's death, Theoderic gained complete control of the Ostrogoths, and, in 484, he was elected to the consulship in Constantinople and given the title Flavius Theodoricus. Soon after, he had Strabo's son assassinated in order to remove any threat to his own power. By 486, Theoderic was able to threaten Constantinople, occupying its outlying areas and cutting off its water supply.

Eager to remove Theoderic as a threat to the Byzantine Empire, Emperor Zeno encouraged the Ostrogothic leader to invade Italy in 488 and expel Odoacer (r. 476–493), the Germanic chieftain who had overthrown the last emperor of the West, Romulus Augustus (r. 475–476), in 476. Conquering Italy would give Theoderic a homeland for his wandering people while also removing him as a threat to Zeno.

Theoderic's forces marched west and challenged Odoacer, defeating him in a series of battles before blockading him in the city of Ravenna in 493. A local bishop finally arranged for a truce between Theoderic and Odoacer. Theoderic, supported by the Church, offered what seemed to be remarkably generous terms. He had no intention of honoring them, however.

Theoderic invited Odoacer, Ocoacer's son, and his chief officers to a banquet. As soon as Odoacer was seated, Theoderic drew his sword and slew his opponent. Odoacer's wife, Sunigilda, was imprisoned and left to die of starvation, and his son, Thelane, was sent to Gaul and murdered there. While violent and unpleasant, Theoderic brought a period of peace and prosperity to Italy. He claimed kingship of Italy in 493, and in 497, he was proclaimed king of the Goths and the Romans by the Byzantine emperor, Anastasius I (r. 491–518).

Theoderic took the surplus wealth from Italy and sent it to his own capital at Ravenna. He spent the remainder of his reign strengthening his new realm. A devout Arian (a Christian sect founded by the North African theologian Arius in the fourth century), Theoderic tolerated all Christian sects, a remarkable policy in an age of religious intolerance. He also promoted the growth of agriculture and commerce in Italy, and he improved public works by repairing Roman aqueducts and baths at Verona and Pavia.

As king of the Ostrogoths in Italy, Theoderic pledged allegiance to the emperor in Constantinople, and he intended to ensure that Italy remained part of the Roman Empire. He respected Roman institutions and laws, allowing Italy to be run by Romans using Roman methods but under Theoderic's administration. The Romans themselves were sufficiently impressed by his power to grant him the title of Augustus.

Theoderic further consolidated his power through marital alliances. He married his daughter to Alaric II (r. 484–507), the Visigoth king of Spain and southern Gaul, and he took for his own wife Audofleda, the sister of the great Frankish king, Clovis I (r. 481–511). When Theoderic died in 526, his daughter Amalasuntha served as regent for her son, Athalaric (r. 526–534).

See also: BYZANTINE EMPIRE; OSTROGOTH KINGDOM; ROMAN EMPIRE.

FURTHER READING

Moorhead, John. *Theoderic in Italy.* New York: Oxford University Press, 1992.

THEODOSIUS I, THE GREAT

(346–395 C.E.)

Roman emperor (r. 379–395) who made Christianity the official state religion of the Roman Empire in 380.

Theodosius was born into an aristocratic Gallo-Roman family in Gallaecia, in modern-day Spain. His father was an accomplished general and politician who was executed by political enemies in 376. After his father's death, Theodosius withdrew from public life and went to his provincial estates in Spain, content to be alive after the rapid change in Roman politics that had brought down his father. Before his father's death, Theodosius had earned a reputation as a skilled soldier and leader of men, as well as a capable and intelligent statesman. At his point in his life, however, he little expected to return to the heights of imperial politics.

Theodosius remained in Spain until 378, when the Emperor Gratian (r. 375–383), ruler of the Western Empire, chose him to rule the Eastern Empire after its ruler, Valens (r. 364–378), was defeated and killed by the Visigoths. Gratian chose Theodosius largely because he was not beholden to any protector at court. Gratian also knew of Theodosius's family and his abilities.

In 379, Theodosius became emperor of the eastern half of the Roman Empire, and he immediately faced a serious challenge. The Roman Empire had always depended upon its military might for stability, but with its defeat by the Visigoths, the Romans lost the military initiative and looked vulnerable. Over the next four years, Theodosius dealt cunningly with the Visigoths, eventually reaching an agreement with them to settle peaceably in the region of Thrace, north of Greece. As part of the agreement, Theodosius also allowed the Visigoths to settle in Pannonia, a Roman province in Central Europe. Although Germanic incursions into the empire did not cease during Theodosius's reign, they did slow to a manageable pace.

Theodosius's great contribution to the empire came when he made Roman Christianity the official state religion in 380. Although Christianity was already a recognized religion in the empire as a result of the conversion of Emperor Constantine I (r. 306–337), Roman Christianity was not the major religion around the Mediterranean. Arianism, a form of Christianity that stressed the human nature of Jesus, claimed more adherents prior to Theodosius's reign.

After Theodosius was baptized into the Roman Christian faith in 380, he issued an edict that banned Arianism. Officially, the laws of Theodosius severely punished unorthodox Christian practice, although, in reality, the laws were never enforced during his lifetime. However, the same set of laws was used to actively repress pagan belief, and many traces of polytheism were wiped out in Egypt, Syria, and Asia Minor. By the time of his death in 395, Theodosius ruled over a truly Christian empire.

See also: ALARIC I; BYZANTINE EMPIRE; CHRISTIANITY AND KINGSHIP; CONSTANTINE I, THE GREAT; ROMAN EMPIRE.

THESEUS. *See* GREEK KINGDOM, ANCIENT

THESSALONIKA KINGDOM

(316 B.C.E.–1430 C.E.)

Kingdom in northeastern Greece, an important power for a brief period in the fourth century B.C.E., that later became a sub-kingdom of the kingdom of Macedonia and the Roman Empire.

During the time of Alexander the Great (r. 336–323 B.C.E.), the Greeks and Macedonians established a number of major trade routes and new trading centers in the eastern Mediterranean and the ancient Near East. One such trading center was founded near the ancient city of Thermes in 316 B.C.E. by Cassander, an officer in Alexander's army who later became king of Macedonia (r. 305–297 B.C.E.).

Situated at the northeastern corner of the Thermaic Gulf, the new city was on the overland trade route from Italy to the East. Trade routes also led north from the city into a vast hinterland and south via the Aegean Sea. Since Cassander founded the new city in the same year that he was married, he named it after his bride, Thessalonika, who was the stepsister of Alexander the Great.

THE MEETING PLACE OF CIVILIZATIONS

Thessalonika's harbor provided a safe port for Macedonia's large merchant fleet and navy. Ships from every part of the Aegean Sea, Syria, Phoenicia, and Egypt brought products and people from foreign lands. With them came elements of new civilizations and religious beliefs. The city had a temple to the Egyptian god, Sarapis, and a crypt was constructed for mystical worship. A small Jewish community developed that, much later, became the basis for an expanding Christian community after that religion was founded.

By the second century B.C.E., Thessalonika had become a crowded city-state that had a vassal-like relationship with the kingdom of Macedonia. Built on a hillside overlooking the sea, it was surrounded by formidable walls and crowned by a spacious acropolis. The government was headed by a king, who consulted with a council of magistrates, a superintendent, and a military governor.

In 168 B.C.E., the last king of Macedonia, Perseus (r. 179–168 B.C.E.), lost the battle of Pydna to the Romans at the end of the Third Macedonian War (171–168 B.C.E.). With this victory, the Romans took control of Macedonia, and Thessalonika was handed over to the Roman consul, Aemilius Paulis.

ROMAN RULE

The Romans divided Macedonia into four districts and named Thessalonika the capital of the second district. They allowed Thessalonika to keep its ancestral laws and have its own officials and privileges, which the city would keep until 1430 C.E., when the Ottoman Turks took control of the region. But the Romans would not permit travel or contact between the districts, hoping to break up further the former Macedonian Empire.

A groundswell of opposition to Roman rule eventually led to a revolt among the Macedonians, which the Romans put down in 149 B.C.E. This time, the Romans formally annexed Macedonia, including Thessalonika, and in 146 B.C.E. it became the first Roman province outside Italy.

Thessalonika grew in importance and wealth when the Romans built a major road, the Via Egnatia, through the region around 145 B.C.E. The Via Regina, a main spur of the Via Egnatia, crossed Thessalonika from west to east, improving the old trade route and increasing east-west trade in the city. The Romans conquered more of the valleys to the north, opening up the Balkans to Thessalonika and making the city the trading center of the ancient world.

Prosperity did not come without danger. The Thracians overran Macedonia in 57–55 B.C.E., but they were no threat to Thessalonika's high walls. A decade later, during Rome's civil war, Thessalonika was threatened again. At the battle of Philippi in 42 B.C.E., the Roman general Marcus Junius Brutus promised his troops they could plunder Thessalonika after the battle. Fortunately, Brutus lost the battle to Mark Antony and Octavian, the heir of Julius Caesar (r. 49–44 B.C.E.). Rome declared Thessalonika a free city, allowing it to mint its own coins and retain its political organization.

Between the first and fourth centuries C.E., Thessalonika grew into one of the great cities of the Roman Empire, becoming a center of intellectual thought and religious worship. These golden years of prosperity ended in the fourth century, at a time when the Byzantine Empire ruled the Balkan region.

CENTURIES OF DECLINE

Under the Byzantines, Thessalonika was the second-most important city of the Eastern Roman Empire, after Constantinople. Byzantine rule, however, marked the beginning of Thessalonika's decline as well as the start of persecution at the hands of other powers.

In 390, thousands of the city's inhabitants were massacred on the orders of the emperor Theodosius I (r. 379–395) after they rioted over a chariot race. In every century thereafter, the Thessalonians were persecuted by conquerors—the Saracens, Bulgarians, Normans, Franks, Romanians, and Venetians all plundered the city.

Finally, in May 1430, the Ottoman Turks, under Sultan Murad II (r. 1421–1451), launched a massive attack on Thessalonika. The Turks plundered the city, removing all evidence of wealth, and turned its Christian churches into mosques. Under the Ottomans, the city was renamed Seanik, and it remained under Turkish control until 1912.

See also: ALEXANDER III, THE GREAT; BYZANTINE EMPIRE; MACEDONIAN EMPIRE; MACEDONIAN KINGDOM; OTTOMAN EMPIRE; ROMAN EMPIRE

THIBAW (1858–1916 C.E.)

The last king of Myanmar and the last ruler of the Alaungpaya dynasty. The younger son of King Mindon (r. 1853–1878), Thibaw (r. 1878–1885) had a relatively short reign that ended with the colonial occupation of upper Myanmar by the British. Throughout his rule, Thibaw was strongly influenced by his wife, Supayalat, and her mother. His reign was accompanied by extensive violence and suffering.

During the reign of King Mindon, the British annexed lower Myanmar. When Thibaw took the throne, he sought to enlist French aid in order to stop any further incursions by the British. In 1883 he sent a mission to Paris in hopes of securing arms from the French. His diplomatic efforts met with some success—a treaty was announced two years later, and a French consul arrived at Mandalay soon after. Although the treaty was described as a commercial agreement, it was also said that Thibaw had granted the French economic incentives in exchange for a political alliance. As a result, it now seemed possible that upper Myanmar would be incorporated into the French Indochina.

The British, meanwhile, growing suspicious of French intentions in the region, saw their own relations with Myanmar collapse. The British Residency in Mandalay had closed down in 1879 because of concerns over security. Upon learning of the French treaty with Thibaw, British officials, owing partly to Chinese and European merchant interests in Rangoon, Calcutta, and London, began demanding the annexation of upper Myanmar. Their demands were now supported by British fears that France would do so first.

Thibaw himself soon presented an opportunity for British involvement and expansion. He accused a British-owned timber firm, the Bombay-Burmah Trading Corporation, which owned a lease to extract teak from the Ningyan forest in upper Burma, with cheating the government. After Thibaw requested and was refused a 250,000-pound loan from the firm, the king demanded a fine of the same amount. The matter was taken up by the British government of India, chiefly Indian viceroy Lord Dufferin, who sent an ultimatum to Thibaw in 1885 requesting that the case be reconsidered. Thibaw refused to allow an appeal of the case outside his own country, but the matter was soon taken up by the British.

Thibaw was disappointed if he was hoping for French support in a showdown with the British. The French, facing a renewal of hostilities with China in 1885 after a misunderstanding over withdrawal of Chinese forces in the region of Tonkin in northern Vietnam, would be able to offer little support to Thibaw. The British used the opportunity to increase pressure on upper Myanmar by demanding a permanent British resident at the capital, the right to trade with the Chinese in Yunnan province, and, perhaps most inflammatory to Thibaw, the right to control Myanmar's foreign relations. Thibaw's rejection of the demands led to a British invasion of upper Myanmar on November 14, 1885.

The British captured Mandalay two weeks later, although sporadic warfare continued throughout much of the rest of the country. Thibaw was deposed, and upper Myanmar was incorporated into the province of British Myanmar, from which it was directly administered until 1897. Siam, acting as a buffer between British and French spheres of influence, survived as an independent state. Thibaw was exiled to India and remained there until his death in 1916.

See also: ALAUNGPAYA DYNASTY; SOUTHEAST ASIAN KINGDOMS.

THRACE KINGDOM (480–345 B.C.E.)

Short-lived rural kingdom in the southern Balkan region, comprising northeastern Greece and southern Bulgaria, that was eventually incorporated within the greater power of the Macedonian kingdom.

The boundaries of Thrace changed continually throughout history. But in the 400s B.C.E., the kingdom of the Odrysae, the leading tribe of Thrace, covered all of Bulgaria, northeast Greece, and parts of Anatolia (present-day Turkey).

The Thracian peoples included warlike tribal dwellers in the mountainous regions and more peaceable counterparts on the plains of Thrace. The latter came into contact with the Greek colonies around the Aegean Sea in the early 300s B.C.E. Thracians lived in open villages and did not develop urban centers until Roman times. Largely as a result, they never achieved a strong sense of national identity.

From the 700s B.C.E., the Greeks colonized the coast of Thrace, but the Thracian people resisted Greek domination. Thrace was conquered by the Persians in 516 B.C.E., and it remained a Persian vassal state until 479 B.C.E. During that time, various Persian customs were introduced into Thrace. In 480 B.C.E., some of the Thracians joined forces with Persia and fought against the Greeks.

Shortly after this conflict, Teres (r. ca. 480–460 B.C.E.), the first king of the Odrysae, attempted to create an independent kingdom for the Thracians out of existing territories occupied by the various Thracian tribes. His son and successor, Sitalkes (r. ca. 460–428 B.C.E.), enlarged this kingdom and declared himself king of the Thracians. Although Sitalkes made a rather bold political move by allying himself with the Athenians against the Macedonians, his invasion of Macedonia in 429 B.C.E. was largely ineffectual.

Sitalkes's Odrysian lineage remained in power in Thrace for several generations. During the reign of Kotys I (r. ca. 384–359 B.C.E.), Thrace declared war against Athens, a campaign in which Kotys was assisted by his Athenian son in-law, Iphicrates. After Kotys's death in 359 B.C.E., the kingdom was split into three parts and ruled by a series of princes, including Kotys's son, Kersouleptes (r. ca. 359–341 B.C.E.).

Odrysian rule came to an end in the mid-300s B.C.E., when King Philip II of Macedon (r. 359–336 B.C.E.) invaded Thrace and made it a tributary of the Macedonian kingdom, thus ending Thracian independence. When Philip died in 336 B.C.E., his son Alexander the Great (r. 336–323 B.C.E.) came to power, but Alexander left Thrace under the control of his generals. After Alexander's death in 323 B.C.E., his general Lysimachus took control of Thrace, which became a protectorate under the rule of Macedonia.

See also: ALEXANDER III, THE GREAT; MACEDONIAN KINGDOM; PHILIP II OF MACEDON.

FURTHER READING

Archibald, Z.H. *The Odrysian Kingdom of Thrace: Orpheus Unmasked.* New York: Oxford University Press, 1998.

Theodossiev, Nikola. *North-Western Thrace from the Fifth to the First Centuries BC.* Oxford: Archaeopress, 2000.

Fol, Alexander, and Ivan Marazov. *Thrace & the Thracians.* Trans. Nevyana Zhelyaskova. New York: St. Martin's Press, 1977.

THREE KINGDOMS (220–266 C.E.)

Period following the fall of the Han dynasty in 220 in which three rival kingdoms ruled China. As the Han dynasty disintegrated in the early third century, three powerful generals emerged as China's new leaders. Initially charged by the Han with suppressing rebel groups, the generals established regional power bases and declared three rival dynasties to replace the Han.

General Cao Cao established control in the north with his base at the city of Luoyang. In 220, his son, Cao Pi (r. 220–226), proclaimed the Wei dynasty (220–266) and forced the last Han emperor to resign. Cao Pi, whose regnal name is Wei Wendi, ruled over a highly centralized, warlike state that was almost constantly in battle with its neighbors. The Wei instituted a system of recruiting for the civil service based on a candidate's merit rather than on family connections. They created large state farms for resettled landless peasants. The Wei also established military colonies for their armies of farmer-soldiers—self-sufficient communities whose members were expected to farm and fight. Although Cao Pi established a strong Confucian state, his successors were all weak rulers plagued by constant attacks from tribes to the north.

A second kingdom was founded in the west by Liu Bei, a relative of the Han imperial family. Liu Bei proclaimed the Shu Han dynasty (221–263), with its capital at Chengdu. Known as Emperor Shu Han Xuande (r. 221–223), Liu Bei presided over a prosperous state centered on Sichuan and the surrounding area. The kingdom also expanded steadily, eventually encompassing Yunnan and parts of present-day Myanmar (Burma).

In the south, the Han general Sun Quan founded the Wu dynasty (222–280). Known as Emperor Wu Wudi (r. 222–252), Sun Quan established his capital at Jianking. Cut off from access to the north and west by its rival dynasties, the Wu looked to the south, establishing contacts with the kingdoms of Southeast Asia and India.

All three kingdoms claimed to be the legitimate rulers of China, but the Wei dynasty, with a much larger population and a more powerful army than its rivals, has generally been considered the true continuation of the imperial line. In 263 the Wei gained the upper hand when Yuandi (r. 260–266), the last Wei emperor, succeeded in conquering the Shu Han dynasty. However, two years later Yuandi was, in turn, ousted by a general, Sima Yuan, who founded the Western Jin dynasty (266–316), also based in Luoyang. In 280, the Jin conquered the Wu dynasty, reuniting China under one rule.

The brief era known as the Three Kingdoms inaugurated a period of disintegration and disorder in China that would last until the Sui dynasty in 589. Known as the Six Dynasties period, it was an era marked by military struggles, the decline of the Confucian social order, and the spread of Buddhism into China from India. The elite, disenchanted with politics, became less interested in the Confucian ideals of public service. Individualism and unconventional behavior became fashionable among the wealthy, while life grew harsher for those at the bottom of the social scale.

The Three Kingdoms was a fruitful period for the arts and especially for poetry. The Wei leaders Cao Cao and Cao Pei were both talented poets. Later Chinese writers would look back on the Three Kingdoms as a chivalrous and romantic era, idealized in *Romance of the Three Kingdoms,* one of China's greatest novels. Written during the Ming dynasty, the work describes imaginary events based on real figures from the Three Kingdoms period, immortalizing their heroic feats in battle. Guan Yu, a real historical figure of the period, became known as Guan Di, god of war.

See also: HAN DYNASTY; SUI DYNASTY.

THUTMOSE III (ca. 1504–1450 B.C.E.)

Among the best known of ancient Egypt's pharaohs (r. 1490–1450 B.C.E.), who left behind a legacy of such important monuments as the Temple of Amon at Karnak and Cleopatra's Needle in Heliopolis.

Thutmose III was born during the Eighteenth dynasty, the son of Pharaoh Thutmose II (r. ca. 1494–1490 B.C.E.) and one of the pharaoh's secondary wives, a woman named Isis. Thutmose II's true wife (his sister) was Queen Hatshepsut (r. 1490–1468 B.C.E.), who had taken over the running of the kingdom from her ineffectual husband years before. When Thutmose II died shortly after the birth of this new son, Hatshepsut assumed the role of regent, maintaining her grip on the throne.

Hatshepsut ordered monuments to be built in her honor throughout Egypt. When Thutmose III was of an age to challenge her claim to power, she sent him off to the military. He became a noted warrior—necessarily so, for his stepmother's preoccupation with self-commemoration and other internal concerns led her to neglect her more distant provinces in Syria and Palestine, which took advantage of her inattention by rebelling. Thutmose managed to regain these possessions and extend Egypt's territory even further. His own commemorative monuments claim that he conquered more than 350 cities before he retired from the field of battle.

Hatshepsut did not relinquish her control over Egypt to Thutmose until after more than twenty years of rule, and there is speculation that Thutmose, tiring of having little power, finally decided to hasten her demise in 1468 B.C.E. The degree to which he resented her control can be measured by the thoroughness with which he set about having her monuments torn down or defaced, replacing them with his own. At the time of Hatshepsut's death, Egypt faced a new challenge to its authority in Syria, and Thutmose III led his army against the insurgents. The ensuing battle of Megiddo (ca. 1468 B.C.E.) took place a little to the southeast of today's Haifa, Israel. It was one of the most famous military campaigns of ancient Egypt.

In accordance with royal traditions, Thutmose took as his queen his half-sister Meryetre, the daughter of Hatshepsut, and together they had a son, Amenhotep II (r. 1438–1412 B.C.E.), who became the heir to the throne. Thutmose III is believed to have died around 1436 B.C.E. His original tomb was looted, as happened with the burial sites of many of Egypt's pharaohs. During the Twentieth dynasty (1185–1070 B.C.E.), his mummy and those of other pharaohs whose tombs had been disturbed were reinterred in the Valley of the Kings, where archaeologists discovered them in 1881.

See also: EGYPTIAN DYNASTIES, ANCIENT (EIGHTEENTH TO TWENTY-SIXTH); FUNERALS AND MORTUARY RITUALS; HATSHEPSUT.

TIBERIUS (42 B.C.E.–37 C.E.)

Roman emperor (r. 14–37 C.E.), whose image as an illustrious military commander was tarnished by the cruelties and perversions he practiced in the last decade of his reign.

Born to the ancient Claudian gens, or clan, Tiberius was embroiled in politics at an early age. His father was Tiberius Claudius Nero, one of Julius Caesar's naval commanders, who advocated the succession of Marcus Antonius (Mark Antony) rather than Octavius after Caesar's assassination in 44 B.C.E. This made the older Tiberius particularly vulnerable when Octavius, soon to be the emperor Augustus (r. 27 B.C.E.–14 C.E.), demanded that he divorce his beautiful, pregnant young wife, Livia Drusilla, so that Octavius could marry her. This marriage brought the young Tiberius and his newborn brother, Drusus, into the royal household to be raised alongside Augustus's nephew Marcellus.

Augustus took Tiberius with him to the Gallic frontier when the boy was only thirteen years old, and gave Tiberius his first major command when he was only twenty-two. This campaign resulted in a major military success, as Tiberius quickly and efficiently subdued the Balkan region of Pannonia. A celebratory triumph was held for Tiberius upon his return to Rome, marking the crest of his tragic life.

Shortly before this military adventure, Tiberius had married Vipsania, an unusual royal union made on the basis of mutual attraction rather than political expediency. Tiberius likewise basked in the love and admiration of his brother, Drusus, who was also pursuing a successful military career.

In 9 B.C.E., Tiberius's brother fell from his horse while on campaign in Germany; Tiberius rode for three days without rest to reach him just as he died.

Returning grief-stricken to Rome, he learned that Roman general Marcus Agrippa, a good friend of Augustus, had also just died and that Augustus had decided that Tiberius must put aside his beloved Vipsania and immediately marry Augustus's only daughter, Julia, the widow of Agrippa.

Urged on by his scheming mother Livia, and fearful of angering the emperor, Tiberius saw no options and complied. However, the worldly, lascivious Julia was unhappy with this match to the taciturn and reluctant Tiberius, and she was soon enjoying affairs with numerous suitors. Tiberius thus found himself in an awkward situation. Augustus had passed a law that mandated death for any adulterous spouse of the noble class. But Tiberius felt certain that the emperor would never forgive anyone who brought the topic of Julia's wandering ways to the emperor's attention. His solution was to have himself assigned to various military duties—as far away from Rome as possible.

Meanwhile, Tiberius's string of military successes recovered the legionary eagles lost by Crassus in Parthia and by Varus in Germany. He returned home to great acclaim, but facing the same domestic problem with Julia, he exiled himself, in 6 B.C.E., to the island of Rhodes and a life of idleness.

During Tiberius's ten years in Rhodes, the affairs of his wife were brought to her father's attention by others and she was exiled for life. Refused permission to return to Rome, Tiberius fell into ever more peculiar and solitary pursuits. Upon the death and disgrace of two more of Augustus's potential heirs, Tiberius was finally recalled to Rome, and Augustus, who had never really liked his stepson, declared Tiberius his adopted son.

In 14 C.E., the emperor Augustus died (some suggest by the hand of Tiberius's mother, Livia), and Tiberius accepted appointment as emperor by the Roman Senate at the age of fifty-four. The first few years of his reign were models of temperance and wise rule. Tiberius abolished gladiatorial games, stopped military expansion of the empire in favor of consolidation and defense, prudently managed state finances, and justly sat in judgment on many complex legal cases.

The kernel of his future excesses, however, could be found even in this early period in the rise of *delatores,* or informers. Tiberius passed a decree whereby any person or informer could accuse any other citizen of treason; if that charge were proved, the informer would receive a significant portion of the accused's estate, the balance passing to the state. The terror and injustice resulting from this rule touched all classes of citizens and stood as a monument to Tiberius's greed and growing paranoia.

Yet, it was not until after the death of his son Drusus in 27 that Tiberius's reign began its descent into monstrous ruthlessness. Tiberius moved to the island of Capri and put the day-to-day running of the empire into the hands of Lucius Aelius Sejanus, the ambitious captain of the Praetorian Guard. For four years, Sejanus ruled Rome in Tiberius's name and with a ruthlessness not seen for many years in that city.

Just as Sejanus was finalizing the consolidation of his power, Tiberius learned that Sejanus had been responsible for the murder of Tiberius's son Drusus. Tiberius smuggled a letter into the Senate that denounced Sejanus as a traitor. Returning to Rome in 31, Tiberius presided over the murder and torture of everyone who had had any positive dealings with Sejanus.

Suffering from numerous ailments, and in search of a successor, Tiberius named his grandnephew Caligula (r. 37–41) as his heir. In doing so, he played a final trick on Rome, perhaps by design, by naming an individual about whom he said, "I am nursing a viper in Rome's bosom."

On March 15, 37, Tiberius slid into a coma after participating in a ceremonial athletic event. Caligula informed the Senate that Tiberius was dead and was quickly proclaimed emperor. The next evening, however, Tiberius awoke, sat up in bed and asked for food. Caligula's henchman, the Praetorian captain who had executed and succeeded Sejanus, moved to the old man's bedside and calmly smothered Tiberius in his blankets.

See also: AUGUSTUS; CALIGULA; JULIO-CLAUDIANS; ROMAN EMPIRE.

TIBETAN KINGDOM

(100s B.C.E.–1949 C.E.)

Central Asian kingdom, dating from as early as the second century B.C.E., that is now part of the People's Republic of China.

The kingdom of Tibet was founded around the second century B.C.E., but it remained relatively obscure and isolated until the seventh century C.E. Around 600, a Tibetan leader named Namri Gampo

(r. ca. 600–627) united a number of small kingdoms within Tibet and established himself as king, founding the Yar-Lyn dynasty. Under this dynasty, Tibet became a powerful and aggressive state, invading both India and China from time to time.

The power of the Tibetan kingdom expanded under Namri's successors, including Songsten Gampo (r. ca. 627–649). Tibetan tradition considers Songsten Gampo to be the reincarnation of Avalokitesvara, a Buddhist *bodhisattva*, or enlightened one. The belief that each Dalai Lama, the Tibetan high priest, is also a reincarnation of this deity provided the monarchy with a sense of legitimacy.

During this early period, Tibet developed its first diplomatic relations with the T'ang dynasty of China, and Songsten Gampo married a T'ang princess. However, like much of early Tibetan history, little more is known about the relation between Tibet and China at this time.

After the reign of Songsten Gampo, a period of indecisive conflict began between Tibet and China

For most of its history, the Kingdom of Tibet has been a religious state, based on a close relationship between Buddhist and secular authorities. The religious leader of Tibetan Buddhism is called the Dalai Lama. The third Dalai Lama, who lived in the sixteenth century, is portrayed in this gilded copper figurine.

that continued for more than two hundred years. By the mid-800s, shortly after the Tibetans made peace with their Chinese neighbors, the kingdom collapsed and broke apart into a series of largely feudal states.

Throughout this early period, Tibet was a religious state closely affiliated with the Mahayana branch of Buddhism, which the Tibetans refined further into their own distinct Buddhist sect. The religious aspect of Tibetan government manifested itself in the close relationship that existed between the higher levels of Buddhist clergy and the secular authorities.

In the 1200s, Tibet was conquered by the Mongols, who reunited the kingdom under a series of religious leaders, the Sakyas. Tibet became a truly religious kingdom in 1254 with the Mongol appointment of Drogon Chogyal Phagpa (r. 1254–1280) as Lama, or priest. In the seventeenth century, the Tibetan kingdom was ruled for the first time by a high priest, or Dalai Lama.

The influence of Mongols in Tibet remained strong until the 1700s, when the Chinese Ch'ing dynasty invaded the kingdom and entered Lhasa, the capital. From this point onward, the Chinese claimed to be sovereign in Tibet, despite the largely nominal nature of their authority in this secluded kingdom.

In 1949, China officially annexed the Tibetan kingdom, an action that was codified in a joint agreement between Tibet and Communist China, which declared Tibet a "national autonomous region" under the leadership of a Chinese-controlled Dalai Lama. Within a decade, as the Chinese infringed on the monarchic privileges and powers of the indigenous Tibetan leadership, Tibetans revolted, prompting the Dalai Lama to flee to India, where a government in exile was established. Although Tibet remains part of China, the Chinese–Tibetan relationship is highly controversial, and there is an active movement among Tibetan exiles and their supporters to free Tibet from Chinese rule.

Throughout Tibetan history, the fortunes of the kingdom generally have been related to its geographic seclusion. In periods of relative independence, Tibet has struggled to maintain itself as a cohesive political unit. At other times, when Tibet has been dominated by other states, the region has been much more successful at maintaining a sense of unity and cohesion.

See also: T'ANG DYNASTY.

TIGLATH–PILESER III

(d. ca. 727 B.C.E.)

Assyrian monarch (r. ca. 744–727 B.C.E.) under whose leadership the Assyrian Empire was restored following decades of decline and reached its greatest extent.

The events surrounding Tiglath-Pileser's rise to power are mysterious. Some evidence suggests that he usurped the throne during a rebellion against the ruling king, Ashur-nirari V (r. 754–745 B.C.E.). Whatever the situation of his succession, Tiglath-Pileser III came to assume power over a state that had gone thirty years without a strong monarch. Weakened by internal unrest, and extended past the limits of its bureaucracy, Assyria was in need of an excellent soldier and administrator if it were to continue as an empire. In Tiglath-Pileser III, it got both.

Tiglath-Pileser demonstrated his administrative abilities by redistricting the Assyrian provinces, giving individual governors less power and less potential for revolt, and by reducing the size of the territory they controlled. He also altered the tax structure of the Assyrian Empire to make its distribution more equitable, and he courted support from the Babylonian priesthood by subsidizing religious building projects.

His restructuring activities were not restricted to the civilian stage. Tiglath-Pileser also created Assyria's first standing army, comprised largely of foreign mercenaries. This proved to be a successful move; as leader of this new kind of army, Tiglath-Pileser conquered the kingdom of Urartu, spread Assyria's borders to encompass Arpad and the urban centers of the Mediterranean coast, and dominated Israel.

In Arpad, Tiglath-Pileser set the pattern for later Assyrian policy toward political annexation; he appointed an Assyrian governor rather than a local king to oversee the city, turning the conquered regions into provinces. Tiglath-Pileser also adopted a policy of forced migrations, or deportations, moving thousands of individuals from the conquered territories. In 728 B.C.E., Tiglath-Pileser seized Babylon by taking advantage of an Aramaean rebellion there and declared himself king, thus linking the two kingdoms of Assyria and Babylon.

In his later years, Tiglath-Pileser retired from campaigning to enjoy the amenities of the palace at Kalakh, which had originally been built by Shalmaneser III (r. ca. 858–824 B.C.E.), but which Tiglath-Pileser remodeled, filling it with examples of Assyrian art and treasures he had collected throughout his reign. Upon his death around 727 B.C.E., Tiglath-Pileser III was succeeded by his son, Shalmaneser V (r. 726–722 B.C.E.), who could not live up to his father's level of administrative or military prowess.

See also: ARAMEAN KINGDOMS; ASSYRIAN EMPIRE; SHALMANESER III; SHALMANESER V.

TIKAR KINGDOM (1600s C.E.–Present)

Also called Bamum (Bamoun, Bamoum), one of the largest of several kingdoms to emerge in the grasslands region of Cameroon in west-central Africa.

The Tikar kingdom was founded in the seventeenth century by a leader named Nshare. Prior to that time, Tikar communities were largely autonomous, each ruled by a local chief. Nshare was the ambitious son of one such chief. However, he was a younger son, and as such, he was not in line to inherit his father's position.

Because Nshare had no hope of inheriting from his father, he recruited a number of followers and set out to create a kingdom of his own in the grassfields region of present-day Cameroon. After establishing a settlement, Nshare led his followers in a series of wars of conquest against the neighboring peoples. He declared himself king (called *fon,* which means "ruler" and can refer to both males and females) and established a capital in the settlement of Fumban, which became famous as a center for highly elaborated court music featuring rattles, flutes, and drums.

The Tikar kingdom had eighteen *fon* in all, beginning with Nshare (r. dates unknown) and ending with Njoya (r. dates unknown), who used the title *fon* from 1885 to 1919 but then took the title of sultan after converting to Islam. Njoya was the last independent king of Tikar, inheriting the throne after his father, Ngungure (r. dates unknown), was killed in battle. Njoya was only about thirteen years old at the time of his accession, so his mother, Nsangu, served as regent until 1895, when Njoya was finally considered old enough to rule on his own.

Tikar independence ended abruptly in 1902, when Germany seized the kingdom as part of its colonial holdings in Africa. Njoya cooperated with German colonial officials, and in return, he was per-mitted to retain a degree of autonomy. During his reign, he introduced a number of innovations to Tikar, including the development of a written alphabet for the Bamum language.

In 1915, the Germans lost their colonial possessions in Africa, and Tikar was claimed by France. Because Njoya had earlier cooperated with the German administrators, the French considered him unreliable. They deposed him in 1924, and around 1930, Njoya was sent into exile. He died in 1933.

The French installed Njoya's son, Njimoluh (r. 1933–1997), as king in 1933. Njimoluh remained on the throne until his death in 1997, but his authority was limited, first by the French and later by the government of the independent Republic of Cameroon. Upon his death, Njimoluh was succeeded on the throne by his son, Mbombo (r. 1997–present).

See also: AFRICAN KINGDOMS; BAMILEKE KINGDOMS.

FURTHER READING

Fowler, Ian, and David Zeitlan, eds. *African Crossroads: Intersections Between History and Anthropology in Cameroon.* Providence, RI: Berghahn Books, 1996.

TIMUR LENG. *See* TAMERLANE

TIMURID DYNASTY. *See* ASIAN

DYNASTIES, CENTRAL; TAMERLANE

TIO KINGDOM (1400s–1891 C.E.)

One of several kingdoms to arise in the Congo region of Central Africa as a result of participation in trade with the Swahili settlements on the East African coast.

Prior to the fifteenth century, the Tio people lived in small, autonomous chiefdoms along the Congo River north of Malabo Pool. Their location along the river brought them into contact with traders, who transported goods to the eastern coast of Africa and the Swahili trade centers there.

At some point during the 1400s, the independent Tio chiefdoms united under a single leader, which made them better able to seize control over the transportation of trade goods. By charging traders for safe passage through their territory, the Tio rulers were able to amass a great deal of wealth. This, in turn, permitted them to develop a superior military with which to conquer neighboring groups.

With their military advantage, the Tio thus came to dominate their region. But they never developed a centralized administration for their state. Instead, Tio rulers depended on the army to collect tribute from all peoples who wanted to pass through Tio territory with trade goods. The actual governance of these peoples was never brought under Tio authority but remained in the hands of traditional leaders.

In the 1600s, Swahili traders from the great coastal cities in the east made their way to the Malabo Pool region, hoping to increase the flow of trade. The traders particularly wanted to increase the traffic in slaves, which were in high demand throughout the Indian Ocean trade territory. The Swahili traders broke the Tio monopoly on trade because they were willing to deal with anyone who had slaves for sale and did not limit their dealings to the Tio.

Peoples who had previously been subject to the Tio king thus were now able to afford to build up their own military forces and to offer more effective resistance to Tio demands for tribute. Over the next two centuries, rebellions became increasingly frequent, as former Tio tributaries broke away and established independent chieftaincies. The Tio kings were forced to expend much of their own wealth on their military, as they struggled to maintain control over the region.

By the early 1800s, European interests were well entrenched throughout much of Africa, with England, France, and Germany each seeking to claim colonies on the continent. In the Congo, France set out to establish a powerful military presence, and by the 1880s it had succeeded in eliminating European rivals for the region. French colonial officials believed that it would be easier to gain control over the indigenous populations by further reducing the power of the Tio kings. To this end, the French provided support for local chiefs in their rebellions against the Tio ruler, ultimately destroying what remained of kingly authority in the region. In 1891, what remained of the Tio kingdom was absorbed into the newly formed French Congo Colony.

See also: AFRICAN KINGDOMS; SWAHILI KINGDOMS.

FURTHER READING

Vansina, Jan. *The Tio Kingdom of Middle Congo: 1880–1892.* New York: Oxford University Press, 1973.

TITUS (39–81 C.E.)

Roman emperor (r. 79–81) who brought to the imperial throne an unflinching and successful history of military service in Britain, Germany, and Judaea, as well as a reputation for debauchery and dissolute living.

Titus Flavius Vespasianus was the eldest son of the emperor Vespasian (r. 69–79) and brother of the emperor Domitian (r. 81–96). The well-favored son of one of the greatest Roman emperors, Titus began his military career stationed in Britain during the bloody Boadiccean Revolt in 60. In 67, the young military commander accompanied his father to Germany and, two years later, commanded a legion in Judaea in Palestine.

Titus actively championed his father's claim to the imperial throne, and, when Vespasian became emperor in 69, one of his first acts was to appoint Titus commander of the war in Judaea. In 70, Titus ruthlessly put down the remaining Jewish revolts and razed Jerusalem to the ground. He returned to Rome with many Jewish religious and secular treasures. Titus's soldiers urged him to challenge the wise and popular Vespasian for supremacy, but Titus declined and entered Rome without his legions to enjoy a co-triumph with his father.

Vespasian rewarded Titus by appointing him commander of the Praetorian Guard. Over the next few years, Titus also was made co-censor with his father and served as consul several times (consul and censor were the highest senatorial positions in Rome).

Titus's popularity with the people of Rome waxed and waned, depending on the nature and success of his military assignments. Moreover, his long relationship with Berenice, the daughter of King Herod Agrippa II of Judaea (r. 49–92), was a source of friction with the Roman populace. They feared a reprise of the strong Asian influence Rome had felt from Queen Cleopatra as a result of her relationship with Julius Caesar and Mark Antony.

In 79, Vespasian died after an enormously successful ten-year reign, and Titus became emperor. Shortly after he succeeded to the throne, it became

The Arch of Titus in Rome commemorates the conquest of Judea and capture of Jerusalem by the Emperor Titus in 66 to 70 C.E. This relief carving on the inside wall of the arch depicts the triumphal procession, with booty from the temple at Jerusalem, including the sacred menorah, or candleholder.

apparent that his new responsibilities had changed the harsh military commander and ladies' man. Whatever the cause of his newfound gentleness and kindness, Titus became greatly loved by the people of Rome during his brief rule.

Unfortunately, Titus's brief time as emperor also witnessed several major natural catastrophes over which he had no control. One of these was the eruption of Vesuvius and the tragedy of Pompeii in 79. That catastrophe was followed by a great fire in Rome in the same year, which destroyed most of the older public buildings still made of wood. Tragedy struck again, in 81, when a horrible plague afflicted the city and the surrounding areas, decimating the population. In response to these events, Titus generously borrowed from the state treasury to provide public and private aid.

The disasters, however, along with Titus's massive public works projects, such as the completion of the Colosseum (the Flavian Amphitheater) and the Flavian Baths, drastically reduced the state treasury. Within a short time, the treasury had sunk to the low level it had been at before his father's scrupulous thrift and economic policies made Rome solvent.

In 81, at the age of forty-one, Titus died in the same farmhouse where his father had died only two years before. His relationship with his younger brother, Domitian, had never been good. Perhaps it is not surprising, then, that several contemporaries attributed Titus's premature death to Domitian, who succeeded his brother to the throne.

See also: ARENAS, ROYAL; BATHS, ROYAL; ROMAN EMPIRE.

TIWANAKU KINGDOM

(ca. 1500 B.C.E.–1200 C.E.)

Ancient empire of Peru and Bolivia, one of the oldest and most splendid civilizations of South America, that reached its peak of power around the 700s C.E.

The Tiwanaku culture started around 1500 B.C.E. in the south-central highlands near Lake Titicaca in Bolivia and gradually spread from there along the highlands and coast of most of Peru. Tiwanaku was one of a number of dynastic states that emerged in the Andean area before the Spanish Conquest, and its power declined well before the Inca Empire began to dominate the region that now includes present-day Peru, Ecuador, Bolivia, and northern Chile.

At its peak, Tiwanaku held power over a large part of present-day eastern and southern Bolivia, northwestern Argentina, northern Chile, and southern Peru. Its influence was largely due to its impressive "raised-field system" of agriculture, which used elevated planting beds separated from each other by small irrigation canals. The canals were designed to keep the crops from freezing on cold nights by preserving the heat from the daytime sun and for growing algae and aquatic plants used as fertilizer.

From the 100s to late 300s C.E., Tiwanaku was a small local state, with little influence beyond its core area around Lake Titicaca in Bolivia. Between about 375 and 725, however, the kingdom began to expand and become a regional power. During this time, Tiwanaku developed a centralized administration and a hierarchy of social classes based primarily on wealth and occupation.

The final stage of the Tiwanaku kingdom, from about 725 to 1200, saw significant territorial expansion and the development of a complex, multiethnic society. Tiwanaku conquests during this period included a large part of the Pacific Coast from central Peru to northern Chile, and highland regions extending into the Andes Mountains. Around 1200, the Tiwanaku kingdom began to decline, and by the next century it had disappeared. Experts are not sure what caused this decline and disappearance, although some attribute it to climate change and extended drought.

Tiwanaku civilization is known primarily from archaeological sites and ruins. The main Tiwanaku archaeological site is located in the high Altiplano area south of Lake Titicaca in Bolivia. The site contains many stone structures, earthen mounds, stairways, plazas, and reservoirs. Building stones at the site, weighing up to 100 tons, were brought from a quarry three miles away. The site's renowned Gateway of the Sun was cut from a 10-foot-high stone and was carved with representations of humans, the condor, and the sun god. These typical Tiwanaku symbols also appear in the region's textile designs and pottery.

Other noteworthy examples of Tiwanaku construction are the Akapana Pyramid, a large earthen platform mound or stepped pyramid faced with fine-grained volcanic rock, and the Kalasasaya, a large rectangular-shaped enclosure built with alternating rectangular blocks and taller stone columns and containing many carved stone figures.

The enormous amount of planning and labor required for such vast and complex construction projects suggests that the Tiwanaku civilization must have been strictly governed and regimented. It is not clear whether the area near Lake Titicaca was the center of Tiwanaku origin or the capital of the empire at its peak, but these remarkable archaeological sites do seem to point to extensive Tiwanaku cultural, and perhaps political, influence.

See also: Huari (Wari) Empire; Inca Empire; Moche Kingdom; South American Monarchies.

TOKUGAWA IEYASU (1543–1616 C.E.)

The last of the three great Japanese warlords (r. ca. 1590–1616) who unified Japan after a century of struggle among *sengoku* (warring clans), who vied for ascendancy following the Onin War (1467–1477). Born Natsudiara Takechiyo, Ieyasu was the founder of the Tokugawa shogunate that ruled Japan from 1603 to the Meiji Restoration of 1868.

Tokugawa Ieyasu learned warfare and negotiation alongside the warriors in feudal Japan. Kidnapped at age four by the Oda family during clan infighting, Ieyasu was eventually freed by Oda Nobunaga when that great warrior of the Oda clan defeated the Imagawa clan in 1560. In the 1570s, Ieyasu fought for Nobunaga, but in 1579, when his family was accused of conspiring against Nobunaga, Ieyasu ordered his son to commit suicide and executed his wife.

In 1585, after initially opposing Nobunaga's successor, Toyotomi Hideyoshi (r. ca. 1590–1598), the year before, Ieyasu paid tenuous homage to Hideyoshi and married Hideyoshi's sister. In 1590, Ieyasu's support was crucial to the Hideyoshi forces at the siege of Odawara castle, a victory that made Hideyoshi dictator of Japan.

During the Odawara siege, Hideyoshi contrived to keep Ieyasu loyal but under control: Hideyoshi granted Ieyasu eight provinces in the Kanto region in eastern Japan near the fishing village of Edo (present-day Tokyo) in place of the five provinces Ieyasu then held near Kyoto. This kept Ieyasu far from Hideyoshi's capital at Kyoto. Though attached to Hideyoshi's headquarters during military campaigns against Korea in 1592 and 1597, Ieyasu provided no troops. Instead, he kept his retainers (soldiers and landowners who fought with him) home to build up his new realms.

Ieyasu was one of five regents sworn to support the Toyotomi succession and the first to plot against it. In October 1600, Ieyasu launched the battle of Sekigahara, a reported gathering of 150,000 warriors; his victory established the supremacy of the Tokugawa clan over Japan for 250 years.

In 1603, Ieyasu persuaded the emperor to name him shogun. Ieyasu retired two years later, passing the shogunate to his third son, Hidetada (r. 1605–1623), thus exploiting the typical Japanese means of legitimizing succession while holding on to power. In 1615, Ieyasu forced Hideyoshi's son, Hideyori, to abandon all claims to power and commit suicide; at the same time, he beheaded Hideyori's seven-year-old son.

As shogun, Ieyasu's main concern was to rebuild Japan after years of civil war. He built upon the policies of both Oda Nobunaga and Toyotomi Hideyoshi, in particular, redistributing captured domains among loyal *daimyo* (feudal lords). Ieyasu also promulgated new laws in 1615 to constrain both the courts and the military clans, instituting rigid policies based on enforced orthodoxy and stability. When Ieyasu died in 1616, his dynasty was intact, and it continued for another 250 years.

See also: ODA NOBUNAGA; TOKUGAWA SHOGUNATE; TOYOTOMI HIDEYOSHI.

TOKUGAWA SHOGUNATE

(1603–1868 C.E.)

A more than 250-year period during which Japan was ruled by the Tokugawa dynasty. The shogunate lasted from the appointment of warlord Tokugawa Ieyasu (1543–1616) as shogun in 1603 until the Meiji restoration in 1868, at which time direct imperial rule was restored in Japan.

In contrast to earlier periods of recurrent and violent civil warfare in Japan, the Tokugawa era was a largely peaceful era of economic expansion. The Tokugawa leaders stabilized Japan under a rigid social structure.

SOCIAL CLASSES

In 1615, Tokugawa Ieyasu decreed a fixed hierarchy of four social classes in Japan: warrior (or samurai), peasant, artisan, and merchant. The samurai, the leading class, represented perhaps only about two million of the thirty million people in Japan at the time. Although shoguns and *daimyo* (feudal landowners) relied on samurai retainers, they no longer needed large armies. No longer needed primarily for their skills as warriors, samurai became the administrators, advisers, teachers, scholars, policemen, guards, and bureaucrats of the Tokugawa shogunate. Ironically, although the role of the samurai as warrior declined drastically, the samurai *bushido* virtues, "the way of the warrior," a type of chivalry and code of conduct, represented the highest ideals of Tokugawa culture.

The bulk of the Japanese population during the Tokugawa shogunate were peasants, who, in the neo-Confucian philosophy of the period, were considered the second most important class because they were essential "producers." Moreover, the income of the Japan-ese ruling classes depended upon carefully regulated taxes on peasant rice production. Forbidden to leave their lands, peasants nonetheless slipped away to the cities during hard times to become tradesmen.

The third class in Tokugawa society were the artisans, who were allowed to sell their goods. The most prestigious craft was swordmaking, since the samurai valued high-quality swords. Below the artisans were the merchants, who, according to Confucian belief, were the lowest of the classes because they lived off the labors of others. Merchants were not considered important enough to be tightly regulated or highly taxed. This gave them considerable leeway to serve as entrepreneurs and moneylenders, and many members of the ruling classes became deeply in debt to merchants.

TOKUGAWA ADMINISTRATION

Tokugawa Ieyasu governed with a delicate balance, ruling with strict authoritarian control yet allowing

Tokugawa Shogunate

IEYASU*	1603–1605
HIDETADA	1605–1623
IEMITSU	1623–1651
IETSUNA	1651–1680
TSUNAYOSHI	1680–1709
IENOBU	1709–1712
IETSUGU	1713–1716
YOSHIMUNE	1716–1745
IESHIGE	1745–1760
IEHARU	1760–1786
IENARI	1787–1837
IEYOSHI	1837–1853
IESADA	1853–1858
IEMOCHI	1858–1866
YOSHINOBU	1867–1868

*Indicates a separate alphabetical entry.

loyal *daimyo* (feudal lords) considerable power and opportunity for gaining wealth within their own realms—as long as they followed the rules and collected and paid their allotted taxes. The system was not so much centralized as institutionalized on the basis of a strict hierarchy.

In 1625, Ieyasu's son and successor, Tokugawa Hidetada (r. 1605–1623), instituted the "alternate attendance" decree, which required *daimyo* to reside every other year at the capital of Edo (present-day Tokyo) while their wives and families resided there year round as virtual hostages. The system stimulated urban growth, for the *daimyo* spent large portions of their agriculturally derived incomes on travel to and from the provinces and the capital and on maintaining stylish residences in Edo.

Throughout the Tokugawa period, the powerless Japanese emperors lived away from Edo in Kyoto, the imperial capital, with virtually no connection to the populace. The imperial court obliged the Tokugawas by bestowing legitimacy of office on the shoguns, and, in return, they were kept in luxury in Kyoto.

URBAN MODERNISM

By 1800, the Tokugawa capital of Edo was the largest city in the world with a population of about a million; Osaka and Kyoto each numbered about half that. These cities sustained the sophisticated and popular culture of the *ukiyo* ("floating world") districts at their outer edges. Upper, lower, and bourgeois classes converged in the *ukiyo* districts to enjoy the ribald pleasures of puppet theater and kabuki drama; to buy easily available titillating novels, haiku, and woodcuts; or to seek out the ritualized commerce with geishas and prostitutes of both sexes.

A CLOSED NATION

The Tokugawa shoguns were wary of foreign influences after their initial encounters with European missionaries. By the 1630s, the shoguns banned Christianity from Japan and forced out most Christian missionaries. By 1639, only the Dutch, the Chinese, and some Koreans were permitted to trade with Japan, and only in tightly proscribed areas. No Japanese could leave Japan upon penalty of death. Only when American Admiral Matthew Perry steamed into Tokyo Bay in 1853 did Japan's self-imposed isolation end.

Although Japan was closed to outside influences, it was not closed to learning. Under the Tokugawa

shoguns, the Japanese literacy rate grew to one of the world's highest, with an estimated 45 percent of males and 15 percent of females able to read and write. Nobles, samurai, and wealthy merchants sent their children to private schools or educated them at home. In villages and towns, priests and samurai taught other children at Buddhist temple schools, which charged little or no tuition.

DECLINE

Despite its efficient administration and progress in education and other fields, the Tokugawa era eventually drew to a close. By the mid-nineteenth century, faced with declining agricultural revenues, the Tokugawa shogunate faced increasing instability and disorder among the peasants and the displaced *ronin* (masterless samurai). The ever-growing strength of the merchant and urban classes further undermined the power base of the shogunate.

The appearance of Western gunboats in Japan's harbors in 1853 signaled the beginning of the end for the Tokugawa rulers. The shogunate was finally brought down in 1868 by young, radical, wealthy *tazama,* or "outer *daimyo*" from the outlying provinces. This group of reformers blamed corrupt shoguns for the humiliating treaties imposed by Western powers following the arrival of U.S. and European ships in the mid-1800s. The reformers expressed a developing Japanese nationalism that rejected "imported" ideas, such as Chinese Confucianism. Instead, they championed the ancient Japanese religion, Shintoism, as well as other aspects of traditional Japanese culture. The reformers successfully "restored" power to the imperial office in 1868, with the accession of the 15-year-old Meiji emperor, Matsuhito (r. 1868–1912) to the throne of Japan. The last Tokugawa shogun, Yoshinobu (r. 1867–1868), relinquished power to the emperor in that same year, bringing the Tokugawa shogunate and era to a close.

See also: Meiji Monarchy; Oda Nobunaga; Tokugawa Ieyasu; Toyotomi Hideyoshi; Yamato Dynasty.

Toltec Empire (900s–1100s c.e.)

One of the principal Mesoamerican civilizations, located in Mexico, which built upon the cultural innovations of the Olmec people and dominated the region from the tenth to twelfth century.

One of the most important deities of the Toltec and Aztec cultures of Mesoamerica was Quetzalcoatl, the feathered serpent. The god of the wind, learning, and the priesthood, as well as a creator and civilizer, he was revered as the patron of arts and inventor of metallurgy.

The Toltec Empire had its beginnings around 900, when a group of Nahuatl-speaking people migrated from the north into the area now known as the Mexican state of Hidalgo. This region had long been under the control of the Teotihuaca, who had themselves taken over the territory once ruled by the Olmec (ca. 1400 B.C.E. to 500 B.C.E.). Around 800 C.E. the Teotihuaca capital was attacked by outsiders, the so-called *chichimec,* or "wild peoples." The attack left the Teoti-

huacas weakened, and their control over their more distant territorial possessions was broken.

From the time of the Olmec kingdom, the peoples of central Mexico were divided into two groups: those who practiced maize agriculture and were therefore "civilized," and those who did not and were thus considered "wild." The Toltec were of the first group, from at least the time of their earliest appearance in the central Mexico region.

The Toltec migration into central Mexico occurred some time after the fall of the Teotihuaca Empire, around 900. Under the leadership of a ruler named Mixcoatl, they took over the Teotihuaca capital city (also called Teotihuaca). The first king of the Toltec, Mixcoatl (r. dates unknown), immediately began a campaign of conquest against neighboring settlements and small states. When Mixcoatl died, apparently murdered by rivals among his kin group, he was succeeded by his son, Ce Acatl Topiltzin (r. dates unknown). The empire begun by Mixcoatl was expanded further by Topiltzin, who took as his royal name Quetzalcoatl, after the feathered serpent god of Toltec (and, previously, Olmec) religion.

Around 780, Topiltzin moved the capital from Teotihuaca to Tula (also called Tollan), which is about eighty miles north of modern-day Mexico City. At Tula, Topiltzin ordered the construction of a major ceremonial center. Tula also became a truly urban settlement with a large resident population. At its peak, the city appears to have been home to about forty thousand inhabitants.

The Toltec Empire, like its predecessors, was com-

ROYAL RITUALS

TOLTEC ART

The influence of Toltec art is evident throughout the Mesoamerican region, and many Toltec motifs were adopted by successor states such as the Aztec. The most ubiquitous motif is the *Chac Mool.* The name *Chac* is Mayan, but the figure predates their empire and is properly attributed to the era of Toltec dominance. *Chac Mool* presents a reclining figure, often carved in basalt or cast in terra cotta, representing the rain god, who was believed to act as a messenger between this world and the supernatural. The *Chac Mool* figure often served as an altar, and atop its chest it clasps a bowl or dish into which offerings could be placed.

posed of a mixture of peoples. The Toltec focused on collecting tribute in the form of maize and slaves, rather than on imposing a unified political structure. This pattern of conquest and demand for tribute, which appears to have been copied from the Olmec by way of the Teotihuaca, constituted a major weakness, for there was great hostility among the various conquered groups, and they rebelled frequently.

In order to quell uprisings, the Toltec developed a professional military, perhaps the first truly professional army to be formed in the region. The military was necessary for another reason as well. Whether or not their predecessor states practiced human sacrifice (a question still unresolved), the Toltec most certainly did. Among the most desirable sacrifices were captive enemy warriors, and since sacrificial ceremonies were held frequently, the army was kept busy acquiring appropriate victims for the rituals.

It was the Toltec who established the custom of offering the living heart of sacrifices to the gods. Although this practice may also have been followed by earlier peoples, the only definitive evidence of its occurrence is linked to the Toltec era. The gods to whom the sacrifices were offered, however, were the same as the gods that had been honored by the earlier civilizations of the region: the "were-jaguar" (essentially human in form but possessing a jaguar's snout) and the feathered serpent, Quetzalcoatl, from whom King Topiltzin took his royal name. The Toltec military was organized into three ritual cults, honoring the jaguar, the coyote, and the eagle.

The Toltec kings controlled the region for only a short time, most likely because they maintained only a loose hold over their subject peoples. The last Toltec king, Huemac (r. ca. ?–1174), died around 1174, four years after the Toltec capital was ransacked and destroyed by his rebellious subjects. Among those who joined in the rebellion to overthrow the Toltec was a powerful upstart group that came to be known as the Aztec (also called Mexica). The Aztec became the next, and last, indigenous empire to rule central Mexico before the arrival of the Spanish conquistadors in the early 1500s.

See also: AZTEC EMPIRE; MAYA EMPIRE; OLMEC KINGDOM; ZAPOTEC EMPIRE.

FURTHER READING

Coe, Michael D. *The Aztecs.* Norman: University of Oklahoma Press, 1973.

———. *The Maya.* 6th ed. New York: Thames and Hudson, 1999.

Davies, Nigel. *The Toltecs.* Norman: University of Oklahoma Press, 1977.

TOMARA DYNASTY (ca. 736–1150 C.E.)

Dynasty that ruled northwest India for several centuries and supposedly founded the modern city of Delhi.

The Tomaras were one of the thirty-six clans of the Rajputs, various princely clans of northern and central India. The Tomaras, who inhabited the Hariyana country in northwestern India, established their capital at Dhillika in 736. Because modern Delhi eventually emerged near this location, some historians credit the Tomaras with founding the city. Even if the Tomaras did not found Delhi, they gained control of the young city in the eleventh century.

Initially, the Pratiharas, another Rajput clan, dominated and ruled the other clans. Jaula, the earliest recorded Tomara leader, held an important position as manager of the king's affairs in the Pratihara court. In the late ninth century, his descendant, Vjarata, attained an even higher position in the Pratihara court. He used this position to increase Tomaran power among the thirty-six clans.

Because the Rajput clans believed that bravery and honor in warfare were admirable characteristics, frequent warfare erupted among the clans. Consequently, Rajput society was also very unstable, and most resources were devoted solely to the military rather than to other social institutions. Consequently, ruling factions could be quickly upended.

Vjarata and his two successors, Jajjuka and Gogga, took advantage of the violent nature of Rajput society and waited patiently while the Pratiharas's strength steadily declined. By the early years of the eleventh century, they had achieved independence from the Pratiharas and had gained control over Delhi.

When Jajjuka died and Gogga became the sole ruler, he tempered the emphasis on military spending. He constructed three magnificent temples on the Sarasvati River that were dedicated to the god Vishnu, and he encouraged Hindu pilgrims to come and worship at Delhi.

The Tomaras were unable to relinquish their violent proclivities, however. One of Gogga's successors, Rudrena, lost a decisive battle to the Chahamanas, one of the earliest group of Muslim invaders in India. After this defeat, the Chahamanas steadily stripped power from the weakening Tomaras. Finally, the last major Tomara monarch, Salavana, suffered a devastating loss to the Chahamanas near the end of the eleventh century. Although the Tomaras managed to maintain control of their homeland in the Hariyana region for another century, their period as an influential power had ended.

See also: INDIAN KINGDOMS; RAJASTHAN KINGDOM.

TOMBS, ROYAL

Burial places and monuments constructed especially for monarchs, often built to represent their power and the glory of their rule.

Throughout history, deceased royalty have been entombed in magnificent and elaborate tombs. The concept of the tomb, a vault constructed either partly or entirely above ground, as a chamber or dwelling place for the dead is widespread. The idea may have originated in the practice, known since prehistoric times and common among so-called primitive peoples of all eras, of burying the dead beneath their place of dwelling. This may account for the recurrence in different periods and places of funeral mounds and chambers: the prehistoric barrow, beehive tomb of Mycenaean civilization, mausoleum of Persian and Roman royalty, Egyptian pyramids, and *stupa* of Asia.

THE MAUSOLEUM

The mausoleum, favored by Persian and Roman royalty, was a sepulchral structure of grand scale and architectural pretension. The term *mausoleum* originates from the monumental tomb of Mausolus of Halicarnassus, the tyrant of Caria in southwestern Asia Minor, built between about 353 and 351 B.C.E. This so-called mausoleum was considered one of the Seven Wonders of the Ancient World.

A noteworthy ancient Roman mausoleum was that of the emperor Hadrian (r. 117–138 C.E.), which was originally a great circular drum sheathed in marble. Perhaps the most celebrated mausoleum, the Taj Mahal, located in Agra in northern India, was built by the Mughal emperor Shah Jahan (r. 1628–1658) in honor of his favorite wife, Mumtaz Mahal.

THE *STUPA*

Buddhist resting places for dead royalty were called *stupas.* The first prototypes appeared around 700 B.C.E. in India and were enormous mounds of earth. The *stupa* became a symbol of the Buddha; more precisely, it became a symbol of his final release from the cycle of birth and rebirth.

Stupas commonly rest on a square pedestal and are carefully aligned with the four cardinal points of the compass. Wooden masts typically embedded in the center of these mounds most likely carried umbrellas that served as a symbol of royalty and authority. Asoka Maurya (268–232 B.C.E.), one of the most famous Buddhist rulers of India, built the world's most well-known *stupa,* the Great Stupa, which stands on the hilltop of Sanchi in India.

THE PYRAMIDS

The monumental pyramids in Egypt were developed around the period of the Fourth dynasty (ca. 2680–2544 B.C.E.) and continued to be the favored form of royal burial through the Sixth dynasty (ca. 2407–2255 B.C.E.). Each Egyptian pharaoh built his own pyramid, often taking many years and massive amounts of raw materials and labor, in which his mummified body would be preserved and protected from sacrilege. The three pyramids of Giza, near Cairo, are the largest and finest of their kind. The Great Pyramid of Cheops was designated one of the Seven Wonders of the Ancient World and is the largest pyramid ever built.

SARCOPHAGI

Sarcophagi, meaning "flesh eaters" in Greek, were used throughout the world as an elaborate burial casket that was not buried in the ground. The name was first used to identify a special marble that the Greeks believed would destroy the entire body, except for the teeth, within a few weeks. The sarcophagus of a deceased ruler was often carved with elaborate scenes and bas reliefs (sculpted figures raised slightly from a flat surface) depicting the deceased's former glory. Among the world's great rulers entombed in sarcophagi are the Egyptian pharaoh Tutankhamen (r. 1334–1325 B.C.E.), Alexander the Great (r. 336–323 B.C.E.), and French emperor Napoleon I Bonaparte (r. 1804–1815).

CHURCHES AS TOMBS

Since the medieval period in Europe, churches have become the preferred final resting place for many deceased kings and royalty. Westminster Abbey, in London, England, is the burial place for eighteen English monarchs. Many kings and queens are buried near the shrine of Edward the Confessor (r. 1042–1066) or in the chapel dedicated to Henry VII (r. 1485–1509). The last king to be buried in Westminster Abbey was George II (r. 1727–1760). The church and Dome des Invalides, in Paris, France, contains the tomb of Napoleon I, while Aachen Cathedral in Germany is the final resting place of Charlemagne (r. 768–814).

See also: FUNERALS AND MORTUARY RITUALS; ICONOGRAPHY.

TONGA, KINGDOM OF

(ca. 1000s B.C.E.–Present)

Located in the southern Pacific northwest of New Zealand, the only existing ancient Polynesian kingdom that has survived uncolonized by the Europeans.

Although the Tongan archipelago may have been lightly populated as early as 3000 B.C.E., modern Tongans are descended primarily from the Polynesian Lapita people who colonized the islands during the first millennium B.C.E. The Norwegian archaeologist and explorer Thor Heyerdahl saw similarities between Lapita oral history and the legends of the Incas of South America: both groups traced the ancestry of their royal house to the sun. Most scholars, however, believe that the Lapita people originated in Asia rather than the Americas and migrated to the islands by sea.

The Tongan system of government, as instituted and maintained by the Lapita, was highly stratified and was centralized around the powerful and semidivine figure of the king, or *tui*. War and conquest were viewed as the proper occupations of men, and the Tongan state was highly aggressive. By the end of the thirteenth century C.E., the Tongan Empire had spread to include parts of Fiji, Samoa, and even the Hawaiian Islands. Over time, the power of the *tui* was dispersed to a number of chiefs, all of whom were related to the *tui* by blood.

Tonga was little affected by European exploration until the early part of the nineteenth century. (Captain James Cook, who called Tonga the Friendly Islands, did not stay long enough to realize that the friendliness of the Tongans was part of a plot to kill him and loot his ship.) In 1826, however, Methodist missionaries established the first Christian mission on the island, and Chief Taufa'ahau, later King George Tupou I (r. 1845–1893), converted to Christianity in 1831. Mass conversions soon followed as individual Tongans followed the example of their native ruler.

Like Queen Pomare of Tahiti, Taufa'ahau utilized guns provided by the Europeans to conquer and unify all of the Tongan archipelago, a process that was completed by 1845. As George Tupou I, he married the daughter of the hereditary *tui* and proclaimed himself the new *tui*. In 1862, he adopted a constitution that made Tonga a constitutional monarchy with a written code of laws. By 1888, Tonga was recognized as an independent state by Great Britain, Germany, and the United States.

When George Tupou I died in 1898, he was succeeded by his great grandson, George Tupou II (r. 1893–1918), who allowed the British to take control of Tongan foreign affairs in return for protection against colonization. Upon his death in 1918, his statuesque daughter, Queen Salote Tupou III (r. 1918–1965), only eighteen at the time, took over the throne. Salote proved a popular ruler, concerned with improving the educational and humanitarian conditions of the populace. Her son and successor, who took the name King Taufa'ahau Tupou IV (r. 1965–) upon his coronation in 1965, has been more controversial, hailed by some as a modern leader but scorned by others as an enemy of democracy.

In 1970, the British released control of Tongan foreign affairs, and the archipelago once more became an independent state.

See also: GEORGE TUPOU I; POMARE IV; SOUTH SEA ISLAND KINGDOMS.

TONKING KINGDOM

(ca. 100s B.C.E.–1873 C.E.)

Also Tonkin or Tongking, a kingdom that included most of present-day northern Vietnam.

In 111 B.C.E., the Chinese conquered the area in the Red River Valley (in present-day northern Vietnam) and divided it into three regions; Tonking, Annam, and Cochin China. The region of Tonking covered the Red River Valley and the Mekong Delta region of Vietnam and shared an eastern border with the Gulf of Tonkin. The Chinese ruled the region as a province until the Vietnamese forced them out in 939 C.E. and established an independent kingdom.

With the conquest of the rival Champa kingdom in the fifteenth century, Tonking began to expand into central Vietnam and then into the south. In 1558, Vietnam was divided under the Le dynasty, and the Trinh family seized control of Tonkin. The capital of the northern half of the Tonking kingdom at this time was named Tonkin (modern Hanoi). Europeans eventually came to use this name to describe all of northern Vietnam.

In 1873, French colonists invaded and occupied the region of Tonkin, calling their newly acquired territory Tonking. During World War II, the region was occupied by the Japanese. After the war, Tonkinese and Annamese nationalist leaders joined in demanding independence for the state of Vietnam, and Tonkin was torn by guerrilla warfare between the French and the Viet Minh nationalists. The Vietnamese never used this name to describe their territory.

See also: FUNAN KINGDOM; LE DYNASTY; NGUYEN (HUE) DYNASTY; TRINH DYNASTY.

TORO KINGDOM (1822 C.E.–Present)

One of four traditional kingdoms (with Nyoro, Ganda, and Ankole) located in what is now the nation of Uganda in central Africa.

The Toro kingdom was established as an independent political entity in 1822. Prior to that, it was an important constituent region of the Bunyoro or Nyoro kingdom. Graced with fertile pasturage, the Toro territory is home to some of Bunyoro's most prosperous pastoralist groups. It also contains important mineral resources, particularly salt. It seceded from Bunyoro primarily because many of the Toro pastoralists were angry with Bunyoro's policy of accommodating European immigrants.

The first king of Toro was Olimi Kaboyo (r. ca. 1830–?), a son of the reigning Bunyoro *omukama* (king), Kyebambe III Nyamutukula (r. 1786–1835). Toro's independence, therefore, did not mark an abrupt break with the state from which it seceded, but was rather an administrative and political arrangement meant to alleviate tensions that were mounting in the region.

Toro's independence was challenged by internal dissension as well as external threat. Internally, the greatest problems arose over succession to the throne. Kaboyo ruled until sometime in the 1860s, and when he died his two sons fought over the right to rule. The succession was assured only when one brother succeeded in killing the other. The successful brother, Nyaiki Kasunga (r. 1866–1870), did not have long to enjoy his success, however. In 1870, a powerful new ruler, Kabarega (r. 1870–1898), rose to power in Bunyoro (Nyoro) and almost immediately launched an invasion of Toro, hoping in this way to restore his empire to some semblance of its past prosperity. Although Kasunga succeeded in forestalling Kabarega, the reprieve was only temporary. Kasunga died sometime during the 1870s.

After Kasunga's death, a series of ten kings held the Toro throne, each briefly, until 1876. First was Kasunga's son, Mukabirere (r. ca. 1872–1875), whom Kabarega again attacked. This time the Bunyoro campaign was more successful, and the new king, who had held the throne for only a year, was captured. His son and successor, Mukalusa, fared no better, for he too was captured almost immediately upon claiming the throne.

With a dearth of male heirs, the next person who attempted to rule Toro was Kasunga's sister, Byanjeru (r. 1875). She was deposed, but this time the threat came from a new source: the neighboring kingdom of Buganda. The Buganda king installed one of his own people on the Toro throne, but once again Kabarega invaded and ousted him in 1876, retaking Toro into the Bunyoro kingdom, where it remained a subordinate territory for the next fourteen years.

The Buganda ruler who had been briefly installed upon the throne was Nyamuyonjo (r. 1876), and he did not survive the violence that removed him from power. However, he had a young brother, Kasagama, who made his way safely back to Buganda. A captain in the British colonial service saw advantages to British interests in the region's political upheaval, so in 1891, he lent the power of his forces to the Kasagama faction, installing the young Kasagama on the Toro throne. Upon becoming king, Kasagama took the royal name of Kyebambe IV. His rule was immediately challenged by a renewed attack by Kabarega's forces, and within two years the king was driven from his palace. He fled into the mountains, where he established a resistance base.

It was only with the establishment of British colonial rule in the early 1890s that the constant violence between Toro and its neighbors was finally brought to an end. Kasagama IV was restored to the throne and became the first of the Toro kings to rule for any appreciable length of time, from 1894 to 1929. Upon his death his son, George Rukidi Kamurasi (r. 1929–1965), assumed the throne without incident. During the reign of these two kings, Toro was able to exploit its resources, especially the salt industry. In later years the Toro economy received further boosts from copper mining, tea plantations, and tourism.

Unfortunately, Toro's hard-won peace and prosperity was abruptly ended with the violence that erupted throughout Uganda during the mid-1960s, as British colonial rule came to a close. In 1965, a new king, Patrick Kaboyo (r. 1965–1966), had taken the throne just as violence throughout the colonial territory reached its peak. Within a year he was forced to flee into exile, and in 1967 the Toro kingdom was abolished by A. Milton Obote, prime minister of the newly independent state of Uganda. In 1993, Uganda's president, Yoweri Museveni, rescinded the order abolishing traditional kingdoms. The current king, Oyo Nyimba Kabamba Iguru Rukidi IV (r. 1995–present), inherited the throne when he was only three years old. As a result, regents administered the kingdom on his behalf during his minority.

See also: AFRICAN KINGDOMS; ANKOLE KINGDOM; GANDA KINGDOM; NYORO KINGDOM.

FURTHER READING
Karugire, Samwiri R. *A Political History of Uganda.* Exeter, NH: Heinemann, 1980.

TOUNGOO DYNASTY (1486–1752 C.E.)

Also called Taungui, generally considered the second dynasty of Burma (present-day Myanmar).

Founded by King Minkyinyo (r. 1486–1531) of Toungoo, a small state in Burma, the Toungoo dynasty united Myanmar by conquering the Shan people in northern Myanmar and the Mon in southern Myanmar. Minkyinyo's successor, King Tabinshwehti (r. 1531–1550), expanded the kingdom by moving south and capturing the Irrawaddy Delta region. After taking the Mon capital of Pegu, Tabinshwehti was crowned king of all Myanmar at the city of Bagan in 1544.

Following defeats against coastal Arakan peoples to the west and Thai forces to the east, Tabinshwehti died in 1550 and was succeeded by his brother-in-law, Bayinnaung (r. 1550–1581). Using a succession of military campaigns, Bayinnaung made Toungoo the most powerful state in the region. He marched twice on the kingdom of Ayutthaya (centered at Bangkok) and by 1569 had conquered the entire Chao Phraya Valley. However, Bayinnaung's wars cost Myanmar dearly, and with his death 1581 the kingdom, exhausted of resources, began to fragment and decline.

Under Bayinnaung's grandson, Anaukpetlun (r. 1605–1628), the country suffered a series of rebellions. During his rule, the Toungoo dynasty also moved its capital to Ava, where it remained until 1752. Through a combination of a weakening political status, French encouragement of Indian encroachment in the region, and the rejuvenation of southern Myanmar by British and Dutch commercial activity, the neighboring Pegu kingdom rose in rebellion against the Toungoo dynasty in the 1700s.

Following a century and a half of gradual disintegration, and besieged both internally and externally, the Toungoo dynasty finally collapsed in 1752 with the fall of the resurrected capital of Ava and the death of the last ruler of the dynasty, King Mahadammayazadipati (r. 1733–1752).

See also: AYUTTHAYA KINGDOM; BURMESE KINGDOMS; PEGU KINGDOMS; SHAN KINGDOMS.

TOYOTOMI HIDEYOSHI

(1536–1598 C.E.)

The Japanese samurai leader (r. ca. 1590–1598) who consolidated control as dictator after the death of the warlord and dictator Oda Nobunaga.

Born into a peasant family, Hideyoshi rose to power as a soldier and gifted military commander in the forces of Oda Nobunaga, becoming Nobunaga's leading general. After Nobunaga's death in 1582, Hideyoshi gradually consolidated his power, and, by 1590 he ruled Japan as a dictator.

Short, thin, and ugly, Hideyoshi had been dubbed "Saru," or monkey, by Nobunaga. Described as cheerful, intelligent, and well liked, he secured his position over Nobunaga's heirs through military prowess and strategic alliances with other warlords. Hideoyoshi shared his wealth with loyal feudal lords and spent it to enhance the image of the imperial court. The emperor thus awarded him the family name Toyotomi, "abundant provider." He was popularly considered a generous and benevolent ruler, particularly during the early years of his rule.

In 1584, Hideyoshi came to terms with his main rival, Tokugawa Ieyasu, the powerful *daimyo*, or hereditary warlord, who later became shogun of Japan. The next year, in 1585, the emperor named Hideyoshi *kampaku*, imperial regent-councilor, thereby enhancing Hideyoshi's stature with a position previously held by the powerful Fujiwara family. As such, Hideyoshi's pronouncements had immediate effect on life in Japan in the period of the Ashikaga shogunate, and this carried into the Tokugawa shogunate that followed.

In 1585, Hideyoshi ordered the "Great Sword Hunt," forbidding Japanese farmers from possessing arms and collecting weapons from them. In 1591, his Edict on Changing Status froze the class structure in Japan by forbidding townspeople from becoming soldiers and samurai from living anywhere but in the castle lands of their lords. As a result of this edict, there would be no more peasant-born rulers like himself who could exploit social mobility to rise to power. Hideyoshi further constrained the populace by reviving the practice of collective responsibility, whereby an entire village group would be punished for the wrongdoing of an individual villager. In 1587, he outlawed Christianity and ordered the expulsion of the Jesuits from the country.

Hideyoshi continued Nobunaga's policy of assigning lands strategically to his retainers, or supporters, swapping realms to move the less trusted further away from his capital at Kyoto. He continued land surveys and the standardization of weights and measures, and completed a public census in 1590.

Hideyoshi was ostentatious in the extreme. He built lavish palaces at Osaka and Momoyama. He was famous for personally serving tea to more than eight hundred people at the Grand Kitano Tea Ceremony in 1585 and for hosting a lavish five-day ceremonial visit by the emperor in 1588. He also starred in his own productions of traditional Japanese Noh dramas, which were performed to audiences of nobles.

After 1590, Hideyoshi appears to have succumbed to his less admirable traits, becoming cruel in his attempt to secure the line of Toyotomi succession and obsessed with the idea of conquering China. The chosen route to China was through the Korean Peninsula. Unfortunately for Japan, Hideyoshi's devastating invasions of the Korean Peninsula in 1592 and 1597 earned Japan centuries of enmity from the Koreans. He directed the invasion from Japan while his forces—between 150,000 and 200,000 men— were repelled by the Koreans. Just before his death in 1598, Hideyoshi ordered the last of his troops to withdraw from Korea.

Hideyoshi's role in history is subject to ongoing debate. Nevertheless, he continues to be one of the most studied men in Japanese history, and he remains a popular historical figure with the Japanese public.

See also: ODA NOBUNAGA; TOKUGAWA IEYASU; TOKUGAWA SHOGUNATE.

TRAJAN (ca. 53–117 C.E.)

Popular and generous emperor of Rome (r. 98–117) whose reign was notable for its stability during a time of Roman territorial expansion.

Marcus Ulpius Trajanus was born in the Roman province of Spain around 53. His family, originally from Northern Italy, was very powerful. Trajan's father, who shared the same name as his son, was a member of the Roman Senate and a war hero. Named consul in 70, when Trajan was seventeen years old, the elder Trajanus was appointed governor of the province of Syria in 75. Trajan followed his father to Syria and distinguished himself in the Roman army there, and in 85 he was given command of a Roman legion and posted in his native Spain.

While serving in Spain, Trajan led his troops northwest to fight against the German tribes that were revolting against then-emperor Domitian (r. 81–96). His service in this action earned him the gratitude of the emperor, and he was elected consul in 91. Domitian, a widely unpopular ruler, was murdered in 96, but his successor, the emperor Nerva (r. 30–98) was equally impressed by the young Trajan. Nerva named Trajan governor of the upper German province in 97.

Nerva's grip on power was shaky at best. He was not well loved by the military, which was prone to foment conspiracies against rulers of whom they did not approve. To shore up the military's support, Nerva looked about for a popular leader to adopt as co-regent and successor. Trajan's family connections, personal reputation, and popularity with the troops made him the perfect choice.

When Nerva died sixteen months later, in 98, Trajan was suddenly called to Rome to take his place on the imperial throne. Instead of hurrying to the capital, however, Trajan took nearly a year to return, using the time to visit the troops stationed in Germany and Gaul, thus assuring the support of the military for the rest of his rule. Upon arriving in Rome, he displayed an equal wisdom in dealing with the often fractious Senate, personally appearing before the senators and according them the greatest respect.

During his administration, Trajan paid equal attention to domestic and imperial matters. At home, he initiated public works, instituted a program to provide support for the poor, and called upon wealthy citizens to give greater public service and investment. Abroad, he initiated several military campaigns, expanding the empire's borders and accumulating a great deal of wealth in the process. Much of this wealth was conspicuously spent to increase Trajan's popularity with the masses, particularly on chariot races, gladiatorial contests, and other great spectacles.

Militarily, Trajan was an aggressive leader. During his reign, Rome added the provinces of Dacia (106), Arabia (106), and Armenia (114) to the growing list of Roman provinces. He also succeeded in wresting control of territories in Asia Minor that had been controlled by a rival power, the Parthians. Trajan personally participated in victory over the Parthians, advancing all the way to the Persian Gulf, but continued unrest in the region drove him to withdraw his troops to Syria in 116. In that same year he suffered a stroke and was forced to begin the return to Rome. But he died en route, on August, 9, 117, and was succeeded by his adopted kinsman, Hadrian (r. 117–138).

See also: HADRIAN; ROMAN EMPIRE.

FURTHER READING

Grant, Michael. *The Roman Emperors.* New York: Scribner's, 1985.

Nardo, Don. *The Roman Empire.* San Diego: Lucent Books, 1994.

Starr, Chester. *A History of the Ancient World.* 4th ed. New York: Oxford University Press, 1991.

TRAN DYNASTY (1225–1400 C.E.)

A Vietnamese dynasty of the Dai Viet kingdom (in present-day northern Vietnam) that succeeded the powerful Later Li dynasty (1009–1225). Tran rule was marked by a series of wars with the Yüan (Mongol) dynasty of China and the Champa kingdom to the south.

The Tran dynasty was established in 1225 as a result of an arranged marriage between a young Tran princess and Li Chieu-Hoang (r. 1224–1225), the last ruler of the Li dynasty. To make the Dai Viet kingdom a powerful force in the region, the Tran monarchs continued many of the land reforms, administrative improvements, and educational policies of their Li predecessors. But in 1257, they had to refocus their attention on the first of three Mongol invasions.

The Mongol armies of Kublai Khan (r. 1260–1284), with the aim of controlling the Red River Delta in northern Vietnam, attacked the Vietnamese three times during the 1200s—in 1257, 1284, and 1287. Each time, the Vietnamese successfully resisted the Mongol incursions, finally defeating the Chinese under the leadership of General Tran Hung Dao, who is considered one of the greatest heroes of Vietnamese history.

Meanwhile, tensions with the Tran's southern neighbors, the Kingdom of Champa, dated back to the early days of Vietnamese independence in the 900s. These tensions culminated in a series of wars with Champa during the thirteenth century. The Tran eventually gained power over much of Champa, but Dai Viet was left drained of its resources and vulnerable to peasant insurrections after decades of fighting.

In 1400, General Ho Quy-ly overthrew the Tran ruler, Tran An (Thieu De), and seized control of the throne, ending Tran rule and establishing the short-lived Ho Dynasty (1400–07). With the fall of the Ho dynasty in 1407, Dai Viet entered a period of Chinese control under China's Ming dynasty.

See also: SOUTHEAST ASIAN KINGDOMS; VIETNAMESE KINGDOMS.

TRASTAMARA, HOUSE OF
(1369–1504 C.E.)

Iberian dynasty descended from Henry of Trastamara, the half-brother of King Pedro I of Castile and

León (r. 1350–1369), which was the last ruling dynasty before most of the Iberian kingdoms were united to form the kingdom of Spain.

Henry of Trastamara was the illegitimate son of King Alfonso XI of Castile (r. 1312–1350), whose eldest son, Pedro, assumed the throne upon Alfonso's death in 1350. After Pedro became king, Henry attempted several unsuccessful uprisings against his half-brother Pedro, who defeated Henry with the assistance of Edward, the Black Prince, the eldest son of King Edward III of England (r. 1327–1377) After the English withdrew, however, Henry ousted and killed Pedro.

In 1369 Henry took the throne as Henry II of Castile and León, establishing the House of Trastamara as the reigning house of the joint kingdoms. Despite opposition from John of Gaunt, another son of Edward III of England and Pedro's son-in-law, Henry II maintained his title, which passed on to his descendants.

When Henry died in 1379, he was succeeded on the throne by his son, John I (r. 1379–1390), who tried unsuccessfully to unite the Crowns of Castile and Portugal. John was also forced to defend his Crown against John of Gaunt, and he arranged a marriage between his son, Henry, and John of Gaunt's daughter to eliminate this threat. Henry took the throne as Henry III (r. 1390–1406) upon his father's death in 1390.

Under Henry III, the Trastamara dynasty consolidated its power against the nobility of the kingdom. Henry III also sponsored the colonization of the Canary Islands, which lay off the northeastern coast of Africa. Henry's successor, his son John II (r. 1406–1454), was a sickly ruler who showed little interest to government, entrusting it to a court favorite, Alvaro de Luna. John II preferred the arts and literature, and during his reign, the Trastamara court became known for its great poetry and brilliant festivals.

Another branch of the Trastamara dynasty ruled the kingdom of Aragón from 1412 to1516. It was founded in that kingdom by Ferdinand I of Antequera (r. 1412–1416), the son of John I of Castile, who was chosen to take the Aragónese throne left vacant when its ruler, Martin of Aragón (r. 1396–1410), died without an heir in 1410. Ferdinand's son and successor, Alfonso V, the Magnanimous (r. 1416–1458), ruled not only Aragón but also Sicily and Naples. Eventually leaving Aragón under the rule of his brother, John II of Aragón (r. 1458–1479), he spent the remainder of his life in Naples, where he attempted to introduce Spanish institutions and played an important role in Italian politics.

The best known Trastamara rulers were Isabella I of Castile (r. 1474–1504) and Ferdinand II of Aragón (r. 1479–1516). Their marriage joined the Crowns of Castile and Aragón and laid the foundations for the united kingdom of Spain. They were also the last Trastamara rulers of their kingdoms and of Spain.

See also: ARAGÓN, KINGDOM OF; CASTILE, KINGDOM OF; IBERIAN KINGDOMS; LEÓN, KINGDOM OF; SPANISH MONARCHIES.

TREASON, ROYAL

Accusations or charges brought against a monarch for acts of disloyalty or for actions that compromise the security or integrity of the state.

Under some unusual circumstances, monarchs throughout history have been charged with treason. Most monarchs who have been accused of treason were defeated claimants or usurpers of the throne. The traitors were defined as never having been legitimate monarchs at all, and their treason was against the legitimate monarch rather than the nation. One of many examples of this type of treason is Lady Jane Grey, who briefly claimed the throne of England after the death of Edward VI (r. 1547–1553) in 1553. Defeated by Edward's half-sister Mary I (r. 1553–1558), Grey was eventually executed, but as a private individual rather than as a queen.

Another type of monarch-traitor is one owed allegiance to a higher monarch. For example, before conquering England, William the Conqueror (r. 1066–1087) treated Harold II Godwinson of England (r. 1066) as an oathbreaker for having violated a feudal oath he allegedly swore to support William's candidacy for the English throne.

Monotheistic religions have sometimes charged individuals rulers with betraying God. The best-known example in the Christian tradition is the Roman emperor Julian the Apostate (r. 360–363), called "apostate" because he was brought up a Christian but later converted to paganism. Christians viewed Julian's death in battle against the Persians in 363 as divine punishment for his act of treason against God.

The idea that a legitimate king could be a traitor

to the people or the nation was slow to emerge. It would have been difficult to even conceive of a traitor-king in societies based on personal monarchy, where treason was a crime committed *against* the king, never by him. Charles I of England (r. 1625–1649) was accused of treason (in his capacity as king) by the victorious Parliamentarians after the English Civil War. The judges at his trial claimed that Charles had committed treason by attempting to exceed his lawful powers and becoming a tyrant, as well as by invoking the aid of foreign princes to do so.

Similar accusations were made against Louis XVI of France (r. 1774–1792) during the French Revolution, when he was accused of undermining the Revolution and plotting with foreigners. In the case of both Charles I and Louis XVI, the execution of the king after a public trial was part of a transition from monarchical to republican rule.

There have been several cases in the twentieth century of monarchs being treated as betrayers of the nation. One involves Pu Yi (r. 1908–1912), the last ruler of the Ch'ing (Qing) dynasty, who became puppet-emperor of the Japanese-controlled state of Manchukuo. As monarchy has become less central to political culture, however, the condemnations of monarchs, whether by trial or otherwise, have not had the impact of those of Charles I and Louis XVI.

See also: CHARLES I; DEACCESSION; DETHRONEMENT; EXECUTIONS, ROYAL; JULIAN THE APOSTATE; LEGITIMACY; LOUIS XVI; OATHS AND OATH-TAKING; REBELLION, RITES OF ROYAL; REGICIDE; SUCCESSION, ROYAL; TYRANNY, ROYAL.

TRIBUTE

Money or other valuable contribution exacted by a ruler from his subject nations; it is often exacted for peace or protection from invasion by other countries.

The practice of paying tribute is found throughout all centuries and all civilizations. In 586 B.C.E., for example, King Zedekiah (r. 598–586 B.C.E.) of Judea ignored the advice of the prophet Jeremiah and rebelled against Nebuchadnezzar II of Babylon (r. 604–562 B.C.E.). As a result, Babylonian armies sacked Jerusalem, taking Zedekiah, the wealth of Jerusalem, and other survivors of the conquest back to Babylon as tribute.

The Roman Empire collected tribute from various peoples under its rule, appointing tax collectors to the conquered regions or provinces. The tax collectors were expected to collect a certain amount of tribute, but whatever they took beyond that was theirs to keep. As a result, the system became corrupt and, not surprisingly, in some provinces tax collectors were particularly hated. In ancient Judea, tax collectors were considered unclean. One reason the Britons revolted against the Romans in 60 B.C.E. was because of the high taxes they were forced to pay to the emperor.

In some empires, particularly in ancient times, emperor-worship was also exacted as a form of tribute. In ancient Rome, for example, the later emperors declared themselves to be gods and demanded to be adored by citizens. Subject nations and Christians who refused to do so were dealt with harshly.

The Vikings extorted tribute in the form of *Danegeld,* an amount of gold or silver demanded of peoples the Vikings threatened. Following the Viking plunder of Paris in 843, Charles the Bald, king of the Franks (r. 843–877), paid Viking warriors seven thousand pounds of silver. *Danegeld* was an easy way to obtain plunder without having to fight for it; the Vikings frequently took the plunder and then reneged on the agreement not to attack again. Such was the case in East Anglia in England: in 865, the Vikings took their *Danegeld* in the form of cavalry mounts, but they returned five years later to raid the area again.

In medieval Europe, serfs paid labor as a form of tribute in exchange for a piece of land, military protection, and other benefits they received from the overlord, such as the use of his mill and his winepress. In return, serfs paid a tribute of as much as three days of labor every week, farming the lord's fields, digging ditches, and repairing roads and bridges.

For hundreds of years, the Barbary pirates, operating from bases in North Africa, plundered ships in the Mediterranean Sea and collected tribute from European powers for protection. In the early 1800s, the United States fought an undeclared war against the Barbary pirates under the slogan "Millions for defense, but not one cent for tribute!"

Demands for tribute often led to disaffection and rebellion among royal subjects and vassal states. For example, the Aztec Empire demanded that its subject peoples give not only part of the harvest but also captives to be sacrificed to the Aztec gods. Consequently, when Spanish conquistador Hernán Cortes landed in Mexico in 1519, he easily found a number of groups that were ready to ally themselves with him to throw off the Aztec yoke.

Similarly, even before the height of its power, the British Empire lost the American colonies over a form of tribute. The trouble began when, to finance the French and Indian Wars in North America, the English government tried to collect tribute in the form of a tax. In 1764, the British tried to enact new taxes with the Revenue Act, called the Sugar Act in the colonies, When that failed, they passed the Stamp Act in 1765. American colonists felt that they were not fairly represented in Parliament and thus should not have to pay any taxes Parliament issued; this became one of the issues behind the American Revolution.

Although the collection of tribute often enriched an empire in the short term, in the long run, tribute usually weakened the empire because it became a source of discontent among subject peoples. In the end, this often caused the empire to lose both territory and power.

See also: TAXATION.

FURTHER READING

Durant, Will. *The Story of Civilization.* New York: Simon & Schuster, 1935.

Leckie, Robert. *George Washington's War.* New York: HarperPerennial: 1992.

TRINH DYNASTY (1545–1787 C.E.)

Dynasty that ruled the northern half of Vietnam, known as the Tonking kingdom, in the name of the Le dynasty from the mid-sixteenth through eighteenth centuries.

The Trinh dynasty ruled northern Vietnam, also known as the Tonking kingdom, in the name of the Le dynasty after the Le rulers lost control of their own territory. In 1527, Mac Dang Dung, a member of the powerful Mac family, usurped the throne from the Le family. Eight years later, the powerful Nguyen family reestablished the Le monarchs and drove the Mac family out of central and southern Vietnam.

The Le dynasty did not have real power in Vietnam from that point on. Instead, power was shared between the rival Trinh and Nguyen families, who each capitalized on the power vacuum created by the weak Le rulers and took control of the northern and southern halves of the country, respectively. Both families claimed loyalty to the Le monarchs, who became mere puppet rulers.

The Trinh rulers spent much of the seventeenth century trying, unsuccessfully, to oust the Nguyen family and regain control of the southern territory. Isolated skirmishes between the two families occurred throughout the 1700s, leaving both the north and the south war-torn and vulnerable to peasant revolts.

In 1771 the Tay Son brothers capitalized on peasant unrest and organized an uprising that sought to redistribute land from the hands of a few wealthy landlords to the poor. The Tay Son brothers took control of Vietnam late in the eighteenth century, ending the Le dynasty and the Trinh family's rule.

See also: LE DYNASTY; NGUYEN (HUE) DYNASTY; VIETNAMESE KINGDOMS.

TROAD KINGDOM. *See* TROJAN KINGDOM

TROJAN KINGDOM

(SECOND AND FIRST MILLENNIA B.C.E.)

Semilegendary kingdom in the eastern Mediterranean, located in Anatolia (present-day Turkey), that was immortalized in the works of the ancient Greek poet Homer.

Prior to 1870, many historians and archaeologists considered the heroic world of Homer's *Iliad* and *Odyssey* to be fantasy. However, the discoveries of German businessman and amateur archaeologist Heinrich Schliemann changed that view. In the late 1800s, Schliemann set out to discover the legendary city of Troy using Homer's epics as a guide. He found the ruins of the city on the northwest coast of Turkey in an area now called Hissarlik.

Despite Schliemann's discovery, much of Troy's history remains shrouded in legend. Other than archaeology, the primary sources for Trojan history are Homer's epics and the *Aeneid,* a work written in the first century B.C.E. by the Roman poet Virgil. The archaeological evidence revealed that Troy was located at the western end of the Hellespont, the narrow waterway connecting the Aegean Sea and Black Sea.

Ruler of the semi-legendary Trojan Kingdom, gentle, old Priam was a central figure in Homer's epic poem of the Trojan War, the *Iliad*. This bas relief frieze depicts a scene from that story, in which Priam begs the Greek hero Achilles for the body of his son Hector, whom Achilles killed in the fighting.

This strategic location gave the city control over any trade between the two areas.

Around 1200 B.C.E., the economically powerful Troy confronted the military might of the Greek Mycenaeans in the Trojan War. According to Homer, the Mycenaeans and Trojans fought this war over Helen, the wife of King Menelalus of Sparta. Helen had either fallen in love with or been kidnapped by Paris, the son of King Priam of Troy. In the *Iliad,* the Trojan war is a conflict between the major powers of the ancient Mediterranean world, as well as between the gods, who disagreed over which side should prove victorious. Historically, however, the war was most likely fought over control of the Hellespont and the economic power that came with it. It is not known whether the war destroyed Troy, although the archaeological record indicates that the last remains of the city were burned to the ground in the twelfth century B.C.E.

The legend of Troy continued to attract interest well after the disappearance of the Trojans and Mycenaeans from history. During the great classical age of Greece, the Greeks regarded Homer's epics as history. In his *Aeneid,* Virgil claimed that the Trojan hero Aeneas founded Rome after he and his people escaped the de-struction of their city at the hands of the Mycenaeans. The continued fascination with Troy generated by the epics of Homer and Virgil eventually resulted in Schliemann's discovery of the city more than three thousand years after its fall to the Mycenaeans.

See also: MINOAN KINGDOMS; MYCENAEAN MONARCHIES; SPARTA, KINGDOM OF.

TSARS AND TSARINAS

Titles used by the rulers of Russia from 1547 to 1918, derived from *Caesar,* one of the designations for the rulers of the Roman and Byzantine empires. *Tsarina* is the feminine form of the title used in English; the Russian form is *tsaritsa.*

The rulers of the state of Muscovy were called grand dukes (*velikiye knyazya*) when they were under the overlordship of the Tatars during the Middle Ages. The title of *tsar* was first taken officially by Ivan IV ("The Terrible") (r. 1533–1584) at a coronation in 1547. The use of the new title was a means of cementing an imperial conception of rulership that had been growing for some time in Russia.

Medieval Russians saw the Byzantine emperor as head of all Orthodox Christians. They called the Byzantine capital *Tsargrad* (the city of Caesar), and often used *tsar* to refer to kings. When the Byzantine Empire fell to the Ottoman Turks in 1453, the imperial leadership came to an end. In 1472, Grand Duke Ivan III of Moscow-Vladimir (r. 1462–1505) married Sofia Palaeologus, the niece of the last Byzantine emperor. Sofia brought an exalted view of imperial rule to her new country. Subsequently, Ivan III sometimes used the title *tsar* in an unofficial capacity, and the head of the Orthodox Church, the Metropolitan, referred to Ivan III as "The New Constantine."

In officially taking the title of tsar, Ivan IV believed he was inheriting the emperor's imperial rule and leadership of the Orthodox Church. The title became part of the official designation of all subsequent Russian rulers.

In 1721, after the Peace of Nystad, Peter I (r. 1682–1725) received the title "The Great." At this time, he also began calling himself the "Emperor and Autocrat of all Russia" and "Tsar of Kazan, Astrakhan and Siberia." Thereafter, tsar remained as a secondary title, equivalent to king, but it remained a popular designation for the Russian ruler.

The terms *tsar* and *tsarina* died out with the last rulers of the Romanov dynasty, Tsar Nicholas II (r. 1894–1917) and his wife, the Tsarina Alexandra, who were deposed and later murdered by the Bolsheviks in 1918, during the Russian Revolution.

The rulers of Bulgaria from the tenth through the fourteenth centuries also called themselves tsars, and the use of the term was revived for the kings of Bulgaria between 1908 and 1946.

See also: BYZANTINE EMPIRE; CAESARS; IVAN IV, THE TERRIBLE; RIURIKID DYNASTY; ROMANOV DYNASTY; RUS PRINCEDOMS.

TSHEKEDI KHAMA (1906–1959 C.E.)

Regent of Bechuanaland (r. 1925–1950) who sought to maintain his country's autonomy from European colonial powers.

Although not a king in his own right, Tshekedi Khama served as regent of Bechuanaland (present-day Botswana) from 1925 to 1950. His father, Khama III (r. 1875–1923), was a ruler of the Bamangwato people, and his older brother, Sekgoma II (r. 1923–1925), was expected to inherit the Bamangwato throne.

Befitting his status as son of a king, Tshekedi Khama received a fine education and was sent to attend college in South Africa. Before completing his studies, however, he was called home to attend the funeral of his brother, Sekgoma II, and to assume the regency for the new king, his nephew Seretse Khama (r. 1925–1966), who was then only four years old.

As regent, Tshekedi's greatest concern was to maintain some semblance of autonomy and integrity for Bechuanaland in the face of ever increasing pressures from encroaching Western interests, such as the British South Africa Company (BSAC), a major mining enterprise. An accomplished politician and diplomat, Tshekedi succeeded in forcing the BSAC to withdraw from Bechuanaland in 1934. His efforts did not always lead to success, however. Bechuanaland was, after all, a colonial possession of Great Britain, and whatever independence he might achieve would always be limited. This was made clear in 1933, when Tsekedi's handling of a criminal case involving a young white man led to a sentence of flogging. This punishment raised the ire of the British, who forced Tshekedi to resign his position as

regent. He was reinstated soon after, however, in the face of great public outcry at his treatment.

In 1948 Tshekedi's regency was drawing to a close, for Seretse was now an adult. Tshekedi's popular support was so high, however, that he had retained his position long after Seretse came of age, permitting the young king to complete his education and to travel. However, support for Tshekedi dropped dramatically when Seretse announced that he intended to marry a white Englishwoman. Tshekedi was strongly opposed to this marriage, in decided contrast to the majority of the populace. He thus fell out of favor with the king and was exiled to Britain in 1950. Yet, he remained active in Bechuanaland politics. He died in London in 1959.

See also: KHAMA III.

TUDOR, HOUSE OF (1485–1603 C.E.)

One of the most powerful ruling families of England, whose monarchs expanded royal power and brought about a great cultural flowering.

The house of Tudor originated with Owen Tudor (ca. 1400–1461), a Welshman of ancient lineage who served as squire to King Henry VI (r. 1422–1471) and fought for the house of Lancaster against the house of York during the so-called Wars of the Roses (1455–1485). Through his service to the king and his marriage to Catherine of Valois, the widow of Henry V (r. 1413–1422), Owen Tudor greatly elevated his fortunes and his social standing.

ATTAINING AND SECURING THE THRONE

Owen Tudor's grandson, Henry Tudor, defeated the Yorkist ruler, King Richard III (r. 1483–1485), at Bosworth Field in 1485, a battle that ended the Wars of the Roses. Henry then assumed the Crown as king Henry VII (r. 1485–1509) through a tenuous genealogical claim to the house of Lancaster. His mother was the great-granddaughter of John of Gaunt, who was the father of the first Lancastrian monarch, King Henry IV (r. 1399–1413)

Henry VII married Elizabeth, the heiress of the house of York, which united the warring houses of Lancaster and York and solidified his claim to the throne. The union did not quell civil unrest, however, and Henry VII's reign was filled with threats to na-

Queen Mary I of the Tudor Dynasty took the English throne upon the death of her younger brother, Edward VI, in 1553. Strong-willed and self-possessed like her father, Henry VIII, Mary I was determined to restore Catholicism to England. Her treatment of Protestants earned her the nickname Bloody Mary.

tional stability, including revolts and rival claimants to the throne. Nevertheless, when Henry died in 1509, the Tudor lineage had been firmly established, and the Crown passed to his son Henry, who became Henry VIII (r. 1509–1547).

Henry VIII was one of the most famous English monarchs, largely because of his many marriages and his role in fostering the English Reformation. By about 1427 Henry, unhappy with the inability of his wife Catherine of Aragón to produce a male heir, and infatuated with the young Anne Boleyn, desired an annulment. When the pope would not grant him one, Henry broke with the Church and married Anne in 1533, ushering in the Protestant Reformation in England.

When Henry VIII died in 1547, the throne went to his only legitimate son, Edward VI (r. 1547–1553), the product of Henry's marriage to his third wife, Jane Seymour. Only nine years old when he became king, Edward never ruled in his own right; instead, a regency was established to rule for him until he came of age. He never got the chance because he contracted tuberculosis and died in 1553.

LATER TUDORS

With the death of Edward VI, Henry's hope for a male heir faltered; the most direct claimants to the throne were all female. In the last months of his life, Edward had decided to pass over his two older half-sisters, Mary and Elizabeth, and name as heir Lady Jane Grey, daughter of Edward's protector, the duke of Northumberland. However, Lady Jane Grey ruled for only nine days before Mary Tudor seized power, becoming Mary I (r. 1553–1558).

Mary was the Catholic daughter of Henry VIII and his first wife, Catherine of Aragón. In 1554, Mary married Philip II of Spain (r. 1556–1598), also a Catholic, and reestablished Catholicism in England. The Church of England had taken hold in the country, however, and bloody religious conflict ensued. Mary earned the nickname "Bloody Mary" as a result of the torture and execution of Protestants that occurred during her reign.

Mary died childless in 1558. Her successor, her younger sister Elizabeth, was the Protestant daughter of Henry VIII and Anne Boleyn. Elizabeth I (r. 1558–1603) reestablished the Church of England and became immensely popular with the people. Throughout her long reign, she displayed remarkable skill as a politician, choosing her advisers wisely and paying close attention to her self-presentation and the way the English people perceived her.

Elizabeth chose never to marry, instead becoming "the Virgin Queen." This was a dangerous political move, however. The closest heir to the throne was Mary, Queen of Scots, the controversial ruler of Scotland (r. 1542–1567). Thus, English Protestants were desperate for Elizabeth to marry and ensure a Protestant dynasty.

Rather than marrying and compromising her power, however, Elizabeth took a different approach. When Mary, Queen of Scots, fell into difficulty in Scotland in 1567 after being suspected of murdering her husband, Lord Darnley, Elizabeth offered her sanctuary in England. That sanctuary turned into imprisonment, however, and Mary was eventually executed for plotting against Elizabeth.

Elizabeth faced other challenges to Protestant stability. Excommunicated by the pope in 1570, she was

Tudor, House of (1485–1603)

Henry VII = Elizabeth of York
(1485–1509)

Arthur, Prince
of Wales

Henry VIII* = Catherine
(1509–1547)   of Aragón[1]

= Anne Boleyn[2] = Jane Seymour[3]

Margaret

Mary

Philip II* of Spain = Mary I (1553–1558)

Elizabeth I*
(1588–1603)

Edward VI*
(1547–1553)

*Indicates a separate alphabetical entry.

the target of repeated assassination attempts, and in the 1580s England engaged in a major military conflict with Spain. Despite the turbulent political and religious situation of the time, Elizabeth's reign, known as the Elizabethan age, was a high point of the English Renaissance, producing brilliant writers including Edmund Spenser, Sir Philip Sidney, and William Shakespeare.

END OF THE DYNASTY AND ITS LEGACY

As Elizabeth approached old age, her choice of successor became a matter of heated speculation. The many civil conflicts of the sixteenth century had left the line of succession vague and disputed, and potential successors courted her favor vigorously. Her choice in the end was surprising to many: James VI of Scotland (r. 1567–1625), the only son of her former enemy Mary, Queen of Scots. James was descended from Margaret Tudor, the sister of Henry VIII. By selecting James as her heir, Elizabeth inaugurated a new English dynasty, the house of Stuart, and effected political consolidation between the former bitter enemies, England and Scotland.

The Tudor era, though a violent and turbulent period in English history, ushered in many important changes. The end of the Wars of the Roses and the as-

cent of the first Tudor monarchs marks the transition from the Middle Ages to the Renaissance in England. Henry VIII inadvertently brought about a major religious change, beginning the process whereby England became one of Europe's most powerful Protestant nations. Under the Tudors, as well, England began promoting exploration of the New World, beginning the country's growth as an imperial power. Literature and the arts flourished under the Tudors, particularly during the Elizabethan period.

See also: EDWARD VI; ELIZABETH I; HENRY VII; HENRY VIII; JAMES I OF ENGLAND (JAMES VI OF SCOTLAND); LANCASTER, HOUSE OF; MARY I, TUDOR; MARY, QUEEN OF SCOTS; RICHARD III; STUART DYNASTY; YORK, HOUSE OF.

FURTHER READING

Griffiths, Ralph A., and Roger S. Thomas. *The Making of the Tudor Dynasty.* New York: St. Martin's Press, 1985.

Mackie, J.D. *The Earlier Tudors.* New York: Oxford University Press, 1994.

Ridley, Jasper. *The Tudor Age.* Woodstock, NY: Overlook Press, 1990.

Williams, Penry. *The Later Tudors: England, 1547–1603.* New York: Oxford University Press, 1995.

TUGHLUQ DYNASTY (1320–1414 C.E.)

Turko-Afgan dynasty, rulers of a sultanate centered in the city of Delhi in India, that created an empire but ultimately was unable to hold it together.

In 1320, a Hindu military leader named Khushraw Khan (r. 1320) murdered Sultan Qutbuddin Mubarak I (r. 1316–1320) and took over the Delhi sultanate. Within the year, the Muslim leader Ghazi Malik attacked and defeated Khushraw. Ghazi Malik took the throne as Ghiyasuddin Tughluq I (r. 1320–1324), the founder of the Tughluq dynasty in Delhi.

Malik's first priority as sultan was to cleanse the countryside of all Mongols, whom he hated and regarded as unruly and a threat to peace. He then set out to build an empire, capturing Telingana and Bengal, kingdoms in central and northeastern India, in the first two years of his reign.

Muhammad II bin Tughluq (r. 1324–1351), who succeeded his father as sultan in 1324, attempted to maintain the political momentum toward empire. A time of continual centralization and expansion, his reign marked the high point of Tughluq power, but decline set in toward the end of his rule.

Under Muhammad II, many non-Muslim Indians rose to high and extremely responsible offices within the sultanate. In an effort to gain the support of the peasants and increase revenue, Muhammad proposed a scheme to improve agricultural output and advanced loans to the villagers. These efforts led to a measure of political unity known previously only in the time of the great Maurya Empire (321–185 B.C.E.)

Muhammad's measures were not sufficient to hold the empire together, however. In the north, he had to contend with Hindu revolts and a new Mongol pressure from Afghanistan. To quell dissent in the southern Deccan region, he moved his capital from Delhi to the city of Deogiri, 700 miles to the south, in 1327, but this made little difference.

While Muhammad spent his time putting down rebellions, a total of twenty-two, Muslim nobles and Hindu leaders continued to revolt. Several small Hindu states were formed, the most important of which was Vijayanagar, which was established in 1336. The sultanate of Madura broke away from Muhammad in 1335, and the rest of the south broke away to form the Bahmani kingdom in 1347.

Firoz Shah Tughluq (1351–1388), a nephew of Tughluq I, moved the capital of the sultanate back to Delhi soon after taking the throne in 1351. A mild and gentle ruler, Firoz established an infrastructure that included the largest network of canals in pre-modern India, as well as many towns, mosques, colleges, and hospitals. Firoz also commissioned Persian translations of some important Sanskrit texts. But despite his efforts, the empire continued to crumble.

When Firoz Tughluq died in 1388, the sultanate was in a state of serious decline. Subsequent succession disputes and palace intrigues only accelerated its pace, as several independent Muslim states arose in former Tughluq territory. In 1398, a Mongol warrior named Tamerlane, who had served with the son of Genghis Khan, swept in with his army from the northwest, defeated the Tughluq army, and sacked the city of Delhi. This defeat marked the end of Tughluq power, although members of the dynasty continued to rule a tiny kingdom until 1414, when the Sayyid dynasty took control of what remained of the Tughluq kingdom, a small district around Delhi.

See also: BAHMANI DYNASTY; DELHI KINGDOM; MAURYA EMPIRE; MONGOL EMPIRE; TAMERLANE (TIMUR LENG).

TULUNID DYNASTY (868–905 C.E.)

The first independent Muslim dynasty of Egypt, which was noted for its fine art and architecture.

The Tulunid dynasty of Egypt was founded in 868 by Ahmad ibn Tulun (r. 868–884). The son of a Turkish slave, Tulun became a soldier and then served as head of the caliph's guard at the court of Caliph al-Ma'mun (r. 813–833) of the Abbasid dynasty. In the 860s, the caliph awarded Tulun's stepfather with the governorship of Egypt, but the older man decided to send the young Tulun in his place as vice-governor.

Tulun arrived at the Egyptian capital of Al-Fustat in 868. Four years later, in 870, his stepfather died and Tulun was granted full governorship of Egypt by the Abbasid caliph. Within a short time, however, Tulun had established an independent military in Egypt and stopped sending taxes to the caliphate. He also established a new capital at Al-Qata'i.

Ahmad ibn Tulun nearly lost control of Egypt around 872 when the Abbasids tried to regain control of the province. But he was able to retain his autonomy by paying them off with gifts. Then, around 875 or 877, Tulun refused to send tribute to Baghdad. The caliph sent an expedition against him, but this was eventually abandoned. In 878, Ahmad ibn Tulun rebelled against the Abbasids and occupied the region of Syria.

The arts flourished in Egypt under Tulun's rule, and in 879 the Mosque of Ahmad ibn Tulun was built in Al-Qata'i to immortalize his name. By 880, Tulun had begun to mint coins in his own name, which had previously been the sole prerogative of the caliphs. He encouraged not only the arts and architecture, but also stimulated agricultural development, industry, trade, and commerce in Egypt. Ahmad ibn Tulun died in 884 after contracting dysentery in Syria while on military campaign there.

Tulun was succeeded by his son, Khumarawayh (r. 884–896), who proved to be a moderately effective ruler. Shortly after his father's death, in 885, he invaded Palestine and defeated an Abbasid army there. Yet, despite this initial success, the financial and military situation of the Tulunid dynasty deteriorated under his leadership.

Khumarawahy's successors—Jaysh (r. 896), Harun (r. 896–905), and Shayban (r. 905)—fared poorly as leaders, and in 905 the Abbasids managed to reconquer Egypt. The Abbasids brought the surviving members of the Tulunid family to Baghdad and destroyed the capital of Al-Qata'i.

See also: ABBASID DYNASTY; CALIPHATES; ISLAM AND KINGSHIP.

TUPAC YUPANQUI (d. 1493 C.E.)

Incan ruler (r. ca. 1471–1493), also known as Topa Inca, who was one of history's most successful conquerors. Through his military exploits, Tupac secured a territory for the Inca comparable to that of the Roman Empire at its height.

The son of the great Inca ruler Pachacuti (r. 1438–1471), Tupac Yupanqui (Topa Inca) began his military exploits under the aegis of his father, who appointed Tupac leader of a campaign to conquer the lands north of the Inca Empire. Tupac did so with extraordinary thoroughness. After defeating the Inca's ancestral enemies, the Chanca, he continued north, attacking and conquering the kingdom of Chimu and extending the borders of the Inca Empire as far north as present-day Quito in Ecuador.

Having extinguished the two greatest military threats to Incan security—the Chanca and Chimu—Tupac returned to the Inca capital of Cuzco. Faced with a state that had increased dramatically in size, Pachacuti and Tupac worked together quickly to institute a number of administrative reforms that would allow the Inca to rule their growing empire more effectively. This included forming a highly centralized bureaucracy and codifying Inca law.

In 1471, Pachacuti chose to abdicate the throne in favor of Tupac, who soon left Cuzco to lead another military campaign—this time attempting to conquer the rain forest lands near the River Tono to the east. While he was gone, a revolt broke out near Lake Titicaca, when it was rumored that Tupac had died in the jungle. The Inca ruler was forced to abort the campaign to quell the unrest.

After successfully putting down the rebellion at Lake Titicaca, Tupac turned his armies southward, adding the highland region of Bolivia, northwestern Argentina, and northern Chile to his empire. In 1476, Tupac turned inward to conquer the coastal region of southern Peru, which, though surrounded by the Inca Empire, had still not been incorporated into it. This proved to be a time-consuming enterprise, as Tupac attacked each valley separately. It took more than three years before all coastal Peru was firmly under Inca rule.

Quenched, perhaps, of his taste for conquest, Tupac devoted the remainder of his rule to improving the administration of the empire. He continued policies of ethnic resettlement, state land ownership, and state-supported religion that he had developed with his father. He also instituted other policies, such as imposing Quechua as the official language, which were designed to strengthen the political unity of the diverse Inca Empire. This unity held for the duration of Tupac's rule and even after his unexpected death in 1493, despite a dispute over the succession. Tupac Yupanqui was succeeded by his son, Huayna Capac (r. 1493–1524), who was the last great Inca to rule over a united Incan empire.

See also: CHIMU EMPIRE; HUAYNA CAPAC; INCA EMPIRE; PACHACUTI; SOUTH AMERICAN MONARCHIES.

TURKIC EMPIRE (552–840 C.E.)

Kingdom located in the Central Asian steppe region that flourished between the sixth and ninth centuries.

The Turks began as a tribal vassal of the Chinese in the mid-sixth century. Their transition from vassal to overlord was initiated by a revolt against Chinese rule in 552. As a result of this revolt, their Turkish chief, Tumin (r. 552–562), was named khan (lord, prince) of Mongolia.

A decade later, the successors to Tumin began to expand their realm by allying with the Sasanid dynasty of Persia to capture the city of Soghia from the Huns. In exchange for the alliance with the Sasanids, the Turks were required to allow the Persians to claim the region of Bactria. However, the Turks soon took Bactria for themselves, once they had assurances that the Byzantine Empire would remain neutral in any relations between the Turks and Persians.

The death of the second Turkic khan, Istemi (r. ca. 562–576), brought a destabilizing element into the ruling house with its new ruler, Tardu (r. ca. 576–603). Despite the benefits reaped as a result of the alliance with the Byzantine Empire, Tardu waged war on the Byzantines over a period of nearly fifteen years. Furthermore, he sought to capitalize on domestic difficulties in the neighboring Chinese Empire by besieging it in 601.

The Chinese eventually pushed back the Turks, and shortly afterward, Tardu died. His death allowed internal dissension within the realm to divide the Turks of the eastern and western portions into separate kingdoms. In addition to the larger Turkic khanate splitting in two, the western Turkish kingdom split into smaller states.

This period of Turkic division was disastrous for the eastern Turks, who eventually fell prey to the Chinese and became a protectorate of the T'ang dynasty. In the west, however, by the late 620s, a semblance of unity began to reemerge. This renewed cohesion made it possible for the Turkic realm to expand west to the Caspian Sea and south to India.

In spite of the success of the western Turks in reintegrating themselves as a political unit, they also fell victim to T'ang maneuvering, as the T'ang encouraged various nomadic groups in the Turkic domains to rebel. As a result, when the reigning khan, T'ung Shih-hu (r. ca. ?–630), was murdered in 630, the western Turkic realm disintegrated once again. It took another half-century for the Turks to liberate themselves from Chinese control.

In 682, the Turks rebelled against the Chinese and successfully liberated themselves. This revolt, led by Tonyukuk (r. ca. 682–691), was made possible by the wide dispersion of the Chinese military throughout the Asian steppes. Once the Chinese had been overthrown, Tonyukuk named himself khan and began the process of joining the various eastern Turkic tribes of Mongolia into a single cohesive empire.

For the next thirty-five years, particularly after the accession of Kapgan (r. ca. 691–716) in 691, the eastern Turks faced continued tension and conflict with the western Turks. They also made unremitting attempts to keep the Chinese destabilized by making repeated incursions into Chinese territory.

Following the death of Kapgan, Tonyukuk's son-in-law, Bilga (r. 716–734), came to the throne. Bilga used the pillaging of Chinese borderlands as a bargaining chip with which he negotiated peace with the T'ang in 722. After Bilga died of poisoning in 734, he was succeeded by Tangri (r. 734–741), who was also murdered. Tangri's death once again destabilized the Turkic Empire, plunging it into a series of domestic conflicts and rebellions. The rebellions ended with the accession of the Uighur tribe to power in Mongolia in 744.

For the next fifty years, the Turks held the Chinese as tributaries. This prestigious status lasted until the death of Baga Tarkan (r. 779–789), and Turkic decline accelerated under the short reign of his successor, Kuluge Bilge (r. 789–790). By 805, the Turkic Empire had begun to disintegrate as it had done in the past. Its decline was furthered by the onset of war with the Turks' northern neighbors, the Kyrgyz. This war, in combination with internal struggles within the Turkic realm, allowed the Turks to be conquered by the Kyrgyz in 840, effectively ending the Turkic khanate.

See also: ASIAN DYNASTIES, CENTRAL; T'ANG DYNASTY.

TUTANKHAMEN (d. ca. 1325 B.C.E.)

Young Egyptian pharaoh (r. ca. 1334–1325 B.C.E.), sometimes referred to as the "boy-king," whose burial site in Egypt's Valley of the Kings was found almost intact in 1922 by English archaeologist Howard Carter.

Very little is known about Tutankhamen's short life and reign. He was only nine years old when he became the twelfth pharaoh of the Eighteenth dynasty, and the realm he inherited was not strong. Tutankhamen reigned only until age eighteen, when he suffered a mysterious death. Medical examination of his mummy indicated that he was most likely a brother of Pharaoh Smenkhkare (r. ca. 1336–1334 B.C.E.) and son-in-law of Pharaoh Akhenaten (r. ca. 1350–1334 B.C.E.), and that he probably became pharaoh after their deaths.

Evidence suggests that Tutankhamen spent his early years in Akhenaten's capital, Akhetaton (Tel el-Amarna). Possibly to make his ascendancy to the throne more certain, Tutankhamen was married to the third daughter of Akhenaten, who was probably the royal family's oldest surviving princess. Since he was so young when he became king, high-ranking officials—especially the vizier Ay and the general Horemheb—governed Egypt during most of his reign. These officials also moved the capital back to Thebes and put a stop to the monotheistic religious cult of Aten that had been established by Akhenaten.

The principal military action during Tutankhamen's reign, led by General Horemheb, was a battle against

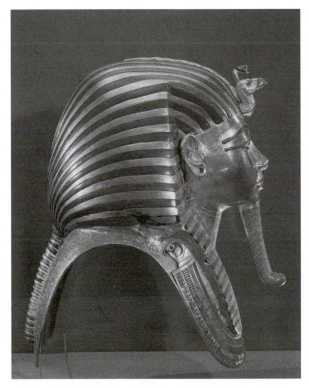

Although only a boy when he ruled, and insignificant in terms of his accomplishments, Tutankhamen is one of the best-known pharaohs of Ancient Egypt. His fame rests largely on the amazing artifacts found in his tomb when it was unearthed in 1922. Among them was this gold death mask inlaid with semi-precious stones.

the Hittites. Tutankhamen died suddenly at the time of a battle against the Mitanni kingdom in northern Syria. Upon his death, the throne passed to the vizier, Kheperkheprure Ay (r. ca. 1325–1321), who apparently also married Tutankhamen's widow, Ankhesenamen.

Like many Egyptian royal tombs, Tutankhamen's tomb had been looted in ancient times, but for some reason not much was taken. The tomb was closed up again and hidden from sight, buried by rock debris from a later construction nearby. When Howard Carter cleared away the debris in 1922, he found steps leading down to the tomb's entry. Archaeologists and scholars have learned a lot about ancient Egyptian civilization from King Tut's tomb, which is considered one of the greatest ever made.

Tutankhamen's mummy was found inside three highly decorative coffins. The innermost one was made of solid gold, shaped like a human with a painted representation of Tutankhamen. A magnificent gold funerary mask covered Tutankhamen's face. The tomb's burial chamber and other rooms contained an enormous amount of gold, jewels, weapons, furniture, statuary, clothes, and other extraordinary objects, such as golden beds and couches from a state chariot, perfume that remained aromatic in sealed pots, and remarkably well-preserved flower garlands. Probably the most magnificent piece was a gold and silver throne covered with jewels. Much of the treasure from Tutankhamen's tomb can now be viewed at the Egyptian Museum in Cairo.

See also: AKHENATEN; HITTITE EMPIRE; MITANNI KINGDOM.

TUTSI KINGDOM (1400s–1890 C.E.)

Kingdom in east-central Africa, located in what is today Rwanda, that was originally inhabited by a people called the Twa and that established a social structure that has colored the history of the region down to the present day.

Sometime in the 1100s, a wave of immigration in east Africa brought Hutu agriculturalists to the region of present-day Rwanda, where they settled in farming communities alongside the Twa people. In the fifteenth century, a new group of immigrants arrived in the region, this time cattle pastoralists coming into the region from the north. These were the ancestral Tutsi people, led by a man named Ruganzu

Bwimba. Ruganzu Bwimba selected an area near present-day Kigali and settled there, establishing the early foundation of the Tutsi kingdom.

The Tutsi had a long tradition of raiding and territorial dominance, which put their new neighbors, the Twa and Hutu, at a disadvantage. Neither of these peoples had any sort of martial tradition, so when the Tutsi clan chiefs began to exert their claims to dominance over the territory, the Twa and Hutu peoples found themselves easily subdued and absorbed. The subjugation of the Hutu was completed in the seventeenth century under the rule of Ruganu Ndori (r. ca. 1600–1624), and the Tutsi kingdom achieved its greatest extent in the nineteenth century under King Kigeri Rwabugiri (r. 1853–1890). In 1890, however, the entire region came under the colonial control of Germany, and the Tutsi kingship was stripped of its authority and autonomy.

The Tutsi kingdom was structured along the lines of a feudal kingship, with leadership roles restricted to those of Tutsi descent, while the Hutu served a subordinate role as serfs. At the head of society was the *mwali,* or king, who ruled with the assistance and advice of a subordinate chiefly class, also drawn from ethnic Tutsis.

Each Tutsi chief controlled an *umusozi,* roughly the equivalent of a fiefdom, which comprised a hilltop settlement and surrounding agricultural fields. Below the chiefs came the ethnic Hutu, who worked the farms of the *umusozi* at the discretion of the Tutsi leadership. These strict social divisions led to the formation of powerful resentments on the part of the Hutu against their Tutsi rulers. These underlying resentments may be seen as the forerunner of much of the ethnic violence that has erupted periodically between the Hutu and Tutsi in Rwanda today.

See also: African Kingdoms.

Tyranny, Royal

The assumption of absolute power by a monarch, also known as despotism or autocracy.

Tyranny has manifested itself at various points throughout the history of virtually every nation, and it is, as some historians have argued, a natural consequence of monarchical forms of government. Though it is common to speak of some rulers as "en-

lightened despots," in reality few royal personages who have enjoyed anything approaching absolute power have wielded such power to the betterment of their people.

Tyranny is generally considered to rival anarchy as the most destructive form of political organization. Historically, tyrannical reigns have rarely been long, as tyrannies are weakened both by internal opposition and by the effect of decisions made by the monarch, which are rarely undertaken for the good of the nation or the people. Fear of, and resistance to, tyranny is one of the primary motivating reasons for the gradual shift away from monarchy and toward democracy.

ORIGINS OF TYRANNY

The history of tyranny is characterized by a fundamental twist in the definition of the word. Ancient Greek society saw the reign of many rulers known as *tyrannos* (tyrants), who were not necessarily despotic or disliked. Greek tyrants were merely those rulers who had seized power through illegal means, such as a military overthrow.

Ancient Greek tyrants generally were able to gain power with widespread support of the people, usually emphasizing one issue or several related issues and claiming to promote some kind of reform. The tyrants would often try to preserve their legacy by declaring their reign hereditary, which moved their tyrannies toward monarchies.

Many Greek tyrants, such as Pisistratus of Athens (r. 560–527 B.C.E.), were actually very capable and generous rulers, who remained well liked throughout their reign. However, the inherently volatile nature of tyrannies—in which the ruler was only as strong as his military—caused this form of government to eventually give way to limited democracy by the third century B.C.E. It was after this point that the word "tyranny" began to acquire a negative connotation, as the democratic Greeks viewed the time of tyranny as a period of virtual anarchy and barbarism.

Tyranny in Rome

Although "tyranny" had not developed into its modern meaning in ancient times, there were many leaders then who would now be called tyrannical. One of the most famous of these was Tarquin the Proud, a semilegendary king who ruled Rome as an absolute monarch in the sixth century B.C.E. until he was overthrown, possibly after the infamous, and possi-

ROYAL RELATIVES

A PERSISTANT TYRANT—PISISTRATUS (ca. 605–527 B.C.E.)

Pisistratus was a tyrant of Athens known for his generally benevolent rule. Little is known of his background, but it is clear that he enjoyed the support and friendship of the great Athenian statesman Solon and that he had distinguished himself in battle as a young man.

In the years immediately before 560 B.C.E., Pisistratus began to agitate against the aristocracy then in power in Athens, and he became an informal leader and representative of the poor. After gathering military strength, Pisistratus attacked Athens, taking charge of the city in 560. Unable to maintain his power, he was exiled almost immediately. Still popular, he returned in 559 B.C.E., this time to rule for three years before being driven out once again by the Athenian aristocracy.

Pisistratus returned to Athens once more in 546 B.C.E., subduing his enemies for good. His reign as tyrant was a prosperous time for Athens, and he was able to lift some of the tax burden on rural farmers, gaining him even greater popularity. Pisistratus encouraged cooperation among the various peoples of the Mediterranean, promoted the literary arts, revived popular religious festivals and groups, and built many temples and monuments. Although he gave preference to friends and family members for government positions and practiced hostage-taking as a political policy, contemporary sources viewed him most favorably.

bly legendary, rape of the virtuous Roman matron Lucretia by his son, Sextus Tarquinius.

It is not known how much of the Tarquin story is true, but Tarquin the Proud is generally considered to have been the last king of Rome, and the Romans used his rule as justification for establishing a new republican form of government. Despite the example of Tarquin, the early Roman Empire would see several figures who ruled despotically, most notably the emperors Caligula (r. 37–41 C.E.) and Nero (r. 54–68 C.E.).

Tyranny and Feudalism

In the first few centuries following the collapse of the Roman Empire in 476 C.E., there was little opportunity for royal tyranny in either Europe or the Near East, as those regions fell under the control of a series of much smaller, less centralized monarchies, and then into feudalism.

In the Far East, in China, the tyranny of the Ch'in (Qin) dynasty had been overthrown in the third century B.C.E., and a feudal system was established that lasted hundreds of years. Similar phenomena would

later occur in Russia and Japan. Monarchs of the feudal period in Europe and Asia were sometimes described as tyrannical, but rarely if ever did any of them gain the amount of political power required for such a designation to be accurate.

TYRANNY RESURFACES

Royal tyranny reemerged at the end of the feudal era, as political philosophies promoting the divine right of kings gained popularity among monarchs. The divine right theory held that monarchs enjoyed their rule as a mandate from God and that their authority thus could not be criticized by human standards.

The first two English kings of the Stuart dynasty, James I (r. 1603–1625) and Charles I (r. 1625–1649), both attempted to put the philosophy of divine right into practice and rule autocratically. Both kings dissolved the British Parliament and ruled alone for brief periods, but neither was able to successfully maintain absolute power.

Seventeenth-century France also succumbed to royal absolutism, under the rule of King Louis XIV (r. 1643–1715). The reign of Louis's predecessor, his father Louis XIII (r. 1610–1643), had seen the monarchy rise in strength thanks to the crafty political schemes of Cardinal Richelieu, and Louis XIV pursued this to its fullest extent.

Using the support of the emerging French middle class to build antagonism toward powerful French nobles, Louis XIV was able to assume almost total control over the government. However, the tyranny of the French monarchy began to wane with Louis's death in 1715. The French Revolution that began in 1789 and led to the death of King Louis XVI (r. 1774–1792) and the establishment of a republic struck a severe blow against royal power throughout Europe.

NAPOLEON AND THE END OF TYRANNY

Despite the democratic uprising of the French Revolution, France quickly fell back under the power of an absolute ruler, this time in the person of Napoleon Bonaparte (r. 1804–1814; 1815).

Though not a monarch in the traditional sense, Napoleon ruled with a royal authority surpassing even that of Louis XIV. Historians continue to debate the value of Napoleon's reign, but it is beyond dispute that he ruled as a vigorous tyrant. Fittingly, Napoleon's brief tenure as absolute ruler helped foster many of the democratic movements that characterized Europe's political development over the next two hundred years.

Although the later nineteenth and twentieth centuries witnessed several governments around the world in which absolute power was effectively invested in one person (such as Nazi Germany), none of these were monarchies in the traditional sense. Indeed, the rapid spread of democracy around the world in the post-Napoleonic era ensured that royal tyranny would remain a thing of the past.

See also: Caligula; Charles I; Divine Right; Feudalism and Kingship; James I of England (James VI of Scotland); Louis XIV; Napoleon I (Bonaparte); Nero; Power, Forms of Royal; Tarquin the Proud.

TWO SICILIES, KINGDOM OF

THE. *See* Naples, Kingdom of; Sicily, Kingdom of

Tz'u Hsi (Cixi), Empress

(1835–1908 C.E.)

Consort to Chinese emperor Xianfeng, who used her role as empress dowager to rule China for nearly fifty years. One of the most powerful women in Chinese history, Tz'u Hsi became a concubine of Ch'ing emperor Xianfeng in 1851. On his death, Tz'u Hsi seized power by claiming the throne for her six-year-old son, Tongzhi, and establishing herself as his regent.

Tz'u Hsi ruled China from behind a screen in the throne room. As a woman, discretion required that she remain hidden when meeting with government ministers. In the early years of her regency, Tz'u Hsi suppressed the anti-Ch'ing Taiping Rebellion and helped restore Ch'ing power after the invasion of Beijing by Western forces in 1860.

Although Tongzhi was the emperor in name, he never had any real power. He led a dissipated life and died in 1875 while still in his teens. After Tongzhi's death, Tz'u Hsi retained power by installing her four-year-old nephew, Guang Xu, on the throne. Guang Xu was intimidated by Tz'u Hsi and remained dominated by her for most of his life.

Tz'u Hsi supported the Boxer movement, which called for removing foreigners from China. The Boxers, believing they possessed magical powers that made them immune to foreign bullets, laid siege to foreign legations in China in 1900. After Western troops defeated the Boxers, Tz'u Hsi was forced to pay a large indemnity to foreign nations.

Tz'u Hsi was out of touch with the empire's problems. The bureaucracy was rife with corruption, while foreign nations constantly encroached on Chinese territory. Tz'u Hsi was also extravagant. In 1893, she diverted money from the navy to build herself a palace, complete with a huge marble boat. China's ill-equipped navy was routed by the Japanese in 1894, losing the war over Korea.

Emperor Guang Xu asserted himself in 1898 by issuing the "Hundred Days' Reform," a series of edicts that called for sweeping reforms to modernize China's institutions. The conservative Tz'u Hsi opposed the reforms and ordered Guang Xu locked up in the summer palace, where he remained a virtual prisoner for the rest of his life.

In her final years, Tz'u Hsi abandoned some of her conservatism, promising to institute constitutional government by 1916. She died in 1908 at age seventy-three. In a highly suspicious coincidence, the thirty-seven-year-old Guang Xu had died the previous day. Tz'u Hsi had chosen a grandnephew, the three-year-old P'u I (Pu Yi), to succeed him.

See also: CH'ING (QING) DYNASTY; PU YI.

UDAIPUR KINGDOM

(ca. 1568–1707 C.E.)

Rajput kingdom that arose in the northeastern Rajasthan region of India during the reign of the Mughal Empire.

Udaipur originally existed as a city in the kingdom of Mewar in the Rajasthan region of India. During the reign of the Mewar king, Udaya Singh (r. 1537–1572), in the mid-sixteenth century, a series of violent Mughal raids razed the Mewar capital at Chitor. In 1568, after the last of these raids, Udaya Singh constructed the city of Udaipur, which would eventually replace Chitor as the capital. Udaipur was built in the mountainous region of Mewar, making it easier to defend than the more exposed Chitor.

Udaya Singh soon utilized this new refuge. In 1568, the Mughal emperor, Akbar the Great (r. 1556–1605), invaded Rajasthan again. Udaya fled Chitor, leaving 8,000 soldiers and 40,000 residents to oppose the Mughals. When Akbar and his massive army approached, the defenders launched a *jauhar,* or a suicidal attack against the more powerful enemy. Akbar slaughtered all of the defenders and completely destroyed all remains of Chitor. Subsequently, Udaipur became the new capital of Mewar.

In 1654, after nearly a century of subservience to the Mughals, Mewar sought to regain its independence. The Mewar ruler at that time, Raja Singh I (r. 1652–1680), deliberately reconstructed the Chitor fortress. But Shah Jahan (r. 1628–1658), the Mughal emperor, discovered this activity and sent an expedi-tionary force to oversee the permanent destruction of the fortress and occupy the region around Chitor. As a result, Raja Singh only retained control of the area surrounding Udaipur. The kingdom thus came to be known as Udaipur instead of Mewar.

Three years later, in 1657, Shah Jahan became extremely ill, and a struggle arose among his sons for control of the empire. Raja Singh wisely allied himself with the emperor's son, Aurangzeb (r. 1658–1707), and helped him to eventually secure the Mughal throne. In return, Aurangzeb gave Raja Singh title to four districts surrounding Udaipur and a large payment of treasure. Under Aurangzeb's beneficence, Udaipur reached the peak of its power.

Soon, however, Aurangzeb extorted his weaker ally. The emperor wished to completely subjugate Rajasthan, and Udaipur offered the quickest path to that goal. To stem the impending invasion, Jaya Singh (r. 1680–1699), Raja Singh's successor, signed a new treaty with the Mughal Empire in 1681. He ceded several strategic districts to the Mughals and pledged military support for the Mughal campaign against Rajasthan. He also swore that his heir would be a Mughal vassal.

The treaty temporarily sustained the stability and autonomy of Udaipur. But it also irrevocably linked Udaipur with the Mughal Empire. When the empire's dominance faded, Udaipur lacked any support. The other Rajasthan states, resentful of Udaipur's alliance with and obedience to the Mughals, attacked and soon crippled the kingdom. In 1770, the British easily overtook the weakened Udaipur kingdom and incorporated it into their expanding Indian colony.

See also: AURANGZEB; INDIAN KINGDOMS; JAHAN, SHAH; MUGHAL EMPIRE; RAJASTHAN KINGDOM.

UIGHUR EMPIRE (744–840 C.E.)

Empire established in western China and Mongolia by the Uighurs, a nomadic people who overthrew the Turkish khanate in Mongolia in the 700s C.E. and established their own state.

In the third century, a group of Turkish tribes moved across Asia and settled in the vast plains of western China. For almost three hundred years, a tribe called the Tuchuehs dominated the others and established a Muslim khanate. During the seventh century, however, the nomadic Uighurs formed an alliance known as the "Nine Clans."

These nine tribes increasingly resisted Turkish control of Mongolia. In 744, their resistance culminated in a fierce battle. The nine clans, led by the Uighurs, emerged victorious and ended Turkish control of the region. Buoyed by their role in the victory, the Uighurs subjugated the other tribes and formed their own empire. Kuli Peilo (Qutlugh Bilga Kul Khan) (r. 744–747), a mighty Uighur warrior, became the empire's first ruler.

In 747 Peilo's successor, Moyencho (Bolmish Bilga Khan) (r. 747–759), constructed a capital named Karabalghasun on the Orkhon River. Attempting to curb the Uighurs' nomadic lifestyle, Moyencho oversaw the cultivation of permanent farmland, formed a variety of artisan guilds, and erected a second city on the Selenga River to serve as a commercial center. He also instituted Manichaeism as the official state religion. Although the Uighurs did not completely abandon their nomadic traditions, they established a culture and literature that were widely admired in Asia.

As the Uighur society developed, the Uighur monarchs established an uneasy relationship with the T'ang dynasty of China. The Chinese had initially attempted to conquer the Uighurs, but the Uighurs possessed a highly skilled cavalry and defeated the attackers. Recognizing their strength, the Uighurs exerted control over the portion of the Silk Road that passed through their territory, exacting heavy taxes from all merchants who passed through their domain. The Chinese ruefully paid these taxes because they knew the Uighurs possessed the power to block all trade along their stretch of the Silk Road.

Eventually, the Uighurs formed a tenuous alliance with the T'ang dynasty because the formidable Tibetan army threatened both groups. With their combined forces, the Uighurs and Chinese were able to deter a potential Tibetan invasion in the mid-eighth century. When the Chinese rebel, An Lu-shan, attempted to overthrow the T'ang dynasty in 755, the Uighurs honored their alliance with the T'ang. The combined forces of the Uighur cavalry with the T'ang army easily defeated An Lu-shan's rebels.

After stopping the rebellion, the T'ang monarch, envious of the Uighur cavalry, negotiated an agreement with the Uighurs under which the Uighurs would provide horses and training in return for Chinese silk. Both kingdoms initially benefited, but by the 780s, the Uighurs increasingly manipulated the arrangement. They provided their weakest horses to the Chinese, yet they still received the choicest silks. They angered the Chinese by treating them with disdain and mocking their military proficiency. Uighur clans also sporadically looted western Chinese communities.

Still, the alliance between the Uighurs and the T'ang dynasty persisted because Tibet posed a constant threat, and the Uighur cavalry, combined with the Chinese army, provided the best deterrent to a Tibetan invasion. In 788, the Tibetan ruler allied with the Pratihara Raja of India and proposed a joint invasion of China. Meanwhile, to fortify the alliance between the Uighurs and the T'ang dynasty, the Uighur *qaghan,* or emperor, married a T'ang princess.

In 821, another marriage occurred between the two royal families, and the Uighur *qaghan* demanded a massive dowry of silk, jewels, pottery, and other handicrafts. The Uighurs continued their unbalanced trade with the Chinese, threatening to blockade the Silk Route if the Chinese refused. Largely as a result of this unbalanced trade, the Uighurs enjoyed their greatest power and prosperity during the early years of the ninth century.

Uighur fortunes rapidly diminished thereafter, however. In the early 830s, internal strife crippled the Tibetan kingdom. Freed from this threat, the Chinese rejected their enforced trade agreement with the Uighurs. At first, the Uighurs threatened to attack the Chinese. But in 840, the last Uighur emperor died without leaving a successor. The absence of a strong leader soon weakened the Uighur Empire, leaving it highly vulnerable.

In 844, the Kirghiz people invaded from the north and overran both the Uighur Empire and Tibet. China, less fearful of the Kirghiz than the Uighur cavalry, refused to aid their former allies. The Uighurs fled to the south and established a new kingdom called Kocho, but they were eventually conquered by the Mongols.

See also: T'ang Dynasty; Tibetan Kingdom.

FURTHER READING

Ben-Adam, Justin. *Oasis Identities: Uighur Nationalism along China's Silk Road.* New York: Columbia University Press, 1997.

Ulster Kingdom (353 b.c.e.–1603 c.e.)

An ancient and medieval kingdom in northern Ireland. At the beginning of the Christian era, most of northern Ireland was ruled by a people called the Ulaid, probably Celts from Britain. (Ulster comes from *Ulaid* plus the Norse *stadhr* or place.)

THE UÍ NEILL KINGS

In the fifth century, the Ulaid were subjugated by the Uí Neill dynasty, who established their rule over the territory. The Uí Neill traced their descent from Eremon, one of the two sons of Míle Easpain, who, according to legend, had arrived in Ireland at the end of the second millennium B.C.E. The name of the dynasty came from a descendant of Eremon named Niall Naoi-Ghiallach (r. ca. 445–452 C.E.), a high king of Ireland. His nickname, "Niall of the Nine Hostages," indicates that he was a powerful ruler and conqueror. According to legend, Niall carried out sea raids along the coasts of England, Scotland, France and Italy.

By Niall's time, Ulster was divided into three kingdoms: Uladh or Ulida (home of the Ulaid), Orghialla or Oriel to the south, and Tir Eóghain or Tyrone to the northwest. Niall's sons set up the northern Uí Neill kingdom in Ulster, while another branch of the family set up the southern Uí Neill kingdoms in the kingdom of Meath.

The dynastic designation Uí Neill became the name O'Neill after the death of high king Niall Glúin Dubh (r. 916–919), when his grandson Domnall (r. 956–980) became the first to adopt this surname.

THE FIGHT AGAINST THE ENGLISH

In 1169, the English conquest of Ulster began when a Norman knight, John de Courcy, invaded Ireland and established an earldom at Ulster. But the Norman invasion met with resistance from Ulster king Aodh Macaemb Toinsleag (r. 1166–1177), who came to the aid of the Irish high king, Rory O'Connor (r. 1166–1186), in his fight against Henry II (r. 1154–1189) of England. Aodh was killed in battle by the Normans in 1177, but the resistance in Ulster continued.

Ulster king Brian O'Neill (r. 1241–1260) was the last native high king of Ireland. He joined an Irish confederacy to drive out the English in 1256 but was defeated and killed by the Normans at the battle of Downpatrick in 1260. Brian's son, Domnall (r. 1283–1325), became king in 1283 but was deposed by the Normans. The Irish restored him in 1295, and he continued to reign until 1325.

In the fourteenth century, the O'Neill divided into two branches: the O'Neill of Tyrone and the O'Neill of Clandeboy. All but two of the subsequent kings of Ulster came from the line of Tyrone.

In 1542, after Henry VIII (r. 1509–1547) of England declared himself king of Ireland, the king of Ulster, Conn Bacach (r. 1520–1559), submitted to the English king in exchange for becoming earl of Ulster, but his outraged people rebelled on his return home. His youngest son, Seán an Díomais (r. 1559–1567), succeeded him and carried on the war against the English. A peace was declared, and Seán went to England to hold a conference with Elizabeth I (r. 1558–1603), in which he defended the rule of the Irish kings. His successor, Tairrdelbach Luimneach O'Neill (r. 1567–1593), defeated Walter, the earl of Essex, and consolidated the peace. He abdicated in 1593 in favor of Aodh Ruadh (Red Hugh) (r. 1593–1603), the last Irish king of Ulster, who carried on the war against the English until he was defeated in battle at Kinsale in 1601 and went into exile in 1603.

See also: CONNAUGHT KINGDOM; LEINSTER KINGDOM; MEATH KINGDOM.

UMAYYAD DYNASTY

(ca. 600–1009 C.E.)

Middle Eastern Islamic dynasty with roots in the pre-Islamic age, whose leaders ruled as caliphs from the ancient city of Baghdad (in present-day Iraq). The Umayyad dynasty originated in pre-Islamic Arabia as a prominent Meccan family called the Banu Umayya, named after a founding ancestor, Ummaya, who was a distant relative of the Prophet Muhammad. As converts to Islam, the Umayyads preserved their power and influence in the new political and religious regime created by the Prophet in the early 600s.

EARLY RULE

In 644, Uthman ibn Affan, a member of the Umayyad dynasty, became the third caliph of Islam (r. 644–656). However, he was assassinated in 656, and Ali ibn Abi Talib, the Prophet Muhammad's son-in-law and cousin, became the fourth caliph (r. 656–661). Uthman's Umayyad kin resented Ali's election as caliph. One of them, Muawiya ibn Ali Sufyan, used his position as governor of Syria to help challenge

One of the oldest Islamic houses of worship in the world, the Great Umayyad Mosque in Damascus, Syria, was built between 705 and 715 C.E. on the site of a former Roman temple and a later Christian basilica. The magnificent interior courtyard is decorated with mosaics and surrounded by dozens of arches.

Ali's rule, resulting in a civil war within the new Islamic community. The two rivals fought at the battle of Siffin in 657 and then decided to negotiate. Ali, whose authority and popularity were undermined by his willingness to agree to arbitration, was assassinated in 661. Muawiya (r. 662–680) then proclaimed himself caliph and made Damascus the capital of the Islamic caliphate.

Muawiya worked to consolidate his rule, making a truce with the Byzantine Empire and relying on family and tribal alliances. His reign is traditionally viewed as the start of a new phase in Islamic history, marking the shift from the reigns of the first four caliphs, regarded as religiously chosen, to a hereditary dynastic caliphate.

Muawiya designated his son Yazid as his successor, but at Muawiya's death in 680, Yazid was challenged by Husayn, the son of Ali ibn Ali Talib and the Prophet's daughter Fatima. Husayn died in the resulting battle at Karbala in Iraq in 680, and Yazid ruled as caliph (r. 680–683).

After Yazid's death in 683, civil war erupted again, and another branch of the Banu Umayya took control, with Marwan I ruling Syria and Egypt (r. 684–685). Marwan's son and successor, Abd al-Malik (r. 685–705), reconquered areas that had split away during the civil wars, including Iraq.

DECLINING POWER

The legacy of civil war and autocratic rule tarnished the image of the Umayyads in many histories, especially those written during succeeding Islamic dynasties. Nonetheless, from their capital of Damascus, the Umayyad caliphs formed a highly successful dynasty. Under the reign of Abd al-Malik and that of his son al-Walid (r. 705–715), Islamic armies conquered North Africa and Spain and nearly took Constantinople from the Byzantines. They also made some headway into India and Central Asia. Abd al-Malik also supervised construction of the Dome of the Rock in Jerusalem and started work on the Umayyad Mosque in Damascus. Under Umayyad rule, the Islamic faith began to spread among the conquered Arab peoples of the eastern Mediterranean, creating a new group of faithful who were distinct from the conquering armies that had originated in the Arabian Peninsula.

Over time, however, increasing territorial expansion and diversity of the empire helped undermine the Umayyad dynasty that had enabled Islam to flourish. In 717, the dynasty suffered a destabilizing defeat by the Byzantine army. Internal tribal feuding and Egypt-based Abbasid opposition to Umayyad rule became stronger, and in 744 Caliph Walid II (r. 743–744) was assassinated. Yet another civil war followed, and in 750 the Abbasid dynasty of Egypt deposed the last Umayyad caliph, Marwan II (r. 744–750), and slaughtered most of his family.

UMAYYAD RULE IN IBERIA

One Umayyad prince, Abd al-Rahman ibn Muawiya, escaped the Abbasid conquest and slaughter and fled Syria for the Iberian Peninsula. In 755 he took control of al-Andalus, the Muslim-ruled region in southern Iberia that the Umayyads had taken from the Visigoths in 711. Abd al-Rahman (r. 756–788) made Córdoba the capital of this new Umayyad dynasty, which became one of the most renowned of all Islamic kingdoms.

Abd al-Rahman began construction of a Great Mosque in the city of Córdoba and started to create a capital to rival Damascus. His descendant and namesake, Abd al-Rahman III (r. 912–961), governed al-Andalus at its peak of power as caliph of Córdoba. During his rule, that city was a great intellectual and religious center where Muslims, Jews, and Christians co-existed peacefully and prosperously.

Islamic Spain continued to flourish under al-Hakam II, who ruled from 961 to 976 and founded a great library in Córdoba. At the beginning of the eleventh century, however, the Umayyad caliphate in Córdoba began to fragment due to financial pressures and war with neighboring states. By the 1010s, al-Andalus had become a collection of smaller kingdoms. These separate kingdoms were not reunited until the 1050s, when the Almoravid dynasty conquered the splinter states and ended Umayyad rule.

See also: ABBASID DYNASTY; ALMORAVID DYNASTY; ISLAM AND KINGSHIP.

UNITED ARAB EMIRATES

(1971–Present)

Country on the eastern Arabian Peninsula, bordering the Persian Gulf and Gulf of Oman, that is a federation of seven sheikdoms: Abu Dhabi (the capital), Dubai, Sharjah, Ajman, Umm al-Qaiwain, Ras al-Khaimah, and Fujairah. The country's diverse geography includes a vast desert interior, coastal lowlands along the shore of the Persian Gulf and the Gulf of Oman, the rocky Hajar Mountains in the north, and nearly two hundred islands in the Gulf. The area has been almost entirely Islamic since the seventh century.

Archaeological evidence indicates that humans first inhabited the area of the present-day United Arab Emirates around 6000 or 5000 B.C.E. By 600 C.E. the area experienced migration mostly from Yemen and Saudi Arabia. The area changed little for centuries. Then, in the early 1500s, Portugal seized control of the rich shipping opportunities that had developed in the Gulf. Great Britain took over about a century later when one of the local tribes, the Qawasim, threatened British maritime dominance in the Gulf. The British forced a series of truces on the native rulers between 1820 and 1892 (when the emirates were called the Trucial States), restricting the area's international trade in return for British protection. Following World War II, Great Britain returned autonomy to the emirates and left the area completely when the federation of the United Arab Emirates was formed in 1971.

Meanwhile, vast quantities of oil had been discovered around 1960 in Abu Dhabi, which became the capital of the new federation. Oil exports brought significant revenue to Abu Dhabi, whose ruler, Sheikh Zayed bin Sultan al-Nahyan (r. 1966–2004), used the new riches to modernize his emirate. He also distributed some of the wealth to the other emirates that did not have major oil reserves. The remarkable guidance of Sheikh Zayed and the rulers of the other emirates, along with an effective new political structure that combined federal jurisdiction with local authority in individual emirates, enabled the United Arab Emirates to become a notable example of Arab unity and political stability.

At the top of the federal government is the Supreme Council, which consists of the rulers of each emirate. Those seven rulers elect the country's president and vice president from among themselves for five-year terms. Abu Dhabi's Sheikh Zayed was elected president for the first term and has been re-elected ever since. The president, in consultation with the Supreme Council, chooses a prime minister to head the Council of Ministers, an executive body with twenty-one members selected from the various emirates.

On the legislative side, the forty-member Federal National Council has the power to amend proposed federal laws and the authority to question the performance of any federal ministry when it receives citizens' complaints. The emirates' members on this council are proportional in number to their population and are chosen by the rulers.

The federal government also has an independent judiciary branch, whose highest court is the Supreme Court, composed of five judges appointed by the Supreme Council. The judges rule on the constitutionality of federal laws and arbitrate disputes between emirates. The lower Courts of First Instance mainly hear commercial and civil cases between the federal government and citizens of the Emirates. Each of the emirates also has a court system for cases that are not under federal jurisdiction.

This governmental structure has served the country well, and the United Arab Emirates has changed from one of the poorest nations in the world to one of the richest. The political leaders also have been astute enough to diversify the economy, taking advantage of agricultural, manufacturing, and mining resources so that the country is not dependent only on oil and natural gas. As a result, the United Arab Emirates has become a leading center of trade and commerce in the Middle East.

Urartu Kingdom

(ca. 1000–600 B.C.E.)

Ancient kingdom located in mountainous regions of eastern Anatolia (present-day Turkey) and Armenia (in the Caucasus region), known for its ongoing provocation of the powerful Assyrian Empire. In the Hebrew Bible, the kingdom of Urartu is referred to as Ararat.

Around 1000 B.C.E., disparate groups of Hurrian tribes in eastern Anatolia united to form the kingdom of Urartu. The most likely explanation for the banding together of the Hurrians was to provide stronger defense against their enemies, most notably the powerful Assyrians of Mesopotamia. The kingdom of Urartu was centered in the highlands surrounding Lake Van, north of the Tigris River. The first king of Urartu was called Arame (r. ca. 1000–? B.C.E.).

The kingdom of Urartu was almost constantly at war with the Assyrians to their south. Unable to defeat the powerful Assyriana in any battles, Urartu nevertheless remained a difficult enemy for Assyria.

Around 850 B.C.E., King Sarduri I of Urartu (r. ca. 850–? B.C.E.) founded a capital city in a well-fortified location at Van, overlooking a lake and surrounded by high mountains. With the Assyrian empire in a period of decline at this time, Sarduri began an expansion of Urartu territory that lasted for the next century.

Urartu became an important and significant power in the region under Menua (r. ca. 810–785 B.C.E.). Its territory grew as far as Lake Urmia in the east and northern Syria in the west. Most importantly, its conquests gave Urartu control of the important caravan trade routes through the area. By the reign of Argitis I (r. ca. 785–750 B.C.E.), Urartu had achieved its greatest stature, rivaling the size and influence of the Assyrians at this time.

The Assyrians regained their strength under Tiglath-pileser III (r. 745–727 B.C.E.), who managed to defeat King Sarduris II of Urartu (r. 750–735 B.C.E.) in a series of campaigns and regain control of much of Assyrian territory in the south. In 736 B.C.E., Tiglath-pileser attempted to capture the Urartian capital at Van. Although Tiglath-pileser failed to capture the capital for his own, the Urartian kingdom never fully recovered from these battles.

It was a badly weakened Urartu that faced Sargon II of Assyria (r. 722–705 B.C.E.) in 714 B.C.E. King Rusas of Urartu (r. 735–714 B.C.E.), the son and successor of Sarduris II, suffered defeat and annexation by Assyria. Despite this victory, however, Urartu remained relatively powerful and prosperous for several decades.

Soon, however, Urartu faced another formidable threat, repeated invasions by warriors from the Caucasus Mountains and beyond in the north—the Cimmerians and Scythians. These invasions further weakened the kingdom, and when the Medes and Babylonians destroyed the Assyrian Empire around 600 B.C.E., the kingdom of Urartu was absorbed by the Medes kingdom and ceased to exist.

See also: ASSYRIAN EMPIRE; MEDES KINGDOM; SARGON II; SCYTHIAN EMPIRE; TIGLATH-PILESER III.

UR-NAMMU (d. ca. 2095 B.C.E.)

Ancient ruler of Ur (r. ca. 2112–2094 B.C.E.), a city-state in Sumer in southern Mesopotamia, and founder of the kingdom's Third dynasty, who some scholars believe was the author of the first recorded set of law codes.

Little is known about the life of Ur-Nammu before he became king of Ur. A successful general, he was made military governor of Ur by King Utukhegal of Uruk (r. ca. 2119–2112 B.C.E.). Upon Utukhegal's death, Ur-Nammu proclaimed himself king, assuming a number of titles, including lord of Uruk, lord of Ur, and king of Sumer and Akkad.

As king, Ur-Nammu set about to extend his influence in southern and central Mesopotamia, largely through diplomacy and negotiation rather than military conquest. One exception to this, however, was his conquest of the rival city-state of Lagash, which Ur-Nammu apparently undertook in order to redirect trade routes in southern Mesopotamia.

Ur-Nammu proved to be a skilled and competent ruler. Under his rule, Ur regained many former territories, and it established trading practices that brought great prosperity, making Ur the wealthiest city-state in Mesopotamia. Ur-Nammu launched a major building program as well, constructing irrigation canals, temples, and other buildings and public works. One of the most magnificent buildings started during the reign of Ur-Nammu was a ziggurat, or tower-temple, built in honor of Nanna, the moon-god of Ur. The remains of this ziggurat still stand today at the site of Ur in present-day Iraq. Ur-Nammu is also is credited with fostering a revival in the arts and in Sumerian literature.

Ur-Nammu was one of the first rulers of the ancient world to write down a code of law for his subjects, although some scholars attribute this codification to his son and successor, Shulgi (r. ca. 2094–2047 B.C.E.). Fragments of these laws have been found written on ancient cuneiform tablets at archaeological sites at Ur. Unusual in a time of harsh punishments such as "an eye for an eye," Ur-Nammu set monetary punishments for most crimes instead.

Ur-Nammu died in battle while waging war against the Gutians, a nomadic people to the east who once ruled Ur but had been driven out by King Utukhegal. Upon his death, the throne passed to his son, Shulgi, during whose fifty-year reign Ur expanded even further to the east and north.

See also: AKKAD, KINGDOM OF; SHULGI.

UTHMAN DAN FODIO (1754–1817 C.E.)

First ruler (r. 1804–1817) of the Sokoto caliphate of northern Nigeria, who is remembered as much for his scholarship as for his political achievements. Pilgrims still travel to his tomb in Sokoto to pay their respects.

Uthman dan Fodio was born to a learned Islamic family in the Fulani town of Gobir, in present-day Nigeria. His full name was Uthman ibn Muhammad Fudi ibn Uthman ibn Salih. Classically educated in Islam, he learned to speak Arabic fluently. Uthman began his adult life in the tradition of his family, first as a scholar and, later, as preacher of Islam. His role as a Muslim teacher took him throughout Fulani territory. As a preacher in rural areas and small towns, he broke with customary practice and spoke in the simple vernacular of the common people.

Before long, Uthman had gathered a large following of students and supporters, which brought him to the attention of the court of the sultan at Gobir, one of the Hausa kingdoms of northern Nigeris. By the end of the eighteenth century, Uthman had spread his message of hope for the poor far and wide. His popularity dismayed the sultan, however, who saw the young Islamic scholar as a potential threat and determined to remove him from the sultanate. But Uthman succeeded in getting himself elected *imam* (religious leader) and declared a *jihad* (holy war) against all who refused to acknowledge his authority. Uthman's call to arms inspired many of his followers to fight in his name.

By 1806, Uthman was ready to extend his *jihad* beyond Fulani territory, into neighboring Hausaland. Within two years, his supporters had taken the powerful city of Zaria, the last stronghold of Hausa resistance against Uthman's expansion. With this conquest, Uthman completed the creation of the Sokoto caliphate. To make his rule more effective, he established four regional districts, and delegated control over them to loyal members of his family. Now approaching age sixty, Uthman retired from rule, becoming once again a teacher. He moved to Sokoto in 1815, and this town became the seat of his government. Uthman died there two years later.

See also: SOKOTO CALIPHATE.

FURTHER READING

Last, Murray. *The Sokoto Caliphate.* New York: Humanities Press, 1967.

UTKALA (ORISSA) KINGDOM

(ca. 1076–1568 C.E.)

Kingdom that existed on India's east coast between Bengal and Vijayanagar from the eleventh through sixteenth centuries.

Around 1076, a tribal leader named Anantavarman Choda Ganga (r. ca. 1076–1118) united the small tribes that inhabited the region south of Bengal in India. He named the new kingdom Orissa (today it is known as Utkala) and installed himself as the kingdom's first monarch. The new ruler vigorously supported the region's Hindu traditions and he erected a large temple at Puri.

Ganga and his successors, most notably Narasimha I (r. ca. 1238–1264), constantly struggled to protect Orissa (Utkala) from Muslim invasion. For two centuries, Muslim control had extended across the Deccan, and only the kingdoms of Orissa and Vijayanagar remained unconquered. However, these two kingdoms failed to unite because of periodic disputes over the small kingdom of Kondavidu, which was located between them.

After the death of Narasimha I in 1264, the Muslims, first during the Tughluq dynasty and then during the Bahmani dynasty, steadily encroached into Orissan territory and eroded the authority of its monarchs. Finally, in 1434, the citizens of Orissa, dismayed by the kingdom's decline, rebelled against the monarchy. A merchant named Kapilendra led the insurrection. With the support of the *vaishyas,* or members of the working class, he overthrew the last ruler of the Ganga dynasty, Bhanudeva IV (r. ca. 1414–1434), and became king.

Kapilendra (r. 1434–1467) established the Suryavamsa dynasty. He immediately sought to reacquire Orissa's lost lands and, in doing so, he expanded the kingdom even further. In 1454 he conquered the kingdom of Kondavidu to the south, while in the north he annexed portions of Bengal, pushing Orissa's border past its traditional boundary at the Ganga River. Kapilendra, however, lacked the diplomatic skill needed to sustain his conquests. Religious differences prevented peaceful relations with Bengal and the Bahmani kingdom, and Kapilendra avoided making an alliance with Vijayanagar because of past disputes with that kingdom.

Consequently, Kapilendra's successors failed to maintain his advances. First, his son, Purushottama (r. 1467–1497), lost Kondavidu to the Bahmanis. His successor, Prataparuda (r. 1497–1540), relinquished much of Orissa's southern territory to Vijayanagar, while the northern conquests were returned to Bengal. During the reign of Prataparuda, Orissa lost its preeminent position.

Prataparuda died in 1540, and the Suryavamsa dynasty, which had originally sprung from civil unrest, succumbed to new unrest. Members of the writer caste, led by a leader named Govind, used the kingdom's misfortunes to incite the public to rebellion. Govind (r. 1541–1549) then seized the throne and formed the Bhoi dynasty.

However, the Bhoi rulers failed to reverse Orissa's misfortunes and yet another revolt erupted. In 1559, an Orissan general, Mukunda Harichandana (r. 1560–1568), staged a coup to prevent an imminent Muslim invasion of the kingdom. But in 1568, despite Mukunda's efforts, Bengal easily overwhelmed the feeble kingdom. Orissa had withstood threats from three stronger enemies for five centuries, but the resulting turmoil finally led to its demise.

See also: BAHMANI DYNASTY; INDIAN KINGDOMS; KONDAVIDU KINGDOM; VIJAYANAGAR EMPIRE.

UZBEK KINGDOM (ca. 1500s–1865 C.E.)

Central Asian kingdom established by the Uzbeks, a nomadic group of people who united under the leadership of Khan Abdullah (r. 1538–1598) in the sixteenth century, who invaded the area now known as Uzbekistan.

The Uzbek people took their name from Uzbeg Khan (r. 1312–1340), a leader from the Golden Horde khanate from whom they claimed dynastic descent. By 1510, after defeating the states controlled by the Timurid dynasty, the Uzbek controlled the area between the Amu-Darya River and the Syr-Darya River to the south and east of the Aral Sea.

The Uzbeki ruler, Khan Abdullah (r. 1538–1598), extended his rule over parts of Persia, Afghanistan, and Turkistan. But his empire broke up into separate principalities—the khanate of Khiva and the khanate of Bukhara (Bulchoro)—around 1586, when Abdullah was defeated in battle by the future Safavid ruler of Iran, Shah Abbas I (r. 1588–1629). By the late sixteenth century, the Uzbek khans controlled much of what is now Central Asia, and they remained in control of that region until the late 1800s.

Of the two Uzbek states, the khanate of Khiva (1511–1920), located in the steppes north and east of present-day Uzbekistan, was ruled by the Arab-Shahid dynasty (ca. 1515–1804) and the Quongrat dynasty (ca. 1763–1920). The khanate of Bukhara (1533–1920), located in the area that includes parts of the present-day republics of Uzbekistan, Turkmenistan, and Tajikistan, was controlled first by the Shaibanid dynasty (1533–1756) and then by the Manghit dynasty (1756–1920).

The Uzbek leader, Khan Shah Rukh Beg (r. ca. 1700–?), established the khanate of Khokand at the beginning of the eighteenth century. It consisted of an area that included part of present-day Turkmenistan. The city of Khokand served as the western capital of the Chinese Ming dynasty from 1777 to 1825.

In the early eighteenth century, the khan of Khiva asked Russian tsar Peter the Great (r. 1682–1725) for help in defending his land against the Turkmen and Kazaks. By the time Russian help arrived in 1717, it was no longer needed because many of the Uzbeks had been massacred.

Tsar Nicholas I (r. 1825–1855) made another effort to enter the area in 1839, with little success. Conflict with Russia started in 1865. By the end of the hostilities, the khanates of Bukhara and Khiva were joined to the Russian Empire in 1868 and 1873, respectively. Kokand was annexed into the Russian Empire in 1876.

Both Khiva and Bukhara remained under their native khans as Russian protectorates until the Red Army conquered the region during the Russian civil war. On February 2, 1920, Soviet troops captured Khiva, resulting in the abolition of the khanate of Khiva. In September 1920, Soviet troops captured Bukhara, and that khanate was abolished. In December 1922, Uzbekistan, the region of the former Uzbek khanates, became one of the republics of the Union of Soviet Socialist Republics.

See also: GOLDEN HORDE KHANATE; SAFAVID DYNASTY.

FURTHER READING

Allworth, Edward A. *The Modern Uzbeks: From the 14th Century to the Present: A Cultural History* (Studies of Nationalities of the USSR). Stanford, CA: Hoover Institution, 1990.

Macleod, Calcum, and Bradley Mayhew. *Uzbekistan: The Golden Road to Samarkand* (Odyssey Guides). New York: Odyssey, 2002.

Soucek, Svatopluk. *A History of Inner Asia.* New York: Cambridge University Press, 2000.

VAKATAKA DYNASTY (ca. 220–520 C.E.)

Dynasty that emerged in the Deccan plateau region of India during the third century.

The Vakataka dynasty assumed control over parts of the Deccan plateau region when the Satavahana dynasty collapsed in the early years of the third century. The Satavahanas had controlled much of the Deccan for nearly three centuries, but they relied upon feudal governors to oversee much of their vast empire. When the dynasty crumbled as a result of internal struggles and external threats from the Maharashtra state, these governors turned their feudal states into autonomous kingdoms.

Vindhyasakti (r. ca. 255–275), the first Vakataka monarch, had been one of these feudal governors, appointed by the Satavahanas to govern the Madhya Pradesh and Berar regions. When the Satavahana dynasty faltered, Vindhyasakti took control of the regions and established the Vakataka dynasty. His accession to the throne was fairly peaceful because the Satavahanas lacked the strength to oppose him and the local inhabitants did not offer any resistance. Some historians believe that Vindhyasakti attacked his former rulers and annexed parts of central India, but textual proof for such speculation is unreliable.

When Vindhyasakti died after a long reign, he was succeeded by his son, Pravarasena I (r. ca. 275–335). Pravarasena I forcefully consolidated his realm, conquering the remaining parts of Madhya Pradesh and Berar and leading several successful invasions into central India. Records describe him as the "universal king" because he gained control over much of the Deccan region. Pravarasena I also vigorously supported the Brahmanical religion, the forerunner of modern Hinduism. Pilgrims from across India journeyed to Madhya Pradesh to witness the massive sacrifices that Pravarasena commissioned for Brahmanical rites.

After the death of Pravarasena's successor, Rudrasena I (r. ca. 335–360), in the mid-fourth century, the Vakatakas increasingly fell under control of the Guptas, a powerful dynasty from western India. The Gupta monarchs arranged repeated marriages between their family and the Vakatakas, and the Vakataka monarchs soon adopted the Gupta ancestry instead of their own.

After the death of the Vakatakan king Rudrasena II (r. ca. 385–390) in the late fourth century, only a young son was left to succeed him. Because Rudrasena's wife, Prabhavati Gupta, was a Guptan princess, the ruler of the Gupta Empire expected to gain even greater control over the Vakatakan dynasty. But Prabhavati protected her son from Guptan influence and raised him to free the Vakatakas from Guptan domination. In 410, when Pravarasena II finally took the throne, he followed his mother's wishes and expelled the Guptas from all Vakataka territory. Pravarasena II also conquered parts of the Malwa Empire of central India.

Freed of Guptan influence, the Vakatakas enjoyed another century of autonomy. Their control over Madhya Pradesh and Berar remained unchallenged until the early part of the sixth century. In 510, the Vakataka monarch, Harishena (r. ca. 480–510), died without leaving any heirs. During the resulting struggle for succession, the Chalukya dynasty of the western Deccan region invaded the Vakataka kingdom and ended nearly three centuries of Vakataka control in western India.

See also: GUPTA EMPIRE; INDIAN KINGDOMS; SATAVAHANA DYNASTY.

VALOIS DYNASTY (1328–1589 C.E.)

French ruling dynasty that began with King Philip VI (r. 1328–1350) and ended in 1589 with the death of Henry III (r. 1574–1589). The Valois dynasty saw the transition of France from the uncertainty of a medieval feudal kingdom to a strong and centralized state. The house of Valois, which took its name from the Valois region of northeastern France, followed the Capetian dynasty and preceded the Bourbon dynasty on the throne.

When the Capetian ruler Charles IV (r. 1322–1328) died without a male heir in 1328, Salic Law (which prohibited female succession) prevented his daughters from inheriting the throne. Thus, Philip of Valois, a first cousin of the king and grandson of Philip III (r. 1270–1285), became Philip VI of France. His succession was disputed by a nephew of Charles IV, Edward III of England (r. 1327–1377), which contributed to the outbreak of the Hundred Years' War (1337–1453).

The first seven Valois monarchs, known as the Capetian Valois (1328–1498), passed the succession from father to son, and later to Valois cousins under the Orleans and Angouleme branches of the family. During the early years of the Valois dynasty, the monarchy was beset by war and crises, including the capture of King John II (r. 1350–1364) by the English at the battle of Poltiers in 1356. During the reign of Charles V (r. 1364–1380), however, the monarchy began to recover. Moreover, during his reign, formalized and theatrical rituals, such as an elaborate coronation ceremony, helped strengthen the idea of the king as an almost sacred figure.

During the reign of Charles VII (r. 1422–1461), France ended its war with England in 1453. Through his willingness to pardon those who had supported the English, Charles VII was able to increase his own support and strengthen the French monarchy at the expense of the feudal lords and the Church. Over the next half-century, the marriages and conquests of Louis XI (r. 1461–1483) and Charles VIII (r. 1483–1498) consolidated the basis for modern France.

The other rulers of the Valois dynasty were Charles VI the Well Beloved (r. 1380–1422), Louis

XII (r. 1498–1515), Francis I (r. 1515–1547), Henry II (r. 1547–1559), Francis II (r. 1559–1560), Charles IX (r. 1560–1574), and Henry III (r. 1574–1589). The dynasty came to an end when Henry III died childless in 1589.

See also: BOURBON DYNASTY; CAPETIAN DYNASTY; CHARLES VII; FRANCIS I; FRENCH MONARCHIES; LOUIS XI.

VANDAL KINGDOM (400s–534 C.E.)

Kingdom of Germanic barbarians that filled the power vacuum caused by the fall of the Roman Empire and eventually located in North Africa.

Originating in southern Scandinavia, the Vandals were one of the many Germanic peoples who migrated to the weakened Roman Empire early in the fifth century. The Vandal rulers were sometimes called Kings of the Vandals and the Alans, since, shortly after their entry into the Roman Empire, they had absorbed a fragment of the Iranian-speaking Alan peoples. The Vandals eventually made their way through Spain, finally settling in North Africa under the leadership of the greatest of their kings, Gaiseric (r. 429–477), who had succeeded his brother, Gunderic (r. 406–428), as the Vandal ruler.

THE REIGN OF GAISERIC

In 429, Gaiseric led the Vandals across the Straits of Gibraltar to the coast of North Africa. After conquering North Africa, the Vandals agreed, in 435, to settle in the area as allies of the Roman Empire, leaving only the North African state of Carthage under direct Roman control. This agreement proved to be only temporary, for the Vandals took Carthage as well in 439. That year became the starting date of the official Vandal calendar, which was dated by the years that the Vandal king had been on the throne rather than by the years of Roman consuls, as was common in other barbarian territories. The Vandals also differed from other barbarians in not putting the head of the current Roman emperor on their coins.

In 442, Rome recognized Gaiseric as the independent ruler of North Africa, rather than as a subordinate ally. Gaiseric fully exploited his highly strategic position. From his North African base, he was able to threaten the heart of the Western Roman Empire in Italy. Gaiseric was the only barbarian leader of the time to build a fleet. In 455, he crowned his anti-Roman career by sacking the city of Rome, a sack so destructive that it gave the current meaning to the word "vandal." After destroying Rome, Gaiseric added Sicily, Sardinia, Corsica, and the Balearic Islands to the Vandal kingdom, and he fended off all Roman attempts at counterattack.

VANDAL NORTH AFRICA

The Vandals were Arian Christians, a Christian sect that denied the Trinity and claimed that Christ had been created by the Father rather than coexisting with the Father and the Holy Spirit. This belief was common among the various Germanic peoples, including the Ostrogoths and Visigoths. Most of the non-Germanic population of North Africa was not Arian, and unlike many other Arian German kingdoms, the Vandals persecuted the non-Arian population.

While Gaiseric regularly plundered and oppressed the Roman population of North Africa, religious persecution aimed specifically at Christians who believed in the Trinity seems to have begun with his son and successor, Hunneric (r. 477–484). The religious distinction between Arians and non-Arians helped the Vandals maintain their separate identity rather than merge with the Romanized North African population they had conquered. Even so, many of the Vandal elite adopted some aspects of the culture of the Roman elite.

END OF THE VANDAL KINGDOM

The Vandal kingdom eventually fell as a result of two main factors: the aggressive policies of Byzantine emperor Justinian I (r. 527–565) in the western Mediterranean, and the division between two claimants for the Vandal throne, Hilderic (r. 523–530) and Gelimer (r. 530–534).

Hilderic, whose mother was the daughter of the Roman emperor Valentinian III (r. 425–455), followed a policy of friendship with Byzantium as well as toleration of his Roman Catholic subjects. When the anti-Byzantine Gelimer deposed and imprisoned Hilderic in 531, the Byzantines called for the overthrow of the usurper. Byzantine forces, landing in North Africa in 533 under the leadership of General Belisarius, were welcomed by the Roman population of the Vandal kingdom.

Belisarius defeated Gelimer at the battle of Tricamarum in late 533, and Gelimer surrendered the following year. (He had already executed Hilderic.)

Gelimer was later paraded around the Hippodrome, or racing arena, in the Byzantine capital of Constantinople. The remaining Vandal nobility were taken from North Africa and settled along the Persian frontier of Byzantium. The defeated Vandal kingdom was no more.

See also: BYZANTINE EMPIRE; JUSTINIAN I.

VARANGIAN KINGDOMS

(ca. 800–1150 C.E.)

Loosely formed kingdoms that preceded the establishment of modern Scandinavian kingdoms such as Sweden and Finland.

Early inhabitants of Russia used the designation Variagi to denote members of the tribes of eastern Scandinavia. They also referred to the Baltic Sea as the Varangian Sea. The term derives from the ancient Scandinavian word *vaeringjar,* which was used to describe Scandinavian warriors who sold their services to the Byzantium Empire.

The Varangians' kingdoms were, in effect, groups of loosely affiliated tribes that populated Scandinavia in the Middle Ages. The tribes were predominantly nomadic, although several sizable settlements developed on the Baltic Sea during the eighth and ninth centuries. These settlements grew into significant economic centers, and Varangian merchants traded both Asian and European goods across northern Europe.

The Varangians received the most recognition, however, for their military prowess. Varangian warriors frequently plundered surrounding countries and often fought one another for the opportunity to attack a specific land. The Varangians also served as mercenaries, protecting the nobility and merchants in lands as distant as Greece, Byzantium, and Armenia. However, they achieved their most lasting fame as the founders of the Rus kingdoms in present-day Russia and Ukraine.

During the ninth century, leaders of the Rus tribes invited the Varangian leader Rurik to inhabit their lands and protect them from the raids of competing Varangian tribes. Rurik accepted and settled his followers in Novgorod in 862, laying the foundation for what came to be known as Kievan Rus. Two of Rurik's subordinates, Askold and Dir, with his consent, moved south and occupied Kiev. When Rurik died in

879, his kinsman Oleg (r. 879–912) assumed control of Novgorod and sought to consolidate the Rus kingdoms under his command. He launched a campaign against Askold and Dir that culminated with their executions in 882. That same year, Oleg transferred his capital from Novgorod to Kiev, which remained the capital of Kievan Rus until 1169.

Oleg and his successors controlled the Rus kingdoms and later the tsardom of Russia until 1598. They greatly expanded the Rus borders and widely subjected the Rus inhabitants to their rule. Because of this control, some historians contend that the Varangians actually founded modern Russia. However, this ignores the fact that the Slavic inhabitants of the Rus kingdoms greatly outnumbered the Varangians and had settled the land nearly two centuries earlier. Although Oleg and his successors did control the Rus kingdoms for centuries, the majority of Rurik's original followers were soon assimilated into the Rus population.

By 980, when Vladimir Sviatoslavich became Grand Prince Vladimir I of Kiev (r. 980–1015), the Varangians no longer controlled the Rus throne. However, their influence over Rus affairs had not entirely dissipated. Both Vladimir and his son, Yaroslav the Wise (r. 1019–1054), who became grand prince in 1019, paid Varangian mercenaries to once again enter the Rus kingdoms. In these instances, however, the Varangians were not asked to repel foreign invaders. Instead, Vladimir and Yaroslav used the Varangians to fortify their power in Rus and unite the competing principalities.

By the early 1100s, the term *Variagi* had begun to disappear across Europe as the Varangian tribes consolidated and developed into the modern Scandinavian nations. Rus writings from this period refer to the *svei,* or Swedes, and the *murmany,* or Norwegians. Variations of these terms also appear in other European historical writings. Ironically, the Russian term *variag* was transformed to describe a peasant class of peddlers, a far removal from the ferocious implications of the term used to describe their predecessors.

Yet the Varangians had a lasting influence on the shape of modern Europe. Their descendants formed the nations of modern Scandinavia, and, although they did not create the Russian state, they helped to preserve it during its earliest years of inception, protecting its Slavic inhabitants and providing them with a governing authority.

See also: KIEV, PRINCEDOM OF; RURIK; RUS PRINCE-DOMS; YAROSLAV I, THE WISE.

FURTHER READING

Freeze, Gregory L., ed. *Russia: A History.* New York: Oxford University Press, 1997.

Martin, Janet. *Medieval Russia: 980–1584.* New York: Cambridge University Press, 1995.

VASA DYNASTY (1523–1654 C.E.)

Family of Swedish rulers in the 1500s and 1600s, one of whom, Gustavus II Adolphus (r. 1611–1632), was a leading commander during the Thirty Years' War (1618–1648).

The Vasa dynasty of Sweden was founded by Gustav Vasa or Gustavus I (r. 1523–1560), who was elected king in 1523 when Sweden rose in revolt against the Kalmar Union (1397–1523). During Gustavus I's reign, Sweden gradually became a Protestant country.

Gustavus I was succeeded by his eldest son, Erik XIV (r. 1560–1568). During much of Erik's reign, Sweden was at war with Poland and Denmark over control of Baltic trade. Mentally unstable, Erik was deposed in 1568 after murdering some of his own nobles. He was succeeded by his brother Johan III (r. 1568–1592).

Johan III married the daughter of the king of Poland, and in 1587 their son Sigismund was elected King Sigismund III of Poland (r. 1587–1632), establishing the Vasa dynasty there. On Johan's death, Sigismund also succeeded to the Swedish throne (r. 1592–1599). But in 1599 he was deposed as king of Sweden in favor of his uncle Carl or Charles IX (r. 1599–1611), as a result of continuing conflicts between Sweden and Poland over Estonia and Sigismund's adherence to Catholicism.

Sigismund was succeeded on the throne of Poland by his sons Wladislaw IV (r. 1632–1648) and John II Casimir (r. 1648–1668). John II Casimir was deposed in 1668, ending Vasa rule in Poland.

The son and successor of Carl IX, Gustavus II Adolphus (r. 1611–1632), made Sweden's armies among the best in Europe, distinguishing himself as a Protestant commander during the Thirty Years' War. When he was killed during the battle of Lützen in 1632, the throne went to his six-year-old daughter Christina (r. 1632–1654), although the country was ruled by a regent, Axel Oxenstierna, until Christina began ruling in her own right in 1644.

Christina abdicated in 1654 in favor of her cousin, Charles X Gustavus (r. 1654–1660). His accession to the throne marks the beginning of the Wittelsbach dynasty. Christina abdicated because of her secret conversion to the Roman Catholic faith. Since 1617, Sweden had required its monarchs to be Lutheran.

During the reign of the Vasas, Sweden went from being a troublesome territory ruled by the Danes to an important power in the Baltic region and a significant player in European politics.

See also: CHRISTINA; GUSTAVUS I (VASA); GUSTAVUS II (ADOLPHUS); SWEDISH MONARCHY.

VENETIAN DOGES (687–1797 C.E.)

Executive officers of the Italian city of Venice from the Middle Ages to the city's defeat by Napoleon in 1797. Elected from among the city's aristocrats, the Doges of Venice were, by law, required to live the remainder of their lives in the Doges' Palace and its surrounding structures and grounds.

Italian merchants and fisherman seeking refuge from the invading Germanic Huns founded the Italian city of Venice in 421. The office of doge first appeared in 687, when the leaders of the city elected a single leader to help defend the city against the Lombards.

In the seventh and eighth centuries, Venice came under the control of the Byzantine Empire, and doges were chosen by imperial decree. By the year 1000, however, Venice was once again independent and increasing its power and influence throughout the Adriatic and Dalmatian coasts.

Venice became exceedingly wealthy during the Crusades, when Venetians provided transport to the Crusaders and helped finance crusading efforts. The ancient Venetian family of Dandolo produced four doges during this period, including Enrico Dandolo (r. 1192–1205), who, in the Fourth Crusade, helped divert the Crusaders in 1202 to Zara and in 1203 to Constantinople. Though aged and blind, Enrico commanded the Crusader fleet in the capture of Constantinople in 1204, ensuring that Venice received the most valuable share of the wealth gained from the effort. Another well-known doge from the Dandolo family, Andrea Dandolo (r. 1343–1354),

The doges of Venice were required by law to live in the Palazzo Ducale (Doges' Palace) after their election. The most impressive secular building in Venice and located in St. Mark's Square, the palace served not only as the doges' residence, but also as the senate house, administrative center, hall of justice, public archives, and prison.

had been a professor of law before his election, and he rewrote Venetian law during his tenure.

By the late 1300s, members of the great council of Venice, made up of leading nobles, had replaced the general citizenry in the election of the doges. The Council of Ten, as the group became known, gained great power, and the doge became largely only a figurehead.

The Republic of Venice reached its peak of power and prosperity in the early 1400s, when it was a great European power, a center of culture and learning, and a wealthy commercial center. By the mid-fifteenth century, however, the city, known as the "queen of the seas," began to decline, in part because of the fall of Constantinople, the capital of the Byzantine Empire, to the Ottoman Turks. The capture of Constantinople reduced Venetian trade with the Levant, thus limiting the city's revenues. In addition, the European discovery of the Americas transferred commercial power to Spain, Portugal, and other nations.

Venice's place in European politics diminished further in the sixteenth century, after the French invaded Italy in 1494. Although Venice escaped the initial onslaught by shrewdly allying itself with France, the city-state could not compete with the larger and growing states of northern and Western Europe.

The doges, who were not monarchs as much as executive officers with limited political power, played an important ceremonial role in Venice. On Ascension Day in 1177, Pope Alexander III had given the city a golden ring to commemorate its mastery of the sea. Every year afterward, the ruling doge threw a golden ring into the Adriatic Sea on Ascension Day in symbolic representation of Venice's marriage with the sea.

The fall of Venetian territories to the Ottoman Turks—Cyprus in 1471, Crete in 1669, and the Peloponnesus of Greece in 1715—effectively ended Venetian dominance in the eastern Mediterranean region. By the eighteenth century, the city's politics were stagnant, the doges merely powerless aristocrats. With the conquest of Italy by Napoleon in 1797, Venice came under the control of Austria, and the political office of the doge effectively ended, as the city fell under Austria's Habsburg rulers.

See also: BYZANTINE EMPIRE; LOMBARD KINGDOM; NAPOLEON I (BONAPARTE); OTTOMAN EMPIRE.

VICTOR EMMANUEL II

(1820–1878 C.E.)

King of Sardinia (r. 1849–1861) and the first ruler of a unified kingdom of Italy (r. 1861–1878). A charismatic leader who was popular for his liberal politics, Victor Emmanuel steadfastly lent his support for a unified Italy in the crucial and turbulent 1850s and early 1860s, thus helping to hold together the struggling nation and secure him as its first king.

A member of the influential and long-lasting house of Savoy, Victor Emmanuel was born in 1820 to Charles Albert (r. 1831–1849) and Maria Teresa, the king and queen of the independent kingdom of Sardinia, which they ruled from the Piedmont region of mainland Italy. Charles Albert, though a controversial ruler, was able to achieve some favor both at home and abroad for his free-trade economic policies and his somewhat reluctant support of a Sardinian constitution. After two unsuccessful wars against Austria, however, Charles Albert exiled himself to Portugal and turned over the kingdom to his son Victor Emmanuel, who became king in 1849.

Victor Emmanuel inspired great loyalty in his people, quickly becoming known as the "Honest King." This was largely due to his continued support of the constitution drafted during his father's rule, and the strong popular appeal he had in the Piedmont. His position as a strong defender of Italian rights was fortified by his choice of the skilled diplomat Camillo Benso di Cavour as his prime minister. Both Cavour and Victor Emmanuel were fervent supporters of Italian unification, and this desire to see the states of Italy joined together put them at the center of an alliance movement known as the "Risorgimento" (revival or rebirth).

In the wake of both the Crimean War (1853–1856) and wars with Austria, many of the independent states of Italy voted to join with Sardinia, and in February of 1861 Victor Emmanuel became the first king of a unified Italy. The final years of his reign were largely spent fortifying his new kingdom and pulling together the few small areas—including the Papal States such as Rome—which had not united with Italy originally. Rome became the capital of the fully unified Italy in 1871, though not without some difficulty and controversy. It was not until 1929 that the question of whether Italy or the pope had proper authority over Rome was settled. When

Victor Emmanuel died in 1878, the Crown passed to his son, Humbert I (r. 1878–1900).

See also: ABDICATION, ROYAL; DIPLOMACY, ROYAL; POWER, FORMS OF ROYAL; SERVANTS AND AIDES, ROYAL.

VICTORIA (1819–1901 C.E.)

Longest reigning monarch of Great Britain, who ruled from 1837 until her death in 1901. Notable for both the allegiance she inspired in her subjects and the practicality with which she oversaw England's rise as the dominant industrial, military, and colonial power of the nineteenth century, Victoria outlasted numerous political uprisings and reforms, the expansion of the British Empire to every continent, twenty changes of prime minister, and seven assassination attempts. The year before Victoria succeeded to the throne, she saw London greet its first railway; by the time of her death, the automobile, the telephone, the subway, and the motion picture had all made their debut.

THE YOUNG QUEEN

The daughter and only child of Edward, duke of Kent, and Victoria, princess of Saxe-Coburg, Victoria came to the throne at the age of eighteen, succeeding Edward's elder brother, King William IV (r. 1830–1837). In contrast to her grandfather, the "mad" King George III (r. 1760–1820), and her uncle, the adulterous and flamboyant George IV (r. 1820–1830), Victoria was conservative in her personal morals and contentedly domestic in her disposition, both qualities which have since come to be identified with the spirit of the age. This apparent reserve, however, concealed a queen who had a fervent desire to be informed of the policies and actions of her government. The prime minister at the time of her accession, Lord Melbourne, encouraged this interest in the young queen and, whether deliberately or not, garnered Victoria's support for the Whigs, his own political party.

Victoria's friendliness toward Whig politics was somewhat tempered after her 1840 marriage to Albert, her first cousin and a member of the royal house of Saxe-Coburg-Gotha, who favored a more conservative political stance and frequently sided with the Tory party. Victoria and Albert, who had nine children together, were deeply devoted to one another despite Albert's relative unpopularity with the British public, which was largely due to nationalist anxiety about his German roots.

THE MIDDLE YEARS

Despite his Tory sympathies, Albert encouraged Queen Victoria to remain above party allegiances, as befits the sovereign in the British system of constitutional monarchy. Although she never completely freed herself from the pull of political factions, both Whig and Tory, Victoria did manage to remain relatively neutral during much of her reign. By choosing to remain informed of the political scene but keeping her own opinions and influence mostly private, Victoria was able to lend credence to the increasingly democratic temper of the period.

The other great influence Albert had on Victoria as a monarch was through his fervent support of the sciences and arts. This interest came to a head with

The last ruler of the House of Hanover in Great Britain, Queen Victoria ruled for sixty-four years. A fervent supporter of the arts and sciences, she ruled during an era that was arguably the social and cultural peak of the British Empire. It came to be known as the Victorian Age.

the 1851 Great Exhibition, a showcase of the artistic and scientific developments that were occurring both in Britain and abroad. Held in an architectural marvel known as the Crystal Palace, the five-month-long Exhibition was a smashing success, drawing visitors from around the globe. The proceeds from the event were so great that they funded a new museum, the Victoria and Albert, which remains to this day one of the most popular public museums in the world. The Great Exhibition was one of the defining moments of Queen Victoria's reign.

Victoria's excitement over the success of the Great Exhibition was short-lived, however, as two events quickly occurred that threw a pall over her reign. The first was the badly bungled Crimean War, which lasted from 1853 to 1856 and cost many unnecessary British casualties due to poor planning and ineffective communications. The second, and much more personally devastating event for Victoria, was the death of Albert in 1861. Her husband's early death—most likely from typhoid fever—sent Victoria into a decades-long period of mourning from which she never completely emerged. After Albert's death, Victoria was rarely seen in public, splitting her time between Balmoral Castle in Scotland and the royal residence of Osborne on the Isle of Wight.

THE LONG END

The final forty years of Victoria's reign were marked by the rapid expansion of the British Empire, which acquired colonies and territories across the globe, most notably in Africa, Australia, and the Indian subcontinent. The development of the empire further solidified Great Britain's place as the dominant economic and political power of the time. Although Victoria herself hated racial prejudice, Britain's imperial growth was largely accompanied by racist beliefs and practices. These attitudes and the resentment they caused came to haunt the British in the twentieth century, which saw the dismantling of the empire.

Victoria died peacefully at Osborne in 1901, having recently celebrated her Diamond Jubilee (sixty years as monarch) in 1897. The nation went into deep mourning as the Crown passed to her eldest son, Edward VII (r. 1901–1910). Victoria had a total of nine children and forty grandchildren, connecting her by blood or marriage to nearly every royal family in Europe.

See also: COLONIALISM AND KINGSHIP; ENGLISH MONARCHIES; GEORGE III; NATIONAL IDENTITY;

QUEENS AND QUEEN MOTHERS; REIGNS, LENGTH OF; SAXE-COBURG-GOTHA DYNASTY.

FURTHER READING

Hibbert, Christopher. *Queen Victoria: A Personal History.* New York: Basic Books, 2000.

Vallone, Lynne. *Becoming Victoria.* New Haven, CT: Yale University Press, 2001.

VIETNAMESE KINGDOMS

(207 B.C.E.–1955 C.E.)

Kingdoms that occupied the area of present-day Vietnam from 207 B.C.E. to the modern era, many of which sought to expand their territory while maintaining independence from their northern neighbor, China.

The first nonlegendary kingdom in Vietnamese history, the kingdom of Nam Viet, was established in 207 B.C.E when former Chinese general Trieu Da (Zhao Tuo in Chinese) overthrew the Chinese overlords in Vietnam and appointed himself ruler of a territory that included present-day southern China and northern Vietnam. This new kingdom of Nam Viet lasted until 111 B.C.E., when it was conquered by the Chinese and renamed the kingdom of Annam, meaning "pacified south." This marked the beginning of a long period of Chinese domination over Vietnam.

In 939 C.E., after more than one thousand years of Chinese rule, a series of uprisings broke out in Vietnam. The Vietnamese people, led by Ngo Quyen, drove out their Chinese overlords and established an independent state, the kingdom of Dai Viet (Great Viet State). This kingdom was based in the fertile Red River Delta region of northern Vietnam. The Dai Viet kingdom thrived politically, economically, and culturally under the Li dynasty (1009–1225) while the powerful kingdom of Champa occupied the central and southern coastal regions of Vietnam.

Established in the second century, the kingdom of Champa dominated central Vietnam for more than one thousand years. The Chams occupied only the central part of the region until the sixth century, when they conquered their neighbors to the south, the kingdom of Funan. With this conquest, the Chams gained control over the Mekong River Delta, making them an even more formidable force against Dai Viet. The kingdoms of Dai Co Viet and Champa

fought several wars during the twelfth and thirteenth centuries under the Li, Tran, and Ho dynasties of Dai Viet.

In 1407, the armies of China's Ming dynasty invaded Vietnam and took control of the kingdom of Dai Viet. However, the Chinese were able to maintain control of the territory for only a brief period of time before a wealthy Vietnamese landowner and rebel leader named Le Loi initiated a rebellion that forced out the Chinese. In 1428, Le Loi founded the Le dynasty (sometimes called the Later Le dynasty) and ruled as Le Thai To (r. 1428–1433). The kingdom of Dai Viet flourished under Le Thai To and his successors, who instituted policies that promoted the arts and improved agricultural techniques.

After regaining its independence from China, the kingdom of Dai Viet began putting increasing pres-

Monarchy in Vietnam ended in 1945, when the last ruler of the Nguyen dynasty, Bao Dai, was forced to abdicate by Vietnamese communists. Shown here with the French army general Raoul Salan, Bao Dai served as chief of state of Vietnam from 1949 to 1955, when he was deposed in a popular referendum.

sure on the kingdom of Champa under a new policy of territorial expansion. Food shortages and limited land resources had begun to hinder the growing population of Dai Viet and, as a result, the kingdom sought to expand its territory. In 1471, under the rule of Le Thanh Tong (r. 1460–1497), Dai Viet defeated the Chams along the central coast and destroyed their kingdom. The Chams were forced to move further south.

Fighting erupted periodically between the north and south for generations. The conflict generally involved the northern Trinh family and southern Nguyen family, each of which sought control of the other's territory. In 1802, the Nguyen family, under the leadership of Nguyen Anh (r. 1788–1820), gained control of the entire country and renamed it Vietnam ("the people of the south"). The Nguyen dynasty continued to rule Vietnam directly until it became a colony of France in the late 1800s and was broken up and merged with other parts of French Indochina. Thereafter, Vietnamese rulers were merely appointed representatives of the French colonial administration. The last Nguyen ruler of Vietnam, Bao-Dai (r. 1926–1955), was deposed by a popular referendum in 1955, which ended the monarchy.

See also: CHAMPA KINGDOM; FUNAN KINGDOM; LE DYNASTY; NAM VIET KINGDOM; NGUYEN ANH; NGUYEN (HUE) DYNASTY; TRAN DYNASTY; TRINH DYNASTY.

VIJAYANAGAR EMPIRE

(1336–1614 C.E.)

Powerful Hindu Empire located in southern India, originally part of the Hoysala kingdom, that was founded in the fourteenth century after the destruction of the Hoysala and Pandya states by Muslim invaders from the north.

In the early fourteenth century, the king of Hoysala, Vir Ballala III (r. ca. 1291–1336), built the city of Anegundi on the Tungabhadra River and appointed two brothers, Harihara and Bukka, to defend it against Muslim incursions. When Ballala died around 1336, the brothers renamed the city Vijayanagar and proclaimed their independence from the Hoysala kingdom.

Harihara became the first ruler of Vijayanagar as Harihara I (r. 1336–1354), designating his dynasty as the Sangama dynasty in honor of his father, Sangama of Warrangal. Harihara I and his successors greatly expanded Vijayanagar's territory, first by conquering the remains of Hoysala and then by expanding into the Kanara, Mysore, Kanchi, and Chingleput regions. By 1406, Vijayanagar controlled nearly all of the southern Indian subcontinent.

To maintain their authority over this wide area, the rulers of Vijayanagar divided the kingdom into six provinces, with a governor appointed to each. These provincial governors enjoyed significant autonomy, but they were required to supply military forces and large tax payments to the central government. In turn, the governors relied on local assemblies, called *panchayat,* to oversee municipal affairs.

The rulers of Vijanagar themselves were fairly generous, and they adopted *dharma* as their primary inspiration. This ancient Hindu moral and religious code asserted that a monarch's foremost concern is the welfare of his people. Each Vijanagar ruler selected a council of ministers, picked from different castes, who were responsible for areas such as defense, trade, agriculture, and taxation.

Despite its increasing prosperity, Vijayanagar faced a constant threat from its northern neighbor, the Bahmani kingdom. The two states frequently battled for supremacy in southern India. With the death of the powerful Vijayangar ruler, Deva Raya II (r. 1422–1446), in 1446, the kingdom lacked a forceful ruler and was left vulnerable. Seizing the opportunity, the Bahmani kingdom invaded and gained control over significant portions of Vijayanagar.

Bahmani control lasted forty years, with Vijanagar rulers serving as mere vassals. Then, in 1486, a Vijayanagar governor named Saluva Narasimha (r. 1486–1491) organized the kingdom's forces, expelled the Bahmani army, and assumed the throne. This transition, known as the First Usurpation, marked the beginning of the Saluva dynasty. Narasimha restored the provincial governments of Vijayanagar and rebuilt the kingdom's economy.

Narasimha died after ruling for only five years. His sons were highly ineffective monarchs, and they quickly squandered their father's success. In 1505, as civil unrest paralyzed the kingdom, an army commander named Vira Narasimha (r. 1505–1509) deposed the Saluvas and took the throne. His action, known as the Second Usurpation, ushered in the Tuluva dynasty.

When Vira Narasimha died in 1509, his younger brother, Krishnadeva Raya (r. 1509–1529), became king. The most successful Vijayanagar monarch, Krishnadeva Raya protected the kingdom from repeated attacks and was never defeated in battle. He also greatly developed the kingdom's economy. Under his authority, all land was assessed as wetlands, dry land, orchards, or forest, and was taxed according to its use, with tax revenue used primarily to finance the military.

Krishnadeva Raya also encouraged industrial expansion, and Vijayanagar soon possessed major textile, mining, fragrance, and metallurgy industries. The kingdom actively traded with numerous Asian nations and maintained a large merchant fleet. Krishnadeva Raya allowed the Portuguese to establish a trading post on Vijayanagar's west coast.

Vijayanagar experienced a cultural explosion under Krishnadeva Raya. He recruited scholars from all areas of India and encouraged them to write in their native languages. The government commonly subsidized poets, philosophers, and historians and financed the construction of temples and public facilities.

Unfortunately, Krishnadeva Raya's successors were weak rulers. In 1542, his nephew Sadasiva (r. 1542–1570) assumed the throne, but he allowed his adviser, Rama Raya, to control the kingdom. Raya envisioned a greatly expanded Vijayanagar in control of all of India. To fulfill this vision, he made shifting alliances with the kingdoms of Ahmadnagar, Golconda, and Bijapur, which were former provinces of the Bahmani kingdom.

In 1543, Vijayanagar joined Golconda and Bijapur in an invasion of Ahmadnagar. But the Vijayanagar forces so badly ravaged the conquered country that the Muslim kingdoms united against Vijayanagar in disgust.

The three kingdoms exacted their revenge in 1565, invading Vijayanagar and massacring Raya and his forces. However, internal dissent again flared among the three allies and prevented them from completely dismantling Vijayanagar. Consequently, the kingdom maintained its autonomy but in a greatly weakened state. Raya's brother, Tirumala (r. 1570–1572), deposed Sadasiva in 1570 and founded the Aravidu dynasty, the last dynasty of Vijayanagar.

After taking control of the kingdom, the Aravidu dynasty struggled to maintain its power. The provincial governors refused to acknowledge any central authority, and the kingdom steadily dissipated. In 1642, the last Vijayanagar monarch, Sriranga III (r. 1642–1670), assumed the throne. Ultimately, Ranga proved unable to resist attacks from Bijapur and Golconda, and he could not convince the provincial governors to supply military forces. The provinces declared their independence, and so the Vijayanagar Empire collapsed and ended.

See also: AHMADNAGAR KINGDOM; BAHMANI DYNASTY; GOLCONDA KINGDOM; INDIAN KINGDOMS.

FURTHER READING

Karashima, Noboru. *Towards a New Formation: Southern Indian Society Under Vijayanagar Rule.* New York: Oxford University Press, 1992.

Stein, Burton. *Vijayanagar.* New York: Cambridge University Press, 1989.

VIKING EMPIRE (ca. 1017–1042 C.E.)

Not an enduring political entity, but rather an eleventh-century union of Denmark, England, and Norway under the rule of Cnut the Great (r. 1013–1035), which did not survive long after his death.

Between the 800s and 1000s, the Vikings founded kingdoms and colonies in places as far-flung as Ireland, Scotland, Normandy, Russia, Iceland, and Greenland, and there is some evidence they may have settled for a time in Newfoundland. However, there was little or no political connection between these colonies and the kingdoms from which they originated. The Viking Empire as such was the work of just one family, the Skjoldung dynasty of Denmark. It lasted but a short time and encompassed little more than Denmark and England.

FOUNDATION BY SVEYN FORKBEARD

King Svend or Sveyn I of Denmark (r. 986–1014), also known as Sveyn Forkbeard, was a son of Harald Bluetooth (r. 940–986), the king who first unified much of Denmark under one crown. In the late tenth century, England suffered much raiding by Viking bands. Sveyn, secure in his control of Denmark, may initially have intended nothing more than similar raids to gain wealth. He first attacked England in 994 but showed no sign of planning to conquer the country at that time. Instead, he returned to Scandinavia to fight Olaf Tryggvason, who had fought in England for both Sveyn and the English king, Ethelred II (r.

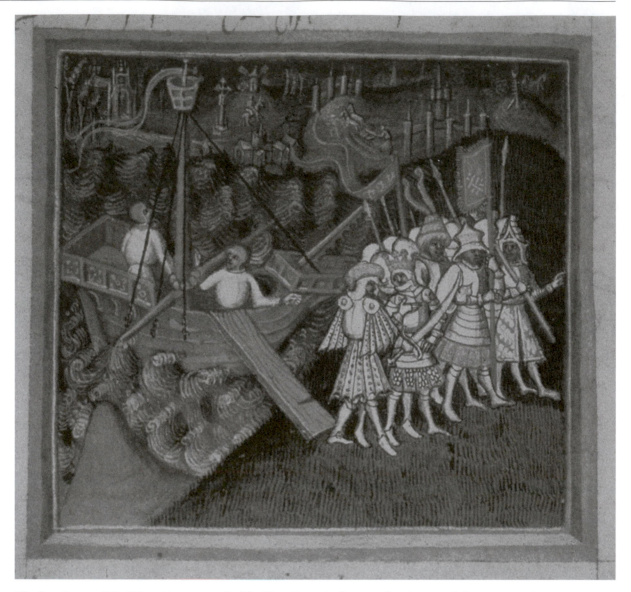

The foundation of the Viking Empire was laid by King Sveyn I of Denmark, who united the Danes under one crown in the mid-tenth century. His attack on England in 994 is depicted in this early illustrated manuscript.

978–1016), and had made himself King Olaf I of Norway (r. 994–999).

Like his father Harald Bluetooth, Sveyn regarded himself as overlord of Norway, and Olaf's kingship was a direct challenge that could not be ignored. Sveyn defeated Olaf in battle in the year 1000. At this time Sveyn was probably also overlord of Sweden, since its king, Olaf Skötkonung (r. 994–1023), was his stepson and "sköt" means tribute (which implies a tributary relationship). The conquered territories of Norway were ruled by Olaf Skötkonung and by Earl Eirik Haakonson of Hladir under Sveyn.

Due to generations of invasions, there was already a large Danish or Norse population in England. This population was concentrated in the area of the Danelaw, the north and east of England, where Norse rather than English customary law prevailed. In 1002, King Ethelred II of England (r. 978–1016) ordered a slaughter of the Danes, known as the St. Brice's Day Massacre; among those killed was Sveyn's sister. Sveyn sought revenge by raiding England extensively between 1003 and 1005. His fleets and armies continued to attack and exact tribute throughout the next decade as well. English districts and towns submitted to him and in December 1013, Ethelred having fled to Normandy, Sveyn was proclaimed king of England. He died just over a month later.

AN EMPIRE UNDER CNUT THE GREAT

Upon Sveyn's death, his son Cnut (also known as Knut or Canute) became king in England, while Cnut's older brother Harald II (r. 1014–1018) ruled in Denmark. The English drove Cnut out in 1014, but with his brother's backing he returned in 1015.

Ethelred II died in 1016, and his son Edmund II Ironside (r. 1016) offered Cnut stiff resistance until Edmund's death later that year. Cnut was then acknowledged king of England. He became king of Denmark in 1018 or 1019, following his brother's death. Sweden, however, withdrew from the sphere of Danish influence. Olaf Skötkonung and his son Anund Jakob (r. 1022–1050) did not offer Cnut the support Olaf had given Sveyn, and their policies often ran contrary to Danish interests.

Cnut's rule of England and Denmark marks the apogee and nearly full extent of a single political entity that could be considered the Viking Empire. Cnut regarded himself as king of England rather than as merely a successful Viking raider with a wealthy territory to plunder. He defended the country against Viking attacks and issued law codes that continued the traditions of English or Anglo-Saxon law. Cnut also issued coins, a traditional method of advertising the legitimacy of one's rule, and modeled his Danish coinage on the longer established English currency.

Cnut's rule was not untroubled. In 1026, his regent in Denmark, his brother-in-law Earl Ulf, revolted against him and united with King Olaf II Haraldsson (Saint Olaf) of Norway (r. 1016–1030) and King Anund Jakob of Sweden (r. 1022–1050). Cnut put down the revolt and maintained control of his two realms of England and Denmark, but he did not win an outright victory.

In 1028, Cnut drove Olaf Haraldsson out of Norway. After Olaf returned and was killed while fighting Norwegian opposition in 1030, Cnut appointed his own son Sveyn and Sveyn's English mother Aelfgifu co-rulers of Norway. However, the Norwegians drove them out in 1035, and both died soon thereafter. Cnut also claimed to be king of Sweden and may have held the allegiance of some Swedish nobles, but there is little evidence for any real overlordship of Sweden on Cnut's part.

THE DISINTEGRATION OF EMPIRE

Cnut had two sons, Sveyn and Harald Harefoot, with Aelfgifu, the daughter of an English nobleman. While married to Aelfgifu, he also married Ethelred's widow, Emma of Normandy. Cnut and Emma agreed that only their sons could inherit the throne of England, excluding Aelfgifu's sons as well as the son of Ethelred and Emma, Edward.

Harthacnut, the son of Cnut and Emma, was raised mostly in Denmark and acted as Cnut's representative there. When Cnut died in 1035, Harthacnut succeeded to the throne of Denmark (r. 1035–1042) while at war with King Magnus I of Norway (r. 1035–1046). Harald Harefoot became king of England (r. 1037–1040) instead of his half-brother Harthacnut after a dispute over the succession, which was never entirely resolved. In 1039 Harthacnut began preparations to invade England.

When Harald Harefoot died in 1040, Harthacnut added the throne of England to his rule. However, the two kingdoms were not destined to remain united. Harthacnut died in 1042 without an heir, and the English elected his half-brother, Edward, son of Emma and Ethelred, as king. Known as Edward the Confessor (r. 1042–1066), Edward proved an ineffectual king, unable to maintain his authority over the English nobles.

Meanwhile, Cnut's nephew Sveyn Estrithson claimed the Crown of Denmark but was rejected by the Danes, who chose instead to be ruled by Magnus of Norway (r. 1035–1046). Upon Magnus's death in 1046, Sveyn Estrithson became king of Denmark. Sveyn was unable to make good on any claim to the English Crown, however, and his hold on Denmark was threatened by Harald Hardraade of Norway.

As Magnus's heir, Harald claimed an inheritance from Harthacnut and made a bid for the English Crown. In 1066 he died fighting against Harold Godwinson at the battle of Stamford Bridge, a few weeks before the English Crown was lost to William the Conqueror, the Norse-descended duke of Normandy.

An attempt to assert a Viking claim to Cnut's empire was made by his nephew Sveyn Estrithson in 1069, when, in response to English pleas for aid, the Danes invaded northern England. The Danes eventually accepted tribute from William the Conqueror and withdrew, leaving their English allies to William's mercy. Danish fleets raided England in 1075, but a planned invasion by Cnut II of Denmark (r. 1080–1086) in 1085 was never carried out. The brief period of the Viking Empire had passed.

The enduring legacy of the Viking Empire founded by Sveyn Forkbeard and ruled by Cnut the Great was its cultural and linguistic contribution to England. Through much of the later Middle Ages, the persistence of a free peasantry in the former Danelaw region, at a time when serfdom was the more common legal status of English peasants, can be attributed to the Viking influence. Speakers of modern English also continue to experience the linguistic heritage of the Vikings, using a variety of words—such as earl, skirt, and skill—that are derived from Old Norse roots.

See also: Anglo-Saxon Rulers; Cnut I; Danish Kingdom; Edward the Confessor; Harald III Hardraade; Harold II Godwinson; Norwegian Monarchy; Olaf II (Saint Olaf); Swedish Monarchy.

FURTHER READING

Garmonsway, G.N., trans. *The Anglo-Saxon Chronicle.* London: Dent, 1953.

Holmes, George, ed. *The Oxford Illustrated History of Medieval Europe.* New York: Oxford University Press, 1988.

Jones, Gwyn. *A History of the Vikings.* 2nd ed. New York: Oxford University Press, 2001.

Lawson, M.K. *Cnut: The Danes in England in the Early Eleventh Century.* New York: Longman, 1993.

Page, R.I. *Chronicles of the Vikings: Records, Memorials, and Myths.* Toronto: University of Toronto Press, 1995.

Sawyer, Peter, ed. *The Oxford Illustrated History of the Vikings.* New York: Oxford University Press, 1997.

Stenton, Sir Frank. *Anglo-Saxon England.* 3rd ed. New York: Oxford University Press, 2001.

VIRACOCHA (d. 1438 C.E.)

Eighth Great Inca (r. ca. 1390s–1438), who ruled during the transitional period when the kingdom of the Incas became a true empire.

Hatun Tapac, son of Yahuar Huacac, took the name Inca Viracocha upon becoming the eighth king to rule over Tahuantinsuyo (the Quechua name for the kingdom and empire of the Incan people). Viracocha is also the name of the creator god upon whom the Incan religion was based. It was the god Viracocha who gave rise to Inti, the sun god, and it is from Inti that the Incan rulers traced their descent.

Viracocha Inca was the first Inca king to assume the title of *Sapa Inca,* which means "supreme ruler."

When Viracocha Inca came to power sometime in the 1390s, his realm extended only throughout the Valley of Cuzco, but Viracocha had grander ambitions. From the Inca capital at Cuzco, he sent his sons out on campaigns of conquest throughout the Andean region. One of these sons, Pachacuti, is credited with extending Incan rule as far north as present-day Ecuador and as far south as the Nazca Plains along the coastal region of present-day Peru. The conquered peoples were assimilated into the Incan state through treaties, marital alliances, and other political means, but were allowed to retain their own local leaders. Quechua became the official language spoken throughout the realm.

Between 1390 and 1420, an external threat arose to challenge the supremacy of the Inca Empire. A people called the Canchos created a rival state to the north, and Viracocha was forced to amass an army to ward off the danger. According to tradition, the Canchos attacked in force in the 1430s. Uncertain that his army could defeat them, Viracocha Inca fled into the mountains with his eldest son and official heir, Urco. Pachacuti, on the other hand, remained behind to face the enemy and was ultimately victorious. When the Canchos were finally defeated, the people turned away from Viracocha Inca and Urco for having abandoned the empire to its fate. Instead, they threw their support behind Pachacuti, who had acquitted himself as a hero.

Around 1438, Pachacuti (r. 1438–1471) became the ninth and, arguably, the greatest of the Inca rulers. Under his reign, the Inca built great roadways linking all the important urban and ritual centers of the empire. Pachacuti also ordered the construction of some of the greatest ceremonial sites of the Inca world, including the city of Machu Picchu deep in the Andes Mountains. By the end of Pachacuti's reign, Tahuantinsuyo had achieved its greatest economic, artistic, architectural, and religious development.

See also: Atahualpa; Huayna Capac; Inca Empire; Pachacuti; South American Monarchies.

VISIGOTH KINGDOM (395–711 C.E.)

Early kingdom established by the Visigoths, a migrating Germanic people who eventually established a kingdom on the Iberian Peninsula in what is present-day Spain.

The earliest Visigoths appear in the historical record as one of the Germanic groups opposing the Roman Empire. Their leaders were elected war-chiefs. Unlike most other Germanic tribes, the Visigoths retained elected leaders, never shifting to a fully hereditary kingship. The first Visigothic leader to be identified as a king is Alaric I (r. 395–410), whose forces sacked Rome in 410.

THE VISIGOTHS IN SOUTHERN FRANCE

From Italy, the Visigoths moved westward to southern France, where they settled as Roman allies—a shift not uncommon in the tulmutuous political period of the later Roman Empire. From that base in France, they migrated into the Iberian Peninsula. The most significant king of this phase of Visigothic history was Euric (r. 466–484), under whom the Visigothic kingdom, with its capital at Toulouse, reached its greatest geographical extent, incorporating most of Iberia along with southern France. Euric also formally renounced Roman sovereignty over the Visigoths, although they had long enjoyed *de facto* independence.

The history of the Visgothic kingdom was marked by religious conflict. The Visigoths, like other Germanic peoples at this time, were Arian Christians. Arians believed that Christ had been created by God rather than being coeternal, as the Roman Church believed. This meant that Visigothic kings could never be fully sure of the loyalty of the Roman church in their dominions, although they did not attempt to destroy it. After defeat by the Franks under Clovis (r. 481–511) in 507 and the death in battle of Euric's successor, Alaric II (r. 484–507), the Visigothic kingdom was driven out of nearly all of its possessions in France, and it reorganized itself on the basis of its Spanish territories.

VISIGOTHIC SPAIN

The most important rulers in sixth-century Visigothic Spain were Leovigild (r. 568–586) and his son Reccared (r. 586–601). Leovigild reinvigorated the Visigothic monarchy, defeated the kingdom of the Suevi in northwestern Spain and incorporated it into the Visigothic kingdom, and drove the Byzantine Empire from all but a few small footholds in the southern part of the Iberian Peninsula. He also established a permanent capital at Toledo. (Previously, Visigothic rulers had traveled throughout their kingdoms rather than living in a central place.)

Leovigild vigorously promoted Arianism, apparently hoping to end the religious division of the Visigothic kingdom by converting large numbers of his Christian subjects to that branch of the faith. This

Visigoth Kingdom	
ALARIC I*	395–410
ATAULF	410–415
SIGERIC	415
WALLIA	415–419
THEODORIC I	419–451
THORISMUND	451–453
THEODORIC II	453–466
EURIC	466–484
ALARIC II	484–507
GESALECH	507–511
AMALARIC	511–531
LEOVIGILD	568–586
RECCARED I*	586–601
SISEBUT	612–621
CHINDASWINTH	642–653
RECCESWINTH (coruler	
with his father	649–653;
CHINDASWINTH)	653–672 (KING)
EGICA	687–702
WITIZA (coruler	
with his father EGICA)	697–702;
	702–710 (KING)
RODERIC*	710–711
*Indicates a separate alphabetical entry.	

project had little success, however. His successor, Reccared, took the opposite approach to attain religious uniformity, converting with his family to the Roman faith and vigorously suppressing Arianism.

The seventh-century Visigothic monarchy was marked by strong cooperation between church and state, with the king making ecclesiastical as well as civil and military appointments and working closely with the bishops. Beginning with Reccared, Visigothic kings adopted the rite of anointment with holy oil at coronations, which gave the kings a particularly sacred status. The Roman Catholic Church in Spain, though in communion with Rome, was more subject to the king than to the pope.

One aspect of the strongly sacral nature of Visigothic kingship was a series of decrees against the Jews. The Catholic Visigothic kings were an exception to the generally tolerant practices of Germanic barbarian kings toward the Jews in the early Middle Ages. King Sisebut (r. 612–621) ordered that Jews be forcibly baptized or exiled from the kingdom. Sisebut was also one of the most learned early medieval kings, writing in Latin a *Life of St. Desiderius* and serving as a patron of the great medieval encyclopedist, Isidor of Seville.

Legislation, as well as war and religious leadership, was an important component of Visigothic kingship. The legal decrees and codes issued by Visigothic rulers show a development away from different laws for different groups toward a single code of law for all peoples in the kingdom. This process of assimilation, encouraged by Reccared's abandonment of a separate Visigothic religious identity, culminated in the *Laws of the Visigoths*, issued in 654 by King Recceswinth (r. 653–672). Recceswinth, following the path laid out by his father king Chindaswinth (r. 642–653), explicitly abolished previous codes of Visigothic and Roman law in favor of a law that applied uniformly over all Visigothic territory.

THE END OF THE VISIGOTHS

Late seventh-century Visigothic kings, though supported by the church, suffered disputed successions, rebellions, and problems with the nobility. A dispute between two claimants to the throne seriously weakened the kingdom prior to the Arab invasion in 711. The Arab Moors also benefited from the Visigothic rulers' alienation of the Jewish population, who welcomed the Muslim invaders as liberators. The last Visigothic ruler, King Rodrigo or Roderic (r. 710–711)—around whom many legends later developed—was killed in battle against the Arabs, bringing the Visigothic kingdom to an end.

See also: ALARIC I; CHRISTIANITY AND KINGSHIP; RECCARED I; RODERIC; SPANISH MONARCHIES.

FURTHER READING
James, Edward, ed. *Visigothic Spain: New Approaches.* New York: Oxford University Press, 1980.

VLACH PRINCIPALITY

(1290–1462 C.E.)

A Balkan principality, also called Walachia, the most famous ruler of which was Vlad Tepes (r. 1448, 1456–1462, 1476), known as Vlad the Impaler and the inspiration for the fictional character Dracula.

The Vlachs are believed to have originally come from Thrace, a remnant of the indigenous population ruled by the Eastern Roman Empire, who were split off from their erstwhile rulers with the disintegration of the empire and the invasion of Slavic tribes into the region. These people established themselves in the mountains, where they maintained a pastoral lifestyle based on sheep herding. For centuries they were subject to one of the various powers of the region, paying tribute in return for being left to themselves. In 1186, however, the demands for tribute became excessive enough to inspire two Vlachian brothers, Ivan and Peter, to lead a revolt. Their aim was to establish an autonomous nation.

The realization of this dream would have to wait until 1290, when Basarab the Great (r. ca. 1290–1352) finally succeeded in uniting the Vlachs into a single political entity. He was the first Vlach prince, establishing the royal house of Basarab and ruling until his death in 1352. The house of Basarab constituted two rival subclans, the Danesti and the house of Mircea the Old (r. 1386–1418). All the Vlach princes (called *voivodes*) came from one of these two clans, selected by a council of nobles called *boyars*.

Vlach politics, both internal and international, were particularly difficult and often bloody. Succession to the throne was a hard-won affair, with assassination a commonly used stratagem to advance a prospective *voivode*'s chances. In addition, dissatisfied *boyars* who felt their king was not attentive enough to their needs were just as quick to display their anger with poison or knives. Beyond the borders of the principality, powerful neighbors contended for control of the region, and Vlach independence required careful attention to strategic alliances with Hungarians on one side and the Byzantine Empire (and later the Ottoman Turks) on the other. Vlach rulers had to be personally powerful and ruthless.

Vlachia's most famous *voivode,* and the last to rule with some semblance of independence, was born in 1431. This was Vlad IV, variously called Vlad Draculea, Vlad Tepes, and Vlad the Impaler. His father, also named Vlad, was frustrated that the house of the Danesti currently held the throne, which he believed rightfully belonged to him as the son of Mircea the Old. True to standard political practice in Vlachia, he ordered the assassination of the ruling prince, Alexandru I (1431–1436), and took over the country, ruling as Vlad II (1436–1442). This action did not go unnoticed by pro-Danesti *boyars,* however, and in 1447 they returned the favor, murdering both Vlad and his eldest son, Mircea, and placing their own candidate, Vladislav II (1447–1448), on the throne.

Vlad Tepes reacted to the murder of his father and brother in the only way he could: He vowed to retake the throne. Accordingly, he enlisted the aid of his powerful neighbors, the Ottoman Turks, and with their support he seized the throne in 1448. This victory was short-lived, however, and a Danesti rival forced him out after only two months. This time Vlad turned to the Hungarians for help in ousting the Danesti king. He succeeded in 1456 and again proclaimed himself prince.

The next six years were epic in their violence, as Vlad demonstrated the obsession that earned him his nickname, the Impaler. This was his chosen method of making a point to foreign powers, and his favorite form of punishment when establishing control within his kingdom. Impalings were conducted on a grand scale, with hundreds of people left hanging on stakes in village courtyards and surrounding his palace. His victims often earned this brutal, deadly punishment by committing only minor crimes.

In 1462 the Vlach principality fell to invading Turks, and Vlad fled to the court of the Hungarian king for safety. Instead, he was imprisoned, and the Hungarian king supported Vlad's brother Radu (called "the Handsome") instead. Radu soon died, however, perhaps assassinated, and a new Danesti prince took the throne. Hungary, however, preferred Vlad over the new *voivod,* and set their prisoner free to try to retake his kingdom.

Vlad struck an alliance with a cousin, Prince Stephen the Great, who ruled the principality of Moldavia. Together they defeated the Danesti faction, but upon seeing Vlad installed as king, Stephen withdrew to his own principality, taking his army with him. The Ottoman Turks saw this moment as an opportunity. Seeing Vlachia helpless and lacking any credible military force, the Ottomans sent their armies pouring over the border. Vlad was forced to take to the battlefield to defend his principality, and was slain in the ensuing battle. His head was carried back to Constantinople as a trophy of war, and was hung on a pike to demonstrate that the cruel king was truly dead.

See also: BYZANTINE EMPIRE; OTTOMAN EMPIRE.

VLADIMIR PRINCEDOM

(1125–1238 C.E.)

A powerful princedom in the Rus kingdoms that flourished from the twelfth to thirteenth centuries.

During the late tenth century, East Slavic tribes from Novgorod (in present-day Russia) migrated into the region between the Oka and Volga rivers and settled an area that eventually became known as Vladimir-Suzdal. Over the next two centuries, the settlers established several key communities, including Rostov, Yaroslavl, Murom, and Suzdal. These cities became known for the highly skilled artisans who inhabited them, and regional merchants sold their pottery and metallic products throughout the Kievan Rus, Bulgaria, and Byzantium.

As the Rus kingdoms became more consolidated under the rule of Oleg (r. 882–912) and his successors in the tenth century, the cities in the region attempted to retain their autonomy by supplying warriors for Oleg's forces and paying an annual tribute to Kiev. However, during the reign of the Kievan grand prince Vladimir I Sviatoslavich (r. 980–1015), the region increasingly succumbed to Kievan authority. Vladimir strengthened the region's ties to Kiev by installing his most loyal supporters as landowners and placing the local farmers under their control. These new feudal servants, the *smerdy,* resented the imposition of a new ruling class. In 1024, during the reign of Vladimir's son, Yaroslav the Wise (r. 1019–1054), the *smerdy* rebelled, but Yaroslav quickly suppressed the revolution.

When Yaroslav died in 1054, the Rus kingdoms were divided among his sons. One of them, Vsevolod

Yaroslavich, was granted Rostov and the surrounding lands. Yaroslav's sons frequently clashed, and the Rus kingdoms gradually dissolved into competing principalities. When Vsevolod's son, Vladimir Vsevolodovich Monomakh, assumed control of Rostov in 1093, he declared Rostov's independence from Kievan control and established the Principality of Suzdal. To protect the new province, he built a powerful fortress, named Vladimir, near the Kliaz'ma River. These actions initiated the Vladimir princedom.

Vladimir Monomakh's son, Yurii Dolgorukii (r. 1149–1157), further solidified Suzdal's independence. He built additional fortresses, repelled a Bulgarian invasion, and quelled a disturbance among his own landowners. Prince Yurii also encouraged an expansion of the artisan class, and their prevalence increased the region's prosperity. In 1155, encouraged by his military and economic successes, Prince Yurii attacked and conquered Kiev.

The victory dramatically reshaped the Rus kingdoms. Yurii's son and successor, Andrei Bogoliubskii (r. 1157–1174), moved the Rus capital to Vladimir and made the Vladimir-Suzdal the center of the Rus realm. Andrei vastly expanded the Rus army. To ensure his soldiers' loyalty, he granted them large amounts of land and gave them complete control over the inhabitants, thereby creating a highly subservient peasant class. Like his father, Andrei also favored the artisan class; his cultivation of their support secured his power.

A cultural explosion also occurred during Andrei's reign. He patronized artists and architects, and he commissioned several historical writings. These writings often served a propagandistic purpose, proclaiming that Vladimir Monomakh had created the principality and introduced Christianity to it. Andrei's control, however, was not complete. In 1174, a group of nobles assassinated him, temporarily disrupting the principality's dominance.

After two years of internecine struggles, Andrei's son Vsevolod (r. 1176–1212) assumed the throne. Over the next twenty years, Vsevolod waged campaigns against the other principalities, and only Novgorod escaped his complete control. Vsevolod also increased his power by defeating the Polovtsians, who had staged frequent, devastating raids on Kiev and southern Rus. A contemporary historical chronicle, the *Song of Igor's Campaign,* extols his victory and designates Vesvolod as the most powerful leader in Rus.

Vsevolod's reign marks the apex of the Vladimir-

Suzdal principality. After his death in 1212, his sons, Konstantin (r. 1212–1218) and Yurii (r. 1212–1238), disagreed on how to rule Vladimir-Suzdal. Konstantin wished to restore the prominence of Rostov; he demanded a separate principality for Rostov with its own government. In 1216, when Konstantin briefly banished Yurii, he divided Vladimir-Suzdal into three separate principalities. Although Yurii regained power in 1218 and forcefully reunited the Valdimir-Suzdal, the decentralization had permanently weakened the region's power. In 1238, the Mongols invaded the Rus kingdoms and devastated the Vladimir-Suzdal principality, initiating over two hundred years of Mongol rule.

Yet the shift of influence from Kiev to Vladimir-Suzdal during this period had lasting implications. The cultural traditions that emerged during Vladimir-Suzdal's ascendancy sustained a sense of Rus nationality during the Mongol occupation. Eventually, the Principality of Moscow would arise from the former Vladimir-Suzdal principality, and its leaders would defeat the Mongols and establish the modern Russian nation.

See also: KIEV, PRINCEDOM OF; RUS PRINCEDOMS.

FURTHER READING

Hartog, Leo de. *Russia and the Mongol Yoke.* New York: British Academic Press, 1996.

Martin, Janet. *Medieval Russia: 980–1584.* New York: Cambridge University Press, 1995.

WALDEMAR I, THE GREAT

(1131–1182 C.E.)

King of Denmark (r. 1157–1182) following a generation of chaos and dynastic war, who established the basis for Denmark's strength and prosperity in succeeding generations.

Waldemar (or Valdemar) the Great was one of three rival claimants to the Danish throne in the mid-twelfth century. After years of conflict, the kingdom was divided between them. One of the three, Sveyn III (r. 1146–1157), held a feast around 1156 or 1157 to celebrate this negotiated peace. At the feast he murdered one rival, but Waldemar escaped in the dark. When Sveyn III was killed by a peasant in Waldemar's territory of Jutland not long afterward, Waldemar became undisputed king of Denmark in 1157.

In the beginning of Waldemar's reign he acknowledged the overlordship of the Holy Roman emperor Frederick I (r. 1152–1190), but in 1165 he reneged on his support of Frederick's chosen anti-pope, and in 1170 had his son, later Cnut IV (r. 1182–1202), anointed co-ruler. With both of these actions, taken without the Holy Roman emperor's approval, Waldemar declared his independence of Frederick's overlordship.

A Slavic people called the Wends from the island of Rügen in the Baltic Sea had been raiding Denmark during the period of civil war between the claimants to the Danish throne. Waldemar's great achievement was his victory over them in 1169. With the support of the Church he invaded Rügen, conquered the island, and destroyed the Wends' pagan shrines. Henry the Lion (r. 1142–1180), duke of Saxony and Bavaria and overlord of the Wends, demanded reparations. At first, Waldemar complied, but he later went to war against the Wends living on the Baltic coast.

Waldemar needed a base from which to command the eastern end of the Oresund, the narrow passage between the North Sea and the Baltic. In 1167, his ally, Archbishop Absalon of Lund, founded Copenhagen, building a fortress where previously only a fishing village existed. This gave Denmark a naval base on the Baltic and, in a time when water was the major route for trade and communications, easy access to Scania, the southernmost part of Sweden. On this strong foundation, Waldemar's son and successor Cnut IV began a period of Danish expansion. When Waldemar I died in 1182, he left a Denmark that was strong, prosperous, and stable, none of which it had been when he took the Crown.

See also: DANISH KINGDOM; FREDERICK I, BARBAROSSA; JUTLAND KINGDOM.

WANG KON (d. ca. 943 C.E.)

Founder of the Koryo dynasty in Korea.

Wang Kon was descended from a local aristocratic family in the Kaesong region of Korea's Silla kingdom. As a young man, he served in the military under General Kungye and was stationed at a fortress on Kanghwa Island, where he helped protect Silla's southwest coast from pirate raids. Wang Kon was rapidly promoted and ultimately selected as Kungye's chief minister.

By the late 800s, the Silla government had begun to deteriorate rapidly. Peasants, forced from their land by intolerable taxes, formed large groups of bandits and terrorized rural communities. The aristocracy was also restless; Silla's rigid bone-rank system (a hierarchical social system) barred many aristocrats from high government positions. Kungye and another general, Kyonhwon, exploited this unrest and organized large groups of bandits into formidable armies.

In 892, Kyonhwon attacked the Silla capital and executed the king. Unwilling to let Kyonhwon gain absolute control, Kungye and Wang Kon blocked his further expansion. In 901, Kungye annexed his own region of Silla and established the Later Koguryo dynasty, named after the former kingdom of Koguryo. But Kungye's extreme cruelty led to his assassination in 918. After his death, Wang Kon assumed control and renamed the kingdom Koryo.

At first, Wang Kon allied himself with Silla to counter Kyonhwon's military strength. In 930, Wang Kon decisively defeated Kyonhwon's forces at Andong. Assured of his strength, Wang Kon then demanded that the Silla king relinquish control of the kingdom. Subsequently, in 935, Wang Kon united the entire Korean Peninsula.

To secure the monarchy, Wang Kon abolished Silla's bone-rank system and actively recruited both the Silla aristocracy and descendants of the original Koguryo monarchy to apply for important government posts. These actions created a new, influential elite social class. To further ease tensions within the new kingdom, Wang Kon married a princess from the Silla royal family and arranged numerous marriages among his family and the Silla aristocratic families. In many cases, Wang Kon even allowed these families to adopt his royal surname.

Many rural landowners, however, still retained

control over groups of bandits and resisted Wang Kon's authority. As a result, Wang Kon failed to achieve complete control of Koryo during his rule. Nevertheless, he had established a kingdom and a dynasty, the Wang dynasty, which would control the Korean Peninsula for more than four centuries—from the early 900s to the late 1300s.

See also: KOGURYO KINGDOM; KORYO KINGDOM; SILLA KINGDOM.

WANLI (1563–1620 C.E.)

Chinese emperor (r. 1573–1620) whose long reign marked the decline of the Ming dynasty. The third son of Emperor Longqing (r. 1567–1572), Wanli began his reign at the height of the Ming dynasty. In the early years of his rule, aided by the capable minister Zhang Zhuzheng, the intelligent Wanli was active in state affairs. However, following Zhang's death, Wanli grew frustrated with squabbles at court among his ministers. Disillusioned, at the age of twenty-five he withdrew completely from his imperial duties and never returned to them, although he remained emperor. Wanli refused to leave the Forbidden City, the royal family's palace and the center of China's government, and for years on end, he did not meet with his ministers. Government posts went unfilled. Foreign visitors kowtowed to an empty throne.

Using state funds, Wanli spent lavishly on clothing, palaces, and other luxuries for himself and his family. Idle and self-indulgent, he grew too fat to stand without help. Only the royal family and the eunuchs—the castrated men who served within the palace—were allowed inside the Forbidden City. Because Wanli refused to leave the palace to meet with his ministers, the eunuchs became the sole source of communication between the emperor and the outside world. This situation gave the eunuchs great power, and a corrupt system dominated by the eunuchs controlled the empire's affairs. During Wanli's reign, more than ten thousand eunuchs lived in Beijing.

Despite Wanli's refusal to govern, his reign was a time of economic growth and prosperity. Increased food production, due to new crops such as maize introduced from the Americas, caused China's population to surpass 100 million. The rise of manufacturing gave birth to a new merchant class and brought new wealth to China. Trade increased as international demand mushroomed for Chinese manufactures like silk and porcelain. This prosperity in turn stimulated cultural and intellectual activity.

Militarily, Wanli's reign faced multiple challenges. Chinese armies had to contend with incursions by tribes from Mongolia, the rebellion of minority tribes in the southwest, and war with Japan over Korea. Meanwhile, the Manchu tribesmen were gathering strength in northeast China, where they invaded and occupied the Liaodong region in 1618.

By the end of Wanli's long, inactive reign, the empire was crumbling from within. In a few decades, the well-organized Manchus would topple the Ming dynasty.

See also: MING DYNASTY.

WARFARE

For most of recorded history, warfare has been an accepted preoccupation of monarchs. Through war, monarchs have extended their power, frightening people into accepting their leadership, and gaining the loyalty of their followers by distributing the spoils. Through the capacity to wage war, monarchs have gained legitimacy in the eyes of their people by promising to protect them in a violent world. In spite of the advocacy of peace by philosophers going back as far as the Chinese scholar Mencius (372–289 B.C.E.), it is really only since World War I (1914–1918) that the inevitability of war has been questioned.

MONARCHS AS CONQUERORS

Because war was always thought of as a necessary part of human life, monarchs since the earliest times have needed to assert themselves as warriors—or as leaders of warriors—in order to have credibility. In fact, many of the earliest written records were made to boast of the conquests of kings. An inscription written at the command of the Assyrian king Shalmaneser I (r. 1274–1245 B.C.E.) celebrates his defeat of his enemies, the Hurrians, in terms that make a virtue of ruthlessness: "I fought a battle and accomplished their defeat. I killed countless numbers of his defeated and widespreading hosts. . . . Their lands I brought under my sway, and the rest of their cities I burned with fire."

On the other side of the world, the Maya kings of the Classic period (25–900 C.E.) had huge stone steles built to memorialize, through pictures in relief and carved hieroglyphic writing, their victories in battle. The great epics of earliest literature—the Sumerian *Epic of Gilgamesh,* the Hindu *Mahabharata,* Homer's *Iliad* and *Odyssey,* the Icelandic sagas—all focus on the wars and fights of kings.

The lesson of literature and written history has consistently been that kings are remembered most of all for their military prowess. Those monarchs who have come to be known as "the Great"—Darius I of Persia (r. 521–486 B.C.E.), Alexander the Great (r. 336–323 B.C.E.), Holy Roman emperor Otto I (936–973 C.E.), Mughal emperor Akbar I (1556–1605), Louis I of Hungary (r. 1342–1382), Frederick II of Prussia (r. 1740–1786)—have mostly earned that epithet by expanding their kingdoms through territorial aggression and military conquest. It is a lesson that ambitious monarchs have found hard to ignore.

For the kings of the Aztecs of Mexico, warfare was actually a prerequisite of kingship. The process of becoming king involved three stages: First there was a four-day period of withdrawal and fasting, during which the new king, dressed only in a loincloth, burned incense to the gods, offered blood pricked from his limbs and earlobes, and contemplated the responsibilities of kingship. Then there was the coronation, when he was invested with the magnificent regalia of kingship and made a public appearance thus attired. After that there was the coronation war:

Unless the new king successfully attacked an enemy and brought back prisoners of war and booty, his legitimacy was felt to be unproven. The final step was confirmation, when gifts were received, honors were distributed, there were feasts and speeches and music, and the prisoners of the coronation war were sacrificed to the principal god, Huitzilopochtli.

MONARCHS AS DEFENDERS

Of course, war is not always a matter of choice. When an outside aggressor threatens a kingdom, a monarch who can lead the defense of the country bravely and effectively, identifying with the people's sufferings, will earn their gratitude. Alfred the Great of England (r. 871–899) earned his title first by defending his country against the Danish invaders and then by cultivating the benefits of peace: literature, scholarship, and the arts.

Elizabeth I of England (r. 1558–1603) was inclined by education and temperament to avoid conflict, but she had no hesitation about adopting a militaristic stance when it was necessary for defense. When in 1588 England was threatened with invasion by the navy of Philip II of Spain (r. 1556–1598)—the great Spanish Armada—Elizabeth made an appearance among her troops as they awaited battle. By her presence, and by making a speech of classic kingly aggression in which she took on the military role, Elizabeth

ROYAL RITUALS

AZTEC CORONATION RITUALS

For the kings of the Aztecs of Mexico, warfare was actually a prerequisite of kingship. The process of becoming king involved three stages: First there was a four-day period of withdrawal and fasting, during which the new king, dressed only in a loincloth, burned incense to the gods, offered blood pricked from his limbs and earlobes, and contemplated the responsibilities of kingship. Then there was the coronation, when he was invested with the magnificent regalia of kingship and made a public appearance thus attired. After that there was the coronation war: Unless the new king successfully attacked an enemy and brought back prisoners of war and booty, his legitimacy was felt to be unproven. The final step was confirmation, when gifts were received, honors were distributed, there were feasts and speeches and music were presented, and the prisoners of the coronation war were sacrificed to the principal god, Huitzilopochtli.

had an electrifying effect on the soldiers' morale. She said: "I am come amongst you at this time, not as for my recreation or sport, but being resolved, in the midst and heat of the battle, to live or die amongst you all; to lay down, for my God, and for my kingdom, and for my people, my honor and my blood. . . . I know I have but the body of a weak and feeble woman; but I have the heart of a king, and of a king of England, too . . . to which, rather than any dishonor should grow by me, I myself will take up arms."

MONARCHS AS NATIONAL SYMBOLS

By the twentieth century, most European monarchs had little real power, but in wartime some of them became important symbols for their countries. In World War II, King George VI of England (r. 1936–1952) or King Christian X of Denmark (r. 1912–1947) could do little against the Nazi terror. But when King George and his wife, the former Elizabeth Bowes-Lyon, refused to leave London during the Blitz, and when they toured bombed areas and talked to people who had lost their homes, they became a focus of affection and comfort for their embattled subjects. When Buckingham Palace was bombed, the queen responded with the comment, "I'm glad we've been bombed, it makes me feel I can look the East End in the face."

King Christian had a much more difficult task, for his country was occupied by Adolf Hitler's army in April 1940. The king refused to leave Denmark or to make concessions to the occupying forces; although he was in his seventies, he continued his habit of a daily horseback ride around the city, without bodyguards, until the Germans placed him under house arrest in 1943. His quiet disregard of the Germans came to symbolize for his people their own secret resistance. Although there was no open revolt against the German invaders, the Danes succeeded in smuggling 7,500 of the 8,000 Danish Jews to safety in Sweden.

See also: CONQUEST AND KINGSHIPS; KINGDOMS AND EMPIRES; MILITARY ROLES, ROYAL; NAVAL ROLES.

WARI. *See* HUARI EMPIRE

WARRI KINGDOM. *See* ITSEKERI KINGDOM

WEDDINGS, ROYAL

The ceremonies by which monarchs marry. Though not a constitutional ceremony like the royal coronation, a royal wedding is important because it is a celebration of the continuation of a dynasty through marriage and children, and therefore the continuance of the state. Royal weddings are usually celebrated with great pomp, demonstrating the symbolic importance of monarchy as the center of power and national identity.

WEDDINGS AND POLITICAL ALLIANCES

A royal marriage is often made to cement an alliance between the countries of the bride and groom, and the accompanying ceremonies celebrate its political importance. A royal wedding was one of the few occasions in many societies in which a queen had real political importance. For example, in 1660, for the wedding of Louis XIV of France (r. 1643–1715) and the Spanish Infanta, María Teresa, which sealed a peace treaty between the two countries, French dramatist Pierre Corneille wrote an allegorical prologue to his drama *The Conquest of the Golden Fleece*. It depicted Hymen (or marriage) holding a shield with the Infanta's face on it to drive away Discord and Envy.

ROYAL COURTSHIP

Even in arranged royal marriages, the fiction is often maintained that the union is personal. In early modern Europe, though marriages to foreign brides were always arranged, the romantic conventions of courtly love were observed. The royal groom would often visit his bride in disguise before the official meeting, as Henry VIII (r. 1509–1547) did with Anne of Cleves.

In the kingdom of Swaziland in southern Africa, the courtship practice is quite public. During the annual Reed Dance performed by the country's young girls, which celebrates the nation's roots and the girls' passage into womanhood, the king examines the young women and chooses his brides from among them.

WEDDING RITES

Royal wedding rites resemble those of most marriages in the society, but with an emphasis on the law of inheritance. During royal wedding ceremonies in later medieval Europe, the royal couple joined right hands.

Royal weddings are generally known for their pageantry, which reinforces the authority and tradition of the monarchy. One of the most celebrated royal weddings of the twentieth century was that of Prince Charles of England and Lady Diana Spencer at St. Paul's Cathedral in London on July 29, 1981.

However, in the case of a morganatic marriage (a union in which the husband was of royal rank, but the bride of lower rank), the groom offered the bride his left hand. Morganatic marriages were thus called marriages of the left hand. The children of morganatic marriages were generally barred from taking the throne.

Royal wedding-night customs in Europe included observing the preparations for the all-important consummation of the marriage and the displaying of blood-spotted sheets as evidence of the bride's virginity. In some societies, where less importance is placed on virginity, a wedding may go through stages. When the Zulu king, Goodwill Zwelithini, married Princess Manitfombi of Swaziland in 1971, the couple had lived together and had children before finalizing the marriage, which took place when the king chose Manitfombi as his main wife among several. The king's gift to the bride's father of 200 cattle legalized the marriage and made the children legitimate. During the ceremony, the bride carried a long spear in her hand and turned the point to the king to show that she chose him as her husband.

ROYAL WEDDINGS AND THE NATION

Since royal weddings are important to the whole country, the celebrations usually contain elements and activities that are intended for the people, such as feasts and dances. At a traditional royal Hindu wedding in Nepal, the royal family would give food and clothing to the needy at the palace gates to ensure the blessing of the gods on the marriage.

A royal wedding can serve a model of marriage for other couples in the nation. In Japan, for example, up until the twentieth century, there had not been any religious component to imperial wedding ceremonies. But the marriage of Crown Prince Yoshishito and Princess Sadako in 1900, celebrated with a newly created Shinto rite, inspired religious and monogamous marriage among the Japanese people, previously known for their high rates of divorce and polygamy.

The ceremonial of a royal wedding provides continuity with the nation's past. But in modern non-Western societies, traditional wedding customs of the country are sometimes combined with Western traditions. At one twentieth-century wedding in the Saudi Arabian royal family, for example, the sisters of the bride wore European designer dresses, while traditional belly dancers entertained the guests.

Royal weddings, such that of Prince Charles and Princess Diana in England in 1981, can project an image of both traditional royal pomp and splendor and fairy tale romance for the world, although that particular romance ended in divorce. Nevertheless, a royal wedding always raises the hopes of many people in the country, because it is not just the wedding of two individuals: it is a national event, more visibly so than ever in the age of mass communications.

See also: BLOOD, ROYAL; CONSORTS, ROYAL; INCEST, ROYAL; MARRIAGE OF KINGS; QUEENS AND QUEEN MOTHERS.

WEI DYNASTIES (386–557 C.E.)

Chinese dynasty of the Sixteen Kingdoms period whose non-Chinese rulers were important patrons of

Buddhist art. Following the collapse of the Han dynasty in 220, China entered a 300-year period of disunity in which the north and south were divided politically. Beginning in the fourth century, the north was ruled by a series of dynasties founded by non-Chinese tribes. Known as the Sixteen Kingdoms (301–439), these dynasties were all short-lived until the emergence of the Northern Wei dynasty in 386. The Northern Wei was founded by a tribal people from southern Manchuria known as the Xianbei or Toba. Having defeated rival kingdoms in the north, the Wei rulers established their capital at the city of Datong.

Vastly outnumbered by their Chinese subjects, the northern rulers relied on Chinese advisers to help them rule. They employed China's traditional government institutions, staffing the bureaucracy with Chinese officials. Lacking a written language, the Wei rulers adopted the Chinese script. In 494 Emperor Xiao Wendi (r. 471–499) moved the capital south to Luoyang. Xiao Wendi advocated assimilation into Chinese society, encouraging intermarriage and requiring that his Xianbei subjects speak Chinese, wear Chinese clothing, and adopt Chinese names.

Aspiring to rule all of China, the Northern Wei strengthened the northern Chinese military. Their rule also saw an improvement in the crippled Chinese economy. In the late fifteenth century, the Wei rulers instituted the "equal-field" system. Designed to prevent land from accumulating in large tax-free estates, the system assigned land to peasants that reverted to the state on their death. The Wei also increased the amount of land under cultivation by resettling large numbers of peasants onto deserted farmland.

Despite the chaos of the Sixteen Kingdoms period, culture flourished. Buddhism spread rapidly and served as a uniting force and an inspiration to artists. Northern Wei rulers, most of whom were Buddhists, commissioned the carving of thousands of magnificent Buddhist sculptures at the famous caves of Yungang and Longmen. The first Chinese encyclopedia was compiled for a Wei ruler in the third century.

In 524, civil war broke out and Luoyang was sacked, but order was restored briefly in 534–535 under two new Wei dynasties, the Eastern and Western Wei. In 550 and 557 they were replaced by the Northern Qi and the Northern Chou dynasties, respectively.

See also: HAN DYNASTY; LIANG DYNASTIES; SUI DYNASTY; THREE KINGDOMS.

WELSH KINGDOMS

(ca. 500s–1200s C.E.)

Series of small kingdoms that developed in Wales following the Roman withdrawal from Britain, which maintained their independence from England until the thirteenth century.

Wales was one of the few parts of Britain not conquered by barbarian invaders after the Roman withdrawal in the fifth century, remaining a British region after the Anglo-Saxon invasion and settlement of neighboring England. The word "Welsh" is derived from the Old English word *wealh* ("foreigner"), which the people of Wales applied to the Britons.

By the sixth century, Wales was divided into a number of small kingdoms or principalities that warred with one another and with the various Anglo-Saxon kingdoms in England. Throughout this period, there was a tendency for larger kingdoms to absorb smaller ones, but these larger territories often broke up again once the influence of the strong ruler who united them had passed.

There were four major kingdoms in Wales during the early medieval period: Gwynedd, Powys, Dyfed, and Deheubarth, and a number of lesser ones, including Ceredigion, Glywysing, and Gwent. Welsh kingship tended to descend within a family group, but strict primogeniture (inheritance by the eldest son) was not adhered to, and legitimacy was not of prime importance for eligibility to the throne.

In the tenth century, Wales was largely united under Hywel Dda (r. ca. 909–949 or 950), who ruled Ceredigion, Dyfed, and Gwynedd. However, Athelstan (r. 924–939), king of Wessex and Mercia, demanded tribute from the Welsh princes. After the Norman conquest of 1066, William I of England (r. 1066–1087) and the Anglo-Norman kings who followed granted fiefs in Wales to English and Normans in an attempt to subdue the Welsh. Campaigns by England to conquer Wales continued throughout the eleventh and twelfth centuries.

In the thirteenth century, the title of "prince" was used more often than "king" for the leading men of the Welsh territories. Llywelyn ap Gruffydd (r. 1246–1282), prince of Gwynedd, who had done homage for his territory to Edward I of England (r. 1272–1307), styled himself prince of Wales, claiming lordship over most of the Welsh principalities.

Llywelyn rebelled unsuccessfully against Edward I

in 1277, but he died in battle during a second rebellion in 1281. Edward I promised the Welsh a prince of their own nation and proclaimed his son, who was born in Caernarvon Castle in Wales, as prince of Wales, a title used ever since to designate the crown prince of England and Great Britain.

Although there were further Welsh rebellions against England, most notably under Owain Glendower between 1402 and 1416, the Act of Union of 1536 established English hegemony over Wales, and the two countries have remained joined up to the present day.

See also: DEHEUBARTH KINGDOM; DYFED KINGDOM; EDWARD I; GLYWYSING KINGDOM; GWENT KINGDOM; GWYNEDD KINGDOM; LLYWELYN AP GRUFFYDD; POWYS KINGDOM.

FURTHER READING

Holmes, George. ed. *Oxford Illustrated History of Medieval Europe.* New York: Oxford University Press, 1988.

Poole, A.L. *From Domesday Book to Magna Carta: 1087–1216.* New York: Oxford University Press, 1993.

Powicke, Sir Maurice. *The Thirteenth Century: 1216–1307.* 2nd ed. New York: Oxford University Press, 1962.

Stenton, Sir Frank. *Anglo-Saxon England.* 3rd ed. New York: Oxford University Press, 2001.

Walker, David. *Medieval Wales.* New York: Cambridge University Press, 1990.

WEN TI (WENDI) (541–604 C.E.)

Chinese emperor (r. 581–604) who founded the Sui dynasty and made Confucianism the state doctrine of China.

Born Yang Chien (Yang Jian), Wen Ti (Wendi) was a member of an aristocratic family from northwestern China. He served as an official for the Northern Chou dynasty (557–581), the last in a series of short-lived dynasties that ruled northern China in the period of political disunity known as the Southern and Northern dynasties.

Wen Ti's daughter married the heir to the Chou throne, who died in 578, leaving a young son to take the throne with Wen Ti as his regent. Wen Ti soon

seized the throne, ordered all of the Chou princes killed, and proclaimed the new Sui dynasty (581–618). He justified his actions as necessary for the defense of his family's religion, Buddhism, which had been attacked by the Chou rulers. From his northern power base, Wen Ti moved his armies south, defeating the southern state of Chen in 589 to reunite China under a single rule for the first time in 300 years.

Wen Ti established the Sui capital at the city of Daxincheng (modern-day Xi'an). A skilled administrator, he centralized the government, broadened the tax system, and improved internal transport. Wen Ti adopted the political institutions of China's first empires, the Ch'in (Qin) and Han dynasties, instituting the examination system that selected scholars to serve in the bureaucracy. He implemented Confucianism as his doctrine of state, avoided extravagance at his court, and instituted the uniform application of laws in which even the nobility were held accountable for crimes.

Wen Ti held regular Buddhist ceremonies at his court and sponsored the building of thousands of Buddhist temples and statues. He also ordered the restoration of Buddhist art defaced by previous dynasties.

Wen Ti's wife refused to allow him to take other consorts, going so far as to kill another woman with whom he fell in love. After Wen Ti died in 604 C.E., he was succeeded by his son, Yang Ti (Yangdi) (r. 604–617).

See also: HAN DYNASTY; LIANG DYNASTIES; SUI DYNASTY; T'ANG DYNASTY; WEI DYNASTIES.

WENCESLAS IV (1361–1419 C.E.)

German king (r. 1378–1400) and king of Bohemia (r. 1363–1419) who was a peace-loving and gifted ruler, but whose administrative neglect and temperamental nature brought his realms to near anarchy at a time when they were facing numerous domestic challenges.

Son of Holy Roman Emperor Charles IV (r. 1346–1378), Wenceslas became king of Germany (although he remained uncrowned as Holy Roman emperor) upon his father's death in 1378. Unfortunately, he succeeded to these thrones at a time when many German princes were in conflict with the larger imperial towns over privileges and other issues. Wenceslas refused to become involved in German affairs, preferring instead to remain in Bohemia, the kingdom he ruled from 1363, when his father handed over power.

In 1380, Wenceslas ignored the request of German princes to appoint a *Reichsverweser* (imperial governor), angering these powerful nobles and leading to a long period of unrest and rebellion. After ten years of near anarchy, including a civil war (1386–1389), and after taking Hungary (1388) with the help of his half-brother, Sigismund, the German conflicts were resolved when Wenceslas sided with the princes against the imperial towns.

His late support did not impress the German princes, however, who plotted against Wenceslas and imprisoned him for a short time in Bohemia in 1394. He angered the German princes again in 1395, when he sold the hereditary fiefdom of Milan to Gian Galeazzo Visconti, placing it further from German control. In 1396, Wenceslaus once again provoked the ire of the princes by appointing Sigismund as *Reichsverweser.*

In 1397, Wenceslas became involved in the Great Schism of the Western Church, a period when there were two, sometimes three, rival popes, all with a claim to the papal throne in Rome. At first, Wenceslas supported Pope Urban VI. Then, possibly because Urban would not officially crown him Holy Roman emperor, Wenceslas allied with Charles VI of France (r. 1380–1422), who suggested that all the current popes should resign and a new one be elected.

Meanwhile, frustrated with Wenceslas's lack of interest in their continuing problems, the four German electors invited him to meet with them. When Wenceslas refused to attend the meeting, they deposed him in August 1400 and elected Rupert (Ruprecht) III (r. 1400–1410), count Palatine of the Rhine, as king of Germany (although he was never crowned as Holy Roman emperor). Wenceslas refused to recognize Rupert, instead considering himself to be the rightful German king for the rest of his life.

In 1402, Sigismund deposed his half-brother Wenceslas as king of Bohemia. Imprisoned once more, Wenceslas was ultimately able to reclaim the Bohemian throne but at the price of yielding any real power to a royal council. After regaining control of Bohemia, Wenceslas withdrew from most state activities. He did become embroiled in religious affairs, however, when he backed the supporters of Bohemian religious reformer John Huss. But he did nothing to prevent the execution of Huss as a heretic in 1415, which angered many of his Bohemian subjects.

When Wenceslas died in 1419, what was left of his power passed to Sigismund, who became king of Bohemia. Sigismund already ruled as German king (r. 1410–1437) and king of Hungary (r. 1387–1437), and in 1433 he was crowned Holy Roman emperor (r. 1433–1437), an official honor that his brother had never achieved.

See also: CHARLES IV; HOLY ROMAN EMPIRE; LUXEMBOURG DYNASTY; SIGISMUND.

WESSEX, KINGDOM OF

(400s–900s C.E.)

Anglo-Saxon kingdom in England that flourished in the early Middle Ages and eventually established dominance over nearly all of the country.

Very little reliable information is available about the kingdom of Wessex. The *Anglo-Saxon Chronicle,* an early source of Anglo-Saxon history, states that the West Saxon kingdom was founded by the Saxon warlords Cerdic and his son Cynric in 495, although recent historians believe the date was probably some forty years later.

Cerdic and Cynric arrived in southern England from the European continent and quickly conquered the Isle of Wight. They expanded from this base, setting up their new kingdom in western England, in the area that now includes the counties of Hampshire, Dorset, Wiltshire, and Somerset.

During the early years of the kingdom of Wessex, power was not always held by a single king but was often shared among family members, and power did not necessarily descend from father to son. For the first centuries of its existence, Wessex battled for dominance with the other Anglo-Saxon kingdoms, particularly Northumbria and Mercia.

The high points of the first centuries of Wessex were the reign of Ceaulin (r. 560–593), who extended the borders of Wessex to the north, and the period in the late seventh century, when Wessex dominated the other Anglo-Saxon kingdoms. King Ine (r. 688–726) was the first ruler of Wessex to set up a code of laws, but after his death, the kingdom fell into a period of anarchy.

In the eighth century, under King Egbert (r. 802–839), Wessex continued to expand, first to the west in the regions of Devon and Cornwall. By 826,

Egbert had conquered the neighboring kingdoms of Kent, Essex, and Sussex, and within three years he had become overlord of the remaining Anglo-Saxon kings. Egbert's successors, however, were faced with defending the realm against powerful outsiders.

In the mid-800s, the armies of the Danes invaded England. Although other Anglo-Saxon kingdoms fell before the Danes, Wessex successfully repelled the Danish threat. Egbert's grandson Alfred (r. 871–899), known to history as Alfred the Great, recaptured the city of London from the Danes in 886 and became ruler of all the English not under Danish control.

In the 900s, Alfred's successors, including his son Edward the Elder (r. 899–924), and grandsons Athelstan (r. 924–939) and Edmund (r. 939–946), gradually regained control over the rest of England from the Danes, including the region known as the Danelaw in eastern England. Alfred's grandson Eadred (r. 946–955) became the first king of Wessex to rule all of England. This unity was threatened and broken by Viking invaders in the eleventh century, but the House of Wessex continued to rule until 1016 with the death of Edmund II, Ironside, the last of Alfred's lineage.

See also: ALFRED THE GREAT; ANGLO-SAXON RULERS; DANISH KINGDOM; KENT, KINGDOM OF; MERCIA, KINGDOM OF; SUSSEX, KINGDOM OF.

WILDERNESS, ROYAL LINKS TO

Relationship of royalty to natural wilderness or the concept of wilderness.

Royalty can be viewed as the uppermost level of the nobility in a realm. Aside from the political functions that are fulfilled by the nobility, royalty also embodies a series of symbolic functions that help to define it as aristocracy. By extension, it is through some of these symbolic functions that royalty is set apart from being merely aristocratic. Royalty's symbolic relationship with the wilderness, as well as the political or legal functions that parallel this relationship, is an excellent example of the function that royals serve in a society.

In many societies, royalty and the aristocracy are viewed as high culture, thereby creating a standard by which the cultural value of a society and its civilization can be judged. The Bourbon dynasty of France, Queen Victoria of England, the emperors of ancient Rome, and the Egyptian pharaohs all served as benchmarks for measuring the culture of their society.

Culture and civility are the symbolic antithesis of the wilderness. The natural world of wild animals, the unrestricted activity of nature, and the inability to restrain unbridled passion and "wildness" are all embodied in the idea of wilderness. It is through the rivalry between the high culture of royalty and the unrestrained wilderness that some of the symbolic functions of royalty and monarchs have developed.

Royalty in England provides a useful illustration. One of the most common and early representations of the wilderness in England was the forest, the place where individuals were forced to confront nature. Only the English monarch had jurisdiction in the forest, and the civil laws of the people were suspended there. Within the forest, English subjects gave up their rights and became wholly subject to royal authority. Symbolically, this gave the English monarch, the highest symbol of civility and culture in society, the right to control the wilderness and impose civilization on it.

This ability to impose civilization on the wilderness was exemplified in the hunt. Until modern times, the hunt occurred in the forest, on royal lands, and individuals could participate only with the permission of the king or a royally appointed protector of the forests. The common people were excluded from taking part in all but the most cursory aspects of the hunt, such as flushing out game.

The European practice of the hunt was also embedded with symbolism, etiquette, and rules of practice, all of which served to elevate the sport to a level applicable to the aristocracy and royalty. The hunt represented a way of acting, a code of civility. Royal participation in the hunt thus reflected a series of symbolic meanings for royal actions. It represented the confrontation between the most refined aspects of society—royalty—and the most unrefined aspects of nature—the forest or wilderness. The success of the hunting party symbolized the victory of civilization over the wilderness.

This symbolic relationship can also be extended to other aspects of royal and aristocratic life. Among the most obvious is the royal garden. The garden symbolized the ability of society to bend the wilderness to its will. Another symbolic example of the royal subjugation of the wilderness was royal encouragement for extending culture and societal norms to areas of the world as yet explored. This included the exploration of the Americas and Africa by Europeans and the granting of royal monopolies to trading companies or religious groups to gain natural resources or convert aboriginals in the name of the monarch.

In the modern era, the decline in the belief that royalty epitomized the highest forms of culture has coincided with a rising dominance of popular culture and changing views about monarchy and democracy, as well as about the nature and function of the wilderness.

See also: BEHAVIOR, CONVENTIONS OF ROYAL; HUNTING AND KINGSHIP; LANDHOLDING PATTERNS; PARKS, ROYAL; RIGHTS TO ANIMALS; RIGHTS, LAND.

WILHELM II (1859–1941 C.E.)

German emperor (r. 1888–1918), whose fervent desire to lead his nation to international greatness helped produce the European tensions that culminated in World War I. In an era of increasing pressure for more democratic forms of government, Wilhelm II ruled as a near autocrat, and his passion for Germany fostered a spirit of strong nationalism and imperial privilege. However, these twin specters of nationalism and imperialism drove Europe into the bloodiest and most destructive war that the world had yet seen, and that ultimately brought about the end of the German Empire.

RISE TO POWER

Born into one of the most powerful families in Europe, the house of Hohenzollern, Wilhelm was the son of German Crown Prince Frederick (later Emperor Frederick III, r. 1888) and Princess Victoria, daughter of Queen Victoria of England. Wilhelm was also the grandson of Wilhelm I (r. 1861–1888), the first emperor of a united Germany, who had led his nation to a position of power in Europe. When Wilhelm I died in 1888, Frederick succeeded him but died of throat cancer only three months into his reign, thereby putting Wilhelm on the throne.

Unlike the popular Frederick, who was a great supporter of cultural development and liberal politics, Wilhelm was deeply authoritarian and interested first and foremost in military growth and imperial expansion. Wilhelm was a strong believer in the divine right of kings, as well as in the greatness of

the German people, beliefs that strongly influenced his politics. Neither Wilhelm's marriage in 1881 to Auguste Victoria of Augustenburg, nor the birth of his son Wilhelm in 1882, did much to calm his passion for military action on Germany's behalf. Some historians believe that Wilhelm's maimed left arm (it was withered when he was born), may have been a factor in his aggressive psychology, though this is certainly debatable.

INTERNATIONAL CONFLICT

Immediately upon his accession to the throne in 1888, Wilhelm came into conflict with Otto von Bismarck, the German chancellor who had run the empire almost single-handedly since its inception. Wilhelm's authoritarian attitude made it impossible for him to share power with Bismarck, and so the chancellor was replaced in 1890. From then on, Wil-

The last emperor of Germany and king of Prussia, Kaiser Wilhelm II (at right) ruled at a time when nationalist feelings were pushing Europe toward armed conflict. A cousin of England's King Edward VII (at left), the kaiser found himself at war with his relative in 1914. Wilhelm II was forced to abdicate after Germany lost World War I.

helm faced little significant internal opposition to his policies.

Related by blood to England's royal family, Wilhelm had a strong interest in staying on good terms with the British. However, his push for German imperial expansion and naval growth drove a wedge between the two nations, leading England to unite with France and Russia in an alliance known as the Triple Entente. The rivalries between the major European powers created a rapid and competitive scramble for imperial dominions (fueled by Germany), commonly known as the "scramble for Africa" because that continent was the focus of most colonial expansion in the 1890s and early 1900s. The enmity between the imperial powers was such that Germany and France nearly went to war several times over Morocco.

The Triple Entente was poised in opposition to the Triple Alliance, which linked Germany, Italy, and Austria-Hungary. Although the Triple Alliance was formed before Wilhelm reached the throne, he continually renewed the pact throughout his reign. The tension between these two great coalitions pushed Europe to the brink of World War I.

DECLINE AND DEFEAT

With most of his attention focused on international affairs, Wilhelm's major domestic concern was the army and navy, which he viewed as essential to German survival. Both military branches underwent great expansion and overhaul during Wilhelm's reign, ostensibly to maintain German security and peace abroad, but also with an eye toward extending the empire. Although Wilhelm promised some liberalizing social reforms, he did little to make good on his promises because his mind was focused on the international scene.

The tense situation in Europe that Wilhelm had helped create was exacerbated by the assassination in 1914 of Franz Ferdinand, heir to the throne of Austria-Hungary, by a Serbian radical. Shortly after Franz Ferdinand's death, Austria-Hungary declared war on Serbia, thus initiating the conflict that became World War I. Because of Germany's alliance with Austria-Hungary, Wilhelm supported the Austrian declaration against Serbia and quickly followed it with declarations of war against Russia and France, which he feared were mobilizing to attack him. Counting on Britain to remain neutral, Wilhelm found himself facing powerful enemies on all fronts when the British government declared war on Germany, citing the German offensive as pretext.

Although nominally at the helm of German forces during the war, Wilhelm exerted very little real military control. By the last years of the war, Germany was run by a council of military and business leaders who held considerable power. After Germany's surrender at the end of World War I, popular pressure forced Wilhelm to abdicate the throne in 1918, and he lived the rest of his life in exile in Holland. With Wilhelm's abdication, the German Empire had come to an end. The desperate economic condition of the country after the war, however, set the stage for the rise of Adolf Hitler and an even more destructive conflict.

See also: AUSTRO-HUNGARIAN EMPIRE; COLONIALISM AND KINGSHIP; HOHENZOLLERN DYNASTY; IMPERIAL RULE; MILITARY POWER, ROYAL; NATIONALISM.

WILHELMINA (1880–1962 C.E.)

Queen of the Netherlands during World Wars I and II, who was beloved by her subjects for her courage and her common sense.

Wilhelmina Helene Pauline Maria Orange-Nassau Waldeck-Pyrmont was born on August 31, 1880, in The Hague, the capital of the Netherlands. She was the only child of then king Willem III (William III) and his second wife, Emma of Walderk Pyrmont. At the time of Wilhelmina's birth, the institution of the monarchy was still somewhat new in the Netherlands. The nation had been a republic until only sixty-five years earlier, when the monarchy was established. Willem III was not a particularly effective ruler and earned little general support for the office of the king. During her fifty-year reign, however, Wilhelmina gained the trust and loyalty of her people to a degree that could not have been anticipated.

King Willem died in 1890, when Wilhelmina was only ten years old. Since there were no suitable male relatives, Wilhelmina was the only legitimate claimant to the throne. As she was still very young, however, her mother was made regent, handling the day-to-day details of administering the country while the young queen was educated in her royal responsibilities. On her eighteenth birthday, Wilhelmina formally assumed her place as ruler of the Netherlands, and her coronation was held in The Hague on September 6, 1898.

Wilhelmina proved to be a practical, level-headed

queen. She understood her role as ruler in a limited monarchy, and was respectful of the authority that properly belonged to the parliament. She saw her role as providing direction and support to her people, and during the early years of her rule she committed herself to initiating policies aimed at developing and improving the nation's economy and institutions.

As with all rulers, Wilhelmina knew that she must provide an heir to the throne, and in 1901, she wed a member of the German nobility, Duke Henry of Mecklenburg-Schwerin. The couple had just one child, a daughter named Juliana, who was born in 1909. Duke Henry never played a role in the Dutch government, and after he died in 1934, the queen never remarried.

Wilhelmina's first real test as leader came with the outbreak of World War I. It is largely through the queen's efforts that the Netherlands succeeded in maintaining neutrality during that conflict, thus sparing the Dutch people much of the destruction experienced by neighboring countries. When the war was ended, Wilhelmina instituted social and economic reforms that strengthened her country's standing among the nations of Europe, earning the respect of her government and the loyalty of her subjects.

Wilhelmina's greatest test, however, came with the onset of World War II. Although she hoped to keep the Netherlands neutral, that proved to be impossible. When Hitler's troops invaded the Netherlands in May 1940, the queen was forced to flee to England to avoid capture. There she established a government in exile.

Though Wilhelmina was safe in England, her mind and heart remained in the Netherlands with her subjects. Throughout the war, she broadcast radio speeches urging courage and denouncing the Nazi occupying forces. Her broadcasts played no small part in strengthening the resolve of the Dutch, and inspired her people to acts of resistance, both small and large, that frustrated their would-be conquerors.

When Allied forces liberated the Netherlands from the Nazis, Wilhelmina made ready to return home. In May 1945, cheering crowds welcomed the queen back to the royal palace in The Hague. Wilhelmina immediately turned her attention to developing a program for restoring the nation's economy and infrastructure, which had been severely damaged during the years of Nazi occupation.

By this time, however, Wilhelmina was in her sixties and suffering from ill health. Recognizing that her country needed a strong ruler to oversee the postwar reconstruction, she abdicated her throne in favor of her daughter, Juliana, in 1948. Wilhelmina then retired to her summer palace, Het Loo, in the city of Apeldoorn, and began writing her memoirs: *Lonely but Not Alone,* which were first published in The Hague in 1959 and translated into English in 1960. She died at Het Loo in 1962.

See also: ORANGE-NASSAU, HOUSE OF.

FURTHER READING

Wilhelmina, Queen of the Netherlands. *Lonely but Not Alone.* Trans. John Peereboom. New York: McGraw-Hill, 1960.

WILLIAM (1650–1702 C.E) AND MARY (1662–1695 C.E.)

King (r. 1689–1702) and queen (r. 1689–1695) of England who ruled jointly after taking the throne in the "Glorious Revolution" of 1688. The accession of William and Mary ended a period of great religious and political controversy in England, and their reign, which took place under a newly ratified Bill of Rights, marked the beginning of modern parliamentary government in Great Britain.

RISE TO POWER

William (who would take the throne as William III) was born in 1650 in the Netherlands to William II, prince of Orange (r. 1647–1650), and Mary, the oldest daughter of King Charles I (r. 1625–1649) of England. As a young man, William distinguished himself in battle and was named the *stadholder,* or chief magistrate, of the Netherlands in 1672, a position his father had held before his death. In 1677 William wed Mary of York.

A member of England's powerful Stuart dynasty, Mary was the oldest daughter of James II (r. 1685–1688) of England and Anne Hyde, his first of two wives. Along with her younger sister Anne (who would later become Queen Anne of England, r. 1702–1714), Mary was raised as a Protestant, even though her father had strong Catholic leanings. Her marriage to William, who was also Protestant, was designed to create a political alliance to defend against Catholic influence in England.

When Mary's father came to the English throne as James II in 1685, controversy engulfed the British populace. Most of the English people, and nearly all of the wealthy and powerful ones, were Protestant and were outraged at the notion of a Catholic king on the throne. Matters came to a head in 1688 when James's staunchly Catholic second wife, Mary of Modena, had a son, thereby securing a Catholic heir to the Crown.

British Parliamentarians, feeling they had no other alternative, asked William of Orange to invade England and claim the throne. In the autumn of 1688, William and a sizable army landed in England and advanced to London without meeting any serious resistance. After taking the city, William ordered safe passage for James out of England. He then accepted the Crown from Parliament in the spring of 1689 and was declared joint-sovereign with his wife Mary. The throne, however, came with a price—Parliament took the opportunity to redefine the relationship between the monarch and the state in a newly drafted Bill of Rights (1689). Along with declaring that James had abdicated and that a Catholic could not occupy the throne, the Bill of Rights shifted the balance of power from the king to Parliament, and declared specific civil rights inalienable, thus marking the first step toward a more democratic form of government. The power of Parliament got another boost in 1701, when William agreed to the Act of Settlement, a measure that forbade English monarchs from leaving the country, using English armies to defend foreign territory, or granting royal pardons without the consent of Parliament.

ON THE THRONE

William and Mary were not particularly well liked in England, although history has judged them somewhat better. William, an immensely skilled diplomat in international affairs, was never able to replicate his success on the domestic front. Seen as coldhearted and even cruel, he was unable to win the trust of the English people, even though he did much to advance both freedom of worship and the press. Mary's unpopularity was in part a corollary of William's and was also owing to the fact that the couple never had children, thus leaving no heir to the throne.

As the arch-enemy of Louis XIV of France (r. 1643–1715), William was deeply involved in foreign affairs, frequently leaving England to confer with other heads of state or to lead his troops into battle against them. Although his side did not fare well militarily in the War of the Grand Alliance (1688–1697), known in America as King William's War, William was able to preserve his coalition with Austria and the Netherlands long enough to keep France in check.

Just before his untimely death in 1702, as England was poised for yet another war with France, William unsuccessfully attempted to push through a peace plan that he believed would provide long-term European security. Many aspects of this plan were later adopted in the treaty known as the Peace of Utrecht (1713), which laid much of the modern foundation of Europe.

Both William and Mary died relatively young, Mary succumbing to smallpox in 1695 and William passing away after a fall from a horse in 1702. Mary's sister Anne, with whom the couple had had a controversial disagreement over money, estates, and the influence of Anne's friends that set the siblings at odds in 1692, took the throne. Anne, also childless, was to be the last monarch of the house of Stuart.

See also: ABDICATION, ROYAL; ANNE; JAMES II; ORANGE-NASSAU, HOUSE OF; QUEENS AND QUEEN MOTHERS; RIGHTS, CIVIL; STUART DYNASTY; SUCCESSION, ROYAL.

FURTHER READING

Hoak, Dale, and Mordechai Feingold, eds. *The World of William and Mary: Anglo-Dutch Perspectives on the Revolution, 1688–89*. Stanford, CA: Stanford University Press, 1996.

Van der Zee, Barbara, and Henri A. Van der Zee. *William and Mary*. New York: Knopf, 1973.

WILLIAM I (1772–1843 C.E.)

First king of the Netherlands (r. 1813–1840), whose refusal to yield to the liberal ideals of his people ultimately cost him the throne. Although his early actions helped modernize the agricultural and industrial sectors of the Dutch economy, William I is remembered primarily for the internal turmoil that gripped the Netherlands under his rule and that eventually led to his abdication.

Born into the powerful House of Orange-Nassau in 1772, William was the son of William V (r. 1751–1795), who was *stadholder* (chief magistrate) of the United Netherlands provinces, and Sophia Wilhelmina, a princess of Prussia. In order to further strengthen the House of Orange-Nassau, William married Frederica Wilhelmina, a cousin of his mother's who was also a Prussian princess.

As the defeat of France in the Napoleonic Wars became increasingly apparent, the major European powers in 1815 convened an international conference, known as the Congress of Vienna, whose purpose was the redesign of Europe for peacetime settlement. The Congress awarded William, who had distinguished himself in battle during both the French Revolutionary and Napoleonic Wars, the kingdom of the Netherlands, which included Belgium and the grand duchy of Luxembourg. He took the throne in 1815 to much popular approval.

Difficulties arose quickly, however, as William was unable to balance the needs of his native Dutch people with those of his Belgian subjects. William's sympathy with the Dutch alienated the Belgians, and this situation was worsened when the king declared Dutch to be the official national language of the kingdom. William's attempts to limit the freedom of the Belgian press proved the breaking point for the Belgians, leading to a revolution in 1830. Caught completely off-guard by this revolt, the Dutch were driven out of Belgium forever.

William's troubles continued throughout the 1830s as the Dutch people lobbied for more democratic political institutions and less monarchical authority. With public pressure for liberalization mounting, the king abdicated the throne in 1840. William spent his remaining years on a family estate in Silesia, a Prussian province, with the Crown of the Netherlands passing to his son, King William II (r. 1840–1849).

See also: ABDICATION, ROYAL; BELGIAN KINGDOM; NETHERLANDS KINGDOM; ORANGE-NASSAU, HOUSE OF.

WILLIAM I, THE CONQUEROR

(1028–1087 C.E.)

Duke of Normandy and first Norman king of England (r. 1066–1087), who was variously known as William the Bastard, William the Conqueror, and William the Great. With the aid of an army of 7,000 Normans, William conducted the last successful invasion of England in 1066.

EARLY LIFE AND CLAIM TO ENGLAND

William was born in 1028 to Duke Robert of Normandy (r. 1027–1035) and to Arlette, a tanner's daughter. Before Duke Robert died in 1035 he designated William as his heir, despite the fact that it was highly unusual for a nobleman to acknowledge an illegitimate child as heir.

At the age of fifteen, William was knighted by King Henry I of France (r. 1031–1060), and he accepted the king as his overlord. By 1047, the young Duke William was fighting skirmishes and battles against this same king in order to maintain the integrity of Normandy's borders. After ten years of such engagements, William had become a hardened and experienced warrior, ready to grasp whatever challenge fate presented him.

Meanwhile, William's distant cousin, King Edward the Confessor of England (r. 1042–1066), had spent many years in Normandy with his mother, Emma of Normandy. In gratitude for the protection he received there, Edward promised in 1051 to make William heir to the English throne. William remembered this promise, but Edward, upon returning to England, changed his mind and declared Harold Godwinson his successor. In any case, the original promise had no real authority unless confirmed by the Anglo-Saxon ruling body, the Witan, who supported Harold.

Encouraged by Harold Godwinson's alienated brother, Tostig, William prepared a large invading force to accompany him to England to claim the English throne. Meanwhile, Tostig persuaded the Norwegian king, Harald III Hardrada (r. 1045–1066), to invade England simultaneously in the north.

INVASION AND CONQUEST OF ENGLAND

William's Norman fleet landed in England at Pevensey, near Hastings, on September 28, 1066, with 4,000 infantry and 3,000 cavalry. He immediately built a camp and began burning and pillaging the surrounding countryside.

Three days earlier, and hundreds of miles to the north, Harold Godwinson—now Harold II of England (r. 1066)—had won the battle of Stamford Bridge against his brother Tostig and Harald Hardrada. Soon afterward, Harold learned of

The conquest of England in 1066 by William the Conqueror of Normandy changed the course of English history and Western civilization. The Bayeux Tapestry, embroidered in France in the eleventh century, recounts the events leading up to and including the Battle of Hastings on October 14, 1066. This detail from the 230-foot-long tapestry shows William the Conqueror directing his troops.

William's landing and, despite all advice against it, force-marched the remnants of his exhausted forces to the south, hoping to surprise William and prevent further destruction of the English countryside.

Harold arrived at Senlac Hill (near Hastings) on October 14, 1066, and faced William and his Norman troops in battle. The battle of Hastings was long and hard-fought. William had three horses killed from under him during the day. The English infantry, with their double-handed axes, were among the toughest foot soldiers of their day. Moreover, Harold had positioned his men at the top of a hill, forcing the Normans to charge upwards, thus reducing much of the advantage that mounted Norman troops might have. However, the Normans had a weapon that the English lacked: the crossbow.

In the end, Harold was shot in the eye with an arrow from a Norman archer's bow. As he fell from his horse, he was cut down by surrounding Normans soldiers. The English broke when they saw Harold's fall, and William's forces won the day, making William's invasion a success.

CONSOLIDATION AND RULE

William I was crowned king of England in the cathedral at Westminster Abbey on Christmas Day, 1066. Even before his coronation, however, William had begun the work of consolidating his new kingdom.

Aptly named "The Conqueror" by posterity, William ruled England as a conquered land. He used its resources as political assets, taking the best properties from their former Saxon owners and giving them to his most trusted Norman aides and favorites. He siphoned off the wealth he collected as taxes to pay for the wars he continued to conduct in England, France, Ireland, and Wales.

William's influence changed the very character of the land he ruled. Throughout England, large tracts

WILLIAM'S LANDING

Although William the Conqueror enjoyed auspicious weather when he crossed the English Channel with his invasion force, an unfortunate mishap occurred when he first stepped from his boat to the shore. He fell face down on the beach. As he fell, a hush went through the entire invading force. These were strong men, ruthless men, but they were also powerfully superstitious, and their leader's mishap seemed a bad omen. William, who had caught himself on his two hands, rose from the ground with his arms raised and cried out, "I thus with both hands lay my grasp on this sod." His men cheered their leader, sure of his quick wits, if not his honesty.

of land were set aside as Crown lands. In one large parcel designated the New Forest, he destroyed all churches, villages, and farms in order to accommodate a private game preserve where only royal hunting parties were allowed (trespassers and poachers were blinded if caught). William responded to rebellions in the north with depredations so great that English agriculture and commerce in that region did not fully recover for many centuries.

William I placed many Normans into positions of power throughout England, but his policy was not limited to the secular world. In 1070, he brought Lanfranc, the bishop of Caen, to England and installed him as the new archbishop of Canterbury. Before long, most of the higher offices in the English church were occupied by Norman clergy.

William separated the ecclesiastical courts from the secular courts, and he employed the secular branch as enforcers of ecclesiastical decrees. Yet, he declared that no papal edict should be decreed nor any papal official enter England without his personal approval. He also declared that the decisions of the national assembly of the bishops of England, which had been a significant part of the Anglo-Saxon Witan, would have no validity unless approved personally by him.

Under William the Conqueror, England was, perhaps, safer for the casual traveler than it had been before the Norman invasion. However, this greater safety came with a price. All the Anglo-Saxon inhabitants of England now dwelt in terror of the vicious exactions and penalties that came with the new Norman laws.

One of the great cultural accomplishments of William's reign, the Domesday Book of 1085, a general census of England, was created for the purpose of facilitating efficient and complete taxation and seizure of property. This census was completed with a thoroughness and speed unsurpassed in medieval history.

DEATH AND LEGACY

Even after the invasion, William spent much of his time in his homeland of Normandy. It was during one of these stays, in 1087, that the French king, Philip I (r. 1060–1108), made a disparaging jest regarding William's substantial girth. In response, William ordered the city of Nantes and its environs burned down. While William was surveying the devastation he had ordered, his horse stumbled, and William suffered grave injuries when he was thrown against the iron pommel of his saddle. He was taken to a nearby abbey at Caen, where he made his confession and then died.

Besides the establishment of autocracy and despotism, William's legacy—the Norman legacy to England—included improved trade with the European mainland, a robust feudalism, and the French language, which blended with Anglo-Saxon to lay the foundations for modern English. Moreover, William's opportunistic adventuring had forever changed the map of Western civilization.

See also: ANGLO-SAXON RULERS; CONQUEST AND KINGSHIPS; EDWARD THE CONFESSOR; ENGLISH

MONARCHIES; HARALD III HARDRAADE; HAROLD II GODWINSON; MILITARY ROLES, ROYAL; NORMAN KINGDOMS.

FURTHER READING

Durant, Will. *The Age of Faith.* New York: Simon & Schuster, 1950.

Douglas, David C. *William the Conqueror: The Norman Impact upon England.* New Haven, CT: Yale University Press, 1999.

WILLIAM II (WILLIAM RUFUS)

(1056–1100 C.E.)

Second Norman king of England (r. 1087–1100), known as Rufus for his reddish complexion, who sought to extend Norman power in France and antagonized the church in England through his policies.

William Rufus was the second surviving son of William, duke of Normandy, and Matilda of Flanders. In 1066, while William Rufus was still a child, his father invaded Anglo-Saxon England and defeated the last Anglo-Saxon ruler, Harold II Godwinson (r. 1066). Duke William took the English throne as king William I (r. 1066–1087), becoming the first Norman ruler of England.

When William the Conqueror died in 1087, he bequeathed the title and lands of his native Normandy in France to his oldest son, Robert. William Rufus, his second and favorite son, received what turned out to be the more valuable bequest, the Crown of England.

The reign of William II was plagued by violence. The other Norman barons tried to oust William in favor of his brother in order to keep England and Normandy under a single ruler. William faced rebellions in 1088 and 1095, each of which was led by Odo of Bayeaux, the earl of Kent, a half-brother of William the Conqueror.

William II attempted to extend his power by leading military campaigns into Wales and Scotland. In 1091, he succeeded in dominating King Malcolm III of Scotland (r. 1058–1093), whom his soldiers killed two years later, in 1093. In 1097, William launched an unsuccessful invasion into Wales. His major military efforts, however, focused on attempting to reclaim Normandy from his brother Robert, a battle that was waged from 1089 to 1096. He also at-

tempted to gain additional territory in France, leading campaigns into the regions of Maine and Vexin. Eventually, Robert left Normandy in the hands of William while he went to the Holy Land on Crusade in 1096.

William ruled England with a firm hand, gaining the antipathy of many of the old Anglo-Saxon barons. He also aroused the anger of the Church by selling Church appointments and taking revenues from abbeys and other Church lands. William's reign ended abruptly in 1100, when he was shot in the back with an arrow while hunting. There is some evidence to suggest that the death was not an accident, but rather a political assassination. The Crown passed to William's younger brother, Henry I (r. 1100–1135), the third surviving son of William the Conqueror.

See also: ANGLO-SAXON RULERS; NORMAN KINGDOMS; WILLIAM I, THE CONQUEROR.

WILLIAM III. *See* WILLIAM AND MARY

WINDSOR, HOUSE OF

(1917 C.E.–Present)

Reigning royal house of Great Britain, which was given the name of Windsor by King George V (r. 1910–1936). The house of Windsor is actually made up of the descendants of Queen Victoria (r. 1837–1901) of the house of Hanover and her husband, Albert of Saxe-Coburg-Gotha. Although perhaps the most visible of any ruling house in British history because of modern communications, the house of Windsor is also the least powerful, having seen the monarchy transformed from a center of political power to a symbolic institution that serves to unite the British people.

ORIGINS

King George V came to the throne in 1910 during a time of widespread nationalist movements throughout Europe, when the very notion of royal power was being called into question. As nationalist pressures and the imperialist conflicts with which they were entwined drove Europe into World War I, Britain found itself facing a powerful enemy in Germany. The British populace developed a hatred of all

England's royal House of Windsor originated with King George V, who changed the dynastic name from the German "Wettin" during World War I. The king (bearded) poses here with his wife, Queen Mary (seated), and his children—the future King Edward VIII, the future King George VI, son Henry, and daughter Mary.

things German, and George V and the royal family came under attack for their German origins. George's grandmother, the venerated Queen Victoria of the German House of Hanover, had married a German prince, Albert of Saxe-Coburg-Gotha. Therefore, the British royal family was, in fact, almost entirely German. Taking the very English-sounding name Windsor from the English royal palace, George issued a declaration in 1917 renaming the descendants of Victoria, and the house of Windsor was born.

DISSOLVING POWER AND CRISIS
Immediately after World War I, the British Empire, still the largest in the world, began to submit to demands for autonomy from its colonies and other territorial possessions. The sheer cost of maintaining the empire became prohibitive as well, and the period from 1920 to 1965 saw the effective dismantling of the British Empire. Simultaneously, the power balance of the constitutional monarchy shifted, and the elected members of the British Parliament became the sole voice in government affairs. The royal family came to be seen in a purely ceremonial light, embodying the British national character but having little say in British politics.

The house of Windsor experienced a major crisis with the death of George V in 1936. George's eldest son and successor, Edward VIII (r. 1936), was deeply in love with an American woman named Wallis Simpson. Mrs. Simpson, to the dismay of many English, not only had no royal blood but also had two ex-husbands. Opposing divorce on any grounds, the Church of England forced Edward into a difficult decision: royal duty or love. Edward, in one of the most famous actions in history, abdicated the throne and

Windsor, House Of

GEORGE V	1910–1936
EDWARD VIII	1936
GEORGE VI	1936–1952
ELIZABETH II*	1952–

*Indicates a separate alphabetical entry.

married Wallis Simpson, giving the Crown to his younger brother, who thus became George VI (r. 1936–1952).

George VI, having neither expected nor desired the throne, was wholly unprepared to rule, and he received a great deal of public criticism early in his reign. A very shy and private man, George did not initially fare well as a public representative of British national identity. With Europe again at war in 1939, the British people needed a strong national leader, and they began to turn from George to Winston Churchill, the prime minister. George, however, quickly proved himself up to the challenge, and his popularity soared when he decided to remain in London during its darkest days, visiting both troops and civilians and promising to defend Buckingham Palace.

CONTEMPORARY STABILITY

George's death in 1952 brought a new era of publicity to the royal family, as his eldest daughter, Queen Elizabeth II (r. 1952–present), took the throne in a ceremony broadcast around the world on television and radio. With her husband Philip of Mountbatten, duke of Edinburgh, Elizabeth had four children, including Charles, prince of Wales, the heir to the throne.

Elizabeth continued the role of British representative established by her father and grandfather, traveling widely around the British Commonwealth and meeting numerous world leaders. She also brought the royal family into charity work, and her efforts to raise money for a variety of causes have been praised extensively. Elizabeth celebrated her Golden Jubilee in 2002, commemorating fifty years on the throne.

The marriage of Elizabeth's son Charles to Diana Spencer in 1981 was one of the most widely viewed events in the history of television, and the marriage was a constant source of interest in the popular press. Their marital difficulties in the 1990s, culminating with a divorce in 1996, were also widely followed. Though the pair's infidelities and lavish lifestyle generated much discussion about the necessity of maintaining the monarchy, Diana's death in an automobile accident in 1997 united the public, both in Britain and around the world, in support and grief. The couple had two sons, Prince Henry and Prince William; William, as first born, is the heir to the throne.

See also: ABDICATION, ROYAL; ELIZABETH II; HANOVER, HOUSE OF; NATIONAL IDENTITY; POWER, FORMS OF ROYAL; QUEENS AND QUEEN MOTHERS; SAXE-COBURG-GOTHA DYNASTY; VICTORIA.

FURTHER READING

Douglas-Home, Charles. *Dignified & Efficient: The British Monarchy in the Twentieth Century.* Brinkworth, Wilts, UK: Claridge Press, 2000.

WITCHCRAFT AND SORCERY

Supernatural activities that have sometimes been thought to affect monarchs and that rulers have worked to eliminate from their realms.

Even the most powerful of monarchs could be considered vulnerable to witchcraft and sorcery. Witchcraft against a monarch had a particularly public aspect, pitting the witch against the community as a whole rather than against a particular individual or family. For example, many traditional African societies distinguish between private witchcraft and witchcraft against a king. In private witchcraft in these societies, it is proper to seek reconciliation between the witch and victim, possibly with the payment of a fine. In witchcraft against the king, however, the prescribed societal response is punishment rather than reconciliation, and the appropriate punishment is death at the king's pleasure.

WITCHCRAFT AT COURT

In the past, kings have used accusations of witchcraft against their enemies, and factions of courtiers have brought such charges against their rivals. Women, less able to use violence or official position to advance their interests, were particularly vulnerable to accusations of sorcery, and sometimes these accusations could reach high up the social scale. For example, the dowager queen of England, Joan of Navarre, was accused of using sorcery to attempt the murder of her stepson, King Henry V (r. 1413–1422), and was imprisoned from 1419 to 1422.

A group of people more likely to be accused of sorcery were those who had come from obscure backgrounds to enjoy the monarch's favor. The rise of the hitherto obscure favorite was often attributed to witchcraft. Guichard of Troyes, a French bishop who had risen from an obscure background, was accused in 1308 of having committed a number of murders by magic, and of preparing a special poison out of adders, scorpions, toads, and spiders for the royal princes. Charges were eventually dropped.

The monarch's sexual or reproductive functioning was commonly involved in accusations of hostile witchcraft. One of the most famous cases was the Affair of the Poisons, which occurred in France under King Louis XIV (r. 1643–1715). The king's mistress, Madame de Montespan, was accused of using magic to keep the king's love and to render the queen sterile. As often happened, the persons actually executed in this case were lower-class magical specialists, while Madame de Montespan was sent to a convent.

It was far rarer for a reigning monarch himself or herself to be accused of witchcraft. One exception was Henri III of France (r. 1574–1589), a very unpopular ruler, who was accused of being a witch and of performing secret magical rituals.

KINGS AGAINST WITCHES

Monarchs who felt threatened by rivals or other opponents could launch witch-hunts extending far beyond the boundaries of the court. James VI of Scotland (r. 1567–1625), for example, encouraged the persecution of a number of witches in North Berwick from 1590 to 1592, advising the legal authorities on tactics of torture and interrogation. James even wrote a book on witchcraft, *Daemonologie* (1597), endorsing the idea that witches were deadly enemies of Christendom. In 1768, the Chinese emperor Ch'ien Lung (Qianlong) (r. 1735–1799) launched a massive, nationwide persecution of wandering monks, vagrants, and other alleged "sorcerers" following reports that some had attempted to conjure up spirit armies that would threaten the regime.

Kings also were perceived as having particular powers against witches and sorcerers. A common

theme of late sixteenth- and early seventeenth-century European masques (court theatrical performances) was how only the monarch could dispel evil enchantments. A common belief among modern Europeans was that magistrates performing their duties were immune from attacks by witches. This "magisterial immunity" was thought to be a result of state officials sharing in the monarch's own divine favor.

KINGS AGAINST WITCH-HUNTERS

The ruler would sometimes claim a particular ability to discern false accusations of witchcraft. After James VI of Scotland ascended the English throne as James I in 1603, he moderated his position on witchcraft, intervening on several occasions to demonstrate the innocence of particular accused persons. He was much less likely to invervene, however, and was more supportive of accusations of witchcraft if the witch was accused of acting against the king.

Shaka Zulu (r. 1816–1828) of the Zulu kingdom once set a trap for professional witch-finders. Shaka secretly smeared blood on his own dwelling, considered by the Zulus to be a hostile magical act, and he then encouraged witch-finders to accuse others of the deed. After revealing the true source of the blood, he massacred the witch-finders.

When monarchs claimed miraculous powers, their supporters were careful to distinguish these powers from those of evil witches. Otherwise, royal opponents might equate the abilities of the monarch with those of witches. Indeed, such was the case in the sixteenth century when the Jesuit demonologist Martin del Rio suggested that when the Protestant Queen of England Elizabeth I (r. 1558–1603) claimed to heal victims of scrofula (a glandular swelling) with her royal touch, she might be a witch using powers derived from Satan.

See also: HEALING POWERS OF KINGS; REGICIDE.

WU TSE-T'IEN (WU ZETIAN) (WU ZHAO) (625–705 C.E.)

Chinese ruler (r. 690–705) of the T'ang dynasty, also known as Wu Hou, who was the only ruling female emperor in Chinese history.

Named Wu Zhao at birth, Wu Tse-t'ien (Wu Zetian) was the daughter of a wealthy family. As a young woman, she was noticed for her beauty and became a concubine of Emperor T'ai Tsung (Taizong) (r. 626–649). Well-read and ambitious, Wu Tse-t'ien later became consort to his son, Emperor Kao Tsung (Gaozong) (r. 649–683) and quickly established great influence over him. She convinced Kao Tsung to remove his current empress, Empress Wang, and make her his new empress.

Beautiful and intelligent, Wu Tse-t'ien was also notoriously ruthless. Once installed as empress, she had the former empress killed and ordered all of her rivals at court executed or exiled, replacing them with her own supporters. Her secret service terrorized the officials and the aristocracy in brutal purges, sniffing out and executing anyone believed to be disloyal.

The strong-willed Wu Tse-t'ien dominated the sickly emperor and eventually became the virtual ruler of China. As empress, she participated in the imperial rites traditionally performed solely by the emperor. In 660 b.c.e., her power increased further when a stroke paralyzed Kao Tsung, leaving Wu Tse-t'ien in total control of the empire.

To maintain power after her husband's death in 683, Wu Tse-t'ien ordered the poisoning of Kao Tsung's son and chosen successor, Li Hung (Li Hong). She then arranged for her own son, Li Che (Li Zhe), to be named heir to the throne. Li Che ascended to the throne as Chung Tsung (Zhongzong) (r. 684, 705–710), but his initial reign lasted a mere six weeks. Angered by the power exerted by Chung Tsung's wife, Empress Wei, Wu Tse-t'ien removed him from the throne and placed him under house arrest. She replaced him with a younger son, Jui Tsung (Ruizong) (r. 684–690, 710–712) but maintained an iron grip on the reigns of power. In 690, Jui Tsung abdicated in Wu Tze'tien's favor, and she proclaimed herself emperor of a new Chou (Zhou) dynasty. This was the first and only time in Chinese history that a woman took the title of emperor.

A gifted ruler, Wu Tze-t'ien surrounded herself with talented administrators chosen from among China's scholar class rather than the local aristocracy. During Kao Tsung's reign, she expanded China's power in Central Asia and defeated Korea. Wu Tze-t'ien was also a skilled propagandist. To win popular support for her rule, she had her supporters circulate a document purported to be an ancient Buddhist text. The document predicted the reincarnation of a female deity, the *Buddha Maitreya,* as a benevolent leader who would come to power in China and rid

the world of suffering. To promote the image of herself as a deity, Wu Tze-t'ien ordered the building of temples throughout the empire in honor of the Buddha Maitreya ("Buddha of the future"). A giant statue of the Buddha Maitreya was carved at the famous caves at Longmen, and its features are said to resemble those of Wu Tze-t'ien.

For decades, first as empress and then as emperor, Wu Tze-t'ien eluded numerous attempts by T'ang princes to dethrone her. She did not falter until old age, when she began to lose public support and her grip on power slipped. In 705, shortly before her death, court officials forced Wu Tze-t'en to abdicate in favor of her son, Chung Tsung, who finally emerged from seclusion to retake the throne.

See also: T'ai Tsung (Taizong); T'ang Dynasty.

XERXES (ca. 518–465 b.c.e.)

Ruler of Persia (r. 485–465 b.c.e.) at the height of its expansion, who was characterized by historians of his day as cruel, vain, and cowardly.

Xerxes is mentioned in the works of both the ancient Greek historian Herodotus and the Greek philosopher Plato. In the Bible he is called Ahasuerus. Born in approximately 518 b.c.e., Xerxes was the son of Darius I (r. 521–486 b.c.e.), then the reigning king of Persia. His mother, Atossa, was of equally royal lineage; she was the daughter of Cyrus the Great (r. 559–530 b.c.e.), the first king of Persia's Achaemenid dynasty.

During his lifetime, Darius was committed to conquering Greece, sending expedition after expedition to invade the powerful city-states of this region. In 485 b.c.e., while preparing to launch the third of these invasions, Darius died. Xerxes duly assumed his father's throne. His first actions were dictated by the unrest in his newly inherited empire. At the time

Persia controlled a vast territory, extending into the Asian steppes and Asia Minor, and including the tributary states of Egypt and Babylon. Rebellions arose in both Egypt and Babylon during the early years of Xerxes's reign. He invaded Egypt in 484 B.C.E. to put down the rebels there, and in 482 B.C.E. he sent forces to reconquer Babylon.

Xerxes also resolved to fulfill his father's dream of conquering Greece, and by 480 B.C.E. he had amassed a huge army for the task. Hoping to surprise his enemies by attacking from an unexpected quarter, he commissioned a massive fleet and then had the ships lashed together to form a bridge that spanned the Hellespont (the narrow strait that separates Asia Minor from the Greek region of Thrace). His bridge of boats was so long, and his army so great, that it took a week for all his soldiers to march into Greek territory. Xerxes himself rode at the head of his army, marching directly toward Athens.

Along the way, Xerxes was forced to bring his troops through mountainous terrain. In a narrow pass called Thermopylae, his army confronted a band of defenders from the Greek city-state of Sparta, which had allied itself with Athens. Xerxes's force had far superior numbers, and he was ultimately victorious in this battle, but the fierce spirit the Spartans exhibited during this battle earned this event a prominent place in history.

Once through the pass at Thermopylae, Xerxes continued his inexorable march on Athens. At the sight of his army, perhaps 300,000 strong, the population of the great city fled, and Xerxes's soldiers looted the wealthy center of Greek culture. Xerxes may have believed that he had finally achieved his father's great dream, but the Greeks had other ideas. With the support of allies throughout the region they took the battle to the sea, where the advantage was to the Greek navy. Xerxes's fleet was destroyed at the battle of Salamis in 480 B.C.E. The following year, the ground troops suffered defeat at the battle of Plataca in central Greece, and Xerxes was ultimately forced to withdraw back into Asia Minor.

Back home, Xerxes found that his empire was crumbling into squabbling factions and that his obsession with conquering Greece had earned him little loyalty and few friends. His personal bodyguard eventually turned against him, and one of their number assassinated him in 465 B.C.E. Xerxes's reign marked the beginning of Persia's decline, and his successors could only watch as other powers in the region came to claim the territories that once belonged to Persia.

See also: Cʏʀᴜs ᴛʜᴇ Gʀᴇᴀᴛ; Dᴀʀɪᴜs I, ᴛʜᴇ Gʀᴇᴀᴛ; Pᴇʀsɪᴀɴ Eᴍᴘɪʀᴇ.

Xɪᴀ (Hsɪᴀ) Dʏɴᴀsᴛʏ

(ca. 2200–1750 B.C.E.)

Traditionally recognized as the first of the ancient dynasties of China, though its existence has been the subject of much debate.

According to legends, beginning around 2500 B.C.E., China was ruled first by the Three Sovereigns and then by the Five Emperors. During the reign of the fifth emperor, Shun, floods devastated the land. Shun asked the engineer Yu to find a way to drain the waters. Yu labored for years, dredging channels that became the rivers leading to the sea in North China and proving his commitment and diligence. As a reward for Yu's efforts, Shun appointed him successor to the throne, and Yu's accession around 2204 B.C.E. marked the establishment of the Xia (Hsia) dynasty.

Although chroniclers of later periods, such as Sima Qian, court historian in the second century B.C.E., provide accounts of the Xia dynasty, the lack of written documentation from the period casts doubt on its existence. Certainly between 3000 and 2000 B.C.E. a complex Bronze Age civilization, the Shang, emerged from the neolithic cultures found in China previously. A stable centralized government, writing, domestication of horses, metal-working, and class distinctions characterized this emerging culture.

Archaeological excavations since the latter part of the twentieth century have attempted to determine whether this more sophisticated civilization could be correlated to an actual Xia dynasty. In 1959, archaeologists digging near Luoyang in eastern China uncovered a settlement with a palace and various bronze, jade, and pottery relics, which was dated 2100 to 1800 B.C.E. Several theories subsequently developed regarding this evidence. Some historians believed that the area could have been a capital of the Xia dynasty. Others argued that the site was an early stage of the Shang dynasty, already known to have been dominant from the mid-eighteenth century B.C.E. until its overthrow by the Chou dynasty around 1022 B.C.E. A third group of historians saw the site as a later neolithic settlement, which made the transition into the Shang dynasty.

In an effort to quell the controversy, the Chinese government in 1996 funded the Hsia-Shang-Chou Chronology Project. Chinese archaeologists and scholars worked at Luoyans and other sites for several years, concluding that the Xia dynasty was founded by mythological Emperor Yu, also called Yu the Great, and endured until the founding of the Shang dynasty.

See also: CHOU (ZHOU) DYNASTY; SHANG (YIN) DYNASTY.

XUANZONG. *See* HSUAN TSUNG

YADAVA DYNASTY (1100s–1300s C.E.)

Ruling family of the Hindu kingdom of Maharashtra, located in central India, which was conquered by the rulers of the Delhi Sultanate in the fourteenth century.

The Yadavas were initially vassals of the Calukyas, a ruling family of Gujarat who were eventually undermined by Hindu feudal states to the south. By the twelfth century, the kingdom of the Yadavas reigned supreme in the Deccan, a large plateau bordered by the mountainous eastern and western Ghats ranges that makes up much of southern India.

Around 1185, a Yadava leader named Bhillama (r. ca. 1185–1192) revolted against the Chalukyas and also attacked the Hoysalas of the Mysore region in the south and the Paramaras of Malwa in the north. He then founded the city of Devagiri (which means "abode of Gods") as his capital. From that point on, the dynasty was known as the Yadavas of Devagiri.

Next in line after Bhillama was Jaitugi (r. ca. 1192–1200), who was forced to recognize the suzerainty of the Hoysalas. But his much more powerful successor, Singhana (ca. 1200–1247), brought the Yadava dynasty to its peak, with military triumphs over the Hoysalas and the Karad Silharas.

The Yadava rulers who followed Singhana, including Krishna (r. ca. 1247–1261) and Mahadeva (r. ca. 1261–1271), did not fare as well with their expansionist policies. Mahadeva's son and successor, Ammana (r. 1271), was deposed by Krishna's son Ramachandra (r. 1271–1311), who had no trouble capturing Devagiri.

Ramachandra's reign went well in the beginning, as he overpowered the Hoysalas and other rival states. However, in 1294, a Muslim army led by the Delhi sultan, Firuz II (r. 1290–1296), attacked the Yadava kingdom and made it a tributary. The Yadavas's attempts to regain Maharashtra were fruitless.

Ramachandra was able to reign until 1311 by paying a heavy ransom to Delhi. But when his son, Sankaradeva (r. 1311–1313), succeeded him in 1311, the new Yadava ruler stopped sending tribute to Delhi; as a result, he was killed in 1313.

Soon afterward, Ramachandra's son-in-law, Harapaladeva (r. 1313–1317), managed to organize a revolt and drive out the Muslims for a while. But the sultanate regained control of the kingdom in 1317 and changed the name of the Yadava capital to Daulatabad. With this defeat, the Yadava dynasty came to an end.

See also: CALUKYA (CHALUKYA) DYNASTY; DELHI KINGDOM; INDIAN KINGDOMS; KHALJI DYNASTY.

YAMATO DYNASTY

(ca. 40 B.C.E.–Present)

The ruling dynasty of Japan, named after the Yamato River and the surrounding region near Kyoto, which is cited as the world's longest surviving dynasty. According to tradition, the Yamato dynasty was founded over 2,500 years ago by the emperor Jimmu Tenno (ca. 40–10 B.C.E.), the semilegendary great-great grandson of the Japanese sun goddess, Amaterasu.

At the end of World War II, the American occupation forces in Japan forced Emperor Hirohito (r. 1926–1989) to give up the traditional claim to divinity that Japanese emperors had claimed for centuries. Nonetheless, the Yamato dynasty remains the symbol of the Japanese state.

Yamato Period

JIMMU*	40–10 B.C.E.
SUIZEI	10 B.C.E.–20 C.E.
ANNEI	20–50
ITOKU	50–80
KOSHO	80–110
KOAN	110–140
KOREI	140–170
KOGEN	170–200
KAIKA	200–230
SUJIN	230–258
SUININ	258–290
KEIKO	290–322
SEIMU	322–355
CHUAI	355–362
OJIN	362–394
NINTOKU	394–427
RICHU	427–432
HANZEI	432–437
INGYO	437–454
ANKO	454–457
YURYAKU	457–489
SEINEI	489–494
KENZO	494–497
NINKEN	497–504
BURETSU	504–510
KEITAI	510–527
ANKAN	527–535
SENKA	535–539
KIMMEI	539–571
BIDATSU	572–585
YOMEI	585–587
SUSHUN	587–592
SUIKO	593–628
JOMEI	629–641
KOGYOKU	642–645
KOTOKU	645–654
SAIMEI	655–661
TENJI	661–672
KOBUN	672
TEMMU	672–686
JITO	686–697
MOMMU	697–707

Nara Period

GEMMEI	707–715
GENSHO	715–724
SHOMU	724–749
KOKEN	749–758
JUNNIN	758–764
SHOTOKU	764–770
KONIN	770–781

Heian Period

KAMMU	781–806
HEIZEI	806–809
SAGA	809–823
JUNNA	823–833
NIMMYO	833–850
MONTOKU	850–858
SEIWA	858–876
YOZEI	876–884
KOKO	884–887
UDA	887–897
DAIGO	897–930
SUZAKU	930–946
MURAKAMI	946–967
REIZEI	967–969
ENYU	969–984
KAZAN	984–986
ICHIJO	986–1011
SANJO	1011–1016
GO-ICHIJO	1016–1036
GO-SUZAKU	1036–1045
GO-REIZEI	1045–1068
GO-SANJO	1068–1073
SHIRAKAWA	1073–1087

Heian Period (continued)

HORIKAWA	1087–1107
TOBA	1107–1123
SUTOKU	1123–1142
KONOE	1142–1155
GO-SHIRAKAWA	1155–1158
NIJO	1158–1165
ROKUJO	1165–1168
TAKAKURA	1168–1180
ANTOKU	1180–1185

Kamakura Period

GO-TOBA	1185–1198
TUSUCHIMIKADO	1198–1210
JUNTOKU	1210–1221
CHUKYO	1221
GO-HORIKAWA	1221–1232
SHIJO	1232–1242
GO-SAGA	1242–1246
GO-FUKAKUSA	1246–1260
KAMEYAMA	1260–1274
GO-UDA	1274–1287
FUSHIMI	1287–1298
GO-FUSHIMI	1298–1301
GO-NIJO	1301–1308
HANAZONO	1308–1318

Period of Dual Dynasties

SOUTHERN IMPERIAL COURT

GO-DAIGO	1318–1339
GO-MURAKAMI	1339–1368
CHOKEI	1368–1383
GO-KAMEYAMA	1383–1392

NORTHERN IMPERIAL COURT

KOGON	1331–1333
KOMYO	1335–1348
SUKO	1348–1351
GO-KOGON	1351–1371
GO-ENYU	1371–1382

Muromachi Period

GO-KAMATSU	1382–1412
SHOKO	1412–1428
GO-HANAZONO	1428–1464
GO-TUSUCHMIKADO	1464–1500
GO-KASHIWABARA	1500–1526
GO-NARA	1526–1557
OGIMACHI	1557–1586

Tokugawa Period

GO-YOZEI	1586–1611
GO-MIZUNOO	1611–1629
MEISHO	1629–1643
GO-KOMYO	1643–1654
GOSAI	1655–1663
REIGEN	1663–1687
HIGASHIYAMA	1687–1709
NAKAMIKADO	1709–1735
SAKURAMACHI	1735–1747
MOMOZONO	1747–1762
GO-SAKURAMACHI	1762–1771
GO-MOMOZONO	1771–1779
KOKAKU	1780–1817
NINKO	1817–1846
KOMEI	1846–1867

Modern Period

MEIJI	1867–1912
TAISHO	1912–1926
SHOWA (HIROHITO*)	1926–1989
AKIHITO	1989–

*Indicates a separate alphabetical entry.

MYTH AND HISTORY

The early dynastic history of Japan is documented in sparse historical and archaeological records. According to two chronicles from the eighth century, the *Kojiki* and *Nihon Shoki,* the imperial line of Japan traces in lineage back to the semilegenday Jimmu in 660 B.C.E. Modern scholars, however, date Jimmu's reign to the late first century B.C.E.

Other early accounts credit Empress Himiko with establishing the Yamato clan. Chinese sources indicate that this was in 238 C.E. Still other legends say that Himiko was the daughter of Emperor Suijin and that she deposited the sacred mirror of Amaterasu at the imperial shrine in Ise in 5 B.C.E. The date on which the dynasty was founded is obviously in conflict. In any event, by about 500 C.E., the Yamato imperial line was secured. Yet, the imperial succession was, historically, under the control of powerful Japanese aristocratic and landowning families.

Except for six or so early reigning female emperors, an empress in 1630, and another in 1762, the line of Yamato succession was male. Given the acceptance of multiple imperial consorts, even into the twentieth century, there was always an available heir to the throne. If the empress did not have suitable sons, she might be pressed to adopt a nephew or the son of an imperial concubine who would then be appointed child emperor under a powerful regent or counselor.

DYARCHY—TITLE VERSUS POWER

More often than not, Japan's emperors were merely puppet rulers. The Yamato dynasty survived an alleged 2,500 years because those leaders who held real power in Japan never actually overthrew the emperor but allowed him to remain on the throne as a puppet. These leaders based their right to rule on the legitimacy of positions sanctioned, however circuitously, by the imperial office. Power might rest with an imperial regent, counselor, or shogun, or with the shogun's regent or counselor. In any of these cases, however, the emperor was the theoretical fountainhead of power.

Power Behind the Throne

Until the late nineteenth century, the scions of five great families—the Soga, Fujiwara, Minamoto, Ashikaga, and Tokugawa—were the true rulers of Japan. From about the mid-400s to the mid-600s, the noble Soga family exercised control, primarily through intermarriage with the imperial family.

Next came the Fujiwara family, which established control in the mid-600s, reaching ascendancy in the mid-800s and lingering until the early twelfth century. The Fujiwara clan supplied generations of daughters as empresses and consorts, and hundreds of fathers, grandfathers, fathers-in-law, and uncles as regents (*sessho*) and counselors (*kampaku*). Rare was the emperor who did not have a Fujiwara mother.

Shogunates

At the end of the twelfth century, Minamoto Yoritomo, a member of a minor branch of the imperial family, triumphed in a series of dynastic struggles and received from the emperor the title of *shogun* (generalissimo). The autocratic rule of the shoguns, maintained with the support of samurai warriors, lasted intermittently for nearly seven hundred years. The Ashikaga shoguns ruled from 1338 to 1573, and the Tokugawa shoguns from 1603 to 1868.

The three shogunates were divided by periods of social unrest and war among the clans. Although the Japanese emperors survived during these seven hundred years, they were often lived in isolation, ignored by the population and periodically reduced to great poverty.

MEIJI RESTORATION

In 1868, a group of young nationalist reformers and samurai *daimyo* (landowners) overthrew the Tokugawa shoguns, moved the imperial court from Kyoto to the shogunal palace in Tokyo, and restored the power of the emperor, in this case, the emperor Mutshihito (r. 1867–1912). This was the beginning of the so-called Meiji Restoration. The Meiji reformers blamed corrupt and incompetent shoguns for cravenly accepting disadvantageous treaties enforced by Western gunboats.

These reformers, the new "powers behind the throne," industrialized and modernized Japan, drawing liberally on Western ideas, which they typically made more Japanese in their application. Under the emperor's decree, the Meiji abolished the *daimyo* feudal land system, set up an educational system that drew from European ideas, set up a parliament (Diet) and a cabinet, and issued a constitution. They also popularized the emperors as a national symbol, emphasizing imperial divinity. By 1920, the imperial myth of divine descent was virtually dogma.

In the mid-twentieth century, the wealthy and military classes of Japan carried the country into a disastrously aggressive military dictatorship that ended with World War II. But Emperor Hirohito, the current Yamato ruler at that time, survived under American protection as a useful icon.

Today, Emperor Akihito (r. 1989–) and Empress Michiko, the first commoner to marry into the Yamato imperial family, serve as national symbols dedicated to serving their nation. No longer considered divine, Japan's emperors also hold almost no real power. They are merely figureheads, as they were during the many centuries of rule by the shoguns.

See also: ASHIKAGA SHOGUNATE; FUJIWARA DYNASTY; HEIAN PERIOD; JIMMU; KAMAKURA SHOGUNATE; MINAMOTO RULERS; NARA KINGDOM, TOKUGAWA SHOGUNATE.

YAROSLAV I, THE WISE

(978–1054 C.E.)

Grand duke of Kiev (r. 1019–1054), who consolidated the power of Kiev and united the Kievan Rus principalities.

Yaroslav was the son of Prince Vladimir I of Kiev (r. 978–1015) and Princess Rogneda of Polotsk. When Yaroslav was ten years old, his father sent him to live with noble families in the principality of Novgorod. This decision had serious repercussions. In 1014, Yaroslav supported the Novgorodians in their decision to withhold tributary payments to Kiev. He then hired the Varangians, mercenary Scandinavian soldiers, to protect Novgorod from a Kievan invasion. Through these actions, Yaroslav successfully wrested control of the principality from his father.

When Vladimir I died in 1015, Yaroslav's brother Sviatopolk (r. 1015–1019) assumed the Kievan throne. Relying again upon his alliance with the Novgorodians and Varangians, Yaroslav attacked his brother's forces in September 1015. With the aid of Polish allies, Sviatopolk repelled Yaroslav's forces for four years. But in 1019, after a mighty attack, Yaroslav gained control of Kiev. Although he faced various threats during the next twenty years, many initiated by his own relatives, Yaroslav managed to consolidate the Kievan kingdoms to a greater degree than any of his predecessors.

Yaroslav also arranged marriages to solidify his control and to gain an international position for Kiev. His sister married the king of Poland, his daughter Anna married King Henry I of France (r. 1031–1060), and Yaroslav himself married Ingegard, the daughter of Olaf Skotkonnung, king of Sweden (r. 995–1022). Consequently, Yaroslav became the first Russian ruler to engage in European affairs. His only foreign misstep was a failed attack against the Byzantine capital of Constantinople in 1043.

Yaroslav oversaw fundamental developments in Kiev's social institutions. Unlike previous rulers, he openly supported Eastern Orthodox Christianity, and he built stunning churches such as the Cathedral of St. Sophia in Kiev. He also encouraged the immigration of Byzantine artisans and teachers, resulting in some of the earliest Russian writings. In 1016, he published the *Justice of Yaroslav*, a new legal code for Kiev.

To ensure that the Rus kingdoms would remain unified after his death and to prevent dissension among his three sons, Yaroslav crafted the *Testament of Yaroslav*. The document urged his sons to sustain a triumvirate and avoid any crippling civil wars. Although his sons managed to maintain Kiev's prominence, civil wars eventually weakened the kingdom, making it vulnerable to an invasion by the Mongols in 1236.

See also: KIEV, PRINCEDOM OF; RUS PRINCEDOMS; VLADIMIR PRINCEDOM.

YA'RUBI DYNASTY (ca. 1625–1743 C.E.)

Islamic dynasty that ruled Oman, on the Arabian Peninsula, during the seventeenth and eighteenth centuries, expelling the Portuguese from the region and creating a strong maritime power that included control over Zanzibar and other areas of the East African coast.

The Ya'rubi dynasty was established around 1625, when Nasir ibn Murshid (r. 1625–1649) was elected imam (guide or leader) of Oman and established a capital at Rustaq. Nasir united the country under the beliefs of Ibadi Islam, a Muslim sect that had been adopted by various Omani tribes as early as the seventh century. He also began a military campaign against the Portuguese in Oman, attacking the trading port of Muscat and capturing the cities of Quriyat, Sur, and Julfar. In 1643, Nasir captured Sohar, but in 1648 he was forced to sign a treaty with the Portuguese allowing them to retain control of Muscat.

Nasir died in 1649 and was succeeded by Sultan I (r. 1649–1679), who immediately broke the treaty with the Portuguese and recaptured Muscat in 1650.

Sultan's expeditions stimulated the creation of an Omani navy and increased the influence of both Oman and its merchants in the region. He moved the capital to Nizwa and rebuilt various towns in the kingdom.

Upon the death of Sultan I in 1669, he was succeeded by Abu al-Arab (r. 1679–1692). Soon after, a power struggle ensued between al-Arab and his brother, Saif ibn Sultan. Saif took the throne in 1692 after his brother committed suicide. During his rule, Saif I (r. 1692–1711) rebuilt the Omani navy and renovated the country's irrigation system, the *falaj,* which had been greatly neglected. Saif also moved the capital back to Rustaq from Nizwa.

Saif died in 1711 and was succeeded by his son, Sultan II (r. 1711–1719). Ya'rubid power declined during his reign, as the treasury was depleted by military campaigns and large building projects. By the reign of Sultan II, hereditary succession had become firmly established in the kingdom. This principle went against the beliefs of Ibadi Islam, however. The resulting tension between religious and tribal leaders resulted in the outbreak of civil war after Sultan II died in 1719 and left a minor, his son, Saif II (r. 1719–1743), on the throne.

Omani tribal leaders backed Saif II as the legitimate successor, but religious leaders chose another individual, Muhanna, to rule. Saif II was eventually proclaimed imam in 1728, but his rule continued to be opposed by a succession of rivals. In 1738, Saif II rebuffed an invasion of Oman by the Persians. But four years later, in 1742, he asked the Persians for assistance during an attempt by opposing factions to depose him. Continuing dynastic disputes greatly weakened the Ya'rubi dynasty. In 1749, an opposition leader, Ahmad ibn Sa'id (r. 1749–1783), became imam and founded the Al-Bu-Sa'id dynasty, bringing an end to rule by the Ya'rubids.

See also: ARABIA, KINGDOMS OF; MIDDLE EASTERN DYNASTIES.

YELLOW EMPEROR. *See* HUANG TI

YEMEN RULERS (ca. 900s B.C.E.–Present)

Rulers of the territory of Yemen, in the southern western corner of the Arabian Peninsula.

From about the tenth century B.C.E., Yemen was the commercial center of ancient Arabian civilization. The fertile land produced an abundance of spices that were much in demand and easily traded throughout the region. Among the ancient kingdoms that prospered at this time were those of the Minaean, Sabaean, and later the Himyarites. Most well known of the rulers of this time was the legendary queen of Sheba, who visited King Solomon of Israel (r. 970–931 B.C.E.).

In the eighth century C.E., northern Yemen became the destination of members of the Shi'ite sect of Islam, who were fleeing from persecution further north. One of their leaders, al-Hadi ilal Haqq, who claimed descent from the Prophet Muhammad, declared himself imam (guide or leader) and founded the Rassid dynasty, which followed a sect of Shi'ite Islam called Zaydism. Although other conquerors would officially claim this territory in succeeding centuries, the Rassid dynasty retained unofficial local control over northern and eastern Yemen until the twentieth century.

In the sixteenth century, Yemen became part of the Ottoman Empire. Qasim the Great (r. ca. 1592–1620), an imam of the Shi'ite Islamic sect called Zaydism, revolted against the Ottomans in the late sixteenth century and gained a period of independence for Yemen. By the eighteenth century, however, Zaydi power had weakened, and the Ottomans regained control. In the nineteenth century, when Great Britain needed to retain access to their vital trading routes to India, they made the strategically situated area of southern Yemen a British protectorate.

The Zaydi imam, Yahya (r. 1904–1948), gained control of northern Yemen from the Ottomans in 1918. Although he tried to gain control over the south, he was thwarted by the British. Yahya was assassinated in 1948 and was succeeded by his son, Ahmad (r. 1948–1962), who also fought against the British over control of the south.

Immediately after Ahmad's death in 1962, a coup led by Colonel Abdullah al-Sallal succeeded in taking power from the monarchy and formed the Yemen Arab Republic in the north, with Sallal as president. Soon thereafter, in 1967, the strongest of the groups opposed to British rule in southern Yemen took control and created the People's Democratic Republic of Yemen.

For over two decades afterward, the two Yemens engaged in periodic fighting, while also working toward the stated goal of unification of both nations. An agreement was reached between the two in 1990, at which time the Yemeni Republic was formed and Ali Abdullah Saleh of the north was chosen by a presidential council to be president. He was reelected by the council in 1994, and in 1999 he became the first leader of Yemen to be elected by a direct vote of the people.

See also: ARABIA, KINGDOMS OF; SABAEAN KINGDOM; SHEBA, QUEEN OF.

YI DYNASTY (1392–1910 C.E.)

Long-lived dynasty that ruled Korea for more than five centuries from medieval times to the modern era.

In 1388, Yi Songgye, a commander in the Koryo army, successfully overthrew the ruler of the kingdom of Koryo and installed a puppet monarch. Four years later, Yi founded the Yi dynasty when he formally proclaimed himself king and took the name T'aejo (r. 1392–1398). He also changed the name of the kingdom to Choson in honor of an ancient kingdom that had once existed on the Korean Peninsula.

To weaken the former Koryo aristocrats who still opposed him, Yi confiscated all privately held land in the kingdom. In 1390, he burned all existing titles to the confiscated land and enacted the Rank Land Law, which divided the land around the capital among the bureaucratic literati, an educated class that supported Yi's ascension. The remaining land throughout Choson was designated as state land. Consequently, the monarchy now held a virtual monopoly over Choson's agricultural economy, and Yi utilized the profits from this monopoly to solidify the new dynasty's power.

With power secured, Yi Songgye's successors shaped a new society in Choson. King Sejong (r. 1418–1450) oversaw the introduction of the Korean alphabet, called the *han'gul.* In 1471, King Songjong (r. 1469–1494) published the *Kyongguk taejon,* a code that dramatically restructured the government bureaucracy by establishing a State Council consisting of three positions: Inspector-General, Censor-General, and Special Adviser. The council not only advised the monarch, but it also possessed a limited veto authority. The code also divided the bureaucracy into six ministries that were responsible for performing all government activities, and it parti-

Yi Dynasty

T'AE-JO	1392–1398
CHONG-JONG	1398–1400
T'AE-JONG	1400–1418
SE-JONG	1418–1450
MUN-JONG	1450–1452
TAN-JONG	1452–1455
SE-JO	1455–1468
YE-JONG	1468–1469
SONG-JONG	1469–1494
YON-SAN	1494–1506
CHUNG-JONG	1506–1544
IN-JONG	1544–1545
MYONG-JONG	1545–1567
SON-JO	1567–1608
KWANG-HAE	1608–1623
IN-JO	1623–1649
HYO-JONG	1649–1659
HYON-JONG	1659–1674
SUK-CHONG	1674–1720
KYONG-JONG	1720–1724
YONG-JO	1724–1776
CHONG-JO	1776–1800
SUN-JO	1800–1834
HON-JONG	1834–1849
CH'OL-CHONG	1849–1864
KO-JONG	1864–1907
SUN-JONG	1907–1910

ROYAL RELATIVES

Taewongun (1821–1898 C.E.)

Grand Prince Taewongun was the father of King Kojong of the Yi dynasty. When Kojong ascended the throne in 1864, he was only twelve years old. Therefore, his father exerted a great deal of influence in the Choson court and helped to stabilize the Yi dynasty at a time when it was faltering. Taewongun epitomized a faction of Choson that had no desire to develop relations with Western countries and opposed any modernization of the Choson society. In 1866, with Taewongun's approval, nine French missionaries to Choson were killed. The murders prompted a French attack that was successfully repelled. Taewongun also despised the increasing prevalence of Chinese and Japanese officials in the Choson court. But King Kojong was increasingly compelled to allow greater foreign control over Choson affairs, and in 1873 he banished his father from the court. Taewongun temporarily resumed power in 1882, but Choson no longer had the power to prevent foreign intrusion. In 1884, Chinese troops forcefully took Taewongun to China, where he died in isolation fourteen years later. However, Taewongun holds a prominent position as the last Choson official to vehemently resist Choson's subjugation to outside powers.

tioned the kingdom into eight provinces that were in turn divided into numerous counties.

Songjong also reformed the civil service examinations that had been instituted during Koryo rule. Under the new format, potential officials had to pass two levels of exams before they could be appointed to a government position. To help students prepare for these exams, the government opened a publicly funded school in each county. For decades, these schools comprised Choson's entire educational system. But in 1542, King Chungjong (r. 1506–1544) allowed the formation of private schools, called *sowon*, to help prepare students for the difficult exam.

Under these reforms, Choson enjoyed nearly two centuries of peace. However, the Yi dynasty acted harshly to suppress any potential threats. Although Confucianism had become the official state religion in the kingdom of Koryo, the Koryo monarchs had not forced the nation's Buddhists to convert. The Yi monarchs, however, viewed Buddhists as insurrectionists. Buddhism was labeled a heresy, and its followers were persecuted repeatedly.

The Yi monarchs also distrusted the literati. Although they recognized the need for the literati to run the bureaucracy, the Yi monarchs believed that a large literati class would be prone to rebellion. Therefore, the monarchy conducted four purges in the 1400s and 1500s, during which large numbers of literati were either executed or banished.

In 1592, a Japanese invasion disrupted Choson's overall peace. The war with Japan lasted six years, ravaging the Choson economy and population. Only the support of the Ming dynasty of China and the outbreak of civil war in Japan prevented Choson's surrender to the Japanese. Choson's reprieve was only temporary, however. In 1627, and again in 1636, invasions of Manchus from north of Korea further crippled the weakened nation. As a result, Choson signed a treaty with Manchuria and renounced its allegiance to China.

To rebuild Choson's devastated economy after the war with Japan, King Sonjo (r. 1567–1608) instituted the Uniform Land Tax Law in Kyonggi province in 1608. The law eliminated taxes on tribute items and required that all taxes be paid in rice. Land assessments determined each individual's tax burden. Consequently, the tax system became much more equitable. The law was so effective that by 1708 it was implemented throughout the entire country.

Agricultural advances also restored Choson's prosperity. During the 1600s, farmers developed a new strain of rice that yielded more abundant crops and grew much more quickly. Choson farmers were thus able to plant two crops a year. The monarchy also allowed farmers to grow commercial crops, such as tobacco and cotton, that could be exported to other countries. Finally, in 1791, King Chongjo (r. 1776–1800) eliminated the requirement that each merchant purchase a government license. This easing of government control led to immediate economic expansion.

After the death of King Chongjo in 1800, the Yi dynasty gradually began to lose power. Chonjo's heir, King Sunjo (r. 1800–1834), was very young when he assumed the throne, and he lacked the skills necessary to rule. Disputes within the royal family erupted, and with no clear leadership, the Choson bureaucracy faltered. Inconsistent tax collections and subsidy payments to farmers developed, and many peasants were bankrupted. In response, many peasants revolted, culminating with the Hong Kyong-nae Rebellion in 1811.

In 1864, when King Kojong (r. 1864–1907) inherited the Choson throne, the Yi dynasty's power was temporarily reasserted. But in an age of imperialism, Choson had become a coveted target for international powers. Russia, France, and the United States all attempted to exert influence over the country, but Japan and China were the most forceful intruders in Choson affairs. In 1876, Japan persuaded Korea to sign the Kanghwa Treaty, which compelled Choson to adopt Japan's plan of adopting Western technology. In response, China pressured Choson to sign a Treaty of Amity and Commerce. Both Japan and China wanted Choson to modernize its society, but each nation wanted to ensure that Choson would rely upon them during the modernization process.

Two events in 1894 gave Japan supremacy in Choson. When the Tonghak Uprising, spurred by the public's displeasure with increasing foreign influence in Choson, threatened the monarchy, King Kojong asked Japanese troops to intervene. Now possessing a foothold on the Korean Peninsula, the Japanese attacked China. Japan's victory in the Sino-Japanese War in 1895 gave Japan unfettered influence over Choson. Subsequently, Japan compelled King Kojong to pass the Kabo Reforms, a series of acts that completely overhauled the Choson government. When Kojong's wife, Queen Min, organized resistance to the reforms, the Japanese government orchestrated her assassination.

Russia's defeat in the Russo-Japanese War in 1905 erased the last impediment to Japanese control of Choson. That same year, Japan forced Kojong to sign the Treaty of Protectorate, which placed Japan in charge of Choson's foreign affairs. When Kojong quietly urged Choson citizens to join rebel groups opposed to Japanese control, the Japanese government forced him to abdicate the throne. Kojong's son, Sunjong (r. 1907–1910), was a weak ruler who was unable to maintain any semblance of Choson independence. The Japanese formally deposed him in 1910 and declared Choson to be a colony of Japan. After five centuries of rule, the Yi dynasty had finally collapsed. Korea would not regain its freedom until 1945, when Japan surrendered at the end of World War II and the new Korean nation emerged.

See also: Choson Kingdom; Koryo Kingdom; Yi Songgye.

FURTHER READING

Eckert, Carter J., et al. *Korea Old and New.* Cambridge, MA: Harvard University Press, 1990.

Yi Songgye (1335–1408 C.E.)

Founder and first king (r. 1392–1398) of the Korean Yi dynasty, which ruled Korea from 1392 to 1910.

Yi Songgye was born in the Hamhung region of the Koryo kingdom. His family had served in the military for several generations, and Yi enlisted at an early age. Shortly after his enlistment, Yi joined a campaign to end the frequent, devastating raids of the Japanese marauders, or *waegu,* that plagued Koryo during the 1300s. The *waegu* pillaged the fertile farm villages that lined the eastern Koryo coast and stole the crops that fueled the kingdom's economy. Yi Songgye and another commander, Choe Yong, successfully halted these attacks. As a result, both men earned rapid promotions and cultivated powerful influence within the Koryo government.

In 1388, the Chinese Ming dynasty threatened to invade the northern portion of Koryo and reclaim land that China had previously lost. Choe Yong convinced the Koryo king to commission a preemptive strike against China, but Yi Songgye disagreed and contended that the best way to preserve Koryo's independence was to pacify the Ming rulers. Unable to convince the king to adopt his plan, Yi Songgye reluctantly agreed to serve as Choe Yong's deputy. But during the army's march toward China, Yi staged a successful coup against Choe Yong, led the army back to the capital, and demanded the king's abdication. After ascending the throne in 1392, Yi Songyye changed the kingdom's name to Choson to commemorate an ancient Korean kingdom.

To secure his power, Yi allied himself with the rapidly growing literati, an educated class in Koryo society. With their support, he seized the vast private estates of both the aristocratic class and the Buddhist monasteries and publicly burned their titles to the land. In 1390, Yi enacted the Rank Land Law, which allocated all land around the capital to the literati and classified all outlying land as government property. The government would now collect the taxes from these areas. Consequently, the aristocratic families lost their rich farms and the financial strength to oppose Yi.

With such actions, Yi Songgye orchestrated a monumental shift in Choson society. He also stripped power away from the aristocratic families who had dominated the Koryo society and gave it to the middle-class bureaucrats who formed the literati class. His reign marked the beginning of the Yi dynasty, which would control the Korean Peninsula for more than five hundred years.

See also: CHOSON KINGDOM; YI DYNASTY.

FURTHER READING
Eckert, Carter J., et al. *Korea Old and New.* Cambridge, MA: Harvard University Press, 1990.

YORITOMO (1147–1199 C.E.)

Also known as Minamoto no Yoritomo, the first Japanese warrior to institutionalize the title *shogun* ("generalissimo"), which was bestowed upon him by the emperor of Japan in 1192.

Yoritomo was born into the Minamoto family, a powerful military clan of imperial descent. When his family rebelled against the rival Taira clan at the imperial court in 1160, Yoritomo and his five siblings had the good luck to be spared when their father was killed for taking part in the revolt. This kindness, displayed by the Taira leader Kiyomori, was atypical of bellicose Japanese warlords in an era of savage personal rivalries. Exiled for his role in the rebellion, Yoritomo later married into the Hojo clan.

In 1180, Yoritomo joined another Minamoto rebellion and established headquarters at the city of Kamakura. His cousin Yoshinaka drove the Taira from the imperial capital at Kyoto in 1183. But when Yoshinaka's forces later caused unrest in Kyoto, Yoritomo and his half-brother, Minamoto Yoshitsune, crushed them. Yoritomo then continued the struggle against the Taira family for control of imperial power, finally smashing the Taira in the naval battle of Dannoura in 1185. He established an independent government at Kamakura that same year.

Yoritomo was now powerful enough to usurp the imperial throne, but he chose not to do so. Instead, in 1192, he took the ancient title of shogun, which gave him the right to act against any rebel that threatened the imperial throne or its interests. As shogun, Yoritomo rewarded loyal supporters with large estates located strategically throughout Japan. These later became the basis of power of the *daimyo,* or heritary nobles of feudal Japan.

Yoritomo established a centralized government at Kamakura. He supported the spread of Zen Buddhism and encouraged samurai to adopt the military virtues of *bushido,* a feudal code of chivalry that emphasized loyalty, courage, and the preference of death to dishonor.

After Yoritomo's death in 1199, his Minamoto clan held power only until 1219, when the line died out. It was replaced by the Hojo clan, into which Yoritomo had married. Yoritomo's clan no longer ruled, but the system of government he established in the Kamakura shogunate (1192–1333) set a pattern of military rule in Japan that lasted until the middle of the nineteenth century.

See also: KAMAKURA SHOGUNATE.

YORK, HOUSE OF (1385–1485 C.E.)

English royal dynasty that produced three kings—Edward IV (r. 1461–1470, 1471–1483), Edward V (r. 1483), and Richard III (r. 1483–1485). The house of York is perhaps best known for the Wars of the Roses (1455–1485), a dynastic struggle for the English Crown that pitted the Yorkists (symbolized by a white rose) against the rival house of Lancaster (symbolized by a red rose).

The house of York, a branch of the Plantagenet dynasty, was founded by Edmund of Langley, a son of

For thirty years, the House of York fought with the House of Lancaster for control of the English crown. The conflict became known as the Wars of the Roses because each house was symbolized by a rose—white for York, red for Lancaster. This 1909–1910 depiction by Henry Arthur Payne depicts a scene from Shakespeare's *Henry IV, Part I,* in which a member of each dynasty plucks a colored rose for its side.

Edward III (r. 1327–1377), who became the first duke of York in 1385. In 1399, Henry of Lancaster, a grandson of Edward III, deposed King Richard II (r. 1377–1399), who had become extremely unpopular among the English nobles and commoners. Henry established himself as King Henry IV (r. 1399–1413). Upon his death, the Crown passed to his son, Henry V (r. 1413–1422), one of the most powerful and popular kings of the medieval period. His only son and successor, Henry VI (r. 1422–1461, 1470–1471), inherited the throne as a child and was a weak and unpopular ruler.

During the reign of the Lancastrian Henry VI, the Yorkists attempted to claim the throne in the name of the deposed Richard II, initiating the War of the Roses. The Yorkist claim to the throne was not any more just than that of the Lancastrians based on genealogy—both houses derived from the sons of Edward III—and there was much dispute over which house was legally entitled to the kingship.

The first Yorkist who aspired to the throne was Richard, third duke of York, who announced his intention to reclaim the throne on behalf of his house

and denounced the weakness of Henry VI's rule. Parliament considered the issue, ruling that Henry would remain on the throne for his lifetime but that the Crown would then pass to the Yorkists. However, Queen Margaret of Anjou, the wife of Henry VI, did not accept this compromise solution, and her followers went to war with the Yorkists. Although Richard was killed in battle, his followers were victorious over the Lancastrians, and Richard's son, Edward IV, became the first king from the house of York.

Upon Edward's death in 1483, his twelve-year-old son took the throne as Edward V. Edward V reigned for less than three months. Perhaps through the machinations of his uncle, Richard, duke of Gloucester, Edward and his younger brother Richard were considered unfit to rule on the grounds that they were probably illegitimate. The English nobles then asked Richard, the next in succession, to assume the throne, and he was crowned Richard III in 1483. The two young princes disappeared, and it is possible that Richard had them murdered.

Richard was the last ruler from the house of York. A rebellion against him broke out in 1483, and he was killed two years later at the battle of Bosworth Field. The rebels had supported Henry Tudor, who now took the throne as Henry VII (r. 1485–1509), the first ruler of the Tudor dynasty. Henry came from a line of the house of Lancaster; his marriage to Elizabeth, a daughter of King Edward IV, united the two sides of the War of the Roses and put an end to a century of civil dispute.

See also: HENRY IV (ENGLAND); LANCASTER, HOUSE OF; PLANTAGENET, HOUSE OF; RICHARD II; RICHARD III; TUDOR, HOUSE OF.

YORUBA KINGDOMS (ca. 500–1820 C.E.)

West African coastal kingdoms centered in the cities of Ife and Oyo, located in what is now Nigeria. Yoruba culture is noted for its achievements in art and literature, its complex religion, and its great cities. In contrast to these achievements, Yoruba also enslaved millions of its own people and sent them to America.

Although the origins of the Yoruba civilization are unknown, archaeologists agree that it is at least 5,000 years old. The Yoruba believe that all life began at the city of Ife. Olorun, God of the Sky, sent five

The Yoruba of West Africa were widely known for their arts and crafts. These colorful beaded items were fashioned for a Yoruba king as regalia, symbolizing his prestige and authority.

beings to earth, with five pieces of iron, a lump of soil, and a chicken. When the party reached Ife, they put down the iron, spread the soil over it, and set the chicken to work spreading out the soil with its feet. This story underscores the Yoruba achievement of carving agricultural land out of the forests in Yoruba territory. Archaeologists also believe that the Yoruba were using iron tools as long as 2,000 years ago. Oduduwa, the leader of the group sent to earth, is regarded as the founding ancestor of the Ife kingdom, and all Yoruba kings, whether at Ife or at any other of the many Yoruba states, claim direct descent from this culture hero.

Beginning around 500 C.E., the Yoruba states were able to grow in power and extent because they could support not only their rulers and courtiers but also their allies. One great advantage they had was the fertility of their territory, which came to include much of the Niger River Delta. The court at Ife was noted for the nobility's patronage of art. Yoruba carvings in wood and ivory, its terracotta sculpture, and its impressive metal casting in bronze, brass, and

copper soon commanded high prices in the trans-Saharan trade. Many religious cults were centered in Ife, all owing allegiance to the divine king and consolidating his power.

As the kingdom grew and became more powerful in trade, settlements arose throughout the territory. One of these villages was Oyo, settled around 1100 and situated at the far north of Yoruba. During the 1500s, the Oyo rulers gained access to horses from traders to the north. The Oyo kings, called *alafins,* were then able to build up a powerful cavalry, giving them a decided advantage in raiding their neighbors for slaves and booty. The cavalry permitted the Oyo to embark on a campaign of expansion by conquest; they accrued such great wealth that, in the seventeenth century, they had eclipsed their own founding state of Ife. Ife remained the center for religion but lost its dominance in trade.

By the late 1600s, Oyo's economy was based primarily on revenues generated by the slave trade, whether through direct participation or through the collection of taxes on slaves that passed through their territory into the larger Saharan and European markets. Between 1680 and 1730, approximately 20,000 slaves per year passed through Oyo. Thus, when Europe brought the traffic in slaves to an end in the nineteenth century, Oyo and all the other regional trading powers suffered a serious loss in revenues. The Oyo kingdom collapsed during the first part of the nineteenth century, setting in motion a period of warfare among the Yoruba that did not end until the British established a protectorate in the region in 1861. With the loss of autonomy, the former Yoruba kingdoms began the process of assimilation into what is now the Nigerian nation.

See also: AFRICAN KINGDOMS.

FURTHER READING

Drewal, Henry John, et al. *Yoruba: Nine Centuries of African Art and Thought.* New York: Harry N. Abrams, 1990.

YUAN DYNASTY (1279–1368 C.E.)

Chinese dynasty whose Mongolian emperors were the first foreigners to rule all of China. Lasting less than a century, the Yuan brought a new cosmopolitanism to the Middle Kingdom (as the Chinese called their empire), opening China to the West for the first time. Although the brutal Mongol rulers often discriminated against the Chinese, it was an era rich in artistic endeavors.

FOUNDING

The Yuan dynasty was founded by Qubilai (Kublai Khan) (r. 1260–1294), grandson of Chingiz (Genghis Khan) (r. 1206–1227) and leader of a vast Mongolian Empire, who ruled under the imperial name Shih Tsu. With their huge cavalry, the Mongols had captured north China from the Chin (Jin) dynasty in 1234. Kublai completed the Mongol conquest of China when he defeated the Southern Sung (Song) dynasty in the south. In 1279 he moved his capital from Mongolia to Beijing and declared the Yuan ("origin") dynasty.

The greatest of the Mongol rulers, Kublai improved communications by extending the Grand Canal north, connecting the Yellow River with Bei-

jing. He introduced the Mongolian postal system, famous for its vast network of stations connected by relays of horsemen. Under Kublai, China's postal system had 1,400 stations and 50,000 horses.

THE CHINESE UNDERCLASS

Many of the Mongol leaders were illiterate and did not speak Chinese. The Yuan dynasty therefore relied on the native Chinese people to help them administer their new empire in China. They established a system in which the Chinese ruled themselves, supervised by the Mongols. To avoid becoming overly dependent on the Chinese bureaucracy, however, the Mongol emperors chose foreigners from other parts of Asia and Europe to serve as their advisers.

The Yuan divided the empire's population into an ethnic hierarchy of four classes. Mongols occupied the first class, followed by their non-Chinese allies and subjects. The lowest ranks were reserved for the Chinese, with northern Chinese classed somewhat higher than the southern Chinese, who ranked at the bottom of the Yuan caste system. Each ethnic group was allowed to keep its own laws for judging and punishing crimes. In addition, the Yuan registered the population according to hereditary classes grouped by occupation.

Under this system, the Chinese constituted a vast underclass. Chinese gentry were not allowed to hold high office. Soldiers in the Chinese military found themselves commanded by Mongol officers. Chinese were forbidden to own weapons or to congregate in public. Many Chinese had their land confiscated, and thousands of others were taken to other parts of the empire to work as slaves.

OPENING TO THE WORLD

Under the Yuan, China was part of a vast region under Mongol control that at its height extended from the Pacific Ocean to Eastern Europe. The Yuan brought a new internationalism to China and instituted a period of unprecedented contact with the West. The Mongol rulers encouraged trade, and a vigorous commerce flourished between China and the West. Chinese inventions, including printing and gunpowder, entered the West at this time. The Yuan court typified the cosmopolitanism of the dynasty, employing advisers from other parts of Asia and a few from Europe. Marco Polo, the famous Italian traveler who lived in China from 1272 to 1292, worked as an official in the Yuan court. When Polo

Yuan (Mongol) Dynasty

T'AI TSU (GENGHIS KHAN*)	1206–1227
T'AI TUNG (OGODEI)	1229–1241
TING TSUNG (GUYUK)	1246–1248
HSIEN TSUNG (MONGKE)	1251–1259
SHIH TSU (KUBLAI KHAN*)	1260–1294
CH'ENG TSUNG	1294–1307
WU TSUNG	1307–1311
JEN TSUNG	1311–1320
YING TSUNG	1320–1323
T'AI-TING TI	1323–1328
WEN TSUNG	1328–1329
MING TSUNG	1329
WEN TSUNG	1329–1332
NING TSUNG	1332
SHUN TI	1333–1368

*Indicates a separate alphabetical entry.

returned to Italy after his sojourn in China, his writings gave Europeans their first detailed descriptions of the Yuan Empire.

The Yuan period marks the beginning of significant numbers of European visitors to China. Starting in the mid-thirteenth century, Europeans came seeking religious converts, trade, and allies against the Muslims. Roman Catholicism first entered China at this time, carried by missionaries who made a small number of converts. The Mongol rulers established religious tolerance in China, allowing Christians, Muslims, Buddhists, and Taoists (Daoists) alike to practice and build temples, churches, and mosques. Kublai, whose mother was a Nestorian Christian, was himself a devotee of Tibetan Lamaism. Although Western contact with China during the Yuan resulted in increased European interest in China, it had the opposite effect on the Chinese, who would become increasingly xenophobic after they expelled their Mongolian rulers in 1368.

In keeping with the Mongolian tradition of constant conquest, the Yuan attempted to extend their empire to incorporate China's neighbors. In 1274 and 1281, thousands of Chinese ships sailed to Japan, each time failing to conquer the island nation. Multiple invasions of Southeast Asia also ended in failure.

A CULTURAL DIVIDE

In an effort to legitimize Mongol rule, Kublai Khan had taken the dynasty's name from the *Book of Changes,* an ancient Chinese classic. The Yuan hoped to gain Chinese acceptance by adopting Confucian ideology as the basis of their political system. However, the Yuan rulers never fully adopted the ancient Chinese traditions required of Confucian emperors and were therefore never completely accepted as China's legitimate rulers.

In addition, the Mongols departed from the ancient pattern of foreign rule in China, in which China's conquerors invariably became assimilated into Chinese culture. The Mongols deliberately resisted assimilation into Chinese culture. They used their own language for governing, discouraged intermarriage with the Chinese, and left Beijing every year for their summer capital at Shangdu. There, outside the Great Wall, they preserved their pastoral way of life. In Beijing, some Mongol princes lived in tents on the palace grounds, preferring their traditional shelters to the capital's grand palaces.

The cultural divide between Chinese and Mongol was wide. The two peoples had different languages, wore different clothing, and had different eating habits. The Mongols were famous for their horsemanship, raising their sons to be disciplined warriors who literally grew up in the saddle. The active, nomadic life of the Mongols bore little resemblance to the sedentary, scholarly life idealized by the Chinese. The Chinese saw the Mongols as uncivilized barbarians and viewed them with suspicion.

A FLOWERING OF CULTURE

Kublai eliminated the traditional Chinese examination system, which had tested knowledge of classical texts and served as a recruiting tool for the civil service. Although the exams were reinstituted in 1315, a quota system gave half the degrees required for government appointment to Mongols and other non-Chinese. This left many of China's scholars without employment and led to a flowering of literature and painting as the educated classes turned to intellectual and artistic endeavors. Novels and plays were written in large numbers. Private academies flourished as centers of Confucian scholarship. Scholars continued to be held in high esteem as respected community leaders. For the most part, the government stayed out of cultural and intellectual affairs.

THE FINAL YEARS

Kublai was succeeded by his grandson, Temur Oljeitu, also known as Ch'eng Tsung (Chengzong) (r. 1294–1307). After the death of Ch'eng Tsung in 1307, the dynasty had seven rulers in just twenty-six years. However, none of Kublai's successors shared his talent for ruling. Constant clashes erupted between those favoring Chinese culture and those who supported Mongol-style rule. Succession was bitterly disputed and almost never peaceful, marked by intrigue and murder.

Tension between Mongols and Chinese remained constant throughout the Yuan period. Treatment as an inferior caste encouraged the growth of Chinese ethnic consciousness. Many saw resistance to the Mongols as the only way to preserve Chinese identity. The Yuan's struggle to effectively rule their vast empire was made more difficult by this cultural divide.

By the end of the Yuan dynasty, the bloated Chinese bureaucracy was riddled with corruption, the population had declined, and crippling taxes damaged the economy. The Yuan's reliance on cruelty and the use of force had introduced a more authoritarian style of rule to China that would influence future dynasties. As with many Chinese dynasties, the end was marked by natural disaster. Floods and epidemics fueled the spread of revolt across China. In the final decades of Yuan rule, civil war raged as warlords vied for control. In 1368, the peasant rebel leader Chu Yüan-Chang (Zhu Yuanzhang) captured the capital at Beijing and proclaimed the Ming dynasty. The last Yuan emperor, Shun Ti (r. 1333–1368), also known as Togun Temur, fled to Mongolia.

See also: GENGHIS KHAN; HUNG WU (HONGWU); KUBLAI KHAN; MING DYNASTY; MONGOL EMPIRE; SUNG (SONG) DYNASTY.

YUNG LO (YONGLE) (1360–1424 C.E.)

Chinese emperor (r. 1403–1424) who presided over the Ming dynasty (1368–1644) at its height.

Born Chu Ti (Zhu Di), Yung Lo (Yongle) was the fourth son of Emperor Hung Wu (Hongwu) (r. 1368–1398), founder of the Ming dynasty. His father made him prince of Yan, granting him military command of China's northern region. Upon Hung Wu's death in 1398, Chu Ti's young nephew, Chien Wen (Jianwen) (r. 1398–1403), became emperor. Three years later, Chu Ti attacked Chien Wen's capital at Nanjing and claimed the throne for himself as Yung Lo ("Perpetual Happiness"). All his rivals and their supporters were executed, but the body of the fifteen-year-old Chien Wen was never found. Suspicious of Chien Wen's advisers, Yung Lo reintroduced eunuchs into the inner circle of power, reversing Hung Wu's policy of forbidding their involvement in politics.

Yung Lo was an intelligent man and a natural leader, experienced in battle from years of defending the Mongolian frontier. In 1421, he moved his capital to Beijing, where he built a city centered on the magnificent Forbidden City. Containing more than nine thousand rooms and covering 250 acres, the Forbidden City's red walls and yellow-tile roofs housed the imperial palaces. Outside its walls, the officials and gentry lived in the Imperial City. The outermost ring contained the Outer City, home of the common people.

Yung Lo reigned over an extremely prosperous China at the height of Ming power. He led five great campaigns against the Mongols, established Korea as a vassal state, and initiated a series of naval missions to distant lands. In 1405 his Grand Eunuch, Cheng He (Zheng He), set out with sixty-three ships carrying 27,000 men on the first of seven naval expeditions that would sail as far as the coasts of India and Africa. These missions were neither commercial nor military, but aimed to establish diplomatic ties with distant lands.

Yung Lo died in 1424 while on a military campaign in Mongolia and was succeeded by his eldest son, Hung Hsi (Hongxi) (r. 1424–1425).

See also: HUNG WU (HONGWU); MING DYNASTY.

ZAND DYNASTY (1750–1794 C.E.)

Short-lived Persian dynasty that reigned in southern Iran, with its capital at Shiraz. The Zands provided a brief era of peace in Iran after decades of civil war.

The first and most important ruler of the Zand dynasty was Muhammad Karim Khan (r. 1750–1779), who had been a general under the Persian ruler Nadir Shah (r. 1736–1747), the founder of the Afsharid dynasty. After the death of Nadir Shah in 1747, Iran plunged once again into civil war. Karim Khan exploited his influence to become regent for Ismail III (r. 1749–1750, the last ruler of the Safavid dynasty. By 1750, however, Karim Khan emerged as the new ruler.

Karim Khan never claimed the title of shah. Instead, he preferred to use the title he had held as regent for Ismail III—*vakil al raaya* ("regent of the people"). Karim Khan, who controlled all of Persia except the region of Khurusan in the northeast, returned peace to the country, which had endured constant warfare for forty years.

As ruler of Iran, Karim Khan constructed many buildings, including a number of monumental mosques, bazaars, and fortifications in his capital city of Shiraz in southern Iran. He supported the arts, inviting many scholars and poets to Shiraz; and he improved the fiscal system, imposing lower taxes on the peasant classes. He promoted agriculture and was responsible for opening trade with Great Britain in 1763, when he let the British East India Company build a base on the Persian Gulf. Karim Khan also relaxed central control, giving northern tribes more autonomy, and he restored official support for the Shi'ite sect of Islam, which had been curtailed under Nadir Shah.

Karim Khan's death in 1779 sparked a succession struggle among various Zand princes. Over the next ten years, six different Zand kings ruled Iran for short periods of time. During this period, a fierce leader of the Turkoman Qajar tribe, Agha Muhammad (r. 1779–1797), gained control of most of northern Iran.

In 1789, Lutf Ali Khan (r. 1789–1794), Karim's grandson, succeeded his father, Jafar Khan (r. 1785–1789), on the throne. Lutf Ali struggled valiantly against the forces of Agha Mohammad, who posed a serious threat to southern Iran. Despite winning a number of victories against the more numerous and better-equipped Qajars, Lotf Ali was finally defeated at Kerman and put to death in 1794. His death marked the end of the Zand dynasty and the ascent of the Qajar dynasty. The Qajars ruled Iran until 1925.

See also: NADIR SHAH; QAJAR DYNASTY; SAFAVID DYNASTY.

ZANZIBAR SULTANATE

(1806–1964 c.e.)

The islands of Zanzibar, Mafia, Lamu, and Pemba, located off the east coast of Africa. These were the possessions of the sultanate of Oman for two centuries and were important outposts of the Indian Ocean trade that linked eastern Africa with Arabia, India, and the Persian Gulf. The islands were settled by Omani traders and by Africans from the eastern coast who came to trade or as slaves.

The Omani originally ruled Zanzibar from their capital city Muscat, relying on appointed officials to oversee their interests in the islands. Seyyid Said (r. 1804–1856), who began the Al-Bu Sa'id dynasty, assumed the Omani sultanate in 1804, and, in 1828, decided to visit his more distant holdings along the east African coast. While the slave trade had long been a staple source of revenue from Zanzibar, Seyyid Said thought to expand his economic interests

in the region. Already having a goodly number of slaves on the island, he put them to work in new ways, most importantly as labor on his newly created Zanzibari clove plantations.

Said's policies met with almost immediate success, helped along by favorable terms of trade with Europe, where his exports were well received. To meet the increasing demand for spices, settlement in Zanzibar, until now concentrated on the coast, rapidly moved into the interior. In addition, Zanzibar became a primary destination for African caravans bringing goods from the interior for trade with Europe.

Even in the early 1800s, day-to-day administration of the sultanate continued through appointed governors who answered directly to the sultan in Muscat. However, Said determined that it would be important to establish a presence near the growing economic center and moved the seat of government to Zanzibar around 1840.

Before his unexpected death (1856) on a voyage between Zanzibar and Muscat, Said had named his youngest son, Thwain, as his heir of Oman and his fourth son, Majid, as heir in Zanzibar. Majid (r. 1856–1870) had already been acting head of state during his father's absence. However, Majid's brothers, Thwain and Barghash, repeatedly tried to oust him from power during the next four years, but they were unsuccessful. Zanzibar's prosperity continued during Majid's reign, and Majid succeeded in breaking free of Oman and becoming an independent sultanate in 1861. Majid died in 1870 without a male heir. The sultanate then went to his closest male relative, his brother Barghash (r. 1870–1888).

During Barghash's rule, the British government prevailed upon Zanzibar to abolish the slave trade, which was nominally suppressed in 1873. During the 1880s, both the Germans and the British reduced the sultanate's territory to the islands and a tiny stretch of African coastline. In 1890, even that small degree of autonomy was lost. Barghash's death in 1888 had left a power vacuum that was filled by the British, and the former independent sultanate became a British protectorate until it was granted independence in 1963.

See also: BARGHASH IBN SA'ID EL-BUSAIDI.

FURTHER READING

Gray, John Milner. *History of Zanzibar, from the Middle Ages to 1856.* Westport, CT: Greenwood Press, 1975.

Nicholls, Christine Stephanie. *The Swahili Coast*. New York: Africana Publishing, 1971.

ZAPOTEC EMPIRE

(ca. 500 B.C.E.–900 C.E.)

Empire established by an indigenous people of southeastern Mexico, which became one of Mesoamerica's most powerful civilizations of the pre-Columbian era.

The earliest archaeological evidence of the Zapotecs dates to about 700 B.C.E., when hunting and gathering peoples first began to establish settlements in the Oaxaca Valley of southeastern Mexico. At that time, there appears to have been no organized political structure unifying the people of the region, but in just 200 years that would change.

The first step toward political organization that led to the Zapotec Empire seems to have been the development of a writing system. This occurred as early as 600 B.C.E. and may have been due to the influence of the Olmec culture, which dominated Mesoamerica up to this time. The Zapotec writing system, which combines phonetic and ideographic elements and consists of carvings in stone, has not been fully deciphered. Nonetheless, incised stones show that the Zapotecs wrote in vertical columns, incorporated numbers in text, and are believed to provide a record of conquests, genealogies, and calendars charting the passage of time and the movement of the sun and moon.

The rise of the Zapotec state seems to have occurred around 500 B.C.E., when the first large, permanent structures began to be built at Monte Alban, some 350 miles southeast of present-day Mexico City. This construction reached its peak around 250 C.E., and came to include governmental and religious centers as well as residential buildings, ball courts, and public plazas. At around this time, the Zapotec also began actively transforming the contours of the countryside by flattening the tops of hills and ridges and terracing the slopes of Monte Alban itself.

As far as can be understood from the stone carvings left behind, Zapotecan kingship seems to have been inherited, at least ideally, by the eldest son of the current ruler upon that ruler's death. This did not always occur, however. Sometimes the reins of government passed to others among the powerful Zapotecan lineages. The right to rule appears to have been validated by religion: the ruler seems to have served as high priest as well as king. Some of the Zapotecan carved stones depict the sacrifice of captives to the gods, chief among which was Cocijo, who controlled such powerful forces of nature as thunder, lightning, and earthquakes.

The Zapotec dominated the region for hundreds of years, and their kings came to rule most of the territory that comprises the modern nation of Mexico. Their urban centers, which came to include secondary sites at Mitla, San Jose Mogote, and elsewhere, expanded immensely. By 700 there may have been as many as 25,000 people living in and around Monte Alban alone, and the total population of the empire numbered in the hundreds of thousands. It is therefore mystifying that, sometime around 750, people began drifting away from these great urban settlements. By 900, the important central administrative sites of the empire were all but deserted.

Archaeologists have advanced several theories as to why the cities declined. Some argue that the very success of the empire led to its downfall: with the elimination of external threats, the citizens saw no need to rely upon a centralized government for protection. They therefore became unwilling to submit to the ritual demands and taxes imposed upon them by the king and the priesthood. Another theory suggests that the population simply became too large to be supported by the local agricultural system. As the lands surrounding the ceremonial centers became depleted and harvests failed, the people began to move away.

Whatever the reason, by 900, the great urban centers of the Zapotec Empire were all but deserted, leaving the region vulnerable to conquest by outsiders. When a new and powerful group, the Mixtecs, began to challenge the Zapotecs for supremacy sometime after 1300, they encountered little resistance and took over the settlement at Monte Alban. The Mixtec were not powerful enough to achieve total conquest of the Zapotecs, however, and the two peoples learned to coexist. By the early 1500s, both the Mixtecs and the Zapotecs faced a powerful new challenge: The Aztec Empire was making incursions into the region. Perhaps recognizing that defiance would achieve nothing, the Zapotecs made an alliance with this newly emergent power and thus managed to maintain control over important trade routes to civilizations in the south. They paid for this privilege by becoming a subordinate state to the new rulers of the region.

The Zapotecs were less fortunate in facing the next threat: the first Spanish conquerors, who arrived in Mexico in 1519. The Spanish quickly conquered the Aztecs, and the Zapotecs found themselves paying tribute to these new masters. Over the next 200 years, the Zapotec population fell victim to the twin devastations of slave labor and European diseases, to which they had no resistance. By 1720, the Zapotec population had fallen from 450,000 (just prior to the arrival of the Spanish) to a mere 35,000.

See also: AZTEC EMPIRE; MAYA EMPIRE; MIXTEC EMPIRE; OLMEC KINGDOM; TOLTEC EMPIRE.

ZARA YA'IQOB (d. 1468)

Emperor of Ethiopia (r. 1434–1468), famed for his military skills and his great devotion to the Ethiopian Orthodox Church, also known as the Coptic Church.

Zara Ya'iqob was a younger son of Ethiopia's emperor Dawit (r. 1380–1412). As befitted a son of royalty and possible future heir to the throne, he received an extensive education that included a solid grounding in the teachings of the Ethiopian Orthodox Church. Upon Dawit's death in 1412, another of the royal sons, Tewodros (r. 1412–1414), briefly took the throne. Zara Ya'iqob was seen as a potential threat to the new king and was thrown into prison. This act did not secure Tewodros's claim to rule, however. Tewodros was unseated within two years of taking the throne and replaced by another brother, Yeshaq (r. 1414–1429).

During this period, Zara Ya'iqob remained in prison, where he cultivated a life of scholarship and devotion to his faith. When Yeshaq died in 1429, the succession was once again thrown into doubt, and a series of minor rulers reigned for short periods of time. Finally, leaders among the Ethiopian nobility called upon Zara Ya'iqob to become king. It is said that the military brought him out of his prison on the very eve of his accession to the throne.

The religion of his fathers was of highest concern to the new emperor. When Zara Ya'iqob came to the throne, the Ethiopian Orthodox Church was split by disputes over certain religious practices, and these disputes threatened the internal peace of the kingdom. One of Ya'iqob's first acts as emperor was to reconcile a thorny question about which of two days was the true Sabbath. Zara Ya'iqob called a council in

1449, at which he decreed that both Sabbaths be honored, thus appeasing both sides of the dispute.

Although willing to compromise on religious matters to end disputes within his church, Zara Ya'iqob showed far less patience or respect for other religions, including the form of Christianity practiced by the Roman Catholic Church. He actively persecuted those whose faiths differed from his own.

Known for his great erudition, Zara Ya'iqob was also a strong military commander. He created an impressively large and well-trained army, with which he imposed his rule over the kingdom of Ethiopia. Zara Ya'iqob remained committed to scholarship throughout his rule as well. He authored several theological tracts that profoundly shaped the traditions of the Ethiopian Orthodoxy.

In his later years, Zara Ya'iqob retired to a stone castle that he had built at Dabra Berhan, and he rarely ventured forth from its walls. Upon his death in 1468, Zara Ya'iqob was succeeded by one of his sons, Ba'eda Maryam (r. 1468–1478).

See also: GALAWDEWOS; HAILE SELASSIE I; SUSENYOS; TEWODROS II.

FURTHER READING

Tamrat, Taddesse. *Church and State in Ethiopia, 1270–1527*. Oxford: Clarendon Press, 1972.

ZHOU DYNASTY. *See* CHOU DYNASTY

ZIMBABWE KINGDOM, GREAT (ca. 500–1600 C.E.)

Kingdom founded by the Shona people around 500, which is perhaps best known for the vast stone enclosure, built starting in the 1100s, which now lies in ruins in the heart of the modern nation of Zimbabwe (a Shona word meaning "house of rock"). This large and impressive ruin was the capital of a great kingdom.

Around 500, the Bantu-speaking Shona people moved into the region of present-day Zimbabwe from an unknown location and began building settlements. Initially, the Shona settlements grew and prospered on the strength of the local economy. The people tended farms and kept cattle, which served as a symbol of wealth and status.

Zimbabwe's earliest territorial expansion in the sixth and seventh centuries was in service of the cattle herds, as more land was needed to provide pasturage for the growing numbers of livestock. Similarly, Zimbabwe military power was probably devoted mostly to raiding neighbors' herds—cattle stealing being a time-honored way of increasing one's own stock of animals.

By the twelfth century, the people of Zimbabwe discovered that their territory was rich in gold deposits, and this gold promised a new source of wealth. The kingdom was fortuitously located at the head of the Sabi River, the best of several routes by which trade goods could be moved from inland regions to the trading settlements being set up by Arab settlers along the east coast of Africa.

Relations were quickly established with Arab traders at the port of Sofala on the coast. By about 1300, nearly all the gold and ivory traded in southern Africa passed through Zimbabwe, which extracted a tax on every shipment that crossed its borders. The kingdom reached its height as a trading center in the 1300s and 1400s.

The monopolization of access to trade gave Zimbabwe great wealth with which to further increase

The stone ruins of Zimbabwe are one of the most impressive archaeological sites in sub-Saharan Africa. Residence of the Zimbabwean royal court, the enclosure has outer walls measuring 32 feet high and up to 17 feet thick. Built without mortar, the entire Great Zimbabwe complex covers nearly 1,800 acres and includes a number of these conical towers.

its power in the region. Zimbabwe extracted tribute from neighboring settlements, and it enforced its dominance militarily as well. Within the kingdom, the rulers embarked on a series of major construction projects, ordering the creation of stone enclosures, much like the great one in the capital, throughout the Sabi River Valley.

The great stone enclosure of Zimbabwe, now in ruins, once housed the king and his courtiers. Its rooms were richly appointed with gold, copper, and fine gems. Excavation of the ruins has turned up evidence that the Zimbabwean court was cosmopolitan in its taste: goods from as far away as Persia and China have been found there. At the peak of its power in the fourteenth and early fifteenth centuries, Zimbabwe enjoyed a thriving economy, supporting a population of as many as 11,000 by the early 1400s.

The great enclosure of Zimbabwe was mysteriously abandoned around 1450, and the people who lived in the surrounding territory moved on to other lands as well. Over the years, experts have put forward various theories to explain the suddenness of the kingdom's decline. It seems clear today, however, that Great Zimbabwe was abandoned because the land around it had been exhausted of its resources. Farms could no longer produce good crop yields, for the soils were depleted, and gold was becoming scarce.

Given the subsequent history of the region, it is perhaps inaccurate to say that Zimbabwe's influence ended with the abandonment of the great enclosure. Refugees from Zimbabwe relocated to other areas, giving rise to new states that continued the traditions and practices of the original Zimbabwe kingdom. To the south, for example, the Torwa state arose just as Zimbabwe fell, and the new kingdom began building stone enclosures that refined and advanced the techniques of the now defunct Zimbabwe state.

Even more closely related to Zimbabwe was the state of Mutapa, which arose to the north just a few years after the great enclosure of Zimbabwe was abandoned. According to Shona oral tradition, the Mutapa kingdom was founded by Nyatsimbe Mutota, a trusted subject of the Zimbabwe king, who was sent north to find new salt reserves. Finding a rich land, Mutota decided to stay. By 1450, he had gained dominance over the region, and when Zimbabwe was abandoned, many of its former residents moved north to Mutapa.

The Portuguese arrived in the region in the early 1500s and tried to take control first of the coastal trading states and then the inland settlements. Having little success gaining control over the coastal Swahili traders, the Portuguese tried to establish direct contact with the kingdom of Mutapa, the primary successor state to Zimbabwe.

Although the Portuguese succeeded in claiming tribute from smaller local states, Mutapa remained autonomous until about 1623, when it was invaded by the Maravi, powerful neighbors to the northeast. This attack marked the beginning of Mutapa's decline as a regional power, and other states rose to take its place.

See also: AFRICAN KINGDOMS.

ZULU KINGDOM (1815–1879 C.E.)

Kingdom in southern Africa that flourished during the nineteenth century.

SOUTH AFRICAN TRIBAL LIFE

Historically, the Zulu and neighboring Bantu tribes based their livelihood on cattle. Individual clans controlled large swaths of territory, enough to support their livestock with adequate pasturage. By the 1700s, both human and livestock populations were growing too large to be supported by the available land. Zulu clans began to expand their lands to the south, displacing the less powerful Khoi Khoi. South Africa's Cape of Good Hope had been a popular trading stop for European ships since the fourteenth century. In the mid-1700s, however, Dutch, German, and Huguenot settlers (known as the Boers) began to claim lands along the coast and then to encroach deeply into Bantu territory, cutting off normal routes of expansion for the indigenous tribes. This situation led to a crisis for all the cattle-keeping Bantu peoples of the region. The only option available for tribes needing more land was to attack their neighbors. For almost a century, warfare raged across the Bantu lands of southern Africa in what came to be known as the Time of Troubles, or *mfecane* (ca. 1795–1870).

THE ZULU TAKE POWER

The Zulu began as one of many African tribes of herders and farmers. At the beginning of the nine-

teenth century, the Zulu were subordinate to the Nguni king, Dingiswayo. The Zulu chief had a son, Shaka, who was something of a hothead. Shaka and his father fought, and Shaka went to serve in the king's court, joined Dingiswayo's army, and rose rapidly through the ranks. In return for his service, Shaka gained the support of Dingiswayo, who named him Zulu clan chief when Shaka's father died in 1815. Shaka and his clan remained subordinate to Dingiswayo for only a little while, however. Dingiswayo was murdered in 1818, and Shaka seized power over his kingdom. With Dingiswayo's warriors at his disposal, Shaka set to work to transform the army into the most powerful military machine ever seen in the region.

Shaka became the fiercest of all the militaristic leaders in the region. He developed an extraordinarily effective mode of fighting and was ruthless in the devastation he wreaked upon his neighbors, even when those neighbors were members of his own Zulu clan. In addition to the traditional throwing spear, Shaka equipped his soldiers with a new shorter spear that gave them an advantage in close combat. He also refined the horn formation battle tactic that allowed the Zulu to surround their enemies.

Shaka's violent campaign was not merely destructive, however. Although he ordered his armies to raze the villages they attacked, and although he was more than willing to slaughter the villagers, he also recruited likely young warriors into his armies, even if that recruitment was more often than not based on coercion. It was by this process of forced recruitment and ever-expanding war that Shaka built up the largest kingdom in the region.

By the mid-1820s, Shaka had a standing army of more than 40,000 soldiers and more than 100,000 people under his rule. Military service was required of all men, and they could not marry until their service was over. Military units were placed throughout the kingdom to ensure Shaka's orders were carried out, but the ultimate power remained in the hands of the king and his court.

ZULU NATIONALISM

Although often brutal in war, Shaka instilled in his people a sense of pride in their traditions. Individuals captured in battle became members of the Zulu kingdom and promised allegiance to the king. Zulu ceremonial and religious traditions became the traditions of the state. During planting and harvesting celebrations, Shaka used the large gatherings of people to further inculcate them with the virtues of the Zulu state. Thus, Shaka was able to unite people from many tribal lines into the Zulu nation.

RIVALS AND REFUGEES

Although the largest and arguably the most powerful kingdom in the region, by the mid-1800s, the Zulu kingdom was one of several militaristic monarchies in southern Africa. The upheaval in Zululand was mirrored in areas as far north as Lake Tanganyika. From among Shaka's own generals, rivals to his power soon arose; for example, Mzilikazi decided not to return after a raid, keeping his cattle and his troops to start his own Ndebele kingdom. Similarly, another of Shaka's subordinates, Zwangendaba, headed north with his regiment to found the Ngoni kingdom and in the process destroyed what was left of the once great kingdom of Zimbabwe.

With all these armies on the march, the entire region was thrown into turmoil, and thousands upon thousands of people became refugees fleeing the violence, settling wherever they could find a king or other leader who was strong enough to provide them with some degree of protection. Thus, the formation of the Zulu kingdom was part of a much larger process of rapid state formation in the region.

THE ZULU AFTER SHAKA

The Zulu kingdom was very much the creation of a single man, Shaka, but he ruled for only ten years. Shaka's son, Dingane, and other conspirators assassinated him in 1828. Dingane (r. 1828–1840) proclaimed himself Shaka's successor, but he was not up to the task. Less capable in military matters than his father, which was after all the basis for the Zulu state, he could not sustain his father's exploits for long. Nor could he stem the tide of Boers, who were on the march north and claiming vast tracts of land for their own settlements. Better armed and with better

leadership, the Boers soon clashed with Dingane's troops. For a while, the Zulus managed to hold their own in this contest, but internal strife in 1840 erupted into civil war in which Dingane was killed. He was succeeded by his brother, Mpande, (r. 1840–1872), who gradually left behind the fierce militarism of Shaka's era. Nonetheless, the kingdom was under constant pressure from the Boers, who wanted their land, and the British, who wanted the wealth of minerals, including gold and diamonds that had been found in the region.

Mpande was succeeded by Cetshwayo (r. 1872–1879). The Zulu faced ever-increasing pressure from the British, who dreamed of controlling the entire region and thus its vast resources. In January of 1872, Cetshwayo sent his entire army against British forces who had come to conquer, and it seemed for a time that this would be enough. The Zulu were resoundingly victorious. The British came back, however, and, although it took eight months, they captured Cetshwayo and defeated the Zulu army. To avoid the possibility of uprisings in their newly conquered territory, the British broke the kingdom up into factions and let factional squabbling take care of the rest. By 1879, the once great Zulu kingdom was no more.

See also: CETSHWAYO; DINGISWAYO; MZILIKAZI; NDEBELE KINGDOM; SHAKA ZULU.

FURTHER READING

Gump, James Oliver. *The Formation of the Zulu Kingdom in South Africa: 1750–1840.* San Francisco: E. Mellen Press, 1990.

Oliver, Roland, and Anthony Atmore. *Africa Since 1800.* 5th ed. New York: Cambridge University Press, 2004.

Parsons, Neil. *A New History of Southern Africa,* 2nd ed. New York: Holmes & Meier, 1994.

Shillington, Kevin. *A History of Africa.* New York: St. Martin's Press, 1989.

BIBLIOGRAPHY

Acton, Harold. *The Bourbons of Naples*. New York: Barnes & Noble, 1974.

Adams, Richard E. W. *Prehistoric Mesoamerica*. Norman: University of Oklahoma Press, 1996.

Adams, Robert M. *The Evolution of Urban Society: Early Mesopotamia and Prehispanic Mexico*. Chicago: Aldine, 1971.

Adams, William Howard. *Nature Perfected: Gardens Through History*. New York: Abbeville Press, 1991.

Ahir, D. C. *Asoka the Great*. Delhi: B. R. Publishing, 1995.

Ajayi, J.F.A., and Michael Crowder, eds. *History of West Africa*. 2nd ed. New York: Columbia University Press, 1976.

Al-Azmeh, Aziz. *Muslim Kingship: Power and the Sacred in Muslim, Christian, and Pagan Polities*. New York: Tauris, 2001.

Alcock, Leslie. *Arthur's Britain: History and Archaeology, 367–634*. New York: Penguin, 2001.

Allan, John Andrew, Wolseley T. Haig, and Henry Dodwell. *The Cambridge Shorter History of India*. New York: Macmillan, 1934.

Allison, Ronald. *The Queen: 50 Years—A Celebration*. London: HarperCollins, 2001.

Ames, Glenn J. *Renascent Empire? The House of Braganza and the Quest for Stability in Portuguese Monsoon Asia, ca. 1640–1683*. Amsterdam: Amsterdam University Press, 2000.

Andaya, Barbara Watson. *Perak, the Abode of Grace: A Study of an Eighteenth-Century Malay State*. New York: Oxford University Press, 1979.

Anderson, Benedict. *Imagined Communities: Reflections on the Origins and Spread of Nationalism*. New York: Verso, 1991.

Anderson, James M. *The History of Portugal*. Westport, CT: Greenwood Press, 2000.

Anderson, M. S. *Peter the Great*. 2nd ed. New York: Longman, 2000.

———. *The Rise of Modern Diplomacy, 1450–1919*. New York: Longman, 1993.

Anderson, Mary M. *Hidden Power: The Palace Eunuchs of Imperial China*. Buffalo, NY: Prometheus Books, 1990.

Andersson, Ingvar. *A History of Sweden*. Trans. Carolyn Hannay. Westport, CT: Greenwood Press, 1975.

Anglo-Saxon Chronicle, The. Trans. and ed. George Norman Garmonsway. Rutland, VT: Tuttle, 1994.

Anglo, Sydney. *Images of Tudor Kingship*. London: Seaby, 1992.

Angold, Michael. *The Byzantine Empire 1025–1204: A Political History*. New York: Longman, 1984.

Anna, Timothy E. *The Mexican Empire of Iturbide*. Lincoln: University of Nebraska Press, 1990.

'Arawi, Abd Allah. *History of the Maghreb: An Interpretive Essay*. Trans. Ralph Manheim. Princeton, NJ: Princeton University Press, 1977.

Archibald, Z. H. *The Odrysian Kingdom of Thrace: Orpheus Unmasked*. New York: Oxford University Press, 1998.

Aristotle. *Politics*. New York: Dover Publishing, 2000.

Armajani, Yahya, and Thomas M. Ricks. *Middle East Past and Present*. 2nd ed. Englewood Cliffs, NJ: Prentice Hall, 1986.

Armstrong, Karen. *Jerusalem: One City, Three Faiths*. New York: Ballantine, 1997.

Arnold, Margot. *Queen Consorts of England: The Power Behind the Throne*. New York: Facts on File, 1993.

Ashe, Geoffrey. *Kings and Queens of Early Britain*. Chicago: Academy Chicago, 1998.

Ashley, James R. *The Macedonian Empire: The Era of Warfare Under Philip II and Alexander the Great, 359–323 B.C.* Jefferson, NC: McFarland, 1998.

Ashley, Maurice. *Great Britain to 1688*. Ed. Allan Nevins and Howard M. Ehrmann. Ann Arbor: University of Michigan Press, 1961.

———. *The House of Stuart: Its Rise and Fall*. London: Dent, 1980.

———. *James II*. Minneapolis: University of Minnesota Press, 1977.

Asimov, Isaac. *The Near East: 10,000 Years of History*. Boston: Houghton Mifflin, 1968.

Asprey, Robert. *The Reign of Napoleon Bonaparte*. New York: Basic Books, 2001.

Auboyer, Jeannine. *Daily Life in Ancient India from 200 B.C. to 700 A.D.* London: Phoenix, 2002.

Augustin, Byron. *United Arab Emirates*. New York: Children's Press, 2002.

Aung-Thwin, Michael. *Pagan: The Origins of Modern Burma*. Honolulu: University of Hawaii Press, 1985.

Aylen, Leo. *The Greek Theater*. Rutherford, NJ: Fairleigh Dickinson University Press, 1985.

Bachrach, Bernard S. *State-Building in Medieval France: Studies in Early Angevin History*. Brookfield, VT: Variorum, 1995.

Baines, John, and Jaromìr Málek. *Atlas of Ancient Egypt*. New York: Facts on File, 1996.

Bak, János M., ed. *Coronations: Medieval and Early Modern Monarchic Ritual*. Berkeley: University of California Press, 1990.

Barasch, Moshe. *Imago Hominis: Studies in the Language of Art*. New York: New York University Press, 1994.

Barlow, Frank. *Edward the Confessor*. New ed. New Haven, CT: Yale University Press, 1997.

———. *William Rufus*. New Haven, CT: Yale University Press, 2000.

Barraclough, Geoffrey. *Crucible of Europe: The Ninth and Tenth Centuries in European History*. Berkeley: University of California Press, 1976.

———. *Origins of Modern Germany*. 3rd ed. Oxford: Basil Blackwell, 1988.

Bartlett, Robert. *England Under the Norman and Angevin Kings, 1075–1225*. New York: Oxford University Press, 2000.

Basak, Radhagovinda. *The History of North-eastern India Extending from the Foundation of the Gupta Empire to the Rise of the Pala Dynasty of Bengal (c. 320–760 A.D.)*. London: K. Paul Trench, Trubner & Co, 1934.

Basham, A. L. *The Wonder That Was India: A Survey of the History and Culture of the Indian Subcontinent Before the Coming of the Muslims*. 3rd rev. ed. New York: Taplinger, 1968.

Bauer, Brian S. *The Development of the Inca State*. Austin: University of Texas Press, 1992.

Beattie, John. *Bunyoro: An African Kingdom*. Fort Worth, TX: Holt, Rinehart & Winston, 1988.

Beaverbrook, Max Aitken. *The Abdication of King Edward VIII*. New York: Atheneum, 1966.

Beckwith, Carol, and Angela Fisher. *African Ceremonies*. New York: Abrams, 1999.

Bede the Venerable. *A History of the English Church and People*. Trans. Leo Shirley-Price. New York: Barnes & Noble, 1993.

Behr, Edward. *The Last Emperor*. New York: Bantam Books, 1987.

Benard, Elisabeth, and Beverly Moon. *Goddesses Who Rule*. New York: Oxford University Press, 2000.

Benn, Charles D. *Daily Life in Traditional China: The Tang Dynasty*. Westport, CT: Greenwood Press, 2002.

Benson, Leslie. *Yugoslavia: A Concise History*. New York: Palgrave Macmillan, 2003.

Berger, Patricia. *Empire of Emptiness: Buddhist Art and Political Authority in Qing China*. Honolulu: University of Hawaii Press, 2003.

Bergeron, David M. *Royal Family, Royal Lovers: King James of England and Scotland*. Columbia: University of Missouri Press, 1991.

Bernard, Paul B. *Joseph II*. New York: Twayne, 1968.

Bernardy, Françoise de. *Princes of Monaco: The Remarkable History of the Grimaldi Family*. London: A. Barker, 1961.

Bertelli, Sergio. *The King's Body: Sacred Rituals of Power in Medieval and Early Modern Europe*. Trans. R. Burr Litchfield. University Park: Pennsylvania State University Press, 2001.

Bettelheim, Bruno. *The Uses of Enchantment: The Meaning and Importance of Fairy Tales*. New York: Alfred A. Knopf, 1991.

Bhatia, Pratipal. *The Paramaras, c. 800–1305 A.D.* New Delhi: Munshiram Manoharlal, 1970.

Bingham, Woodbridge. *The Founding of the T'ang Dynasty: The Fall of Sui and the Rise of T'ang, A Preliminary Survey*. New York: Octagon Books, 1975.

Birley, Anthony Richard. *Hadrian, the Restless Emperor*. New York: Routledge, 2000.

———. *Marcus Aurelius: A Biography*. New York: Barnes & Noble, 1999.

Birmingham, David. *A Concise History of Portugal*. New York: Cambridge University Press, 1993.

Birn, Raymond. *Crisis, Absolutism, Revolution: Europe, 1648–1789*. Fort Worth, TX: Harcourt Brace Jovanovich, 1992.

Bix, Herbert. *Hirohito and the Making of Modern Japan*. New York: HarperCollins, 2000.

Black, Antony. *The History of Islamic Political Thought: From the Prophet to the Present*. New York: Routledge, 2001.

Black, Jeremy. *A New History of England*. Stroud, Gloucestershire: Sutton, 2000.

Bled, Jean-Paul. *Franz Joseph*. Trans. Teresa Bridgeman. Cambridge, MA: Blackwell, 1992.

Bloch, Marc. *Feudal Society*. New York: Routledge, 1989.

———. *The Royal Touch, Monarchy and Miracles in France and England*. Trans. J. E. Anderson. New York: Dorset Press, 1990.

Blöndal, Sigfús. *The Varangians of Byzantium: An Aspect*

of Byzantine Military History. Trans. Benedikt S. Benedikz. New York: Cambridge University Press, 1978.

Bluche, François. *Louis XIV.* New York: Watts, 1990.

Bluhm, William T. *Theories of the Political System. Classics of Political Thought and Modern Political Analysis.* 3rd ed. Englewood Cliffs, NJ: Prentice Hall, 1978.

Blunden, Carolina, and Mark Elvin. *Cultural Atlas of China.* New York: Checkmark Books, 1998.

Boardman, John, Jasper Griffin, and Oswyn Murray. *The Oxford History of the Classical World.* New York: Oxford University Press, 1988.

Bombay Subaltern, A. *History of Mandu: The Ancient Capital of Malwa.* Bombay: Education Society's Press, Byculla, 1879.

Bonner, Philip L. *Kings, Commoners, and Concessionaires: The Evolution and Devolution of the Nineteenth-Century Swazi State.* New York: Cambridge University Press, 1983.

Bonney, Richard. *The European Dynastic States: 1494–1660.* New York: Oxford University Press, 1991.

Boose, Donald W., and Richard A. Gabriel. *The Great Battles of Antiquity: A Strategic and Tactical Guide to Great Battles That Shaped the Development of War.* Westport, CT: Greenwood Press, 1994.

Bossuet, Jacques-Bénigne. *Politics Drawn from the Very Words of Holy Scripture.* Trans. and ed. Patrick Riley. New York: Cambridge University Press, 1990.

Botsford, George Willis. *A History of Greece for High Schools and Academies.* New York: Macmillan, 1917.

Bournoutian, George. *A History of the Armenian People.* Costa Mesa, CA: Mazda Publishers, 1994.

Boussard, Jacques. *The Civilization of Charlemagne.* New York: McGraw-Hill, 1976.

Bowle, John. *Charles I: A Biography.* Boston: Little, Brown, 1976.

Bowring, Richard, and Peter Kornicki, eds. *The Cambridge Encyclopedia of Japan.* New York: Cambridge University Press, 1993.

Braswell, George W. *Understanding World Religions: Hinduism, Buddhism, Taoism, Confucianism, Judaism, Islam.* Nashville, TN: Broadman & Holman, 1994.

Braude, Benjamin, and Bernard Lewis. *Christians and Jews in the Ottoman Empire: The Functioning of a Plural Society.* New York: Holmes & Meier, 1982.

Breasted, James H. *A History of Egypt from the Earliest Times to the Persian Conquest.* New York: Bantam Books, 1964.

Brendel, Otto, and Francesca R. Serra Ridgway. *Etruscan Art.* New Haven, CT: Yale University Press, 1995.

Brendon, Piers, and Phillip Whitehead. *The Windsors: A Dynasty Revealed 1917–2000.* London: Pimlico, 2001.

Brenner, Louis. *Shehus of Kukawa: A History of the al-Kanemi Dynasty of Bornu.* Oxford: Clarendon Press, 1973.

Briggs, Lawrence Palmer. *The Ancient Khmer Empire.* Philadelphia: American Philosophical Society, 1974.

Brion, Marcel. *Alaric the Goth.* Trans. Frederick H. Martens. New York: R. M. McBride, 1930.

Broers, Michael. *Napoleonic Imperialism and the Savoyard Monarchy, 1773–1821: State Building in Piedmont.* Lewiston, NY: Mellen, 1997.

Brookes, John. *Gardens of Paradise: The History and Design of the Great Islamic Gardens.* New York: New Amsterdam, 1987.

Brown, Roslind Varghese. *Tunisia.* New York: Marshall Cavendish, 1999.

Browning, Robert. *The Byzantine Empire.* Rev. ed. Washington, DC: Catholic University of America Press, 1992.

—————. *Justinian and Theodora.* New York: Thames and Hudson, 1987.

Bryce, Trevor. *The Kingdom of the Hittites.* New York: Oxford University Press, 1998.

Bugbee, Bruce W. *Genesis of the American Patent and Copyright Law.* Washington, DC: Public Affairs Press, 1967.

Bukdahl, Jørgen, et al. *Scandinavia Past and Present: From the Viking Age to Absolute Monarchy.* Odense, Denmark: Arnkrone, 1959.

Bulei, Ion. *A Short History of Romania.* 2nd ed. Bucharest: Meronia Publishers, 1998.

Bullough, Vern L., and Bonnie Bullough. *Cross Dressing, Sex, and Gender.* Philadelphia: University of Pennsylvania Press, 1993.

Bunnens, Guy, ed. *Essays on Syria in the Iron Age.* Sterling, VA: Peeters Press, 2000.

Burney, Charles. *The Ancient Near East.* Ithaca, NY: Cornell University Press, 1977.

Butler, Ewan. *The Horizon Concise History of Scandinavia.* New York: American Heritage, 1973.

Byrne, Francis John. *Irish Kings and High-Kings.* 2nd ed. Portland, OR: Four Courts Press, 2001.

Cadogan, Gerald. *Palaces of Minoan Crete.* New York: Routledge, 1991.

Cady, John F. *Southeast Asia: Its Historical Development.* New York: McGraw-Hill, 1976.

Campbell, James, Eric John, and Patrick Wormald. *The Anglo-Saxons.* New York: Penguin, 1991.

Cannadine, David, and Simon Price, eds. *Rituals of Royalty: Power and Ceremonial in Traditional Societies.* New York: Cambridge University Press, 1992.

Cantor, Norman F. *The Civilization of the Middle Ages.* New York: HarperCollins, 1993.

Caraman, Philip. *The Lost Empire: The Story of the Jesuits in Ethiopia, 1555–1634.* Notre Dame, IN: University of Notre Dame Press, 1985.

Carey, Hilary M. *Courting Disaster: Astrology at the English Court and University in the Later Middle Ages.* New York: St. Martin's Press, 1992.

Carlin, Norah. *The Causes of the English Civil War.* Malden, MA: Blackwell, 1999.

Carneiro, Robert L. *A Theory of the Origin of the State.* Menlo Park, CA: Institute for Human Studies, 1977.

Carr, Raymond. *Spain, 1808–1975.* Oxford: Clarendon Press, 1982.

Carrère d'Encausse, Hélène. *Nicholas II: The Interrupted Transition.* Trans. George Holoch. New York: Holmes & Meier, 2000.

Cassin, Elena, Jean Bottéro, and Jean Vercoutter, eds. *The Near East: The Early Civilizations.* New York: Delacorte Press, 1967.

Casson, Lionel. *Ancient Egypt.* Alexandria, VA: Time-Life Books, 1978.

Casson, Stanley. *Macedonia, Thrace and Illyria; Their Relations to Greece from the Earliest Times Down to the Time of Philip Son of Amyntas.* Westport, CT: Greenwood Press, 1971.

Castleden, Rodney. "People and Life in Minoan Crete." In *Ancient Civilizations,* vol. 1, ed. Don Nardo. San Diego: Greenhaven Press, 2000.

———. *Minoans: Life in Bronze Age Crete.* New York: Routledge, 1993.

Caton, Mary Anne. *Fooles and Fricassees: Food in Shakespeare's England.* Washington, DC: The Folger Shakespeare Library, 1999.

Cavendish, Richard. *The Great Religions.* New York: Arco, 1980.

Ceram, C. W. *The Secret of the Hittites: The Discovery of an Ancient Empire.* New York: Dorset Press, 1990.

Chandler, David. *History of Cambodia.* 3rd ed. Boulder, CO: Westview Press, 2000.

Chapuis, Oscar. *The Last Emperors of Vietnam: From Tu Duc to Bao Dai.* Westport, CT: Greenwood Press, 2000.

Cheesman, Clive, and Jonathan Williams. *Rebels, Pretenders and Impostors.* New York: St. Martin's Press, 2000.

Cheetham, Anthony. *The Life and Times of Richard III.* New York: Welcome Rain Publishers, 1998.

Ching, Julia. *Mysticism and Kingship in China: The Heart of Chinese Wisdom.* New York: Cambridge University Press, 1997.

Chirenje, J. Mutero. *Chief Kgama and His Times, c. 1835–1923: The Story of a Southern African Ruler.* London: R. Collings, 1978.

Chrétien de Troyes. *The Complete Romances of Chrétien de Troyes.* Bloomington: Indiana University Press, 1993.

Christian, David. *Imperial and Soviet Russia.* New York: St. Martin's Press, 1997.

Chu, Daniel, and Elliot P. Skinner. *A Glorious Age in Africa: The Story of Three Great African Empires.* Trenton, NJ: Africa World Press, 1990.

Clark, Christopher. *Kaiser Wilhelm II.* New York: Longman, 2000.

Clark, Stuart. *Thinking with Demons: The Idea of Witchcraft in Early Modern Europe.* New York: Oxford University Press, 1999.

Clayton, Peter. *Chronicle of the Pharaohs.* New York: Thames & Hudson, 2001.

Coe, Michael D. *The Aztecs.* Norman: University of Oklahoma Press, 1973.

———. *The Maya.* 6th ed. New York: Thames & Hudson, 1999.

Coedés, George. *Angkor: An Introduction.* New York: Oxford University Press, 1970.

———. *The Indianized States of Southeast Asia.* Ed. Walter F. Vella; trans. Susan Brown Cowing. Canberra: Australian National University Press, 1975.

Cohen, Ronald. *The Kanuri of Bornu.* New York: Holt, Rinehart & Winston, 1967.

Collcutt, Martin, Marius Jansen, and Isai Kumakura. *Cultural Atlas of Japan.* New York: Facts on File, 1988.

Collins, James. *The State in Early Modern France.* New York: Cambridge University Press, 1999.

Collins, Roger. *The Basques.* 2nd ed. Cambridge, MA: Basil Blackwell, 1990.

———. *Early Medieval Spain: Unity in Diversity, 400–1000.* 2nd ed. New York: St. Martin's Press, 1995.

Comay, Joan. *The Hebrew Kings.* New York: William Morrow, 1977.

Comnena, Anna. *The Alexiad of Anna Comnena: Being a History of the Reign of Her Father, Alexis I, Emperor of the Romans, 1081–1118 A.D.* Trans. Elizabeth A. S. Dawes. New York: Kegan Paul, 2003.

Congressional Quarterly, Inc. *The Middle East.* 9th ed. Washington, DC: CQ Press, 2000.

Conrad, Geoffrey W., and Arthur Andrew Demarest. *Religion and Empire: The Dynamics of Aztec and Inca Expansionism.* New York: Cambridge University Press, 1984.

Conti, Flavio. *Homes of Kings.* Trans. Patrick Creagh. New York: HBJ Press, 1978.

Cook, J. M. *The Persian Empire.* New York: Barnes & Noble, 1993.

Cope, Christopher. *Phoenix Frustrated: The Lost Kingdom of Burgundy.* New York: Dodd, Mead, 1987.

Coquet, Michèle. *African Royal Court Art.* Trans. Jane Marie Todd. Chicago: University of Chicago Press, 1998.

Costa, Emilia Viotti da. *The Brazilian Empire: Myths and Histories.* Rev. ed. Chapel Hill: University of North Carolina Press, 2000.

Costain, Thomas. *A History of the Plantagenets.* 4 vols. Cutchogue, NY: Buccaneer Books, 1994.

Craig, Albert M., et al. *The Heritage of World Civilizations.* 6th ed. Upper Saddle River, NJ: Prentice Hall, 2003.

Crankshaw, Edward. *The Fall of the House of Hapsburg.* New York: Penguin, 1983.

———. *Maria Theresa.* New York: Atheneum, 1986.

———. *The Shadow of the Winter Palace: Russia's Drift to Revolution, 1825–1917.* New York: Da Capo Press, 2000.

Cressy, David. *Birth, Marriage and Death: Ritual, Religion and the Life Cycle in Tudor and Stuart England.* New York: Oxford University Press 1999.

Croutier, Alev Lytle. *Harem: The World Behind the Veil.* New York: Abbeville Press, 1989.

Cuming, G. J. *A History of Anglican Liturgy.* 2nd ed. New York: St. Martin's Press, 1969.

Cunningham, Michelle. *Mexico and the Foreign Policy of Napoleon III.* New York: Palgrave, 2001.

Curtis, Edmund. *A History of Medieval Ireland from 1086 to 1513.* New York: Barnes & Noble, 1968.

Dagens, Bruno. *Angkor: Heart of an Asian Empire.* New York: Abrams, 1995.

Dako, Christo A. *Zogu, the First, King of the Albanians: A Sketch of His Life and Times.* Tirana, Albania: K. Luarasi Printing Press, 1937.

Daniel, Elton L. *The History of Iran.* Westport, CT: Greenwood Press, 2001.

Dann, Uriel. *King Hussein and the Challenge of Arab Radicalism: Jordan 1955–1967.* New York: Oxford University Press, 1991.

———. *King Hussein's Strategy of Survival.* Washington, DC: Washington Institute for Near East Policy, 1992.

David, A. Rosalie. *Discovering Ancient Egypt.* New York: Facts on File, 1994.

Davies, Glyn. *A History of Money from Ancient Times to the Present Day.* 3rd rev. ed. Cardiff: University of Wales Press, 2002.

Davies, Nigel. *The Ancient Kingdoms of Mexico.* New York: Penguin, 1990.

Davies, Norman. *Europe: A History.* New York: HarperPerennial, 1998.

———. *God's Playground: A History of Poland.* New York: Columbia University Press, 1982.

Davis, R. H. C. *A History of Medieval Europe: From Constantine to Saint Louis.* 2nd ed. New York: Longman, 2000.

Daws, Gavan. *Shoal of Time: A History of the Hawaiian Islands.* New York: Macmillan, 1974.

Day, Upendra Nath. *Medieval Malwa: A Political and Cultural History.* Delhi: Munshi Ram Manohar Lal, 1965.

Decaux, Alain. *Monaco and Its Princes: Seven Centuries of History.* Paris: Perrin, 1997.

"The Declaration of Right." (February 1689). In J. H. Robinson, ed. *Readings in European History.* Boston: Ginn, 1906.

Denieul-Cormier, Anne. *Wise and Foolish Kings: The First House of Valois 1328–1498.* Garden City, NY: Doubleday, 1980.

Desai, Vishakha N., B. N. Goswamy, and Ainslie T. Embree. *Life at Court: Art for India's Rulers, 16th–19th Centuries.* Boston: Museum of Fine Arts, 1985.

Di Scala, Spencer M. *Italy: From Revolution to Republic: 1700 to the Present.* 3rd ed. Boulder, CO: Westview Press, 2004.

Diamond, Jared. *Germs, Guns, and Steel: The Fates of Human Societies.* New York: W. W. Norton, 2003.

Dijkstra, Henk, ed. *History of the Ancient & Medieval World: Egypt and Mesopotamia.* New York: Marshall Cavendish, 1996.

Dix, Gregory. *The Shape of the Liturgy.* New York: Continuum, 2001.

Douglas, David C. *William the Conqueror: The Norman*

Impact upon England. New Haven, CT: Yale University Press, 1999.

Douglas-Home, Charles. *Dignified & Efficient: The British Monarchy in the Twentieth Century.* Brinkworth, Wilts, UK: Claridge Press, 2000.

Drekmeier, Charles. *Kingship and Community in Early India.* Stanford, CA: Stanford University Press, 1962.

Drucker-Brown, Susan. *Ritual Aspects of the Mamprusi Kingship.* Leiden: Afrika-Studiecentrum, 1975.

Duby, Georges. *France in the Middle Ages, 987–1460: From Hugh Capet to Joan of Arc.* Trans. Juliet Vale. Cambridge, MA: Basil Blackwell, 1996.

Duby, Georges, and Robert Mandrou. *A History of French Civilization: From the Year 1000 to the Present.* Trans. James Blakely Atkinson. New York: Random House, 1964.

Duff, Mabel. *The Chronology of Indian History: From the Earliest Times to the 16th Century.* Delhi: Cosmo Publications, 1972.

Duffy, James P., and Vincent L. Ricci. *Czars: Russia's Rulers for More Than One Thousand Years.* New York: Barnes & Noble, 2002.

Dunbabin, Jean. *France in the Making 843–1180.* New York: Oxford University Press, 2000.

Durant, Will, and Ariel Durant. *The Story of Civilization.* New York: Simon & Schuster, 1935.

Duus, Peter, ed. *The Cambridge History of Japan.* Cambridge: Cambridge University Press, 1988.

Dyer, T. F. Thiselton. *Royalty in All Ages: The Amusements, Eccentricities, Accomplishments, Superstitions, and Frolics of the Kings and Queens of Europe.* New York: Scribner, 1903.

Ebrey, Patricia Buckley. *The Cambridge Illustrated History of China.* New York: Cambridge University Press, 1999.

———. "The Interaction of Yin and Yang." In *Chinese Civilization and Society: A Sourcebook.* New York: Free Press, 1981.

Eckert, Carter J., et al. *Korea Old and New.* Cambridge, MA: Harvard University Press, 1990.

Edwards, I.E.S., C. J. Gadd, and N.G.L. Hammond, eds. *The Cambridge Ancient History.* New York: Cambridge University Press, 1977.

Eliade, Mircea. *Patterns in Comparative Religion.* Trans. Rosemary Sheed. Lincoln: University of Nebraska Press, 1996.

Ellis, Peter Beresford. *Erin's Blood Royal: The Gaelic Noble Dynasties of Ireland.* New York: Palgrave Macmillan, 2002.

Ellwood, Robert S. *The Feast of Kingship: Accession Ceremonies in Ancient Japan.* Tokyo: Sophia University, 1973.

———. *Many Peoples, Many Faiths.* 7th ed. Upper Saddle River, NJ: Prentice Hall, 2002.

Embree, Ainslie, ed. *Encyclopedia of Asian History.* New York: Scribner, 1988.

Engel, David M. *Law and Kingship in Thailand During the Reign of King Chulalongkorn.* Ann Arbor: Center for South and Southeast Asian Studies, University of Michigan, 1975.

Engnell, Ivan. *Studies in Divine Kingship in the Ancient Near East.* Oxford: Basil Blackwell, 1967.

Erasmus, Desiderius. *Education of a Christian Prince.* Trans. Neil M. Cheshire and Michael J. Heath. New York: Cambridge University Press, 1997.

Erickson, Carolly. *Alexandra: The Last Tsarina.* New York: St. Martin's Griffin, 2002.

———. *Bloody Mary.* New York: St. Martin's Press, 1998.

———. *To the Scaffold: The Life of Marie Antoinette.* New York: William Morrow, 1992.

Esposito, John L. *Islam and Politics.* 4th ed. Syracuse, NY: Syracuse University Press, 1998.

Evans-Pritchard, Edward E. *Divine Kingship of the Shilluk of the Nilotic Sudan.* Cambridge: Cambridge University Press, 1948.

———. *The Political System of the Anuak of the Anglo-Egyptian Sudan.* New York: AMS Press, 1977.

———. *Witchcraft, Oracles and Magic Among the Azande.* Oxford: Clarendon Press, 1968.

Fairbank, John King. *China: A New History.* Enlarged ed. Cambridge, MA: Belknap Press of Harvard University Press, 1992.

Fawtier, R. *The Capetian Kings of France: Monarchy and Nation 967–1328.* New York: St. Martin's Press, 1969.

Faxian. *The Travels of Fa-hsien (ca. A.D. 399–414), or, Record of the Buddhistic Kingdoms.* Trans. Herbert Allen Giles. Westport, CT: Greenwood Press, 1981.

Feigin, Samuel I. *Legal and Administrative Texts of the Reign of Samsu-iluna.* New Haven, CT: Yale University Press, 1979.

Fenton, William N. *The Great Law and the Longhouse: A Political History of the Iroquois Confederacy.* Norman: University of Oklahoma Press, 1998.

Fichtenau, H. *The Carolinigian Empire.* New York: Harper & Row, 1964.

Figgis, John Neville. *The Divine Right of Kings.* Gloucester, MA: P. Smith, 1970.

Finer, S. E. *The History of Government from the Earliest Times.* New York: Oxford University Press, 1997.

Fischer-Lichte, Erika. *History of European Drama and Theatre.* New York: Routledge, 2002.

Fisher, Sydney Nettleton, and William Ochsenwald. *The Middle East: A History.* 6th ed. Boston: McGraw-Hill, 2004.

Fletcher, Richard. *Moorish Spain.* Berkeley: University of California Press, 1993.

Fol, Aleksandur, and Ivan Marazov. *Thrace & the Thracians.* Trans. Nevyana Zhelyaskova. New York: St. Martin's Press, 1977.

Fouracre, Paul. *The Age of Charles Martel.* New York: Longman, 2000.

Fowler, Ian, and David Zeitlyn, eds. *African Crossroads: Intersections Between History and Anthropology in Cameroon.* Providence, RI: Berghahn Books, 1996.

Franz, Marie-Luise von. *An Introduction to the Psychology of Fairy Tales.* Irving, TX: Spring Publications, 1978.

Fraser, Antonia. *King James VI of Scotland, I of England.* New York: Alfred A. Knopf, 1975.

———. *Mary Queen of Scots.* New York: Delta Trade Paperbacks, 2001.

———. *Royal Charles: Charles II and the Restoration.* New York: Dell, 1980.

Frazer, Sir James George. *The Golden Bough: A Study in Magic and Religion.* Abridged ed. Mineola, NY: Dover Publications, 2002.

Freemann, Charles. *The Greek Achievement.* New York. Viking, 1999.

Freestone, Basil. *Osei Tutu: The Leopard Owns the Land.* London: Dobson, 1968.

Freeze, Gregory L., ed. *Russia: A History.* New York: Oxford University Press, 1997.

Freyre, Gilberto. *Order and Progress: Brazil from Monarchy to Republic.* Trans. Rod W. Horton. Berkeley: University of California Press, 1986.

Frye, Richard Nelson. *Islamic Iran and Central Asia (7th–12th Centuries).* London: Variorum, 1979.

Fuhrmann, Horst. *Germany in the High Middle Ages, c. 1050–1200.* Trans. Timothy Reuter. New York: Cambridge University Press, 1992.

Fujitani, T. *Splendid Monarchy: Power and Pageantry in Modern Japan.* Berkeley: University of California Press, 1996.

Gaekwad, Fatehsinhrao P. *Sayajirao of Baroda.* London: Sangam, 1989.

Gager, John G., ed. *Curse Tablets and Binding Spells from the Ancient World.* New York: Oxford University Press, 1999.

Galliou, Patrick, and Michael Jones. *The Bretons.* Cambridge, MA: Basil Blackwell, 1996.

Ganshof, F. L. *The Carolingians and the Frankish Monarchy.* Ithaca, NY: Cornell University Press, 1971.

Gardiner, Alan Henderson. *Egypt of the Pharaohs.* Oxford: Clarendon Press, 1961.

Gerutis, Albertas, ed. *Lithuania 700 Years.* Trans. Algirdas Budreckis. 6th ed. New York: Manyland Books, 1984.

Gesick, Lorraine, and Michael Aung-Thwin, eds. *Centers, Symbols and Hierarchies: Essays on the Classical States of Southeast Asia.* New Haven, CT: Yale University Southeast Asian Studies, 1983.

Gillingham, John. *The Angevin Empire.* 2nd ed. New York: Oxford University Press, 2001.

———. *Richard Coeur de Lion: Kingship, Chivalry and War in the Twelfth Century.* Rio Grande, OH: Hambledon Press, 1994.

———. *The Wars of the Roses: Peace and Conflict in Fifteenth-Century England.* Baton Rouge: Louisiana State University Press, 1981.

Gillis, John, R. ed. *Commemorations: The Politics of National Identity.* Princeton, NJ: Princeton University Press, 1994.

Giurescu, Constantin C., et al. *Chronological History of Romania.* 2nd ed. Bucharest: Editura enciclopedica română, 1974.

Glatt, John. *The Royal House of Monaco: Dynasty of Glamour, Tragedy and Scandal.* New York: St. Martin's Press, 2000.

Gluckman, Max. *Essays on Lozi Land and Royal Property.* Manchester, England: Manchester University Press, 1968.

Golding, Brian. *Conquest and Colonisation: The Normans in Britain, 1066–1100.* New York: Palgrave, 2001.

Goldschmidt, Arthur. *A Concise History of the Middle East.* 7th ed. Boulder, CO: Westview Press, 2002.

———. *Modern Egypt.* 2nd ed. Boulder, CO: Westview Press, 2002.

González-Wippler, Migene. *The Complete Book of Amulets & Talismans.* St. Paul, MN: Llewellyn Publications, 1991.

Goodblatt, David. *The Monarchic Principle: Studies in Jewish Self-Government in Antiquity.* Tubingen: J.C.B. Mohr (P. Siebeck), 1994.

Goodwin, Jason. *Lords of the Horizons: A History of the Ottoman Empire.* New York: Picador, 2003.

Goubert, Pierre. *The Ancien Régime: French Society, 1600–1750*. New York: Harper and Row, 1973.

Grant, Michael. *Herod the Great*. New York: American Heritage Press, 1971.

————. *History of Rome*. New York: History Book Club, 1997.

————. *The Roman Emperors: A Biographical Guide to the Rulers of Imperial Rome, 31 B.C.–A.D. 476*. New York: Scribner's, 1985.

Graves, Robert. *The Claudius Novels*. New York: Penguin, 1999.

Gray, John Milner. *History of Zanzibar from the Middle Ages to 1856*. Westport, CT: Greenwood Press, 1975.

Greengrass, Mark. *France in the Age of Henri IV: The Struggle for Stability*. 2nd ed. New York: Longman, 1995.

Gregg, Edward. *Queen Anne*. New Haven, CT: Yale University Press, 2001.

Gregg, Pauline. *King Charles I*. Berkeley: University of California Press, 1984.

Gregory of Tours. *The History of the Franks*. Trans. Lewis Thorpe. New York: Penguin Books, 1974.

Grewal, J. S. *The Sikhs of the Punjab*. New York. Cambridge University Press, 1991.

Grey, Ian. *Ivan III and the Unification of Russia*. New York: Collier, 1972.

————. *The Romanovs: The Rise and Fall of a Russian Dynasty*. New York: Doubleday, 1970.

Griffiths, Ralph A., and Roger S. Thomas. *The Making of the Tudor Dynasty*. New York: St. Martin's Press, 1985.

Grimal, Nicolas-Christophe. *A History of Ancient Egypt*. Trans. Ian Shaw. Oxford: Basil Blackwell, 1992.

Gubser, Peter. *Historical Dictionary of the Hashemite Kingdom of Jordan*. Metuchen, NJ: Scarecrow Press, 1991.

Guldescu, Stanko. *The Croatian-Slavonian Kingdom, 1526–1792*. The Hague: Mouton, 1970.

Gump, James Oliver. *The Formation of the Zulu Kingdom in South Africa: 1750–1840*. San Francisco: E.Mellen Press, 1990.

Hale, Matthew. *The History and Analysis of the Common Law of England*. Union, NY: Lawbook Exchange, 2000.

Halecki, Oskar. "Casimir the Great, 1333–70." In W. F. Reddaway, J. H. Penson, O. Halecki, and R. Dyboski, eds. *The Cambridge History of Poland: From the Origins to Sobieski (to 1696)*. New York: Octagon Books, 1978.

————. *Jadwiga of Anjou and the Rise of East Central Europe*. Boulder, CO: Social Science Monographs, distributed by Columbia University Press, 1991.

Hall, D.G.E. *A History of South-East Asia*. 3rd ed. New York: St. Martin's Press, 1981.

Hall, John G. *North Africa*. Philadelphia: Chelsea House, 2002.

Hall, John Whitney. *Japan from Prehistory to Modern Times*. Ann Arbor: Center for Japanese Studies, University of Michigan, 1991.

Hallam, Elizabeth M., and Judith Everard. *Capetian France 987–1328*. 2nd ed. New York: Longman, 2001.

Hamer, Mary. *Signs of Cleopatra: History, Politics, Representation*. New York: Routledge, 1993.

Hamilton, Carolyn, ed. *In Pursuit of Swaziland's Precolonial Past*. Manzini, Swaziland: Macmillan Boleswa, 1990.

Hamilton, Keith, and Richard Langhorne. *The Practice of Diplomacy: Its Evolution, Theory, and Administration*. New York: Routledge, 1995.

Hammond, Mason. *The Antonine Monarchy*. New York: De Gruyter, 1975.

Hammond, Nicholas G. L. *The Miracle That Was Macedonia*. New York: St. Martin's Press. 1991.

Hammond, P. W., and Anne F. Sutton. *Richard III: The Road to Bosworth Field*. London: Constable, 1985.

Hampe, Karl. *Germany Under the Salian and Hohenstaufen Emperors*. Trans. Ralph Bennett. Totowa, NJ: Rowman and Littlefield, 1988.

Hanfmann, G.M.A. *From Croesus to Constantine: The Cities of Western Asia Minor and Their Arts in Greek and Roman Times*. Ann Arbor: University of Michigan Press, 1975.

Hansen, Valerie. *The Open Empire: A History of China to 1600*. New York: W. W. Norton, 2000.

Harding, Bertita. *Amazon Throne: The Story of the Braganzas of Brazil*. Indianapolis and New York: Bobbs-Merrill, 1941.

Hardman, John. *Louis XVI: The Silent King*. New York: Oxford University Press, 2000.

Harris, Marvin. *Cannibals and Kings: The Origins of Cultures*. New York: Vintage Books, 1991.

Harrison, Brian. *South-East Asia: A Short History*. 3rd ed. New York: St. Martin's Press, 1966.

Hartley, Janet M. *Alexander I*. New York: Longman, 1994.

Hartog, Leo de. *Genghis Khan: Conqueror of the World*. New York: Barnes & Noble, 1999.

————. *Russia and the Mongol Yoke: The History of the*

Russian Principalities and the Golden Horde, 1221–1502. New York: British Academic Press, 1996.

Harvey, John. *The Plantagenets.* New York: John Wiley, 1967.

Harvey, L. P. *Islamic Spain, 1250 to 1500.* Chicago: University of Chicago Press, 1992.

Haverkamp, Alfred. *Medieval Germany, 1056–1273.* 2nd ed. Trans. Helga Braun and Richard Mortimer. New York: Oxford University Press, 1992.

Hawkes, Jacquetta. *The First Great Civilizations: Life in Mesopotamia, the Indus Valley, and Egypt.* New York: Alfred A. Knopf, 1973.

Haynes, Sybille. *Etruscan Civilization: A Cultural History.* Los Angeles: J. Paul Getty Museum, 2000.

Haywood, John. *The Penguin Historical Atlas of the Vikings.* New York: Penguin, 1995.

Heer, Friedrich. *The Holy Roman Empire.* New York: Praeger, 1968.

Heinl, Robert Debs, Nancy Gordon Heinl, and Michael Heinl. *Written in Blood: The Story of the Haitian People, 1492–1971.* Lanham, MD: University Press of America, 1996.

Henderson, Isabel. *The Picts.* New York: Praeger, 1967.

Henriksen, Vera. *Saint Olav of Norway: King, Saint, and Enigma.* Oslo: Tano, 1985.

Henshall, Kenneth G. *A History of Japan: From Stone Age to Superpower.* New York: St. Martin's Press, 2001.

Herodotus. *The Penguin Herodotus.* Trans. George Rawlinson. New York: Penguin, 1991.

Heusch, Luc de. *The Drunken King; or, The Origin of the State.* Trans. Roy Willis. Bloomington: Indiana University Press, 1982.

Hevia, James. *Cherishing Men from Afar: Qing Guest Ritual and the Maccartney Embassy of 1793.* Durham, NC: Duke University Press, 1995.

Hibbert, Christopher. *George III: A Personal History.* New York: Penguin, 1999.

———. *The House of Medici: Its Rise and Fall.* New York: Perennial, 1999.

———. *Queen Victoria: A Personal History.* New York: Basic Books, 2000.

Higgins, Reynold. *Minoan and Mycenaean Art.* New rev. ed. New York: Thames & Hudson, 1997.

Hillenbrand, Carole. *The Crusades: Islamic Perspectives.* New York: Routledge, 2000.

Hilton, Anne. *The Kingdom of Kongo.* New York: Oxford University Press, 1985.

Hindley, Geoffrey. *The Royal Families of Europe.* New York: Carroll & Graf, 2000.

Hingley, Ronald. *The Tsars: Russian Autocrats, 1953–1917.* New York: Macmillan, 1968.

Hiro, Dilip. *The Middle East.* Phoenix, AZ: Oryx Press, 1996.

Hitti, Philip K. *History of Syria, Including Lebanon and Palestine.* Piscataway, NJ: Gorgias Press, 2002.

———. *History of the Arabs: From the Earliest Time to the Present.* Rev. 10th ed. New Preface by Walid Khalidi. New York: Palgrave Macmillan, 2002.

———. *The Near East in History: A 5000 Year Story.* Princeton, NJ: Van Nostrand, 1961.

Hoak, Dale, and Mordechai Feingold, eds. *The World of William and Mary: Anglo-Dutch Perspectives on the Revolution of 1688–89.* Stanford, CA: Stanford University Press, 1996.

Hocart, A. M. *Kings and Councillors: An Essay in the Comparative Anatomy of Human Society.* Ed. and with an Introduction by Rodney Needham. Chicago: University of Chicago Press, 1970.

———. *Kingship.* London: Oxford University Press, 1969.

Hodgkin, Thomas. *Italy and Her Invaders, 376–814.* New York: Russell & Russell, 1967.

Hoffman, William. *Queen Juliana: The Story of the Richest Woman in the World.* New York: Harcourt, Brace, Jovanovich, 1979.

Holborn, Hajo. *A History of Modern Germany, 1648–1840.* Princeton, NJ: Princeton University Press, 1982.

Holderness, Graham. *Shakespeare: The Histories.* New York: St. Martin's Press, 2000.

Holmes, George, ed. *The Oxford History of Italy.* New York: Oxford University Press, 1997.

———. *Oxford Illustrated History of Medieval Europe.* New York: Oxford University Press, 1988.

Homans, Margaret. *Royal Representations: Queen Victoria and British Culture, 1837–1876.* Chicago: University of Chicago Press, 1998.

Homer. *The Iliad.* Trans. Robert Fitzgerald. New York: Farrar, Straus & Giroux, 2004.

———. *The Odyssey.* Trans. Robert Fitzgerald. New York: Farrar, Straus & Giroux, 1998.

Hooker, Mark T. *The History of Holland.* Westport, CT: Greenwood Press, 1999.

Hornblower, Simon, and Antony Spawforth, eds. *The Oxford Companion to Classical Civilization.* New York: Oxford University Press, 1998.

Hornung, Erik. *History of Ancient Egypt: An Introduction.* Trans. David Lorton. Ithaca, NY: Cornell University Press, 1999.

Horrox, Rosemary. *Richard III: A Study of Service*. New York: Cambridge University Press, 1989.

Hourani, Albert H. *A History of the Arab Peoples*. Cambridge, MA: Belknap Press of Harvard University Press, 2002.

Houston, Stephen D., and Takeshi Inomata. *Royal Courts of the Ancient Maya*. Boulder, CO: Westview Press, 2000.

Howarth, Thomas E. B. *Citizen-King: The Life of Louis-Philippe, King of the French*. New York: White Lion Publishers, 1975.

Hoyt, Edwin P. *Hirohito: The Emperor and the Man*. New York: Praeger, 1992.

Hucker, Charles O. *China's Imperial Past: An Introduction to Chinese History of Culture*. Stanford, CA: Stanford University Press, 1997.

Hufton, Olwen. *Historical Change and Human Rights*. New York: Basic Books, 1995.

Hughes, Kristine. *The Writer's Guide to Everyday Life in Regency and Victorian England from 1811–1901*. Cincinnati, OH: Writer's Digest Books, 1997.

Hughes, Michael. *Law and Politics in Eighteenth-Century Germany: The Imperial Aulic Council in the Reign of Charles VI*. Wolfeboro, NH: Boydell Press, 1988.

Hull, Anthony. *Charles III and the Revival of Spain*. Washington, DC: University Press of America, 1980.

Hunt, Lynn, et al. *The Making of the West, Peoples and Cultures*. Boston: Bedford/St. Martin's, 2003.

Hunter Blair, Peter. *An Introduction to Anglo-Saxon England*. 3rd ed. With a new Introduction by Simon Keynes. New York: Cambridge University Press, 2003.

Huntingford, G.W.B. *The Galla of Ethiopia: The Kingdoms of Kafa and Janjero*. London: International African Institute, 19869.

Jacques, Edwin E. *The Albanians: An Ethnic History from Prehistoric Times to the Present*. Jefferson, NC: McFarland, 1995.

James, Edward. *The Franks*. Cambridge, MA: Basil Blackwell, 1991.

———, ed. *Visigothic Spain: New Approaches*. New York: Oxford University Press, 1980.

James, T.G.H. *A Short History of Ancient Egypt: From Predynastic to Roman Times*. Baltimore, MD: Johns Hopkins University Press, 1998.

Jaski, Bart. *Early Irish Kingship and Succession*. Portland, OR: Four Courts Press, 2000.

Jenkins, Earnestine. *A Glorious Past: Ancient Egypt, Ethiopia and Nubia*. New York: Chelsea House, 1995.

Jenkins, Elizabeth. *Elizabeth the Great*. New York: Berkley, 1972.

Jessup, Helen I., and Thierry Zephir, eds. *Sculpture of Angkor and Ancient Cambodia: Millennium of Glory*. Washington, DC: National Gallery of Art, 1997.

Johnson, David G. *The Medieval Chinese Oligarchy*. Boulder, CO: Westview Press, 1977.

Johnson, Lonnie. *Introducing Austria: A Short History*. Riverside, CA: Ariadne Press, 1989.

Johnson, P. A. *Richard, Duke of York, 1411–1460*. New York: Oxford University Press, 1988.

Johnson, Paul. *The Civilization of Ancient Egypt*. Updated ed. New York: HarperCollins, 1999.

———. *Elizabeth I: A Study in Power and Intellect*. London: Weidenfeld & Nicolson, 1988.

Jones, Colin. *The Cambridge Illustrated History of France*. New York: Cambridge University Press, 1999.

Jones, Gwyn. *A History of the Vikings*. 2nd ed. New York: Oxford University Press, 2001.

Jordan, David. *The King's Trial: The French Revolution vs. Louis XVI*. New York: Notable Trials Library, 1993.

JPS Hebrew-English Tanakh: The Traditional Hebrew Text and the New JPS Translation. 2nd ed. Philadelphia: The Jewish Publication Society, 2000.

Kadam, V. S. *Maratha Confederacy: A Study of Its Origin and Development*. New Delhi: Munshiram Manoharlal Publishers, 1993.

Kagan, Donald, et al. *The Western Heritage*. Upper Saddle River, NJ: Prentice Hall, 2002.

Kagwa, Apolo, and M.S.M. Semakula Kiwanuka. *The Kings of Buganda*. Nairobi: East African Publishing House, 1971.

Kantorowicz, Ernst. *The King's Two Bodies: A Study in Mediaeval Political Theology*. With a New Preface by William Chester Jordan. Princeton, NJ: Princeton University Press, 1997.

Kaplan, Marion. *The Portuguese: The Land and Its People*. New York: Viking Penguin, 1991.

Kaul, Ranjana. *Constitutional Development in the Indian Princely States*. New Delhi: Vikas Publishing House, 1998.

Keatinge, Richard W., ed. *Peruvian Prehistory. An Overview of pre-Inca and Inca society*. New York: Cambridge University Press, 1988.

Keay, John. *India, a History*. New York: Atlantic Monthly Press, 2000.

———. *Into India*. Ann Arbor: University of Michigan Press, 1999.

Keene, Donald, comp. *Anthology of Japanese Literature from the Earliest Era to the Nineteenth Century.* Rutland, VT: Tuttle, 1991.

Kelly, Amy. *Eleanor of Aquitaine and the Four Kings.* New York: Book of the Month Club, 1996.

Kennedy, Hugh. *Muslim Spain and Portugal: A Political History of al-Andalus.* New York: Longman, 1996.

Kenyon, J. P. *The Stuarts: A Study in English Kingship.* London: Severn House, 1977.

Kern, Fritz. *Kingship and Law in the Middle Ages.* Trans. S. B. Chrimes. Westport, CT: Greenwood Press, 1985.

Kibler, William W. *Eleanor of Aquitaine: Patron and Politician.* Austin: University of Texas Press, 1976.

Kinross, Patrick Balfour. *The Ottoman Centuries: The Rise and Fall of the Turkish Empire.* New York: William Morrow, 1979.

Kirby, D. G. *Northern Europe in the Early Modern Period: The Baltic World, 1492–1772.* New York: Longman, 1990.

Knecht, R. J. *The Rise and Fall of Renaissance France 1483–1610.* 2nd ed. Malden, MA: Basil Blackwell, 2001.

Knight, Judson, Stacy A. McConnell, and Lawrence W. Baker, eds. *Ancient Civilizations: Biographies.* Detroit: UXL, 2000.

Koenigsberger, H. G. *Medieval Europe, 400–1500.* New York: Longman, 1987.

Köhne, Eckart, Cornelia Ewigleben, and Ralph Jackson. *Gladiators and Caesars.* Berkeley: University of California Press, 2000.

Kossmann, E. H. *The Low Countries, 1780–1940.* New York: Oxford University Press, 1978.

Kostiner, Joseph, ed. *Middle East Monarchies: The Challenge of Modernity.* Boulder, CO: Lynne Reinner, 2000.

Kottak, Conrad P., ed. *Madagascar: Society and History.* Durham, NC: Carolina Academic Press, 1986.

———. *The Past in the Present: History, Ecology, and Cultural Variation in Highland Madagascar.* Ann Arbor: University of Michigan Press, 1980.

Kramer, Samuel Noah. *Cradle of Civilization.* Alexandria, VA: Time-Life Books, 1978.

Krejci, Jaroslav. *Before the European Challenge: The Great Civilizations of Asia and the Middle East.* Albany: State University of New York Press, 1990.

Kulke, Hermann. *Kings and Cults: State Formation and Legitimization in India and Southeast Asia.* New Delhi: Manohar, 2001.

———, and Dietmar Rothermund. *A History of India.* 3rd ed. New York: Routledge, 1998.

Kuper, Hilda. *The Swazi: A South African Kingdom.* New York: Holt, Rinehart & Winston, 1986.

Kurlansky, Mark. *Salt: A World History.* New York: Penguin, 2003.

Lagorio, Valerie M., and Mildred Leake Day, eds. *King Arthur Through the Ages.* New York: Garland, 1990.

Laistner, M.L.W. *A History of the Greek World from 479–323 B.C.* 3rd ed. New York: Barnes & Noble, 1962.

Lamberg-Karlovsky, C. C., and Jeremy A. Sabloff. *Ancient Civilizations: The Near East and Mesoamerica.* 2nd ed. Prospect Heights, IL: Waveland Press, 1995.

Lane Fox, Robin. *Alexander the Great.* New York: Penguin, 1994.

Lanning, Edward P. *Peru Before the Incas.* Englewood Cliffs, NJ: Prentice Hall, 1967.

Lapidus, Ira M. *A History of Islamic Societies.* 2nd ed. New York: Cambridge University Press, 2002.

Large, Stephen S. *Emperor Hirohito and Showa Japan: A Political Biography.* New York: Routledge, 1992.

Larsen, Karen. *A History of Norway.* Princeton, NJ: Princeton University Press for the American-Scandinavian Foundation, 1948.

Last, Murray. *The Sokoto Caliphate.* New York: Humanities Press, 1967.

Lawson, M. K. *Cnut: The Danes in England in the Early Eleventh Century.* New York: Longman, 1993.

Le Goff, Jacques. *Medieval Civilization: 400–1500.* Trans. Julia Barrow. New York: Barnes & Noble, 2000.

Le Roy Ladurie, Emmanuel, and Jean François Fitou. *Saint-Simon and the Court of Louis XIV.* Trans. Arthur Goldhammer. Chicago: University of Chicago Press, 2001.

Lee, Ki-baik. *A New History of Korea.* Trans. Edward W. Wagner, with Edward J. Schulz. Cambridge, MA: Harvard University Press, 1984.

Lee, Maurice, Jr. *Great Britain's Solomon: James VI and I in His Three Kingdoms.* Urbana: University of Illinois Press, 1990.

Leeper, Alexander Wigram Allen. *A History of Medieval Austria.* New York: AMS Press, 1978.

Leick, Gwendolyn. *Who's Who in the Ancient Near East.* New York: Routledge, 2002.

Lemarchand, René, ed. *African Kingships in Perspective: Political Change and Modernization in Monarchical Settings.* London: Cass, 1977.

Leveque, Pierre. *The Greek Adventure*. Cleveland: World, 1968.

Levi-Strauss, Claude. *The View from Afar*. Chicago: University of Chicago Press, 1992.

Levtzion, Nehemia. *Ancient Ghana and Mali*. New York: Africana Publishing, 1980.

Levy, Patricia. *Sudan*. New York: Marshall Cavendish, 1997.

Lewcock, Ronald. *Wadi Hadramawt and the Walled City of Shibam*. Paris: UNESCO, 1986.

Lewis, Bernard. *The Arabs in History*. 6th ed. New York: Oxford University Press, 2002.

————. *Islam and the Arab World: Faith, People, Culture*. New York: Alfred A. Knopf, 1976.

————. *The Middle East: A Brief History of the Last 2,000 Years*. New York: Scribner, 2003.

————. *Race and Slavery in the Middle East: An Historical Inquiry*. New York: Oxford University Press, 1992.

Lewis, Jayne Elizabeth, ed. *The Trial of Mary Queen of Scots: A Brief History with Documents*. Boston: Bedford/St. Martin's Press, 1999.

Lewis, P. S. *Later Medieval France: The Polity*. New York: St. Martin's Press, 1968.

Lewis, W. H. *The Splendid Century: Life in the France of Louis XIV*. Prospect Heights, IL: Waveland Press, 1999.

Leyser, Karl. *Medieval Germany and Its Neighbours: 900–1250*. London: Hambledon Press, 1982.

Lincoln, W. Bruce. *The Great Reforms: Autocracy, Bureaucracy and the Politics of Change in Imperial Russia*. DeKalb: Northern Illinois University Press, 1990.

————. *Nicholas I: Emperor and Autocrat of All the Russias*. DeKalb: Northern Illinois University Press, 1989.

————. *Sunlight at Midnight: St. Petersburg and the Rise of Modern Russia*. New York: Basic Books, 2002.

Lindemann, Mary. *Medicine and Society in Early Modern Europe*. New York: Cambridge University Press, 1999.

Livermore, H. V. *A New History of Portugal*. 2nd ed. New York: Cambridge University Press, 1976.

Lloyd, Alan. *The Maligned Monarch: The Life of King John of England*. Garden City, NY: Doubleday, 1972.

Lloyd, Seton. *Early Highland Peoples of Anatolia*. New York: McGraw-Hill, 1967.

Loach, Jennifer, G. W. Bernard, and Penry Williams. *Edward VI*. New Haven, CT: Yale University Press, 2002.

Lockot, Hans Wilhelm. *The Mission: The Life, Reign, and Character of Haile Sellassie I*. Bridgetown, Chesapeake, VA: ECA Associates Press, 1993.

Lockyer, Roger. *The Early Stuarts: A Political History of England, 1603–1642*. 2nd ed. New York: Longman, 1999.

Loewe, Michael, and Edward L. Shaughnessy, eds. *The Cambridge History of Ancient China: From the Origins of Civilization to 221 B.C.* New York: Cambridge University Press, 1999.

Longford, Elizabeth, ed. *The Oxford Book of Royal Anecdotes*. New York: Oxford University Press, 1991.

Loprete, Carlos A. *Iberoamerica: Historia de su civilización y cultura*. 4th ed. Upper Saddle River, NJ: Prentice Hall. 2000.

L'Orange, Hans Peter. *Studies on the Iconography of Cosmic Kingship in the Ancient World*. New Rochelle, NY: Caratzas Brothers, 1982.

Lukowski, Jerzy, and Hubert Zawadzki. *A Concise History of Poland*. New York: Cambridge University Press, 2001.

Lynch, Michael. *Scotland: A New History*. London: Pimlico, 1992.

Mabbett, Ian, and David Chandler. *The Khmers*. Cambridge, MA: Basil Blackwell, 1996.

Macalister, R.A.S. *Tara: A Pagan Sanctuary of Ancient Ireland*. New York: Scribner, 1931.

Macartney, C. A. *The Habsburg Empire, 1790–1918*. New York: Macmillan, 1969.

Macaulay, Neill. *Dom Pedro: The Struggle for Liberty in Brazil and Portugal (1798–1834)*. Durham, NC: Duke University Press, 1986.

Macgowan, J. *The Imperial History of China*. 2nd ed. New York: Barnes & Noble, 1973.

Machiavelli, Niccolò. *The Prince*. Trans. George Bull. New York: Penguin, 2003.

Mackey, Sandra. *The Iranians: Persia, Islam and the Soul of a Nation*. New York: Plume, 1998.

Mackie, John Duncan. *The Earlier Tudors*. New York: Oxford University Press, 1994.

————. *A History of Scotland*. New York: Penguin, 1984.

Macnamara, Ellen. *The Etruscans*. Cambridge, MA: Harvard University Press, 1991.

Macqueen, J. G. *The Hittites and Their Contemporaries in Asia Minor*. Rev. ed. New York: Thames & Hudson, 1986.

Madden, Annette. *In Her Footsteps: 101 Remarkable*

Black Women from the Queen of Sheba to Queen Latifah. New York: Gramercy Books, 2001.

Magnus, Philip. *King Edward the Seventh*. New York: Penguin, 1979.

Mahajan, Vidya. *Ancient India*. New Delhi: S. Chand, 1976.

Majumdar, Ramesh Chandra, ed. *The History and Culture of the Indian People*. 6th ed. Bombay: Bharatiya Vidya Bhavan, 1990.

Malory, Sir Thomas. *Malory's Le Morte d'Arthur: King Arthur and the Legends of the Round Table: The Classic Rendition*. With an Introduction by Robert Graves. New York: New American Library, 2001.

Manchen-Helfen, Otto. *The World of the Huns, Studies in Their History and Culture*. Berkeley: University of California Press, 1973.

Manich Jumsai, M. L. *History of Laos, Including the History of Lannathai, Cheingmai*. New York: Paragon Book Gallery, 1967.

Mann, Kenny. *Ghana, Mali, Songhay: The Western Sudan*. Parsippany, NJ: Dillon Press, 1996.

Mansfield, Peter. *A History of the Middle East*. New York: Penguin, 1992.

Marcus, Harold G. *The Life and Times of Menelik II: Ethiopia 1844–1913*. Lawrenceville, NJ: Red Sea Books, 1995.

Marcus, Joyce. *Zapotec Religion*. New York: Academic Press, 1983.

———, and Kent V. Flannery. *Zapotec Civilization: How Urban Society Evolved in Mexico's Oaxaca Valley*. New York: Thames & Hudson, 1996.

Marques, A. H. de Oliveira. *History of Portugal*. 2nd ed. New York: Columbia University Press, 1976.

Martin, Janet. *Medieval Russia: 980–1584*. New York: Cambridge University Press, 1995.

Marvick, Elizabeth Wirth. *Louis XIII: The Making of a King*. New Haven, CT: Yale University Press, 1986.

Mason, John Alden. *The Ancient Civilizations of Peru*. Baltimore, MD: Penguin, 1964.

Mason, John W. *The Dissolution of the Austro-Hungarian Empire, 1867–1918*. 2nd ed. New York: Longman, 1997.

Massie, Robert K. *Nicholas and Alexandra*. New York: Random House, 1995.

———. *Peter the Great: His Life and World*. New York: Wings Books, 1991.

———. *The Romanovs: The Final Chapter*. New York: Ballantine, 1996.

May, Arthur. *The Hapsburg Monarchy: 1867–1914*. Cambridge, MA: Harvard University Press, 1989.

Mayo, Patricia Elton. *The Roots of Identity: Three National Movements in Contemporary European Politics*. London: Allen Lane, 1974.

Mazour, Anatole G. *Rise and Fall of the Romanovs*. Princeton, NJ: Van Nostrand, 1960.

Mazower, Mark. *The Balkans: A Short History*. New York: Modern Library, 2000.

McConnell, Allen. *Tsar Alexander I: Paternalist Reformer*. New York: Crowell, 1970.

McCormick, Donald. *The Incredible Mr. Kavanagh*. New York: Devin-Adair, 1961.

McCoy, Richard C. *Alterations of State: Sacred Kingship in the English Reformation*. New York: Columbia University Press, 2002.

McKay, Derek. *The Great Elector*. New York: Longman, 2001.

McKenzie, Steven L. *King David: A Biography*. New York: Oxford University Press, 2001.

McKissack, Pat, and Frederick McKissack. *The Royal Kingdoms of Ghana, Mali, and Songhay: Life in Medieval Africa*. New York: Henry Holt, 1995.

McLeod, Malcolm D. *The Asante*. London: British Museum Publications, 1981.

McNamara, Jo Ann, and John E. Halborg, eds. *Sainted Women of the Dark Ages*. Durham, NC: Duke University Press, 1992.

McNeill, William H., and Jean W. Sedlar. *Classical India*. New York: Oxford University Press, 1969.

Metz, Helen Chapin, ed. *Egypt: A Country Study*. 5th ed. Washington, DC: Federal Research Division, Library of Congress, 1991.

———. *Iran: A Country Study*. 4th ed. Washington, DC: Library of Congress Federal Research Division, 1989.

Meyer, Carolyn. *Mary, Bloody Mary*. San Diego, CA: Harcourt Brace, 2001.

Michael of Kent, Princess. *Crowned in a Far Country: Portraits of Eight Royal Brides*. New York: Weidenfeld & Nicolson, 1986.

Middleton, John. *Africa: An Encyclopedia for Students*. New York: Scribner, 2001.

———. *The World of the Swahili: An African Mercantile Civilization*. New Haven, CT: Yale University Press, 1992.

Miksic, John, ed. *Indonesian Heritage: Ancient History*. Vol. 1: *Ancient History*. Singapore: Archipelago Press, 1996.

Millar, Fergus. *The Emperor in the Roman World, 31*

BC–AD 337. Ithaca, NY: Cornell University Press, 1992.

Miller, John. *James II.* Rev. ed. New Haven, CT: Yale University Press, 2000.

Miller, Townsend. *The Castles and the Crown: Spain, 1451–1555.* New York: Coward-McCann, 1986.

Minahan, James. *Nations Without States: A Historical Dictionary of Contemporary National Movements.* Westport, CT: Greenwood Press, 1996.

Moffat, Abbott Low. *Mongkut, the King of Siam.* Ithaca, NY: Cornell University Press, 1968.

Molnar, Miklos. *A Concise History of Hungary.* Trans. Anna Magnar. New York: Cambridge University Press, 2001.

Monmouth, Geoffrey. *History of the Kings of Britain.* With an Introduction by Lewis Thorpe. New York: Penguin, 1978.

Monod, Paul. *The Power of Kings: Monarchy and Religion in Europe, 1589–1715.* New Haven, CT: Yale University Press, 1999.

Moorhead, John. *Justinian.* New York: Longman, 1994.

———. *Theoderic in Italy.* New York: Oxford University Press, 1992.

Morby, John. *Dynasties of the World: A Chronological and Genealogical Handbook.* Oxford University Press, 1990.

Mordecai, Carolyn. *You Are Cordially Invited to Weddings: Dating and Love Customs of Cultures Worldwide, Including Royalty.* Phoenix: Nittany Publishers, 1999.

Morris, Ivan. *The World of the Shining Prince: Court Life in Ancient Japan.* New York: Kodansha International, 1994.

Morton, W. Scott. *China: Its History and Culture.* 3rd ed. New York: McGraw-Hill, 1995.

———. *Japan: Its History and Culture.* 3rd ed. New York: McGraw-Hill, 1994.

Moseley, Michael E., and Alana Cordy-Collins, eds. *The Northern Dynasties: Kingship and Statecraft in Chimor: A Symposium.* Washington, DC: Dumbarton Oaks Research Library and Collection, 1990.

Moss, Henry St. Lawrence. *The Birth of the Middle Ages, 395–814.* Westport, CT: Greenwood Press, 1980.

Mote, Frederick W. *Imperial China.* Cambridge, MA: Harvard University Press, 1999.

Mullen, Richard, and James Munson. *Victoria: Portrait of a Queen.* London: BBC Books, 1988.

Murra, John V. *The Economic Organization of the Inca State.* Greenwich, CT: JAI Press, 1980.

Myers, Henry A. *Medieval Kingship.* Chicago: Nelson-Hall, 1982.

Nadel, S. F. *A Black Byzantium: The Kingdom of Nupe in Nigeria.* New York: Oxford University Press, 1973.

Nardo, Don. *The Roman Empire.* San Diego: Lucent Books, 1994.

Nelson, Harold D., ed. *Morocco: A Country Study.* 5th ed. Washington, DC: American University, 1986.

———. *Sudan: A Country Study.* 3rd ed. Washington, DC: Foreign Area Studies, American University, 1982.

Nelson, Walter Henry. *The Soldier Kings: The House of Hohenzollern.* New York: Putnam, 1970.

Niane, D. T. *Sundiata: An Epic of Old Mali.* Trans. G. D. Pickett. London: Longman, 1965.

Nicholls, Christine S. *The Swahili Coast: Politics, Diplomacy and Trade on the East African Littoral, 1798–1856.* New York: Africana Publishing, 1971.

Nicolson, Harold. *The Evolution of Diplomatic Method.* Westport, CT: Greenwood Press, 1977.

———. *Kings, Courts and Monarchy.* New York: Simon & Schuster, 1962.

Nilakanta Sastri, N. K. *Age of the Nandas and Mauryas.* Delhi: Motilal Banarsidass, 1988.

Niles, Susan A. *The Shape of Inca History: Narratives and Architecture in an Andean Empire.* Iowa City: University of Iowa Press, 1999.

Nordstrom, Byron J. *Scandinavia Since 1500.* Minneapolis: University of Minnesota Press, 2000.

Northcutt, W. *The Regions of France: A Reference Guide to History and Culture.* Westport, CT: Greenwood Press, 1996.

Norton, Mary Beth, et al. *A People and a Nation: A History of the United States.* 6th ed. Boston: Houghton Mifflin, 2003.

Norwich, John Julius. *Byzantium: The Decline and Fall.* New York: Alfred A. Knopf, 1996.

O Corrain, Donnchadh. *Ireland Before the Normans.* Portland, OR: Four Courts Press, 2004.

Ó Cróinín, Dáibhí. *Early Medieval Ireland 400–1200.* London: Longman, 1995.

O'Brien, Jacqueline, and Peter Harbison. *Ancient Ireland: From Prehistory to the Middle Ages.* New York: Oxford University Press, 1996.

O'Fahey, Rex S. *State and Society in Dar Fur.* New York: St. Martin's Press, 1980.

Oliver, Roland, and Anthony Atmore. *Africa Since 1800.* 5th ed. New York: Cambridge University Press, 2004.

———, and J. D. Fage. *A Short History of Africa*. 6th ed. New York: Penguin, 1995.

———, and G. N. Sanderson, eds. *Cambridge History of Africa: From 1870 to 1905*. New York: Cambridge University Press, 1985.

Ollard, Richard. *The Image of the King: Charles I and Charles II*. New York: Atheneum, 1979.

Osborne, Milton E. *Sihanouk: Prince of Light, Prince of Darkness*. Honolulu: University of Hawaii Press, 1994.

Otetea, Andrei, ed. *The History of the Romanian People*. New York: Twayne, 1974.

Owen, Francis. *The Germanic People: Their Origin, Culture, and Expansion*. New York: Barnes & Noble, 1993.

Pachai, Bridglal. *Malawi: The History of the Nation*. London: Longman, 1973.

Page, R. I. *Chronicles of the Viking: Records, Memorials and Myths*. Toronto: University of Toronto Press, 1995.

Painter, Sidney. *French Chivalry: Chivalric Ideas and Practices in Mediaeval France*. Ithaca, NY: Cornell University Press, 1969.

Pakula, Hannah. *The Last Romantic: A Biography of Queen Marie of Romania*. New York: Simon & Schuster, 1985.

Palampal, Ve. *Studies in Chola History*. Delhi: Kalinga Publications, 1998.

Palmer, John. *England, France and Christendom, 1377–99*. Chapel Hill, NC: University of North Carolina Press, 1972.

Palmer, Tony. *Charles II: Portrait of an Age*. London: Cassell, 1979.

Paludan, Ann. *Chronicle of the Chinese Emperors: The Reign-by-Reign Record of the Rulers of Imperial China*. New York: Thames & Hudson, 1998.

Park, Thomas K. *Historical Dictionary of Morocco*. New ed. Lanham, MD: Scarecrow Press, 1996.

Parsons, Neil. *A New History of Southern Africa*. 2nd ed. New York: Holmes & Meier, 1994.

Pasztory, Esther. *Aztec Art*. Norman: University of Oklahoma Press, 1998.

Patnaik, Naveen. *A Second Paradise: Indian Courtly Life, 1590–1947*. Garden City, NY: Doubleday, 1985.

Paul the Deacon. *History of the Lombards*. Trans. William Dudley Foulke, ed. Edward Peters. Philadelphia: University of Pennsylvania Press, 1974.

Payne, Stanley G. *A History of Spain and Portugal*. Vol. 1. *Antiquity to the Seventeenth Century*. Madison: University of Wisconsin Press, 1973.

Pecora, Vincent P., ed. *Nations and Identities: Classic Readings*. Malden, MA: Basil Blackwell, 2001.

Pelenski, Jaroslaw. *The Contest for the Legacy of Kievan Rus'*. New York: Columbia University Press, 1998.

Pemberton, John, and Funso S. Afolayan. *Yoruba Sacred Kingship: A Power Like That of the Gods*. Washington, DC: Smithsonian Institution Press, 1996.

Perkins, Dorothy. *Encyclopedia of China: The Essential Reference to China, Its History and Culture*. New York: Facts on File, 1999.

Perry, Glenn E. *The Middle East: Fourteen Islamic Centuries*. 3rd ed. Upper Saddle River, NJ: Prentice Hall, 1997.

Perry, John Curtis, and Bardwell L. Smith. *Essays on T'ang Society: The Interplay of Social, Political, and Economic Forces*. Leiden: E. J. Brill, 1976.

Perry, John Weir. *Lord of the Four Quarters: The Mythology of Kingship*. New York: Paulist Press, 1991.

Petrie, Charles. *King Charles III of Spain: An Enlightened Despot*. New York: J. Day, 1971.

Pickel, Margaret Barnard. *Charles I as Patron of Poetry and Drama*. Folcroft, PA: Folcroft Library Editions, 1974.

Pirenne, Henri. *The Economic and Social History of Medieval Europe*. San Diego, CA: Harcourt Brace, 1989.

Pitard, Wayne T. *Ancient Damascus: A Historical Study of the Syrian City-State from Earliest Times until Its Fall to the Assyrians in 732 B.C.E.* Winona Lake, IN: Eisenbrauns, 1987.

Plato. *The Republic*. Trans. Benjamin Jowett. Mineola, NY: Dover, 2000.

Polish, David. *Give Us a King: Legal-Religious Sources of Jewish Sovereignty*. Hoboken, NJ: Ktav, 1989.

Pollard, Helen Perlstein. *Tariácuri's Legacy. The Prehispanic Tarascan State*. Norman: University of Oklahoma Press, 1993.

Poole, Austin Lane. *From Domesday Book to Magna Carta: 1087–1216*. 2nd ed. New York: Oxford University Press, 1993.

Potter, David. *A History of France, 1460–1560: The Emergence of a Nation State*. New York: St. Martin's Press, 1995.

Power, Brian. *The Puppet Emperor: The Life of Pu Yi, Last Emperor of China*. New York: Universe Books, 1988.

Powicke, Sir Maurice. *The Thirteenth Century:*

1216–1307. 2nd ed. New York: Oxford University Press, 1962.

Prakash, Vidya. *Khajuraho: A Study in the Cultural Conditions of Chandella Society.* New York: Distributed by Apt Books, 1982.

Prestwich, Michael. *The Three Edwards: War and State in England, 1272–1377.* 2nd ed. New York: Routledge, 2003.

Price, Roger. *A Concise History of France.* New York: Cambridge University Press, 1993.

———. *The French Second Empire: An Anatomy of Political Power.* New York: Cambridge University Press, 2001.

Radzinskii, Edvard. *The Last Tsar: The Life and Death of Tsar Nicholas II.* Trans. Marian Schwartz. New York: Doubleday Anchor Books, 1993.

Raglan, Fitzroy Richard Somerset. *The Hero: A Study in Tradition, Myth and Drama.* Mineola, NY: Dover, 2003.

Ramankutty, P. V. *Curse as a Motif in the Mahabharata.* Delhi: Nag Publishers, 1999.

Rank, Otto. "The Myth of the Birth of the Hero." In *Quest of the Hero.* Introduction by Robert A. Segal. Princeton, NJ: Princeton University Press, 1990.

Rankov, Boris. *The Praetorian Guard.* London: Osprey, 1994.

Ratchnevsky, Paul. *Genghis Khan: His Life and Legacy.* Trans. and ed. Thomas Nivison Haining. Cambridge, MA: Basil Blackwell, 1993.

Read, Jan. *The Moors in Spain and Portugal.* Totowa, NJ: Rowman & Littlefield, 1975.

Redgate, Anne Elizabeth. *The Armenians.* Malden, MA: Basil Blackwell, 2000.

Redman, Charles L. *The Rise of Civilization: From Early Farmers to Urban Society in the Ancient Near East.* San Francisco. W. H. Freeman, 1978.

Reeves, Carl Nicholas. *Akhenaten: Egypt's False Prophet.* New York: Thames & Hudson, 2001.

Regan, Geoffrey. *Elizabeth I.* New York: Cambridge University Press, 1988.

Reid, Anthony, ed. *Indonesian Heritage: Early Modern History.* Vol. 3. Singapore: Archipelago Press, 1996.

Renfrew, Colin. "Trade as Action at a Distance." In *Approaches to Social Archaeology.* Cambridge, MA: Harvard University Press, 1984, pp. 86–134.

Reyna, S. P. *Wars Without End: The Political Economy of a Pre-African State.* Hanover, NH: University Press of New England, 1990.

Riasanovsky, Nicholas V. *A History of Russia.* 6th ed. New York: Oxford University Press, 2000.

Richardson, Hugh E. *Tibet and Its History.* Boulder, CO: Shambhala, 1984.

Richardson, Jerusha D. *The Doges of Venice.* New York: Doran, 1914.

Ricklefs, M. C. *A History of Modern Indonesia Since c. 1200.* Stanford, CA: Stanford University Press, 2001.

Ridley, Jasper. *Bloody Mary's Martyrs: The Story of England's Terror.* New York: Carroll & Graf, 2002.

———. *The Tudor Age.* Woodstock, NY: Overlook Press, 1990.

Riley-Smith, Jonathan. *The Crusades: A Short History.* New Haven, CT: Yale University Press, 1987.

Riphenburg, Carol J. *Oman: Political Development in a Changing World.* Westport, CT: Praeger, 1998.

Risso, Patricia. *Oman & Muscat: An Early Modern History.* New York: St. Martin's Press, 1986.

Roberts, J.A.G. *A Concise History of China.* Cambridge, MA: Harvard University Press, 1999.

———. *A History of China.* Vol. 1, *Prehistory to c. 1800.* New York: St. Martin's Press, 1996.

Roberts, John L. *Lost Kingdoms: Celtic Scotland and the Middle Ages.* Edinburgh: Edinburgh University Press, 1997.

Roberts, Michael. *The Early Vasas: A History of Sweden, 1523–1611.* New York: Cambridge University Press, 1968.

Roberts, Richard. *Warriors, Merchants, and Slaves: The State and the Economy in the Middle Niger Valley, 1700–1914.* Stanford, CA: Stanford University Press, 1987.

Robertson, Ian. *A Traveller's History of Portugal.* New York: Interlink Books, 2002.

Robinson, Francis, ed. *The Cambridge Illustrated History of the Islamic World.* New York: Cambridge University Press, 1998.

Robinson, I. S. *Henry IV of Germany, 1056–1106.* New York: Cambridge University Press, 1999.

Roche, Daniel. *France in the Enlightenment.* Cambridge, MA: Harvard University Press, 2000.

Rochon, Thomas R. *The Netherlands: Negotiating Sovereignty in an Interdependent World.* Boulder, CO: Westview Press, 1999.

Ross, Charles D. *The Wars of the Roses: A Concise History.* New York: Thames & Hudson, 1977.

Ross, Stewart. *Monarchs of Scotland.* New York: Facts on File, 1990.

Rostworowski de Diez Canseco, María. *History of the Inca Realm.* New York: Cambridge University Press, 1999.

Roux, Georges. *Ancient Iraq.* 3rd ed. New York: Penguin, 1992.

Roy, Jyotirmoy. *History of Manipur.* Calcutta: Firma KLM, 1999.

Rubenson, Sven. *King of Kings: Tewodros of Ethiopia.* Addis Ababa: Haile Sellassie I University, 1966.

Ruiz, Ana. *The Spirit of Ancient Egypt.* New York: Algora, 2001.

Runes, Dagobert D. *Despotism: A Pictorial History of Tyranny.* New York: Philosophical Library, 1963.

Ryder, Alan. *The Kingdom of Naples Under Alfonso the Magnanimous: The Making of a Modern State.* New York: Oxford University Press, 1976.

Saeed, Mian Muhammad. *The Sharqi Sultanate of Jaunpur.* Karachi, Pakistan: University of Karachi, 1972.

Saggs, H. W. F. *Civilization Before Greek and Rome.* New Haven, CT: Yale University Press, 1989.

Sandars, Thomas Collett. *The Institutes of Justinian.* Holmes Beach, FL: Gaunt, 1997.

Sanders, Andrew. *A Deed Without a Name: The Witch in Society and History.* Washington, DC: Berg, 1995.

Sandmel, Samuel. *Herod, Profile of a Tyrant.* Philadelphia: Lippincott, 1967.

Sansom, George Bailey. *A History of Japan.* Stanford, CA: Stanford University Press, 1996–2000.

————. *Japan, A Short Cultural History.* Stanford, CA: Stanford University Press, 1978.

Santosuosso, Antonio. *Soldiers, Citizens, and the Symbols of War: From Classical Greece to Republican Rome, 500–167 B.C.* Boulder, CO: Westview Press, 1997.

SarDesai, D. R. *Southeast Asia, Past and Present.* 5th ed. Boulder, CO: Westview Press, 2003.

Sasson, Jack M., Editor-in-Chief. *Civilizations of the Ancient Near East.* Peabody, MA: Hendrickson, 2000.

Sauvigny, G. de Bertier de, and David H. Pinkney. *History of France.* Trans. James Friguglietti. Arlington Heights, IL: Forum Press, 1983.

Sawyer, Peter. *Kings and Vikings: Scandinavia and Europe, A. D. 700–1100.* New York: Methuen, 1982.

————. *The Oxford Illustrated History of the Vikings.* New York: Oxford University Press, 1997.

Sayyid, Marsot, and Afaf Lutfi. *A Short History of Modern Egypt.* New York: Cambridge University Press, 1996.

Scarre, Christopher. *Chronicle of the Roman Emperors: The Reign-by-Reign Record of the Rulers of Imperial Rome.* New York: Thames & Hudson, 1995.

Schama, Simon. *A History of Britain.* New York: Hyperion, 2002.

Schele, Linda, and David Freidel. *A Forest of Kings: The Untold Story of the Ancient Maya.* New York: William Morrow, 1992.

Scholz, Piotr O. *Eunuchs and Castrati: A Cultural History.* Trans. John A. Broadwin and Shelley L. Frisch. Princeton, NJ: Markus Wiener Publishers, 2001.

Schom, Alan. *Napoleon Bonaparte.* New York: HarperCollins, 1998.

Scott, Otto J. *James I.* New York: Mason/Charter, 1976.

Scott, Ronald McNair. *Robert the Bruce, King of Scots.* New York: Carroll & Graf, 1999.

Seagrave, Sterling, and Peggy Seagrave. *The Yamato Dynasty: The Secret History of Japan's Imperial Family.* New York: Broadway Books, 2001.

Sealey, Raphael. *A History of the Greek City States ca. 700–388 B.C.* Los Angeles: University of California Press, 1977.

Seaman, Gary, and Daniel Marks. *Rulers from the Steppe: State Formation on the Eurasian Periphery.* Los Angeles: Ethnographics Press, Center for Visual Anthropology, University of Southern California, 1991.

Sedlar, Jean W. *India and the Greek World: A Study in the Transmission of Culture.* Totowa, NJ: Rowman & Littlefield, 1980.

Segal, Robert A. *Theorizing about Myth.* Amherst: University of Massachusetts Press, 1999.

Seisanu, Romulus. *Rumania.* Miami Beach, FL: Romanian Historical Studies, 1987.

Seligman, C. G. *Egypt and Negro Africa: A Study in Divine Kingship.* New York: AMS Press, 1978.

Service, Elman R. *Origins of the State and Civilization: The Process of Cultural Evolution.* New York: W. W. Norton, 1975.

————. *Primitive Social Organization: An Evolutionary Perspective.* 2nd ed. New York: Random House, 1971.

Seward, Desmond. *The Bourbon Kings of France.* New York: Barnes & Noble, 1976.

————. *The Hundred Years' War: The English in France, 1337–1453.* New York: Penguin, 1999.

————. *Marie Antoinette.* New York: St. Martin's Press, 1981.

Shaffer, Lynda Norene. *Maritime Southeast Asia to 1500.* Armonk, NY: M. E. Sharpe, 1996.

Shapiro, Ian. *The Evolution of Rights in Liberal Theory.* New York: Cambridge University Press, 1986.

Shastri, Ajay Mitra. *The Age of the Satavahanas.* New Delhi: Aryan Books International, 1999.

Shaw, Ian, ed. *The Oxford History of Ancient Egypt.* New York: Oxford University Press, 2002.

Shaw, Stanford J., and Ezel Kural Shaw. *History of the Ottoman Empire and Modern Turkey.* New York: Cambridge University Press, 1995.

Sherwin-White, Susan, and Amelie Kuhrt. *From Samarkhand to Sardis: A New Approach to the Seleucid Empire.* Berkeley: University of California Press, 1993.

Shillington, Kevin. *History of Africa.* New York: St. Martin's Press, 1989.

Shinoda, Minoru. *The Founding of the Kamakura Shogunate, 1180–1185.* New York: Columbia University Press, 1960.

Shreshtha, Kusum. *Monarchy in Nepal: Tribhuvan Era: Imprisonment to Glory.* London: Sangam Books, 1984.

Shulgi, King of Ur. *Sumerian Royal Hymns Glorifying King Šulgi of Ur.* Ed. Jacob Klein. Ramat-Gan, Israel: Bar-Ilan University Press, 1981.

Shuter, Jane. *Egypt.* Austin, TX: Raintree Steck-Vaughn Publishers, 1999.

Sicker, Martin. *The Islamic World in Ascendancy: From the Arab Conquests to the Siege of Vienna.* Westport, CT: Praeger, 2000.

———. *The Pre-Islamic Middle East.* Westport, CT: Praeger, 2000.

Sihanouk, Norodom. *My War with the CIA: The Memoirs of Prince Norodom Sihanouk,* as related to Wilfred Burchett. New York: Pantheon, 1973.

Silverman, David P., general ed. *Ancient Egypt.* New York: Oxford University Press, 2003.

Simms, Peter and Sanda. *The Kingdom of Laos: Six Hundred Years of History.* Surrey: Curzon Press, 1999.

Sinor, Denis, ed. *The Cambridge History of Early Inner Asia.* New York: Cambridge University Press, 1990.

Skeet, Ian. *Oman Before 1970: The End of an Era.* Boston: Faber and Faber, 1985.

Skinner, Elliott P. *The Mossi of Burkina Faso: Chiefs, Politicians, and Soldiers.* Prospect Heights, IL: Waveland Press, 1989.

———. *The Mossi of the Upper Volta: The Political Development of a Sudanese People.* Stanford, CA: Stanford University Press, 1968.

Slavin, Michael. *The Book of Tara.* Foreword by Conor Newman. Dublin: Wolfhound Press, 1996.

Smith, Bradley. *Japan: A History in Art.* Rev. ed. New York: Doubleday, 1979.

Smith, David. *Russia of the Tsars.* London: Ernest Benn, 1971.

Smith, Denis Mack. *A History of Sicily.* New York: Dorset, 1988.

———. *Italy and Its Monarchy.* New ed. New Haven, CT: Yale University Press, 1992.

———. *Victor Emanuel, Cavour, and the Risorgimento.* New York: Oxford University Press, 1971.

Smith, Lacey Baldwin. *Elizabeth Tudor: Portrait of a Queen.* Boston: Little, Brown, 1975.

Smith, Rhea Marsh. *Spain: A Modern History.* Ann Arbor: University of Michigan Press, 1965.

Smith, Richard J. *Fortune-Tellers and Philosophers: Divination in Traditional Chinese Society.* Boulder, CO: Westview Press, 1992.

Smith, Vincent A. *The Oxford History of India.* Ed. Percival Spear. 4th ed. New York: Oxford University Press, 1981.

Smith, William H. C. *Napoleon III: The Pursuit of Prestige.* London: Collins and Brown, 1991.

Snellgrove, David, and Hugh Edward Richardson. *A Cultural History of Tibet.* Boston: Shambhala, 1995.

Soucek, Svatopluk. *A History of Inner Asia.* New York: Cambridge University Press, 2000.

Speck, Paul. *Understanding Byzantium: Studies in Byzantine Historical Sources.* Brookfield, VT: Variorum, 2003.

Spellman, W. M. *Monarchies, 1000–2000.* London: Reaktion Books, 2001.

Spence, Jonathan D. *The Search for Modern China.* 2nd ed. New York: W. W. Norton, 1999.

Spielman, John P. *Leopold I of Austria.* New Brunswick, NJ: Rutgers University Press, 1977.

Spores, Ronald. *The Mixtecs in Ancient and Colonial Times.* Norman: University of Oklahoma Press, 1984.

Srinivasan, Radhika. *India.* 2nd ed. New York: Marshall Cavendish, 2002.

Srivastava, Ashirbadi Lal. *The History of India: 1000 A.D.–1707 A.D.* Jaipur: Shiva Lal Agarwala, 1964.

Stafford, Pauline. *Queens, Concubines, and Dowagers: The King's Wife in the Early Middle Ages.* Washington, DC: University of Leicester Press, 1998.

Starkey, David, ed. *The English Court from the Wars of the Roses to the Civil Wars.* New York: Longman, 1987.

Starr, Chester. *A History of the Ancient World.* 4th ed. New York: Oxford University Press, 1991.

Stavrianos, Leften Stavros. *The Balkans Since 1453.* New York: New York University Press, 2000.

Stavro, Skendi. *The Albanian National Awakening, 1878–*

1912. Princeton, NJ: Princeton University Press, 1981.

Steed, Henry W. *The Habsburg Monarchy.* New York: Howard Fertig, 1969.

Steedman, Scott. *Ancient Egypt.* 2nd ed. New York: DK Publishing, 2003.

Stein, Rolf A. *Tibetan Civilization.* Stanford, CA: Stanford University Press, 1972.

Stenton, F. M. *Anglo-Saxon England.* 3rd ed. New York: Oxford University Press, 2001.

Stiebing, William H. *Ancient Near Eastern History and Culture.* New York: Longman, 2003.

Storey, R. L. *The End of the House of Lancaster.* Wolfeboro, NH: A. Sutton, 1989.

Storry, Richard. *A History of Modern Japan.* Rev. ed. New York: Penguin, 1990.

Strong, Roy C. *Gloriana: The Portraits of Queen Elizabeth I.* New York: Thames & Hudson, 1987.

Stuart-Fox, Martin. *A History of Laos.* New York: Cambridge University Press, 1997.

———. *The Lao Kingdom of Lan Xang: Rise and Decline.* Bangkok: White Lotus Press, 1998.

Sturluson, Snorri. *Heimskringla: History of the Kings of Norway.* Trans. Lee M. Hollander. Austin: University of Texas for the American-Scandinavian Foundation, 1992.

Suetonius, Gaius. *The Lives of the Twelve Caesars.* Trans. Robert Graves, ed. Michael Grant. New York: Welcome Rain Publishers, 2001.

Sugar, Peter F., ed. *A History of Hungary.* Bloomington: Indiana University Press, 1994.

Swaminathan, S. *The Early Cholas: History, Art and Culture.* Delhi: Sharada Publishing House, 1998.

Symcox, Geoffrey. *Victor Amadeus II: Absolutism in the Savoyard State, 1675–1730.* Berkeley: University of California Press, 1983.

Syme, Ronald. *Roman Papers.* New York: Oxford University Press, 1979.

Tacitus, Cornelius. The *Annals; and The Histories.* Trans. Alfred John Church and William Jackson Bodribb. New York: Modern Library, 2003.

Tamrat, Taddesse. *Church and State in Ethiopia: 1270–1527.* Oxford: Clarendon Press, 1972.

Tanner, Stephen. *Afghanistan: A Military History from Alexander the Great to the Fall of the Taliban.* New York: Da Capo Press, 2002.

Tarn, William W. *Hellenistic Civilization.* 3rd rev. ed. New York: World, 1971.

Taylor, A. J. P. *English History: 1914–1945.* New York: Oxford University Press, 2001.

Taylor, Keith W. *The Birth of Vietnam.* Berkeley: University of California Press, 1983.

Taylor, Lou. *Mourning Dress: A Costume and Social History.* Boston: Allen & Unwin, 1983.

Temperley, Harold W. *History of Serbia.* New York: AMS Press, 1970.

Thapar, Romila. *Asoka and the Decline of the Mauryas.* Rev. ed. New York: Oxford University Press, 1997.

———. *A History of India.* New York: Penguin, 1985.

Theodossiev, Nikola. *North-Western Thrace from the Fifth to First Centuries B.C.* Oxford: Archaeopress, 2000.

Thomas Aquinas, Saint. "On Kingship." In Dino Bigongiari, ed., *The Political Ideas of St. Thomas Aquinas: Representative Selections.* New York: Free Press, 1997.

Thomas, Hugh. *Conquest: Montezuma, Cortes, and the Fall of Old Mexico.* New York: Simon & Schuster, 1993.

Thompson, E. A. *The Huns.* Oxford: Basil Blackwell, 1996.

Thompson, Leonard M. *Survival in Two Worlds: Moshoeshoe of Lesotho, 1786–1870.* Oxford: Clarendon Press, 1975.

Thomson, John A. F. *The Transformation of Medieval England: 1370–1529.* New York: Longman, 1983.

Tierney, Brian, and Sidney Painter. *Western Europe in the Middle Ages, 300–1475.* 6th ed. New York: McGraw-Hill, 1999.

Todd, Malcolm. *The Early Germans.* Cambridge, MA: Basil Blackwell, 1992.

Totman, Conrad D. *A History of Japan.* Malden, MA: Basil Blackwell, 2000.

———. *Tokugawa Ieyasu, Shogun: A Biography.* San Francisco: Heian Press, 1983.

Toynbee, Arnold. *Constantine Porphyrogenitus and His World.* New York: Oxford University Press, 1973.

Toyne, Stanley M. *The Scandinavians in History.* 1948. Reprint, New York: Barnes & Noble, 1996.

Trevelyan, George Macaulay. *A Shortened History of England.* Baltimore, MD: Pelican Books, 1970.

Trevor, Meriol. *The Shadow of a Crown: The Life Story of James II of England and VII of Scotland.* London: Constable, 1988.

Tsvetkov, Plamen S. *A History of the Balkans: A Regional Overview from a Bulgarian Perspective.* San Francisco: EM Text, 1993.

Twitchett, Denis, ed. *Sui and T'ang China, 589–906.*

Vol. 3 of *The Cambridge History of China*. New York: Cambridge University Press, 1979.

Urton, Gary. *Inca Myths*. Austin: University of Texas Press, 1999.

Vakalopoulos, Apostolos E. *A History of Thessaloniki*. Trans. T. F. Carney. Thessalonike: Institute for Balkan Studies, 1993.

Vallone, Lynne. *Becoming Victoria*. New Haven, CT: Yale University Press, 2001.

Van der Zee, Barbara, and Henri A. Van der Zee. *William and Mary*. New York: Alfred A. Knopf, 1973.

Vardys, Vytas Stanley, and Judith B. Sedaitis. *Lithuania: The Rebel Nation*. Boulder, CO: Westview Press, 1997.

Vasiliev, Alexander A. *History of the Byzantine Empire 324–1453*. Madison: University of Wisconsin Press, 1952.

Vekony, Gabor. *Dacians-Romans-Romanians*. Toronto: Matthias Corvinus Publishing, 2000.

Venturi, Franco. *The End of the Old Regime in Europe, 1768–1776: The First Crisis*. Trans. R. Burr Litchfield. Princeton, NJ: Princeton University Press, 1989.

Vernadsky, George. *A History of Russia*. New Haven, CT: Yale University Press, 1987.

———. *Kievan Russia*. New Haven, CT: Yale University Press, 1973.

Vierhaus, Rudolph. *Germany in the Age of Absolutism*. Trans. Jonathan B. Knudsen. New York: Cambridge University Press, 1988.

Wakefield, David Fenjia. *Household Division and Inheritance in Qing and Republican China*. Honolulu: University of Hawaii Press, 1998.

Walker, David. *Medieval Wales*. New York: Cambridge University Press, 1990.

Wallace-Hadrill, J. M. *The Barbarian West: 400–1000*. 3rd rev. ed. New York: Barnes & Noble, 1998.

Walzer, Michael, ed. *Regicide and Revolution: Speeches at the Trial of Louis XVI*. Trans. Marian Rothstein. New York: Columbia University Press, 1992.

Ward, Christine Gailey. *Kinship to Kingship: Gender Hierarchy and State Formation in the Tongan Islands*. Austin: University of Texas Press, 1987.

Warnicke, Retha M. *The Marrying of Anne of Cleves: Royal Protocol in Early Modern England*. New York: Cambridge University Press, 2000.

Watson, Francis. *India: A Concise History*. Rev. ed. New York: Thames & Hudson, 2002.

Webb, Robert N. *Attila, King of the Huns*. New York: Watts, 1965.

Webber, Carolyn, and Aaron B. Wildavsky. *A History of Taxation and Expenditure in the Western World*. New York: Simon & Schuster, 1986.

Wedgwood, C. V. *A Coffin for King Charles: The Trial and Execution of Charles I*. Pleasantville, NY: Akadine Press, 2001.

Weigall, Arthur. *The Life and Times of Cleopatra, Queen of Egypt*. New and rev. ed. New York: Putnam, 1996.

Weinfurter, Stefan. *The Salian Century: Main Currents in an Age of Transition*. Trans. Barbara M. Bowlus. Philadelphia: University of Pennsylvania Press, 1999.

Weinstein, Brian, and Aaron Segal. *Haiti: Political Failures, Cultural Successes*. New York: Praeger, 1984.

Weintraub, Stanley. *Victoria: An Intimate Biography*. New York: Truman Talley/Plume, 1992.

Weir, Alison. *Lancaster and York: The Wars of the Roses*. London: Pimlico, 1998.

———. *The Wars of the Roses*. New York: Ballantine, 1996.

Westwood, J. N. *Endurance and Endeavour: Russian History, 1812–2001*. 5th ed. Oxford: Oxford University Press, 2002.

Wheatcroft, Andrew. *The Habsburgs: Embodying Empire*. New York: Penguin, 1996.

———. *The Ottomans: Dissolving Images*. New York: Penguin, 1993.

White, T. H. *The Once and Future King*. New York: Putnam, 2002.

Wiebe, Robert H. *Who We Are: A History of Popular Nationalism*. Princeton, NJ: Princeton University Press, 2002.

Wilentz, Sean. *Rites of Power: Symbolism, Ritual and Politics Since the Middle Ages*. Philadelphia: University of Pennsylvania Press, 1999.

Wilhelmina, Queen of the Netherlands. *Lonely but Not Alone*. Trans. John Peereboom. New York: McGraw-Hill, 1960.

Wilkins, Frances. *Egypt*. Philadelphia: Chelsea House, 1999.

Willetts, R. F. *The Civilization of Ancient Crete*. New York: Barnes & Noble, 1995.

Williams, Jonathan, Joe Cribb, and Elizabeth Errington, eds. *Money: A History*. New York: St. Martin's Press, 1998.

Williams, Neville. *The Life and Times of Elizabeth I*. New York: Welcome Rain Publishers, 1998.

Williams, Penry. *The Later Tudors: England, 1547–1603*. New York: Oxford University Press, 1995.

Williams, Stephen, and Friell, Gerard. *Theodosius:The Empire at Bay.* New Haven, CT: Yale University Press, 1995.

Winnifrith, Tom. *The Vlachs: The History of a Balkan People.* New York: St. Martin's Press, 1987.

Winstedt, Richard O. *Malaya and Its History.* 3rd ed. New York: Hutchinson's University Library, 1953.

Wirsing, Robert, and Nancy Wirsing. *Ancient India and Its Influence in Modern Times.* New York: Watts, 1973.

Wisniewski, Richard A. *The Rise and Fall of the Hawaiian Kingdom: A Pictorial History.* Honolulu: Pacific Basin Enterprises, 1979.

Wittfogel, Karl A. *Oriental Despotism: A Comparative Study of Total Power.* New York: Vintage Books, 1981.

Wolpert, Stanley. *A New History of India.* 7th ed. New York: Oxford University Press, 2003.

Wolters, O. W. *Early Indonesian Commerce: A Study of the Origins of Srivijaya.* Ithaca, NY: Cornell University Press, 1967.

Wolverton, Lisa. *Hastening Toward Prague: Power and Society in the Medieval Czech Lands.* Philadelphia: University of Pennsylvania Press, 2001.

Wormald, Jenny. *Mary Queen of Scots: Passion, Politics and a Kingdom Lost.* New York: Distributed by St. Martin's Press, 2001.

Wright, Arthur F., and Denis C. Twitchett, eds. *Perspectives on the T'ang.* New Haven, CT: Yale University Press, 1973.

Wyatt, David K. *The Politics of Reform in Thailand: Education in the Reign of King Chulalongkorn.* New Haven, CT: Yale University Press, 1969.

———. *Thailand: A Short History.* New Haven, CT: Yale University Press, 1984.

Wynaden, Jo, and Ronald Cherry. *Welcome to Thailand.* Milwaukee: Gareth Stevens Publishing, 2001.

Xuanzang, Ibn Batuta, and François Bernier. *Three Travellers to India: Being a Simple Account of India as Seen by Yuan Chwang (Huien Tsiang), Ibn Batuta and Bernier.* Lahore: Al-Biruni, 1978.

Yorke, Barbara. *Kings and Kingdoms of Early Anglo-Saxon England.* New York: Routledge, 1997.

Young, Robert J. C. *Postcolonialism.* New York: Oxford University Press, 2003.

Zanger, Abby E. *Scenes from the Marriage of Louis XIV: Nuptial Fictions and the Making of Absolutist Power.* Stanford, CA: Stanford University Press, 1997.

Zehavi, A.M., ed. *Handbook of the World's Religions.* New York: Watts, 1973.

Zéphir, Thierry. *Khmer: The Lost Empire of Cambodia.* New York: Abrams, 1998.

General Index

Note: Page references in italics indicate photographs.

A

Aachen, Germany, **1:**97
Abbas the Great, **1:**1; **3:**815
Abbasid Dynasty, **1:**1–2, 3
Abdication, royal, **1:**3–5
  political factors, **1:**4
  religion and, **1:**3–4
Abu Bakr, **1:**5
Accession of kings, **1:**5–7
  King Baudouin, **1:**6
  modern changes, **1:**6
Achaeans. *See* Mycenaean monarchies
Achaemenid Dynasty, **1:**7–8
  Artaxerxes I, **1:**57
  Artaxerxes II, **1:**57–58, *57*
  Artaxerxes III, **1:**58
Acheh Kingdom, **1:**8–9
Adolph of Nassau, **1:**24
Adud ad-Dawlah, **1:**134
Aethelred the Unready. *See* Anglo-
  Saxon rulers; Edward the
  Confessor
Afonso I, **1:**9–10
Afonso I, Nzinga Mbemba, **1:**10–11
African Kingdoms, **1:**11–15, *12, 13,*
  17–18
  Assante Kingdom, **1:**60–61
  Azande Kingdoms, **1:**82
  Bemba Kingdom, **1:**101–102
  Benin Kingdom, **1:**102–103, *102*
  modern kingdoms, **1:**15
  polygynous monarchs, **1:**11
  regalia, **1:**14
  rise of, **1:**12–14
  royal advisors, **1:**14–15

African Kingdoms (*continued*)
  Sa'id, Sayyid ibn, **3:**816–817
  Shaka Zulu, **3:**846–847
  Shilluk Kingdom, **3:**853
  Sobhuza I, **3:**867–868
  Sobhuza II, **3:**868, *868*
  Sokoto Caliphate, **3:**869
  Songhai Kingdom, **3:**870–871
  Sotho (Suto) Kingdom, **3:**872–873
  succession to throne, **1:**14–15
  Swazi Kingdom, **3:**917–918
  symbolism of, **1:**14
  Tikar Kingdom, **3:**945
  Tio Kingdom, **3:**945–946
  Toro Kingdom, **3:**955–956
  Tutsi Kingdom, **3:**969–970
Ahab, **1:**15–16
Ahmadnagar Kingdom, **1:**16–17
Ahmose I, **1:**17
Akan Kingdoms, **1:**17–18
  impact of trade, **1:**18
  rise of strong leaders, **1:**18
Akbar the Great, **1:**18–20, *20. See also*
  Mughal Dynasty
Akhenaten, **1:**20–21
  Tutankhamen, **3:**968–969, *969*
Akkad, Kingdom of, **1:**21–22
  Sargon of Akkad, **3:**826
Aksum Kingdom, **1:**22
  Amhara Kingdom, **1:**39–40
  prosperity and decline, **1:**22
  rise, **1:**22
Al Hajj, **1:**90
Al-Hamid, Abd II, **1:**2–3
Al-Mansur, **1:**2
Al-Rahman, Abd, **1:**3
Al-Sharif, Ahmad, **3:**824
Alan I, Bretangne, **1:**124
Alaric I, **1:**23

Alaungpaya, **1:**23, 133
Alaungpaya Dynasty, **1:**23–24
  Thibaw, **3:**939
Albert I, **1:**24–25; **3:**831
Albert II, **1:***100,* 101
Alexander I, **1:**25, 116
Alexander I, Tsar, **1:**25–27, *26*
Alexander II, **1:**27–28
Alexander III. *See* Romanov Dynasty
Alexander III, the Great, **1:**28–31, 48,
  208; **3:**921
  divinity signs, **3:**811
  Macedonian Empire, **1:**28–31;
    2:559–560
  Seleucid Dynasty, **3:**839
Alexandra, **1:**31
Alexius I, **1:**140
Alfonso V, the Magnanimous, **1:**31–32
Alfonso X, the Wise, **1:**32–33
Alfred the Great, **1:**33, 43–44
Alienation, of royal subjects, **3:**904
Almohad Dynasty, **1:**33–35
Almoravid Dynasty, **1:**33–35
  caliphates, **1:**34–35
Amadeus VIII, **3:**829
Ambassadors, **1:**35–36
Amenhotep IV. *See* Akhenaten
American Kingdoms, central and
  north, **1:**37–39
Amhara Kingdom, **1:**39–40
Amorian Dynasty, Byzantine Empire,
  1:136
Amum, **1:**20–21
Anawrahta, **1:**133
Andhra Kingdom, **1:**40–41
Andhras Dynasty. *See* Satavahana
  Dynasty
Angelus Dynasty, **1:**137
Angevin Dynasties, **1:**41–42, 44–45

Angkor Kingdom, **1:**42–43;
  3:886–887
Anglo-Dutch Treaty, **1:**9
Anglo-Saxon rulers, **1:**43–44
  Alfred the Great, **1:**33
  Sussex and, **3:**916
Anjou, House of. *See* Angevin
  Dynasties
Anjou Kingdom, **1:**41–42, 44–45
Ankole Kingdom, **1:**45
Annam, Kingdom of. *See* Vietnamese
  Kingdoms
Anne, **1:**46; **3:**903
Antanavaratra Rahena, **1:**105
Antigonid Dynasty. *See* Hellenistic
  Dynasties
Antiochus III, the Great, **1:**46–47;
  3:839
Antonine Dynasty, **1:**142
Aquitaine Duchy, **1:**41–42, 47
Arabia, Kingdoms of, **1:**48
Arabian Peninsula, **3:**811
Arachosia Kingdom, **1:**48–49
Aragón, House of, **1:**49–50
Aragón, Kingdom of, **1:**50–51
  Alfonso V, the Magnanimous,
    1:31–32
Aramean Kingdoms, **1:**51–52
Ardashir I, **3:**826
Arenas, royal, **1:**52–53
Argead Dynasty, **2:**558
Arles Kingdom, **1:**53–54
Armenian Kingdoms, **1:**54–55
Arpad Dynasty, **1:**55–56
  Angevin Dynasties, **1:**41–42
  Stephen I, **3:***899,* 899–900
Art
  Byzantine Empire, **1:**140
  portraits, **1:**56–57
  Sung (Song) Dynasty, **3:**913–914
  Toltec Empire, **3:**951
Artaxerxes I, **1:**57
Artaxerxes II, **1:***57,* 57–58
Artaxerxes III, **1:**58
Arthur, King, **1:**58–60, *59*
Aryans
  Brahmarsi-Desa Kingdom, **1:**123
  South Asian Kingdoms, **3:**877, 879
Ashikaga Shogunate, **1:**61–62; **3:**854,
  854, 855–856
Ashurbanipal, **1:**62–63

Asia
  Bhutan Kingdom, **1:**106–107
  landholding patterns, **2:**520
Asia Minor
  Byzantine Empire, **1:**134
  Macedonian Empire, **2:**559
Asian Dynasties, Central, **1:**63–64
  Turkic Empire, **3:**967–968
Asoka, **1:**64–66, *65*
Assante Kingdom, **1:**60–61
Assyrian Empire, **1:**66–67
  Aramean Kingdoms, **1:**51–52
  Ashurbanipal, **1:**62–63
  Sargon II, **3:**825–826
  Scythian Empire, **3:**836
  Sennacherib, **3:**842
  Shalmaneser III, **3:**847
  Shalmaneser V, **3:**848
  Shamshi-Adad I, **3:**848
  Tiglath-Pileser III, **3:**944–945
Asturias Kingdom, **1:**67–68
Atahualpa, **1:**68
Athaliah, **1:**69
Athens, Kingdom of, **1:**69–71
  Sparta and, **3:**895–896
Attalid Dynasty. *See* Hellenistic
  Dynasties
Attila, **1:**71–73, *72*
Augustus, **1:***73,* 73–74; **3:**942
Aurangzeb, **1:**74–75
Austro-Hungarian Empire, **1:**75–77
  Serbian Kingdom, **3:**842–844
Ava Kingdom, **3:**886
Avadh Kingdom. *See* Oudh (Avadh)
  Kingdom
Avanti Kingdom, **1:**77–78
Aviz Dynasty, **1:**78–79
Avongara. *See* Azande Kingdoms
Awan Dynasty, **1:**79
Aymara Kingdom, **1:**79–80
  South American monarchies, **3:**875–876
Ayudhya Kingdom, **3:**887
Ayutthaya Kingdom, **1:**80
  Angkor Kingdom, **1:**42–43
  Siam, Kingdoms of, **3:**858
Ayyubid Dynasty, **1:**80–82
  Saladin, **3:**818–819
Azande Kingdoms, **1:**82
Aztec Empire, **1:**37, 82–85, *84, 85*
  baths, royal, **1:**96
  Toltec Empire, **3:**952

B

Babar. *See* Babur
Babenberg Dynasty, **1:**86
Babur, **1:**18–20, 86–87, *87*
Baburnama (Babur), **1:**87
Babylonian Empire, **3:**822
Bacatá rulers, **3:**875
Bactrian Kingdom. *See* Indo-Greek
  Kingdoms
Bagirmi Kingdom, **1:**88
Bagyidaw, King, **1:**134
Bahmani Dynasty, **1:**88–89
Bakufu, shoguns, **3:**855–856
Baldwin I, **1:**89. *See also* Crusader
  Kingdoms
Balkan Peninsula, Byzantine Empire,
  1:134
Balkan Wars, **1:**129
Bambara Kingdom, **1:**89–91
  Songhai Kingdom, **3:**870–871
Bamileke Kingdoms, **1:**91–92
  formation, **1:**91
  society, **1:**91
  Tikar Kingdom, **3:**945
Bangkok Kingdom, **1:**92; **3:**887
Banu Khurasan, **1:**92–93
Banum Kingdom. *See* Tikar Kingdom
Barcelona, county of. *See* Catalonia,
  county of
Barghash ibn Sa'id el-Busaidi, **1:**93
Baridshahi Dynasty, **1:**109
Baroda Kingdom, **1:**93–94
Basil I, **1:**94
Basil II, **1:**94–95
Basque Kingdom, **1:**95–96
Baths, royal, **1:**96–97, *97*
Bathsheba, **3:**869
Batu Khan, **1:**97–98. *See also* Genghis
  Khan
Baudouin, **1:**6, 98
Behavior, conventions of royal,
  1:98–99
Belgian Kingdom, **1:**99–101
  Baudouin, **1:**98
  Burgundy Kingdom, **1:**131–132
  expansion, **1:**100–101
  origins, **1:**99–100
  Saxe-Coburg-Gotha Dynasty,
    3:830–831
  stability, **1:**100–101

Bemba Kingdom, **1:**101–102

Benin Kingdom, **1:**102–103
  decline, **1:**103
  expansion, **1:**103
  origins, **1:**102–103
  wealth, **1:**103

Berar Kingdom, **1:**103–104
  fall, **1:**104
  independence, **1:**103–104
  relations with other states, **1:**104

Berengar, Raymond. *See* Catalonia, County of

Bernadotte Dynasty, **3:**919

Betsimisaraka Kingdom, **1:**104–105

Beyezid I, **3:**910

Beyezid II, **1:**105

Bhagnagar Kingdom. *See* Hyderabad Kingdom

Bharatpur Kingdom, **1:**105–106

Bhutan Kingdom, **1:**106–107
  Buddhism, **1:**106
  Chinese and British dominance, **1:**106–107
  early period, **1:**106
  modern times, **1:**107

Bible, The, **3:**814

Biblical kings, **1:**107–109
  Aramean Kingdoms, **1:**51–52
  Athaliah, **1:**69
  commerce, **1:**108
  corruption, **1:**108
  David, **1:**107–108
  end of kingdoms, **1:**108–109
  Saul, **1:**107–108
  Solomon, **1:**108
  succession, **1:**108
  Zedekiah, **1:**109

Bidar Kingdom, **1:**109

Bimbisara. *See* Magadha Kingdom

Bindusara. *See* Asoka

Birth. *See* Sacral birth and death

Blois-Champagne Dynasty, **1:**110–111
  cultural and literary center, **1:**110
  descendants, **1:**110–111
  families, **1:**110
  Henry I, **1:**110
  union with France, **1:**111

Blood, royal, **1:**111–112

Bodawpaya, King, **1:**134

Bodhisattva, **1:**127

Bodies, politic and natural, **1:**112–114

Bonapartist Empire, **1:**114–116, *116*
  empire collapse, **1:**116
  empire expands, **1:**114–115
  imperial administration, **1:**115–116
  Marie Louise, **1:**115
  origins, **1:**114

Boris I Michael, **1:**128

Borneo, **1:**125–126

Bornu Empire. *See* Kanembu-Kanuri Kingdom

Boru, Brian, **1:**117

Boudicca (Boadicea), **1:**117–118

Bourbon Dynasty, **1:***118,* 118–121
  beginnings, **1:**118
  French kings, **1:**120
  Henry IV, **1:**118–119
  Italian kings, **1:**120, 121
  Louis XIV, **1:**119
  Louis XVIII, **1:**120–121
  Parma kings, **1:**120, 121
  Spanish kings, **1:**120, 121

Bragança Dynasty, **1:**122

Brahmarsi-Desa Kingdom, **1:**122–123

Brazil
  Bragança Dynasty, **1:**122
  Portuguese monarchy of, **1:**123–124

Bretagne Duchy, **1:**124–125

Brittany. *See* Bretagne Duchy

Brooke, Sir James (Rajah), **1:**125–126

Buddhism and kingship, **1:***126,* 126–128
  Bhutan Kingdom, **1:**106
  bodhisattva, **1:**127
  chakravartin, **1:**127
  councils, **1:**126–127
  devaraja, **1:**127
  dharmaraja, **1:**127
  elements of, **1:**127
  sacred texts, **3:**814–815
  Sailendra Dynasty, **3:**817
  spread of Buddhism, **1:**126–127
  Srivijaya-Palembang Empire, **3:**896–897

Buganda Kingdom. *See* Ganda Kingdom

Bulgarian Monarchy, **1:**94–95, 128–129
  beginnings, **1:**128
  fall of kingdom, **1:**128
  modern Bulgaria, **1:**129

Bulgarian Monarchy *(continued)*
  return of kingdom, **1:**128
  Saxe-Coburg-Gotha Dynasty, **3:**831
  third kingdom, **1:**128–129

Bulgarian Orthodox Exarchate, **1:**128

Bundi Kingdom, **1:**129–130

Bunyoro Kingdom. *See* Nyoro Kingdom

Bureaucracy, royal, **1:**130–131
  bureaucrats, **1:**130–131
  censorship, **1:**130
  origins, **1:**130
  religion, **1:**130
  revenue, **1:**130
  surveillance, **1:**130

Bureaucrats, **1:**130–131

Burgundy duchy, **1:**132

Burgundy Kingdom, **1:**131–132
  duchy, **1:**132
  Juane-Burgundy, **1:**132
  origins, **1:**131

Burmese Dynasty
  Alaungpaya Dynasty, **1:**23–24
  Ayutthaya Kingdom, **1:**80

Burmese Kingdoms, **1:**132–134
  British conflicts, **1:**134
  Konbaung Dynasty, **1:**133
  Mon Kingdom, **1:**133
  origins, **1:**132–133
  Pagan Kingdom, **1:**133
  Shan Kingdom, **1:**133
  Shan Kingdoms, **3:**848–849
  Southeast Asian Kingdoms, **3:**886
  Toungoo Dynasty, **1:**133; **3:**956

Busaid Dynasty. *See* Barghash ibn Sa'id el-Busaidi

Buyid (Buwayhid) Dynasty, **1:**134

Byzantine Empire, **1:**94, 134–141, *135*
  Amorian Dynasty, **1:**136
  Angelus Dynasty, **1:**137
  Armenian Kingdoms, **1:**54–55
  art, **1:**140
  Christianity, **1:**135
  Conmenian Dynasty, **1:**137, 138
  culture, **1:**140
  demise, **1:**134–135
  Ducas Dynasty, **1:**137
  Eastern Empire, **1:**140
  Heraclius Dynasty, **1:**136
  imperial power, **1:**139–140
  Justin Dynasty, **1:**136, 138

Byzantine Empire (continued)
  Lascarid Dynasty, **1:**137
  Latin Empire rules, **1:**137
  Leo Dynasty, **1:**136
  Macedonian Dynasty, **1:**136–137
  military, **1:**138–139
  origins, **1:**134–138
  Palaeologan Dynasty, **1:**137, 138
  relations with west, **1:**140–141
  religion, **1:**139
  sacred kingships, **3:**813
  Syrian Dynasty, **1:**136
  Theoderic the Great, **3:**936–937
  Theodora I, **3:**935–936
  Theodosius Dynasty, **1:**136
  Thessalonika Kingdom, **3:**938–939

C

Caesars, **1:***141*, 141–142
  arenas, royal, **1:**52–53
  Augustus, **1:***73*, 73–74
  Flavian and Antonine Dynasties,
    1:142
  Julio-Claudian Dynasty, **1:**141–142
  as subordinate rulers, **1:**142
Caligula, **1:**142–143; **3:**943
Caliphates, **1:**143–146
  Almoravid Dynasty, **1:**34–35
  growth and decline, **1:**145–146
  origins and early years, **1:**143–145
  Sokoto Caliphate, **3:**869
Calukya (Chalukya) Dynasty, **1:**146
Cambodian Kingdoms, **1:**146–148, *147*
  Angkor Kingdom, **1:**42–43, 147
  earliest kingdoms, **1:**146–147
  foreign domination, **1:**147
  Southeast Asian Kingdoms,
    3:886–887
Cambyses II, **1:**148
Canute I, the Great. *See* Cnut I
Capet, Hugh, **1:**148–149
Capetian Dynasty, **1:**149–150
Caracalla, Emperor, **1:**96, *97*. *See also*
    Roman Empire
Carl XVI, **3:***919*
Carolingian Dynasty, **1:**150–153, *152*
  after Charlemagne, **1:**151
  gaining legitimacy, **1:**150
  kingdom divided, **1:**151–152
  maintaining stability, **1:**150–151

Carolingian Dynasty (continued)
  in west, **1:**152
Carthage, Kingdom of, **1:**153–154
  culture, **1:**153
  founding of, **1:**153
  relationship with Rome, **1:**153–154
Casimir III, **1:**154
Casimir IV, **1:**154–155
Caste systems, **1:**155–156
Castile, Kingdom of, **1:**156–157
  Alfonso X, the Wise, **1:**32–33
  Aragón, Kingdom of, **1:**50–51, 157
  autonomy and mergers, **1:**156
  and León, **1:**156–157
Catalonia, county of, **1:**157–158
Catherine II, the Great, **1:**25–27,
    158–159, *159*
  early life, **1:**158–159
  as monarch, **1:**159
  Stanislas II, **3:**898
  theater and, **3:**933
Censorship, bureaucracy and, **1:**130
Central America, **1:**37–38
Central Asia, **2:**559
Cera (Chera) Dynasty, **1:**160
Cetshwayo, **1:**160–161
Chahamanas Dynasty. *See* Chauhan
    Dynasty
Chakravartin, **1:**127; **2:**397
Chakri, **1:**92
Chakri Dynasty, **1:**161; **3:**858–859
Chaldean Empire. *See* Nebuchadrezzar II
Chalukya Dynasty. *See* Calukya Dynasty
Champa Kingdom, **1:**161–162
Champagne Dynasty. *See* Blois-
    Champagne Dynasty
Champassak Kingdom, **1:**162–163
Chandella Dynasty, **1:**163–164
Chandragupta Maurya, **1:**164–165
Chao Dynasties, **1:**165
Charlemagne, **1:**165–168, *167*
  accomplishments, **1:**167
  Byzantine Empire, **1:**138
  commanding an empire, **1:**166–167
  early life and rule, **1:**166
  royal baths and, **1:**97
  Saxon Kingdoms, **3:**833
Charles the Bold, **1:**132
Charles I, **1:**121, 168–169; **3:**777,
    861, 902
Charles II, **1:**169; **3:**902

Charles III, **1:**169–170
Charles IV, **1:**170
Charles V, **1:**170–171
Charles VI, **1:**171–172
Charles VII, **1:**172
Chauhan Dynasty, **1:**172–173
Chavin Empire, **1:**173–174
Chefs. *See* Cooks, royal
Chenla Empire, **1:**174
  Angkor Kingdom, **1:**42–43
  Southeast Asian Kingdoms, **3:**886
Chera Dynasty. *See* Mysore Kingdom
Chiangmai, **1:**174–175
Chibchas, **3:**874–875
Ch'ien Lung, **1:**175–176
  conquest and prosperity, **1:**176
  corruption and decay, **1:**176
  Manchu and, **1:**175–176
Childeric I. *See* Clovis I
Chilufya Mulenga, **1:**102
Chimú Empire, **1:**176–177
  autonomous rulers, **1:**177
  economic and social organization,
    1:177
  Incas conquest, **1:**177
Ch'in (Qin) Dynasty, **1:**177–179, *179*
  Shih Huang Ti (Shihuangdi),
    3:852–853
Chinese sacred texts, **3:**814
Ch'ing (Qing) Dynasty, **1:**179–181,
    180
  establishing authority, **1:**180
  rebellion and invasion, **1:**181
  stability, **1:**180–181
Chola Dynasty. *See* Mysore Kingdom
Chola Kingdom. *See* Cola Kingdom
Choson Kingdom, **1:**182–183, *183*
Chou (Zhou) Dynasty, **1:**183–185
  eastern Chou, **1:**184–185
  golden age of philosophy, **1:**185
  life under the Chou, **1:**185
  Shang (Yin) Dynasty, **3:**849–851
  western Chou, **1:**184
Christianity and kingship, **1:**185–188,
    187
  Byzantine Empire, **1:**135
  Byzantine kingship, **1:**187
  Christian ideas of kingship,
    1:185–187
  renaissance and post-reformation
    kingship, **1:**187–188

Christianity and kingship *(continued)*
  Sancho III, the Great, **3:**824
  Theodosius I, the Great, **3:**937
Christina, **1:**188–189; **3:**920
Chulalongkorn, **1:**189–190; **3:**858
Churches as tombs, **3:**954
Cixi. *See* Tz'u Hsi
Class systems and royalty, **1:**190–191
  ancient Egypt, **1:**190
  collapse of monarchy, **1:**191
  middle class, **1:**191
  origins and background, **1:**190
  Roman Empire and feudal state,
    1:190
Claudian Dynasty. *See* Julio-Claudians
Claudius, **1:**191–192, *192*
Cleisthenes, **1:**70
Cleopatra VII, **1:**192–194, *193*
Clovis I, **1:**194–195
Cnut I, **1:**195–196
  achievements as king, **1:**196
  conquest of England, **1:**195
  rule in Scandinavia, **1:**195–196
  Viking Empire, **3:**993
Code Napoléon, **1:**115–116
Coinage, royal, **1:**196–197
  Europe, **1:**197
  middle ages, **1:**197
  modern era, **1:**197
  origins, **1:**196–197
  Satavahana Dynasty, **3:**828
Cola Kingdom, **1:**197–198
  fall, **1:**198
  further expansion, **1:**198
  maintaining power, **1:**198
Colonialism and kingship, **1:**198–202,
    199, 200
  effect of indirect rule, **1:**201
  empires in new world, **1:**199
  imperial experience, **1:**200–201
  North America, **1:**201
  other European powers, **1:**200–201
  Portuguese and Spanish,
    1:199–200
Commerce and kingship, **1:**202–203
  Biblical kings, **1:**108
  commercial revolution, **1:**203
  early commerce and trade, **1:**202
  means of exchange, **1:**202–203
  Satavahana Dynasty, **3:**828
  taxation, **3:**931–932

Comnenian Dynasty, **1:**137, 138,
    203–204
Competition, fraternal, **1:**204–205
Concubines, royal, **1:**205–206
  concubine or mistress, **1:**205
  Lady Nijo, **1:**206
  Madame De Pompadour, **1:**206
  Yang Guifei, **1:**205–206
Confucius, **3:**814
Congo Kingdom. *See* Kongo
    Kingdom
Connaught Kingdom, **1:**206–207
  early rulers, **1:**206
  O'Connors, **1:**207
  struggle with England, **1:**207
Conquest and kingships, **1:**207–209
  Alexander the Great, **1:**208
  historical notion, **1:**207–208
  modern notion, **1:**209
  Mongol conquest, **1:**208–209
  Norman conquests, **1:**208
Conrad I, **3:**831–832
Conrad II, **1:**209; **3:**819–820
Conrad III, **1:**209–210
Consorts, royal, **1:**210–211
Constantine I, the Great, **1:***211,*
    211–212
  conversion to Christianity, **1:**212
  reforms and policies, **1:**212
  rise to power, **1:**211
Cooks, royal, **1:**212–213
Córdoba, caliphate of, **1:**213
  Taifa rulers, **3:**925
Corruption, Biblical kings, **1:**108
Councils and counselors, royal,
    1:214–215
  early royal councils, **1:**214
  revolution and decline, **1:**214–215
  witenagemot and emergence of
    democracy, **1:**214
Courts and court officials, royal,
    1:215–216, *216*
  court hierarchy, **1:**215
  court life, **1:**215–217
Croatian Kingdom, **1:**217–218
  Alexander I, **1:**25
Croesus, **1:**218
Crowning of kings, **1:**5–7
Crusader Kingdoms, **1:**218–219
  Angevin Dynasties, **1:**41–42
  Ayyubid Dynasty, **1:**80–82

Crusader Kingdoms *(continued)*
  elsewhere in the Mediterranean,
    1:219
  Outremer, **1:**218
  Saladin, **3:**819
  Syrian Kingdoms, **3:**921–922
Culture
  Byzantine Empire, **1:**140
  Maori Kingdoms, **2:**574
  Satavahana Dynasty, **3:**828
  Yuan Dynasty, **3:**1034
Curses, royal, **1:**220–221
Cyaxares, **1:**221
Cyrus the Great, **1:**7, 221–222;
    3:846

D

Da Monzon, **1:**90
Dacia Kingdom, **1:**223
  early kings, **1:**223
  struggle with Rome, **1:**223
Dacomba Kingdom, **1:**224
Dai Viet, Kingdom of. *See* Vietnamese
    Kingdoms
Dalai Lama, **3:***943,* 943–944
Danish Kingdom, **1:**224–225
  Alfred the Great, **1:**33
Dar Fur sultinate. *See* Fur Kingdom
Darius I, the Great, **1:**7, *8,* 48,
    225–227, *226*
  empire, **1:**226–227
  western struggles, **1:**226
Darius II (Ochus), **1:**227
Darius III (Codommanus),
    1:227–228
Davaravati Kingdom. *See* Siam,
    Kingdoms of
David, **1:***228,* 228–229; **3:**869
  Biblical kings, **1:**107–108
  sacred kingships, **3:**813
David I, **1:**229
David II, **1:**230
Deaccession, **1:**230–231
  institutionalized retirement,
    1:230
  involuntary loss of rulership,
    1:230–231
  voluntary retirement, **1:**230
Death. *See* Sacral birth and death
Deheubarth Kingdom, **1:**231

Delhi, 3:881

Delhi Kingdom, 1:231–233
  Khalji Dynasty, 1:232
  Slave Dynasty, 1:231
  sultanate's decline, 1:233
  Tughluq Dynasty, 1:232; 3:966

Delhi sultanate. See Delhi Kingdom

Delian League, 1:71

Descent, royal, 1:233–234
  gender and, 1:234
  legitimate and illegitimate, 1:234

Dessalines, Jean-Jacques, 1:234–235

Dethronement, 1:235–236
  of monarchy, 1:235–236
  rights, 1:235

Devaraja, 1:127

Dewas Kingdom, 1:236

Dharmaraja, 1:127

Dido. See Carthage, Kingdom of

Dinga Cisse, 3:871–872

Dingiswayo, 1:237

Diocletian, 1:237–238
  gaining throne, 1:237
  last years, 1:238
  political and economic reform,
    1:237–238

Diplomacy, royal, 1:238–239
  monarchs and diplomatic protocol,
    1:239
  personal and national diplomacy,
    1:239

Disease and royalty, 1:239–241

Divination and diviners, royal,
    1:241–242
  African society, 1:241–242
  astrology, 1:241
  attitudes toward, 1:241
  examples of, 1:241
  penalties against, 1:242

Divine right, 1:242–243
  ages of decline, 1:243
  origins, 1:242

Divinity of kings, 1:243–246
  divinity manipulated, 1:245
  fundamentals, 1:244–245
  lasting concept, 1:245–246

Djoser, 1:246

Dmitri, Grand Prince, 1:246–247

Domitian, 3:957

Dravidians, 3:880

Dual monarchies, 1:247–248

Dual monarchies (continued)
  Biblical times, 1:247
  medieval and Renaissance Europe,
    1:247–248
  modern era, 1:248

Ducas Dynasty, 1:137

Dutch Kingdoms. See Netherlands
  Kingdom

Dyfed Kingdom, 1:248–249

E

Earth and sky, separation of,
    1:250

East Asian Dynasties, 1:250–255,
    251, 252–253
  Buddhism, 1:255
  conflicts, 1:251–253
  Confucianism, 1:254–255
  cultural values, 1:253–254
  land and taxes, 1:254
  post-fifteenth century, 1:253
  social organization, 1:254

East Asian Kingdoms
  Shih Huang Ti (Shihuangdi),
    3:852–853

Eastern Empire, 1:140

Eastern Orthodox Church, 1:139

Eastern Roman Empire. See Byzantine
  Empire

Ebna Hakim, 3:852

Edo Kingdom. See Benin Kingdom

Education of kings, 1:255–257
  appointed tutors, 1:256
  Christian kings, 1:256–257
  divine descent, 1:256
  heredity or election, 1:257
  social contract, 1:256

Edward I, 1:257–259, 258

Edward II, 1:259–260

Edward III, 1:260–261
  early life and rule, 1:260
  final years, 1:260–261
  war, plague, parliament, 1:260

Edward VI, 1:262

Edward VIII, 1:4

Edward the Confessor, 1:261
  Anglo-Saxon rulers, 1:43–44

Egypt, 1:12, 17
  Akhenaten, 1:20–21
  sacred texts, 3:814

Egyptian Dynasties, Ancient (before
    Eighteenth Dynasty), 1:262–264,
    263
  early dynastic period, 1:262
  first intermediate period, 1:263
  great pyramids, 1:263
  Hyskos, 1:263–264
  middle kingdom, 1:263–264
  nomes and monarchs, 1:263
  old kingdom, 1:262
  second intermediate period, 1:264

Egyptian Dynasties, Ancient
    (Eighteenth to Twenty-sixth),
    1:264–270, 265, 266–267
  Amarna revolution, 1:265–268
  empire, 1:264–265
  Late Period, 1:269–270
  new kingdom, 1:264–265, 268–269
  Seti I, 3:845–846
  Third Intermediate period, 1:269
  Thutmose III, 3:941–942

Egyptian Dynasties, Persian,
    Hellenistic, Roman, 1:270–273,
    271
  Alexander III, the Great, 1:28–31
  Hellenistic period, 1:270–271
  Persian rule, 1:270
  Roman rule, 1:272

Egyptian Kingdom, modern, 1:273

El Escorial, 3:894

Eleanor of Aquitaine, 1:47, 274; 2:439

Election, royal, 1:274–275
  Anglo-Saxon and early England,
    1:274–275
  Holy Roman Empire, 1:275
  other elective monarchies, 1:275

Elizabeth I, 1:112, 275–277, 276;
    3:964–965
  Elizabethan Age, 1:276–277
  life and reign, 1:276–277

Elizabeth II, 1:277, 277–278

Emissary letters, 1:278–279

Emperors and empresses, 1:279–280

Empire, 1:280–281

England
  English Bill of Rights, 3:786–787
  sacred kingships, 3:813

English Bill of Rights, 3:786–787

English monarchies, 1:281–285,
    282–283, 284
  Anne, 1:46

English monarchies *(continued)*
  history, **1:**281
  power, **1:**281–284
  responsibilities, **1:**284–285
  Stephen, **3:**898–899
Enthronement rites, **1:**285–286
  symbolism of thrones, **1:**285
Esarhaddon, **1:**286–287
  Sennacherib, **3:**842
Ethelred II, the Unready. *See* Anglo-
    Saxon rulers; Edward the Confessor
Ethiopia
  Susenyos, **3:**915–916
  Tewodros II, **3:**932
Ethiopian Orthodox (Coptic) Church,
    3:916
Etiquette, royal, **1:**287
Etruscan Kingdoms, **1:**288–291, *289*
  decline, **1:**290
  Etruscan civilization, **1:**288–290
  government and social structure,
      1:288–289
  language and writing, **1:**288
  leisure, **1:**289–290
  origin, **1:**288
  religion, **1:**288
  Roman rule, **1:**290
  Tarquin Dynasty, **3:**929–930
  Tarquin the Proud, **3:**929, 930
  war and trade, **1:**290
Eunuchs, royal, **1:**291–292; **3:**844–845
  roles, **1:**291
  slave eunuchs in Turkey, **1:**291–292
  system in China, **1:**291
European kingships, **1:**292–294
  democracy and modern monarchy,
      1:294
  early modern period, **1:**293–294
  England and constitutionalism,
      1:293–294
  France and absolutism, **1:**294
  medieval origins, **1:**292
  other monarchies, **1:**294
  rise of centralized state, **1:**292–293
Ewyas, Kingdom of. *See* Gwent
    Kingdom
Exchange, means of. *See* Coinage, royal
Executions, royal, **1:**295
Expansion
  Belgian Kingdom, **1:**100–101
  Benin Kingdom, **1:**103

F

Faisal I, **1:**295–296
Fan Shih-Man, **1:**296
Fante Kingdom. *See* Akan Kingdoms
Farouk, **1:**296–297
Fatimid Dynasty, **1:**297–298
Ferdinand I, **1:**121, 129, 298
Ferdinand II, **1:**298–299, 299–301,
    300
Ferdinand IV, **3:**861
Feudalism and kingship, **1:**301–303,
    302
  landholding in Europe, **2:**520
  royal subjects, **3:**904
  royal tyranny, **3:**971
Five Dynasties and Ten Kingdoms,
    1:303–304
  T'ai Tsu (Taizu), **3:**923
Flanders, County of, **1:**304–305
Flavian Dynasty, **1:**142
Folklore and myths. *See* Myth and
    folklore
Folkung Dynasty, **1:**305–306; **3:**919
Fon Kingdom, **1:**306
France
  Blois-Champagne Dynasty, **1:**111
  Bonapartist Empire, **1:**114–116, *116*
  Bretagne Duchy, **1:**124–125
  Burgundy Kingdom, **1:**131–132
  Savoy Dynasty, **3:**829–830
Francis I, **2:**307
Franconian Dynasty, **2:**307–308
Frankish Kingdom, **2:**308–309
  Lombard Kingdom, **2:**540
  Saxon Kingdoms, **3:**833
Franz Ferdinand, **1:**75, 76
Franz Josef, **1:**76–77; **2:**309–311,
    310
Frederick I, **1:**86
Frederick I, Barbarossa, **2:**311–312;
    3:833
Frederick II, the Great, **1:**86;
    2:312–316, *315;* **3:**866
Frederick William, the Great Elector,
    2:316
French monarchies, **2:**316–322, *317.*
    See also Bourbon Dynasty
Fuad, **2:**322
Fujiwara Dynasty, **2:**322–324
Funan Kingdom, **2:**324; **3:**886

Funerals and mortuary rituals,
    2:324–326, *325*
Funerary temples, **3:**934–935
Fur Kingdom, **2:**326–327

G

Gaddafi, Muammar, **3:**825
Gaekwar Dynasty. *See* Baroda Kingdom
Gaelic Kingdoms, **3:**834–835
Gahadvalas Dynasty, **2:**327–328
Gaiseric reign, **3:**983
Galawdewos, **2:**328
Ganda Kingdom, **2:**328–329
Gaodi. *See* Liu Bang
Gaozong. *See* Kao Tsung
Gascony, **1:**95–96
Gauda Kingdom, **2:**329–330
Gautama Siddhartha, **1:**126
Gautamiputra Satakarni, **3:**828
Gender and kinship, **2:**330–332
Genealogy, royal, **2:**332–333
Geneva Bible, **3:**814
Genghis Khan, *2:334,* 334–335
Geoffrey of Monmouth, **1:**58
George I, **2:**335–336
George II, **2:**336
George III, **2:**336–337
George Tupou I, **2:**337; **3:**954
Germany
  Salian Dynasty, **3:**819–820
  Saxe-Coburg-Gotha Dynasty,
      3:830–831
  Saxon Kingdoms, **3:**832–833
Ghana Kingdom, Ancient, **2:**337–339,
    338
  Almoravid Dynasty, **1:**34–35
  Mali, Ancient Kingdom of,
      2:565
  Songhai Kingdom, **3:**870–871
  Soninke Kingdom, **3:**871–872
  Sundjata Keita, **3:**910–911
Ghaznavid Dynasty, **2:**339–340
Ghur Dynasty, **2:**340
Gideon, **1:**107–108
Glywysing Kingdom, **2:**340–341
Godfrey of Bouillon, **1:**89
Golconda Kingdom, **2:**341
Golden Horde Khanate, **2:**341–342
Götaland Monarchy, **2:**342
Granada, Kingdom of, **2:**342–343

Great Britian. *See also* England
  Burmese Kingdoms, **1:**134
  landholding patterns, **2:**520
  Leinster Kingdom, **2:**524
  Napoleon I (Bonaparte), **1:**114
  Saxe-Coburg-Gotha Dynasty,
    3:830–831
  Ulster Kingdom, **3:**975
Greco-Roman Dynasties, **2:**611–612
Greece
  Byzantine Empire, **1:**134
  Macedonian Empire, **2:**558–559
Greek Islands of Aegean, **1:**134
Greek Kingdoms, Ancient, **2:**343–346,
  344
  Alexander III, the Great, **1:**28–31
Greek Monarchy, **2:**346–347
Grimaldi Dynasty, **2:**347–349, *348*
Grooms of the stool, **2:**349–350
Guang Wudi. *See* Kuang Wu Ti
Guang Xu. *See* Kuang Hsü
Gudea, **2:**350
Guise, House of. *See* Lorraine Dynasty
Gujarat Kingdom, **2:**350–351
Gundobad, **1:**131
Gupta Dynasty, **3:**878
Gupta Empire, **2:**351–352
Gurjara-Pratihara Dynasty, **2:**352–353
Gustavus I (Vasa), **2:**353
Gustavus II (Adolphus), **2:**353–354
Gwalior Kingdom, **2:**354–355
Gwent Kingdom, **2:**355
Gwynedd Kingdom, **2:**356
Gyges. *See* Lydia, Kingdom of

H

Haakon VI, **2:**356–357
Habsburg Dynasty, **2:**357–362, *358*
  Austro-Hungarian Empire, **1:**75–77
Hadramawt Kingdoms, **2:**362–363
Hadrian, **2:**363–364, *364;* **3:**958
Hafsid Dynasty, **2:**364–365
Haihaya Dynasty, **2:**365
Haile Selassie I, **1:**39; **2:***366,*
  366–367
Haiti, **3:**873–874
Hammurabi, **2:***367,* 367–368
  Samsu-Iluna, **3:**822
Han Dynasty, **2:**368–370
  Three Kingdoms, **3:**940–941

Hanover, House of, **2:**370–372, *371*
Hapsid Dynasty, **1:**33–34
Harald III Hardraade, **2:**372
Harappan States. *See* South Asian
  Kingdoms
Harems, **2:**373–375
Harold II Godwinson, **2:**375–376
Harun al-Rashid, **1:**145; **2:**376
Hasan Zafar Khan, **1:**88
Hashemite Dynasty, **2:**376–378, *377*
Hasmonean Kingdom, **2:**378
Hassan II, **2:**378–379
Hatshepsut, **2:**379–380, *380;* **3:**811,
  941
Hawaiian Kingdoms, **2:***381,* 381–382;
  3:883–884, *884*
Healing powers of kings, **2:**382–383
Heavens and kingship, **2:**383–384
Hebrew kings, **1:**107–109; **2:**384–385;
  3:869–870
Heian Period, **2:**385–387
Hellenistic Dynasties, **1:**270–271;
  2:389
  Alexander III, the Great, **1:**28–31
  Antiochus III, the Great, **1:**46–47
Henry I, **1:**110
Henry II, **1:**96; **2:**389–391, *390;* **3:**899
Henry III, **3:**820
Henry IV (England), **2:**391–392; **3:**820
Henry IV (France), **1:***118,* 118–119;
  2:392–393
Henry V, **3:**820
Henry VIII, **2:**393–395, *394*
Heraclius Dynasty, **1:**136
Herod, **2:**395–396
Hinduism and kingship, **2:**396–399,
  397
Hirohito, **2:***399,* 399–401
Hittite Empire, **2:**401–402
  Shuppiluliuma I, **3:**857
Hohenstaufen Dynasty, **2:**403–404
Hohenzollern Dynasty, **2:**404–407,
  405
Holy Roman Empire, **2:**407–410. *See
  also* Roman Empire
  Albert I, **1:**24–25
  Arles Kingdom, **1:**53–54
  Salian Dynasty, **3:**819–820
  Saxon Dynasty, **3:**831–832
  Saxon Kingdoms, **3:**832–833
  Sigismund, **3:**861–862

Homer, **3:**962
Homosexuality and kingship,
  2:410–412
Hong Bang Dynasty, **2:**412
Hongwu. *See* Hung Wu
Hsia Dynasty, **2:**412–413
  Shang (Yin) Dynasty, **3:**849–851
Hsuan Tsung (Xuanzong), **2:**413–414;
  3:928
Huang Ti (Huangdi) (Yellow Emperor),
  2:414
Huari (Wari) Empire, **2:**414–415
Huascar, **2:**415–416
Huayna Capac, **2:**416–417
Hulagu. *See* Il-Khan Dynasty
Humbert I, **3:**829
Hun Empire, **2:**417–418
  Attila, **1:**71–73, *72*
Hung Wu (Hongwu), **2:**418–419
Hungary
  Arpad Dynasty, **1:**55–56
  Stephen I, **3:***899,* 899–900
Hunting and kingship, **2:**419–420
Hussein I, **2:**420–421
Hyderabad Kingdom, **2:**421–422
Hyksos Dynasty, **1:**264; **2:**422

I

Iberian Dynasty
  Almohad Dynasty, **1:**33–34
  Umayyad Dynasty, **3:**977
Iberian Kingdoms, **2:**423–424
  Aviz Dynasty, **1:**78–79
  Transtamara, House of, **3:**958–959
Ibn Saud, **2:**424–425, *425*
Iceni, **1:**117–118
Iconography, **2:**425–426
Ieyasu Tokugawa. *See* Tokugawa Ieyasu
Ikhshidid Dynasty, **2:**426–427
Il-Khan Dynasty, **2:**427–428
Illyria Kingdom, **2:**428
Inca Empire, **2:**429–433, *430*
  Atahualpa, **1:**68
  rulers, **3:**875, 876
  Tupac Yupanqui, **3:**967
Incest, royal, **2:**433–434
Indian Kingdoms, **2:**434–437
  Andhra Kingdom, **1:**40–41
  Avanti Kingdom, **1:**77–78
  Berar Kingdom, **1:**103–104

Indian Kingdoms (continued)
  Bharatpur Kingdom, **1:**105–106
  Bidar Kingdom, **1:**109
  Brahmarsi-Desa Kingdom,
    1:122–123
  Bundi Kingdom, **1:**129–130
  Burmese Kingdoms, **1:**132–134
  Macedonian Empire, **2:**559–560
  Muslim, **3:**881–883
  Satavahana Dynasty, **3:**827–828
  Sikkim Kingdom, **3:**862–863
  Sunga Dynasty, **3:**914–915
  Tomara Dynasty, **3:**952–953
Indo-Greek Kingdoms, **2:**437–438
  Sunga Dynasty, **3:**914–915
Inheritance, royal, **2:**438–440
Insignia, royal, **3:**773–775, *774*
Iran
  Buyid (Buwayhid) Dynasty,
    1:134
  Safavid Dynasty, **3:**815
  Saffarid Dynasty, **3:**815–816
  Samanid Dynasty, **3:**821
Iraq
  Buyid (Buwayhid) Dynasty, **1:**134
Ireland, high kings of. *See* Irish kings
Irene, **2:**440
Irish kings, **1:**117; **2:**440–442
Isabella I, **1:**299–301, *300;* **3:**744
Isfahan, **1:**1
Iskander Muda, **1:**9
Islam and kingship, **2:**443–445, *444*
  jizya tax, **1:**19
  Middle Eastern Dynasties, **2:**612
  sacred texts, **3:**814–815
  Samudera-Pasai, **3:**822–823
  Sokoto Caliphate, **3:**869
  sultanates, **3:**909–910
  Sunni Ali, **3:**915
Israel, Kingdoms of, **1:**15–16;
  2:445–446
  Athaliah, **1:**69
  Biblical kings, **1:**107–109
  Shalmaneser III, **3:**847
  Solomon, **3:**869–870
Iterbide, Agustín de, **2:**447
Itsekeri Kingdom, **2:**446–447
Ivan III, the Great, **2:**447–448
Ivan IV, the Terrible, **2:**448–449, *449;*
  3:807–809
Ivar, **1:**117

J

Jagiello Dynasty, **2:**450–451
  Angevin Dynasties, **1:**41–42
Jahan, Shah, **2:***451,* 451–452
Jahangir, **2:**452–453
James I of Aragón, **2:**453
James I of England (James VI of
  Scotland), **2:***454,* 454–455; **3:**902
  theater and, **3:**933
James II, **2:**455–456; **3:**902
James II of Aragón, **2:**456–457
James IV, **3:**900
Janggala Kingdom, **2:**457–458
Japan
  sacred kingships, **3:**812–813
  siblings, royal, **3:**860
Jaunpur Kingdom, **2:**458
Javan Kingdoms, **2:**458–461
  Srivijaya-Palembang Empire,
    3:896–897
Jean de Montfort, **1:**125
Jeanne d'Albert. *See* Bourbon Dynasty;
  Henry IV (France)
Jerusalem, **1:**89; **3:**819
Jezebel, Queen, **1:**16
Jigme Singye Wangchuk, **1:**107, *107*
Jimmu, **2:**461–462
Jizya tax, **1:**19
João (John) VI, **1:**123–124, *124;*
  2:462–463
João the Great, **2:**463–464, *464*
Jodhpur Kingdom, **2:**464–465
John I, **2:**465–466
John III (John Sobieski), **2:**466
John the Fearless, **1:**132
Johnson, Charles Anthony, **1:**125–126
Jordan, **1:**89
Joseph II, **2:**467
Juan Carlos, **2:**467–468; **3:**893
Juane-Burgundy Kingdom, **1:**132
Judah, Kingdom of, **2:**468–469
  Athaliah, **1:**69
  Biblical kings, **1:**107–109
Judaism and kingship, **2:**469–470
  Athaliah, **1:**69
Julian the Apostate, **2:**470–471
Juliana, **2:**471
Julio-Claudians, **2:**471–472
  caesars, **1:**141–142
  Caligula, **3:**943

Julio-Claudians (continued)
  Tiberius, **3:**942–943
Julius Caesar, **2:**472–474
Jurane-Burgundy Kingdom. *See*
  Burgundy Kingdom
Justin Dynasty, **1:**136, 138
Justinian I, **2:**474–475
  Theodora I, **3:**935–936
Jutland Kingdom, **2:**475–476

K

Kabarega, **2:**476
Kafa Kingdom, **2:**476–477
Kaiser Wilhelm II, **1:**4; **3:**844
Kalacuri Dynasties, **2:**477–478
Kalakaua, **3:**883
Kalinga Kingdom, **2:**478–479
Kalmar Union, **2:**479–480
Kamakura Shogunate, **2:**480–481;
  3:854, 855
Kamehameha I, the Great, **2:**481–483;
  3:883–884
  conquest and rule, **2:**481–482
  Europeans in Hawaii, **2:**482
  successors, **2:**482–483
Kandy Kingdom, **2:**483–484
Kanembu-Kanuri Kingdom,
  2:484–485
  end, **2:**485
  expanded kingdom, **2:**484
  trade, **2:**484
Kanemi, Muhammad Al-Amin Al,
  2:485
Kang Xi, **2:**485–486
Kantorowicz, Ernest H., **1:**112
Kanva Dynasty, **2:**486
  Sunga Dynasty, **3:**914–915
Kao Tsung (Gaozong), **2:**487
Kashmir Kingdom, **2:**487–488
Kassites, **2:**488–489
Kathiawar Kingdom, **2:**489
Kenneth I (Kenneth MacAlpin),
  2:489–490; **3:**834
Kent, Kingdom of, **2:**490–491
  Alfred the Great, **1:**33
  Anglo-Saxon rulers, **1:**43–44
Kertanagara Empire, **2:**491
Khalji Dynasty, **2:**491–492;
  3:878
Khama III, **2:**492

Khatti Kingdom. *See* Hittite Empire
Khattushili I, **2:**493
Khazar Kingdom, **2:**493–495
  building, **2:**494
  conversion to Judaism, **2:**494–495
  early history, **2:**493–494
  end, **2:**495
Khmer Empire, **2:**495–498, *496*
  Angkor Era, **2:**496–497
  Angkor Kingdom, **1:**42–43
  Angkor Thom, **2:**496–497
  Angkor Wat, **2:**496
  decline, **2:**497
  rise, **2:**495
  Siam, Kingdoms of, **3:**857–859
Khufu, **2:**498
Khusrau I, **3:**827
Khwarazm-Shah Dynasty, **2:**498–499
Kiev, Princedom of, **2:**499–500
Killing. *See* Regicide
Kingdoms and empires, **2:**500
Kingly body, **2:**500–502
  beauty and ugliness, **2:**500–501
  gendered royal body, **2:**501–502
  royal corpses and their powers, **2:**502
Kings and queens, **2:**502–503
  early evidence of kingship, **2:**502
  hereditary basis of kingship, **2:**503
  military basis of kingship, **2:**503
  religious basis of kingship, **2:**503
  women rulers, **2:**503
King's Two Bodies, The (Kantorowicz),
  1:112
Kipchak Khanate. *See* Golden Horde
  Khanate
Knut. *See* Cnut I
Koguryo Kingdom, **2:**503–506
  China conflict, **2:**505–506
  conflict and recovery, **2:**504–505
  emerging power, **2:**504
  Silla Kingdom, **3:**863–865
Kondavidu Kingdom, **2:**506–507
Kongbaung Dynasty. *See also*
  Alaungpaya Dynasty
  Burmese Kingdoms, **1:**133
  Southeast Asian Kingdoms, **3:**886
Kongo Kingdom, **1:**10–11; **2:**507–508
Koryo Kingdom, **2:**508–510
  changes in Koryo society, **2:**508
  dictatorship and foreign rule,
    2:508–509

Koryo Kingdom *(continued)*
  regained power and final collapse,
    2:509–510
Kosala Kingdom, **2:**510
Kösem, **3:**746
Kota Kingdom, **2:**510–511
Kuang Hsü (Guang Xu), **2:**511–512
Kuang Wu Ti (Guang Wudi), **2:**512
Kuba Kingdom, **2:**512
Kublai Khan, **2:***513,* 513–514
Kulasekhara Dynasty. *See* Cera (Chera)
  Dynasty
Kumaon Kingdom, **2:**514–515
Kusana Dynasty, **2:**515
Kush, Kingdom of, **2:**515–517
Kyanzittha, **1:**133

L

Labor, forms of, **2:**517–518
  alternative labor systems, **2:**517
  foundations of, **2:**517
  guilds and birth of democracy, **2:**518
  labor reform, **2:**517–518
Lady Nijo, **1:**206
Lake Titicaca, **3:**947–948
Lakhmid Dynasty, **2:**518
Lancaster, House of, **2:**518–519, *519*
Land rights. *See* Rights, land
Landholding patterns, **2:**519–521
  English landholding, **2:**520
  feudal landholding in Europe, **2:**520
  landholding in early Asia, **2:**520
Landscape painting, Sung (Song)
  Dynasty, **3:**913
Lang Chang, **3:**887–888
Lascarid Dynasty, **1:**137
Later Roman Empire. *See* Byzantine
  Empire
Latin Empire, **1:**137
Le Dynasty, **1:**136; **2:**521; **3:**888–889
  Trinh Dynasty, **3:**961
Legitimacy, **2:**521–522
  absolutist basis, **2:**522
  figurehead monarchy, **2:**522
  monarchy and revolution, **2:**522
  other bases of legitimacy, **2:**522
  religious basis, **2:**521
Leinster Kingdom, **2:**522–524
  coming of English, **2:**524
  early history, **2:**522–524

Leinster Kingdom *(continued)*
  later history, **2:**524
Leo III. *See* Byzantine Empire
León, Kingdom of, **2:**524–525
Leopold I, **1:**86; **2:**525–526
Leopold II, **1:**101; **2:**526; **3:**830
Leopold III, **1:**86, 101
Leopold V, **1:**86
Li Yuan, **3:**926–927
Liang Dynasties, **2:**527
Liang Wu Ti, **2:**527–528
Liao Dynasty, **2:**528
Libya, Sanusi Dynasty, **3:**824–825
Liliuokalani, **2:***529,* 529–530
Literature and kingship, **2:**530–534,
  531, 533
  Alfred the Great, **1:**33
  changing portrayals, **2:**532–533
  ideal king, **2:**531–532
  present and future, **2:**533–534
Lithuania, grand duchy of,
  2:534–535
  expansion, **2:**534–535
  origins, **2:**534
  union with Poland, **2:**535
Liu Pang (Gao Ti), **2:**535–536
Llywelyn ap Gruffydd, **2:**536
Lobengula, **2:**536–537
Lodi Dynasty, **3:**879
Lodi Kingdom, **2:**537–538
Lombard Dynasty, **2:**538–539
Lombard Kingdom, **2:**539–540
  creation, **2:**539–540
  establishment of Lombard Dynasty,
    2:539
  Frankish control, **2:**540
Long reigns, **3:**778
Lords of the Isles, **2:**540
Lorraine Dynasty, **2:**540–541
Lothair I, **2:**541
Louis Napoleon. *See* Napoleon III
Louis I, the Great, **2:**541–542
Louis I, the Pious, **2:**542–543
Louis IV, the Bavarian, **2:**543–544
Louis VII, **2:**544
Louis IX (St. Louis), **2:**544–545
Louis XI, **2:**545–546
Louis XIV, **1:**119; **2:***546,* 546–548;
  3:866
  Bourbon Dynasty, **1:**119
  childhood, **2:**546–547

Louis XIV (continued)
  France at war, **2:**548
  matters of faith, **2:**548
  religion and war, **2:**547–548
Louis XV, **2:**548–550
Louis XVI, **2:**550–551, *551;* **3:**777
  early years, **2:**550
  revolution, **2:**550–551
  trouble begins, **2:**550
Louis-Philippe, **2:**551–552
Lovedu Kingdom, **2:**552–553
Lozi (or Rotse) Kingdom, **2:**553
Luang Prabang Kingdom, **2:**553–554;
  3:888
Luba Kingdom, **2:**554
Lunda Kingdom, **2:**554–555
Lusignan Dynasty, **2:**555
Luxembourg Dynasty, **2:**556–557;
  3:861–862
Lycurgus, **3:**895
Lydia, Kingdom of, **2:**557–558

M

Mac Dynasty, **3:**889
Maccabees. *See* Hasmonean Kingdom
Macedonian Dynasty, **1:**136–137
Macedonian Empire, **2:**558–561
  Alexander III, the Great, **1:**28–31;
    2:559–560
  Argead Dynasty, **2:**558
  Asia Minor, **2:**559
  Central Asia, **2:**559
  decline, **2:**560–561
  Eastern Mediterranean, **2:**559
  Greece, **2:**558–559
  India, **2:**559–560
  Mesopotamia, **2:**559
  Philip II of Macedon, **2:**558–559
Macedonian Kingdom, **2:**561
  Thrace Kingdom, **3:**940
Madagascar Kingdoms, **2:**562
  Betsimisaraka Kingdom, **1:**104–105
  Sakalava Kingdom, **3:**817–818
Madame De Pompadour, **1:**206
Magadha Kingdom, **2:**562–563
  Avanti Kingdom, **1:**77–78
Magna Carta, **3:**786–787
Maharashtra Kingdom. *See* Yadava
  Dynasty
Mahmud of Ghazna, **2:**563

Ma'In Kingdom, **2:**563–564
Majapahit Empire, **2:**564; **3:**823
Makeda, **3:**852
Malcolm III, **3:***834*
Mali, Ancient Kingdom of, **2:**564–566,
  565
  confederation, **2:**566
  decline, **2:**566
  Ghana, **2:**565
  Songhai Kingdom, **3:**870–871
  Soninke Kingdom, **3:**871–872
  Sundjata Keita, **2:**565–566;
    3:910–911
  Sunni Ali, **3:**915
Malory, Thomas, **1:**59
Malwa Kingdom, **2:**567–568
Mamari Kulubali, **1:**90
Mamluk Dynasty, **2:**568–569
  Ayyubid Dynasty, **1:**80–82
  decline, **2:**569
  origins and early rule, **2:**568
  policies and achievements,
    2:568–569
  Selim I, the Grim, **3:**840
  sultanates, **3:**909–910
Mamprusi Kingdom, **2:**569–570
Mamun, al-, **2:**570–571
Manchu Dynasty. *See* Ch'ing (Qing)
  Dynasty
Mangbetu Kingdom, **2:**571
Manikongo, **1:**10
Manipur Kingdom, **2:**572
Mansa Musa, **2:**572–573
Mansur, Ahmad al-, **2:**573
Maori Kingdoms, **2:**574–575
  European conflict, **2:**574–575
  Maori culture, **2:**574
Marcus Aurelius, **2:***576,* 576–577
Margaret of Denmark, **2:**577–578
Maria Theresa, **2:**467, *578,*
  578–579
Marib, **3:**811
Marie Antoinette, **2:**579–580
Marie de France, **1:**110
Marie Louise
  Bonapartist Empire, **1:**115
Marquesas Kingdoms, **2:**580–581
Marriage of kings, **2:**581–582
  love, **2:**582
  political reasons, **2:**581–582
Martel, Charles, **2:**582

Martha Confederacy, **1:**93–94;
  2:575–576
  establishment, **2:**575–576
  kingdom, **2:**575
Mary, Queen of Scots, **2:**584–586,
  585; **3:**901, 965
  court intrigue and scandal,
    2:584–585
  England and the final years,
    2:585–586
  marriage and early rule, **2:**584
Mary I, Tudor, **2:**582–584
Mary II. *See* William and Mary
Mataram Empire, **2:**586
  first Mataram Kingdom, **2:**586
  second Mataram Kingdom, **2:**586
Matrilineal succession, **3:**905
Maurya Dynasty, **3:**878
Maurya Empire, **2:**589
  Andhra Kingdom, **1:**40–41
  Asoka's ascendency, **2:**588–589
  Chandragupta's reign, **2:**587–588
  decline of the empire, **2:**589
  Satavahana Dynasty, **3:**828
  Sunga Dynasty, **3:**914–915
Mausolea, royal. *See* Funerals and
  mortuary rituals
Mausoleums, **3:**953
Maximilian, **2:**589–590
Maximilian I, **2:**590–591
Maya Empire, **2:***591,* 591–593
  classic period, **2:**592–593
  postclassic period, **2:**593
  pre-classic period, **2:**591–592
Mayors of palace. *See* Carolingian
  Dynasty
Mbang, **1:**88
Mbembe, Nzinga. *See* Afonso I
Mbundu Kingdoms, **2:**593–594
Meath Kingdom, **2:**594–595
Mecca, Sanusi Dynasty, **3:**824–825
Medes Kingdom, **2:**595–596
  Scythian Empire, **3:**836
Medici family, **2:**596–598, *597*
  challenges of maintaining power,
    2:596–598
  consolidation of family power, **2:**596
  decline, **2:**597–598
  origins and early years, **2:**596
Mehmed II, the Conqueror,
  2:598–599; **3:**859

Meiji Monarchy, 2:*599*, 599–601
  Tokugawa Shogunate, 3:949–950
Menander, 2:601
Menelik II, 1:39; 2:*602*, 602–603
  King of Shewa, 2:602
  rule as emperor, 2:602
Menes, 1:11; 2:603
Mercia, Kingdom of, 2:603–604
  Anglo-Saxon rulers, 1:43–44
Merina Kingdom, 2:604–605
Meroe, Kingdom of, 1:22
Merovingian Dynasty, 2:605–606
  king of all Franks, 2:605–606
  mayors of palace, 2:606
Merovingian-Frankish Kingdom,
    2:606–608
  decline of Merovingians, 2:608
  division and rivalry, 2:606–607
  Merovingian kings, 2:607–608
Mesopotamia
  Macedonian Empire, 2:559
  Samsu-Iluna, 3:822
  Shulgi, 3:856
Mewar Kingdom. *See* Udaipur
    Kingdom
Mexican Monarchy, 2:608–610, *609*
  Iturbide's rule, 2:608–609
  Maximilian's rule, 2:609–610
Midas, 2:610–611
Middle Eastern Dynasties, 2:611–613
  ancient Middle East, 2:611
  Greco-Roman and Persian dynasties,
    2:611–612
  Islamic Age, 2:612
  modern Middle East, 2:612
  Shamshi-Adad I, 3:848
Milan, Duchy of, 2:613–614
  Sforza, 2:613–614
  Visconti, 2:613
Military
  Byzantine Empire, 1:138–139
Military roles, royal, 2:614–615
Milutin, 3:843
Minamoto rulers, 2:615–616
  disturbances, 2:616
  Minamoto shoguns, 2:616
  rise, 2:615
  shogunate, 3:*854*, 854–855
Minangkabau Kingdom, 2:616–617
Ming Dynasty, 2:617–620
  arts and culture, 2:618–619

Ming Dynasty *(continued)*
  isolation and collapse, 2:619–620
  return to Chinese rule, 2:617–618
  strength and prosperity, 2:618
Minoan Kingdoms, 2:620–622, *621*
Miru, 3:883
Mississippian culture, 2:622–623
  early life, 2:622
  economic growth, 2:622–623
Mitanni Kingdom, 2:623
Mixtec Empire, 2:623–624
Moche Kingdom, 2:624–625, *625*
Moctezuma, 2:626–627
Mon Kingdom, 2:627; 3:890
  Burmese Kingdoms, 1:133
  Siam, Kingdoms of, 3:857–859
Monarchs, ages of, 2:627–629
  dangers to young monarchs,
    2:627–628
  successful young monarchs, 2:628
  young monarchs and regents, 2:628
Monarchy formation, myths of,
    2:629–630
Mongkut (Rama IV), 2:630; 3:859
Mongol Dynasty. *See* Yuan Dynasty
Mongol Empire, 2:631–633
  Batu Khan, 1:97–98
  early development, 2:631
  Genghis Khan and his sons,
    2:631–632
  Kublai Khan and Tamerlane,
    2:632–633
  Tamerlane (Timur Leng),
    3:925–926, *926*
Monivong, King, 2:633
Monopolies, royal, 2:633–634
  economic monopolies, 2:634
  fostering trade and colonization,
    2:634
  generating revenue, 2:634
  as government function, 2:633–634
Monotheistic societies
  sacred kingships, 3:813
Montenegro Kingdom, 2:634–635
  Alexander I, 1:25
Monzon Jara, 1:90
Morea, principate of, 2:635–636
Mortuary rites. *See* Funerals and
    mortuary rituals
Moshoeshoe I, 2:636–637
Moshoeshoe II, 3:873

Mossi Kingdoms, 2:637–638
Mughal Dynasty, 3:*880*
  Babur, 1:86–87
Mughal Empire, 2:638–642, *639*
  Aurangzeb, 1:74–75
  Bundi Kingdom, 1:129–130
  decline, 2:640–641
  government and society, 2:639–640
  intial challenges, 2:638
Muhammad Ahmad, 2:642
Muhammad Ali, 2:642–643
  Selim III, the Great, 3:841
Muhammad I, 1:88–89
Muhammad III, 1:89
Muhammad V, 2:643
Muhammad XII (Boabdil), 2:643–644
Mu'izzi (Slave) Dynasty, 2:644–645
  South Asian Kingdoms, 3:878
Munster Kingdom, 2:645–646
  early history, 2:645
  later history, 2:646
  partition of kingdom, 2:645–646
Music and song, 2:646–647
  in afterlife, 2:646
  monarchs as music lovers,
    2:644–647
  monarchs as musicians, 2:647
Muslim
  invasion of India, 3:881–883
  sacred kingships, 3:813
Mutesa I, 2:647–648
Mutsuhito. *See* Meiji Monarchy
Myanmar, 1:23–24, 132; 3:848–849
Mycenaean monarchies, 2:648–650,
    649
  Trojan Kingdom, 3:961–962, *962*
Mysore Kingdom, 2:650
Myth and folklore, 2:651–653
  kings and queens in folklore and fairy
    tales, 2:652–653
  King Arthur, 1:58–60, *59*
  kings and hero myths, 2:651
  legendary kings and god-kings,
    2:651
  mythical motifs, 2:651–652
Mzilikazi, 2:653; 3:947

N

Nabataean Kingdom. *See* Arabia,
    Kingdoms of

Nabopolassar, **3:**654

Nadir Shah, **3:**654–655, 846

Nam Viet Kingdom, **3:**655–656

Nanchao Kingdom, **3:**656

Naples, Kingdom of, **3:**656–657
  Alfonso V, the Magnanimous,
    1:31–32
  Anjou Kingdom, **1:**44–45
  Normans, Germans, and French,
    3:656–657
  Spanish rule, **3:**657

Napoleon I (Bonaparte), **1:**114;
    3:657–660, *658*
  absolute power, **3:**658–659
  decline and defeat, **3:**660
  the home front, **3:**660
  military might, **3:**658
  rise to power, **3:**657–658
  success to the East, **3:**659
  trouble with Britain, **3:**659–660
  tyranny, royal, **3:**972

Napoleon II, **1:**115

Napoleon III, **3:**660–662
  foreign policy, **3:**661
  modernization of Paris, **3:**661
  Second Empire, **3:**837–838, *838*
  vying for power, **3:**660

Napoleonic Empire. *See* Bonapartist
    Empire

Nara Kingdom, **3:***662,* 662–664
  the ritsuryo system, **3:**662–663
  uneasy rule, **3:**663–664

Narai, **3:**664–665

Naram-Sin, **3:**665

Nasrid Dynasty, **3:**665–666

National identity, **3:**666–668
  early formations, **3:**666
  flags and anthems, **3:**667
  the medieval period, **3:**666–667
  the modern era, **3:**667–668
  religion, history, and the arts,
    3:667–668

Nationalism, **3:**668–669
  Austria-Hungary, **3:**669
  China, **3:**669
  Germany, **3:**668
  Japan, **3:**669
  nationalism reconsidered, **3:**669
  origins, **3:**668
  two centuries of nationalism,
    3:668–669

Naval roles, **3:**669–670
  ceremonial power, **3:**669–670
  he who rules the sea, **3:**670

Navarre, Kingdom of, **1:**95–96;
    3:670–671
  foreign rule, **3:**671
  period of greatness, **3:**671
  rise of the kingdom, **3:**670–671
  Sancho III, the Great, **3:**823–824

Nazca Kingdom, **3:**671–672

Ndebele Kingdom, **3:**672–673
  European threat, **3:**673
  formation of the kingdom,
    3:672–673

Nebuchadrezzar II, **3:**673–675, *674*

Nefertiti, **3:***675,* 675–676
  the Amarna revolution, **3:**675–676
  decline and fall, **3:**676

Nepal, Kingdom of. *See* Shah Dynasty

Nero, **3:***676,* 676–677

Nerva, **3:**957–958

Netherlands
  Burgundy Kingdom, **1:**131–132

Netherlands Kingdom, **3:**677–678

Nevsky, Alexander, **3:**678

Ngolo Jara, **1:**90

Ngonde Kingdom, **3:**678–679

Nguyen Anh, **3:**679

Nguyen (Hue) Dynasty, **3:**679–680

Nguyen Dynasty of Hue, **3:**889

Nicholas I, **1:**27; **3:***680,* 680–682

Nicholas II, **3:**682–684

Nigeria
  Benin Kingdom, **1:***102,* 102–103

Nkosi Dlamini, **3:**918

Norman Anonymous, **1:**113

Norman Kingdoms, **3:**684–685
  Anglo-Saxon rulers, **1:**43–44
  expansion of the realm, **3:**684
  formation by the Normans, **3:**684
  French and Spanish rule, **3:**685
  German rule, **3:**685
  period of decline, **3:**684–685

Norodom Sihanouk, **3:**685–686

North Africa
  Sanusi Dynasty, **3:**824–825
  Vandal Kingdom, **3:**983

North America, **1:**38–39

Northern Sung Dynasty
  Sung (Song) Dynasty, **3:**911–912,
    912

Northumbria, Kingdom of, **3:**686–687
  Anglo-Saxon rulers, **1:**43–44

Norwegian Monarchy, **3:**687–689, *688*

Novgorod, principality of. *See* Rus
    princedoms

Nubian Kingdoms, **3:**689–690

Nupe Kingdom, **3:**690

Nyikang, **3:**853

Nyoro Kingdom, **3:**690–691
  Ankole Kingdom, **1:**45
  colonial and postcolonial era, **3:**691
  origins and aspects of kingship,
    3:690–691
  the rise of the Ganda Kingdom, **3:**691
  Toro Kingdom, **3:**955–956

O

Oaths and oath-taking, **3:**691–692

Oceania, **3:**883

O'Connor, Turloch, **1:**207

O'Connors, **1:**207

Oda Nobunaga, **3:**692–694, 957
  dictatorial rule, **3:**693–694
  end of his rule, **3:**694
  family and character, **3:**692–693
  leadership, **3:**693

Oldenburg Dynasty, **3:**694–695

Olmec Kingdom, **3:***695,* 695–696

Orange-Nassau, house of, **3:**696–697

Orissa Kingdom. *See* Utkala (Orissa)
    Kingdom

Osei Tutu, **3:**697

Osman I, **3:**697–698

Ostrogoth Kingdom, **3:**698–699
  Theoderic the Great, **3:**936–937

Otto I, the Great, **3:**699–700
  Saxon Dynasty, **3:**832

Ottoman Empire, **1:**2–3; **3:**700–705
  Beyezid II, **1:**105
  Bulgarian Monarchy, **1:**128
  the empire in decline, **3:**704
  expansion and consolidation,
    3:701–704
  a fractious ruling family, **3:**702–703
  life within the empire, **3:**703–704
  rise of the empire, **3:**700–701
  Seleucid Dynasty, **3:**839–840
  Selim I, the Grim, **3:**840
  Selim III, the Great, **3:**840–841
  Serbian Kingdom, **3:**842–844

Ottoman Empire (continued)
  Suleyman I, the Magnificent, 3:908, 909
  sultanates, 3:909–910
  Thessalonika Kingdom, 3:938–939
Ottonian Dynasty, 3:705–706
Oudh (Avadh) Kingdom, 3:706

P

Pacal, 3:706–707
Pachacuti, 3:707
Paekche Kingdom, 3:708–709
  Silla Kingdom, 3:863–865
Pagan Kingdom, 3:709–710
  Burmese Kingdoms, 1:133
  Southeast Asian Kingdoms, 3:886
Pahlavi Dynasty, 3:710, 710–711
  shahs, 3:846
Pala Dynasty, 3:711
Palaces, 3:711–714, 712, 713
  Egyptian Age, 3:712
  modern palaces, 3:713–714
  origins and ancient palaces, 3:712–713
  Post-Egyptian Age, 3:712–713
Palaeologan Dynasty, 3:714–715
  Byzantine Empire, 1:137, 138
Palestine, 1:89
Palestine, Kingdoms of, 3:715–716
  ancient Jewish kingdoms, 3:715
  Jewish kingdoms and foreign rule, 3:715
  Muslims and Christians, 3:716
Pallava Dynasty. See Mysore Kingdom
Pandya Dynasty, 3:716–718
  cultural heritage, 3:716–717
  defeat, containment, and foreign rule, 3:717
  early contact with Greece and Rome, 3:716
  end of the Pandya Dynasty, 3:717–718
  military expansion, 3:717
Panjalu Kingdom, 3:718
Papal States, 3:718–719, 719
Paramara Dynasty, 3:719–720
Parks, royal, 3:720–721
Parthian Kingdom, 3:721–722
Patent letters, royal, 3:722
Paulinus, 1:118

Peace of Utrecht, 3:829
Pedro I, 3:722–723
Pedro II, 1:122, 124; 3:723–724
Pegu Kingdoms, 3:724
Peisistratus, 1:70
Pelayo. See Asturias Kingdom
Peloponnesian League, 3:895
Penda. See Mercia, Kingdom of
Pepin Dynasty, 3:724–726, 725
Pepin the Short (Pepin III), 3:726
Perak Kingdom, 3:726
  British and the present, 3:727
  independence and early history, 3:726–727
  relations with the Dutch, 3:727
Pergamum Kingdom, 3:727–728
Perlak Kingdom. See Acheh Kingdom
Persepolis, 1:8
Perseus, 3:938
Persia, 1:1, 7–8
Persian Dynasties, 2:611–612
Persian Empire, 3:728–731, 730
  Alexander III, the Great, 1:28–31
  building the Empire, 3:728–729
  governing a vast empire, 3:729
  trouble with the Greeks, 3:729–731
Persian rule
  Egyptian Dynasties, Persian, Hellenistic, and Roman, 1:270
Peter I, 3:843–844
Peter I, the Great, 3:731, 731–732, 962
  accomplishments, 3:731–732
  influences, 3:731
  northern war and founding of St. Petersburg, 3:732
  rise to power, 3:731
Philip the Bold, 1:132
Philip the Good, 1:131
Philip II, 3:732–734, 733, 893, 940
Philip II of Macedon, 3:734–735
  dealing with the Greeks and Persians, 3:735
  Macedonian Empire, 2:558–559
  reforms of the military, 3:734–735
  taking control, 3:734
Philip II, Augustus, 3:735–736
Philip IV of Spain, 1:122
Philip IV, the Fair, 3:736–737
Phoenician Empire, 3:737–738
  Phoenician rule, 3:737–738

Phoenician Empire (continued)
  Phoenician trade and colonization, 3:737
  relations with Persia, 3:738
Phrygia Kingdom, 3:738–739
Piast Dynasty, 3:739–740
  early state, 3:739–740
  high point and decline, 3:740
Picts, Kingdom of, 3:740–741
  decline of the Picts, 3:741
  early medieval period, 3:740–741
  Picts and Northumbria, 3:741
  Scottish Kingdoms, 3:834
Piedmont Kingdom, 3:741–742
Pisistratus, 3:971
Pizzarro, Francisco, 3:876
Plantagenet, House of, 3:742–745, 743
  origins, 3:743
  strife at home, 3:744–745
  struggles for the Crown, 3:743–744
  troubles with France and decline, 3:745
Plowden, Edmund, 1:112
Poland
  Stanislas I, 3:897
  union with Lithuania , 2:535
Political system
  Satavahana Dynasty, 3:828
Polygamy, royal, 3:746–748
  ancient China, 3:747
  Ch'ing Dynasty, 3:747
  Inca Empire, 3:747
  modern Swaziland, 3:748
  Ottoman Empire, 3:746–747
Polygynous monarchs, 1:11
Pomare IV, 3:748, 922, 922–923
Pompeii, 3:947
Pope Boniface VIII, 1:24
Pope Gregory VII, 3:820
Pophung, King, 3:865
Portraits, 1:56–57
Portugal, 1:9–10
  Bragança Dynasty, 1:122
  Brazil, Portuguese monarchy of, 1:123–124
  Saxe-Coburg-Gotha Dynasty, 3:831
Postcolonial States, 3:748–749
  characteristics, 3:749
  independence and governance, 3:749

Power, forms of royal, **3:**750–751
  absolute monarchy, **3:**750
  limited monarchy, **3:**750–751
  postfeudal absolute monarchy,
      3:750
  prefeudal absolute monarch,
      3:750
Powys Kingdom, **3:**751
Prasutagus, **1:**118
Premysl Dynasty, **3:**751–752
Priam, **3:**962
Priests, royal, **3:**752–754
  changing roles for priests,
      3:753–754
  priestly rulers, **3:**753
Primogeniture, **3:**754
Prophets, royal, **3:**754–755
Ptolemaic Dynasty, **3:**755–756,
      756
Ptolemy I, **3:**756–757
Pu Yi, **3:***757, *757–758
Punjab Princely States, **3:**758–760
  Punjab in independent India,
      3:759–760
  Punjab under the British, **3:**759
  Sikhism and the Punjab, **3:**759
Purépechas, **1:**37–38
Pusyamitra, **3:**914
P'ya Taksin, **1:**92
Pyraminds
  tombs, royal, **3:**953
Pyu Kingdom, **3:**760

Q

Qajar Dynasty, **3:**761–762
  challenges and successes, **3:**761
  increasing foreign influence,
      3:761–762
  origins and early rule, **3:**761
  shahs, **3:**846
Qianlong. *See* Ch'ien Lung
Qin Dynasty. *See* Ch'in Dynasty
Qing Dynasty. *See* Ch'ing Dynasty
Quaraysh. *See* Hashemite Dynasty
Queens and queen mothers,
      3:762–763
  Anne, **1:**46
Qur'an, The, **3:**814
Qutb Shahi Dynasty. *See* Golconda
      Kingdom

R

Radama I, **3:**763–764
Radama II, **3:**764
Rajasthan Kingdom, **3:**764–766
  before the Rajuts, **3:**764–765
  Bundi Kingdom, **1:**129–130
  Guhilots of Mewer and Harsha, **3:**765
  Katchawaha and Bahti Rajputs, **3:**765
  Rajasthan and the Mughals, **3:**766
  Rajput princes, **3:**765
  Rathors of Marwar, **3:**765–766
  Tomara Dynasty, **3:**952–953
Rama Dynasty. *See* Bangkok Kingdom
Rama Khamheng, **3:**766–767, 907
Rama I, **1:**92
Rama V. *See* Chulalongkorn
Ramses II, the Great, **3:**767–769, *768*
  building projects, **3:**767–768
  Egypt and the Hittites, **3:**767
  Seti I, **3:**846
  succession, **3:**768
Ranavalona I, Mada, **3:**769
Ranjit Singh Bahadur, **1:**106
Rastrakuta Dynasty, **3:**769–770
Ravahiny, Queen, **3:**818
Realms, types of, **3:**770–771
  city-state, **3:**770–771
  imperial realms of ancient world,
      3:771
  medieval, **3:**771
  nation-states, **3:**771
Rebellion, **3:**771–773
Reccared I, **3:**773
Regalia and insignia, royal, **3:**773–775,
      774
  seats and thrones, **3:**774–775
Regencies, **3:**775–776
Regicide, **3:**776–778
  Charles I, **3:**777
  and the good of the people,
      3:776–777
  literary regicide, **3:**778
  Louis XVI, **3:**777
  Nepal, **3:**777–778
  politics of regicide, **3:**776
  ritual regicide, **3:**776
  Russia, **3:**777–778
Reigns, length of, **3:**778–779
  long, **3:**778
  short, **3:**779

Religion
  basis of kingship, **2:**503
  bureaucracy, royal, **1:**130
  Byzantine Empire, **1:**139
  Etruscan Kingdoms, **1:**288
  royal behavior and, **1:**99
  Scottish Kingdoms, **3:**834
  Theodosius I, the Great, **3:**937
Religious duties and powers,
      3:779–780
Reports (Plowden), **1:**112
Revenue
  bureaucracy, royal, **1:**130
Revolt
  subjects, royal, **3:**904
Richard I, Lionheart, **3:**780–782,
      781
Richard II, **3:**782–783
Richard III, **3:**783–785, *784*
  reign, **3:**784–785
  rise to power, **3:**783–784
Rights, civil, **3:**786–787
  English Bill of Rights, **3:**786–787
  Magna Carta, **3:**786–787
  origins, **3:**786
Rights, land, **3:**787–788
  feudal system, **3:**788
  land reforms, **3:**788
  origins, **3:**787–788
Rights to animals, **3:**785–786
  animal husbandry and kingship,
      3:785–786
  domestication of animals, **3:**785
  hunting, **3:**785
Ritual, royal, **3:**788–789
Riurikid Dynasty, **3:**788–789
Robert Guiscard. *See* Naples, Kingdom
      of; Norman Kingdoms
Robert I (Robert the Bruce), **3:**790,
      790, 901
  Scottish Kingdoms, **3:**835
Roderic, **3:**790
Roger II, **3:**860–861
Roman Empire, **3:**791–795, *795. See
      also* Byzantine Empire; Holy
      Roman Empire
  Armenian Kingdoms, **1:**54–55
  Athens and, **3:**896
  Augustus, **1:***73,* 73–74
  Boudicca (Boadicea), **1:**117–118
  Caligula, **3:**943

Roman Empire (continued)
  class systems and royalty, **1:**190
  royal baths, **1:**96, 97
  Tarquin Dynasty, **3:**929–930
  Tarquin the Proud, **3:**929, 930
  Theoderic the Great, **3:**936–937
  Theodosius I, the Great, **3:**937
  Thessalonika Kingdom, **3:**938–939
  Tiberius, **3:**942–943
  Titus, **3:**946–947, 947
  Trajan, **3:**957–958
  tyranny, royal, **3:**970–971
Roman Empire, Holy. See Holy Roman
    Empire
Roman rule
  Egyptian Dynasties, Persian,
      Hellenistic, and Roman, **1:**272
Romanian monarchy, **3:**796–797
Romanov Dynasty, **3:**797, 797–798
  Alexander I, Tsar, **1:**25–27, 26
  Alexander II, **1:**27–28
  Alexandra, **1:**31
Romanov, Michael, **3:**798–799
Romanovs
  Russian Dynasties, **3:**809–810
Rotsie Kingdom. See Lozi Kingdom
Royal abdication. See Abdication, royal
Royal behavior. See Behavior,
    conventions of royal
Royal families, **3:**799–801
  concubines and mistresses,
      3:800–801
  marriages, **3:**799–800
Royal imposters, **3:**801
Royal line, **3:**801–802
Royal pretenders, **3:**802–803
Rudolph I, **3:**803
Rudolph III, **1:**53, 132
Rurik, **3:**803–804
Rus princedoms, **3:**804–805
Russian Dynasties, **3:**805, 805–810,
    806–807
  Alexandra, **1:**31
  changing monarchy, **3:**810
  growth of Russian Kingdoms,
      3:805–807
  internal conflict and external threat,
      3:807
  Ivan the Terrible, **3:**807–809
  new dynasty, **3:**810
  powerful women on throne, **3:**810

Russian Dynasties (continued)
  revolution, **3:**809–810
  Romanovs, **3:**809–810
  time of troubles, **3:**809–810
  tsardom, **3:**807–809
Russian Kingdoms, **3:**805–807
Rwanda, **3:**969–970

S

Saba, **3:**811
Sabaean Kingdom, **3:**811
  Arabia, Kingdoms of, **1:**48
  Solomon, **3:**869–870
Sacral birth and death, **3:**811–812
  divinity signs, **3:**811–812
Sacred kingships, **3:**812–814
  Byzantine Empire, **3:**813
  England, **3:**813
  intermediaries between human and
      divine, **3:**812–813
  Japan and, **3:**812–813
  King David, **3:**813
  monotheistic societies, **3:**813
  Muslim, **3:**813
Sacred texts, **3:**814–815
  ancient Egypt, **3:**814
  Bible, **3:**814
  Buddhist, **3:**814–815
  Chinese, **3:**814
  Islamic, **3:**814–815
Safavid Dynasty, **1:**1; **3:**815
  shahs, **3:**846
Saffarid Dynasty, **3:**815–816
Sa'id, Sayyid ibn, **3:**816–817
Sailendra Dynasty, **3:**817
Sakalava Kingdom, **3:**817–818
Saladin, **3:**818–819
  Crusades, **3:**819
  Jerusalem, **3:**819
Salian Dynasty, **3:**819–820
  Conrad II, **3:**819–820
  Henry III, **3:**820
Samanid Dynasty, **3:**821
Samoan Kingdoms, **3:**821–822
Samsu-Iluna, **3:**822
Samudera-Pasai, **3:**822–823
Sancho III, the Great, **1:**95; **3:**823–824
  Christianity, **3:**824
Sanusi Dynasty, **3:**824–825
Sarawak, Rajah of, **1:**125–126

Sarcophagi, **3:**953
Sargon II, **3:**825–826, 848
  Sennacherib, **3:**842
Sargon of Akkad, **1:**21–22; **3:**826
Sasanid Dynasty, **3:**826–827
  Ardashir I, **3:**826
  Khusrau I, **3:**827
  Shapur I, **3:**826
Satavahana Dynasty, **3:**827–828
  Andhra Kingdom, **1:**40–41
  commerce, **3:**828
  culture, **3:**828
  Gautamiputra Satakarni, **3:**828
  political system, **3:**828
Saul
  Biblical kings, **1:**107–108
Saurashtra Kingdom. See Kathiawar
    Kingdom
Savoy Dynasty, **3:**829–830
Saxe-Coburg-Gotha Dynasty,
    3:830–831
  Belgian line, **3:**830–831
  British line, **3:**831
  Bulgaria, **3:**831
  Portugal, **3:**831
Saxon Dynasty, **3:**831–832
  Otto I, the Great, **3:**832
  Stanislas I, **3:**897
Saxon Kingdoms, **3:**832–833
  Charlemagne, **3:**833
  Frankish Kingdom and, **3:**833
  Frederick I Barbarossa, **3:**833
Sayyid Dynasty
  South Asian Kingdoms, **3:**878–879
Sayyid Muhammad al-Mahdi, **3:**824
Scottish Kingdoms, **3:**834–835,
    900–901
  ancient Scotland, **3:**834
  Gaelic Kingdoms, **3:**834–835
  Kenneth I (Kenneth MacAlpin),
      3:834
  Picts, Kingdom of, **3:**834
  Robert I (Robert the Bruce), **3:**835
  Stewart Dynasty, **3:**835
  Strathclyde Kingdom, **3:**901
Scythian Empire, **3:**835–836
  Andhra Kingdom, **1:**40–41
Seclusion of monarch, **3:**837
Second Empire, **3:**837–839
  Napoleon III, **3:**837–838, 838
  Prussia and, **3:**838–839

Segu state. *See* Bambara Kingdom

Seleucid Dynasty, **3:**839–840
  Antiochus III, the Great, **1:**46–47
  Arachosia Kingdom, **1:**48–49

Seleucus I, **3:**839

Selim I, the Grim, **3:**840, 908
  Mamluk Dynasty, **3:**840

Selim III, the Great, **3:**840–841

Seljuq Dynasty, **3:**841–842
  sultanates, **3:**909–910

Sennacherib, **3:**842

Serbian Kingdom, **3:**842–844
  Alexander I, **1:**25

Servants and aides, royal, **3:**844–845

Seti I, **3:***845,* 845–846

Severus, Septimius, **3:**859

Seyyid Sa'id, **1:**93

Shah Dynasty, **3:**846

Shaka
  Zulu Kingdom, **3:**1041

Shaka Zulu, **3:**846–847, 873

Shalmaneser III, **3:**847

Shalmaneser V, **3:**848

Shamshi-Adad I, **3:**848

Shan Kingdoms, **3:**848–849
  Burmese Kingdoms, **1:**133

Shan states. *See* Alaungpaya Dynasty

Shang (Yin) Dynasty, **3:**849–851

Shapur I
  Sasanid Dynasty, **3:**826

Sharqi Dynasty. *See* Jaunpur Kingdom

Sheba, Queen of, **3:**851–852
  Sabaean Kingdom, **3:**811

Shih Huang Ti (Shihuangdi),
  3:852–853

Shilluk Kingdom, **3:**853

Shogunate, **3:***854,* 854–855

Shoguns, **3:**855–856
  bakufu, **3:**855–856

Short reigns, **3:**779

Shulgi, **3:**856

Shuppiluliuma I, **3:**857

Siam, Kingdoms of, **3:**857–859

Siblings, royal, **3:**859–860

Sicily, Kingdom of, **3:**860–861
  Alfonso V, the Magnanimous,
    1:31–32
  Anjou Kingdom, **1:**44–45
  Aragón, House of, **1:**49–50
  Aragón, Kingdom of, **1:**50–51
  Savoy Dynasty, **3:**829–830

Sigismund, **3:**861–862

Sihanouk. *See* Norodom Sihanouk

Sikkim Kingdom, **3:**862–863

Silla Kingdom, **3:**863–865
  Koguryo Kingdom, **3:**863–865

Simeon, **1:**128

Simeon II, **1:**129

Sisters, royal, **3:**866

Slave dynasty. *See* Mu'izzi (Slave)
  Dynasty

Slavery, royal, **3:**866–867

Sobhuza I, **3:**867–868

Sobhuza II, **3:**868, *868*

Sobieski, John. *See* John III (John
  Sobieski)

Social classes
  Tokugawa Shogunate, **3:**949

Sokoto Caliphate, **3:**869

Solomon, **3:**869–870
  Biblical kings, **1:**108
  Sheba, Queen of, **3:**851–852

Solon, **1:**70

Song Dynasty. *See* Sung Dynasty

Songhai Kingdom, **3:**870–871
  Mali, Ancient Kingdom of,
    3:870–871
  Sunni Ali, **3:**915

Soninke Kingdom, **3:**871–872
  Mali, Ancient Kingdom of,
    3:871–872

Sorcery. *See* Witchcraft and sorcery

Sotho (Suto) Kingdom, **3:**872–873

Soulouque, Faustin Elie,
  3:873–874

South African tribal life, **3:**1040

South American monarchies,
  3:874–877
  Atahualpa, **1:**68
  Aymara Kingdoms, **1:**79–80
  Aymaras, **3:**875–876
  Bacatá rulers, **3:**875
  Chibchas, **3:**874–875
  Hunza rulers, **3:**875
  Inca rulers, **3:**875, 876
  Tiwandku Kingdom, **3:**947–948
  Tupac Yupanqui, **3:**967
  Vilcabamba state rulers, **3:**875

South Asian Kingdoms, **3:**877–883
  Aryans, **3:**877, 879
  Gupta Dynasty, **3:**878
  Khalji Dynasty, **3:**878

South Asian Kingdoms *(continued)*
  Lodi Dynasty, **3:**879
  Maurya Dynasty, **3:**878
  Mu'izzi Dynasty, **3:**878
  Sayyid Dynasty, **3:**878–879
  Suri Dynasty, **3:**879
  Tughluqid Dynasty, **3:**878

South Sea Island Kingdoms,
  3:883–884, *884*
  Samoan Kingdoms, **3:**821–822
  Taufa'ahau Tupou IV, **3:**930–931
  Tonga, Kingdom of, **3:**954

Southeast Asian Kingdoms,
  3:885–891
  Samudera-Pasai, **3:**823
  Sarawak, Rajah of, **1:**125–126
  Shan Kingdoms, **3:**848–849
  Srivijaya-Palembang Empire,
    3:896–897
  Sukhothai Kingdom, **3:**907–908
  Tagaung Dynasty, **3:**886
  Thibaw, **3:**939
  Tran Dynasty, **3:**958

Southern Sung Dynasty, **3:**912

Spain
  Basque Kingdom, **1:**95–96
  Spanish Conquest, **1:**38

Spanish monarchies, **3:**892–894, *893*
  Aviz Dynasty, **1:**78–79
  Bonaparte, **3:**892
  Bourbon, **3:**892, 893–894
  Hapsburg, **3:**892–893
  Savoy, **3:**892
  Transtamara, House of, **3:**958–959

Sparta, Kingdom of, **1:**70; **3:**895–896
  founding, **3:**895
  law and government, **3:**895
  war, **3:**895–896

Srivijaya Kingdom, **3:**890

Srivijaya-Palembang Empire,
  3:896–897

Stability
  Belgian Kingdom, **1:**100–101

Stanislas I, **3:**897

Stanislas II, **3:**897–898

Stephen, **3:**898–899

Stephen I, **3:***899,* 899–900

Stewart Dynasty, **3:**900–901
  Scottish Kingdoms, **3:**835

Strathclyde Kingdom, **3:**901
  Viking Empire, **3:**901

Stuart Dynasty, **3**:*902,* 902–904
  Anne, **1**:46
Stupas, **3**:953
Subjects, royal, **3**:904–905
  alienation, **3**:904
  ancient times, **3**:904
  feudal, **3**:904
  monarchs and, **3**:904
  revolt, **3**:904
Succession, royal, **3**:905–906
  Biblical kings, **1**:108
  high priests and judges, **1**:108
  laws, **3**:905
  matrilineal succession, **3**:905
Sudanic Empires. *See* African Kingdoms
Sui Dynasty, **3**:906–907
  Three Kingdoms, **3**:940–941
Sukhothai Kingdom, **3**:907–908
  Siam, Kingdoms of, **3**:858
  Southeast Asian Kingdoms, **3**:887
Suleyman I, the Magnificent, **3**:908,
    909
Sultanates, **3**:909–910
  Mamluk Dynasty, **3**:909–910
Sumatran Kingdoms, **1**:8–9. *See also*
    Acheh Kingdom; Sailendra
    Dynasty
  Samudera-Pasai, **3**:822–823
Sumer. *See* Akkad, Kingdom of
Sumeria
  Shulgi, **3**:856
Sundjata Keita, **3**:910–911
  Mali, Ancient Kingdom of,
    2:565–566; **3**:910–911
Sung (Song) Dynasty, **3**:911–914
  arts, **3**:913–914
  landscape painting, **3**:913
  Northern Sung Dynasty, **3**:911–912,
    912
  Southern Sung Dynasty, **3**:912
  T'ai Tsu (Taizu), **3**:923
Sunga Dynasty, **3**:914–915
Sunni Ali, **3**:871, 915
  Mali, Ancient Kingdom of, **3**:915
Suri Dynasty
  South Asian Kingdoms, **3**:879
Surveillance
  bureaucracy, royal, **1**:130
Susenyos, **3**:915–916
Sussex, Kingdom of, **3**:916
  Alfred the Great, **1**:33

Sveyn Forkbeard
  Viking Empire, **3**:991–992
Swahili Kingdoms, **3**:916–917
  Tio Kingdom, **3**:945–946
Swazi Kingdom, **3**:917–918
  Sobhuza I, **3**:867–868
Swaziland
  Sobhuza II, **3**:868, *868*
Swedish monarchy, **3**:918–920, *919*
Syria, **1**:89
Syrian Dynasty
  Byzantine Empire, **1**:136
Syrian Kingdoms, **3**:920–922
  Aramean Kingdoms, **1**:51–52
  Crusader Kingdoms, **3**:921–922

T

Tabinshwehti, **1**:133
Tagaung Dynasty, **3**:886
Tahitian Kingdom, **3**:*922,* 922–923
T'ai Tsu (Taizu), **3**:923
T'ai Tsung (Taizong), **3**:924, 927
Taifa rulers, **3**:925
  Almoravid Dynasty, **1**:34–35
Taizong. *See* T'ai Tsung (Taizong)
Taizu. *See* T'ai Tsu
Takauji Ashikaga. *See* Ashikaga
    Shogunate
Tamerlane (Timur Leng), **3**:925–926,
    926
T'ang Dynasty, **3**:926–929, *927*
  Sui Dynasty, **3**:906–907
  T'ai Tsung (Taizong), **3**:924
  Tibetan Kingdom, **3**:*943,*
    943–944
Tara High Kingship. *See* Irish kings
Tarascos, **1**:37–38
Tarquin Dynasty, **3**:929–930, 930
Tarquin the Proud, **3**:929, 930
Taufa'ahau Tupou IV, **3**:930–931
Taxation, **3**:931–932
  early forms, **3**:931
  feudal eras, **3**:931–932
  modern eras, **3**:931–932
  tribute, **3**:960–961
Tay Son Dynasty, **3**:889
Temple of Amun, **3**:933
Temple of Karnak, **3**:933
Temple of Luxor, **3**:934
Temuchin. *See* Genghis Khan

Teres, **3**:940
Tewodros II, **3**:932
Thailand
  Siam, Kingdoms of, **3**:857–859
  Southeast Asian Kingdoms,
    3:887–888
Thalun, King, **1**:133
Theater, royal, **3**:932–933
Thebes Kingdom, **3**:933–935, *934*
  funerary temples, **3**:934–935
  Seti I, **3**:845–846
  Temple of Amun, **3**:933
  Temple of Karnak, **3**:933
  Temple of Luxor, **3**:934
  Valley of the Kings, **3**:935
Theoderic the Great, **3**:936–937
Theodora I, **3**:935–936
Theodosius Dynasty, **1**:136
Theodosius I, the Great, **3**:937
Theseus. *See* Greek Kingdoms, Ancient
Thessalonika Kingdom, **3**:938–939
Thibault I, **1**:110
Thibault IV, **1**:111
Thibaw, **3**:939
Thrace Kingdom, **3**:940
Three Kingdoms, **3**:940–941
Thutmose III, **3**:941–942
Tiberius, **3**:942–943
Tibetan Kingdom, **3**:*943,* 943–944
Tiglath-Pileser III, **3**:944–945
Tikar Kingdom, **3**:945
Timur Leng. *See* Tamerlane (Timur
    Leng)
Timurid Dynasty. *See* Asian Dynasties,
    Central; Tamerlane
Tio Kingdom, **3**:945–946
Titus, **3**:946–947, *947*
Tiwandku Kingdom, **3**:947–948
Tokugawa Ieyasu, **3**:948–949
Tokugawa Shogunate, **3**:854–856,
    949–950
  administration, **3**:949
  social classes, **3**:949
  Tokugawa Ieyasu, **3**:948–949
Toltec Empire, **3**:950–952, *951*
  art, **3**:951
Tomara Dynasty, **3**:952–953
Tombs, royal, **3**:953–954
  churches as tombs, **3**:954
  mausoleum, **3**:953
  pyramids, **3**:953

Tombs, royal *(continued)*
  sarcophagi, **3:**953
  stupas, **3:**953
Tonga, **3:**884
  Taufa'ahau Tupou IV, **3:**930–931
Tonga, Kingdom of, **3:**954
Tonking Kingdom, **3:**954–955
Toro Kingdom, **3:**955–956
  Ankole Kingdom, **1:**45
Toungoo Dynasty, **3:**956
  Burmese Kingdoms, **1:**133
  Southeast Asian Kingdoms, **3:**886
Toyotomi Hideyoshi, **3:**956–957
Trajan, **3:**957–958
Tran Dynasty, **3:**888, 958
Trastamara, House of, **3:**958–959
Treason, royal, **3:**959–960
Tribute, **3:**960–961
  taxation, **3:**931–932
Trinh Dynasty, **3:**889, 961
Troad Kingdom. *See* Trojan Kingdom
Trojan Kingdom, **3:**961–962, *962*
Troy, **3:**961–962
Tsars and tsarinas, **3:**962–963
Tshedkedi Khama, **3:**963
Tudor Dynasty, **3:**859
Tudor, House of, **3:**963–965, *964*
Tughluq Dynasty, **3:**966
Tughluqid Dynasty, **3:**878
Tughril Beg, **3:**841
Tulunid Dynasty, **3:**966–967
Tupac Yupanqui, **3:**967
Turkic Empire, **3:**967–968
  Seljuq Dynasty, **3:**841–842
Tutankhamen, **3:***934,* 935, 968–969, *969*
Tutsi Kingdom, **3:**969–970
Two Sicilies, Kingdom of the. *See*
  Naples, Kingdom of; Sicily,
  Kingdom of
Tyranny, royal, **3:**970–972
  feudalism and, **3:**971
  Napoleon I and, **3:**972
  origins, **3:**970–971
Tz'u Hsi (Cixi), Empress,
  3:972–973

U

Udaipur Kingdom, **3:**973
Uí Neill kings
  Ulster Kingdom, **3:**975

Uighur Empire, **3:**973–974
Ulster Kingdom, **3:**974–975
  English fight, **3:**975
  Uí Neill kings, **3:**975
Umayyad Dynasty, **1:**3; **3:**975–977,
  976
  declining power, **3:**976–977
  early rule, **3:**976–977
  Iberia rule, **3:**977
  Taifa rulers, **3:**925
United Arab Emirates, **3:**977–978
Ur-Nammu, **3:**856, 979
Urartu Kingdom, **3:**978–979
Uthman dan Fodio, **3:**869, 979–980
Utkala (Orissa) Kingdom, **3:**980
Uzbek Kingdom, **3:**980–981
Uzbeks, **1:**1

V

Vakataka Dynasty, **3:**981–982
Valens, **3:**937
Valley of the Kings, **3:**935
Valois Dynasty, **3:**982–983
Vandal Kingdom, **3:**983–984
  end, **3:**983–984
  Gaiseric reign, **3:**983
  North Africa, **3:**983
Varangian Kingdoms, **3:**984–985
Vasa Dynasty, **3:**919–920, 985
Vedas, **3:**814
Venetian Doges, **3:**985–986, *986*
Versailles, **1:**119
Vespasian, **3:**946
Vesuvius, **3:**947
Victor Emmanuel II, **3:**987
Victoria, **1:**31, 287; **3:**987–989, *988*
  end, **3:**988
  middle years, **3:**988
  royal servants and aides, **3:**844
  seclusion, **3:**837
  young queen, **3:**987–988
Vien Chang, **3:**888
Vietnamese Kingdoms, **3:***989,*
  989–990
  Angkor Kingdom, **1:**42–43
  Southeast Asian Kingdoms,
    3:888–889
  Tonking Kingdom, **3:**954–955
  Tran Dynasty, **3:**958
  Trinh Dynasty, **3:**961

Vijayanagar Empire, **3:**990–991
Viking Empire, **3:**991–994, *992*
  Brian Boru, **1:**117
  Cnut the Great, **3:**993
  disintegration of empire, **3:**993–994
  Strathclyde Kingdom, **3:**901
  Sveyn Forkbeard, **3:**991–992
Vilcabamba state rulers, **3:**875
Viracocha, **3:**994
Virgil, **3:**962
Visigoth Kingdom, **3:**994–996, 996
  Alaric I, **1:**23
  in Southern France, **3:**995
Visigothic Spain, **3:**995–996
Vlach Principality, **3:**996–997
Vladimir Princedom, **3:**997–998

W

Waldemar I, the Great, **3:**998–999
Wang Kon, **3:**999–1000
Wangchuk
  King Jigme Singye Wangchuk, **1:**107,
    107
Wanli, **3:**1000
Warfare, **3:**1000–1002
  monarchs as conquerors,
    3:1000–1002
  monarchs as defenders, **3:**1001–1002
  monarchs as national symbols,
    3:1002
Wari. *See* Huari Empire
Warri Kingdom. *See* Itsekeri
  Kingdom
Warrior societies
  royal behavior and, **1:**99
Wealth
  Benin Kingdom, **1:**103
Weddings, royal, **3:**1002–1003, *1003*
  and the nation, **3:**1003
  political alliances and, **3:**1002
  rites, **3:**1002–1003
  royal courtship, **3:**1002
Wei Dynasties, **3:**1003–1004
Welsh Kingdoms, **3:**1004–1005
Wen Ti (Wendi), **3:**906, 1005
Wenceslas IV, **3:**862, 1005–1006
Wenceslaus III of Bohemia, **1:**24
Wessex, Kingdom of, **3:**1006–1007
  Alfred the Great, **1:**33
  Anglo-Saxon rulers, **1:**43–44

Western relations
  Byzantine Empire, **1:**140–141
Wetting, House of, **3:**830
Wilderness, royal links to,
    3:1007–1008
Wilhelm II, **3:***1008,* 1008–1009
  decline and defeat, **3:**1009
  international conflict,
      3:1008–1009
  rise to power, **3:**1008
Wilhelmina, **3:**1009–1010
William and Mary, **3:**1010–1011
  rise to power, **3:**1010–1011
  on throne, **3:**1011
William I, the Conqueror, **3:**898,
    1011–1015, *1013*
  consolidation and rule, **3:**1013–1014
  death and legacy, **3:**1014
  early life and claim to England,
      3:1012
  invasion and conquest of England,
      3:1012–1013
William II (William Rufus), **3:**1015
William III. *See* William and Mary
Windsor, House of, **3:**830,
    1015–1017, *1016*
  contemporary stability, **3:**1017
  origins, **3:**1015–1016
  power and crisis, **3:**1016–1017
Witchcraft and sorcery, **3:**1017–1018
  kings against witch-hunters, **3:**1018
  kings against witches, **3:**1018
  witchcraft at court, **3:**1017–1018
Women rulers
  kings and queens, **2:**503

Wu Tse-t'ien (Wu Zetian) (Wu Zhao),
    3:1018–1019

X

Xerxes, **3:**1019–1020
Xia (Hsia) Dynasty, **3:**1020–1021
Xuanzong. *See* Hsuan Tsung

Y

Yadava Dynasty, **3:**1021
Yamato Dynasty, **3:**1021–1025
  dyarchy—title *versus* power,
      3:1024
  Meiji restoration, **3:**1024–1025
  myth and history, **3:**1024
  power behind the throne, **3:**1024
  shogunates, **3:**1024
Yang Guifei, **1:**205–206
Yaqub ibn Layth al-Saffar, **3:**816
Yaroslav I, the Wise, **3:**1025
Ya'rubi Dynasty, **3:**1025–1026
Yellow Emperor. *See* Huang Ti
Yemen, **3:**851
  rulers, **3:**1026–1027
Yi Dynasty, **3:**1027–1029
Yi Songgye, **3:**1029–1030
Yoritomo, **3:**1030
York, House of, **3:**1030–1031, *1031*
Yoruba Kingdoms, **3:**1031–1032,
    1032
Yoshinobu, **3:**855
Yuan Dynasty, **3:**1032–1035
  Chinese underclass, **3:**1033

Yuan Dynasty *(continued)*
  cultural divide, **3:**1034
  culture, **3:**1034
  final years, **3:**1034–1035
  founding, **3:**1033
  opening to world, **3:**1033–1034
Yugoslavia
  Alexander I, **1:**25
Yung Lo (Yongle), **3:**1035

Z

Zand Dynasty, **3:**1035–1036
  shahs, **3:**846
Zanzibar, **1:**93
  Sa'id, Sayyid ibn, **3:**816–817
Zanzibar sultanate, **3:**917,
    1036–1037
Zapotec Empire, **3:**1037–1038
Zara Ya'iqob, **3:**1038
Zedekiah
  Biblical kings, **1:**109
Zhou Dynasty. *See* Chou Dynasty
Zhu Xi, **3:**914
Zimbabwe Kingdom, Great,
    3:1038–1040, *1039*
Zulu Kingdom, **3:**1040–1041
  after Shaka, **3:**1041
  nationalism, **3:**1040–1041
  power, **3:**1040
  rivals and refugees, **3:**1041
  Shaka Zulu, **3:**846–847
  Sotho (Suto) Kingdom, **3:**872–873
  South African tribal life, **3:**1040
  Swazi Kingdom, **3:**917–918

BIOGRAPHICAL INDEX

Note: Page references in italics indicate photographs.

A

Abbas the Great, **1:**1; **3:**815

Abu Bakr, **1:**5

Adolph of Nassau, **1:**24

Adud ad-Dawlah, **1:**134

Aethelred the Unready. *See* Edward the Confessor

Afonso I, **1:**9–10

Afonso I, Nzinga Mbemba, **1:**10–11

Ahab, **1:**15–16

Ahmose I, **1:**17

Akbar the Great, **1:**18–20, *20*

Akhenaten, **1:**20–21

Al Hajj, **1:**90

Al-Hamid, Abd II, **1:**2–3

Al-Mansur, **1:**2

Al-Rahman, Abd, **1:**3

Al-Sharif, Ahmad, **3:**824

Alan I, Bretangne, **1:**124

Alaric I, **1:**23

Alaungpaya, **1:**23, 133

Albert I, **1:**24–25; **3:**831

Albert II, **1:***100,* 101

Alexander I, **1:**25, 116

Alexander I, Tsar, **1:**25–27, *26*

Alexander II, **1:**27–28

Alexander III, the Great, **1:**28–31, *30,* 48, 208; **3:**921

  divinity signs, **3:**811

  Macedonian Empire, **1:**28–31; **2:**559–560

  Seleucid Dynasty, **3:**839

Alexandra, **1:**31

Alexius I, **1:**140

Alfonso V, the Magnanimous, **1:**31–32

Alfonso X, the Wise, **1:**32–33

Alfred the Great, **1:**33, 43–44

Amadeus VIII, **3:**829

Amum, **1:**20–21

Anawrahta, **1:**133

Anne, **1:**46; **3:**903

Antanavaratra Rahena, **1:**105

Antiochus III, the Great, **1:**46–47; **3:**839

Ardashir I, **3:**826

Artaxerxes I, **1:**57

Artaxerxes II, **1:***57,* 57–58

Artaxerxes III, **1:**58

Arthur, King, **1:**58–60, *59*

Ashurbanipal, **1:**62–63

Asoka, **1:**64–66, *65*

Atahualpa, **1:**68

Athaliah, **1:**69

Attila, **1:**71–73, *72*

Augustus, **1:***73,* 73–74; **3:**942

Aurangzeb, **1:**74–75

B

Babar. *See* Babur

Babur, **1:**18–20, 86–87, *87*

Baburnama (Babur), **1:**87

Bagyidaw, King, **1:**134

Baldwin I, **1:**89

Banu Khurasan, **1:**92–93

Barghash ibn Sa'id el-Busaidi, **1:**93

Basil I, **1:**94

Basil II, **1:**94–95

Bathsheba, **1:**869

Batu Khan, **1:**97–98. *See also* Genghis Khan

Baudouin, **1:**6, 98

Beyezid I, **3:**910

Beyezid II, **1:**105

Bodawpaya, King, **1:**134

Boris I Michael, **1:**128

Boru, Brian, **1:**117

Boudicca (Boadicea), **1:**117–118

Brooke, Sir James (Rajah), **1:**125–126

C

Caligula, **1:**142–143; **3:**943

Cambyses II, **1:**148

Canute I, the Great. *See* Cnut I

Capet, Hugh, **1:**148–149

Caracalla, Emperor, **1:**96, *97*

Carl XVI, **3:***919*

Casimir III, **1:**154

Casimir IV, **1:**154–155

Catherine II, the Great, **1:**25–27, 158–159, *159*

  early life, **1:**158–159

  as monarch, **1:**159

  Stanislas II, **3:**898

  theater and, **3:**933

Cetshwayo, **1:**160–161

Chakri, **1:**92

Chandragupta Maurya, **1:**164–165

Charlemagne, **1:**165–168, *167*

  accomplishments, **1:**167

  Byzantine Empire, **1:**138

  commanding an empire, **1:**166–167

  early life and rule, **1:**166

  royal baths and, **1:**97

  Saxon Kingdoms, **3:**833

Charles I, **1:**121, 168–169; **3:**777, 861, 902

Charles II, **1:**169; **3:**902

Charles III, **1:**169–170

Charles IV, **1:**170

Charles V, **1:**170–171

Charles VI, **1:**171–172

Charles VII, **1:**172

Charles the Bold, **1:**132

Ch'ien Lung, **1:**175–176
  conquest and prosperity, **1:**176
  corruption and decay, **1:**176
  Manchu and, **1:**175–176

Childeric I. *See* Clovis I

Chilufya Mulenga, **1:**102

Christina, **1:**188–189; **3:**920

Chulalongkorn, **1:**189–190; **3:**858

Cixi. *See* Tz'u Hsi (Cixi), Empress

Claudius, **1:**191–192, *192*

Cleisthenes, **1:**70

Cleopatra VII, **1:**192–194, *193*

Clovis I, **1:**194–195

Cnut I, **1:**195–196
  achievements as king, **1:**196
  conquest of England, **1:**195
  rule in Scandinavia, **1:**195–196
  Viking Empire, **3:**993

Confucius, **3:**814

Conrad I, **3:**831–832

Conrad II, **1:**209; **3:**819–820

Conrad III, **1:**209–210

Constantine I, the Great, **1:***211,*
    211–212
  conversion to Christianity, **1:**212
  reforms and policies, **1:**212
  rise to power, **1:**211

Croesus, **1:**218

Cyaxares, **1:**221

Cyrus the Great, **1:**7, 221–222; **3:**846

D

Da Monzon, **1:**90

Dalai Lama, **3:***943,* 943–944

Darius I, the Great, **1:**7, *8,* 48,
    225–227, *226*
  empire, **1:**226–227
  western struggles, **1:**226

Darius II (Ochus), **1:**227

Darius III (Codommanus), **1:**227–228

David, **1:***228,* 228–229; **3:**869
  Biblical kings, **1:**107–108
  sacred kingships, **3:**813

David I, **1:**229

David II, **1:**230

Dessalines, Jean-Jacques, **1:**234–235

Dinga Cisse, **3:**871–872

Dingiswayo, **1:**237

Diocletian, **1:**237–238
  gaining throne, **1:**237
  last years, **1:**238
  political and economic reform,
    1:237–238

Djoser, **1:**246

Dmitri, Grand Prince, **1:**246–247

Domitian, **3:**957

E

Ebna Hakim, **3:**852

Edward I, **1:**257–259, *258*

Edward II, **1:**259–260

Edward III, **1:**260–261
  early life and rule, **1:**260
  final years, **1:**260–261
  war, plague, parliament, **1:**260

Edward VI, **1:**262

Edward VIII, **1:**4

Edward the Confessor, **1:**43-44, 261

El Escorial, **3:**894

Eleanor of Aquitaine, **1:**47, 274; **2:**439

Elizabeth I, **1:**112, 275–277, *276;*
    3:964–965
  Elizabethan Age, **1:**276–277
  life and reign, **1:**276–277

Elizabeth II, **1:***277,* 277–278

Esarhaddon, **1:**286–287; **3:**842

Ethelred II, the Unready. *See* Edward
    the Confessor

F

Faisal I, **1:**295–296

Fan Shih-Man, **1:**296

Farouk, **1:**296–297

Ferdinand I, **1:**121, 129, 298

Ferdinand II, **1:**298–299, 299–301, *300*

Ferdinand IV, **3:**861

Francis I, **2:**307

Franz Ferdinand, **1:**75, *76*

Franz Josef, **1:**76–77; **2:**309–311, *310*

Frederick I, **1:**86

Frederick I, Barbarossa, **2:**311–312;
    3:833

Frederick II, the Great, **1:**86;
    2:312–314, 314–316, *315;* **3:**866

Frederick William, the Great Elector,
    2:316

Fuad, **2:**322

G

Gaddafi, Muammar, **3:**825

Galawdewos, **2:**328

Gaodi. *See* Liu Pang (Gao Ti)

Gaozong. *See* Kao Tsung

Gautama Siddhartha, **1:**126

Gautamiputra Satakarni, **3:**828

Genghis Khan, *2:334,* 334–335

Geoffrey of Monmouth, **1:**58

George I, **2:**335–336

George II, **2:**336

George III, **2:**336–337

George Tupou I, **2:**337; **3:**954

Gideon, **1:**107–108

Godfrey of Bouillon, **1:**89

Guang Wudi. *See* Kuang Wu Ti

Guang Xu. *See* Kuang Hsü

Gundobad, **1:**131

Gustavus I (Vasa), **2:**353

Gustavus II (Adolphus), **2:**353–354

H

Haakon VI, **2:**356–357

Hadrian, **2:**363–364, *364;* **3:**958

Haile Selassie I, **1:**39; **2:***366,* 366–367

Hammurabi, **2:***367,* 367–368; **3:**822

Harald III Hardraade, **2:**372

Harold II Godwinson, **2:**375–376

Harun al-Rashid, **1:**145; **2:**376

Hasan Zafar Khan, **1:**88

Hassan II, **2:**378–379

Hatshepsut, **2:**379–380, *380;* **3:**811,
    941

Henry I, **1:**110

Henry II, **1:**96; **2:**389–391, *390;*
    3:899

Henry III, **3:**820

Henry IV (England), **2:**391–392; **3:**820

Henry IV (France), **1:***118,* 118–119;
    2:392–393

Henry V, **3:**820

Henry VIII, **2:**393–395, *394*

Herod, **2:**395–396

Hirohito, **2:***399,* 399–401

Homer, **3:**962

Hsuan Tsung (Xuanzong), **2:**413–414;
    3:928

Humbert I, **3:**829

Hussein I, **2:**420–421

I

Ibn Saud, **2:**424–425, *425*
Ieyasu Tokugawa. *See* Tokugawa Ieyasu
Irene, **2:**440
Isabella I, **1:**299–301, *300;* **3:**744
Isfahan, **1:**1
Iskander Muda, **1:**9
Iterbide, Agustín de, **2:**447
Ivan III, the Great, **2:**447–448
Ivan IV, the Terrible, **2:**448–449, *449;*
    3:807–809
Ivar, **1:**117

J

Jahan, Shah, **2:***451,* 451–452
Jahangir, **2:**452–453
James I of Aragón, **2:**453
James I of England (James VI of Scotland),
    2:*454,* 454–455; **3:**902, 933
James II, **2:**455–456; **3:**902
James II of Aragón, **2:**456–457
James IV, **3:**900
Jean de Montfort, **1:**125
Jeanne d'Albert. *See* Henry IV (France)
Jezebel, Queen, **1:**16
Jimmu, **2:**461–462
João (John) VI, **1:**123–124, *124;*
    2:462–463
João the Great, **2:**463–464, *464*
John I, **2:**465–466
John III (John Sobieski), **2:**466
John the Fearless, **1:**132
Johnson, Charles Anthony, **1:**125–126
Joseph II, **2:**467
Juan Carlos, **2:**467–468; **3:**893
Julian the Apostate, **2:**470–471
Juliana, **2:**471
Julius Caesar, **2:**472–474
Justinian I, **2:**474–475; **3:**935–936

K

Kabarega, **2:**476
Kaiser Wilhelm II, **1:**4; **3:**844
Kamehameha I, the Great, **2:**481–483;
    3:883–884
   conquest and rule, **2:**481–482
   Europeans in Hawaii, **2:**482
   successors, **2:**482–483

Kanemi, Muhammad Al-Amin Al,
    2:485
Kang Xi, **2:**485–486
Kantorowicz, Ernest H., **1:**112
Kao Tsung (Gaozong), **2:**487
Kenneth I (Kenneth MacAlpin),
    2:489–490; **3:**834
Khama III, **2:**492
Khattushili I, **2:**493
Khufu, **2:**498
Khusrau I, **3:**827
Knut. *See* Cnut I
Kösem, **3:**746
Kuang Hsü (Guang Xu), **2:**511–512
Kuang Wu Ti (Guang Wudi), **2:**512
Kublai Khan, **2:***513,* 513–514
Kyanzittha, **1:**133

L

Lady Nijo, **1:**206
Lang Chang, **3:**887–888
Leopold I, **1:**86; **2:**525–526
Leopold II, **1:**101; **2:**526; **3:**830
Leopold III, **1:**86, 101
Leopold V, **1:**86
Li Yuan, **3:**926–927
Liang Wu Ti, **2:**527–528
Liliuokalani, **2:***529,* 529–530
Liu Pang (Gao Ti), **2:**535–536
Llywelyn ap Gruffydd, **2:**536
Lobengula, **2:**536–537
Lothair I, **2:**541
Louis I, the Great, **2:**541–542
Louis I, the Pious, **2:**542–543
Louis IV, the Bavarian, **2:**543–544
Louis VII, **2:**544
Louis IX (St. Louis), **2:**544–545
Louis XI, **2:**545–546
Louis XIV, **1:**119; **2:***546,* 546–548;
    3:866
   Bourbon Dynasty, **1:**119
   childhood, **2:**546–547
   France at war, **2:**548
   matters of faith, **2:**548
   religion and war, **2:**547–548
Louis XV, **2:**548–550
Louis XVI, **2:**550–551, *551;* **3:**777
   early years, **2:**550
   revolution, **2:**550–551
   trouble begins, **2:**550

Louis-Philippe, **2:**551–552
Lycurgus, **3:**895

M

Madame De Pompadour, **1:**206
Mahmud of Ghazna, **2:**563
Makeda, **3:**852
Malcolm III, **3:***834*
Malory, Thomas, **1:**59
Mamari Kulubali, **1:**90
Mamun, al-, **2:**570–571
Mansa Musa, **2:**572–573
Mansur, Ahmad al-, **2:**573
Marcus Aurelius, **2:***576,* 576–577
Margaret of Denmark, **2:**577–578
Maria Theresa, **2:**467, *578,*
    578–579
Marie Antoinette, **2:**579–580
Marie de France, **1:**110
Marie Louise, **1:**115
Martel, Charles, **2:**582
Mary I, Tudor, **2:**582–584
Mary II. *See* William and Mary
Mary, Queen of Scots, **2:**584–586,
    585; **3:**901, 965
   court intrigue and scandal,
    2:584–585
   England and final years, **2:**585–586
   marriage and early rule, **2:**584
Maximilian, **2:**589–590
Maximilian I, **2:**590–591
Mbembe, Nzinga. *See* Afonso I
Mehmed II, the Conqueror,
    2:598–599; **3:**859
Menander, **2:**601
Menelik II, **1:**39; **2:***602,* 602–603
   King of Shewa, **2:**602
   rule as emperor, **2:**602
Menes, **1:**11; **2:**603
Midas, **2:**610–611
Milutin, **3:**843
Miru, **3:**883
Moctezuma, **2:**626–627
Mongkut (Rama IV), **2:**630;
    3:859
Monivong, King, **2:**633
Monzon Jara, **1:**90
Moshoeshoe I, **2:**636–637
Moshoeshoe II, **3:**873
Muhammad Ahmad, **2:**642

Muhammad Ali, **2:**642–643; **3:**841
Muhammad I, **1:**88–89
Muhammad III, **1:**89
Muhammad V, **2:**643
Muhammad XII (Boabdil), **2:**643–644
Mutesa I, **2:**647–648
Mzilikazi, **2:**653; **3:**947

N

Nabopolassar, **3:**654
Nadir Shah, **3:**846
Napoleon I (Bonaparte), **1:**114;
  3:657–660, *658*
  absolute power, **3:**658–659
  decline and defeat, **3:**660
  the home front, **3:**660
  military might, **3:**658
  rise to power, **3:**657–658
  success to the East, **3:**659
  trouble with Britain, **3:**659–660
  tyranny, royal, **3:**972
Napoleon II, **1:**115
Napoleon III, **3:**660–662
  foreign policy, **3:**661
  modernization of Paris, **3:**661
  Second Empire, **3:**837–838, *838*
  vying for power, **3:**660
Narai, **3:**664–665
Naram-Sin, **3:**665
Nebuchadrezzar II, **3:**673–675, *674*
Nefertiti, **3:***675*, 675–676
  the Amarna revolution, **3:**675–676
  decline and fall, **3:**676
Nero, **3:***676*, 676–677
Nerva, **3:**957–958
Nevsky, Alexander, **3:**678
Nguyen Anh, **3:**679
Nicholas I, **3:***680*, 680–682
Nicholas II, **3:**682–684
Norodom Sihanouk, **3:**685–686

O

O'Connor, Turloch, **1:**207
O'Connors, **1:**207
Oda Nobunaga, **3:**692–694, 957
  dictatorial rule, **3:**693–694
  end of rule, **3:**694
  family and character, **3:**692–693
  leadership, **3:**693

Osei Tutu, **3:**697
Osman I, **3:**697–698
Otto I, the Great, **3:**699–700

P

Pacal, **3:**706–707
Pachacuti, **3:**707
Pedro I, **3:**722–723
Pedro II, **1:**122, *124*; **3:**723–724
Pepin the Short (Pepin III), **3:**726
Persepolis, **1:***8*
Peter I, the Great, **3:***731*, 731–732
  accomplishments, **3:**731–732
  influences, **3:**731
  northern war and founding of St.
    Petersburg, **3:**732
  rise to power, **3:**731
Philip the Bold, **1:**132
Philip the Good, **1:***131*
Philip II, **3:**732–734, *733*, 893, 940
Philip II of Macedon, **3:**734–735
  dealing with the Greeks and Persians,
    3:735
  reforms of military, **3:**734–735
  taking control, **3:**734
Philip II, Augustus, **3:**735–736
Philip IV of Spain, **1:**122
Philip IV, the Fair, **3:**736–737
Pomare IV, **3:**748, *922,* 922–923
Pope Boniface VIII, **1:**24
Ptolemy I, **3:**756–757
Pu Yi, **3:***757,* 757–758

Q

Qianlong. *See* Ch'ien Lung

R

Radama I, **3:**763–764
Radama II, **3:**764
Rama Khamheng, **3:**766–767, 907
Rama I, **1:**92
Rama V. *See* Chulalongkorn
Ramses II, the Great, **3:**767–769, *768*
  building projects, **3:**767–768
  Egypt and the Hittites, **3:**767
  Seti I, **3:**846
  succession, **3:**768
Ranavalona I, Mada, **3:**769

Ranjit Singh Bahadur, **1:**106
Ravahiny, Queen, **3:**818
Reccared I, **3:**773
Richard I, Lionheart, **3:**780–782, *781*
Richard II, **3:**782–783
Richard III, **3:**783–785, *784*
  reign, **3:**784–785
  rise to power, **3:**783–784
Robert I (Robert the Bruce), **3:**790,
  790, 835, 901
Roderic, **3:**790
Roger II, **3:**860–861
Romanov, Michael, **3:**798–799
Rudolph I, **3:**803
Rudolph III, **1:**53, 132
Rurik, **3:**803–804

S

Sa'id, Sayyid ibn, **3:**816–817
Saladin, **3:**818–819
  Crusades, **3:**819
  Jerusalem, **3:**819
Samsu-iluna, **3:**822
Samudera-Pasai, **3:**822–823
Sancho III, the Great, **1:**95;
  3:823–824
Sarawak, Rajah of, **1:**125–126
Sargon II, **3:**825–826, 842, 848
Sargon of Akkad, **1:**21–22; **3:**826
Saul, **1:**107–108
Sayyid Muhammad al-Mahdi, **3:**824
Seleucus I, **3:**839
Selim I, the Grim, **3:**840, 908
Selim III, the Great, **3:**840–841
Sennacherib, **3:**842
Seti I, **3:***845,* 845–846
Severus, Septimius, **3:**859
Seyyid Sa'id, **1:**93
Shaka Zulu, **3:**846–847, 873
Shalmaneser III, **3:**847
Shalmaneser V, **3:**848
Shamshi-Adad I, **3:**848
Shapur I, **3:**826
Sheba, Queen of, **3:**811, 851–852
Shih Huang Ti (Shihuangdi),
  3:852–853
Shulgi, **3:**856
Shuppiluliuma I, **3:**857
Sigismund, **3:**861–862
Sihanouk. *See* Norodom Sihanouk

Simeon, **1:**128

Simeon II, **1:**129

Sobhuza I, **3:**867–868

Sobhuza II, **3:**868, *868*

Sobieski, John. *See* John III (John Sobieski)

Solomon, **1:**108; **3:**851–852, 869–870

Stanislas I, **3:**897

Stanislas II, **3:**897–898

Stephen, **3:**898–899

Stephen I, **3:***899,* 899–900

Suleyman I, the Magnificent, **3:**908, *909*

Sunni Ali, **3:**871, 915

Susenyos, **3:**915–916

T

Tabinshwehti, **1:**133

T'ai Tsu (Taizu), **3:**923

T'ai Tsung (Taizong), **3:**924, 927

Taizong. *See* T'ai Tsung (Taizong)

Taizu. *See* T'ai Tsu (Taizu)

Tamerlane (Timur Leng), **3:**925–926, *926*

Tarascos, **1:**37–38

Tarquin the Proud, **3:**929, 930

Taufa'ahau Tupou IV, **3:**930–931

Temuchin. *See* Genghis Khan

Teres, **3:**940

Tewodros II, **3:**932

Thalun, King, **1:**133

Theoderic the Great, **3:**936–937

Theodora, **3:**935–936

Theodosius I, the Great, **3:**937

Thibault I, **1:**110

Thibault IV, **1:**111

Thibaw, **3:**939

Thutmose III, **3:**941–942

Tiberius, **3:**942–943

Tiglath-Pileser III, **3:**944–945

Timur Leng. *See* Tamerlane (Timur Leng)

Titus, **3:**946–947, *947*

Tokugawa Ieyasu, **3:**948–949

Toyotomi Hideyoshi, **3:**956–957

Trajan, **3:**957–958

Tshedkedi Khama, **3:**963

Tughril Beg, **3:**841

Tupac Yupanqui, **3:**967

Tutankhamen, **3:***934,* 935, 968–969, *969*

Tz'u Hsi (Cixi), Empress, **3:**972–973

U

Ur-Nammu, **3:**856, 979

Uthman dan Fodio, **3:**869, 979–980

V

Vespasian, **3:**946

Vesuvius, **3:**947

Victor Emmanuel II, **3:**987

Victoria, **1:**31, 287; **3:**987–989, *988*

  end, **3:**988

  middle years, **3:**988

  royal servants and aides, **3:**844

  seclusion, **3:**837

  young queen, **3:**987–988

Viracocha, **3:**994

Virgil, **3:**962

W

Waldemar I, the Great, **3:**998–999

Wang Kon, **3:**999–1000

Wangchuk, **1:**107, *107*

Wanli, **3:**1000

Wen Ti (Wendi), **3:**906, 1005

Wenceslas IV, **3:**862, 1005–1006

Wenceslaus III of Bohemia, **1:**24

Wilhelm II, **3:***1008,* 1008–1009

  decline and defeat, **3:**1009

  international conflict, **3:**1008–1009

  rise to power, **3:**1008

Wilhelmina, **3:**1009–1010

William and Mary, **3:**1010–1011

  rise to power, **3:**1010–1011

  on the throne, **3:**1011

William I, **3:**1011–1012

William I, the Conqueror, **3:**1012–1015, *1013*

  consolidation and rule, **3:**1013–1014

  death and legacy, **3:**1014

  early life and claim to England, **3:**1012

  invasion and conquest of England, **3:**1012–1013

William II (William Rufus), **3:**1015

William III. *See* William and Mary

Wu Tse-t'ien (Wu Zetian) (Wu Zhao), **3:**1018–1019

X

Xerxes, **3:**1019–1020

Xuanzong. *See* Hsuan Tsung

Y

Yang Guifei, **1:**205–206

Yaqub ibn Layth al-Saffar, **3:**816

Yaroslav I, the Wise, **3:**1025

Yi Songgye, **3:**1029–1030

Yoritomo, **3:**1030

Yoshinobu, **3:**855

Yung Lo (Yongle), **3:**1035

Z

Zara Ya'iqob, **3:**1038

Zedekiah, **1:**109

Zhu Xi, **3:**914

Photo Credits Volume Three

p. 658, Musée National du Château de Malmaison, Rueil-Malmaison, France/Lauros/Giraudon/Bridgeman Art Library; p. 662, Jeff Hacker; p. 674, British Museum, London, UK/Bridgeman Art Library; p. 675, Bode Museum, Berlin, Germany/Bridgeman Art Library; p. 676, Museo Capitolino, Rome, Italy/Bridgeman Art Library; p. 680, Brown Brothers; p. 688, AP/Wide World Photos; p. 695, Jean-Pierre Courau/Anthropologico de Xalapa, Veracruz, Mexico/Bridgeman Art Library; p. 710, Brown Brothers; p. 712, Jeff Hacker; p. 713, The Stapleton Collection/Bridgeman Art Library; p. 719, Lobkowicz Collections, Nelahozeves Castle, Czech Republic/Bridgeman Art Library; p. 725, Lauros/Giraudon/Bridgeman Art Library; p. 731, Hermitage, St. Petersburg, Russia/Bridgeman Art Library; p. 733, Prado, Madrid, Spain/Giraudon/Bridgeman Art Library; p. 734, Fitzwilliam Museum, University of Cambridge, UK/Bridgeman Art Library; p. 743, Bridgeman Art Library; p. 756, Hermitage, St. Petersburg, Russia/Bridgeman Art Library; p. 757, Brown Brothers; p. 768, Bridgeman Art Library; p. 774, Weltliche und Geistliche Schatzkammer, Vienna, Austria/Bridgeman Art Library; p. 781, Brown Brothers; p. 784, Brown Brothers; p. 790, Private Collection/Bridgeman Art Library; p. 797, Private Collection/Bridgeman Art Library; p. 805, Bridgeman Art Library; p. 834, Derrick E. Witty/National Trust Photographic Library/Bridgeman Art Library; p. 838, Château de Versailles, France/Lauros/Giraudon/Bridgeman Art Library; p. 845, Louvre, Paris, France/Giraudon/Bridgeman Art Library; p. 851, Museo dell'Opera del Duomo, Florence, Italy/Bridgeman Art Library; p. 854, Ali Meyer/Bridgeman Art Library; p. 858, Private Collection/Bridgeman Art Library; p. 868, AP/Wide World Photos; p. 880, Bridgeman Art Library; p. 884, Scott Stewart/AP/Wide World Photos; p. 893, Bridgeman Art Library; p. 899, Magyar Nemzeti Galeria, Budapest, Hungary/Bridgeman Art Library; p. 902, Philip Mould, Historical Portraits Ltd., London, UK/Bridgeman Art Library; p. 909, Topkapi Palace Museum, Istanbul, Turkey/Giraudon/Bridgeman Art Library; p. 912, Bibliotheque Nationale, Paris, France/Bridgeman Art Library; p. 919, Soren Andersson/AP/Wide World Photos; p. 922, Musée des Arts d'Afrique et d'Oceanie, Paris, France/Lauros/Giraudon/Bridgeman Art Library; p. 926, British Museum, London, UK/Bridgeman Art Library; p. 927, Denman Waldo Ross Collection/Museum of Fine Arts, Boston, Massachusetts/Bridgeman Art Library; p. 934, Bridgeman Art Library; p. 943, Hermitage, St. Petersburg, Russia/Bridgeman Art Library; p. 947, Private Collection/Bridgeman Art Library; p. 951, Biblioteca Nazionale Centrale, Florence, Italy/Bridgeman Art Library; p. 962, Ancient Art and Architecture Collection Ltd./Bridgeman Art Library; p. 964, Brown Brothers; p. 969, Egyptian National Museum, Cairo, Egypt/Giraudon/Bridgeman Art Library; p. 976, Umayyad Mosque, Damascus, Syria/Bridgeman Art Library; p. 986, Sarah Quill/Venice Picture Library/Bridgeman Art Library; p. 988, Forbes Magazine Collection, New York, New York/Bridgeman Art Library; p. 989, AP/Wide World Photos; p. 992, British Library, London, UK/Bridgeman Art Library; p. 1003, AP/Wide World Photos; p. 1008, Ken Welsh/Private Collection/Bridgeman Art Library; p. 1013, Musee de la Tapisserie, Bayeux, France/With Special Authorization of the City of Bayeux/Bridgeman Art Library; p. 1016, Brown Brothers; p. 1031, Birmingham Museums and Art Gallery/Bridgeman Art Library; p. 1032, University of California Museum of Cultural History/Bridgeman Art Library; p. 1039, Great Zimbabwe, Masvingo Region, Zimbabwe/Bildarchiv Steffens/Bridgeman Art Library; Map credits (all): IMA for BOOK BUILDERS LLC.

WORLD MONARCHIES,
PRESENT DAY

LEGEND

Non-Monarchies

Monarchies